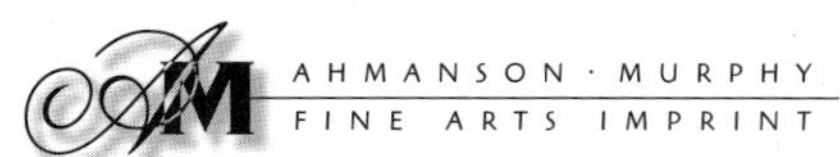

THE AHMANSON FOUNDATION
has endowed this imprint
to honor the memory of
FRANKLIN D. MURPHY
who for half a century
served arts and letters,
beauty and learning, in
equal measure by shaping
with a brilliant devotion
those institutions upon
which they rely.

The publisher gratefully acknowledges the generous contribution to this book provided by the Art Endowment Fund of the University of California Press Foundation, which is supported by a major gift from the Ahmanson Foundation.

CRITICAL READINGS IN

Impressionism and Post-Impressionism

CRITICAL READINGS IN

Impressionism and Post-Impressionism

AN ANTHOLOGY

Edited by MARY TOMPKINS LEWIS

University of California Press
Berkeley Los Angeles London

University of California Press, one of the most distinguished university presses in the United States, enriches lives around the world by advancing scholarship in the humanities, social sciences, and natural sciences. Its activities are supported by the UC Press Foundation and by philanthropic contributions from individuals and institutions. For more information, visit www.ucpress.edu.

University of California Press
Berkeley and Los Angeles, California

University of California Press, Ltd.
London, England

Library of Congress Cataloging-in-Publication Data

Critical readings in Impressionism and Post-Impressionism : an anthology / edited by Mary Tompkins Lewis.
p. cm.
Includes bibliographical references and index.
ISBN 978-0-520-24010-0 (cloth : alk. paper) —
ISBN 978-0-520-25022-2 (pbk. : alk. paper)
1. Impressionism (Art)—France. 2. Post-impressionism (Art)—France. 3. Painting, French—19th century. 4. Painting, French—20th century. I. Lewis, Mary Tompkins.
ND547.5.I4C75 2007
759.05'4—dc22 2006034879

Manufactured in the United States of America

16 15 14 13 12 11 10 09 08 07
10 9 8 7 6 5 4 3 2 1

The paper used in this publication meets the minimum requirements of ANSI/NISO Z39.48-1992 (R 1997) (*Permanence of Paper*).

Contents

Preface

IN THE SCANT three decades since the publication of the fourth and final edition of John Rewald's authoritative *History of Impressionism,* a wealth of new documents, critical approaches, and scholarly exhibitions has significantly enlarged our perception of French Impressionist painting. Historians, critics, and curators have sought to place this perennially popular body of work in wider social and historical contexts and to examine the art world in which it emerged from new perspectives. In the process, the conventional history of Impressionism has been rewritten. The heroic young rebels who banded together to defy the art and institutions of the past in bold paintings of modern life and landscapes have emerged as far more nuanced and conditioned voices, and the Impressionist movement itself has been revealed as increasingly complex. New explorations of the ambitions and strategies of the Impressionists, of the critical reception and modern criteria their painting engendered, and of problematic questions concerning the movement's historical legacy and role in the formation of an avant-garde tradition have shaped both recent blockbuster exhibitions and the critical literature. Amidst it all, the public and scholarly appetite for Impressionism seems not only to endure but to grow.

Many of the new surveys that have supplanted Rewald's text seek to assimilate and synthesize this vastly expanded discipline. However, useful as these surveys are, they can reflect only in abridged form the theoretical breadth and scholarly rigor that now define the field. This book, which is intended not as a primary text on Impressionism but as a supplemental volume to such broader general studies, hopes to redress that fundamental and pedagogical imbalance. On a practical level, it offers an alternative to the cumbersome course packs of photocopied articles that educators have been forced to use as complements to more general course texts (recent legal decisions about duplication in educational contexts make this especially problematic). It should also, however, find a place on the bookshelves of more general readers, those legions of museum visitors who have long suspected that more serious issues and deeper questions lie beneath the fleeting vistas and leisurely spectacles of the popular Impressionist canvas.

The essays collected here represent the dynamic range of the recent criticism that has transformed the study of Impressionism; selection has been made from a wide array of materials—monographs, journals, and museum publications—that form the underpinnings of current scholarship in the field. They have also been chosen because they provide students with instructive models of in-depth critical analysis, of competing, rather than monolithic, art historical methodologies, and also access to the vital and organic unfolding of ideas. Finally, an attempt was made to represent both senior and midcareer scholars, to include both academic articles and scholarly exhibition essays, and, in some cases, to highlight a handful of studies that have not yet been widely reproduced or distributed. Nonetheless, the selection process was marked by both painful choices and practical concerns. Because the scope of the volume could not include every eminent scholar of Impressionism (and there are many), nor address every aspect, artist, or approach in current Impressionist scholarship, a select bibliography of primary materials and recent Impressionist studies and exhibition catalogues is also included.

The anthology is structured along both chronological and thematic lines. After an introductory overview of the movement's critical history, the first group of essays engages broader questions of how and why the movement took root when it did. Robert Herbert's short but prescient article argues for a thorough revision of the history of Impressionism from a sociohistorical viewpoint. His clarion call sets the tone for much recent scholarship and is echoed in several of the subsequent chapters. For example, Nicholas Green situates the aesthetic developments of the later nineteenth century within its evolving economic infrastructure. His emphasis on how entrepreneurial art dealers, such as Paul Durand-Ruel, and a new cadre of speculative art buyers transformed the late nineteenth-century art market underscores not only the expansion of French capitalism in this era but the triumph of individualism that is celebrated in its new art as well. Martha Ward's study of how both new collaborative and individual exhibitions affected the reception of Impressionist art complements Green's highly original essay. Both are crucial to understanding the strategies the Impressionists employed to most effectively harness the dramatically altered economic and social landscape into which Impressionism was born.

The second section of the book, entitled "Landscapes of Modernity," showcases two scholars who have mapped the urban, suburban, and rural territory of modernity as reflected or refracted on the Impressionist canvas, allowing us to see deeper relationships between the visual motifs, social contexts, and pictorial formats inscribed in their art. In his essay from the exhibition catalogue *Impressions of France: Monet, Renoir, Pissarro, and Their Rivals*, John House situates the often subversive Impressionist landscape within the wide-ranging debate about nineteenth-century landscape painting as a whole. His study positions Impressionism within the cultural and popular experience of the French landscape as it was known to artists and tourists alike and within the shadow of the more traditional landscape painting on view at the annual state-sponsored Salons, each of which contexts helps to measure the originality and transgressive boldness of the Impressionist painters. In a chapter from his groundbreaking book of 1985, *The Painting of Modern Life*, T. J. Clark relocates the origins of the movement—aesthetically and geographically—in Edouard Manet's painting of the 1860s and in the suburbs of Paris, where so many of Claude Monet's later canvases would take shape. In pointing to Manet's random, ambivalent spaces as metaphors of dislocation and uncertainty, Clark also helps to extend the movement's critical vocabulary and sociohistorical reorientation.

After this wide-ranging selection of broad, issue-based approaches, the third segment of the anthology draws from recent monographic studies and exhibition-related essays to focus more closely on the critical climate of the period. Stephen Eisenman's seminal essay from the exhibition catalogue *The New Painting* frames Impressionism's early critical fortunes by exploring the movement's evolving, charged, and often highly political terminology. Two additional essays, which focus on the work and reception of individual artists, also broaden our perception of the movement's complex critical reception in its era. Carol Armstrong's study of Edmond Duranty's *La Nouvelle Peinture* of 1876 and its relevance to the work of Edgar Degas reveals a contemporary critic's attempt to articulate a theory of realism against which Degas's Realist practice, so often at odds with that of his Impressionist peers, could be measured. Offering both a vivid contextual reading of one of the pioneering critical texts on Impressionism and a model of how to approach primary sources through the lens of contemporary theory, Armstrong's incisive essay establishes Degas's defiance of pictorial legibility in his art as one of the key factors of his "outsider" modernist aesthetic. Likewise, in her study of the contemporary response to Berthe Morisot's painting, Tamar Garb outlines the broader, gendered terrain of nineteenth-century scientific, social, and aesthetic theory that surrounded both critical and popular perceptions of Impressionist painting.

Many recent Impressionist scholars and scholarly exhibitions have emphasized the potent political contexts in which Impressionism emerged in the immediate and haunting aftermath of the Franco-Prussian War and the Paris Commune of 1870–71. Not only some of the subjects and the shape of Impressionist painting but the strategies employed by its painters have been characterized as deeply inscribed with, or formed in reaction to, the repressive atmosphere of that decade's regime of "moral order." As Eisenman establishes, it was this political and often incendiary context from which the Impressionists struggled to distance their art, though such political readings of Impressionism would resurface, as a survey of its later critical history reveals, in subsequent periods of national peril. An early essay in this now widespread political vein, reflecting the author's own political orientation, Michel Melot's study of Camille Pissarro's graphic work in light of the artist's socialist and anarchist theories provides a fascinating analysis of both the techniques and iconography of Impressionist prints. Paul Tucker's essay on Monet's new art of the 1880s depicts the evolution of his painting and of Impressionism itself against the backdrop of the often-described artistic (but also political) "crisis" of that decade and, in terms of the painter's own burgeoning ambition, the new competitive art market and the powerful tide of nationalism that swept late nineteenth-century France.

The anthology concludes with a group of essays on the Post-Impressionists Georges Seurat, Vincent van Gogh, Paul Gauguin, and Paul Cézanne, not only because these four major painters were well integrated into the Impressionist milieu and crucial conveyers of its influence on later art but because these readings significantly enlarge the critical and contextual scope, and thus usefulness, of the book. Linda Nochlin's landmark piece on Seurat's *La Grande Jatte*, which argues that the painter produced visual codes for the anti-utopian experience of modern life in the formal strategies of the work itself, offers a new perspective on both Seurat and the construction of modernity in subsequent avant-garde painting. In the equally important essay that preceded her recent book on Van Gogh, Gauguin, and Symbolism, Debora Silverman contrasts these two painters' disparate religious backgrounds and contrasting approaches to the physical surface of the canvas to reveal yet another perspective on the development of modern visual form. The volume's final work is Richard Shiff's wide-ranging, requisite discussion of Cézanne's influence on later art, which focuses specifically on the unique, additive character of Cézanne's brushstroke and more generally on the essential pictorialism (or abstraction) of his mode of representation. This compelling recent study further defines the critical criteria and vocabulary of Impressionism and Post-Impressionism and gives solid form to their legacy in twentieth-century painting.

A note of gratitude is due to the contributors, who generously offered their work for publication, and to the numerous colleagues in the field who responded to requests from the editor and from UC Press about the need and scope for such a project. Jim Rubin and Richard Shiff were two of many who offered valuable suggestions. I am grateful as well to my editors at UC Press, to Sarah Montague, Fronia W. Simpson, David Savage, Ryan Jensen, and Jim Lewis, and also to Brian and Bridget Lewis for patient technical support. The staff at the Frick Art Reference Library, and especially Suz Massen, Jacqueline Rogers, and Lydia Defour, were generous with their time and assistance. I am also indebted to Trinity College for financial (and moral) support: none of my colleagues complained when this project overflowed the department office. No doubt a number of my former students will recognize in this book the syllabi and photocopied articles they inherited in past courses on late nineteenth-century art, and they are also to be thanked. But I am above all grateful to Judith Gilligan, without whose endless patience, superb organizational skills, and constant good cheer this volume would never have come to light.

Mary Tompkins Lewis

Introduction

The Critical History of Impressionism

An Overview

MARY TOMPKINS LEWIS

For Jack Ready

FOR MUCH OF the twentieth century French Impressionism was broadly defined as an art of objective, visual truth. Its painters were seen as having worked without past or passion, and without aesthetic consideration or concern for the motifs they captured spontaneously on canvas. Their painting seemed to be given over to the rapid recording of transient, fleeting nature. The strong Positivist spirit of the age, moreover, was often evoked as the most crucial context for Impressionism's presumed basis in material, visual fact.[1] As framed by Auguste Comte and disseminated by his followers, the Positivist philosophy declared that only the tools of science—direct observation and empirical analysis—provided the means to credible knowledge. But to see Impressionism only through such a limited lens is to ignore aspects of the movement that were recognized even by contemporaries. Some of Impressionism's earliest chroniclers suggested the richer and more nuanced vision that recent scholars have rediscovered in Impressionist painting. In some important and fascinating ways, our understanding of Impressionism has come full circle.

When they banded together in 1874 to organize their first independent exhibition on the fashionable boulevard des Capucines in Paris, the young Impressionists shared, above all, a vision of truth in painting that was twofold. Their approach encompassed a sense of naturalism based not only on close observation of nature but also on each painter's subjective vision (or temperament), often expressed in highly individual techniques. Impressionist painting celebrated a sense of freedom that underpins many of the subjects and spectacles it offers. By rejecting line to work directly in color to produce quick, sketch-like views of modern life and landscapes, Impressionist painters more broadly rejected the Salon's traditional criteria, and even its exhibition walls, as formative modes and contexts for their art. A number of the essays in this anthology explore the ways in which Impressionist painting has come to define not so much a specific style, movement, or even clear artistic affiliation as a premise of individual freedom, inseparable from our understanding of modern art. Impressionism has long represented a resonant historical phenomenon, as even a brief survey of the fluctuating, sometimes narrow, and often contentious century of critical debate over its merits, objectives, and influences shows.[2]

The Early Critical History

In 1863 the French critic Jules-Antoine Castagnary coined the term "naturalist" to separate the vanguard of young artists (a group that would include, by his 1866 Salon review, the twenty-six-year-old Claude Monet) from such earlier Realists as Gustave Courbet. Emphasizing their works' passionless objectivity in front of the motif, the critic wrote that their "sole aim is to reproduce nature. . . . It is truth balanced with science."[3] But a decade later, as Richard Shiff has shown in his watershed essay "The End of Impressionism," Castagnary realized the inadequacy of the "naturalist" term when he saw the first Impressionist exhibition, in 1874, at Nadar's gallery.[4] It was that show that led to the conservative critic Louis Leroy's infamous, mocking description of Monet's loosened, sketch-like technique in such paintings as *Impression: Sunrise* (plate 1), which gave popular currency to the term "Impressionism," though its widespread adoption would soon dilute Leroy's original pejorative connotations.[5] Later that year Castagnary employed the Impressionist label in an essay that captured the paintings' deeply expressive character: "They are 'impressionists' in the sense that they render not the landscape, but the sensation produced by the landscape."[6] This vision, he elaborated, was individual and imaginative—far more than a painted, optical truth. Even the writer and critic Emile Zola, himself the leading figure in the Naturalist movement in literature and a staunch defender of the Realist painter Edouard Manet in the 1860s, allowed that a degree of subjective truth shaped the individual artistic visions of Manet and the later Impressionists.[7] Given such early readings of Impressionism as embodying "a kind of intensely subjectified naturalism" (although Castagnary did articulate reservations about painters who, like Cézanne, pursued their personal visions to an excessive "degree of romanticism without bounds"),[8] it is perhaps surprising that the myth of Impressionism's objectivity endured for so much of the twentieth century. Early critics seemed already attuned to the qualities that have now come to be most prized—a luminous rendering of both the subject and the act of perception.

The critic Félix Fénéon, a supporter of Georges Seurat, questioned Impressionist naturalism in his writings of the 1880s and helped to shape the narrow view of the movement that persisted into the twentieth century.[9] However, as Shiff has argued, other critics of the period echoed Castagnary's assessment, and the work's inherent duality continued to elicit divergent critical strands. In the 1890s, the decade when the overtly subjective Symbolist movement prevailed, many historians saw artists' orientation shifting away from the Impressionist mode, but others, conversely, saw the two movements as flowing seamlessly one into the other. The earlier paintings were cited as models for the new: the critic and Symbolist advocate Albert Aurier praised Impressionism's "attempts at expressive synthesis."[10] In his review of 1891, another critic, Gustave Geoffroy, cited both the universal, symbolic content and the transient natural effects of Monet's recent painting.[11] The following year the Symbolist artist and critic Maurice Denis struggled to distinguish between the *idéaliste* and *naturaliste* elements in Pierre-Auguste Renoir's art as well.[12] Although later critics and historians would portray them as polar opposites even in their mid-careers, to many writers in the 1890s Monet and Renoir shared a good deal of common ground. Both artists were repeatedly lauded for achieving in their recent work not only a highly personal vision but a signatory painting technique that allowed for emotional expressiveness. Thus, in the critical landscape of the 1890s the celebrated Impressionist brushstroke—which has so often been interpreted as a sign of fierce independence and dedication to a radically uninflected, "scientific" truth—helped tie Impressionism to the more openly expressive mode of Symbolist painting. The various explorations of subjective and Symbolist strains in Impressionist art point to a growing sense that Impressionism itself was not so much a reaction against earlier nineteenth-century Romanticism but, like Symbolism, a fluid continuation of that earlier age and sentiment. By the end of the 1890s, in fact, much of the original controversy surrounding Impressionism had subsided: all of the Impressionists were represented in the Musée du Luxembourg (the museum for living French artists); Renoir received the prestigious Légion d'Honneur; and Monet was proclaimed "the most significant painter of the century."[13] And in the fine arts section of the Paris world's fair of 1900, where the nation's cultural heritage was on view, the once outcast band of young painters was rewarded with their own exhibition gallery. This tranquil state of affairs, however, did not last.

Nationalism and Historical Contexts: The Early Twentieth Century

In the early twentieth century the positioning of French Impressionism in its own era and within the grand tradition of French painting as a whole became problematic and hotly contested. As Norma Broude and Tamar Garb have argued, it was also a habitually gendered issue.[14] And, to complicate matters, a handful of the Impressionists continued to paint. Monet and Renoir, for example, worked for two decades after the turn of the century, unlike Seurat, Van Gogh, Gauguin, and Cézanne, who were by then acknowledged as the masters of the Post-Impressionist generation but were not as long-lived. In his essay Stephen Eisenman aptly describes how, despite the Impressionists' attempts to evade any radical affiliations, their painting had been, at its inception, framed in potently political terms, and so it was again. Though Impressionism was no longer at the forefront of the artistic avant-garde, critical assessment of this movement became highly politicized as France took careful stock of its imposing cultural history.

As epitomized by the work of J. A. D. Ingres and Pierre Puvis de Chavannes and by academic painting at the Paris Salons, the nineteenth-century French classical tradition was perceived by contemporary French critics and historians, and even by some of the French populace, as having evolved from Latin antiquity. The painting of Nicolas Poussin, the father of French Baroque Classicism in seventeenth-century Rome, was widely promoted in this era by French Nationalists anxious to substantiate their country's ancient Mediterranean roots.[15] Impressionism, however, could be credited with a far more recent lineage, one built upon a modern legacy of innovation that originated in the work of Manet.[16] To many Frenchmen, this constituted an artistic heritage in its own right and one that contemporary French artists had to recognize. Yet with the appearance of the first histories of the movement, such as Camille Mauclair's *L'Impressionnisme: Son histoire, son esthétique, ses maîtres* (1904) and Théodore Duret's *Histoire des peintres impressionnistes* (1906), a somewhat longer view of Impressionism's historical locus took shape. To such resolute Republicans as Mauclair, who adamantly rejected the idea of even distant Latin origins for French culture, Impressionism represented the culmination of centuries of painterly refinement in French art. Recasting Jean-Antoine Watteau's *Cythera* as an Impressionist painting, Mauclair embraced the eighteenth-century Rococo, rather than Poussin's Baroque Classicism, as the true national style and, in the same vein, pronounced Renoir one of the great, truly French painters.[17] A close friend and colleague of the Symbolist poet and theoretician Stéphane Mallarmé, Mauclair also emphasized Impressionism's subjective and Romantic elements and so further solidified its place within a continuous, rather than a combative, history of French art. Though he would decry the intersection of Nationalist politics and art and later criticize the Impressionists' inordinate concern with the themes of modern life and the capturing of fleeting atmospheric effects, Mauclair's early enthusiasm for Impressionism as an extension of an eighteenth-century French style gave the movement, if only briefly, a needed historical and national pedigree.[18]

By the early twentieth century, however, the ongoing debate in French circles over preferred period styles and national schools reflected an increasingly precarious political situation, and Nationalist sentiments and fears found echoes in every facet of French society. Still reeling from the destructive polarization of the Dreyfus scandal (a dark moment of anti-Semitic sentiment that reverberated for years after Zola's famous "J'Accuse" of 1898) and increasingly threatened by a burgeoning German war machine, France struggled both as a nation and as a cultural entity to redefine its intellectual patrimony and future.[19] Conciliatory efforts may have shaped even some of its most radical new art. In his study of Fauvist painting and politics, James Herbert argues that the Fauves reconciled the competing Latinate and innovative Impressionist traditions by reiterating classical themes and compositions while adopting Impressionist (and Post-Impressionist) sites and devices.[20] Thus, André Derain painted, as had Monet, on the banks of the Thames in London, Maurice de Vlaminck followed Renoir's path to Chatou, and Georges Braque painted the landscape of Cézanne's L'Estaque. And Henri Matisse transformed the Impressionists' tourist landscapes of the south into timeless pastorals. Yet, though heir to the Impressionist (and Post-Impressionist) motifs and methods, the Fauves pointedly rejected the aura of studied refinement that critics had perceived in the later paintings of Monet and especially Renoir. Instead, they employed such virulent palettes and willfully crude techniques that they earned the appellation "Wild Beasts" at the Salon d'Automne of 1905. The distance they deliberately established between their own art and that of their Impressionist forebears reflected a growing sense in many quarters that the "delicate sensations" (as Matisse noted in the paintings of Monet and Alfred Sisley), the ephemeral effects, and the Romantic tendencies of the Impressionists represented, as one critic wrote in 1905, "extremely civilized painting, very decadent, very degenerate."[21]

World War I and the *Rappel à l'Ordre*

Echoes of such harsh critical judgments of Impressionism grew louder as France moved closer to the brink of war. Although its classical heritage was variously defined, the efforts to establish the nation's cultural origins in a secure historical past became, at times, a rallying point and unifying crusade for Nationalists and Republicans alike, as both sides became increasingly anxious to restore a sense of stability, permanence, and order in a time of escalating national peril. Impressionism's perceived Romantic strain, which, as seen in Fénéon's and Mauclair's writings, had once given it a place in a tidy, evolving history of French art, now became part of its critical undoing.[22] In the new atmosphere of *rappel à l'ordre*, the Romantic tradition was offered as damning evidence of the culture's enfeebled, less cerebral side, and Impressionism became its most recent self-indulgent offspring. As the painter and conservative critic André Lhote noted in 1916: "The Romantic wave, of which Impressionism was the outcome, renewed the poorly harnessed deliquescences of the eighteenth century, provoked the disfavor of all precise teaching . . . and led to a pictorial empiricism based on feeling alone."[23]

Impressionist and Symbolist painting and music had often been tied to German Romanticism, specifically to the circle and aesthetics of Richard Wagner, and this now seemed abhorrent, further undermining the movement's reputation in this period of rampant nationalism.[24] Finally, while earlier Romantic art in France and the anti-academic painting of the Realists were only distant memories, historians still easily recalled the Impressionists' initial audacity, their defiance of authority and established artistic practice, and, perhaps above all, their emergence on the Parisian art scene in the charged historical moment immediately following the humiliation of the Franco-Prussian War and Paris Commune. As Kenneth Silver describes, "Although the history of Impressionism would later be written as essentially the triumph of formal values over subject matter, it is clear that, at least during World War I, the visual flux of Impressionism was often understood as being the objective correlative of the fluctuating society from which it issued."[25] Not surprisingly then, on the left, right, and center in war-torn France, Impressionism became a special bête noire; almost any other artistic manifestation was preferable.

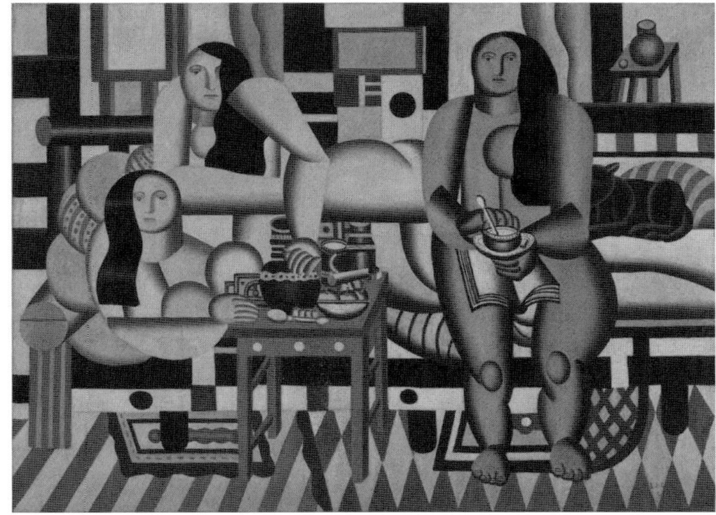

FIGURE I.1. Fernand Léger, *Le Grand Déjeuner (Three Women)*, 1921. The Museum of Modern Art, New York; Mrs. Simon Guggenheim Fund. © 2007 Artists Rights Society (ARS), New York/ADAGP, Paris. Digital image © The Museum of Modern Art/Licensed by Scala/Art Resource, NY.

Antidotes to the decadence implied by the ephemeral forms, seemingly capricious subjects, and sensuous, virtuoso brushwork of the Impressionists already existed in the paintings of the Post-Impressionists, especially Cézanne and Seurat. Not surprisingly, their work was reevaluated and newly lauded in this period by critics hoping to restore to French painting a sense of structure and classical authority. Even before Cézanne's death in 1906, his two disciples, Emile Bernard and Maurice Denis, had anointed him the Poussin of modern French art and argued that Cézanne's painting reflected the seventeenth-century master's careful balance between style and nature and between tradition and originality.[26] While their definition of Cézanne's classicism was often arbitrary and their criteria sometimes seemed closer to Symbolism, their association of Cézanne and Poussin and the notion of a revived classicism in Post-Impressionist painting drew many adherents.[27] By the onset of war, as the Swiss writer Charles Ferdinand Ramuz suggested in a 1914 essay, the traditional and classical character of Cézanne's art superseded all others in the minds of many critics and historians.[28] And Cézanne remained the modern embodiment of the French classical tradition for some time, even though his popularity wavered. At the 1937 Paris world's fair, where the lineage and hegemony of French culture were again strategically argued, a massive exhibition of more than thirteen hundred works of French art traced its origins to the Greco-Roman period and closed with Cézanne.[29]

In the 1920s, however, it was Seurat's reputation that soared. At the time, many saw him as the Post-Impressionist artist most closely aligned with the French classical tradition because of his even more palpable efforts to reform Impressionism along stable and structured lines. Although the formal strategies in Seurat's paintings may well have been conceived, as Linda Nochlin argues in her essay here, as reflections of the problematic (or anti-utopian) conditions of modern urban life in the 1880s, the artist's methodical, architectonic, and highly finished paintings provided French viewers in the 1920s with an oddly comforting vision. As Silver argues, "In the midst of France's post-war reconstruction, Seurat's pictures offered the French an image of the world that they found reassuringly ordered, geometric, and much like the world that they themselves hoped to reconstruct on their own devastated territories."[30] In perhaps a rare confluence of audience perceptions and artists' imperatives, such modernist painters as Fernand Léger looked to Seurat's paintings (e.g., plate 5) for the architectonic classicism of their own figural styles (fig. I.1).[31]

Fry and Formalist Criticism

In the early twentieth century it was not only in France that Post-Impressionist painting was showcased as an antidote to Impressionism and as a vital wellspring in the evolutionary flow of modern art. Among its most influential advocates were the German art historian Julius Meier-Graefe, whose 1904 history of modern art was translated into English in 1908, and Roger Fry, one of the most important British art critics of his generation.[32] Fry coined the umbrella term "Post-Impressionism" to describe the works featured in the 1910 and 1912 shows he organized at the Grafton Galleries in London. These exhibitions had emphasized the importance of Van Gogh, Gauguin, and especially Cézanne, but after Fry saw Seurat's work in Paris during the war, it replaced the work of Van Gogh and Gauguin in his new canon.[33] Influenced by Meier-Graefe's denunciation of Impressionism, Fry's early hostility to the movement set him apart from many of his British colleagues, including the "New Art Critics," as they were called, whose critical approach was largely defined by their long-standing support of Impressionism.[34] Many of their circle vehemently rejected Fry's new Post-Impressionist pantheon. But his impassioned belief that the most significant art—old and new—emphasizes the formal beauty of the medium itself and also endows it with deeper meaning struck a chord, and his critical writings became vastly influential. While Clement Greenberg, a later formalist, would substantially revise Fry's modernist canon and even admit Monet's late work to it, Fry's emphasis on the aesthetic value of an artist's handling of the medium vaulted Cézanne to the top of his own list of modernists. Fry's formalist aesthetic permeated twentieth-century criticism and its frequent backward glances at the Impressionists, resonating long after he himself had been relegated to a more anecdotal position.

As we have seen, in the charged critical landscape of the teens and early twenties, earlier and more subtle distinctions (e.g., between Impressionism, Post-Impressionism, and Fauvism) tended to disappear as the deeply politicized avant-garde art world fell into two opposing camps:

> There remains today only two possible orders of thought . . . on the one side, the Impressionist ideal (to which are attached the bad imitators of Cézanne, the lazy disciples of Sisley and Monet, and those "fauves" now enraptured by their comfortable cage)—and on the other, the Cubist ideal embracing all those painters who renounce the direct [Impressionist or naturalist] language.[35]

Since at least 1910 Cubist painting was portrayed as a reaction against Impressionism and its followers and Cubism's emphasis on mass, volume, and form and concomitant devaluation of color and brushstroke offered a calculated and deeply intellectual, if not always fixed, alternative to the sensual, Impressionist-influenced work of many early twentieth-century painters. Jean Cocteau's declaration "Make no mistake here, Cubism was a classicism after the Romanticism of the Fauves" was characteristic.[36] (Cocteau, of course, was a friend of Picasso's, and his distaste for Impressionism, which would have disappointed his sense of irony, was legendary.)

The first historians of the Cubist movement pursued the notion of its classical basis, connecting it to Cézanne as well as Latin and native genealogical traditions to establish its rightful position in the French cultural matrix (and, in the process, laying aside Picasso's Spanish origins).[37] The old model of opposing styles (or of a dialogue between sensibility and reason) was resurrected to describe the relationship of Matisse and Picasso, who had emerged as the leaders of the Fauves and the Cubists, respectively. Such broad and avidly articulated dichotomies left little room for the conflicting nuances that complicate the wartime production of both painters—for example, Matisse's austere formulations from 1908 to 1918, when he clearly distanced himself from the Impressionist heritage (though after 1918 an Impressionist sensibility returned to his art, and his critical stature fell accordingly), or the splashes of brilliant color and stippled (Neo-) Impressionist brushwork that enliven some of Picasso's and Georges Braque's Cubist canvases from the teens.[38] On the whole, however, though Picasso came to appreciate Renoir's painting, he openly rejected the legacy of the Impressionist landscape and even more the shimmering surface effects that shaped the art of more recent colorists, such as the Nabi painter Pierre Bonnard, who later proclaimed himself the last of the Impressionists. Matisse, while always less demonstrative about his critical shifts, nevertheless might well have spoken for Picasso at this point when he said, "A rapid translation of the landscape can only give a moment in its life duration. By insisting on its character, I prefer to risk losing some of its charm."[39]

Postwar Reassessments: Renoir's and Monet's Late Work

By 1920 another artistic discourse was taking shape, one on which Matisse and Picasso would largely agree, and it would help determine the critical fortunes of Impressionism in the postwar era. During the harsh war years, both Monet and Renoir had seen their work devalued by critics. Monet, as the quintessential painter of the Impressionist landscape, had suffered more at their hands. As Romy Golan argues, the French landscape had acquired a new moral dimension through vivid memories and photographs of the trenches and bloodied battlefields, and the potent new meaning of landscape as a subject was evident in the preponderance of landscape paintings at postwar exhibitions and Salons.[40] Even some of the most vanguard landscape painters of prewar Paris, such as the Cubist Roger de la Fresnaye, turned to a postwar landscape style of legible, ordered forms and blatantly Poussinesque compositions.[41] Likewise, the new preference for images of rural villages and rugged provincial landscapes refuted the sunlit tourist sites and aura of urban leisure that had proliferated in Impressionist painting. Against the backdrop of this politicized restructuring of the French landscape, in art and in reality, Monet's unending stream of canvases from his idyllic garden at Giverny unleashed harsh critical attacks like those he had received as a young painter. Although some critics tried to redeem his evanescent late paintings by proclaiming Monet to be no longer a painter of trite Impressionist motifs but a great patron of the terrain of the Ile-de-France, "to which he was tied as a peasant is to his turf," the artist was not easily recast.[42] As Lhote summarized the conservative backlash: "Indifferent to all the landscapes that only begged to be copied to enter the museums for posterity . . . the century's greatest eye and hand, preferring the pond of Giverny, committed one of the most frightful artistic suicides. Can our times produce nothing but mutilated geniuses?"[43] Thus, while few challenged Monet's secure place in the history of French art—and the installation of his *Waterlilies* (see fig. I.6) at the Musée de l'Orangerie in 1927, at the behest of the former prime minister Georges Clemenceau, would solidify it—his contemporary influence and relevance were far more open to question.

The critical fortunes of Renoir's painting in postwar France followed a decidedly different track. After the artist's death on the Riviera in 1919, a series of exhibitions, critical notices, and monographs did much to restore Renoir's reputation in French art circles. Within only a few years—and boosted in part by a boom in the art market—his auction prices exceeded their prewar levels; Matisse and Picasso each acquired his works.[44] For Matisse, who visited the aged painter several times just before his death, Renoir's painting proved to be a crucial factor in reshaping his own work after the war. Describing Renoir as "second only to Cézanne" and crediting him with rescuing contemporary art "from the atrophying effect of pure abstraction through his example," Matisse pointedly evoked Renoir's early Impressionist *Odalisque* of 1871 (fig. I.2) in his own orientalist fantasies of 1921–22 (fig. I.3).[45]

Many of the posthumous tributes to Renoir emphasized how the painter's late style had evolved away from his earlier Impressionist mode. In a number of exhibitions, as well as in the massive retrospective at the Salon d'Automne of 1920, the significance of Renoir's final period was underscored. In

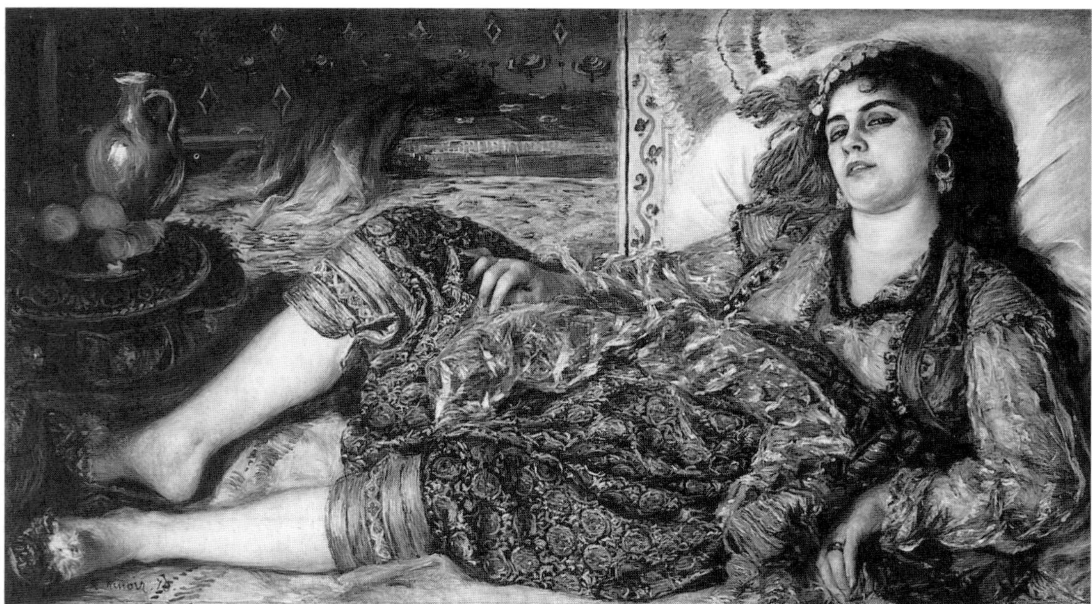

FIGURE I.2. Pierre-Auguste Renoir, *Odalisque*, 1871. National Gallery of Art, Washington, Chester Dale Collection. Image © 2007 Board of Trustees, National Gallery of Art, Washington.

his ample, roseate female figures and late paintings of bathers, Renoir reconciled his painterly brushstroke and opulent palette with a revived classical figure style, drawing the admiration of many. Though in 1918 Cocteau dismissed Renoir's painting as part of the "Impressionist decadence" he abhorred, soon afterward Picasso was embracing both Renoir's art and his example. Picasso's occasional retreats from Cubism in the early 1920s to a personal brand of Neoclassicism, as seen in his colossal nudes and vaguely antique figures, were informed not only by the painting of Ingres, which many avant-garde painters had recently rediscovered, but by Renoir's late work as well.[46] And in a 1919 drawing after a photograph of the aging artist, Picasso emphasized the older painter's infirmity and hands crippled by arthritis to create a poignant portrait and homage.[47] Braque, too, looked to Renoir's late classical figures when he abandoned his Cubist mode in the postwar years to create large, sensual and idealized female figures, such as his *Basket Carrier* (1922; Centre Georges Pompidou, Paris).[48]

Recent historians have ascribed the widespread enthusiasm in this period for Renoir's late colossal nudes and the surge of new paintings of sensual female figures in similarly idealized, natural states by vanguard and traditional artists alike to the conservative tenor of the postwar *rappel à l'ordre*.[49] This moralizing period was shaped by reactionary forces seeking to restructure society along premodern lines and to return women to their "preordained" roles as procreators and keepers of the home. As Golan notes, a parallel vogue for images of the heroic French peasant, rooted in the rustic countryside and indicative of its imminent renewal, reflected the same regressive climate.[50] But for artists such as Braque, Picasso, and even some of their more conservative peers, Renoir's late painting held a different appeal, as it pointed toward an ordered art that did not need to be austere. His exquisite color, generous, dappled brushstroke, sensualized classical forms, and vaguely arcadian milieus suggested, in a time of bleak retrenchment on every front, a new future for French art based on what the scholar Christopher Green

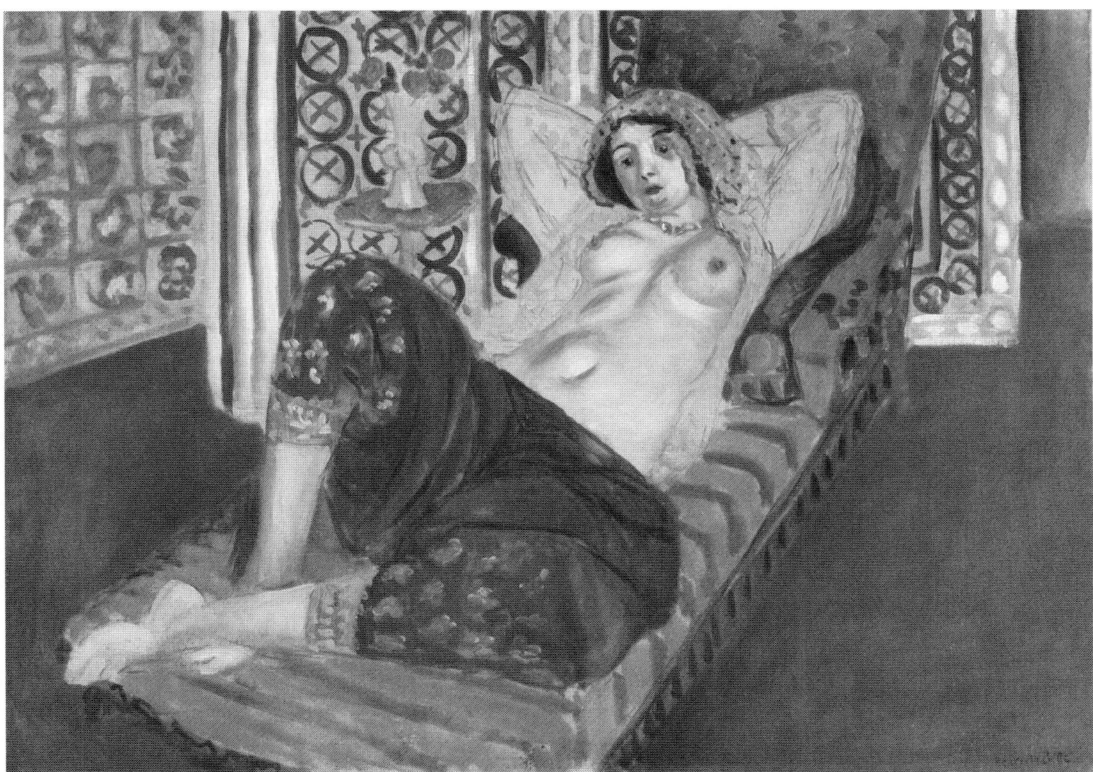

FIGURE I.3. Henri Matisse, *Odalisque in Red Culottes*, 1921. Musée National d'Art Moderne, Centre Georges Pompidou, Paris. © 2007 Succession H. Matisse, Paris/Artists Rights Society (ARS), New York. Photo: CNAC/MNAM/Dist. Réunion des Musées Nationaux/Art Resource, NY. Photographed by Philippe Migeat.

calls "a structured hedonism of great refinement."[51] In 1943, when the Surrealist René Magritte was seeking a new sensibility for his art that would counter the misery of life in Occupied Europe, he briefly adopted both the technique and subject matter of Renoir's late period. A series of more than seventy paintings—many of which combine Renoir's brilliant palette, lush technique, and late figure style with oddly surreal images (e.g., fig. I.4)—stands pointedly apart from what Magritte described as the darker "disturbing poetry" of most of his oeuvre. Even in parodic form, Renoir's example (fig. I.5) offered "a new poetic effectiveness which would bring us both charm and pleasure."[52]

A critical vocabulary soon emerged to legitimize these painters' choices. The critic Waldemar George, who strongly supported Cubism but urged a broader base for the renewal of French art after World War I, saw the legacy of Impressionist color, and especially Renoir's palette, as key. In an essay of 1922, he urged living French painters to embrace the Impressionist color revolution:

> There will be no question of taking up for ourselves the ideas of Claude Monet and his contemporaries. The painter of today has no intention of representing the ephemeral and superficial aspect of a view, submitted to the external action of lighting, but he can, he must even, benefit from the experience in the realm of color acquired by his seniors.[53]

In the late 1920s Mauclair, who had argued in his earlier criticism that Impressionism represented a truly

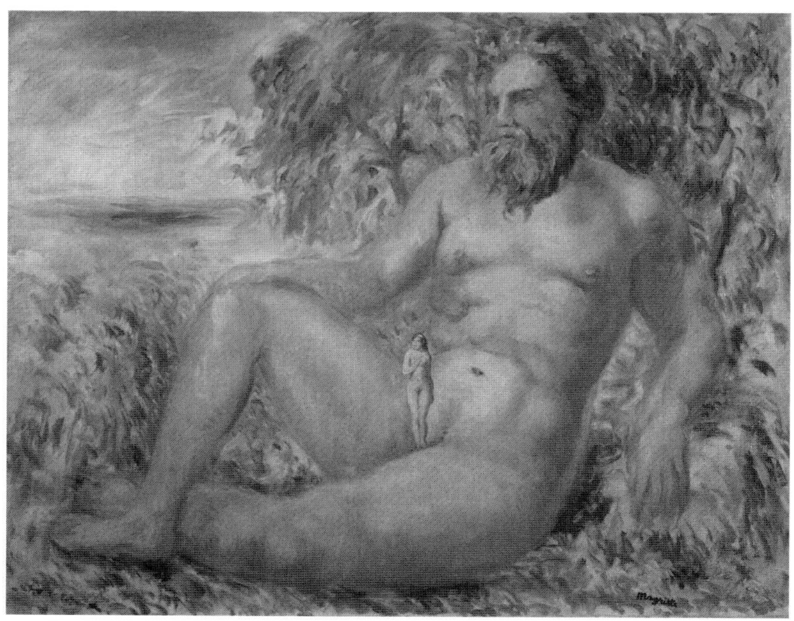

FIGURE I.4. René Magritte, *The Ocean*, 1943. Private collection. © 2007 C. Herscoviel, Brussels/ Artists Rights Society (ARS), New York. Photo: The Bridgeman Art Library.

national style in modern form, and George became leading cultural figures in a growing xenophobic movement, which persisted into the Vichy regime. Even though George was a Polish Jewish immigrant, his writings, along with those of Mauclair, reflected the underlying Nationalist, and often anti-Semitic, bias that colored critical discourse between the wars.[54] Not surprisingly, in this context the questions of national schools and historical pedigrees were brought up again. As so often happens in such debates, in which concepts of style and tradition are used to exclude rather than embrace, the issue was raised most pointedly to condemn the painting of the new, so-called "Ecole de Paris," produced by largely foreign-born artists, many of whom were Jews living in the Montparnasse quarter of Paris. Thus, for example, the works of Chaim Soutine and Marc Chagall were widely criticized for their non-French sensibilities, though the allegations of "hasty" or "weak" character, overdone "painterliness," and signs of latent Romanticism echoed some of the criticisms hurled at the French-born Impressionists a half century earlier.[55] Ironically, the memory of the work of the Impressionists, especially Renoir, now stood as the national antithesis to this invading foreign school. Once threatened with marginalization because of their ephemeral subjects, the Impressionist painters had become monumental. As the critic Louis Vauxcelles wrote in 1925, in a passage that vividly captures the jingoistic tenor of the times:

> A barbarian horde has rushed like a plague, like a cloud of locusts, upon Montparnasse. . . . These are people from "somewhere else" who ignore and, in the bottom of their hearts, look down on what Renoir has called the gentleness of the French School, that is, the virtue of tact, the nuanced quality of our race. . . . This painter [Renoir] shows the misled the good old French route to follow. The peril has been exorcised and safe is the honor of the French School.[56]

Yet again, Monet proved hard to conscript into the service of this new critical war. His death at Giverny in December 1926 did not occasion the kind of immediate, wholesale reevaluation of his work and reputation that Renoir had posthumously enjoyed. Following years of struggle by the increasingly solitary painter—who continued to work on his enormous *Waterlilies* paintings in his studio until his death—and

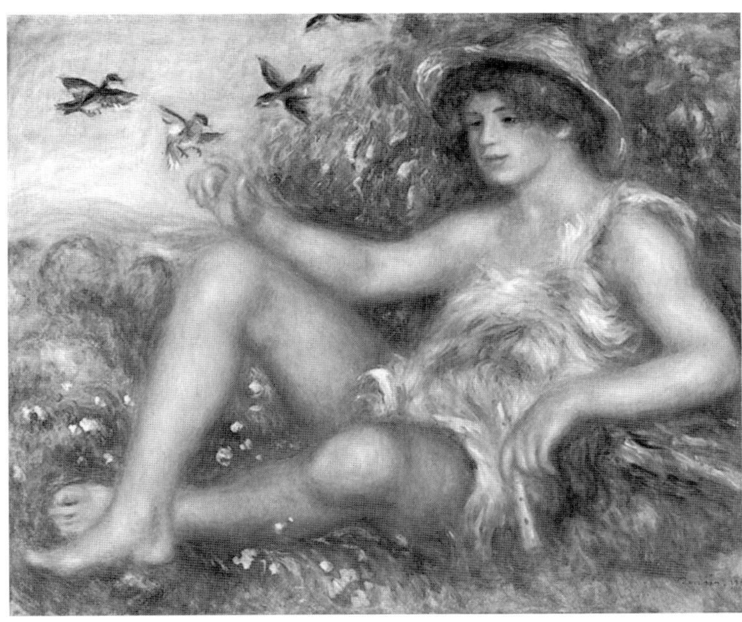

FIGURE I.5. Pierre-Auguste Renoir, *Young Shepherd in Repose*, 1911. Rhode Island School of Design; Museum Works of Art Fund. Photo: Cathy Carver.

his old friend and loyal supporter Clemenceau, the twenty-two canvases that make up his *Grandes Décorations* were permanently installed on the walls of the Musée de l'Orangerie in the center of Paris and unveiled to the public in May 1927 (fig. I.6). In a book published a year later to mark the event, and perhaps in reaction to the critical fire the panels had drawn, Clemenceau argued for their rational sequence and extolled their "delicate construction" and "luminous order."[57] Other old friends of the painter, including the circle of now aged critics who had long promoted his work, also responded with tributes to Monet's ambitious, evanescent late painting and legacy to the nation.[58] (One of them, François Thiébault-Sisson, had earlier advocated the public installation of the *Water-lilies* to bolster the postwar prestige of France, and this had been Clemenceau's hope as well.) But to younger critics and painters, who had the ear of the avant-garde and were still enmeshed in the moralizing mind-set of the postwar culture, Monet's late work, with its dematerialized forms and ephemeral sensory effects, revived the old balance between observed nature and the "sensation" of nature on canvases so lushly negotiated as to require critical alignment. As Paul Tucker describes, to them it celebrated "the shifting, incalculable world of nature, instead of the disciplined one of [a] rational, rebuilt France."[59]

Monet's magnificent decorative ensemble languished in virtual oblivion in its subterranean, cryptlike galleries for almost two decades, as did the critical stature of not only his later painting but to some degree Impressionism itself. In the catalogue to the single exhibition of his work mounted by a French museum between the wars, a retrospective in 1931 at the Musée de l'Orangerie, Paul Jamot, the senior curator at the Louvre, applauded Monet's early career but did little to foster interest in his later work.[60] And in the handful of reviews the show elicited, the criticism of the late painting was particularly unforgiving: "How empty this work is, what a misunderstanding this strange and truly pitiful crowning of Monet's career. What kind of vanity seduced him into this sort of monumental decoration when the man had no talent for this kind of work?"[61] Thus, unlike Renoir, Monet was seen as tied, even in his late, increasingly autonomous and mural-sized paintings, to an outdated Impressionist mode. Only after yet another war and an accompanying sea change in

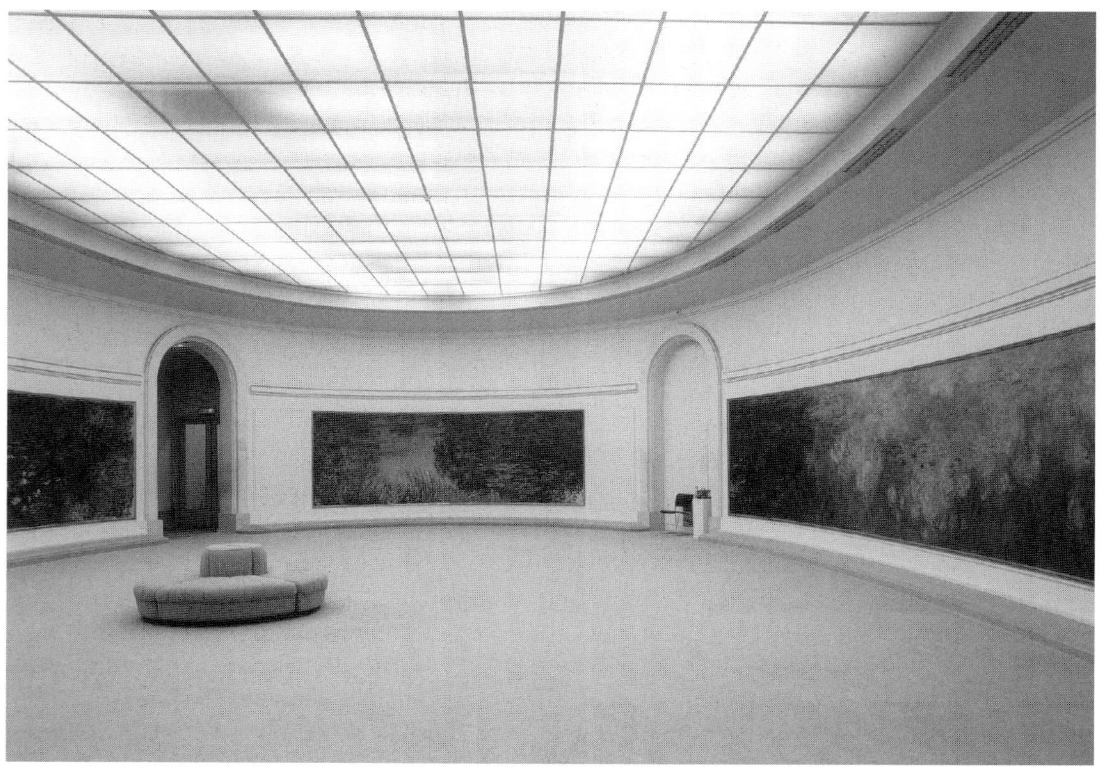

FIGURE I.6. Claude Monet, *Les Nymphéas (Waterlilies)*. Musée de l'Orangerie, Paris. Photo: Réunion des Musées Nationaux/Art Resource, NY.

critical thinking and contexts would both Monet and Impressionism emerge in a more favorable light.

By the 1930s Fry's formalist reading of Impressionism as a kind of impassive, retinal realism had become entrenched in the critical literature, and it shaped the predominant understanding of the movement for almost half a century. Writing in 1927, long after he had dismissed the Impressionists, and especially Monet, for offering only the last development in the science of representation in their art, Fry explained: "They failed to see that the only value of facts of appearance for an artist lies in what constructions his imaginative apprehension of them is capable of creating. That its value lies in the power of these constructions to express profound feelings and to transmit these feelings to the spectator."[62] Against the backdrop of Surrealist painting and literature, which dominated vanguard culture in the 1930s and cultivated the rich, imaginary world of dreams and the subconscious, Fry's discrediting of Impressionism for its emphasis on objectivity was particularly damning. However, the same decade also witnessed the first revisionist studies, which would ultimately challenge the widespread authority of Fry's views.

Schapiro's Sociohistorical Approach and Abstract Expressionism

In 1932, in his pioneering study "Matisse and Impressionism," Meyer Schapiro argued for the intrinsic subjectivity, however implicit, of Impressionist painting, in which the painter's aesthetic vision and choice of subject were "entirely his own."[63] Moreover, Schapiro suggested, this aspect of Impressionist painting "may be paralleled in other aspects of modern life. It corresponds to the steadily increasing subjectivity of art since the Renaissance and the decreasing firmness and objectivity of the external world."[64] Pierre Francastel resurrected a more traditional view of the subjective and emotional content in the painting of Monet, Renoir, and Degas in his 1937 monograph, *L'Impressionnisme: Les Origines de la peinture moderne de Monet à Gauguin*, which may have been influenced, as Shiff has suggested, by his reading of the earlier Symbolist critics Geoffroy and Denis.[65] But it was Schapiro's groundbreaking essay "The Nature of Abstract Art" of that same year that proved most influential over time in dislodging formalist methodology. Adopting a bold sociohistorical approach, Schapiro declared that Impressionist subject matter not only celebrated the urban idyll of bourgeois recreation but also reflected the underlying "freedom for an enlightened bourgeois detached from the official beliefs of his class."[66] In addition, Schapiro argued, the unregulated vision of the Impressionist painter, marked by changing, momentary perceptions, was deliberate, inherently modern, and could be shared by the viewer: "In enjoying realistic pictures of his surroundings as a spectacle of traffic and changing atmospheres, the cultivated rentier was experiencing in its phenomenal aspect that mobility of the environment, the market and of industry to which he owed his income and freedom."[67]

It took at least a generation for the full impact of Schapiro's critical thinking to be felt, but its influence was unmistakable. In his 1985 study, *The Painting of Modern Life: Paris in the Art of Manet and His Followers* (from which his essay here is excerpted), T. J. Clark traced the origins of his own methodology to Schapiro and described the few lines devoted to Impressionism in Schapiro's 1937 tract as still "the best things on the subject, simply because they suggest so tellingly that the form of the new art is inseparable from its content."[68] Likewise, Robert Herbert's body of scholarship (see, for example, chapter 1) focuses on the social and political perspectives inscribed in Impressionist painting, and Paul Tucker's numerous studies (as in chapter 10) set Monet's art against the backdrop of the sweeping social currents of his time. They represent just three of the prominent scholars who have continued to explore the significance to Impressionism of subject matter, social history, and modes of perception, as first outlined by Schapiro.

At the popular level, however, the reevaluation of Impressionism came from other perceptions. Ironically, perhaps, Monet's painting was "rediscovered" (and, to a lesser extent, Impressionism reexamined) by an interim coterie of American curators and critics who were seeking a heroic modernist canon for recent American art. In their view, the amorphous quality, mural-sized scale, and lush, painterly surfaces of Monet's ethereal, late canvases made them especially promising as formal antecedents for the Abstract Expressionist painting that had burst onto the New York art scene in the late 1940s and transformed the city into the new hub of avant-garde art.[69] This new American interest in Monet's late work—which soon spread to France and helped to dislodge a longstanding preference for Cubist-derived abstraction—may also have been precipitated in part by the French painter and former Surrealist André Masson, who had lived in the United States during the war and promoted just such a reappraisal in his seminal essay of 1952, "Monet le fondateur."[70] Declaring famously that the Orangerie was "the Sistine Chapel of Impressionism" and "one of the peaks of French genius," Masson urged French painters to explore the possibilities Monet's late work offered. However, as Michael Leja and other scholars have shown, some American critics believed American painters were far ahead of the game.[71] It was indeed through the lens of Abstract Expressionist painting that esteem for Monet's art and especially his late painting was revived, allowing this work to be historically repositioned as a fountainhead for postwar American abstraction. When, in 1955, the Museum of Modern Art purchased one of the late *Waterlilies* panels and cited its importance "for the young abstract painters of our mid-century," the new genealogy seemed indisputable.[72] As Hilton Kramer would remark the following year, Monet's name "has now replaced that of Cézanne on the lips of many painters. . . . The process of reconstructing Monet into an avant-garde master of heroic dimensions is now in full swing."[73] New takes on the earlier formalist and symbolist readings of Monet's art, and of Impressionism in general, further redefined the critical discourse.

Throughout the 1950s, American interest in Impressionism became increasingly palpable. The publication in 1946 of John Rewald's *History of Impressionism*, which substantially enlarged on earlier monographs on the movement and included a wealth of fresh documentary and illustrated material, provided a crucial backdrop for popular and scholarly attention. A series of important American exhibitions of the work of Camille Pissarro, Monet, Renoir, and the Impressionist-influenced Nabi painters Bonnard and Edouard Vuillard, as well as major purchases of Impressionist masterpieces by American private collectors and museums, further encouraged a widespread reconsideration of Impressionism and its legacy.[74]

Clement Greenberg and William Seitz were key forces among the many critics helping to reshape one landscape in the context of another. Originally, in the early and mid-1940s, Greenberg voiced his preference for Cubist-inspired abstraction, but this slowly gave way to a taste for its antithesis, the chromatic-field branch of Abstract Expressionism he identified with the work of Clyfford Still, Barnett Newman, and Mark Rothko and traced back to the influence of Impressionism.[75] Greenberg's valuation of Monet's art also came full circle. Writing in 1945, the critic described Monet as an artist who "in his last period offered the mere texture of color as adequate form in painting . . . [even though] his design disintegrated progressively and his color thinned out and lost its juice."[76] But by 1955, Greenberg heralded the essence of Monet's late painting as far more radical than the Cubist legacy and admitted: "Recently . . . some of the late Monets began to assume a unity and power they never had before."[77] A committed formalist, Greenberg underscored how, in his view, Monet's two-dimensional images and horizontal formats—in his late *Waterlilies*, for example—had allowed purely formal values to triumph over nature in his art and thus had stylistic affinities with the chromatic-field painters. Later, the art historian William Rubin posited an even closer connection, arguing that Impressionism's influence could be found even on the dripped surfaces of Jackson Pollock's canvases.[78] Another scholar and critic who allied himself with this view was Leo Steinberg. In 1956 he lauded the "spiritual courage" and marveled at the infinite, flattened space of MoMA's newly purchased Monet canvas.[79] A decade later, Steinberg returned to the subject, suggesting the *Waterlilies* as an important precedent for the concept of the "flatbed picture plane" as embodied in the 1950s combines of Robert Rauschenberg.[80]

Just as the debate about Impressionism's "modern" and classical character had polarized nineteenth-century critics, not all contemporary painters and critical interpreters agreed with Greenberg. Deploring the theoretical paternity Greenberg and his disciples had structured for Abstract Expressionism, some opponents pointed to this group's refusal to address the role of Surrealism and other influences on the new painting, and they noted that few of the original New York group had direct access to Monet's late work during their formative years.[81] Still, it was Greenberg's revised assessment of Monet's achievement and influence that held sway at the time, crucially altering the critical stature not only of Monet and Impressionism but of many of the Abstract Expressionists as well.[82]

While the art historian William Seitz (who called MoMA's purchase of the *Waterlilies* "clairvoyant") also argued for Monet's significance for later abstract painting, he situated Monet's art in a much broader continuum. For Seitz, a kind of abstraction that found its origins in a lyrical nature could be seen in works by not only Monet but also Wassily Kandinsky and Piet Mondrian as well as midcentury artists.[83] In contrast to Greenberg's emphasis on formalism, Seitz stressed the evocative, Symbolist elements he saw in Monet's art: the bleak solitude of some of his landscapes from the mid-1880s, the inner illumination of a Japanese footbridge that seemed to glow like a late painting by Rembrandt, the "life-rhythms" of his Orangerie paintings (fig. I.6) that were all but stilled in their enveloping darkness. In the catalogue to the Monet show he curated for MoMA in 1960, Seitz codified his profoundly moving vision of Monet as a pantheistic poet of nature—a view that later found numerous adherents and was reflected in contemporaneous discussions of the so-called "Abstract Impressionists."[84] This group of painters, which included Philip Guston, Joan Mitchell, and Sam Francis, was distinguished from the Abstract Expressionist school by their paintings' evocations of calmer, meditative landscape elements. Their art was often likened by critics to the work of Monet, Pissarro, Sisley, and Renoir.

The Monet revival was only one of the more pronounced expressions of the fluctuating interest in Impressionist painting during the past half century. Throughout the later twentieth century, Impressionism continued to attract attention, surviving the vicissitudes of popular taste, shifting academic allegiances, and the art market. Certainly, it is fascinating to discover how Impressionism could be employed as an established canon to validate the vanguard art of a new, French (and transatlantic) style. But it seems more significant that even more than a century after its bold arrival on the precipitous stage of modern French painting, Impressionism continues to inspire a richly divergent critical discourse, one that is still evolving, as the essays assembled in this volume demonstrate.

Notes

1. For discussions of Positivism and Impressionism, see Norma Broude, *Impressionism: A Feminist Reading* (New York, 1991); Richard Shiff, *Cézanne and the End of Impressionism* (Chicago, 1984), 13; see also Meyer Schapiro, "The Concept of Impressionism," in *Impressionism, Reflections, and Perceptions* (New York, 1997), 21–42; and James Rubin, *Impressionism* (London, 1999), chap. 1.
2. See, for example, the discussion of Impressionism in James D. Herbert's *Fauve Painting: The Making of Cultural Politics* (New Haven, 1992); Kenneth E. Silver, *Esprit de Corps: The Art of the Parisian Avant-Garde and the First World War* (Princeton, 1989); Christopher Green, *Cubism and Its Enemies: Modern Movements and Reactions in French Art, 1916–1928* (New Haven, 1987); and Romy Golan, *Modernity and Nostalgia: Art and Politics in France between the Wars* (New Haven, 1995). For the extensive literature on Impressionism, Monet, and postwar painting in the United States, see notes 69, 71–84 below.
3. Jules-Antoine Castagnary, "Salon des Refusés" (1863), in *Salons (1857–1879)* (Paris, 1892), vol. 1.
4. Richard Shiff, "The End of Impressionism," in Charles Moffett et al., *The New Painting: Impressionism, 1874–1886*, exh. cat. (San Francisco: Fine Arts Museums of San Francisco, 1986), 61–89. See also Shiff's earlier version, "The End of Impressionism: A Study in Theories of Artistic Expression," *Art Quarterly*, new series, 1 (Autumn 1978): 338–78, and his expanded discussion in *Cézanne and the End of Impressionism*.
5. Louis Leroy, "L'Exposition des impressionnistes," *Le Charivari*, 25 April 1874, 79–80; reprinted in Ruth Berson, ed., *The New Painting: Impressionism 1874–1886: Documentation*, vol. 1: *Reviews* (San Francisco: Fine Arts Museums of San Francisco, 1996), 25–26.
6. Jules-Antoine Castagnary, "L'Exposition du boulevard des Capucines: Les Impressionnistes," *Le Siècle*, 29 April 1874; quoted by Shiff, *Cézanne and the End of Impressionism*, 3.
7. On this aspect of Zola's critical reaction to Impressionism, and his related, famous quotation that a work of art is "a bit of nature seen through a temperament," see Shiff, *Cézanne and the End of Impressionism*, 88–89, 189, 260 n. 73.
8. Castagnary, "L'Exposition," 265; quoted in Shiff, *Cézanne and the End of Impressionism*, 4, 232 n. 8.
9. Félix Fénéon, "Le Néo-Impressionnisme," *Art moderne* 7 (1 May 1887): 139; quoted and discussed by Robert Herbert in "Impressionism, Originality, and Laissez-Faire," *Radical History Review* 38 (1987): 7 (reprinted as chapter 1 in this volume).
10. A. Aurier, "Les Peintres symbolists" (1892); quoted by Shiff, "The End of Impressionism," 63.

    In *Cézanne and the End of Impressionism*, Shiff also discusses Aurier's extension of Zola's awareness of the subjective element in Impressionism and quotes him further on this: "In sum, for Aurier, impressionism amounted to the 'translation of instantaneous sensation, with all the distortions of a rapid subjective synthesis.'" (37–38, 189). Recognition in the 1890s of Symbolist qualities in Monet's art has also been discussed by Steven Z. Levine in *Monet and His Critics* (New York, 1976); Grace Seiberling in *Monet's Series* (New York, 1981); and, to a lesser degree, by Robert Goldwater in his *Symbolism* (New York, 1979).

11. G. Geoffroy, "Les Meules de Claude Monet," *La Vie artistique*, no. 1 (1 May 1891): 26–29.
12. M. Denis, "Le Salon du Champ-de-Mars; L'Exposition de Renoir," *Revue blanche* (25 June 1892), reprinted in *Théories, 1890–1910: Du symbolism et de Gauguin vers un nouvel ordre classique* (Paris: Rouart and Watelin, 1920 [1st ed. 1912]), 19; cited and discussed by Shiff, *Cézanne and the End of Impressionism*, 8, 235 n. 30.
13. Monet may also have been offered the Légion d'Honneur and turned it down: on this, and the international repute of Monet and the Impressionists c. 1900, see Paul Tucker, "The Revolution in the Garden: Monet in the Twentieth Century," in Tucker et al., *Monet in the 20th Century*, exh. cat. (London: Royal Academy of Arts; Boston: Museum of Fine Arts, 1998), 14–15, 285 n. 1.
14. Broude, *Impressionism: A Feminist Reading*.
15. The Nationalists' drive to secure for French culture an antique heritage (and its effect on Fauvist painting) has been discussed extensively by J. Herbert, *Fauve Painting*, 9–14, 112–45. The literature on this subject is immense, however. For a more recent study of the Nationalist movement and its effect on late nineteenth- and early twentieth-century painting, see Margaret Werth, *The Joy of Life: The Idyllic in French Art, circa 1900* (Berkeley, 2002).
16. J. Herbert, *Fauve Painting*, 9.
17. C. Mauclair, *L'Impressionnisme: Son Histoire, son esthétique, ses maîtres* (Paris, 1904), 134; cited by J. Herbert, *Fauve Painting*, 186 n. 20. Herbert further cites Mauclair's "De Fragonard à Renoir (Une Leçon de nationalisme picturale)," *Revue bleue*, 5th series, 2 (9 July 1904). The literature on nineteenth-century and early twentieth-century revivals and recastings of the Rococo is also quite extensive; see especially D. L. Silverman, *Art Nouveau in Fin-de-siècle France* (Berkeley, 1989).
18. C. Mauclair, "La Réaction nationaliste en art et l'ignorance de l'homme de letters," *La Revue*, no. 54 (15 January 1905): 162; J. Herbert, *Fauve Painting*, 127, 202 n. 48. For Mauclair's later complaints regarding Impressionism, which he would come to see as a dangerous negation of authority, see his *L'Avenir de France* (Paris, 1918), 518; discussed by Silver, *Esprit de Corps*, 210, and cited 444 n. 40.
19. For the fullest discussion of the Dreyfus Affair and its reflection in art, see Norman L. Kleeblatt, ed., *The Dreyfus Affair: Art, Truth, and Justice* (Berkeley, 1987). It is also discussed in specific relation to Monet's late career in Tucker, "Revolution in the Garden," 20–23.
20. J. Herbert, *Fauve Painting*, 9 ff.
21. "The impressionist painters, especially Monet and Sisley, had delicate sensations, quite close to each other: as a result their canvases all look alike." From Matisse's "Notes du'un peintre," *La Grande Revue* 52, no. 24 (25 December 1908): 731–45; translated in Jack Flam, *Matisse on Art* (Berkeley, 1995), 39; Georges Lanoë on Monet's painting in *Histoire de l'école française de paysage depuis Chintreuil jusqu'à 1900* (Nantes, 1905), 290; cited by J. Herbert, *Fauve Painting*, 186 n. 25.
22. On the wartime extension of the term "Romanticism" into descriptions of late nineteenth-century art and its implications, see Silver, *Esprit de Corps*, 210 ff.
23. A. Lhote, "Totalisme," *L'Elan*, no. 9 (February 1916): 3–4; quoted by Silver, *Esprit de Corps*, 210, 444 n. 38.
24. As Silver notes, "The art of Richard Wagner as well as the French cult of Wagner symbolized for many nationalists the total domination of France by Germany since the time of the Franco-Prussian war. . . . We already know that Wagnerian aesthetics were considered anathema to the French precisely because, in the wake of 1870, their impact had been so great. Wagner's French popularity was the proof of the power of those noxious later-Romantic vapors" (ibid., 22, 208). For an earlier, extended discussion of Wagnerism, see David Large and William Weber, eds., *Wagnerism in European Culture and Politics* (Ithaca, 1984).
25. Silver, *Esprit de Corps*, 214.
26. E. Bernard, "Paul Cézanne," *L'Occident* 6, no. 32 (July 1904): 17–30; M. Denis, "Cézanne," *L'Occident* 12, no. 41 (September 1907); reprinted in Denis, *Théories*, 245–61.
27. Bernard's and Denis's writings and formulations of Cézanne's classicism have been studied extensively by Shiff in *Cézanne and the End of Impressionism*. For a study of the "naturalistic classicism" another writer, the Provençal poet Joachim Gasquet, attributed to Cézanne, see Shiff's introduction to *Joachim Gasquet's Cézanne: A Memoir with Conversations* (New York, 1991), 15–24.
28. C. F. Ramuz, *L'Exemple de Cézanne, suivi de pages sur Cézanne* (Lausanne, 1951); this is noted by Lionello Venturi in *Cézanne* (New York, 1978), where he wrote,

"In his conviction that Cézanne was a classicist and traditionalist, Ramuz reflects the taste of his time" (47).

29. This is discussed at length by James Herbert in *Paris 1937: Worlds on Exhibition* (Ithaca, 1998), 99 ff.

30. Silver, *Esprit de Corps*, 337. The author quotes Gustave Coquiot's telling postwar description of Seurat's landscapes:

> Seurat gives us a solemn image of a naked landscape, which has come into the world with no gnashing of teeth, with no devastation, with no barrel-organ obbligato. Everything there is well established for living: very straight white walls, a very rigid chimney; and above all, the wasteland only waits—indifferent—for an industrialist to build a vast shed for work and production. . . . This, then, is a graphic definition of style! [*Seurat* (Paris, 1923), 195–96.]

31. This is discussed by Silver, *Esprit de Corps*, 340–44. See also R. Herbert's discussions of Léger's new art of the 1920s in *Léger's "Le Grand Déjeuner,"* exh. cat. (Minneapolis, 1980), 9–37; and "Léger, the Renaissance and 'Primitivism,'" in *Hommage à Michael Laclotte* (Paris, 1994), 642–47. Both are reprinted in R. Herbert, *From Millet to Léger: Essays in Social Art History* (New Haven, 2002).

32. J. Meier-Graefe, *Entwicklungsgeschichte der modernen Kunst: Ein Beitrag zur modernen Ästhetik*, 3 vols. (Stuttgart, 1904); English edition: *Modern Art, Being a Contribution to a New System of Aesthetics* (London, 1908).

33. On Fry's reassessment of Seurat, see C. Green, *Art Made Modern: Roger Fry's Vision of Art* (London, 1999), 208–10.

34. Elizabeth Prettejohn, "Out of the Nineteenth Century: Roger Fry's Early Art Criticism, 1900–1906," in ibid., 37–38. See also Shiff's discussions of Denis's influence on Fry and of Fry's own vision of Cézanne's classicism in *Cézanne and the End of Impressionism*, 143–52.

35. A. Lhote, "Tradition et troisième dimension," *La Nouvelle Revue française* 15, no. 85 (1 October 1920): 620; quoted (and discussed) in C. Green, *Cubism and Its Enemies: Modern Movements and Reactions in French Art, 1916–1928* (New Haven, 1987), 168 ff., 311 n. 4.

36. Quoted (without original source indicated) by P. Pool, "Picasso's Neo-Classicism: Second Period, 1917–1925," *Apollo* 85, no. 61 (March 1987): 200–202; and cited by Silver, *Esprit de Corps*, 211, 444 n. 44.

37. A recent discussion of this phenomenon can be found in Mark Antliff and Patricia Leighten, *Cubism and Culture* (London, 2001), 111 ff., where the authors describe both the Celtic (or Gothic) and Latin (or classical) origins claimed for the Cubist movement before 1914 by its first historians in a markedly politicized discourse.

38. Flam, *Matisse on Art*, 5; see also Matisse's interview in 1919 with Ragner Hope (Flam, 75–76), in which the artist discusses the return to his recent art of some characteristics from his Impressionist-influenced period. On "the odd sparkle of Neo-Impressionist painting" in Picasso's and Braque's art from 1914 to 1917, see Green, *Cubism and Its Enemies*, 176.

39. Matisse, "Notes d'un peintre" (1908); quoted in Flam, *Matisse on Art*, 39.

40. R. Golan, "France Revisited: Landscape as *Lieu de Mémoire*," in *Modernity and Nostalgia*, 1–17.

41. Ibid., 2–3, and fig. 2. Silver (*Esprit de Corps*, 237–38) also discusses the postwar figural art and "thorough perusal of *la grande tradition*" of La Fresnaye, "whose actual uses of the artistic past seem to have begun in earnest in Tours, when he was hospitalized there at the very end of the war in October 1918, after having been gassed in the trenches."

42. Florent Fels, *Monet* (Paris, 1925), 5; quoted in Golan, *Modernity and Nostalgia*, 40, and cited 176 n. 77.

43. A. Lhote (review of Monet's show at the Galerie Paul Rosenberg), *La Nouvelle Revue française* (1919): 810; quoted in Golan, *Modernity and Nostalgia*, 40, and cited 176 n. 77.

44. Picasso acquired a painting entitled *Woman Reading* and a large *Bather Seated in a Landscape*. On these and also Matisse's acquisition, see Elizabeth Cowling et al., *Matisse Picasso*, exh. cat. (London: Tate Modern, 2002), 191–93.

45. Théodore Duret and Walter Halvorsen, *Den Franske Udstilling (Corot à Matisse)*, exh. cat. (Oslo: Kunstnerforbundet, 1918), with texts by Matisse on Renoir and Cézanne; quoted in *Matisse Picasso*, 192. See also Jed Perl's discussion of Matisse's odalisques in *Paris without End: On French Art Since World War I* (San Francisco, 1988), 13–18. Matisse also visited Monet in spring 1917. Paul Tucker suggests that his memory of Monet's Giverny garden may have helped to shape the richly painted, luxuriant view of nature glimpsed out the window in Matisse's *The Music Lesson* (Barnes Foundation), of 1917 ("Revolution in the Garden," 71).

46. This is discussed at length in Michael Fitzgerald, *Making Modernism: Picasso and the Creation of the Market for Twentieth-Century Art* (New York, 1995), 99–107. On the rediscovery of Ingres by Picasso, Matisse, and Roger de la Fresnaye among others, see Silver, *Esprit de Corps*, 139–40, 244–46, 252, 258, and fig. 169.

47. Fitzgerald, *Making Modernism*, 99–100 and fig. 36 (Musée Picasso, Paris).

48. Green, *Cubism and Its Enemies*, 56 and fig. 71. Silver (*Esprit de Corps*, 291–94), however, suggests a wide range of classicizing influences for Braque's series of *Canephores*, including Picasso's recent work, Michelangelo's Sistine Sibyls, and the recent sculpture of Antoine Bourdelle.
49. Golan specifically ties the new currency of images of "women as nature" to the widespread fears in postwar France regarding a decline in the population and new hope for the nation's rebirth and growth (*Modernity and Nostalgia*, 17–21).
50. Ibid., 45.
51. Green, *Cubism and Its Enemies*, 57.
52. This is noted in William Rubin's *Dada, Surrealism and Their Heritage*, exh. cat. (New York: MoMA, 1968), 193 n. 8; and documented in *René Magritte: Catalogue Raisonné*, ed. D. Sylvester, vol. 2 (London, 1993), 91 ff.; and in *CNAC Archives* (Paris, 1972), no. 7. See also, for example, no. 521 in the catalogue raisonné, Magritte's *Le Traite de la lumière* of 1943, based on Renoir's *Les Grandes Baigneuses* of c. 1918–19 (Musée d'Orsay, Paris).
53. W. George, "Robert Delaunay et le triomphe de la couleur," *La Vie des lettres* (August 1922): 332; quoted in Green, *Cubism and Its Enemies*, 83, and cited 306 n. 56.
54. This is discussed in R. Golan, "From Fin de Siècle to Vichy: The Cultural Hygenics of Camille (Faust) Mauclair," in *The Jew in the Text: Modernity and the Construction of Identity*, ed. Linda Nochlin and Tamar Garb (London, 1995), 167 ff.
55. R. Golan, "The *Ecole Française* vs. the *Ecole de Paris:* The Debate about the Status of Jewish Artists in Paris between the Wars," in *The Circle of Montparnasse: Jewish Artists in Paris, 1905–1945*, exh. cat., ed. C. Green (New York: Jewish Museum, 1985), 83.
56. L. Vauxcelles (under the pseudonym Pinturicchio), "Le carnet des ateliers," *Le Carnet de la semaine* (1925), file 5, Fonds Vauxcelles; quoted in Golan, "From Fin de Siècle," 167, and cited 319 n. 33.
57. G. Clemenceau, *Les Nymphéas* (Paris, 1928).
58. On their critical reception by older critics, see Tucker, "Revolution in the Garden," 85, 290 n. 278.
59. Ibid., 85.
60. On this exhibit, the fate of Monet's Orangerie panels, and his critical stature in this period, see R. Golan, "Oceanic Sensations: Monet's *Grandes Decorations* and Mural Painting in France from 1927 to 1952," in Tucker et al., *Monet in the 20th Century*, 86–97.
61. A. Benoit, "Alexandre Benoit réfléchit" (1931); quoted in Golan, "Oceanic Sensations," 92, and cited 290 n. 29.
62. Fry papers in Modern Archive, King's College Library, University of Cambridge, 1/117; quoted in Green, *Art Made Modern*, 178.
63. M. Schapiro, "Matisse and Abstraction: A Review of the Retrospective Exhibition of Matisse at the Museum of Modern Art, New York; November 1931," *Androcles* 1, no. 1 (February 1932): 21–36.
64. Ibid., 29.
65. P. Francastel, *L'Impressionnisme: Les Origines de la peinture moderne de Monet à Gauguin* (Paris, 1937), 92–94; Shiff, *Cézanne*, 237 n. 43.
66. M. Schapiro, "The Nature of Abstract Art," *Marxist Quarterly* 1, no. 1 (1937): 8.
67. Ibid., 8.
68. T. J. Clark, *The Painting of Modern Life: Paris in the Art of Manet and His Followers* (New York, 1985), 5.
69. The extensive early literature on this is discussed by Irving Sandler in *The New York School: The Painters and Sculptors of the Fifties* (New York, 1978), 52–57, and notes 19–21. See also Sandler's "The Influence of Impressionism on Jackson Pollock and His Contemporaries," *Arts* 53, no. 7 (March 1979): 110–11. And even very recent writers have added to this body of literature. See, for example, Robert Storr, "A Piece of the Action," especially 38 and 68 n. 24, and Rosalind Krauss, "The Crisis of the Easel Picture," both in *Jackson Pollock: New Approaches*, ed. K. Varnedoe and P. Karmel (New York, 1998).
70. A. Masson, "Monet le fondateur," *Verve* 7, nos. 27/28 (December 1952): 68–70.
71. M. Leja, "The Monet Revival and New York School Abstraction," in Tucker et al., *Monet in the 20th Century*, 98–108, 291–93.
72. Quoted by Leja from a number of MoMA documents, including press releases announcing the acquisition (101 and nn. 19–20).
73. H. Kramer, "Month in Review," *Arts* 31, no. 2 (November 1956): 52.
74. On this, see especially Sandler, *New York School*, 52.
75. For a similar viewpoint, see Robert Rosenblum's discussion of Impressionism's "unexpected analogies to recent developments" in "Varieties of Impressionism," *Art Digest* 29, no. 1 (1 October 1954): 7.
76. C. Greenberg, "Art," *The Nation* 160, no. 18 (5 May 1945): 526; quoted in I. Sandler, *The Triumph of American Painting* (New York, 1970), 272.
77. C. Greenberg, "'American-Type' Painting," *Partisan Review* 22, no. 2 (Spring 1955): 192–94.
78. W. Rubin, "Jackson Pollock and the Modern Tradition," *Artforum* 5, no. 6 (February 1967): 14–22.
79. L. Steinberg, "Month in Review," *Arts* 30, no. 5 (Feb-

ruary 1956): 46–48; reprinted as "Monet's *Waterlilies*" in L. Steinberg, *Other Criteria* (New York, 1972), 235–39.

80. L. Steinberg, "Other Criteria," based on a lecture given at MoMA (March 1952); reprinted in Steinberg, *Other Criteria*, 55–91; see especially 85.
81. In his discussion cited above (note 78), Rubin would include Surrealist influences among others, including late Monet, in Pollock's early art, but many of the painters argued against the influence of Monet and Impressionism on their work. On this, and especially on Barnett Newman's often misrepresented discussion of Monet, see Leja, "Monet Revival," 101–2. Also, see W. Seitz, "The Relevance of Impressionism," *Art News* 67, no. 9 (January 1969), where the author wrote, "Aside from its powerfully original components, it is now recognized that Abstract Expressionism was more than anything else a meeting of Surrealist imagery and automatism with Cubist form. This view must be augmented in retrospect to recognize the Impressionist component of the mixed currents to which the New York School painters responded, either in sympathy or in self-defense" (58); cited in Sandler, *Triumph of American Painting*, 57 n. 21.
82. On this, see Leja, "Monet Revival," 102.
83. W. Seitz, "Monet and Abstract Painting," *Art Journal* 16, no. 1 (1956): 34–46.
84. W. Seitz, *Claude Monet: Seasons and Moments*, exh. cat. (New York: MoMA, 1960). On this new "branch" of the New York School, see especially Louis Finkelstein, "New Look: Abstraction-Impressionism," *Art News* 55, no. 1 (March 1956): 36–39, 66–68.

PART ONE

Background Studies

Economic Landscapes and Exhibition Strategies

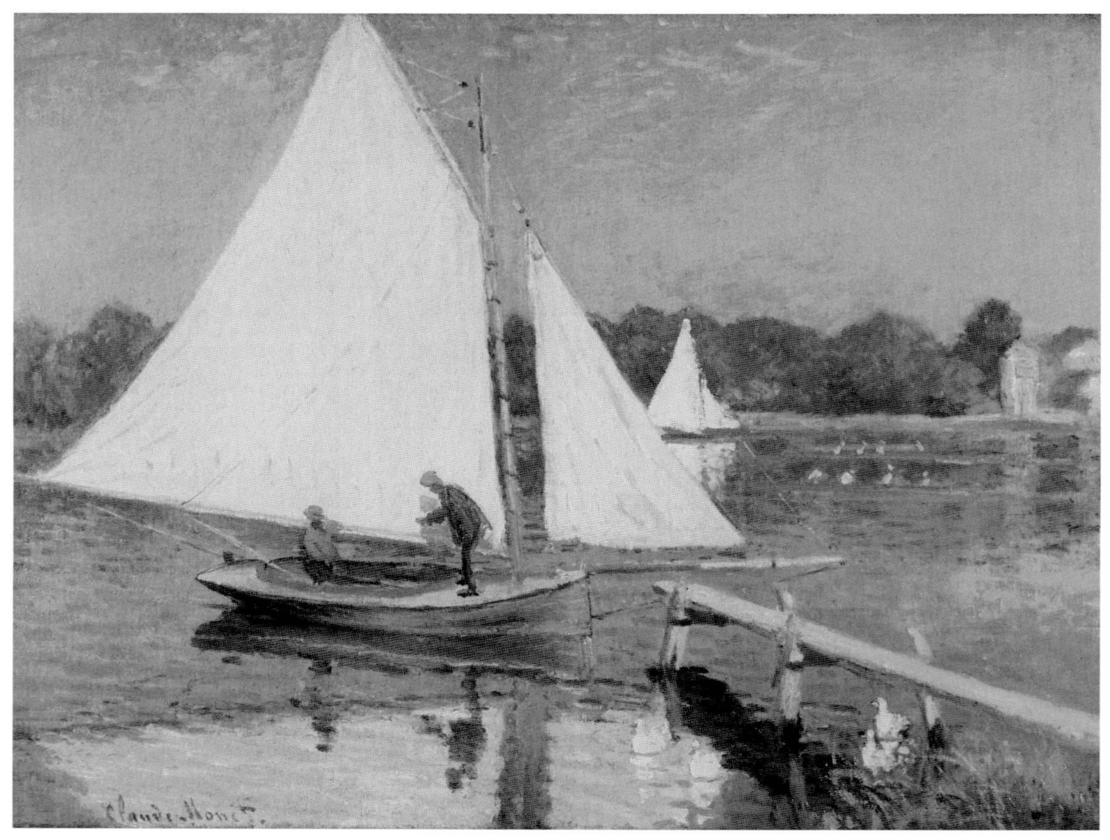

FIGURE I.1. Claude Monet, *Sailing at Argenteuil*, c. 1874. Private collection. Photo: The Bridgeman Art Library.

1

Impressionism, Originality, and Laissez-Faire

ROBERT L. HERBERT

WITH THE ADVENT of Symbolism in the late 1880s, and the growth of an antinaturalist current in the paintings of younger artists (Seurat, Van Gogh, Gauguin), Impressionist art came to be regarded as an unthinking form of naturalism. The Symbolist critics praised the new painters by claiming that their art was rich in intellectual, expressive, and decorative ideas, as opposed to Impressionism which, they believed, merely added a heightened color sense to the old Renaissance tradition of verisimilitude. Impressionist naturalism was dismissed by Félix Fénéon, Seurat's chief defender, in these derisive terms:

> The spectacle of the heavens, the water, greenery, varies from moment to moment, professed the first Impressionists. To imprint one of these fugitive appearances on the retina was their goal. Thus arose the necessity to paint a landscape in one séance and a tendency to make nature grimace in order to prove that the moment was unique and that one would never again see it.[1]

This view became commonplace in the twentieth century, and until the 1940s it was generally believed that in their mature work Morisot, Degas, Monet, Renoir, Cassatt, and Manet were depicting their own society without analyzing it. They enjoyed theaters and promenades in the country and simply represented these innocent pleasures. Praise for them therefore fell not on their images of contemporary life, but on their innovations in color, brushwork, and other aspects of "pure painting," so congenial to the era of abstraction, given the premium it has placed on the formal components of painting.

Since the 1940s this view has been discredited, and scholars have expanded the range of issues eligible for analysis to include complicated interrelationships among painting, literature, and the history of Paris from 1848 to the 1880s.[2] We now know that Impressionism was not a simple-minded representation of color-light, and we are constantly reminded of the painters' innovations, for which the words "radical" and "revolutionary" are frequently used (especially by corporate sponsors of the recent spate of "blockbuster" Impressionist exhibitions). We have learned that Impressionism really was born of adversity and miscomprehension; its new brushwork, color, and spatial organization were subversive; its devotion to the immediate present was profoundly shocking; its subjects and attitudes undermined the whole concept of what art was, what art schools should teach, and how art exhibitions should be organized.

All this is well worth pointing to, but were the Impressionists radicals? On the surface of it, no. Caillebotte, Degas, Manet, and Morisot were upper-class Parisians who can readily be assimilated with their peers, and who demonstrated no wish to make profound alterations of their society. Monet was the upstart son of a shopkeeper, eager to be accepted, and Renoir, the only Impressionist of artisan-class origins, was critical of the ruthlessness of urban-industrial society, but wanted to return to a premodern patrician order.[3] Pissarro was the only political radical among the painters, but he remains a special case, and he dealt with rural life, not with the urban and suburban society the others preferred.

What is needed in order to assess the label "radical" are inquiries along new lines. Further investigation of the artists' subjects, especially their preference for themes of leisure and entertainment, should be revealing.[4] Systematic study of the artists' clients and dealers, not yet undertaken, would certainly be rewarding. Many of their early patrons, for example, were not long-established members of high society, but wielders of new money: the financier Ernest May, the banker Albert Hecht, the retailer and speculator Ernest Hoschedé, the renowned baritone Jean-Baptiste Faure. The links between the new money and the new painting are doubtless there, but will remain speculative until someone does the work. In addition to these aspects of social history, we should look more deeply into the often discussed issues of the "caught moment," the hedonistic indulgence in natural light and out-of-doors living, the pronounced individualism of the painters, and their concern for originality. This chapter concentrates on the last two of these.[5]

The Impressionists' devotion to contemporary phenomena is now recognized as one of the key elements of their art. They looked to Paris and its suburbs for most of their subjects; even when they turned to the countryside, they represented it as though it were newly seen, free of the literary, historical, and moral overlays that had characterized the work of the preceding generation. They dealt in what are, after all, slight events in the history of humankind, mere ephemeral moments seized from the pleasure of leisure-time activities. Not only did they turn toward present-day subjects, they also emphasized features that pointed to the immediate and the momentary. There are many ways to represent a moored sailboat or a ballet rehearsal, but Monet and Degas used broken brushwork, indistinct contours, bright colors, and striking compositional geometry to induce in the viewer a sense of the spontaneous, the unresolved, that which is just now being seen. Impressionism, wrote César Graña,

> assumes a world in which *moments* can exist as total units of experience: where self-feeling, as well as the perception of others, has a new swiftness and, within that, a new, flickering poignancy; where the ephemeral and the unguarded can be memorable and must be followed and scanned by the painter with a flashing perceptivity of his own.[6]

Graña's words point to the combination of external observation and subjectivity that marked Impressionism. When the painters concentrated upon the illusion of what could be seen in the flash of a moment, they seemed to reduce experience to the self, unsupported by references to other moments, to other experiences. This was upsetting to many, for the viewer, required to concentrate on this one moment, was denied contact with other moments—with memory, in effect.

Denial of memory meant denial of history, a pervasive consequence of the Impressionists' orientation. "History" was not simply the discarded subjects of earlier painting, but the means by which they were rendered, particularly the structure of light and dark that gave conventional painting the satisfactory illusion of three dimensions. The exaltation of bright color and patchy brushwork was the Impressionists' way of presenting what one could see, without recourse to what one "knows" by virtue of traditional artistic training. This was only an *apparent* spontaneity, for Impressionism was just as artfully constructed as earlier painting. However, to many observers, then and later, the concentration on spontaneous vision and the absence of memory-trained techniques condemned the Impressionists to a superficial indulgence in pleasures. Max Friedländer, gifted historian of Lowlands art, could not grant profundity to Impressionism because he believed that seeing was not just looking with the eyes, but with the judgments provided by memory and history:

> The man who knows most sees most; he sees more than is actually visible to him in a given instant and from a given standpoint. The Impressionists, however, were at pains to forget what they knew so as to notice only what fell within their field of vision. . . .
>
> The Impressionists, deliberately forgoing all criticism and judgment in respect of the phenomenal world, appealing neither to sentiment nor to sense of humor, absorbing the prismatic glitter of things with a positive neutrality, mark the visual art off from the art of poetry, from history, from satire, as also from the affecting, entertaining, instructive or informative type of narrative. The picture is no longer the exemplar of an idea, does not point beyond the visible, strikes us as something unique, individual, like a portrait.[7]

For this reason, Friedländer denied the label "genre" to Impressionism. It lacked the moral ideas that he required for his definition. Similarly, Graña, while admiring the Impressionists, said that they cannot be called "naturalistic" because their art is one of "amiable lyricism" that mirrors but does not interpret contemporary life.[8]

The Impressionists' disavowal of memory and of history was one symptom of the gulf between present and past that opened ever wider with the spread of the urban-industrial revolution. History, mythology, and religion, for centuries the chief points of reference for painting, were discarded with surprising rapidity during the third quarter of the nineteenth century, first by the Barbizon artists in the second halves of their careers, then by the Impressionists (after youthful essays in traditional subjects). An education in Greek and Latin, in Homer and Virgil, and in the Bible had little real function for the entrepreneurs of industrial capitalism: "If you're so smart, why ain't you rich?" These premodern subjects, which had been attached to monarchy, nobility, and theocracy, eventually ceased to underpin public education (private schools, out of class solidarity, retained the old curriculum for much longer). The Impressionists were ahead of most of their contemporaries when they denounced the Academy and its *retardataire* allegiance to those traditional sources.

To uproot the past was no easy step for the painters to take, and this is evident when we reflect on the upheavals it caused. Manet's mocking of history in his *Déjeuner sur l'herbe* and *Olympia* (both Musée d'Orsay, Paris), as well as in other pictures of the 1860s, was linked to his defiance of the government's guardians of history—the directors of fine arts, the Academy, the juries of official exhibitions. The other Impressionists did battle with the government by organizing their own exhibitions, a step which effectively, by the end of the century, demoted the Academy's shows to minor status, and set the pattern for twentieth-century exhibitions, so often sponsored by independent artists' societies. A number of the Impressionists had only perfunctory periods of training in the Ecole des Beaux-Arts, and their example led to its rapid decline, if we are to judge by the pattern of artists who dominated early modernism. Few of them studied in sanctioned ways, and by ignoring government exhibitions, prizes, and fellowships, rendered them obsolete. The whole world of official painting came tumbling down, at least as far as alert young artists were concerned.

Because they turned toward contemporary subjects, the Impressionists had to disavow tradition and its institutions—hence their constant demands for freedom. Critics close to them made a virtual litany of this demand. Manet's friend Théodore Duret wrote of all "true artists" that they

> are vigorous persons, profoundly original, most often obeying in their methods of production a kind of instinct and inherent natural strength. Let all these individuals develop instead of trying to restrict them, let them freely express the outstanding aspects of their nature. Everything that will contribute towards assuring the individual his freedom of action will contribute to the development of the artist.[9]

The Impressionists and their supporters in the press demanded freedom from the restraints of official art policies. In this context, the term "freedom" has political meaning, for it paralleled the freedom from prior restraints that entrepreneurs were pleading for. Duret's words (including the phrase "methods of production") could have served the cause of a Parisian businessman trying to market a product in the face of government restrictions that survived from an earlier era. Edmond Duranty, another friend of the Impressionists, after invoking the word "liberté" several times, used the famous economic phrase "laissez-faire, laissez-passer" to initiate a plea for freedom from "this bureaucracy of the mind, steeped in rules, that weighs on us in this country."[10]

Freedom, quite logically for the artists, was required both for the sake of producing their works (art historians recognize this) and for marketing them (most art historians avoid this). The laissez-faire market they fought for is the most obvious comparison with the commercial world. Having rebelled against the subjects of a prior age, they had excluded themselves from the patronage of government and church, and were forced to develop their own market. The role of private dealers greatly expanded in their era, and some of the painters, particularly Monet and Degas, were very clever in manipulating their markets. They played one dealer off another, learned various maneuvers to keep their prices up, and bypassed commercial galleries when they could reach clients directly. In December 1873 the Impressionists formed their own exhibition society, duly incorporated as a cooperative business, and began displaying their wares in rented quarters in the fashionable center of Paris.

Forced to seek their own outlets, the painters had to claim value for their product. This value was located in their originality, in the very way their works were produced. Their paintings were said to be the result of the creative individual working in freedom. Creativity, that is, was identified with the individual, not within the social, and originality was the precise locus of value. Originality in the business world was equated with invention, and it is revealing that both words are used repeatedly by the defenders of the Impressionists. Real artists, according to Duret, "are inventors, men who have an unusual character, an original way of feeling and, if they are painters, a touch, a sense of color, a way of drawing that are entirely personal." Their works are original because they do not imitate existing ones. They earn their way, furthermore, because they succeed "by painful labor, a tension of all their faculties, in giving form to their conceptions." And these forms are like other products whose originality guarantees their value: "new forms, original creations."[11]

By using the phrases "painful labor" and "original creations," Duret was crediting the Impressionists with two kinds of entrepreneurial virtue: hard, steady work and brilliant flashes of genius. These two values were often separated. Horatio Alger's boy heroes made it the hard way, with patience and dutiful attention to the boss's wishes. Victor Appleton's Tom Swift also made it by the end of each of his books, but it was invariably thanks to his remarkable inventive powers, such as building a giant searchlight in his garage. The Impressionists were more like Swift than like Alger's heroes, but Duret and other critics had to allay bourgeois fears by showing that genius was accompanied by hard work and skill.

The Impressionists' originality was based upon individuality and craftsmanship, and was therefore free of the monotonous effects of that unimaginative kind of work that emulates the perfectly finished product, that is, the industrial artifact. This product was equated with clever academic art, so that Duranty, in distinguishing the Impressionists from their imitators, again used the vocabulary of commerce. In France, he wrote, "the inventor disappears in favor of the one who takes out a patent on perfecting; virtuosity wins out over naïve awkwardness, and the vulgarizer absorbs the value of the man who has innovated."[12] The Impressionists' famous brushwork was cited constantly as proof of their "naïve awkwardness," of their honest and empirical response to nature, as distinct from the hated polish of conventional painting, where brushwork was suppressed, the smooth result constituting a sign of "skill." Mere polish in painting was equated with the despised values of the bourgeoisie, who confused skill with talent, and who valued mass production over the rare, imaginative, and hand-wrought piece.

What happened over the course of the nineteenth century was simply this: artists who remained within the sanctioned institutions of art did not have to cultivate very much originality (only enough to be noticed), because the system of prizes, government purchases, and church commissions gave them a living. The requirement was to conform enough to these institutions to guarantee continued subsidies and commissions—observing tradition was literally a way to make a living. How could artists outside this closed market earn their way? Like upstart businessmen, they had to develop a new product, and in the process they had to assert its newness, its originality. Their battles with tradition were a means of establishing this essential quality or originality that a few years later was translated into market value. "Radical" or "revolutionary" in relation to the dominant institutions, they were taken up at first by a handful of patrons, usually men of new fortunes, and therefore joined the advanced thrust of the rising bourgeoisie.[13] Their enemy was not the bourgeoisie as a whole, but its stodgiest representatives who were still mired in the past, whose protectionist attitudes thwarted progress. The painters, like other advanced entrepreneurs, had difficulty making their way at first, but this very difficulty was a sign of their originality, and a half-generation later (for most, when they reached their mid-forties) their originality was the very proof of their genius to a larger segment of the middle class, who then provided the income.

Thorstein Veblen, in *The Theory of the Leisure Class* (1899), offered an analysis of this phenomenon that should be applied to artistic originality:

> Hand labor is a more wasteful method of production; hence the goods turned out by this method are more serviceable for the purpose of pecuniary reputability; hence the marks of hand labor came to be honorific, and the goods which exhibit these marks take rank as of higher grade than the corresponding machine product. Commonly, if not invariably, the honorific marks of hand labor are certain imperfections and irregularities in the lines of the hand-wrought article. . . . The ground of the superiority of hand-wrought goods, therefore, is a certain margin of crudeness. This margin must never be so wide as to show bungling workmanship, since that would be evidence of low cost, nor so narrow as to suggest the ideal precision attained only by the machine, for that would be evidence of low cost.[14]

Veblen then went on to say that the "honorific" mark is not appreciated by the ordinary mortals who prefer the perfection of the machine-made, and therefore its appreciation is a way of distinguishing oneself from the common herd.

Originality and handcraft gave distinction and, eventually, great value to the Impressionists' paintings. They were not, therefore, radicals seeking the overthrow of their society, despite their flirtations with gypsies, urban itinerants, and other marginals. They were more like other aggressive members of the bourgeoisie, doing battle with outmoded institutions in order to push themselves and their culture in new directions. Nineteenth-century industrial society thrived on its critics, using them to lurch forward, to shed old ideas, painfully and awkwardly, in a process that bound together critic and target, each requiring the other.[15] The Impressionists were the vanguard of the bourgeoisie, not of any revolution. Of course it did not seem so at the time, not just because their work was new or "radical," but also because the world of entertainment and leisure that they favored was so opposed to the work ethic and the other moral underpinnings of the bourgeoisie.

From the vantage point of over a century later, it is easy to see this. Even so, historians have paid too little attention to the undercurrents flowing beneath the brilliant surfaces of Impressionist paintings. Their innovations have been largely seen in terms of style, and the social meanings of their forms and their subjects have remained too seldom explored. The history of Impressionism should be rewritten by integrating style and subject, individual and society. The whole history of modernism suffers still from formalism, including its latest manifestation, a trendy combination of semiotics and structuralism that gives a false veneer of newness, but that preserves the erroneous idea that art is somehow "pure," elevated above history into a realm of its own. Impressionism is a good place to start the necessary reevaluation; it has replaced Renaissance painting as the art most widely admired and most sought after, because it built the foundations for the experience of modern life as it is comprehended and given structure in visual form.

Notes

Originally published in *Radical History Review* 38 (1987): 7–15.

1. Félix Fénéon, "Le Néo-Impressionnisme," *Art moderne* 7 (1 May 1887): 139.
2. The key work in the revision of Impressionism is T. J. Clark's *The Painting of Modern Life: Paris in the Art of Manet and His Followers* (New York, 1985), a brilliant, original, and often tendentious interpretation (incorporating, amended, two influential earlier articles). My regret is that he pays insufficient attention to Degas, and little at all to Monet and Renoir. See also my *Impressionism: Art, Leisure, and Parisian Society* (New Haven, 1988).
3. See my *Nature's Workshop: Renoir's Writings on the Decorative Arts* (New Haven, 2000).
4. Among the rare studies of the art market in late nineteenth-century art are Nicholas Green, "Dealing in Temperaments: Economic Transformation of the Artistic Field in France during the Second Half of the Nineteenth Century," *Art History* 10 (March 1987): 59–75 [reprinted as chapter 2 in this volume], and Robert Jensen, *Marketing Modernism in Fin-de-siècle Europe* (Princeton, 1994).
5. Only after the original publication of this essay did I find Michel Melot's article "La Notion d'originalité et son importance dans la définition des objets d'art," in *Sociologie de l'art*, ed. Raymonde Moulin (Paris, 1986), 191–202. Melot's incisive article concentrates on the relation of the quantitative rarity of an object to "originality," demonstrating that its value as property lies behind metaphysical, aesthetic, and other considerations of the term.
6. César Graña, "Impressionism as an Urban Art Form," in *Fact and Symbol* (New York, 1971), 83–84. Welcome though this view was in 1971, it has been superseded by Clark's *Painting of Modern Life*. Clark embeds the idea of "flickering poignancy" in the social history of Haussmannian Paris, particularly well in his first chapter.
7. Max Friedländer, *Landscape, Portrait, Still-Life* (1949; repr. New York, 1963), 224–26.
8. Graña, "Impressionism," 74 and passim.
9. Théodore Duret, "Les Peintres français en 1867," cited in George H. Hamilton, *Manet and His Critics* (1954; repr. New York, 1969), 110.
10. Edmond Duranty, *La Nouvelle Peinture* (1876), ed. Marcel Guérin (Paris, 1946), 50–51.
11. Théodore Duret, "Edouard Manet," in his *Critique d'avant-garde* (Paris, 1885), 121–22. Richard Shiff, *Cézanne and the End of Impressionism* (Chicago, 1984), offers by far the most incisive analysis of the new marks and forms of Impressionism, and he deals extensively with the issues of originality in artistic processes. He limits his discussion to aesthetics, however, and does not incorporate social history.
12. Duranty, *Nouvelle Peinture*, 54.
13. See Albert Boime, "Entrepreneurial Patronage in Nineteenth-Century France," in *Enterprise and Entrepreneurs in Nineteenth- and Twentieth-Century*

France, ed. E. C. Carter, R. Forster, and J. N. Moody (Baltimore, 1976), 137–207.

14. Thorstein Veblen, *The Theory of the Leisure Class* (1899; repr., New York, 1934), 159–60.

15. In addition to Marx, this process has been studied by Georg Simmel, especially in his essay "Conflict," in *Georg Simmel on Individuality and Social Forms*, ed. Donald N. Levine (Chicago, 1971), 70–95. See also Siegfried Kracauer, *Orpheus in Paris: Offenbach and the Paris of His Time* (New York, 1938); Jerrold Siegel, *Bohemian Paris* (New York, 1986); and Green, "Dealing in Temperaments."

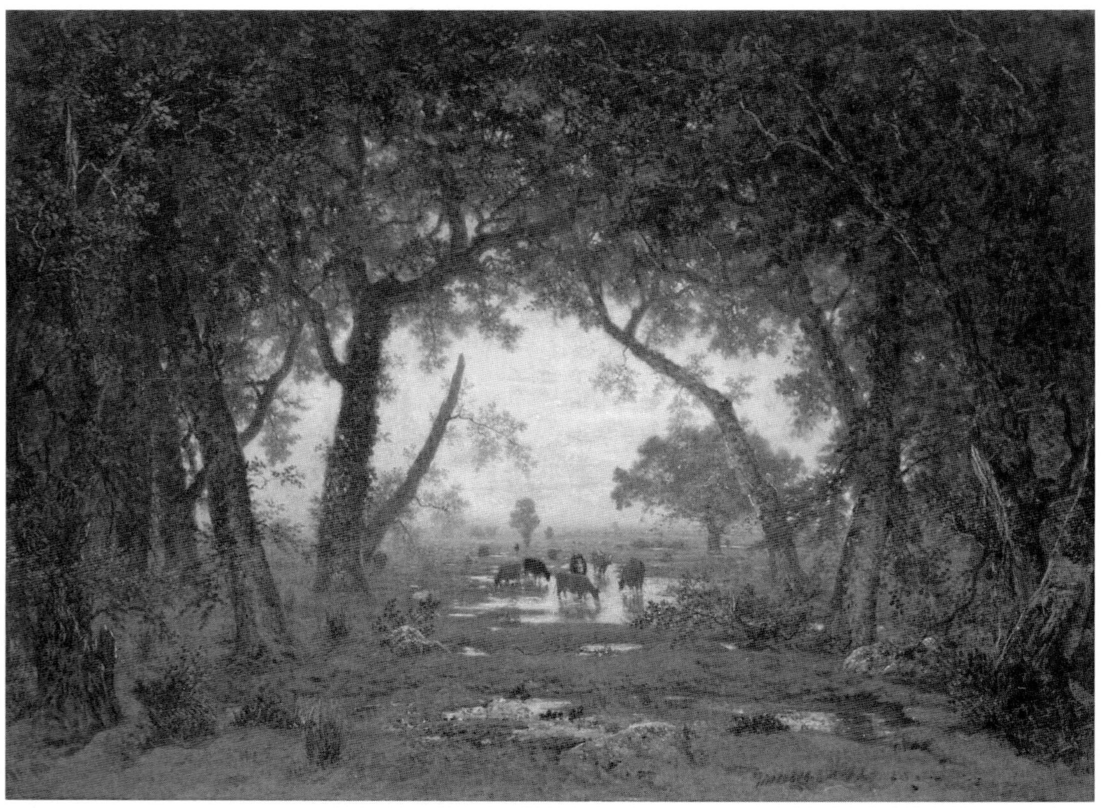

FIGURE 2.1. Pierre Etienne Théodore Rousseau, *Lisière de forêt: Effet de matin (The Forest at Fontainebleau: Morning)*, 1850. Reproduced by permission of the Trustees of the Wallace Collection, London.

2

Dealing in Temperaments

Economic Transformation of the Artistic Field in France during the Second Half of the Nineteenth Century

NICHOLAS GREEN

FROM FEBRUARY 13 TO 27, 1870, large-scale advertisements in the *Chronique des arts,* the art news supplement to the *Gazette des beaux-arts,* trumpeted the sale of a major collection of contemporary pictures at the Hôtel Drouot.[1] In another art periodical, the *Revue internationale de l'art et de la curiosité,* a preview article lavished praise both upon the connoisseur concerned, Charles Edwards, and upon the school of painting he favored, which included artists like Delacroix, Decamps, Dupré, and Théodore Rousseau.[2] Six pictures by Rousseau were to be in the auction, and the writer of the piece, Jean Ravenal, complimented their owner on his perspicacious taste: "They have all been chosen by a real amateur; six of them have been judged worthy of appearing as reproductions in the *Oeuvre de Rousseau,* which the executors of his will are publishing." Each work was evocatively described in terms of cultural associations that assigned it the status of a masterpiece: one was compared to the lyrical prose of George Sand, another to the resplendent chiaroscuro of Rembrandt, while a third was validated via the view of Rousseau's friend, the well-known critic and historian Théophile Thoré, who "considered this one of Rousseau's most astonishing pictures."

Three years later this last painting cropped up again in the sale of the Laurent-Richard collection, selling for 33,500 francs, more than double its 1870 price.[3] The writer of the sale catalogue, Armand Silvestre, set the tone for this important event with a quote from the learned Thoré: "Théodore Rousseau [there were eleven works by him in the sale] is heading straight for posterity, leading the pleiade of contemporary landscapists."[4] Other works by Rousseau achieved similar or even higher sale prices, prices unheard of in the artist's lifetime and previously reserved for the "old masters." At a third major auction of modern work in 1881, composed primarily of Delacroix and the Barbizon group, some of the same Rousseaus reappeared, reaching even more impressive figures of between 46,000 and 49,000 francs.[5] One commentator remarked on this as "one of those great sales—so rare nowadays—which enthuse the connoisseurs." He characterized the anonymous seller, Monsieur E., as a true collector, "a gourmet, whose collection has been built up over many years with great finesse."[6]

This little narrative serves to introduce many of the elements featured in this essay: the rapid rise in price of particular forms of modern art—and especially nature painting by the likes of Rousseau; the role of journalism and historical expertise in securing the cultural and investment value of artworks; and, crucially, the strategic alliances between speculative collectors, critics, and dealers. In fact, though unnamed, the operations of the latter were ever-present throughout all this enthusiastic hype and precious connoisseurship. For it was the dealer Paul Durand-Ruel (see fig. 2.2) who constituted the lynchpin of the whole network of publicity and sales campaigns. A quick glance at his contemporary activities, especially vis-à-vis Rousseau, is revealing.

In 1866, along with his colleague Brame, he made a huge investment in Rousseau's production, scooping up much of his studio contents—unfinished works, preparatory sketches, and youthful studies—for a grand total of around 140,000 francs.[7] Two years later at the auction following the artist's death, Durand-Ruel and Brame acted as valuing experts but also entered into the sale to purchase more work for themselves. Between 1869 and 1871 the dealer funded the *Revue internationale de l'art et de la curiosité* with a view to promoting his activities and "his" artists. One of the regular contributors was Alfred Sensier, who used the journal to publish a preliminary version of his mammoth biography of Rousseau. But Sensier also participated under another name, that of the enthusiastic Jean Ravenal.[8] To finance supportive publicity and large-scale investment projects like the near-monopolization of Rousseau, Durand-Ruel negotiated an arrangement with the financier Edwards, who loaned him considerable amounts of capital. Edwards and Monsieur E. of the 1881 auction were one and the same—less a speculative collector than the much-needed financial backing for ambitious entrepreneurial dealing.

Paul Durand-Ruel has often been hailed—and indeed he represented himself—as a knightly crusader for the modern tradition in art, first with the so-called Barbizon school of 1830 and then with the Impressionist generation.[9] His financial strategies have been widely recognized as effectively initiating norms of dealer operations still familiar today. Yet surprisingly, given his own frankness in discussing many of his transactions in an autobiographical memoir, little real awareness of the formation and implications of such economic "innovations" has penetrated mainstream art historical literature. All too often, accounts of the period segregate aesthetic developments from any economic infrastructure, and even where economic determinants have been brought into play, their significance has been blunted by the commitment to an evolutionary history of modern art—a problematic which structures out broader issues.[10]

This essay aims to break open part of that history. It will argue that from being one minor element in the repertoire of urban consumerism earlier in the century, dealing in contemporary art had emerged by the end of the 1860s as a highly distinctive economic practice with clear-cut business codes and financial protocols. The biggest operators were becoming entrepreneurial capitalists, based internationally and backed by considerable financial resources. Their metamorphosis from the status of small artisans and shopkeepers kept pace with many other areas of industry and commerce which boomed during the dynamic decade of the 1850s. For Napoleonic autocracy provided key political conditions for the take-off of industrial capitalism generally. In other words, dealers were now well on the way to becoming the central mechanism shaping the economic relations of the artistic field in France. Free-market principles and speculative investment intervened in and regulated the production and circulation of art products on a massive scale.

But that is not to push for a reductionism; it is neither to lament the metamorphosis of art into speculative commodity nor to lambaste it for complicity with capitalism. The aim of our account is rather different. It is, first, to chart the structural features of art dealing as an emergent economic practice and, then, to demonstrate how the success of big speculative ventures in modern painting depended upon particular discourses of individualism grounded in the dominant ideology of the Third Republic. What

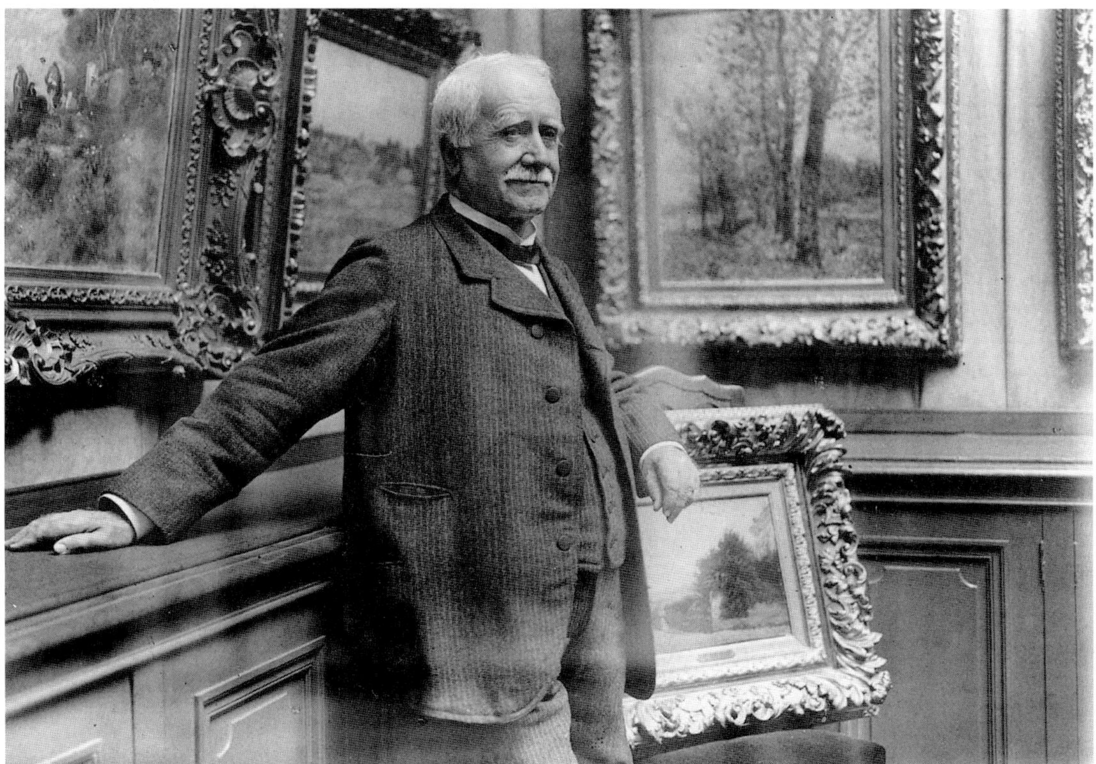

FIGURE 2.2. Paul Durand-Ruel, 1910, photograph. Archives Durand-Ruel. Photo: Dornec, all rights reserved.

is insistent is the historically precise and complex ways in which economic structures worked in conjunction with professional art discourses of critics and historians, class specific definitions of leisure and science, and even contradictory political ideologies, often with mutually reinforcing effects. However, if the mode of production is not to be elevated to an a priori principle of explanation, nor will art and aesthetic expression figure as the starting point or central object of focus. In that respect what needs to be foregrounded is the distance of the approach adumbrated here from the conceptual landscape of art history. At the risk of repeating the obvious, a brief review of some familiar positions will draw this out.

It is by now a standard criticism of traditional histories of nineteenth-century art that their inherent formalism allows little space for examination of the relation between art and society. The "social" enters only in an abbreviated form as the biographical tracing of artists' lives or an impressionistic sketch of historical context. That absence has been addressed with increasing acuity by what has come to be termed the "revisionist" approach. In particular, writings by Francis Haskell, Albert Boime, Harrison White and Cynthia White, and Linda Whiteley have usefully illuminated technical and social dimensions of nineteenth-century dealing and patronage.[11] Yet do such accounts substantially transform the underlying terms of the debate? On the contrary, it can be argued that the ghost of formalism has a nasty habit of haunting these more socially oriented inquiries. How history in general is to be understood still remains a problem. Displacing the focus on painting and sculpture by discrete studies of art criticism, buyers, or institutions fails to shift the subordination of society and social relations to the causal exploration of art. The centrality of art as that which is to be explained remains unchallenged. This preserves a hierarchization of priorities, it reproduces an epistemological order of knowledge which writes out questions, problems, and relations outside its field of visibility. The trajectory is always ultimately circular, returning us to those aesthetic objects and values from which we began. What is argued for here is a radically different model of cultural history: one in which the artistic—its discourses and institutions—occupies a place, but not a preordained privilege *qua* art. One in which the terms of reference are set by a wider debate about the contradictory forces molding social relations. Yet the impact—if you like, the politics—of cultural representations and practices does lie at the heart of our concerns. For a major issue posed in this essay involves the work of cultural formations in furnishing key conditions of possibility for economic transformations at specific historical moments. The implications of this have less to do with revising art history than revising the questions we ask of history.

Into the Auction House

In mapping the field, the first step is to come to grips with the mechanics of modern art dealing. But the most self-evident points of entry—gallery archives and records—do not necessarily offer the clearest perspective. The developing market had no single unifying principle, and it operated across a range of institutions, the art magazine as well as the dealer gallery/shop or the auction house. Arguably, it was the last which from the 1850s became the fulcrum of the system and the site, if not the sole source, of an emergent speculative strategy.

Speculation was nothing new in the art world. Throughout the nineteenth century and before, public sales were classic terrain for gambling on the investment value of "old masters" and, to a lesser extent, *curiosités* like Sèvres porcelain and Italian Renaissance faience. Auctioneers had been instituted as an official body to preside over all public sales of property as part of the legislation to protect and control private property stemming from the 1789 revolution.[12] Though they were expected to stamp out abuses, auctioneers were themselves soon complicit in dubious practices. Legally, for instance, only sales following bankruptcy or judicial confiscation could be held in public premises as opposed to private households. Yet by the 1840s, if not before, many posthumous collector sales took place in the auction houses, as did those organized by professional middlemen. That shift facilitated deals between auctioneers and sellers to fix prices beforehand to the disadvantage of those bidding. It also enhanced the prestige of auctioneers, some of whom, like Charles Pillet, won respected reputations and a regular public following. After 1852 the powerful Parisian association was concentrated at one impressive base, the Hôtel Drouot, which hosted a wide diversity of auctions. Physical proximity to the stock exchange now linked it both literally and metaphorically to the fortunes of finance capitalism. As Philippe Burty put it: "Its success corresponded to that financial surge which for ten years made the Bourse a speculator's paradise."[13]

Equally important in stoking the speculative circuit were the activities of the valuing expert—a figure of ambivalent standing. The term *expert* in this context requires careful decoding. Strictly speaking it referred to the process of financially assessing the objects on sale to fix their reserve prices. Given the range of property coming up at auction—from art and antiques to household knickknacks—and the complete absence of legal restrictions, the field was wide open for all kinds of sharp practice.[14] It was common knowledge that just about anyone could and did become an expert, since "the auction house demands no diplomas."[15] Which explained, another commentator sneered, but did not excuse the continual errors and false attributions that littered their sale catalogues.[16] However, with respect to art the role of expert was largely the province of "old master" dealers—middlemen who prided themselves on the connoisseurship of their knowing eye and combined financial acumen with historical knowledge.[17] As we shall see, the market in modern art was to depend upon the separation and greater specification of different forms of expertise—financial and cultural—*and* their reintegration through the alliance between dealers and art historians.

By the 1860s awareness of the Hôtel Drouot extended beyond specialist journals to semidocumentary journalism and comic literature. In texts by Champfleury and Henri Rochefort the "popular capitalism" of the auction house was incorporated into the pageant of metropolitan life and entertainment as an object both of exotic curiosity and active interest for a broad bourgeois readership.[18] The character types of auctioneer, collector, dealer, and expert were wittily delineated, though interestingly the personas of the last two categories were differentiated—a distinction which would have made little sense to the middlemen themselves. In these popular literary representations the dealer was sympathetically described as a true connoisseur without a fortune rather than a grasping profiteer. The golden age of dealing was now in the past, or so it seemed, due in part to the very proliferation of all kinds of dealers and because of the "collector/speculators [who] comprise the vast majority of those regularly frequenting the Drouot rooms and wage a competition with the dealers which is all the more dangerous as it is covert."[19] The auction house—that stock exchange of art products—was compared to a gambling hall with the speculators as roulette players. Drawing on extensive financial backing, big business could easily outbid the competition so that "it is no longer the dealers who thwart the acquisitions of the bourgeois, it is the bourgeois who silences the dealer."[20] A case in point arose in 1861 when the banking and industrial syndicate of Seillière bought Prince Soltykoff's collection *en bloc* and then proceeded to sell it off piecemeal at a huge profit.[21]

Two features of this literature deserve note. First, there is the clear perception that speculation is rife: dealers failing and experts faking in a diminishing market where too many investors are chasing too few commodities. Second, less evident here but equally insistent throughout the texts is the focus on "old masters" and antiques—all that which is old—as the only viable speculative material. What popular coverage of the 1860s fails to register are the structural moves already afoot to exploit the investment potential of modern art. In that process many of the same operations and personas were to recur but often in changed combinations and proportions.

Until the 1840s sales of contemporary pictures were relatively few and far between. When they did occur, they were unglamorous and uncelebrated affairs. Unlike the "old master" middlemen, dealers in this material were primarily shop-based and had little direct contact with the auction house. They had emerged out of artisan trades like printing, framing, and gilding, and they catered to an expansive Parisian market for leisure and luxury commodities, with few pretensions to connoisseurship or status.[22] The turning point came in the early 1850s.[23] One factor was growing interest from collectors disenchanted with the high prices and dubious quality of mainstream collecting areas, another, the recycling of commodities which had first passed through the dealers' hands twenty or thirty years before. Most important for our present purpose was the establishment of a new generation of gallery-based dealers at the first buoyant moment of economic expansion under the Napoleonic regime. Cutting loose from the artisanal roots of the trade, these dealers tended to specialize in modern artwork, and the most enterprising became actively involved in public auctions. By adopting the role of valuation, they twinned the previously modest but secure shop trade with the risks of the speculative market. This represented a successful adaptation of the techniques of their "old master" colleagues, while avoiding, for the present at least, the problems that beset the latter.

The case of Francis Petit was characteristic. From the beginning of his career around 1852, he operated as a valuing expert at auctions.[24] At first he used the description *appréciateur* rather than *expert*, suggesting hesitancy over the acceptability of valuing recent art products. Such diffidence had disappeared by 1855, when he valued the collection of the opera singer Paul Baroilhet, a noted buyer of contemporary work. Earlier established traders like Alexis Febvre rose to the challenge. A decade before, Febvre's business—located in the old commercial heart of the city—had been as much concerned with gilding as with selling pictures. By 1852 he had moved upmarket to the exclusive rue de Choiseul and advertised his services for the "direction of public sales," as well as publicizing his "gallery of pictures ancient and modern." [25] An obituary of the dealer claimed that it was involvement in important auctions of the 1850s that made his reputation.[26] By means of this mediating role, dealers were better able to manipulate the prices of painters whose work they stocked, and to mold the tastes and interests of their clientele. Burty insinuated that the task of the modern art dealer was an especially delicate one. Not only did he have to certify the authenticity of the objects in his care but to steer them through the pitfalls of the market, including low bidding at auction and the extravagant pretensions of collectors. According to this gently ironic account, a major function was to act as doctor to the ailments of collectors—boredom and lassitude—by frequently swapping the contents of their collections without them appearing to be speculators. Francis Petit excelled in this kind of confidential treatment: "He knows precisely the moral temperature of his clientele. To one who is weary of his Troyons he proposes a Jules Dupré; to another who can no longer bear the name of Isabey he offers Jongkind; he will swap a Théodore Rousseau for a Millet. . . ."[27]

At the same time dealers worked to inflate the cultural capital of art at auction by a variety of devices. They organized sales in their own right, assuming a cloak of anonymity or the front of a collector like Edwards. The act of collecting itself invested these commodities with a cachet not present in material which came straight from the artist's studio or the gallery/shop. Further, they exploited the presentation and content of sale catalogues to supply supportive publicity. Illustrations began to appear, as in the catalogue for the Deforge sale of 1857 "adorned with eleven wood engravings illustrating the principal pictures on sale."[28] And rather than the customary brief and eulogistic preface by the valuing expert, reputable art writers and historians such as Charles Blanc and Burty—themselves part of a rapidly proliferating breed—were now commissioned to write introductions and notes. Such texts enhanced the prestige and authenticity of the art on offer both by building on the weight of historical evidence and by testifying to personal knowledge of the painters and their work. Here was the beginning of a cultural alliance between dealers and art writers which was to be long and fruitful, and to which we shall return later.

Let us pause for a moment to ask: what about those key agents in the process of cultural production, the artists themselves? It would be quite wrong to assume that the producers were passive dupes of an exploitative system—which is of course what they often claimed, taking on the personas of martyrs and outcasts. Indeed, such complaints have been incorporated all too literally into the mythology of the artist as suffering hero which permeates many standard art historical narratives. Rousseau, for example, was one successful painter who liked to declare his oppression yet who had extensive and useful connections with dealers in the 1850s and 1860s.[29] From his personal correspondence it emerges that he was skilled at playing one dealer against another to fend off debts or to squeeze out a better price.[30] But Rousseau preferred to work through friendly intermediaries like Gustave Coûteaux or Sensier rather than directly with trader and client. Which introduces another participant in the system. Sensier, the civil servant, friend and loyal biographer of Rousseau and of Millet, carried out all sorts of useful services.[31] He paid off creditors, watched over pictures in auctions, and had work framed, delivered, or displayed to buyers. In the process he managed to accumulate a major collection of his own, including unsold Salon pieces. But Sensier's role and importance should not be overestimated. Small-scale middlemen working in active alliance with artists thrived only briefly during the transitional moment at which capital began to realize steady profits from speculation but before serious expenditure by big business forced out small investors. And Sensier's involvement with Barbizon painters was multifaceted; it certainly cannot be separated from his own economic interests, yet it was equally a mark of identification with a particular artistic culture and the point of access to a role as art writer and historical researcher.

By the early 1870s things had begun to change again—partly as a result of the deaths of many of the artists concerned. From the memoir of Durand-Ruel it is evident that wealthy industrialists, entrepreneurs, and professionals were now entering the field of modern art as overtly speculative buyers. Among them were the deluxe tailor Laurent-Richard, the opera singer Jean-Baptiste Faure, and Ernest Hoschedé, financier and department store magnate.[32] Like traditional "old master" collectors they had at their disposal funds sufficient to outbid not just small middlemen but also the new generation of dealers. But while their intentions were undoubtedly to make a financial killing, this did not preclude a powerful cultural investment as "generous" patrons and vanguardist arbiters of taste; witness Hoschedé's close personal relations with Monet and other Impressionists. All three patrons bought extensively from Durand-Ruel, putting their acquisitions on the market at strategic intervals, with the dealer usually doubling as valuer *and* buyer. The stratagem did not always come off. All three were badly caught out by the general slump at the end of the 1870s, for the Hôtel Drouot closely followed the barometer of the stock exchange, fluctuating in tune with political tension and economic reverses. Nonetheless, the constant circulation of work by particular artists through successive sales held by speculators and dealers initiated a sharp upturn in their prices. With every auction, with every new catalogue entry, the provenance, the critical history, and unique character of the commodity was enriched. The spiraling cycle of cultural capital fed into new and unexpected price levels, which in turn set the parameters for future reserve prices. Entrepreneurial commerce in modern art was entering its most dynamic phase to date, with massive capital investment providing impetus for constant growth and high profitability.

It is in this context that we can better understand the strategy developed by Durand-Ruel (fig. 2.2). By borrowing from Edwards he obtained backing equivalent to that of his collectors and avoided being squeezed out of the market in "top quality" work. His long-term loan policy represented a belated imitation of the ambitious banking schemes pioneered by the Pereire brothers in the early years of the Second Empire.[33] While traditional bankers like the Rothschilds were unwilling to gamble on bold entrepreneurial ventures, the Pereires' *Credit Mobilier*, through taking a controlling share interest in a range of businesses and promoting mergers, enabled riskier enterprises to be supported by solid investments. In the arrangement with Durand-Ruel, the role of Edwards was less that of a direct speculator than that of a silent partner earning a steady income from the steep rate of interest on his capital, invested where the dealer saw fit. It was still a high-risk operation, as ensuing conflicts made clear. The dealer was burdened with an onerous rate of interest repayments, while the financier risked losing his whole capital outlay if the dealer failed.

The advantages, however, were striking and manifold. As already noted, Durand-Ruel benefited from Edwards's name, using it as a front to put gallery stock on the market in the guise of a famous collection. Then, the money came in handy for financing his publicity machine, first with the *Revue internationale de l'art et de la curiosité* and in 1873 with a massive but abortive illustrated catalogue of his stock.[34] Though such advertising devices were commonplace in other economic areas—both banking and commercial—the dealer was able to draw on and expand the dialogue with art writers and historians. In his periodical, blatant panegyrics boosting the dealer, his gallery, and his collectors were juxtaposed with contributions by eminent art historians on anything from the Renaissance to the present. This literary and academic backup was not solely functional, it also helped to mold cultural definitions of the dealer as a disinterested patron of art and a sponsor of serious learning. Third, and most important of all, large-scale financial reserves empowered him to pursue a two-pronged buying policy. On the one hand, he aimed to accumulate holdings in a young and cheap generation of rising artists (among them the Impressionists), who, with careful presentation, would become profitable in the long run—effectively a sort of speculating in "futures." On the other, he specialized in established artists like Rousseau, dead or nearly so, building up an exclusive stock in this safer but more expensive material.

Specialization and monopolization were the keynotes, allowing dealers to inflect the direction of prices by reducing or increasing the flow of an artist's work onto the market. In 1878, for example, Durand-Ruel organized a noncommercial showing of the Barbizon group—Rousseau, Millet, Corot, and others—in response to the state's art exhibition at the Exposition Universelle, where these "major masters" were poorly represented. He assembled 380 paintings, borrowing mainly from patrons to whom he had sold work. The effect was dramatic. The prices of artists seen here were boosted to record heights in the auctions of the Hartmann and Wilson collections in 1881.[35]

Durand-Ruel is probably the best known but he was by no means the only or the most successful representative of new entrepreneurial dealer strategies. Others like Georges Petit also cultivated reputations as connoisseurs and published lavish illustrated catalogues for auctions and gallery exhibitions. Their texts were produced both as deluxe objects of consumption—part of the metropolitan repertoire on show at the Hôtel Drouot—and, overlapping with art historical literature, as lasting contributions to scholarly historical knowledge. Equally, monopolization was becoming widespread by the end of the 1870s. It was manifest in contractual arrangements between artists and dealers and in the use of the single-artist retrospective exhibition.[36] And it was placed center stage in the kind of approach taken up by such "avant-garde" dealers as Vollard and Kahnweiler at the end of the century.

The argument so far could be read as crudely economistic. The fuse of modern art speculation was, so it seemed, ignited by the dynamic combustion of investment capital—deriving from industrial expansion under Napoleon—with commercial strategies adapted from "progressive" finance capitalism. Different sectors at the level of the mode of production combined to transform the operation and meaning of art, shifting it from a commodity—aesthetic, moral, entertaining—to an exchange value. But that would be a very partial and inadequate explanation. For only certain types of art and artists enjoyed the dubious privilege of participating in the new structure. It was landscape, or more precisely nature painting in the broadest sense, which formed the prime object of focus for speculation. And it was painters like Corot, Millet, and Rousseau who, at the time of their deaths, first became the cult figures of the auction house. Understanding why this was so involves an examination of those cultural languages and alliances which have only been hinted at so far. Specifically, it means scrutinizing the distinctive dynamic and organization of forms of contemporary art history. Cultural definitions, I shall argue, were an intrinsic facet in the transformation of the economic relations of the artistic field. Such definitions are not reducible to economic determinants; they have their own structuring logic and discursive effects. But nor are they wholly autonomous. Their conditions are to be found both in the specific institutional nexus through which art history was channeled and more general ideological currents. Tracing that formation uncovers a tissue of connections between the marketplace and the early Third Republic state.

Biographical Explanations

From the 1820s, pictures of nature—whether Gothic ruins, "imitative" landscape, or peasant genre scenes—had formed a basic component of dealer stock. Relatively low on the hierarchy of genres, nature pictures were widely marketed not so much as art as inexpensive luxury commodities for an urban public. Such images were prized for *what* they represented rather than their mode of representation. They locked into the pleasures of the diorama and the boulevard theaters with their dramatic light effects, urban curiosity for distant and primitive provinces stoked by a plethora of illustrated travel literature, and the growing vogue for actually experiencing the countryside for the sake of one's health, both physical and moral. By the late 1840s the crystallization of metropolitan bourgeois ideologies of nature both drew on and reinforced pictorial/poetic readings of landscape. Under Napoleonic dictatorship that process was institutionalized as much in the picturesque Parisian parks, like Buttes Chaumont, of Haussmann's henchman Alphand, as in the gradual rise of nature painting up the artistic hierarchy. At the first moment of contemporary dealer expansion into the Hôtel Drouot in the 1850s, nature commodities—if still ambiguously placed on the official scale of artistic values—were in a commanding position to dominate the commercial market in modern work.

However, from the 1860s, the speculative potential of such imagery was to reside less in the ongoing identification with ideologies of the natural world than in novel modes of biographical interpretation. Developing over the next two decades, this analytical structure worked hand in glove with the commercial publicizing of public auctions and dealer stock. Already in the 1850s, as we have seen, reputable art writers like Blanc were willing to contribute to sale catalogues. At the same time they seized the opportunity to advance their own cultural status by extensive coverage of art news. For much of the 1850s and 1860s, when Napoleonic censorship made criticism of official art politics a sensitive issue, public sales constituted an important part of that news.

With the deaths of many of the Romantic/Barbizon generation from the late 1860s, biographies proliferated, ranging from detailed monographs to brief magazine vignettes. Sensier's *Souvenirs sur Théodore Rousseau*, 1872, was one early example. Others included Burty on Paul Huet, 1870, Frédéric Henriet on Antoine Chintreuil, 1873, Henri Dumesnil on Corot, 1875, Louis Gonse on Fromentin, 1881, and Louis de Fourcaud on Bastien-Lepage, 1885, as well as collections of essays by Burty, Ernest Chesneau, and Jules Claretie.[37] The texts formed part of a two-way dialogue between art writers and the dealing market. Biographical activity was underpinned, at least in part, by commercial interest; likewise dealer and collector investment was stimulated by the writing of artists into history. In some instances, as between Sensier and Durand-Ruel, the objectives of the alliances were explicit. With one exception Sensier's "loving" monographs were devoted to painters exclusively collected by the dealer—Rousseau, Millet, and Georges Michel. Generally, the relationship was far less manipulative though equally fruitful to both parties, secured through informal contact in the auction house and through art reporting for newspapers and specialist journals.

Take the example of Philippe Burty, a noted habitué of the Hôtel Drouot, who edited the *Chronique des arts* in the 1860s. [While he was] a politically engaged art critic—he wrote for Gambetta's *La République française* from the 1870s—this did not inhibit his enthusiastic participation in the commercial art world, to which he contributed numerous sale catalogues. Simultaneously, he developed a reputation for art history, with special interests in contemporary, applied, and Japanese art. His biographical writings on the Barbizon group complemented their commercial success at auction, while he was also prepared to back the "futures" of risky trends like the Impressionists.[38] Eventually in 1881 his political loyalty was rewarded and his expertise recognized with an official position as inspector of fine arts with special responsibility for lectures.[39] That was a mark of the growing profile of art history as a definable professionalism. But what makes Burty's career worth investigating—and it was typical of many—is its elasticity. Part popular journalist, part political polemicist, part learned scholar, part financial broker; such institutional suppleness oiled the wheels of cultural exchanges between different agents in the circuit of cultural production.

Along with other forms of art historical writing, biographies enriched the historical and aesthetic texture in which the cultural capital of the speculative commodity was grounded. But the widespread *production* of biographies does not in itself explain why nature art became so financially privileged. Rather, it was their *discursive organization*, the particular interpretative framework that they established that supplied the vital ingredient. Here was a quite new formulation of creative individuality—one all too familiar

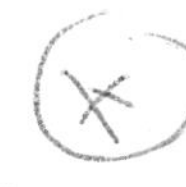

today—which carried distinct implications not just for the meaning but also for the valuation of art products.

Look at any of the early biographies of Corot, Rousseau, or Millet. There we find in varying proportions a kaleidoscope of personalized observation, anecdote, and reminiscence juxtaposed with carefully gathered empirical documentation. Although the overall intention is to praise, unlike official obituaries of academicians which sternly eschewed the low ground of the personal, these texts revel in a detailed exposé of painters' lives. Birth certificates, wills, private letters, lists of exhibitions and patrons, and color charts jostle with touching vignettes of the artists on their deathbed, wife or mistress hysterical with grief, or in happier mood, imparting their most secret emotions before nature to the author (notebook in hand!). Such different—even antithetical—devices point to structural and highly productive tensions in the particular mode of writing. For art biography and its conceptual repertoire currently hovered in a kind of no-man's-land, part popular journalism, part historical science.

Over the last thirty years of the nineteenth century, art history was to take shape as a professionalized discipline institutionally recognized by the state, mainly under the rubric of empirical history. The discreet but essentially nationalistic methodology of Fustel de Coulanges or Gabriel Monod delivered a history in tune with the aims and ambitions of the Third Republic state.[40] Biography as practiced by Hippolyte Taine and Ernest Renan and even art biography with Louis de Fourcaud in the 1890s won some acceptance as a recognized component of the empirical and scientific approach. But its seriousness was frequently undermined by long-standing associations with anecdotal journalism, the muckraking scandalmongering of populist biographers like Eugène de Mirecourt or, in the case of art, fresh links with commerce and sharp financial practices.[41] The more intimate and personal the observation, the more the text smacked of "light" entertainment rather than "serious" science. It is not coincidental that where other dimensions of art history were becoming rapidly specialized, biography was an area where the relative amateur, like Sensier, or the witty dilettante, like Clarétie, could still flourish.

These deep-rooted institutional ambiguities were intrinsic conditions framing the way biographies functioned as a mode of interpretation. Together, diversified anecdote and careful documentary "fact" worked to evoke a graphic and sometimes complex picture of the life and character of the artist, while having little to say—apart from description—about the meaning and message of the art images. It was in biographies of nature painters specifically that this formula took on the real force of explanation, for critical interpretation had traditionally concentrated on these artists' "naïve" and "sincere" dialogue with the world in opposition to the academic (and noble) preoccupation with style. In other words, the given absence of stylistic analysis for nature painting—of a vocabulary which could engage with the formal structure of the image—opened up space for the full-blooded entry of biographical explanation. Implicitly, the artworks were to be read as the reflection or expression of the temperament descriptively explored in the written texts. Nature was the ground on which the plethora of creative individualities was inscribed.

The choice of motif, weather, and viewpoint, the manner in which they had been transcribed into paint, all could be traced back to the complex unity of the painter's personality. Rousseau's volatile and yet stubborn spirit was revealed in blasted oaks or stagnant pools beneath fervid sunsets, his "scientific" pantheism in the meticulous enumeration of detail, his spiritual quest for the unknown and the infinite in the unusual angle, the bizarre effect, or even the bold reworking of a hackneyed compositional cliché. Likewise "papa" Corot's dreamy and gentle character was reflected in the limpid ponds of Ville d'Avray, the silvery screens of trees and dancing nymphs, while Millet's earthy and intense religiosity found its equivalent in the rude peasants and barren plain of Barbizon.

A number of points need to be clarified, for much of this may seem embarrassingly obvious or banal. It is of course usually argued that the language of temperament and personal sensation was, if not forged by, then registered in the writing of such contemporary art critics as Castagnary and Zola, or indeed even earlier in the 1840s generation of Thoré and Baudelaire. It is usually assumed that self-expression referenced an avant-garde tradition from Delacroix or Courbet onward and its innovative reaction against stultifying officialdom. Again, the cult of personality is often claimed for the kind of psychological individualism which is seen to have its roots in Romanticism and which is still germane to much art practice *and* art history today. The argument of our account moves in quite another direction. It proposes that the individualizing schema was formulated from the 1860s through the discursive twinning of biographical narrative with a preexistent aesthetic code in which the relation between the painter and that which was rendered into paint was constructed as transparent. The vocabulary of perception, sensation, expression permeating contemporary critical and theoretical art writing consistently registered the transparency of the artist/nature couplet, drawing on the currency of experimental science to come to terms with it.[42] Here was an epistemology that brought art close to physiological theories of perception underpinning the formation of experimental psychology at the very same period.[43] But the use of such language was not simply a question of discursive homologies, it was materially located in the push for scientific status by the professionalizing art historian. Under the impact of scientific definitions, the artistic conception of nature was steadily enlarged from its standard fields of reference—landscape and peasants—to encompass other genres and eventually the artist's total relationship with the world—external *and* internal. In the process, the biographical approach and its corollary, the cult of creative individualism, became dominant throughout the late nineteenth-century art worlds, official as well as avant-garde.[44]

Further, the degree to which art discourse operated psychologically, as we would understand it, is much in doubt. For the individualism laid down made sense only in terms of the overall ideological framework concerning the individual and the state within which it was positioned. That framework was shaped in the early decades of the Third Republic by experimental science certainly, but also by traditional Sorbonne moral philosophy and crucially by a secular educational obsession with turning out patriotic and dutiful citizens.[45] Artistic individualism was backed by such differing definitions around citizenship, which, unevenly combined, produced the ideological cement for bourgeois republican hegemony from the late 1870s. But it also actively fed into that repertoire through the incorporation of art historical expertise into official initiatives. Countless statues, monuments, and place-names dedicated to (nature) artists pay tribute to its evident contribution. From the early 1880s the cultural policy of the central state took individuality on board as a useful unit of measurement for the nation's aesthetic wealth, and exhibitions were organized around the thematic at the Exposition Universelle of 1889 and of 1900,[46] while local authorities adopted resident and visiting artists as heroes who demonstrated regional participation in French civilization.[47]

There is also a more general analytical issue here. Discussion of temperament, personality, and the like among art critics and writers does not in and of itself necessarily point us to psychological individualism. Too often even the most perceptive art historical accounts remain fixated by the level of the text in isolation, paying scant attention to the material sites and structures through which languages are circulated and validated. Like standard hermeneutic explorations of art images, such readings, however sophisticated the linguistic analysis, cannot escape their text-based problematic. But to plot the genealogy of knowledge is to engage with systems of signification both in the materiality of their institutional networks and effects and on the ground of their broader conditions of existence. Certainly, the "truth effect" of biographical individualism lay less in any internal conceptual coherence than in the effectiveness of its institutional operation. Though biographers like Burty or Chesneau were well acquainted with the philosophical concepts of Taine and Renan, their approach with its epistemological slippage between empirical description and analytical explanation produced individualism by default as much as by design. In sum, the articulation of creative personality within art discourse was the result of a historically specific shift in the organization of knowledge, sustained on the one hand by internal conditions—the transparency traditionally accredited to nature painting, the institutional pull between entertainment literature and professional science—and on the other by the dominant ideological forces molding republican citizenship.

Aesthetic criteria deriving from the new discursive model had a direct input into contemporary dealing. Central to the market in "old masters" was the rarity value of "great" works. Through the specification of an individualized personality expressed in art, the biographical approach transformed the means of measurement from the rarity of the object to the uniqueness of the artist. The market in modern art was reoriented around the buying and selling of individual *painters*. This was ideal for the promotion of nature painting, where high productivity had been one of the mainstays of the earlier shop trade but a handicap in an investment market revolving around rarity. Now the great artist could be simultaneously prolific and unique. Traditional emphases on rarity were reconciled with large-scale commodity capitalism.

The principle was firmly grasped by those like Durand-Ruel who sought to corner certain artists' work and who actively encouraged art historical literature. But perhaps the tie-up can be most dramatically demonstrated in the changing attitudes to sketches. From midcentury, sketches and studies had occasionally been sold to friends or on the open market, yet their value remained fixed by the status of the tools of the trade, the mechanical and artisanal aspect of artistic production. According to the biographical model, all kinds of sketches and unfinished work could be incorporated into the painter's oeuvre, reclassified as "first thoughts," "truly personal expressions," "developing ideas." Though smaller and more modest than exhibition machines, they ceased to be qualitatively distinct. In staking out a claim over Rousseau, whose output of Salon pieces was limited but whose studio was littered with the debris of many years' experimentation, Durand-Ruel made full use of the redefinition of aesthetic priorities. Included in the studio sale of 1866 were many tiny oil sketches on paper dating from the painter's youth. Mounted on board or canvas, cut down or even expanded to suitably attractive shapes, framed in rich gilt Rococo frames, this material was now transformed into standard dealer stock.[48] Similarly, in his 1873 catalogue, *Recueil des estampes gravées à l'eau-forte*, no attention was drawn by the presentation of the text to massive differences in scale or function between small practice studies, memory notes, sizable but unfinished canvases, and worked-up Salon/collector pictures. They all stood as representations of Rousseau's rich and complex individuality.

To sum up: it has been argued that a dealer system rooted in expanding capitalism was able to rework the economic relations of the artistic field insofar as it drew on and exploited constructions of individualism ultimately validated by the Third Republic ideology of citizenship. In that process art biographers played a central part. It was they who forged the language naturalizing the ongoing relation between entrepreneurial capitalism and the perceived progress of art. It was they who were instrumental in establishing dialogue between the commercial marketplace and state policy. But, as we have seen, they were neither the dupes nor the subaltern agents of capital. Biographical discourse had its own logic, its own institutional conditions and its own, often contradictory, rationale. The writers themselves, while frequently acceding to the demands of capital, inhabited a distinct economic and cultural milieu. In fact, what is perhaps as interesting about this semiprofessionalized cadre of cultural agents as their obvious links with dealing is the carefully guarded compartmentalizations between the different sites in which they operated. In the role of historical specialists Burty and Blanc were careful to blank out the current state of art investments as largely irrelevant and unworthy of the integrity of their subject. We might speculate on the disjunctions and awkwardnesses which they experienced in terms of their personal identities as they shifted fluidly across from one context to another.

Contradictions in Personal Lives

Economic analyses by themselves do not satisfactorily explain the nexus of practices making up contemporary art dealing. Equally if we turn from general structures to particular lives, it emerges that the economic activities of dealers were personally lived out through distinctive cultural identities. As entrepreneurial capitalists pushing modern art, we might expect them to be, if not republicans, then supportive of "progress" and "modernity" in other respects. A couple of thumbnail sketches puts paid to any such straightforward assumptions, demonstrating surprising tensions between economic, political, and cultural alignments.

Georges Petit, successful son of a successful father, was one of the foremost dealers of the late nineteenth century with an international clientele and reputation. An erudite writer and noted sales expert, Petit fostered amicable relations with living artists, hosting both group and single-artist exhibitions.[49] Yet there are indications that Petit eschewed the sordid terrain of trade by cultivating associations with a blue-blooded elite and by posing as the disinterested benefactor of charities. In June 1883, for example, his exhibition of a hundred masterpieces from Parisian collections brought together pictures mainly by Delacroix and the Barbizon school.[50] The steering committee—few of whom were actually collectors—included a glamorous cross section of eminent aristocrats, and the proceeds went to the *écoles libres*—Catholic schools currently under attack from republican legislation. More of the social ambiance sought by Petit could be glimpsed at the Prince Narishkine sale of "old masters" and contemporary work also in 1883.[51] This was held at the dealer's own sumptuous gallery rather than at the Hôtel Drouot, and Petit published an exclusive illustrated catalogue. Moreover, half the room was reserved for specially invited guests. In the "egalitarian" 1880s, such an ostentatious display of exclusivity—transforming a very public sale into a select soirée-like occasion—effectively signaled identification with those right-wing notables displaced from political power by the republican settlement of the late 1870s. For Petit, the affirmation of a traditional (and increasingly marginalized) social hierarchy was perhaps one way by which his capitalist enterprise could be distinguished from the "vulgarity" of commerce, opening up recognition for his cultural persona as a guardian of civilization. That was a language not always available to republican businessmen and meritocrats.

Finally, back to Durand-Ruel. His memoir presented a self-image of the altruistic crusader for the pure interests of art; a representation deeply bound up with his own political views and social values. For Durand-Ruel, the "progressive" capitalist and champion of "innovative" painting, was a militant Catholic and monarchist, who believed the Third Republic to be a canker poisoning the health and sapping the moral temper of the age. He wrote to *Le Figaro* in 1873, claiming that "Trade is slack for the sole reason that we fear falling into the hands of the republicans and we all of us aspire to the reestablishment of the hereditary monarchy, both as Frenchmen and as businessmen."[52] A decade later, when tipped for the *légion d'honneur* for services to modern art, his all-too-active protests in favor of religious teaching orders lost him the favor of the state.[53] And Durand-Ruel never rallied. Even in the First World War he used his profits to produce a religious brochure to be distributed among the troops in the trenches. To his daughter Marie he wrote in 1917: "It is to combat and destroy the evil effect of the campaign waged by Gambetta, in favor of anti-clericalism. They have done enough harm to France with this campaign, led on and bribed by satanic Germany. Now we are seeing the result of it."[54]

What to make of these apparent contradictions? Or are they only contradictions if it is assumed that economic positions prescribe political and cultural attitudes? In fact it may be said that the fervor of Durand-Ruel's religious views forged a language and a subjective sense of mission which underpinned his activities as speculative art dealer. Missionary zeal found an outlet in the espousal of risky aesthetic trends and furnished him with a combative discourse that harnessed all the mechanisms of the market to the "valiant" struggle for civilization. Clearly two such accounts cannot be taken as typical of dealers as a whole. Yet the interesting connections they display do have general implications for the way we think through class and class formation. Though too massive an issue to broach in this essay, the message is clear. Economic positions do not deliver predetermined political alignments and cultural values. The distinctive cultural formations of dealers like Petit and Durand-Ruel had an undeniable impact on their actions as economic agents of capitalism.

Conclusion

Much of this essay has worked well-worn ground. Neither the expansion of French capitalism during the second half of the nineteenth century nor the growing importance of individualism within art are in any sense new themes. But in attempting to map changing economic relations in the artistic field, my intention has been to reposition the terms of the debate, to shuffle the pack, in order to move toward a different kind of cultural history. Three principles have been established. First, it is important to differentiate the enterprise from a history *of art*. If, that is, we are concerned to explore the social processes and relations in which cultural practices are engaged. For the conceptual privileging of art as the category to be explained orders history and society in the distorting mirror of its own preoccupations. Economic factors, for instance, are considered as conditions for or barriers to art's development; they are not seen as the springboard for opening up wider historical and theoretical issues. Here, on the contrary, the emergence of modern art dealing has been examined as a particular subdomain of capitalism, but one which sloughed off its artisanal skin by integrating financial strategies of the auction house *with* the cultural repertoire of art writers and historians.

Second, a major task has been coming to grips with the discursive logic of individualism as it was specified across biographical writing. It is important to engage with the specific codes and protocols at work in cultural formations. But texts are never free-floating. They are always underpinned by professional allegiances and institutional structures. Focusing on the conceptual range of biographical individualism is meaningless unless it is set in the context of a professionalizing art history and bourgeois republican ideology. It is through those material sites and structures that we can plot a network of precise yet mediated connections between the free-market principles of entrepreneurial dealing and state policy in the 1870s and 1880s.

Finally, and most urgently, what has been insistent throughout is the proposition that economic processes and changes can rarely if ever be understood in purely economic terms. This throws up difficult questions for historical accounts which isolate economic determination as the ultimate motor of history. The analysis of dealing shows how both at the structural level and in the lives of individual agents distinctive cultural languages supplied integral conditions of existence. In putting the case for these complex configurations, the cultural historian has important insights to offer outside the boundaries of the discipline to others such as economic and social historians. In a climate when the relevance of our studies is in dispute, that is a challenge it would be inexcusable to refuse.

Notes

Originally published in *Art History* 10, no. 1 (March 1987): 59–78.

1. See, for example, *Chronique des arts et de la curiosité*, no. 7 (13 February 1870): 28; also Lionello Venturi, *Les Archives de l'impressionnisme*, vol. 2 (Paris, 1939): 165 n. 3, which references a report on the sale catalogue by Théophile Gautier in the *Journal officiel*, 14 February 1870.
2. Jean Ravenal, "Vente Edwards," *Revue internationale de l'art et de la curiosité* 3 (1870): 105–16.
3. *Vente Laurent-Richard*, 7 April 1873, 49, no. 47. The copy of the catalogue in the Bibliothèque Nationale is annotated with prices later confirmed by Hippolyte

Mireur, *Dictionnaire des ventes d'art faites en France et à l'Etranger pendant les XVIIIème et XIXème siècles,* vol. 6 (Paris, 1901–12), 331. Mireur gave the price for the same picture in the Edwards sale as 13,600 francs.

4. *Vente Laurent-Richard,* 111.
5. Paul Eudel, *L'Hôtel Drouot et la curiosité en 1881,* vol. 1 (Paris, 1882), 36.
6. Ibid., 36, 39.
7. Alfred Sensier, *Souvenirs sur Théodore Rousseau* (Paris, 1872), 327. Durand-Ruel recorded spending only 130,000 francs (Venturi, *Archives de l'impressionnisme,* vol. 2, 166).
8. For this identification, see M. Tourneux, *Salons et expositions d'art à Paris (1801–1876)—Essai bibliographique* (Paris, 1919), 176; and Neil McWilliam and Christopher Parsons, " 'Le Paysan de Paris': Alfred Sensier and the Myth of Rural France," *Oxford Art Journal* 6, no. 2 (1983): 57 n. 82.
9. This image was consistently presented throughout the dealer's autobiographical accounts, "Mémoires de Paul Durand-Ruel," published in vol. 2 of Venturi, *Archives de l'impressionnisme.* John Rewald's influential *The History of Impressionism,* first published in the United States in 1946, crystallized the Durand-Ruel crusader myth.
10. A useful statistical analysis of the spectacular rise and then fall in the prices of Barbizon pictures by Anne Reverdy, *L'Ecole de Barbizon—évolution des prix des tableaux de 1850–1960* (Paris, 1973), made no attempt to relate such shifts to an analysis of dealing or of other artistic developments—the flip side to neglect of economic issues in most accounts of art movements. By far the most lucid analysis of dealing is still H. C. White and C. A. White, *Canvases and Careers: Institutional Change in the French Painting World* (New York, 1965), but even their fruitful sociological insights are yoked to an implicit celebration of Impressionism as somehow genuinely "progressive" (124–29).
11. Francis Haskell, *Rediscoveries in Art: Some Aspects of Taste, Fashion and Collecting in England and France* (Ithaca, N.Y., 1976); Albert Boime, "Entrepreneurial Patronage in Nineteenth-Century France," in *Enterprise and Entrepreneurs in Nineteenth- and Twentieth-Century France,* ed. E. C. Carter (Baltimore, 1976); White and White, *Canvases and Careers*; and Linda Whiteley, "Art et commerce d'art en France avant l'époque impressionniste," *Romantisme,* no. 40 (1983).
12. Laws of 27 ventôse, year IX—for Paris—and 28 April 1816—for the provinces (*Larousse Dictionnaire du XIX siècle,* vol. 4 [Paris, 1896], 730). There was no academic qualification for auctioneers, but they had to be French citizens over twenty-five and able to provide a security of between 4,000 and 20,000 francs depending on the size of their district. They could also name their successors. See also Claude Marie, "Les Ventes publiques," *Cabinet de l'amateur et de l'antiquaire* 1 (1842): 570 ff., for auctioneers' involvement in dubious deals.
13. Philippe Burty, "L'Hôtel des Ventes et le commerce des tableaux," *Paris Guide,* vol. 2 (Paris, 1867), 953.
14. See the legal tirade against abuse of the term *expert* in Edmond Copper, *Art et la loi* (Paris, 1903), 494–95.
15. Champfleury, *L'Hôtel des Commissaires-Priseurs* (Paris, 1867), 128.
16. Henri Rochefort, *Les Petits Mystères de l'Hôtel des Ventes* (Paris, 1862), 15–16.
17. See Haskell, *Rediscoveries in Art,* 26–37, on the fortunes of Jean-Baptiste-Pierre Lebrun around the period of the 1789 revolution. By the 1840s some like George, former *commissaire expert* at the Louvre, still retained an untarnished reputation (Charles Blanc, *Trésors de la curiosité,* vol. 2 [Paris, 1857], 500), but others, typified by Charles Pillet, were fiercely attacked for their duplicity (*Cabinet de l'amateur et de l'antiquaire* 1 [1842]: 520 and 528; 2 [1843]: 380).
18. Rochefort, *Les Petits Mystères;* and Champfleury, *L'Hôtel des Commissaires-Priseurs.* Also see the vaudeville play *Les Mystères de l'Hôtel des Ventes* (Paris, 1863), by Rochefort and Albert Wolff, first performed at the Théâtre du Palais Royal.
19. Rochefort, *Les Petits Mystères,* 31; and for similar arguments Champfleury, *L'Hôtel des Commissaires-Priseurs,* 153–54.
20. Rochefort, *Les Petits Mystères,* 49.
21. *Cabinet de l'amateur,* n.s. (April 1861): 2.
22. Whiteley, "Art et commerce," 68 and 71–72.
23. Burty, "L'Hôtel des Ventes," 952. The *Cabinet de l'amateur* had noted increasing interest by collectors in modern work back in 1845 ("Bulletin-Chronique," vol. 4, [1845], 331). Blanc, *Trésors de la curiosité,* included no collection devoted to modern art before the Thévenin sale of 1851 and the Collot sale of 1852. Further, by 1852 seventy-one dealers, a number of whom specialized in modern art, were listed in the commercial almanacs as opposed to forty-four ten years before.
24. Petit was first listed in the *Didot Annuaire du commerce* of 1853, but his name appeared as *appréciateur* in the catalogues for the anonymous JK sale of March 20, 1852, and the Van Isaaker sale of May 15, 1852 (British Library, ref. SC 182). *Appréciateur* was the title regularly adopted by the print seller Schroth, one of few to value modern art at auction during the 1840s.

25. *Didot Annuaire du commerce* (Paris, 1852), 851.
26. Eudel, *L'Hôtel Drouot*, vol. 2 (Paris, 1883), 238 ff.
27. Burty, "L'Hôtel des Ventes," 962.
28. Blanc, *Trésors de la curiosité*, vol. 2, 518.
29. Rousseau's paranoid attitudes toward collectors and dealers by whom he frequently felt betrayed are well represented in a series of letters concerning the dealer Arthur Stevens and the selling of Rousseau's major work, the *Chêne de Roche*, 1860 (unpublished correspondence of Théodore Rousseau, Cabinet des Dessins, Louvre, packet 1); similarly, see the draft of a letter to Baroilhet, who was accused of spreading "imputations calumnieuses" among his friends (ibid., packet 5). Sensier, *Souvenirs*, 261–62, published a draft statement by the artist which attacked the system for destroying true creators like himself. Yet the same unpublished correspondence reveals a network of connections with the following dealers: Weyl, Tedesco, Febvre, Détrimont, Moureau, Bouffier, Beugniet, and Thomas. Of these, only Febvre had been established before the 1850s.
30. Again, this emerges in the unpublished correspondence, especially with Sensier (*Souvenirs*, packet 1). For example, he was known to postpone the delivery of finished pictures to dealer or buyer in order to add a last and perfect touch to the work, urging Sensier to extract an advance of one thousand to two thousand francs, which effectively raised the overall price. A letter of 1857 requested Sensier to tell the dealer Thomas that he had brought his painting to Paris "qui est ravissant" and on this basis to ask for an extra five hundred to a thousand francs. Artists like Rousseau also arranged auctions of their own work. The most astute businessman was Diaz, who held eleven sales between 1849 and 1868.
31. On Sensier, see Paul Mantz, *Vente Sensier* (Paris, 1877); and McWilliam and Parsons, " 'Le Paysan de Paris,' " 38–39.
32. Venturi, *Archives de l'impressionnisme*, vol. 2, 204–5; Boime, "Entrepreneurial Patronage," 154. Laurent-Richard was probably the "tailleur du roi" based at 2, rue Laffitte (*Didot Annuaire du commerce* [Paris, 1854], 959 and 1172–73).
33. Hippolyte Castille, "Les Frères Pereire," in *Portraits politiques (et historiques) du dix-neuvième siècle* (Paris, 1856–58); Guy Palmade, *French Capitalism in the Nineteenth Century*, trans. Graeme Holmes (London, 1972), 129–31.
34. *Recueil des estampes gravées à l'eau-forte*, preface by Armand Silvestre, 3 vols. (Paris, 1873). It consisted of three hundred illustrations, the largest contingent of Delacroix and the Barbizon group. Among the younger generation there are not only Degas, Monet, and Pissarro but also Puvis de Chavannes, Gustave Moreau, Ferdinand Roybet, Léon Lhermitte, and Emile Van Marcke. Although the catalogue exists in several museums, it seems never to have been put into general circulation, possibly due to the dealer's financial difficulties.
35. Venturi, *Archives de l'impressionnisme*, vol. 2, 208–9.
36. From the late 1820s, the print firm of Goupil had signed contracts with its regular artists like Delaroche and Gérôme (Whiteley, "Art et commerce," 74), but this was primarily to maintain control over the engravings market. Arthur Stevens drew up a contract with Millet in 1860, backed by his industrialist relation Emile Blanc, but the arrangement was soon in chaos and was terminated by 1866 (Alfred Sensier, *La Vie et les oeuvres de J. F. Millet* [Paris, 1881], 205; and Arts Council of Great Britain, *Jean-François Millet*, text by R. L. Herbert [London, 1976], 26). By the 1870s Brame had some kind of contractual and domestic arrangement with Roybet (Eudel, *L'Hôtel Drouot*, vol. 4 [Paris, 1885], 339), while Gustave Tempelaere signed a contract with Bonvin and protected Fantin-Latour (White and White, *Canvases and Careers*, 108; and Ambroise Vollard, *Recollections of a Picture Dealer* [Boston, 1936], 67). More than Durand-Ruel, Georges Petit used the single artist exhibition, promoting Meissonier, Dumoulin, Monet, and Rodin in this way in the 1880s and 1890s.
37. Philippe Burty, *Paul Huet: Notice biographique et critique* (Paris, 1869); Frédéric Henriet, *Vie et l'oeuvre de Chintreuil* (Paris, 1874); Henri Dumesnil, *Corot: Souvenirs intimes* (Paris, 1875); J. Rousseau, *Camille Corot* (Paris, 1884); Sensier, *Millet;* Louis Gonse, *E. Fromentin: Biographie critique* (Paris, 1881); E. Gros-Kost, *Courbet, Souvenirs intimes* (Paris, 1880); Edmond Bazire, *Manet* (Paris, 1884); Louis de Fourcaud, *Bastien-Lepage: Sa Vie et ses oeuvres* (Paris, 1885). For collections, see Philippe Burty, *Maîtres et petits maîtres* (Paris, 1877); Charles Blanc, *Les Artistes de mon temps* (Paris, 1876); Ernest Chesneau, *Peintres et statuaires romantiques* (Paris, 1880); and Jules Clarétie, *Peintres et sculpteurs contemporains* (Paris, 1882–84), 1880, 1882.
38. He provided the text for the first auction of Impressionist work in 1875 and also for Courbet's posthumous sale in 1881—both organized by Durand-Ruel. Other catalogues included a noncommercial exhibition of eighteenth-century pictures from private collections organized by Francis Petit in 1860 and Delacroix's posthumous auction in 1864.

39. *Courrier de l'art*, no. 4 (1881), 1 December, 57, and 22 December, 108.
40. On the flowering of French empirical history in the last decades of the nineteenth century, see George Gooch, *History and Historians in the Nineteenth Century* (London, 1961 [1913]), 198–204; Claude Digeon, *La Crise allemande de la pensée française (1870–1914)* (Paris, 1959), passim; and George Lefebvre, *La Naissance de l'historiographie moderne* (Paris, 1971), 216–20. On the links with art history, see André Michel, *Histoire de l'art*, book 1, vol. 1 (Paris, 1905), 10–11; and Samuel Rocheblave, *Louis de Fourcaud et le mouvement artistique en France de 1875 à 1914* (Paris, 1926), 64. Rocheblave also stresses the importance of nationalism (ibid., 63–65).
41. Eugène de Mirecourt, *Histoire contemporaine: Portraits et silhouettes au XIX siècle*, nos. 1–140 (1867–71); David Madelenat, *La Biographie* (Paris, 1984), 59–61.
42. Richard Shiff, "The End of Impressionism: A Study in Theories of Artistic Expression," *Art Quarterly* 1, no. 4 (1978): 338–78, offered a sophisticated analysis of Impressionism in terms of a language of subjective responses to nature which drew on Taine's philosophical theories. The problem with this account is that it sets up too neat and narrow an equivalence between Impressionist "crisis" and Taine's ideas, failing to locate both in the broader framework of those experimental scientific codes which were hegemonizing truth and knowledge.
43. Physiology as practiced and publicized by Claude Bernard was to stand as the key signifier for the methodology of the experimental sciences from the 1860s (*Introduction à l'étude de la médecine expérimentale* [Paris, 1865]; Reino Virtanen, *Claude Bernard and His Place in the History of Ideas* (Lincoln, Neb., 1960); and Georges Canguilhem, *Idéologie et rationalité* [Paris, 1977], 10 and 44–45). Experimental psychology focusing on the individuality of the subject via a physiological exploration of the nervous system and its relation to attention, sensation, and intelligence was developed from the 1880s by Théodule Ribot, Pierre Janet, and Alfred Binet among others (G. Lamarque, *Théodule Ribot: Choix de texts et l'étude de l'oeuvre* [Paris, undated], especially the preface by Pierre Janet; and Guy Avanzani, *La Contribution de Binet à l'élaboration d'une pédagogie scientifique* [Paris, 1969]).
44. Mrs. C. H. Stranahan in *A History of French Painting* (New York, 1888), 262, claimed that the dominant tendency in art since 1848 was toward individuality, a result of the success of Romanticism in official circles. At the *Ecole du Louvre*, Louis Courajod's lectures on medieval and Renaissance sculpture (1887–96) drew on an expansive definition of naturalism as a distinctive mark of the French spirit to claim the birth of the Renaissance for the north (Wallace K. Ferguson, *The Renaissance in Historical Thought: Five Centuries of Interpretation* [Boston, 1948], 316–19).
45. Discussion of the components feeding into the dominant ideology of the early Third Republic and especially educational policy can be found in Antoine Prost, *Histoire de l'enseignement en France, 1800–1967* (Paris, 1968), 335–45; and Katherine Auspitz, *The Radical Bourgeoisie: The Ligue de l'Enseignement and the Origins of the Third Republic* (Cambridge, 1982), 20–48. Formulations around civic individuality also lie at the heart of the second half of my Ph.D. thesis, "The Nature of the Bourgeoisie: Nature, Art, and Cultural Class Formation in Nineteenth-Century France" (CNAA [Council of National Academic Awards], 1986).
46. Antonin Proust, *L'Art sous la République* (Paris, 1892), 49–57 and 164–74; and Fritz Marcou, Roger Marx, and Emile Molinier, *Histoire de l'art français des origines jusqu'à 1900*, vol. 2 (Paris, 1900), 10–12.
47. Chantel Martinet, "Les Historiens et la statue," *Le Mouvement Social* (April–June 1985): 127. Also see the final chapter of my thesis (see note 45).
48. Sainsbury Centre for Visual Arts, Norwich, *Théodore Rousseau*, exh. cat., text by Nicholas Green (London, 1982), 43.
49. Petit hosted the first exhibition of the *Société internationale des peintres et sculpteurs* in 1882. This was an avowedly modern grouping including Bastien-Lepage, Béraud, Cazin, Dagnan, Duez, Liebermann, and Sargent. He also gave his gallery over to the *Société d'aquarellistes français*, 1882–86 and the *Société des pastellistes français*, 1885–86.
50. *Cent Chefs d'oeuvre des collections parisiennes*, 1883. This catalogue did not mention the destination of the profits as a Catholic charity; a wise precaution considering the current secular climate. But it [this fact] was referenced in the catalogue to a second exhibition, *Cent Chefs d'oeuvre des écoles françaises et étrangères*, July 1892.
51. Eudel, *L'Hôtel Drouot*, vol. 3 (Paris, 1884), 179–81.
52. Georges Lecomte, ed., *Lettres d'un grand-père* (Paris, 1933), 21.
53. Ibid., preface, viii–ix.
54. Ibid., 38.

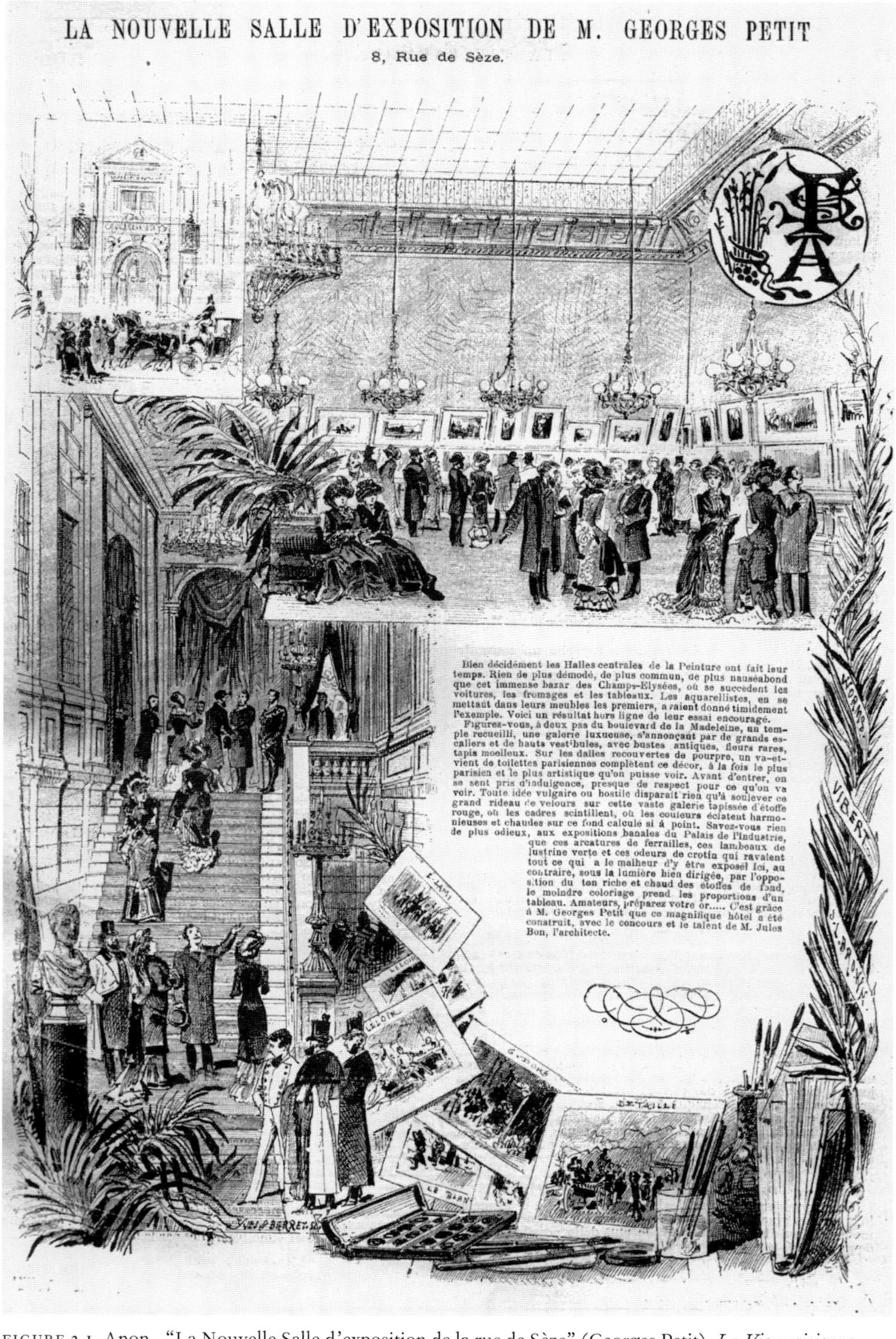

LA NOUVELLE SALLE D'EXPOSITION DE M. GEORGES PETIT

8, Rue de Sèze.

Bien décidément les Halles centrales de la Peinture ont fait leur temps. Rien de plus démodé, de plus commun, de plus nauséabond que cet immense bazar des Champs-Elysées, où se succèdent les voitures, les fromages et les tableaux. Les aquarellistes, en se mettant dans leurs meubles les premiers, avaient donné timidement l'exemple. Voici un résultat hors ligne de leur essai encouragé.

Figurez-vous, à deux pas du boulevard de la Madeleine, un temple recueilli, une galerie luxueuse, s'annonçant par de grands escaliers et de hauts vestibules, avec bustes antiques, fleurs rares, tapis moelleux. Sur les dalles recouvertes de pourpre, un va-et-vient de toilettes parisiennes complètent ce décor, à la fois le plus parisien et le plus artistique qu'on puisse voir. Avant d'entrer, on se sent pris d'indulgence, presque de respect pour ce qu'on va voir. Toute idée vulgaire ou hostile disparait rien qu'à soulever ce grand rideau de velours sur cette vaste galerie tapissée d'étoffe rouge, où les cadres scintillent, où les couleurs éclatent harmonieuses et chaudes sur ce fond calculé si à point. Savez-vous rien de plus odieux, aux expositions banales du Palais de l'Industrie, que ces arcatures de ferrailles, ces lambeaux de lustrine verte et ces odeurs de crotin qui ravalent tout ce qui a le malheur d'y être exposé! Ici, au contraire, sous la lumière bien dirigée, par l'opposition du ton riche et chaud des étoffes de fond, le moindre coloriage prend les proportions d'un tableau. Amateurs, préparez votre or..... C'est grâce à M. Georges Petit que ce magnifique hôtel a été construit, avec le concours et le talent de M. Jules Bon, l'architecte.

FIGURE 3.1. Anon., "La Nouvelle Salle d'exposition de la rue de Sèze" (Georges Petit), *La Vie parisienne* (February 25, 1882): 119. Main Library, University of Illinois at Urbana-Champaign.

3

Impressionist Installations and Private Exhibitions

MARTHA WARD

THE EXPANSION OF THE ART market and the liberal government policies of the early Third Republic encouraged a remarkable proliferation of "independent" exhibitions in Paris, shows that were mounted separately from the huge State-sponsored jamboree, the annual Salon.[1] Dealers, art societies, enterprising painters, and groups like the Impressionists sought out new venues and experimented with installations so as to present their works in the best circumstances. In selecting sites and decor, exhibition organizers did not have recourse to anything like today's specialized techniques of display; they began to develop only toward the end of the century and then primarily for shop merchandise. Instead, the practices and innovations in this period seem to have been prompted by more intuitive judgments about the social connotations of a variety of spaces and audiences and about the appropriate place and role of art in relation to these. By considering a range of shows and focusing on the Impressionists, this essay examines how installations and venues corresponded to or affected understandings of contemporary painting in late nineteenth-century Paris.

In contrast to the diversity of the sites that I have just remarked, Rosalind Krauss has argued that nineteenth-century aesthetic discourse increasingly developed around a generalized exhibition space, characterized by the exclusivity of a wall reserved for showing art and nothing else. Modernist works internalized this medium of display and exchange, Krauss suggests, as landscapes flattened, expanded laterally, and came thus to resemble the exhibition wall itself.[2] My essay investigates this generalized "exhibitionality," but tracks its elaborations across culturally differentiated spheres. Rather than stress how the proliferation and variation of exhibition walls essentially served to provide an increasingly uniform medium of exchange, I emphasize the social and aesthetic distinctions that contemporaries experienced as significant and held to be definitive.[3]

Among the social expectations that affected the presentation and reception of art in nineteenth-century France, the delimitation of the boundaries between the public and the private was especially crucial, although deeply problematic. This distinction depended in the art world on the separation between the Salon and the independently sponsored shows, or, more precisely, on the perception that the latter drew audiences that were not only much smaller but more artistically cultivated. (Hence the separation was both real and ideological.) As art was shown and viewed in diverse places—the Salon, the gallery, the club, the bookstore, the studio, the apartment, the home—the distinction between public and private served to create finely gradated nuances of refinement, and the ideal private exhibition came to be represented as a haven for aesthetic appreciation that was removed from the crass commerce of the art market, the divisive polemics of criticism, and the sensationalized tastes of the "public." Regardless of the fact that the purpose of shows was to sell works or to introduce artists to patrons, creating a noncommercial ambiance was important, and this seems often to have required that the decor and installations of exhibitions be clearly distinguishable from the large rooms stacked with paintings in the Salon or the halls glutted with commodities in Universal Expositions and other late nineteenth-century spectacles. In addition to size and scale, the character of the actual place of exhibition and the composition of the audience suggested what would be an appropriate installation in the private show and, accordingly, what modes of viewing would be encouraged. But there was no certainty in these matters, for during this period venues and their social connotations changed quickly. While the "dealer and critic system" expanded rapidly, artists also increasingly took the initiative for their own promotion, and Salon organizers began to adopt practices from the private domain. The distinction between public and private proved to be chronically unstable and required constant renegotiation with the actual conditions of artistic production and consumption.[4]

Exhibition decor and installation provided organizers with an interface between their conceptions of the special qualities of the art on view and their projections of the expectations of audiences and collectors. Most important, artists or dealers had to determine how a single work should best be contextualized, that is, how it should be positioned in relation to other works and the environment. Installations often had to balance the increasing importance of the individual artist and the integrity of his or her production, on the one hand, against the explanatory or polemical potential afforded by installation according to school, genre, or style, on the other. Similarly, organizers had to define implicitly the status of the small easel painting, which was the type of work most frequently exhibited: was it to be evaluated as an autonomous object addressing the public or as a potentially decorative complement to a domestic space?

Despite the articulation of such problems of definition, many of the key decisions in arranging shows—the selection of site, the choice of wall color, the ordering of picture frames, the hanging of works—were often treated by organizers as simply practical matters and left to the last minute, not to be dictated by elaborate artistic principles or subjected to close critical scrutiny. That such decisions remained relatively untheorized in the day-to-day practice of presenting works—so that changes were not seen to be the result of newly articulated "definitions of art" so much as they seemed to be responses to different material circumstances—makes the history of these exhibition presentations particularly valuable as a register of the variety of assumptions that conditioned production and consumption during this period.

My purpose in this study is to explore the vicissitudes of late nineteenth-century installations in relation to understandings of contemporary art, and to describe the appearances of some of the shows. In the absence of many visual records or sustained discussions, my project has mainly entailed piecing together offhand remarks in critical commentaries and artists' letters. I make no effort to survey all of the types of shows of the early Third Republic or even to treat a representative sample, a project beyond the scope of a single article and one whose unfeasibility as a research endeavor points up the pressing need for a synthetic study of dealers and art institutions of this period. Instead, I concentrate on the presentations at the Impressionist exhibitions and the early shows of the Société des Indépendants, already well documented as events but not systematically considered as installations.

I have adopted a roughly chronological approach, but not because there is a story of development to tell. Rather, by moving between descriptions of Impressionist practices and analyses of other exhibitions—the Salon of the Second Empire, artistic circles and societies, dealers' shows and publications—I want the juxtapositions to demonstrate that for contemporaries, sustaining the separation of public and private spheres in the face of the unprecedented expansion of the art market proved to be not only difficult but crucial.

Criticism of the Salon and Practices of the Early Impressionist Shows, 1874 to 1877

If the history of Impressionist installations has a beginning, it is not with actual practices but with published complaints. In a letter of 1870 that appeared in the newspaper *Paris-Journal*, Edgar Degas described what was wrong with the Salon and advised how to fix it.

Rather than crowd works up, down, and across the walls, the Salon should install only two rows, Degas recommended. Paintings should be separated by at least twenty to thirty centimeters and positioned according to their own demands instead of those preordained by traditional patterns of symmetry. Because not all paintings were made to be viewed from the same vantage point, Degas continued, the artist should specify upon submitting a piece for consideration where it should be displayed, on either the higher or lower level. Furthermore, rather than divide works by medium, the Salon should mix drawings and paintings and should include large and small screens to provide additional space, like those the British had employed in their Fine Arts section at the Paris Universal Exposition of 1867.[5]

Degas aimed his modest reforms at adapting the public forum of the Salon to the needs of exhibitors, and he assumed that the primary concept determining installation should be the integrity of the individual artist and the individual work. Just as authorship should override distinctions in medium, so the autonomy of the work—the particular requirements of a single piece (here as assessed by the artist)—should override the desires of the installer for decorative ensembles. The Salon should not interfere with the right of each individual to determine his or her own best place on the wall.

Degas's privileging of the individual actually conformed to the logic of recent Salon reforms, which had essentially reordered the relative importance of the competing conceptions of how a work should be presented in an exhibition for the public. Starting in 1861, Salon installations had in most cases abandoned allegiance to the central academic concept of the hierarchy of genres (history painting had heretofore often assumed pride of place in the public show for its didactic and inspirational possibilities). Except for several rooms given over to official and patriotic paintings, the alphabet and the artist's name determined where oils hung. Even though the Salon continued to weigh alternative conceptions, the propriety of the individual author had, by the time of Degas's complaints, triumphed over two potentially competing notions: the desire for public instruction and the aesthetics of decorative integration.[6]

In addition to the rights or needs of the individual artist, other points in Degas's letter had also been rehearsed many times in the preceding decade (if not before), including admiration for the spacious installations of the English, who had abolished "skying" at the Royal Academy in the 1860s and who were generally held in France to be commercially and aesthetically more advanced in the arrangement of dealers' galleries and other exhibition spaces. The most commonly made accusation of all against the Salon was that the State-sponsored exhibition was principally a marketplace rather than a forum of public enlightenment, fears that each nineteenth-century generation seems to have rekindled anew. As Patricia Mainardi has shown, the distinction between art exhibition and industrial fair was considerably lessened after 1855 by the location of the Salon in the vast spaces of the Palais de l'Industrie, whose calendar of events was booked with marketable goods. Depending on the month, the visitor might encounter cows, plants, or paintings.[7] In 1867 *La Vie parisienne* demanded special treatment for art, and its commentator concluded his report, as was typical, by recommending that exhibitors take over the shows and find suitably dignified places and appropriate conditions for displaying works of art.[8]

By 1874, for Degas and the other artists who mounted the Impressionist exhibitions, finding appropriate conditions meant withdrawing from the principal public forum, with its continual debates over the commercial or didactic connotations of exhibitions, and exploring the possibilities of more intimate and in that sense more private areas. Their shows were situated in the midst of Haussmann's newly constructed city blocks: in 1874 they mounted an exhibition in the photographer Nadar's recently vacated studios and in 1876 in the art dealer Durand-Ruel's gallery; in 1877 they rented and adapted a domestic apartment for the show. In such spaces, the artists had the opportunity to cultivate conditions appropriate to the appreciation of small easel paintings. Still, the concept of the integrity of the individual's production continued to govern most practical decisions regarding the installations of these ventures: the individual oeuvre became a standard feature of the exhibition wall, almost regardless of domain in the late nineteenth century. However, some reviewers, responsive to the connotations of the sites as well as the appearance of the art, thought that the shows suggested a new and different understanding of the relation between viewer, painting, and exhibition space.

Aspects of the exhibition in 1874 must have been reassuringly familiar to Paris collectors, audiences, and critics. The brownish-red linen, favored by Nadar, was left on the walls as a ground against which the paintings were hung. It marked a departure from the red of the official walls of the Salon and Universal Expositions, but its apparent neutrality must have made it similar to the subdued tones that critics had praised in art society exhibitions of the early 1860s, such as those mounted in elaborate dwellings by Louis Martinet and Alphonse Jame, exhibitions where discretion was the sign of distinction in decor: not too bright the red, not too shiny the gold, not too ostentatious the setting.[9] In 1874 the artists had draperies hung in Nadar's studio, prompting the critic Philippe Burty to remark favorably on its similarity to the appearance of a private gallery.[10] To take advantage at night of their proximity to the theater district, they adopted late hours for the show, a schedule employed for exhibitions in England and also regularly used for shows mounted by French art circles and societies of the 1860s (with a short memory, some French critics hailed these hours as an innovation).

How works were arranged at the exhibition in 1874 remains somewhat unclear, even though such matters were of sufficient concern that they were mentioned in critical reviews, and the catalogue itself carried as a sort of epithet a single line of installation policy: "Once arranged by size, draw determined their placement."[11] The display was spacious, with works hung in two horizontal rows and with larger works placed on the upper level. Jules Castagnary said that the works were arranged by artist and hung in alphabetical order, with the beginning letter of the arrangement established by draw.[12] Different media were exhibited but no mention was made of their location, a fact that suggests that the entire show was probably rigorously governed by the progression of artists' names. Little effort seems to have been made to fashion decorative ensembles.

In contrast to the fair treatment of the individual on the exhibition wall, we get a different sense of the effect of the installation from the comments of the reviewer who was most sensitive to the intimacy of the setting and its implications for the understanding of the paintings: Degas's friend, Philippe Burty, who was a well-known figure on the Paris and London art scenes, an ardent Republican, Japonist, and Anglophile, and a major print collector and critic. In a review that Burty composed for the English audience of *The Academy*, he offered an analogy for the exhibition space of the first Impressionist exhibition:

> The chief object of these gentlemen, whose views, temperament, and education are very dissimilar, was to present their paintings almost under the same conditions as in a studio, that is, in a good light, isolated

> from one another, in smaller numbers than in official exhibitions, which are like docks of painting and sculpture, without the neighbourhood of other works either too bright or too dull.[13]

For the French audience of *La République française*, Burty evoked another comparison: the paintings were "lit rather as in an average apartment, isolated, not too numerous."[14] The favorable connotations of personalized space that informed Burty's descriptions of the proper lighting and viewing conditions pointed toward values that he confirmed by praising the painters for coming in person to the show to greet visitors and to meet amateurs. And these were values that clearly complemented or advanced his assessment of the nature of the painting of the nascent Impressionist group, which must be understood in relation to the artists' withdrawal from the spaces and trappings of "officialdom":

> They renounce success, medals, decorations, and even the esteem of their fellows to pursue a purely artistic end. They depend upon elements of interest strictly aesthetic, and not social or human—lightness of colouring, boldness of masses, blunt naturalness of impression. . . . [B]ased on the swiftest possible rendering of physical sensation, it [their art] considerably narrows the domain of painting. It scarcely leaves room for any but decorative motives; it forbids itself the stirring representation of those complex situations in which the mind collects its forces and takes possession by analysis of places, situations, sentiments.[15]

Indirectly, Burty found in the general aspects of much of the painting on display—in its distance from history painting and from the intellectual and analytical complexity of adequately representing the external world—a link with what he termed the decorative, which he in turn associated with the privately sponsored exhibition. Such a loose but suggestive counterplay between definitions of public and private, autonomous and decorative, intellectual and sensual, was indicative to Burty of the nature of the aesthetic experience in the intimate interior and would continue to be seen, in his reviews, as part of Impressionist shows.

The installations of the next two Impressionist exhibitions did not substantially deviate from that of the first. However, the show of 1877 was mounted by the group in a bourgeois apartment, the type of site that would later provide the spaces for the most decorative of the Impressionist installations, that is, those in which works were most thoroughly integrated with and subordinated to the environment. In 1877 the five rooms of the centrally located apartment on the rue Le Peletier were subdivided by panels, a common practice, which created both more intimate areas and more hanging surfaces. Once again, to judge from reviews, the individual functioned as the primary motif of the installation, although the desire to distribute the largest works ceremonially among rooms and to create harmonious and thematic juxtapositions also affected the arrangement.[16]

Over and against the individual artist or the autonomous work, however, Burty insisted in his reviews on the decorative aspects of both shows, perceiving a relation between the character of the paintings on view and the manner in which they were presented: "The dominant interest of this group being the effects of light and open air, irisation and color, this painting will benefit from being enframed in the vast panels of a high gallery," he wrote in one article of 1876.[17] For his English public, Burty offered similar observations in a later review: "The rooms are very spacious and well lighted, both important requisites for the kind of paintings now exhibited there, which is characterized by a kind of decorative freedom and demands blank spaces between the respective frames."[18] Burty was once again concerned in 1877 with certain implications of seeing works in relation to their setting, finding the paintings effective only when considered as *décors* rather than as completely independent or autonomous works of art *(tableaux)*: "They offend as paintings *[tableaux]* because of their sketchy appearance and indications of scumbling. Seen in place and as *décors*, they have a brightness and frankness which are undeniable."[19] Viewed in relation to the surroundings and from a certain distance, the paintings were effective in creating a sense of light; the otherwise incomplete works possessed expansive qualities of "decorative freedom," which demanded a spacious and well-lit setting. Here lack of autonomy or self-sufficiency and apparent intellectual complexity became a virtue, allowing the successful integration into the interior of a work that appeared decorative without becoming (mere) decoration.

Notions of the decorative and of completeness were frequently employed critical concepts in the discussion of Impressionist painting in the 1870s.[20] In deploying these, however, Burty was the reviewer who was most attentive to the installations of the early Impressionist exhibitions and the most concerned with the implications that the privacy of the setting might have for the perception and, in that respect, the status of the paintings being exhibited. Still, his connections remained vaguely formulated: metaphorical conjunctions of visual appearances and social spaces. More fully developed conceptions of the place of art in the private domain, as well as the characteristics of art to be valued in the intimate show, were to be found elsewhere, in responses to exhibitions other than the Impressionist ventures. When compared to these exhibitions where a more or less coherent logic of the private show emerged in installations and publications, it becomes evident that the walls at the early Impressionist shows failed to secure convincingly the values associated with either the public or private space but constructed instead a rather awkward site.

Installations in Art Circles and Societies in the 1870s and 1880s

Simultaneously with the Impressionist exhibitions in the mid-1870s, other privately sponsored shows were mounted by artistic circles and societies, groups that generally included both artists and amateurs as members. Art circles and societies had been organized during earlier periods, and they thrived in the 1870s and 1880s, when they afforded increasingly professionalized artists direct access to collectors and to financial backing for shows, while allowing amateurs to buy without the intermediary of a dealer and on occasion to exhibit their own works. As Tamar Garb has recently emphasized, these often entirely male institutions and their elaborate houses served as a noncommercial forum for leisure and business contacts outside the home, establishing a site that extended well beyond the demands of the art world to service more generally the needs of mid-nineteenth-century bourgeois society for forms of sociability reliant on gendered and financial exclusivity.[21] Here the cultivation of aesthetic appreciation relied, in part, upon the assurance that one was removed from the competition of the market and shared a space with amateurs and artists of compatible sensibility.

Creating the right ambiance was essential to the success of the enterprise of the circles. The standards were set by the first and most famous of the "petits salons," the Cercle de l'Union Artistique, familiarly known as the Mirlitons, which began in the 1850s and counted among its members in the 1870s such artists as Carolus-Duran, Edouard Detaille, and Ernest Meissonier. The Mirlitons held exhibitions in the 1870s in the elaborate top-floor galleries of the building owned by the circle in the place Vendôme. Such extensive facilities were generally associated with the elite circles, although some dealers, such as Denman Tripp, whose galleries opened in a *hôtel* in 1883, sought to encourage shared activities by providing special rooms for viewing prints, reading about art, and talking and socializing.[22]

Contemporary illustrations and critical reviews reveal that in installing shows in their main room, which also served for concerts and theater performances, the Mirlitons generally avoided vast spaces reminiscent of the Louvre or Salon and favored more intimate settings constructed in part by easels and screens. Following the common practice at the Salon and in dealers' galleries, the room at the place Vendôme was further subdivided by divans and plants, which also served to diversify a coloration otherwise dominated by the dull red of tapestried walls and the muted gold of frames. Daytime illumination came through an iron and glass skylight, and for evening sessions (which sometimes ran as late as 11 P.M.), the room was hung with gaslight chandeliers, carefully distanced from the walls and ceilings to avoid shadowing and equipped with cup-shaped reflectors to direct light laterally. Although in the event of a sizable exhibition, installations might depart from the norm of two or three rows to fill the wall, rarely, if ever, were paintings displayed in a single row, an arrangement that some critics recommended for adoption in the 1870s but that must have seemed to exhibition organizers altogether impractical given the general expectation that shows should contain at least one to two hundred works.[23] Similarly revelatory of the mode of viewing in the intimate yet sociable spaces of the Mirlitons is the fact that although skirts beneath dados went out of fashion for exhibitions in the 1870s, these rooms retained the waist-high railing that allowed the viewer to balance his or her weight while closely inspecting a work to appreciate the detail of the depiction or the execution of the surface. Totally oblivious to one's surroundings, carefully poised against the railing, with nose pressed against the painting, and with catalogue dangling in hand: this is the stock viewing posture that incessantly appears in representations of all sorts of midcentury exhibitions, public and private. Yet conditions conducive to such engagement seem to have been most often realized in exclusive spaces like those of the Mirlitons.

The Mirlitons was the sort of aristocratic milieu where, unlike the Salon or a dealer's gallery or an Impressionist show, men were likely to remove their top hats and lower their voices. Ernest Chesneau, Inspector of Fine Arts during the Second Empire, a well-informed critic and enthusiastic supporter of independent shows (including the Impressionist endeavors), felt ill at ease performing his public role at the Mirlitons, where the privacy of the locale made the directness of art journalism inappropriate:

> To tell the truth, the Mirlitons' show presents only one inconvenience, but it is serious. One is in the midst of interested parties, invited by them to their dwelling: one is their guest. As a result, it is appropriate to express one's opinion of the exhibited works only with discretion, to speak only at half voice, sometimes to be altogether silent. Only admiration can be shown expansively.[24]

The exclusivity of the site did not preclude publicity (the shows were reviewed), but the milieu did apparently quiet criticism *sur place*. Criticism was understood here as a "public" discourse about art that had been painted for the "public" and, as such, it was out of place at the circles. This was the representation that ill-at-ease reviewers provided as they wrote about the shows without the justification of serving the public interest, a justification readily provided by the Salon, and without the need to fulfill such higher functions of criticism as assessing the state of art in France, encouraging unknown talent, educating the tastes of viewers, or even presuming to speak for a readership. The art critic and historian Henry Houssaye put it well: at the circles, the reviewer had nothing to diagnose in the present and nothing to predict for the future.[25]

When reviewers noted that their judgments had been inappropriate at the show but then expressed their opinions in newspapers, they exploited a perhaps contradictory set of expectations among their readers. On the one hand, protests against the privacy of the circles bolstered the image of the critic's allegiance and responsibility to a public readership, and reinforced the notion that criticism informed and represented the views of readers, perhaps even transforming them into audiences for art. On the other hand, the reviewer's description of private milieus advanced the chief characteristic of the shows that appealed to amateurs and no doubt to the social imaginations of many newspaper readers as well: namely, that the private space was the preserve of a truly experienced aesthetic, a relation between art and viewer that was in its very essence noncritical, perhaps even nonverbal.

Critics' descriptions of the privacy of these shows, and their simultaneous circumvention or transgression of that privacy, reveals that exhibition walls like those at the Mirlitons could be simultaneously situated in different places—an elite Paris address and the columns of the press—and subjected to conflicting expectations of art with relative ease. The separateness of the private domain and its removal from the market were reinforced in principle even as they were denied in practice.

By the end of the 1870s, such "private" settings as the Mirlitons had come to be praised by favorable reviewers for providing a haven where artists could disclose their most "natural" or spontaneous aspects, the personal sides of their individuality, their incomplete works. Here the artist sent work that escaped professional definitions of genre, medium, or finish but that the amateur, as the acquaintance of the artist, would understand and treasure for what it revealed of the private side of the individual. For those who developed the logic of the private exhibition to its fullest, the expressions of individuality among members of the circles and societies did not result in the discord that characterized the Salon, whose competitive and democratic forum forced heightened displays of self-promotion. Because members had to be voted into circles, a similarity or compatibility of sentiments—a certain level of taste—was assured. Thus, explained the reviewer of *La Paix*, the viewer of these shows could pass from one work to the next and appreciate the nuances of the person, without experiencing too much of a jolt in moving between neighbors on the wall.[26]

The formation of societies based on media, especially following the example of the successful Société d'Aquarellistes Français in 1879, underscored the nonpublic character of the exhibitions.[27] To the intimacy of the space was joined the intimacy of the technique and materials. Like pastels or prints, watercolor was treated in specialized journals as an art of the connoisseur, an art removed from the glaring public pronouncements produced in oil for Salon consumption. The space reserved for watercolors and pastels at the Palais de l'Industrie in the 1870s and 1880s was celebrated by Raoul dos Santos, then critic of the *Moniteur des arts*, as a place where only artists and true lovers of art ventured, a place whose intimacy could be measured by the absence of history or anecdotal painting.[28] Cardon similarly maintained that "private" light was necessary for the proper appreciation of works on paper: "It's a delicate, intimate, lovable art that one can only appreciate well in a choice, elegant, distinguished milieu; it needs some care and installation; it needs a discreet light; the light of the street or the public place does not suit it at all."[29] It was to these associations that the Société d'Aquarellistes appealed in the reticently decorated exhibition premises that it maintained on the rue Le Peletier, in the same building, in fact, as the galleries of Durand-Ruel.

What is revealed when the shows of these circles and societies are juxtaposed with the Impressionist exhibitions is that the values that came to shape the contents and organization of the former—the nonprofessional and nonfinished, the informal and personal, the aristocratic and cultivated, the private and the nondiscursive—were also values called upon in the evaluation of Impressionist painting. The Impressionist exhibitions failed to engender among many reviewers expectations similar to those shaped by the circles (i.e., that here was a proper haven for the artist's expression of self and for the viewer's cultivation of aesthetic sensibility, *hors Salon*). An explanation may be found in the art displayed at the Impressionist shows, to be sure, but the failure must also have resulted from the nomadic appearances of the group and their insecure definition in relation to the spaces and practices that structured the private domain, especially when they temporarily renovated apartments for shows open to the public. Moving from place to place, the Impressionists clearly lacked the financial solidity, established premises, and informed amateur membership of other associations. In 1880 Victor Champier identified the group as "this society that doesn't have a place of its own."[30] Rather than appearing to escape the public domain and to provide a refuge for refining the senses, their exhibitions seemed to some commentators to be designed for posturing in public: their stylistic experimentation was polemical and factional; their expression of individuality, forced; their lack of finish, an affront. In accord with the hybrid character of the exhibitions, responses varied widely, and favorable critics like Burty found aspects of the shows especially satisfying as a private domain where the senses delighted in decorative ensembles. No critic removed his top hat at the Impressionist shows, however, and none deemed the business of criticism inappropriate. Chez les Mirlitons, intimacy meant one thing; at an Impressionist show, quite another.

Decorative Impressionist Installations, 1879 to 1881

It was from 1879 to 1881 that the Impressionist exhibitions, all held in apartment-like spaces, assumed an especially intimate character. Innovations at this time seem to have been directed toward exploiting associations with the private domain. In particular, this involved renegotiating through practice the definition and interrelation of media, decoration, and individuality. Degas seems to have provided the motivation necessary for these endeavors; with his absence from the show in 1882, innovation ceased.

The most overt manifestation of the new tendencies at the Impressionist shows came with the use of colored frames and walls. Already at the exhibition of 1877 Pissarro and Degas had used white frames, thus marking the first appearance among the Impressionists of what would, after a decade of pervasive use by the group, be called the "Impressionist frame."[31] From 1879 to 1881, Pissarro, Degas, and Cassatt paid considerable attention to the possibilities of employing color to redefine the relationship of work and environment, to enhance decorative appeal, and to code through color relations the individual character of their work. Degas and Cassatt used colored frames for some of their pieces at the show of 1879, but unfortunately no reviewer mentioned how the colors may have been cued to the paintings or surroundings. In his review of the Impressionist exhibition of 1880, J.-K. Huysmans noted that Pissarro's prints were exhibited with yellow mats and bordered by purple frames. These experiments gave rise at the show in 1881 to a profusion of individually designed frames. Huysmans was again the most enthusiastic as well as the most descriptive reviewer:

> What variety in the frames, which carry varied tones of gold and which are bordered with margins painted with the color complementary to the frames! The series of Pissarro is, this year, surprising above all. It's a variety of water- and veronese-green, of corn and peach skin, of unguent yellow and wine-colored purple, and you have to see with what tact the colorist has sorted out all his tints to make his skies recede and his foregrounds come forth. It's the sharpest refinement; and, even though the frame can't add anything to the talent of a work, it's still a necessary complement, an addition that brings out value. It's the same thing as the beauty of a woman which requires certain surroundings.[32]

The border of complementary color made evident one new role that the frame was assuming. It was now to be seen not just as a complement to a painting, or as a zone of transition between the worlds of the painting and the viewer. While serving as a *repoussoir*, it was also to be perceived as entering into an expansive, active, and coloristic relation with the painted surface.[33]

Like colored frames, tinted exhibition rooms served the end of subordinating the autonomy of the work to a decorative display and to an identity compatible with or fostered by the surroundings. Burty deplored the crowded conditions at the 1880 exhibition but nevertheless praised the artists for making the best of their limited circumstances by painting the various rooms in those tones that they felt were best suited to the effect *(effet)* of their works. Just to prove that they were not prejudiced, Burty said, the artists had set one room aside (labeled the Salon d'Institut) and in homage to official practice had painted it antique red. The landscapes of Charles Tillot and Henri Rouart, whom Burty called "les sages," were hung there.[34] It is very likely that this was the exhibition that Pissarro and his son Lucien recalled in 1883 in an exchange of letters about exhibition decoration and specifically about Whistler's installations. Lucien wrote from London that Whistler, whose show with yellow interiors and butterfly signatures he had just seen, had stolen the Impressionist idea for tinted exhibition rooms. Pissarro lamented in his response that the Impressionists had generally lacked the means to realize fully their ideas for decoration, although he had once had a lilac room with a yellow border, albeit *sans papillons*.

Whistler had created his first one-man show in 1874 by reconstructing and recoloring a dealer's gallery to suggest how his works would appear on the walls of patrons' homes. This and his later installations provided an important precedent for the Impressionist experimentation with domestic spaces and colored rooms and frames, although they were not a source Pissarro later remembered or was at any rate willing to acknowledge. Still, the similarities are striking: the interest in innovative borders, the decorative coordination of painting and environment through complementary contrasts or color pairs, the integration of various media, and (possibly) the mounting of deliberately asymmetrical displays. However, Pissarro indicated his distrust of totally harmonized ensembles in 1883, when he responded to Lucien's descriptions of Whistler's exhibition rooms with an attack on aestheticism. Even though the decorative installation might seem to provide a refuge from the anonymity and commodification of art in the public exhibition space, its complete realization—its complete absorption of the work in the fully unified effect of an aestheticized ensemble—seems to have struck Pissarro as a promotional gimmick, for in his letter he associated aestheticism with *puffisme*.[35]

Although much less insistently or successfully than Whistler, the Impressionists who had tinted rooms of their own at these shows still contextualized art in ways that resonated with models for the domestic domain. To enhance the appearance of their works, the artists exploited in part the feminine pursuit of expressing personal identity through interior arrangement. At the 1881 show, for example, settees and rocking chairs were put in the crowded mezzanine apartment, and Degas's works inhabited the cabinet, the most secluded area of the show, which he distinguished as his own by hanging it in yellow. The practice anticipates the advice to be offered in manuals on how to decorate intimate spaces, the private rooms where one is face to face with oneself. Here one should avoid ostentation in ornamentation and banish overly gilt surfaces, and instead, Henry Havard advised the female readers of his work on interior decoration, *L'Art dans la maison* of 1882, "Choose the color that is yours, morally and physically, and then, to go with it, give preference to tones and nuances that harmonize."[36] Just as a domestic space personalized through color harmony should provide an area "naturally" coded for the complexion of the owner and her more intimate possessions, so the works of a single artist at an exhibition might best be comprehended in the expressive cast of an appropriately tinted room.

The gendered aspects of the model remained mute in most criticism, however, and it was only when Huysmans and Jules Laforgue evoked the common analogy of decorative frames and women's toilettes that the implications of establishing personal taste through color preference were extended. Writing in 1883, Laforgue marveled at the Impressionist borders and relied upon this analogy to reinforce his description of the highly personalized nature of their decorative enterprise:

> A sunny green landscape, a bright winter scene, an interior twinkling with polishes and fashions require different frames, which only their respective authors know how to devise, just as a woman knows better than anyone else the nuances of materials and powders and boudoir hangings that will bring out her color, the expression of her face, her manners. We've seen frames that were flat, white, pale pink, green, jonquil yellow, and others variegated to the extreme with a thousand tones and in a thousand manners.[37]

Similarly accentuating the intimacy of the installations during these years was the artists' inclusion of different media and their alteration of the surface appearances of oil paintings. In his review of the show in 1879, Havard wrote that he felt certain that both

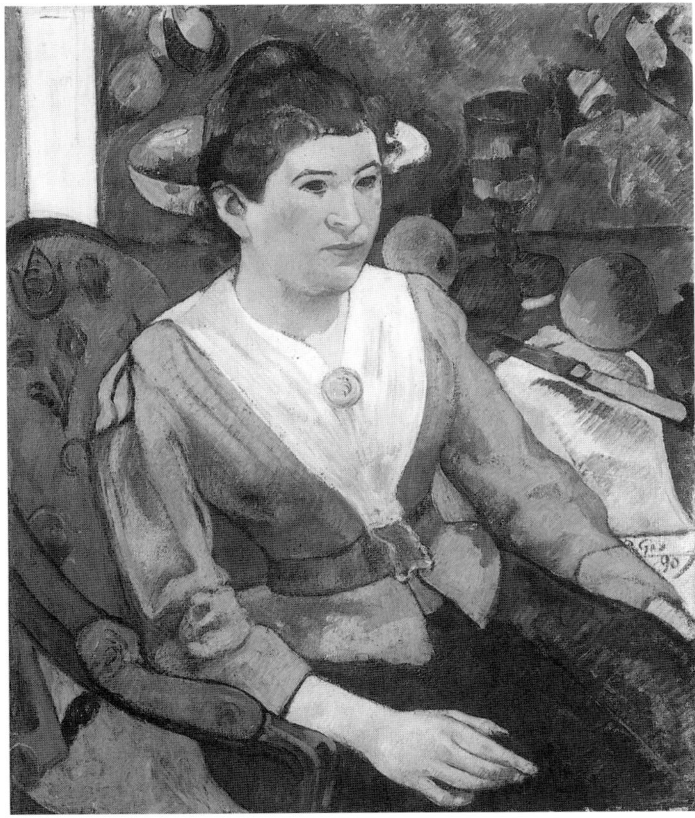

FIGURE 3.2. Paul Gauguin, *Portrait of a Woman in Front of a Still Life by Cézanne*, 1890. The Art Institute of Chicago, The Joseph Winterbotham Collection, 1925.753. Photo © The Art Institute of Chicago.

Degas's and Cassatt's colored borders were somehow connected with their interest in gouache, chalk, and distemper.[38] Pissarro also shared their concern to explore the possibilities of media such as gouache and pastel, whose dry, opaque surfaces were inherently mat. In fact, critics seem to have felt an irresistible impulse to compare the effect of Impressionist paintings in general, but particularly the works of Pissarro, Degas, and Cassatt during these years, to pastels or frescoes.[39] The mat surface was an appearance that this group associated with a sense of brightness in the phrase reoccurring in letters by Pissarro and others as a desideratum, "faire mat et clair," which involved making a surface seem luminous in its own right, without the reflection of external light. Given the setting of the decorative exhibition and the scale of the works, such techniques must also have suggested a Rococo-like confection and a delicacy of effect far removed from the glaring "public" surfaces of Salon oils.

The widespread recognition that the Impressionists had manipulated oils to resemble pastel and gouache was probably facilitated by the type of frame the artists employed. As far as we know from contemporary descriptions, the most common Impressionist frame was a hybrid mat frame that was relatively flat, roughly parallel to the wall, and facing the spectator more than sloping inward toward the painting; usually it was rather plain with only a few bands of different woods, colors, or gilt, and little projecting ornamentation (see, for example, the frame in fig. 3.2). It was a border that nineteenth-century manuals recommended for use with already matted works (gouaches, distempers, drawings, etc.), where the frame did not have to encourage the illusion of depth or to establish an appropriately oblique transition between the world of the image and that of the viewer.[40]

Also contributing to the intimate mode of viewing suggested by the evocation of domestic space was the use of glass for the display of oil paintings. Pissarro was singled out among the exhibitors in 1881 and 1882 for placing sheets of glass over oils, an unusual practice in France (it would be forbidden at the Salon in 1888) but more common in England and quickly associated by reviewers with the *mode anglaise*.[41] On separate occasions, the critic Félix Fénéon and Pissarro remarked on the advantage in placing glass over a work, an advantage that reveals the more subtle processes of perception and association at work: essentially glass served as a filter to alter one's sense of the physical nature of the surface which, when viewed "naked," both artist and critic considered to be too rough and irregular.[42] Apparently glass acted to elide material irregularities in the painting, thus enhancing perception of the luminous, expansive qualities of a mat surface while simultaneously inviting the precious inspection of a delicate pastel. The *toilette* suited well the character of the exhibition, both decorative and intimate.

These shows went further than any other ventures of the Impressionist group in subordinating the autonomy of the work and the individuality of the artist to the harmonies of a private environment. Still, as comparison with several literary enterprises of the period makes plain, the Impressionist experiments were tentative, and certain latent tensions within them suggest a considerable reluctance on the part of the artists to define their paintings entirely in the terms of the decorative and nondiscursive modes of the domestic interior.

It was in literature that the most striking and notorious development of the gendered and classed implications of male decorative enterprises occurred. In Edmond de Goncourt's *La Maison d'un artiste* (1881) and Huysmans's *A Rebours* (1884), these were given a decidedly decadent and aristocratic allure.[43] Here, primary divisions of responsibility for the appearances of the bourgeois interior—the roles of the man as collector and the woman as decorator—were collapsed as men of leisure inhabited womanless spaces. In a curious newspaper article of the late 1880s, Maurice de Fleury described at length the house of an almost certainly imaginary collector, an aristocrat who expressed himself and his modernity through decoration with new materials and recent art. In his "*maison sans femme*" (emphasis mine), Duke X had positioned Impressionist and Symbolist works in an environment embellished with the architectural materials he advocated for the creation of a *style troisième République* (the piece was dedicated to Charles Garnier, the most vocal opponent of iron and glass construction). The house had among its many ensembles a *salle de bain* lined with pastels of women by Degas, a *salle de gymnastique* outfitted with energetic posters by Chéret, and a *chambre à coucher* complete with interiors by Caillebotte and Forain, a Whistler vision, and a Redon nightmare. The "maison d'un moderniste" pastiched for the amusement of the newspaper reader the notoriously decadent behavior of Huysmans's des Esseintes, now rendered less eccentric and more modern, converted to a taste for glass and Impressionism.

These parodic installations far outdid what the Impressionist shows might have suggested about the function or definition of art in a private ensemble. The interiors by Duke X were built on the assumption that the domestic installation of one's collection should completely subsume the works to the quotidian activities and moods of the resident, and vice versa. What is striking about the decorative Impressionist installations of the early 1880s, in comparison, is how much the works exhibited in the tinted settings must have disrupted or, in any case, resisted assimilation into the personalized environment or appreciation through analogy with experiences of the interior. I find it frankly difficult to imagine the effect in 1881 of seeing displayed in Degas's small cabinet, suffused with yellow, his portraits of notorious criminals; or of seeing set against lavender walls, correlated to the tints of frames and placed discreetly under glass, Pissarro's stiffly jointed and roughly brushed peasants.[44] Here, the connotations of the depictions and the decorativeness assumed by the installation must have resulted in a bizarrely contradictory display.

Whatever motivated the decorative experiments from 1879 to 1881, they seem as much an attempt to contextualize the exhibition wall in accord with its apartment setting as an effort to suggest a mode of perception entirely appropriate for the art. The exhibitors I have discussed drew their installations from gendered and classed practices of decoration, but they stopped far short of enhancing or even endorsing these with the types of works they chose for display. Certainly, it was not the case that they were unsure of how to translate their art into decoration for the interior: in the early 1870s Pissarro had painted above-the-door landscapes of the seasons and in the mid-1880s Monet created door panels of flowers for the *grand salon* of Durand-Ruel's apartment.[45] Nor was it the case that the decorative installations of the walls at these Impressionist exhibitions compromised the more pictorially specific (and less overtly gendered) conception of the "decorative" that had led Burty and others to praise landscapes in the early Impressionist shows, for such appreciation continued to greet appropriate works from 1879 to 1881. Instead, the odd assortment of forms and subjects that showed up in the colored frames, tinted walls, and close spaces of the Impressionist expositions of these years suggests, I think, that the artists were ultimately unable to accept the possibility that their own installations evinced: art might be subordinated to or subsumed by an emerging (feminine) sense of interior decoration.

Dealers' Exhibitions in the 1880s

Economic conditions in the French art market changed in the early 1880s. The depression that began in 1882 heightened competition for a share of the market in contemporary paintings, a market that seemed to be diminishing and was certainly threatened. The Salon, which the State handed over to the artists themselves in 1881, had already begun to experiment with modest innovations in décor, arrangement, and hours. But it was dealers who took the lead at this time and gained more control over artists partly by structuring new possibilities for exhibition while simultaneously affecting expectations about shows with new sites and strategies.

The new stage was set by the opening of Georges Petit's premises on the rue de Sèze in February of 1882, the same month as the collapse of the Catholic bank, the Union Générale. Critics declared the site unprecedented among Paris exhibition spaces for splendor (see fig. 3.1) and only a glance at galleries of an earlier generation is needed (fig. 3.3) to establish the difference in milieu. A high vestibule, lined with antique busts on marble bases, old tapestries, and fresh exotic flowers, gave way to a ceremonially broad and gently sloped staircase, stationed with attendants, clad in red. Passing under a thickly draped velvet curtain, the visitor turned right into the grand *salle*, measuring sixteen by twenty-six meters. Here works hung in two or three rows on draped walls of warm chestnut red. Softly filtered daytime illumination came from the iron and glass skylight that extended the entire length of the room. For evening viewing, the regiment of twenty or so regularly spaced chandeliers, equipped with gas bulbs and copper reflectors, added still more warmth to the *salle*, effects that reviewers found marvelous. Everywhere the decor was plush, some thought a bit to excess.[46]

Despite what another critic called the "vastitude" of the "Petit(e) *salle*," provisions were made for the desire for intimacy in viewing. An elaborate wooden skirting and dado supported works propped upon it for close inspection. The predictable divans and plants were present, although somewhat ineffective as spatial dividers in the *salle* Petit, and an ample supply of portable chairs was provided to help offset the officialness of the room by permitting spontaneous conversations and facilitating comfortable observation. Petit had it both ways: the grandeur of the space could suggest Garnier's Opera, but the flexibility of the

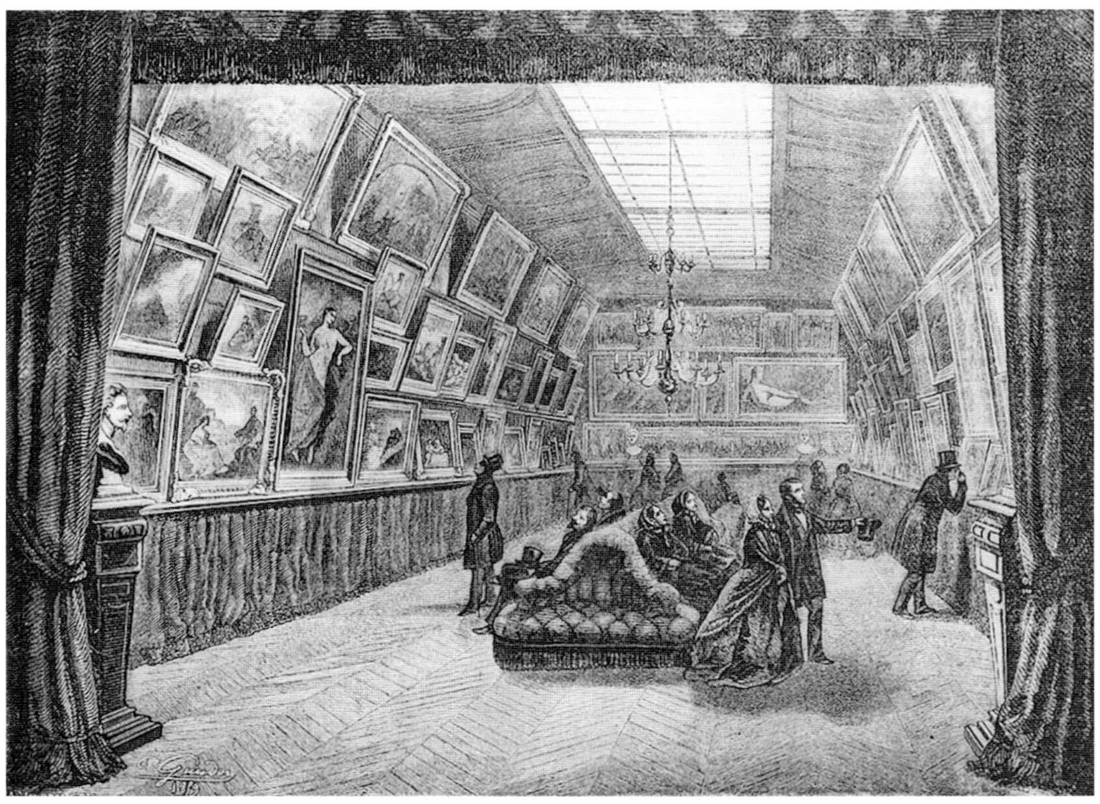

FIGURE 3.3. Anon., Galerie Goupil, *L'Illustration* 35 (March 10, 1860): 155. Bibliothèque nationale de France, Paris.

arrangement could accommodate a range of shows and purposes. Although unique in Paris, it was roughly the same size as the main room of the Grosvenor Gallery in London, and it must have seemed less imposing if compared to that most modern and elaborately outfitted place of merchandizing, to which Emile Zola among others noted its resemblance, the Paris department store.[47]

Hurt by the crash of the stock market, Durand-Ruel responded to the palace of his rival (as well as to Petit's bid for Impressionist business) not in kind but with a new tack, one that exploited the already tested virtues of the intimate space, the individual artist, and the wealthy amateur. In the spring of 1883 Durand-Ruel transformed a mezzanine apartment at 9 boulevard de la Madeleine into a gallery and mounted there a series of one-person exhibitions, beginning with Boudin and followed by Monet, Renoir, Pissarro, and Sisley. We know little about the appearances of the gallery-apartment on the boulevard de la Madeleine except that it was small and very lavish: four rooms, hung in garance [madder]-colored cloth, furnished with tables and twelve red-clad chairs.[48] "Fort bien ornée, ma foi!" was one critic's not atypical reaction.[49] Another noted the thick carpets and wall hangings and set the social register accordingly: "One goes there discreetly and speaks softly."[50] Some critics understood the gallery to be a permanent home for the Impressionists, perhaps a resolution to questions of stability raised by the roving appearances of the group shows and the need to have a place of their own.[51] A survey of the gallery's records reveals that 9 boulevard de la Madeleine was, in fact, an address reserved exclusively for Impressionism: except for Boudin, there was apparently nothing else in the place. Sisley described the moment to Durand-Ruel as one when the Impressionists had ceased to be nomads.[52]

The boulevard de la Madeleine was apparently a good move made at the wrong time; despite the enormous expenditure on its decoration, no shows were mounted after those of the inaugural spring season, and the gallery closed its doors at the end of the year. Following this venture, Durand-Ruel remained content to compete with Petit in Paris from his premises on the rue Laffitte. And even though he could on occasion mount shows in specially designed decors, such as that created in 1893 for the Bing-sponsored show of Japanese art, with exotic pink and green hangings and spare, asymmetrical designs on the walls, Durand-Ruel seems to have decided that it was best not to be too adventurous in Paris but to subscribe to the norm: red tapestried surfaces, gilt frames, a spacious arrangement with some easels and a few palms. Installed in one or more of his gallery rooms, an Impressionist show could still appeal here to an audience's imagination of the preferred milieu for experiencing modern art. In 1891 the critic Emile Bergerat condemned the Salon and its commercialism and recommended instead that his readers go to see Monet's series paintings at Durand-Ruel's: a "truly private and intimate space."[53]

Durand-Ruel extended the decorative tendencies of Impressionist paintings not so much through the practices he instituted in his gallery as in the publication he devoted to the experience of Impressionist painting in his home. He produced his own version of the "maison d'un moderniste" in a deluxe edition of 1892, *L'Art impressionniste d'après la collection privée de M. Durand-Ruel.* Skillfully composed by Pissarro's close friend, the gifted young *littérateur* and critic Georges Lecomte, the book describes the possessions of the dealer in a multitude of mini-chapters, curiously bracketed between an introductory account of the development of Impressionism and a concluding note on the future of the movement. Thus framed by a narrative of the historical importance of Impressionism, the titles and contents of the middle chapters shift dizzyingly from the names and attitudes of individual artists to the titles of individual works to the appearances of the rooms of the *maison* Durand-Ruel. The apotheosis of decoration and description occurs in the chapter on the *petit salon* of the dealer's home:

> We enter into the drawing room of M. Durand-Ruel. The lowered blinds create delicate shadows and already on the walls appear reflections, glimmers, mysterious glares. The lightness of cool tones illuminates. We could say that these radiant colors are being seen in the confusion of a dream, such is the joy of this dawn attenuated by subtle fog. . . . All the joys of nature are condensed in this small space.[54]

Lecomte proceeded to evoke paintings by Monet, Renoir, and Pissarro in a dense and reflexive prose which suggested the decorative possibilities of the art, stretching actions from sentences across paragraphs and hues from two-dimensional surfaces across three. His celebration of the Durand-Ruel *petit salon* ended with a note on the thick draperies, tapestries, and carpets that enclosed the room and protected its silent drama from the harshness of the tumultuous exterior. Here the private domestic space became a pantheistic microcosm, encompassing nature and artist, painting and resident, indeed submerging these merely material qualities in the dream of a higher unity.

Such a vision of wholeness, domestically sheltered, answered to deeply felt needs to preserve the integrity of the private domain and to secure there the truth and the purity of aesthetic experience. The thick curtains in Durand-Ruel's house seem metaphorically to shut out a host of evils—competitive markets, divisive politics, unsuitable publics, critical polemics, and perhaps even words themselves—in order to secure at "home" (Lecomte's term) a space where unity can be recovered through the senses. Even a narration of the history of Impressionism would only be, to judge from the ordering of Lecomte's chapters, an intrusion on the sensual immediacy of the *petit salon.*[55]

In the end, the *maison* Durand-Ruel dealt shrewdly with competition from the *salle* Petit.

Impressionist and Independent Shows of the Late 1880s

In the late 1880s, some avant-garde circles reacted against the implications of decorative installations and the values of intimacy that had so contributed to the appeal of privately sponsored exhibitions.[56] While the efforts of the Neo-Impressionists were informed by a more hermetic and insistent aestheticism than the decorative and more commercially practical impulses that characterized Impressionist installations, because the younger group mainly participated in public shows, their reassertion of the autonomy of easel painting possessed the power of critique.

A preliminary manifestation of these tendencies occurred at the last Impressionist exhibition, which was held in the late spring of 1886 in a splendidly situated, five-room apartment. Each of the seventeen participants had his or her own panel on which to mount an unlimited number of works in any manner. However, as a result of what started as personal quarrels and became polemical divides, the Neo-Impressionist faction installed its work as a group in the last room of the show. This exhibition lacked the amenities of some of the earlier Impressionist ventures: no hangings, draperies, plants, or Algerian settees. "So much the better," said the militantly avant-garde Belgian critic Octave Maus: "All attention is directed toward the works."[57] That insistent focus on the works themselves, along with an allegiance to group presentation, subsequently emerged as the guiding principles of Neo-Impressionist installations.

Many of the Neo-Impressionists adopted as their primary forum not a privately sponsored venue but a decidedly public one: the Société des Artistes Indépendants, which had been founded in 1884 and which held its exhibitions from 1887 onward in the Pavillon de la Ville de Paris, supported with city funds. Ranging in size at this time from roughly four hundred to seven hundred works, the shows were jammed into four large rooms, and entries might be mounted in three or four horizontal rows. Participants could submit as many works as desired and could specify which should be placed higher or lower, relative to the others in their own submission. The individual was the primary installation concept, but rather than follow alphabetical order on the wall, organizers sought to situate each artist within a compatible group. Thus, at the show opening in August 1886 and at each exhibition thereafter, the Neo-Impressionists and other avant-garde artists appeared together in the final room. The arrangement encouraged critical polemics.

It was principally in this forum over the course of the late 1880s that the Neo-Impressionists developed an installation aesthetic, one that addressed the public nature of their exhibition site. The autonomy of the work came foremost: the separation of the painting from its environment and its exclusive claim on the viewer's attention were essential to secure. Having endorsed the white frames that the group favored in 1886 and 1887, the politically and artistically radical critic who was the principal defender of the Neo-Impressionists, Félix Fénéon, introduced the concern for autonomy when he claimed that the artists' experiments in 1888 with frames of complementary color were misconceived: had the frame been painted to put the painting *en valeur,* he asked, or vice versa?[58] This same year in the radical paper *Le Cri du peuple*, Paul Signac defended the Neo-Impressionists' rejection of the red of the walls at the Independents and their decision to hang the walls of their space, the last room, with gray coverings. When works were displayed here with white or other achromatic frames, he claimed, the effect was to make the colors of the paintings more vibrant.[59] In another piece published in the same newspaper in 1888, Signac mounted a diatribe against the viewing conditions created by the deep-red walls and frames "dripping with gold" at the *galerie* Durand-Ruel and the *salle* Petit: it would be up to the Neo-Impressionists to establish the definitively normal (neutral) exhibition environment.[60] It was in this year that Pissarro expressed his preference for

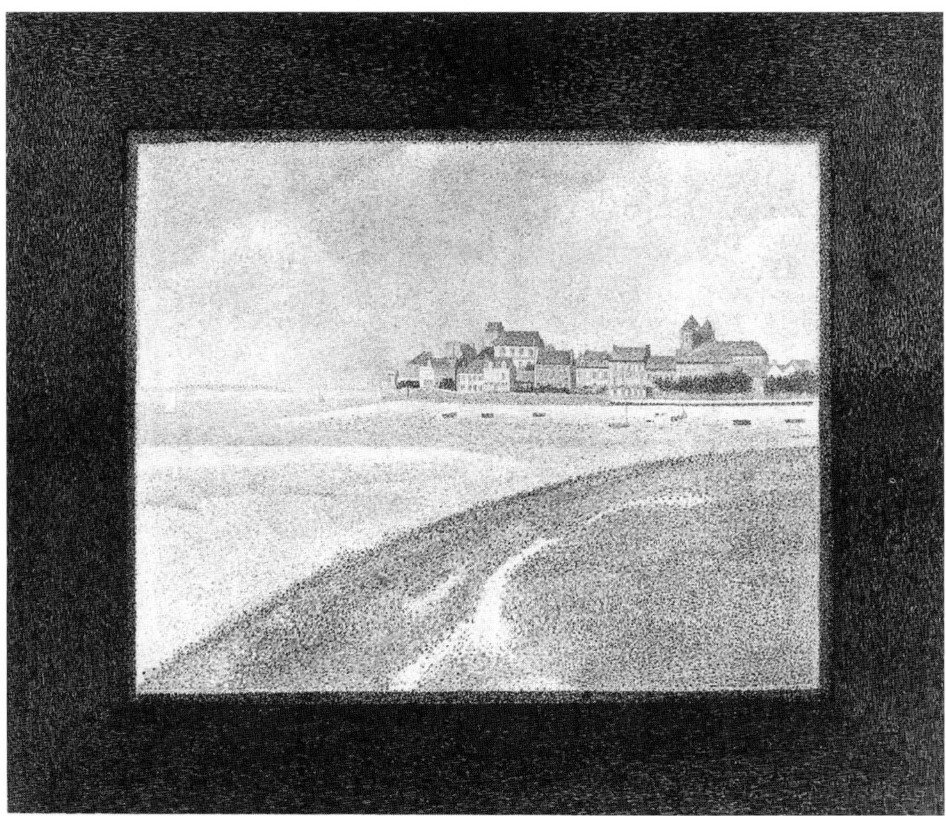

FIGURE 3.4. Georges Seurat, *View of Le Crotoy from Upstream* (with painted frame), 1889. The Detroit Institute of Arts, Bequest of Robert H. Tannahill. Photo © 1990 The Detroit Institute of Arts.

gray frames, and the following year that Seurat, too, showed his paintings with gray borders at the Independents' exhibition. In subsequent framing experiments Seurat and others established marked contrasts between frame and painting (fig. 3.4)—contrasts of material, tone, and shape—which reinforced a key principle of the Neo-Impressionists' attitude toward exhibition installation at this time by moving further away from any implied decorative connection of painting, frame, and wall to concentrate instead on the emphatic presentation of the painting as a self-sufficient work in an ideally neutral (and I should add, public) space.

With definitive pronouncements, the Neo-Impressionist group and its critics posed as experts who determined norms for public display, norms sometimes justified as simultaneously aesthetic and social. In a review of 1890, for example, Signac complained about the conditions at the shows mounted by the Belgian group, Les XX. Held in a former museum, the exhibitions were plushly installed, noted Signac, beginning with the ushers and the vestiary and continuing through to the marble bases for sculpture, the door draperies of red velvet, the green wall hangings, and the palms. His conclusion about the effects combined condemnation of the injurious effects of such splendor with some (deliberately) hyperbolic aestheticism:

> [These objects are] certainly decorative but because of their complementaries [i.e., the color reactions they produce] they are destructive of the harmonies

of the paintings, which are the victims of this luxury. The normal exhibition of paintings will be that where, to the exclusion of all colored objects (catalogue, wall hanging, flowers, frames, even women's hats), only the colors of the painting will sing the triumph of their undisturbed harmonies.[61]

Still, these seem now to be minor adjustments to prevailing conventions: small shifts of definition and acts of resistance. The painters' nearly exclusive reliance on color relations and balances to justify their practice (the playful absurdity of Signac's recommendation of a totally monochrome environment) all but reduced to a minute optical calculus the issue of how socially defined spaces might determine an exhibition aesthetic. Insofar as the Neo-Impressionist practices and pronouncements stood counter to dominant Impressionist tendencies of the day, however—to the tendency to interiorize painting as private decor in the *maison* Durand-Ruel or to float *objets* across the aristocratic red of the *salle* Georges Petit—their concerns to establish a normative and public mode held open at least the possibility that vanguard painting might occupy different social places and address broader audiences.[62]

Despite obvious points of resemblance, the neutrality and autonomy sought by the Neo-Impressionists are historically quite distinct from late twentieth-century modes of display. Our familiar experience of confronting in an exhibition a wall of paintings, spaciously hung in a single row, each work positioned to be viewed straight on and to be approached so that it might fill the visual field of the beholder and (ideally) consume his or her attention, has so conditioned us that we are hard-pressed to imagine why, except for lack of space or gross insensitivity, it should have ever been otherwise. By the same token, the pervasiveness of this norm makes it difficult to recapture the historical conditions in which attempts to establish the neutrality of exhibition spaces or the autonomy of easel paintings might have been as much statements against particularly powerful conjunctions in the art market, of definitions that conjoined aesthetics and private spaces, as promotions of absolute (and like our spaces, seemingly context-less) norms. Restoring the social dimensions to installation practices makes clear that the Neo-Impressionist insistence on autonomy in the late 1880s, as distinct from other moments in the history of the *tableau* in modernist practice, might have carried with it, or might even have been generated by, a commitment to establishing a place for avant-garde painting in a domain that was defined and experienced as public, and to accepting the distractions and diversions of such domains as conditions to be faced. (Such a commitment is underscored by Seurat's investigation in his works of what Meyer Schapiro called the "aesthetic aspects of popular experience"—the spectacles or spectators that Seurat painted, Schapiro noted, on a "public as opposed to a private, intimate scale."[63]) The recent tendency to see assertions of the autonomy of art as always and simply amounting to severances of art from social life—to the ensconcement of art within museum-like spaces for aesthetic appreciation—can obscure or miss the complex history of artists' and audiences' responses to the variety of social spaces that constituted the nineteenth-century institutional nexus. In that premier age of "exhibitionality," distinctions among walls still mattered to experiences of art, and the historical significance of any particular practice, including efforts to secure the autonomy of the *tableau*, must be established in relation to the system of differences at play at the time.

I have paid far more attention in this account to the ways that sites and installations shaped aesthetics and defined art than to how they may have been selected to bring out the characteristics of particular paintings or movements. It may also have seemed at times in this essay that nineteenth-century paintings themselves played no role in structuring an appropriate relation with the viewer or in provoking a critical discourse (an absurd position). My strong emphasis has partly resulted from a desire to set right the imbalance in art historical studies by examining the operations of the context rather than those of the object. But, as the following and final example of installation practices is meant to suggest, such an emphasis may also be in line with the experience of artists during this period. The possibilities, polemics, and politics of painting could be subdued (practically ignored) if transplanted into a properly hushed domain.

In the spring of 1887, Pissarro responded to the pressures on his finances, which he attributed to his recent adoption of the Neo-Impressionist style, and accepted an invitation from Monet and Renoir to participate in the Exposition Internationale, an annual spring event on the calendar of the *salle* Petit. Pissarro stipulated that his works should be bordered not in gold but in white. Petit apparently accepted the paintings (or the name of Pissarro) but refused the frames. From the point of view of the dealer and the exhibition committee, caution was in order. The white frames that Pissarro employed at an exhibition in Nantes the previous year had been compared by a critic to the "sides of crude packing cases."[64] And although Pissarro proposed in letters the use of what became a Neo-Impressionist favorite—a modest white frame with narrow bands of gold at the external edges—it was apparently feared that these would disrupt the harmonies of the *salle* Petit.[65]

For Pissarro, the presentation of works was one place where distinctions could still be drawn in 1887. No doubt, for him, it was as much the social definition of a debut at Petit's as it was the optical advantage of the white frame that provoked the crisis. The recognition that Neo-Impressionist painting might be marketed and desired in such luxurious circumstances—quasi-aristocratic, quasi-*grand magasin*—must have pushed him to see what it would take to be rejected. The radical connotations of painting style, it seems, were less consequential than the establishment of value by display.

Pissarro succumbed in the end, but made sure that critic-friends pushed the point in the press, explaining that the gold enframing his Neo-Impressionist paintings at the *salle* Petit prohibited their proper perception. As a historical event, the episode is too minor to count. As a testimony of why installation had come to matter so much, it is painfully instructive.

Notes

Originally published in a longer version in *Art Bulletin* 73, no. 4 (December 1991): 599–622.

My thanks go to Hollis Clayson for her comments on a version of this essay, and to all those who have helped with the research for this project, including Ruth Berson, Filiz Burhan, Karen Carter, Mlle France Daguet, Katherine Haskins, John House, Patricia Mainardi, and Bart Schultz. All translations are the author's.

1. This expansion has been well analyzed by T. Garb, "Revising the Revisionists: The Formation of the Union des Femmes Peintres et Sculpteurs," *Art Journal* 48, no. 1 (1989): 63–70; and by P. Vaisse, "Salons, expositions et sociétés d'artistes en France 1871–1914," in *Saloni, gallerie, musei e loro influenza sullo sviluppo dell'arte dei secoli XIX e XX* (*Atti del XXIV Congresso Internazionale di Storia dell'Arte*, VII), ed. F. Haskell (Bologna, 1981), 141–55. In this same volume, there is a detailed survey of art venues in previous periods: J. Whiteley, "Exhibitions of Contemporary Painting in London and Paris 1760–1860," 69–87.
2. R. Krauss, "Photography's Discursive Spaces," in her *The Originality of the Avant-Garde and Other Modernist Myths* (Cambridge, Mass., 1985), 133.
3. Another important account showing that structures of exclusion and exclusivity were essential to the production and exhibition of nineteenth-century modernism is Y-A. Bois, "Exposition: Esthétique de la distraction, espace de démonstration," *Les Cahiers du Musée National d'Art Moderne*, no. 29 (Fall 1989): 57–79.
4. I have used "public" and "private" in the way that these appeared in contemporary art criticism to describe exhibitions. For an analysis of art production in terms similar to these, but emphasizing the gendered character of the spaces, see A. Higonnet, "Secluded Vision: Images of Feminine Experience in Nineteenth-Century Europe," *Radical History Review*, no. 38 (1987): 16–36. The basic text on the development of the "dealer-critic" system and the role of exhibitions within it remains H. C. White and C. A. White, *Canvases and Careers: Institutional Change in the French Painting World* (New York, 1965). The most important recent work on the opera-

tions of the late nineteenth-century art market is Nicholas Green, "Dealing in Temperaments: Economic Transformation of the Artistic Field in France during the Second Half of the Nineteenth Century," *Art History* 10, no. 1 (1987): 59–78 [reprinted as chapter 2 in this volume]. See also his "Circuits of Production, Circuits of Consumption: The Case of Mid-Nineteenth-Century French Art Dealing," *Art Journal* 48, no. 1 (1989): 29–34.

5. E. Degas, "A propos du Salon," *Paris-Journal*, 12 April 1870, as quoted by T. Reff, "Some Unpublished Letters of Degas," *Art Bulletin* 50 (1968): 87–93.
6. A discussion of the alphabetical arrangement (concentrating mainly on its disadvantages) can be found in R. de Mergy, "Quelques observations à propos des expositions officielles," *Le Courrier artistique*, 15 February 1863, 65–66. The Marquis de Chennevières's recollections of the origins of the alphabetical system are in "Le Salon de 1880," *Gazette des beaux-arts*, series 2, 22 (May 1880): 393–407. A brief history and an analysis of issues regarding Salon installations are provided by M. Vachon, "Études administratives, 1: Le Salon," *Gazette des beaux-arts*, series 2, no. 23 (February 1881): 121–34.
7. On the changes that accompanied the moving of the Salon from the Louvre to the Palais de l'Industrie, as well as an extremely useful history of Salon practices, see P. Mainardi, "The Eviction of the Salon from the Louvre," *Gazette des beaux-arts*, series 6, 112 (July–August 1988): 31–40. For artists' organization of their own installations during the Second Empire, see P. Mainardi, *Art and Politics of the Second Empire: The Universal Expositions of 1855 and 1867* (New Haven, 1987), especially 49–61.
8. "A l'exposition anglaise," *La Vie parisienne*, 20 April 1867, 276–77.
9. On Alphonse Jame, see *Gazette des beaux-arts*, series 1, no. 9 (1861): 189–92. On Martinet, see "Inauguration de la nouvelle galerie de la Société nationale des beaux-arts," *Le Courrier artistique*, 19 February 1865.
10. P. Burty, "Exposition de la Société anonyme des artistes," *La République française*, 25 April 1874; repr. in *Centenaire de l'impressionnisme* (Paris, 1974), 261–62.
11. "Une fois les ouvrages rangés par grandeur, le sort décidera de leur placement." For reprints of the Impressionist exhibition catalogues and essays on the shows, see C. S. Moffett, ed., *The New Painting: Impressionism, 1874–1886* (San Francisco, 1986).
12. J. Castagnary, "L'Exposition du boulevard des Capucines," *Le Siècle*, 29 April 1874; repr. in *Centenaire*, 264–65. In contrast, Burty said the privilege of the picture rail *(cimaise)* on each panel had been decided by lot; *Centenaire*, 261.
13. P. Burty, "The Paris Exhibitions: Les Impressionnistes—Chintreuil," *The Academy*, 30 May 1874, 616–17.
14. "Eclairées à peu près comme dans un appartement moyen, isolées, pas trop nombreuses"; *Centenaire*, 261.
15. Burty, "Paris Exhibitions," 616.
16. See R. Brettell's elaborate reconstruction and discussion in "The 'First' Exhibition of Impressionist Painters," in Moffett, ed., *New Painting*, 189–98.
17. "La donnée qui domine dans ce groupe étant la recherché de la lumière et des effets du plein air, de l'irisation, de la couleur, cette peinture gagne à être encadrée dans les vastes panneaux d'une haute galerie"; P. Burty, "Chronique du jour," *La République française*, 1 April 1876.
18. P. Burty, "The Exhibition of the 'Intransigeants,'" *The Academy*, 15 April 1876, 363.
19. "Elles heurtent comme tableaux, par leur aspect d'ébauches, par leurs indications de frottis. Elles ont, en place et comme décors, une valeur de clarté, de franchise d'effet qui ne sont pas niables"; P. Burty, "Exposition des impressionnistes," *La République française*, 25 April 1877.
20. For an analysis of these concepts in the criticism and practice of Monet, see S. Z. Levine, "Décor/Decorative/Decoration in Monet's Art," *Arts Magazine* 51 (February 1977): 136–39; see also his *Monet and His Critics* (New York, 1976).
21. Garb, "Revising the Revisionists," 66–67. The emergence and significance of circles and societies in the history of French forms of sociability are analyzed by M. Agulhon, *Le Cercle dans la France bourgeoise, 1810–1848* (Paris, 1977). A particularly clear explanation of the advantages that art circles offered to both artists and collectors can be found in the anonymous article, "Le Cercle de l'union artistique," *La Paix*, 16 February 1883. J.-P. Bouillon has carefully examined the relationship of art circles and societies to economic developments, aesthetic definitions, and representations of the power of the state: "Sociétés d'artistes et institutions officielles dans la seconde moitié du XIXe siècle," *Romantisme*, no. 54 (1986): 88–113.
22. On the Denman Tripp gallery, see the description in *L'Illustration* 81 (12 May 1883): 301; see also J. Sillevis, "Lettres de Josef Israëls à Arnold et Tripp, marchands de tableaux à Paris (1881–1892)," *Archives de l'art français: Correspondances d'artistes des XVIIe, XVIIIe,*

XIXe et XXe siècles, appartenant à la Fondation Custodia et conservées à l'Institut Néerlandais à Paris, new series, 29 (1988): 154.

23. As an indication of how unusual the practice of single-row installation must have been, consider the comments of Degas's and Pissarro's friend Diego Martelli on the display of works for the Laurent-Richard sale of 1878, in Martelli, *Les Impressionnistes et l'art moderne* (Paris, 1979), 78–83.
24. "A vrai dire, elle [the show of the Mirlitons] ne présente qu'un inconvénient, mais il est grave. On y est au milieu des intéressés; invité par eux, chez eux, on est leur hôte; par conséquent, il est de stricte convenance de n'y exprimer qu'avec discrétion son sentiment sur les oeuvres exposées, de n'y parler qu'à demi voix, parfois même de se taire tout à fait. Seule l'admiration peut s'y montrer expansive"; E. Chesneau, "Cercle de l'union artistique: Exposition de 1873," *Paris-Journal*, 25 February 1873. Chesneau repeated the same objections nearly a decade later in "Les Cercles artistes," *Paris-Journal*, 11–12 February 1882.
25. H. Houssaye, "Les Petites Expositions de peinture," *La Revue des deux mondes*, no. 38 (March 1880): 193–202.
26. Anonymous, "Cercle de l'union artistique."
27. The founding of numerous societies based on technique, medium, genre, or aesthetic allegiance in the 1880s and 1890s and the change that this orientation marks from the basis for association in the 1860s have been noted by Bouillon, "Sociétés d'artistes," 96–97.
28. R. dos Santos, "Un Coin du Salon: Aquarelles et pastels," *Moniteur des arts*, 16 May 1884.
29. "C'est un art délicat, intime, aimable, qu'on ne peut bien apprécier que dans un milieu de choix, élégant, distingué; il demande quelque soin et un peu de mise-en-scène; il lui faut une lumière discrète; le grand jour de la rue ou de la place publique ne lui convient pas"; E. Cardon, "Aquarellistes chez Petit," *Moniteur des arts*, 18 January 1889.
30. "Cette société, qui n'a point de local à elle"; V. Champier, *Chronique de l'année*: *L'Année artistique* (Paris, 1880), 140.
31. G. Lecomte, who got the information for his short biography of Pissarro from conversations with the artist, recorded that Pissarro first used white frames in 1877; "Camille Pissarro," *Les Hommes d'aujourd'hui*, vol. 8 (Paris, n.d. [1890]). A reviewer of the 1877 show noted white frames around Degas's series of cafés-concerts and likened them to "passe-partouts" (Jacques, "Menus propos," *L'Homme libre*, 12 April 1877). Another reference to white frames during this year occurs in the play *La Cigale* about the imaginary Impressionist painter Marignon; L. Tannenbaum first called attention to this reference in "Degas: Illustrious and Unknown," *Art News* (January 1967): 76. For a very informative history of Impressionist and late nineteenth-century framing experiments, see I. Cahn, *Cadres de peintres* (Paris, 1989). Monet's practices, which differed significantly from those of some other Impressionists, are discussed by J. House, *Monet: Nature into Art* (New Haven, 1986), especially 180, 214. Additional documentation concerning the use of white frames by Cassatt, Manet, Morisot, and Gauguin is provided by I. Horowitz, "The Picture Frame, 1848–1892: The Pre-Raphaelites, Whistler, Paris" (M.A. thesis, Queens College, City University of New York, 1974), 108–15.
32. "Puis quelle variété dans les encadrements qui revêtent tous les tons variés de l'or, toutes les nuances connues, qui se bordent de liserés peints avec la couleur complémentaire des cadres! La série des Pissarro est, cette année, surtout, surprenante. C'est un barriolage de véronèse et de vert d'eau, de maïs et de chair de pêche, d'amadou et de lie de vin, et il faut voir avec quel tact le coloriste a assorti toutes ses teintes pour mieux faire s'écouler ses ceils et saillir ses premiers plans. C'est le raffinement le plus acéré; et, encore que le cadre ne puisse rien ajouter au talent d'une oeuvre, il en est cependant un complément nécessaire, un adjuvant qui le fait valoir. C'est la même chose qu'une beautée de femme qui exige certains atours"; J.-K. Huysmans, "L'Exposition des indépendents," *L'Art moderne / Certains* (repr. Paris, 1975), 251. On Pissarro's frames at these exhibitions and on the principle of complementary contrasts, see also Lecomte, "Camille Pissarro."
33. The decorative border reversed the rationale of the traditional gilt frame. The academician, critic, and widely read author Charles Blanc had carefully defined in his work on decorative arts why shiny or mat gold was preferred for framing: shiny or mat surfaces "both adapt themselves to the framing of paintings where light, concentrated toward the center, is stifled at the margins. Gilt has the additional advantage of casting warm reflections onto the painting and lighting it a little, if of course the frame is located well in front of the canvas and creates a concavity favorable to casting these reflections." (The shiny or mat surfaces "s'adaptent l'un et l'autre à l'encadrement des tableaux où la lumière, concentrée vers le milieu, est étouffée sur les bords. La dorure a ici de plus l'avantage de jeter des

reflets chauds sur le fond de la peinture et de l'éclaircir un peu, à la condition, toutefois, que le cadre sera bien en avant de la toile, et présentera une concavité favorable au renvoi de ces reflets"); C. Blanc, *Grammaire des arts décoratifs* (Paris, 1882), 190. Because light values in Impressionist paintings were generally not concentrated at the center but tended to be more evenly distributed across the surface, and because in composition the painters often preferred contrasts of color to those of value, Blanc's rationale for the use of gold was no longer pertinent.

34. P. Burty, "Exposition des oeuvres des artistes indépendants," *La République française*, 10 April 1880.
35. On Whistler's show in 1874, see R. Spencer, "Whistler's First One-Man Exhibition Reconstructed," in *The Documented Image: Visions in Art History*, ed. G. P. Weisberg and L. S. Dixon (Syracuse, 1987), 27–49. For Pissarro's comments, see letter no. 120, *Correspondance de Camille Pissarro*, ed. J. Bailly-Herzberg, vol. 1 (Paris, 1983), 177–78.
36. "Choissions-là de la couleur qui vous convient le mieux moralement et physiquement, et, pour les marier avec elle, donnons la préférence aux tons et aux nuances qui s'harmonisent"; H. Havard, "L'Art dans la maison: La Chambre à coucher," *L'Illustration* 80 (4 November 1882): 307.
37. "Un paysage vert soleil, une page blonde d'hiver, un intérieur papillotant de lustres et de toilettes exigent des cadres différents que leurs auteurs respectifs sauront seuls confectionner, comme une femme sait mieux que personne quelles nuances d'étoffes et quelles poudres, et quelles tentures de boudoir feront valoir son teint, l'expression de son visage, ses manières. Nous avons vu des cadres plats, blancs, rose-pâle, verts, jaune jonquille, d'autres bariolés à outrance de mille tons et de mille façons"; "L'Impressionnisme," in *Jules Laforgue: Textes de critique d'art*, ed. M. Dottin (Lille, 1988), 174.
38. H. Havard, "L'Exposition des artistes indépendants," *Le Siècle*, 27 April 1879.
39. For example, three reviews remarked in 1882 that Pissarro's oil paintings resembled pastels: Fichtre, "L'Actualité: L'Exposition des peintres indépendants," *Le Réveil*, 2 March 1882; A. Sallanches, "L'Exposition des artistes indépendants," *Le Journal des arts*, 3 March 1882; G. Vassy, "L'Actualité: Les Peintres impressionnistes," *Gil Blas*, 2 March 1882.
40. J. Saulo and de Saint-Victor *[sic]*, *Nouveau Manuel complet du fabricant de cadres* (Paris, 1896), 8.
41. Huysmans remarked upon the use of glass by the Impressionists as a group at the exhibition of 1882, but for one reason or another, critics consistently noted only Pissarro's paintings in this respect, perhaps because more of his paintings were displayed under glass. Pissarro either continued this practice or returned to it in the mid-1880s when he probably helped to inspire the Neo-Impressionists as well to exhibit their paintings under glass, which they began in 1886. By 1889, if not before, however, the practice seems to have been abandoned, as may be judged from the critic Félix Fénéon's comment that year that Seurat's marines needed glass to complete their *toilettes* at the Independents' exhibition; "Tableaux," *La Vogue*, September 1889; repr. in *Félix Fénéon: Oeuvres plus que complètes*, ed. J. U. Halperin, vol. 1 (Geneva, 1970), 165.
42. F. Fénéon, "L'Impressionnisme aux Tuileries," *L'Art moderne*, 19 September 1886; repr. in *Fénéon: Oeuvres*, vol. 1, 55–56. Letter from Pissarro to Esther Isaacson of 1889, no. 561 in *Correspondance de Camille Pissarro*, ed. J. Bailly-Herzberg, vol. 2 (Paris, 1986), 318–19. Degas also commented on this advantage, while Burty remarked in his review of the exhibition of 1882 that Pissarro's oils looked like velvety pastels precisely because they were seen under glass (*Lettres de Degas*, ed. M. Guérin [Paris, 1945], 60; P. Burty, "Les Aquarellistes, les indépendants et le cercle des arts libéraux," *La République française*, 8 March 1882). There were, of course, other obvious advantages to placing a sheet of glass over an oil: it protected the painted surface from dirt without incurring the disadvantages of a layer of varnish which might discolor with age. Also, because varnish adhered directly to the surface's unevenly painted terrain, it might result in irregular and distracting reflections of light. This was the principal explanation Huysmans offered when he saw paintings displayed under glass in 1882. Glass also allowed the painting's surface to be left mat and thus made it seem less like an oil.
43. On *La Maison d'un artiste* and the Goncourts' model home at Auteuil, see the analysis by Debora L. Silverman, *Art Nouveau in Fin-de-Siècle France* (Berkeley, 1989), 17–39.
44. For an interpretation of Degas's installations that accounts for the framing experiments as scientific investigation, see D. W. Druick and P. Zegers, "Scientific Realism 1874–1881," in *Degas*, exh. cat. (Paris: Grand Palais; Ottawa: National Gallery of Canada; New York: Metropolitan Museum of Art, 1988–89), 197–211.
45. L. R. Pissarro and L. Venturi, *Pissarro: Son Art—son oeuvre*, vol. 1 (Paris and New York, 1939), nos. 183–86; D. Wildenstein, *Monet, biographie et catalogue raisonné*, vol. 2 (Lausanne, 1979), nos. 937–42.

46. A. Baignères, "Société d'aquarellistes français," *Gazette des beaux-arts*, series 2, 25 (1882): 433. A. Dalligny, "L'Exposition de la rue de Sèze," *Le Journal des arts*, 24 February 1882, 1. J.-E. Blanche, *Les Arts plastiques: La Troisième République* (Paris, 1931), 111–15. Quotations from Blanche and other information about the gallery are provided by R. T. Dunn, "The Monet-Rodin Exhibition at the Galerie Georges Petit in 1889" (Ph.D. diss., Northwestern University, 1978).
47. Zola's description of Petit's gallery as "les magasins du Louvre de la peinture" is quoted in *Camille Pissarro: Lettres à son fils Lucien*, ed. J. Rewald (Paris, 1950), 102 n. 1. It appears in Zola's manuscript for his 1886 novel about the art world, *L'Oeuvre* (NAF 10316, p. 354; Département des Manuscrits, Bibliothèque Nationale, Paris).
48. These details are drawn from the *brouillards* and *grand livre* in the Durand-Ruel gallery: I would like to express my gratitude to the gallery for allowing me to consult these materials. The recorded expenditures show that the gallery at 9 boulevard de la Madeleine was an expensive undertaking: during the period from July 1882 to December 1883, Durand-Ruel spent at least 11,615 francs on decoration (including some minor remodeling) and 18,000 on rent.
49. F. Henriet, "L'Exposition des oeuvres de C. Pissaro *[sic]*," *Le Journal des arts*, 25 May 1883.
50. P. Gilbert, "Exposition de M. P. A. Renoir," *Journal des artistes*, 13 April 1883.
51. For example, the critic Hustin remarked that the rooms had been "affecté spécialement depuis quelques temps à l'exhibition des impressionnistes"; "Exposition d'Eugène Boudin," *Moniteur des arts*, 9 February 1883. See also the similar remarks by P. Burty, "Les Paysages de Eugène Boudin," *La République française*, 4 February 1883.
52. Sisley made the remark in the context of arguing in favor of a group exhibition, rather than individual exhibitions, for the new site: "Ce n'est pas il me semble au moment où nous cessons d'être des nomades, que nous avons un local définitif, bien placé, que nous devons songer à inaugurer un autre genre d'expositions"; Letter of 5 November 1882, in L. Venturi, ed., *Les Archives de l'impressionnisme*, vol. 2 (Paris, 1939), 56.
53. E. Bergerat, "Chronique parisien," *Gil blas*, 17 May 1891; as quoted by M. J. Aquilino, "The Decorating Campaigns at the Salon du Champs-de-Mars and the Salon des Champs-Elysées in the 1890s," *Art Journal* 48, no. 1 (1989): 82. It is worth noting that Durand-Ruel later complained that his main gallery on the rue Laffitte, although subdivided into several rooms, was too large for good business: "One sees too many things at once, one hesitates, one listens to the opinions of other visitors and puts off purchases until later. In addition, in large rooms all objects look smaller, and as a result the prices that one asks for paintings seem more elevated than if one showed the works in a small locale" ("On voit trop de choses à la fois, on hésite, on écoute les avis des visiteurs et on remet les achats à plus tard. En outre, dans les grandes salles tous les objets paraissent plus petits et par suite les prix que l'on demande des tableaux semblent plus élevés que si on les montre dans un petit local"); "Mémoires de Paul Durand-Ruel," in Venturi, ed., *Archives de l'impressionnisme*, vol. 2, 174–75. For an early description of the rue Laffitte gallery, see J. Raffey, "Galerie de M. Durand-Ruel," *Revue internationale de l'art et de la curiosité* 2 (15 December 1869).
54. "Nous entrons dans le petit salon de M. Durand-Ruel. Les stores baissés le tiennent en une pénombre délicate, et déjà ce sont, sur les parois, des chatoiements, des lueurs, de mystérieux éblouissements. L'allégresse des tons frais s'illumine. On dirait de radieuses couleurs entrevues dans la confusion d'un rêve, telle la joie d'une aurore atténuée par une brume subtile. . . . Toutes les joies de la nature sont condensées en ce court espace"; G. Lecomte, *L'Art impressionniste d'après la collection privée de M. Durand-Ruel* (Paris, 1892), 117–18. In a graduate seminar, Katherine Haskins first noted the strange separation of history from house in Lecomte's text. (The first and last chapters of the book are texts that Lecomte had published elsewhere as separate articles.) For an analysis of the compatibility of notions of the decorative and the natural in the 1880s and 1890s, see R. Herbert, "The Decorative and the Natural in Monet's Cathedrals," in *Aspects of Monet: A Symposium on the Artist's Life and Times*, ed. J. Rewald and F. Weitzenhoffer (New York, 1984), 160–79.
55. It is important to observe the difference between Lecomte's domestication of Impressionism and the attitude of the traditional collector, who would most likely prize the art in *his* home for its historical value or its contribution to his collection. An interesting suggestion of how an ideal of the collector and his home could have been translated into installation practices in this period is suggested by the remarks on Paris museum reform by Charles Saunier, a critic and historian whose enthusiasms at this time included vanguard art, like the Neo-Impressionists, Japanese artifacts, and the patrimony of the French Gothic. Saunier recommended that paintings in museums should be grouped

with objects and furniture of the same period and placed in small rooms, fashioned like domiciles, so that the visitor would sense that a man of taste and discrimination had collected them there: "Make the visitor forget that he is in a museum, give him the illusion that he is at his home, that the objects belong to him and are part of his life, that his fantasy has recently placed them like this; teach him to love beauty, to understand it, give him time for reflection" ("Faire oublier au visiteur qu'il se trouve dans un musée, lui donner l'illusion qu'il est chez lui, que les objets lui appartiennent, font partie de sa vie, que sa fantaisie les place naguère ainsi; lui apprendre à aimer le beau, à le comprendre, lui laisser le temps de la reflexion"); "La Parure des oeuvres d'art," *Ermitage* 10 (1895): 257–60. Although Lecomte and Saunier each ultimately appeal to the home as the site of the authentic experience of art or the exercise of taste, the viewer-resident in Saunier's account is clearly meant to emulate the self-consciousness and historical sensibility of the collector and not, as in Lecomte's text, to exclude history so that self and painting can mingle in a "natural" (achronological) interior. For a discussion of the relationship of history and interior decoration, to which my remarks here are indebted, see Silverman, *Art Nouveau*.

56. For the relationship between the Neo-Impressionists and dealers, see M. Ward. "The Rhetoric of Independence and Innovation," in Moffett, ed., *New Painting*, 421–28. Complaints about the growing number of private exhibitions and praise for public shows, accessible to all, appeared in the Socialist paper *Le Parti ouvrier;* see P. Buquet, "Le Salon," 3 May 1889.
57. "Toute l'attention est dirigée sur les oeuvres"; O. Maus, "Les Vingtistes parisiens," *L'Art moderne*, 27 June 1886, 201.
58. F. Fénéon, "Le Néo-impressionnisme," *L'Art moderne*, 15 April 1888; repr. in *Fénéon: Oeuvres*, vol. 1, 84.
59. P. Signac, "Au minuit," *Le Cri du peuple*, 29 March 1888.
60. "Aux néo-impressionnistes sera réservée la gloire d'établir l'exposition normale où dans un milieu achromatique, les toiles seules viberont dans la splendeur de leurs contrastes." These remarks are from a letter by Signac that P. Alexis published in his column "Au minuit" in *Le Cri du peuple*, 29 May 1888.
61. These objects are "certainement décoratifs mais déstructeurs par leurs complémentaires de l'harmonie des toiles victims de ce faste. L'exposition normale d'oeuvres peintes sera celle où, à l'exclusion de tout objet colorant (catalogue, tenture, fleurs, cadres, même chapeaux de dames), seules les teintes des toile chanteront dans le triomphe de leurs harmonies inviolées"; P. S. [P. Signac], "Catalogue de l'exposition des XX," *Art et critique*, 1 February 1890, 76–77. Consider also Signac's similar description of the "normal museum," where he thought there should be a single and well-spaced row of paintings, with works by the same artist hung together, in bright rooms on panels without ornaments; diary entry of 10 December 1894, in J. Rewald, ed., "Extraits du journal inédit de Paul Signac, I," *Gazette des beaux-arts*, series 6, 36 (July–September 1949): 110. These conditions seem to have been at least partly realized at the Neo-Impressionist gallery on the rue Laffitte, which opened in 1893. A reviewer of a show there in 1895 provided a rare description of the site and praised the spacing of the works for not speeding the eye through the show: "As soon as one enters the Neo-Impressionist sanctuary, one is struck by its impeccable attire: dark blue cloth applied to the wall has happily replaced the sumptuous red fabric, commonly used in galleries or official exhibitions. On this blue cloth, bright frames and few of them—just what's needed so that each work is not blocked by those around it: frames placed in a single row, at picture-rail height" ("Dès qu'on pénètre dans le sanctuaire néo-impressionniste, l'on est frappé tout d'abord par sa tenue impeccable: de l'étoffe bleue foncé appliquée au mur, a heureusement remplacé le 'somptueux Andrinople' usité d'ordinaire dans les galeries ou expositions officielles. Sur cette etoffe bleue, des cadres clairs, peu nombreux, 'juste ce qu'il en faut' pour que chaque toile ne soit point gênée par celles qui l'entourent: cadres placés sur un seul rang, à hauteur de cimaise"). The reviewer went on to note that most of the frames were brightly tinted or had been painted to harmonize with individual works; three or more easels, he observed, were included to display drawings and small works. Tiphéreth, "Les Récentes Expositions: . . . Néo-impressionnistes," *Le Coeur*, no. 8 (July 1895): 8–9.
62. It might be argued that the type of engagement sought by the Neo-Impressionists and Fénéon was not all that different from the private ideal for Impressionism as described by Lecomte and situated in the domestic sphere of the *maison* Durand-Ruel: the total absorption of the viewer in the light and color and rhythm that seemed to emanate from or be generated by the painting, a condition of viewing that was only to be secured by shutting out or darkening the surrounding environment (drawing the heavy draperies in Durand-Ruel's *petit salon;* imposing a thick and somber frame around a thinly painted surface at the Independents

show). As much as the friends Lecomte and Fénéon shared an emphasis on the sensual immediacy of painting, however, the differences between their accounts are more important here. As described by Lecomte, the extension and dissolution of Impressionist painting into the surroundings is a spatially disorienting experience for the reader and viewer, who is simultaneously surrounded and distracted by the flickering action and ambiance created by the works. If we estimate the probable effects of Neo-Impressionist installation, the viewer seems to be distinctly separated from the image, and especially in the case of Seurat's landscapes, the depicted scene itself is made to seem remote and otherworldly by virtue of the contrast with the heavy and dark frame. Seurat reportedly wanted to simulate in these experiments the effects of lowering the house lights at Wagner's theater at Bayreuth, whereby the spotlit stage became the unique center of attention; E. Verhaeren, "Georges Seurat," *Société nouvelle* 7 (April 1891): 433. As a model of how to create a sense of intimacy with the individual viewer and to concentrate his or her attention on a work to the exclusion of the distractions of a public place, Wagner's theater no doubt appealed to Seurat.

The points made here and elsewhere on the relationship of viewer to painting are fundamentally indebted to the work of Michael Fried: see especially his *Absorption and Theatricality: Painting and Beholder in the Age of Diderot* (Berkeley, 1980); and his *Courbet's Realism* (Chicago, 1990).

63. M. Schapiro, "Seurat and 'La Grande Jatte,'" *Columbia Review* 17 (November 1935): 13.

64. "Exposition des beaux-arts," *L'Espérance du peuple* (Nantes), 21 December 1886. The satirical reviewer also noted the use of glass by Seurat and Pissarro at this show.

65. For the controversy, see especially Pissarro's letter of 17 March 1887, in *Correspondance*, vol. 2, 144–45. The Petit exhibition committee was not very dictatorial in handling the problems posed in the 1880s by displays that were increasingly individualized. Consider that the Salon began in 1884 to forbid all but wood, black, or gilt frames and in 1888 to prohibit the use of glass over oils. (Regulations are printed in the Salon catalogues.)

PART TWO

Landscapes of Modernity

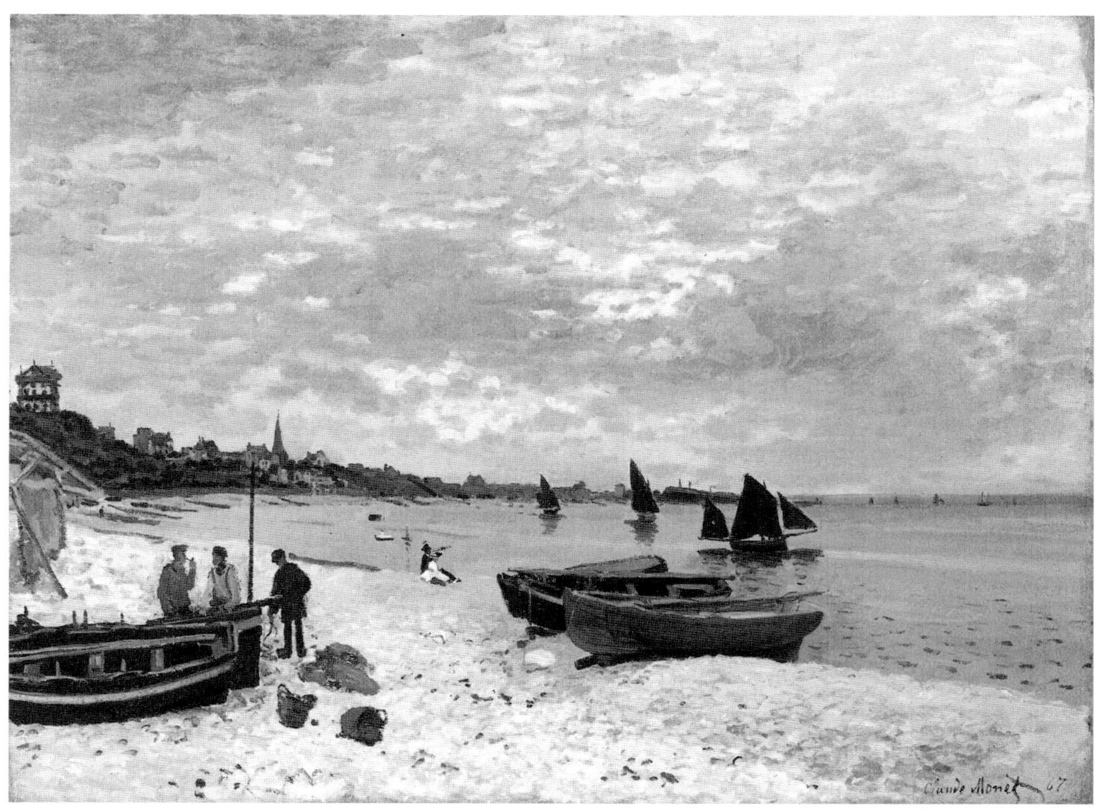

FIGURE 4.1. Claude Monet, *The Beach at Sainte-Adresse*, 1867. The Art Institute of Chicago, Chicago, Mr. and Mrs. Lewis Larned Coburn Memorial Collection, 1933.439. Photo © The Art Institute of Chicago.

4

Framing the Landscape

JOHN HOUSE

THE FRENCH WORD *PAYSAGE*, like the English word "landscape," refers to two things: the visual representation of an outdoor scene and the scene itself. In writings about landscape painting in nineteenth-century France, these two meanings were often deliberately merged. When discussing the landscapes exhibited at the Paris Salon, critics would write as if the paintings had transported them from the exhibition halls into the open air:

> The critic feels a sense of joy and refreshment when, having examined the history paintings, the mythologies, the sentimental scenes and the portraits, he sees, in the middle of his voyage through the exhibition, these green meadows, these deep woods, these solitary valleys where the landscapists allow him to stroll and to breathe at leisure.[1]

The experience of landscape in France in the later nineteenth century was rooted in these ambiguities: paintings viewed as if they were actual scenes and the countryside viewed as if it were a picture. Yet many commentators were worried by this, arguing that the higher aims of fine art could not be fulfilled by paintings that they saw as mere portraits of particular places.

The "Landscape"

What is a landscape painting? The standard nineteenth-century answer was that it was a view of the countryside without figures in it or one where they played a subordinate role.[2] However, the place of figures in the landscape was more than a question of classification. In 1864 the critic Léon Lagrange explained why he preferred landscapes without figures: "Reduced to its very own elements, nature still speaks to anyone who wishes to listen to it in a language full of elevation. The absence of man seems to lend nature's voice yet more resonance."[3] In 1861 Maxime du Camp was still more explicit about why he wanted to cleanse the landscape of its human occupants:

> The painters of landscapes and marines do not generally realize how much they harm their pictures by

loading them with useless little people. What one loves in the forests, in the meadows, by the edge of the sea, is the absolute solitude which allows one to be in direct communion with nature; if a peasant or a sailor appears, the spell is broken, and one is grasped again by the humanity that one had wanted to escape; what is true in reality is also true in fiction; a landscape only has grandeur if it is uninhabited.[4]

This is "nature" stripped of signs of human life and labor, presented as a spectacle for solitary contemplation.

Du Camp's comments show that the notion of landscape itself, like that of landscape painting, is not simply a question of subject matter but involves a particular way of seeing—one that views the outdoor scene as a landscape. The "landscape" itself, as W. J. T. Mitchell has recently insisted, is "already a representation in its own right."[5] Du Camp's wish to banish the figure was an attempt to defuse the threat of other, potentially potent, ways of seeing the countryside. The distinction appears most starkly in a passage by the American writer Ralph Waldo Emerson (1836):

The charming landscape which I saw this morning, is indubitably made up of some twenty or thirty farms. Miller owns this field, Locke that, and Manning the woodland beyond. But none of them owns the landscape. There is a property in the horizon which no man has but he whose eye can integrate all the parts, that is, the poet. This is the best part of these men's farms, yet to this their warranty-deeds give no title . . . you cannot freely admire a noble landscape, if laborers are digging in the field hard by.[6]

Jean-François Millet's *End of the Village of Greville* (c. 1865–66; Museum of Fine Arts, Boston), first shown at the Salon, attempts to bridge this division between "landscape" and the owned, worked countryside; Claude Monet wittily played on the contrast between the two in *The Beach at Sainte-Adresse* (1867; fig. 4.1), where the fishermen in the foreground turn their backs on the "landscape" that we and the bourgeois couple on the beach (the man with his telescope) are looking at.

Through the elimination or subordination of the figure, the landscape sought to distance itself from contemporary social issues. Yet, amid the dramatic social and political transformations of the period, the position of landscape painting was inevitably scrutinized within wider contexts. A central issue was the contrast between the image of the rural landscape and the modern city. Art critics repeatedly speculated on the reasons for the popularity of landscape. Whatever their analysis of contemporary art and society, one theme recurred: the love of landscape was seen in opposition to the experience of modern urban life—as a refuge from its mental and physical pressures.[7]

By the later nineteenth century, landscape was essentially an urban art form. It was exhibited and sold in cities, primarily in Paris. In contrast to eighteenth-century England, few of the viewers and buyers of landscape in nineteenth-century Paris belonged to the rural landowning classes, and few would have had firsthand experience of the changing conditions in the countryside. Their idea of landscape stood in contrast to their own experiences of life in the city. Countryside and "landscape" were commodities that could be consumed in many forms: through antiquarian and geographical treatises; through popular magazines and novels; through topographical prints and exhibition paintings; and through actual travel and tourism.

Viewing the Landscape

There were two stages in the development of interest in the French countryside in the nineteenth century. From the 1820s onward, the country's picturesque sites and monuments began to be visited and studied, and guidebooks began to popularize their beauties. Later in the century the horizons opened further as travel was transformed by the development of the railway. The *grandes lignes* from Paris to the main French cities were mostly completed by the mid-1850s; a web of local lines that linked even remote regions to the national network were built from the 1880s on.[8]

The study of provincial France was pioneered by the volumes of *Voyages pittoresques et romantiques dans l'ancienne France* from 1820 onward. In the first volume, on Normandy, Charles Nodier insisted on the national significance of France's monuments, not only as objects of beauty but also as salutary reminders of the imprint of French history. His was not a work of antiquarianism but rather "a voyage of impressions, if one may describe it like this."[9] Nodier recognized that the "superb countryside" might appeal to the landscapist, but the Normandy volume focused on historical monuments because it was the monuments that were then at risk from destruction; the countryside would remain for future generations to enjoy and paint.[10] By the end of the century Nodier's priorities had been reversed. For the most part the monuments were safe, but the countryside was now at risk from modernization and agricultural decline.

In contrast to the lavish volumes of the *Voyages pittoresques,* Abel Hugo's *France pittoresque* of 1835 surveyed the whole country in one dense tome. The purpose of the book was blatantly nationalistic, insisting that France was as worthy of study as foreign countries such as Italy that had, until then, been favored by travelers and painters: "France contains all the riches of nature, combined with the treasures of intelligence and industry. . . . France, by its position, by its nature and by the character of its inhabitants, is the land of civilization."[11] The book's many illustrations include both monuments and natural sites.

Books such as these mark the beginnings of a type of travel not confined to the pre-Revolutionary elite of the Grand Tour, but in principle accessible to a wider range of the middle classes. Nicholas Green has noted a shift during these same years to a new style of writing about travel: away from a primary concern with literary and philosophical associations and toward a "nature tourism" that focused on the sensory experience of the sites themselves.[12] This new conception of travel, Green argues, was inseparable from changing perceptions of Paris: fears of the city's infected old quarters and anxieties about its burgeoning boulevard consumer culture. However, historical monuments remained a central focus in travel writing and for travel itself throughout the century, and accounts of any site might expound on its historical associations.

The nineteenth century saw the emergence of a key distinction in the history of modern travel: between the tourist and the traveler. Travelers see themselves as solitary, independent, free-ranging, and fascinated by the unknown, while tourists stick in groups and follow prescribed paths, seeking only what can be accommodated within familiar frameworks. We all like to think of ourselves as travelers, while dismissing our fellow travelers as mere tourists.

However, self-styled travelers are also outsiders, engaging with the "Other"; they may better be labeled "anti-tourists," since the uniqueness and authenticity they claim for their own experiences are the direct opposite of what they reject in "tourism."[13] Likewise, the claim to independence does not necessarily entail traveling independently. Even when traveling in groups, they may seek to separate themselves from the shared experience; and the tourist may momentarily assume the position of traveler. The advertising for package tours today makes much of the possibility of the unique, "authentic" experience that may be found just off the beaten track.[14]

The same distinctions were central to landscape painting. The landscape painter presented himself as the ultimate "anti-tourist," traveling alone in search of sites and understanding them in a way that no one else could; yet the painter encountered the landscape as an outsider, and the painted landscapes were viewed and judged in the city.

In the nineteenth century the term "tourist" was not necessarily used pejoratively: in 1838 Stendhal entitled his volume of travels around France *Mémoires d'un touriste*. But, even before the age of rail, "tourist" was used to designate the visitor who focused on the superficial attractions of a place. The stereotypes were already in place in 1841, in Roger de Beauvoir's essay on the tourist in the series *Les Français peints par eux-mêmes:* tourists travel only to confirm their preconceptions, while the writer sets himself apart, since he alone is able to see beyond the tourists around him to appreciate the *paysage*.[15] This process was accelerated by the railway, which created a new class of traveler whose experiences literally followed a rigid, immovable track; contemporary guidebooks likewise followed the paths of the railway.

The same years witnessed the rapid development of the holiday resort and of travel not for exploration but for rest and recreation. Even before the railway reached the Channel Coast, resorts such as Etretat and Trouville were becoming popular, but the arrival of the train gave easy access to fashionable Parisians; it was this beach life that formed the subject of Eugène Le Poittevin's *Sea Bathing at Etretat* (1866; fig. 4.2) and Eugène Boudin's most celebrated paintings.[16]

The train also brought the day tripper, even lowlier than the tourist in esteem. The stereotype of the day tripper was the worker, artisan, or petit bourgeois, either exploring the pleasures and entertainments of the city's fringes or pursuing a naïve and uninformed notion of "nature" and the countryside.

Apart from tourism, there were other reasons why city dwellers might travel to the French countryside. Many Parisians had migrated from the provinces or were the children of migrants, retaining a sense of their *pays* and ties with their relatives there. The wealthier might own substantial country properties and farms that were worked by tenants. These groups all differed from the tourist in one way: they had a stake in a particular place.

The same is true of the city dwellers who owned or rented a *maison de campagne*. By the 1840s, as Nicholas Green has argued, this was used primarily as a rural refuge, though it also needed to be within easy reach of Paris.[17] This combination of retreat with access shows again how inseparable the experience of countryside and landscape was from the city and the concerns of urban living.[18] In this respect the position of the landscapist who regularly painted a single area was very similar to that of the owner of a *maison de campagne;* although he had a stake in the place, his vision of it, and the paintings he produced there, were geared not toward the local community but to the interests of the Parisian public.

The new modes of travel were accompanied by changes in the ways in which travel and remote places were promoted in Paris. The mass of illustrated material that became available from the 1840s onward, in guidebooks and magazines, offered a vast range of information to the prospective traveler and the armchair tourist.[19] Many other types of publication also discussed the countryside and the French provinces. Ideas of "nature" were central to contemporary religious, philosophical, and scientific discussions. Today we tend to see these as specialized types of writing, but in mid-nineteenth-century France there were no such boundaries. Semi-specialist essays on geology and metaphysics might appear in periodicals and popular series of books designed for a general educated audience; and celebrated authors such as Jules Michelet published successful books on themes like the sea and the mountains, which offered a hybrid synthesis of philosophy, geology, natural history, and sociology.[20]

There has been much discussion of how to characterize the engagement of tourists and travelers with the sites they visit. The physical access to unfamiliar places and the tourist "gaze" have often been described in terms of the predator or of penetration, implying some sense of invasion and violation. However, this model is not always applicable. The package tourist generally encounters the "Other" prepackaged: the tourist industry itself may irreversibly alter the cultural patterns of the places it colonizes, but the tourist is protected from the disorientation of the truly "Other." Even the solo traveler in France is invited to follow certain tracks—no longer the train tracks of the nineteenth-century Joanne guides, but the recommended sites and itineraries of the green Michelin guides, with their carefully indicated starred viewpoints.

Travelers engage with what they see in different ways. Someone seeking to buy a *maison de campagne* will view places differently from a group following a Michelin itinerary.[21] Among these ways of seeing is the one that views a place as "landscape." Although the process of finding a prospect, of seeking out a viewpoint for a landscape, may be an intrusion, the landscape "gaze" itself claims not to be invasive, since it depends on a process of distancing and framing. In

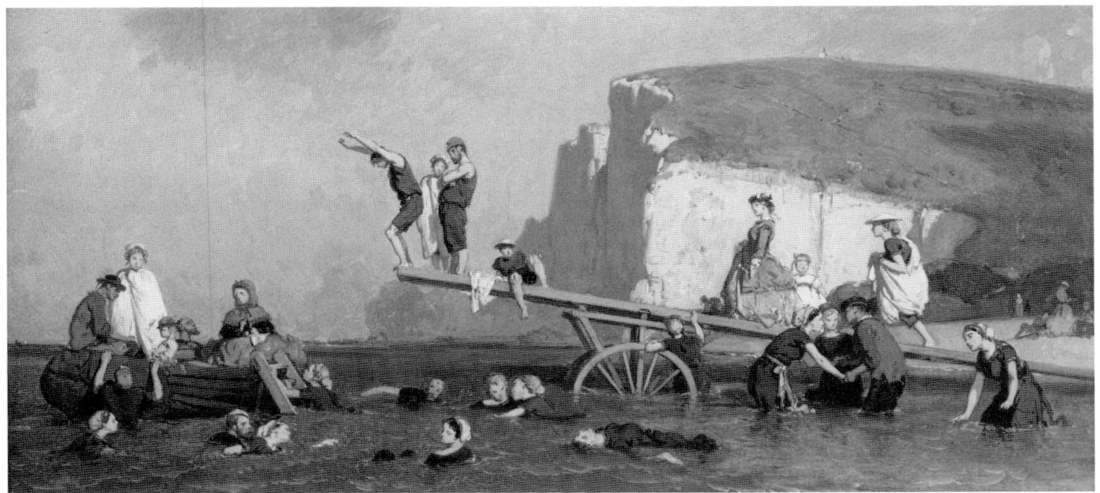

FIGURE 4.2. Eugène Le Poittevin, *Sea Bathing at Etretat*, 1866. Association Peindre en Normandie, Caen. Photo: Bridgeman-Giraudon.

a broader sense, the "landscape" view of nature is not about the site itself, but about the image that is made of it, whether a memory, a photograph, a verbal description, or a painting.

The Painter in the Landscape

Landscape painting was viewed in terms of both art and nature. It was judged in relation to its subject—for the significance of the subject itself and for its apparent truthfulness—but it also had to justify itself as fine art. The history of nineteenth-century landscape painting is the history of successive attempts to reconcile these apparently conflicting requirements.

The landscape painter was expected to have special insight into "nature," particularly after the invention of photography, which superseded the purely reproductive function of landscape painting. But there was much disagreement about what the landscapist's involvement in his subject should be.[22] Was the artist's vision justified by some generalized notion of "truth to nature" that had little to do with the particular site, or was truth more specific, more local? And if so, how might the landscapist claim special insight into that place?

Jean-Baptiste-Camille Corot was consistently praised in the years after 1860 as a painter who understood the "truths of nature." Yet his paintings ranged from artificial pastorals such as *Souvenir of Italy* (1873; Glasgow Museums, Kelvingrove), through more informal images of particular places—sometimes but not always entitled *souvenir*—to small studies, often executed in front of the subject. But whatever site he treated, whether an Italian lake or a corner of northern France, his art tended to be discussed in terms of mood, reverie, and poetry.

In general, though, landscapists were expected to engage more directly with their subjects. In 1862 Théophile Thoré spelt out his requirements for a true landscapist:

> The true artist is an indissoluble fusion of nature and humanity, a visionary and a thinker at the same time. . . . [Such artists] see what they need to see, experience a corresponding impression of it, and then translate it without any other concern. I have lived with them in the woods, often with Rousseau for example, and the man interested me as much as the painter: his heart was always involved, and his eye, too; his hand followed. When the whole man is absorbed like this in his work, when he lives in it and

makes it live within him, it is not surprising that his work has expressive virtues.[23]

In part, Théodore Rousseau's vision is here justified by his personality: by the unity of heart, eye, and hand. In part, the justification is external: Rousseau lives where he paints, in the Forest of Fontainebleau (see fig. 2.1), and Thoré has witnessed his immersion in it.

Such testimonies recurred throughout the period and played a significant part in the attempts of painters to distinguish themselves from photographers. In 1872, writing from New Orleans to a friend, Edgar Degas explained why he was painting so little there: "One can't just arrive in Louisiana and make art as easily as one can in Paris; that would be just like *Le Monde illustré*. It's only a long stay that can reveal to you the habits of a race, that is to say its charm. The instantaneous is photography, nothing more."[24]

Yet even an extended period of familiarization might not be considered enough. For Alfred Sensier, writing in 1870, the painter's birthplace was all-important:

> A continual source of trouble, doubt and despair for our contemporary artists is the imbalance that has led them to be born in Paris, in Lyon, or in Marseille, and has made them children of an unreasonable and pernicious atmosphere, and has led them to a love of nature through their loathing for cities. Their childhood impressions have not been frank, simple, and "animal," and they always feel themselves embarrassed by the thorns of the rustic soil. . . . Throughout his life Rousseau expiated the misfortune of being born in the Place des Victoires; nothing has been able to free him from the doubts of his vision, his timidity as a painter, and the profusion of his invention.[25]

Sensier's was an extreme position and a form of special pleading on behalf of Jean-François Millet.[26] Yet the links between a painter's birthplace and the paintings he produced were more complex than Sensier's account implies. Although Millet exhibited one landscape of his birthplace on the Normandy coast at the Salon, his reputation as a "peasant painter" was founded on his paintings of the Barbizon region near the Fontainebleau Forest, where he lived and worked. Moreover, Sensier's arguments obscure the fact that Millet's paintings, and the accounts he propagated of his origins, were designed for a Parisian audience; his images of rural life found their meanings in urban culture.

The issue of the relationship between the landscapist and the peasant population recurred for Camille Pissarro in 1892. The anarchist theorist Piotr Kropotkin had argued in *La Conquête du pain* that only someone who had lived as a peasant could paint peasants truthfully and without sentimentality. Pissarro responded: "Certainly one must be involved in one's subject in order to render it well, but is it necessary to be a peasant? Let us, rather, be artists, and we will be able to experience everything, even a *paysage* without being *paysan*."[27]

Another way by which artists might promote the authenticity of their knowledge was circulating stories of their heroics in immersing themselves in their subjects. Monet, in particular, used these tactics. In the winter of 1866–67 he ensured that a reporter saw him painting deep in a snowdrift near Honfleur; in the 1880s accounts reported him braving waves, gales, and rain in order to paint the French coasts.[28] This image was confirmed by his paintings of extreme weather effects (see fig. 10.7), and by his sedulously propagated (and unjustified) reputation as a painter who only worked out of doors.[29]

Images emerged of the distinctive lifestyle of the landscapist, its principal feature being solitary contemplation. In 1886 Guy de Maupassant presented the landscapist out of doors from morning to evening, living by his eyes alone, seeking out the nuances of color that the studio education of the Ecole denied him.[30] Frédéric Henriet, a close associate of Charles-François Daubigny, described the escape to the country of "the landscapist who desires silence and solitude." The artist reconnoiters for sites, seeking "to penetrate the intimate meaning, the unique accent, the essential character of this nature . . . whose secret he searches out," and stops to paint where instinct leads him. The painter is set apart both from the local peasants and farmers and from the bourgeois tourists: we see how little those who work the land understand the landscapist's art, and a mocking aside introduces the ladies of the village who encourage him to paint the most obvious picturesque sites in the area—"a real little Switzerland."[31]

Yet Henriet's book shows that, as for the tourist, Paris was the necessary repoussoir for the landscapist's retreat from the city:

> [In the country] how far away Paris is! And what does the echo of the boulevard . . . mean to him now that he has cut the mooring that tied him to real life in order to sail off into the true ideal! . . . In these periods of work and contemplation, . . . I do not want to know about the controversies that divide men.[32]

There is no sense here that the countryside might have its own "real life"!

Daubigny's more down-to-earth vision of the landscapist's life made the links to Paris still more explicit. In his sequence of etchings entitled *Voyage en bateau* of 1862, a visual narrative of his travels in his studio boat along the rivers Seine and Oise, we see him painting in communion with nature. He and his son fish in the river, eat and sleep in the local inns, but socialize with friends who have come down from Paris by train, not with the local children whom they watch from a safe distance. This is an image of urban bohemianism transported to the countryside.

The interdependence of city and country in the life of the landscapist emerges most vividly in the growing popularity of artists' colonies from the mid-century onward. Barbizon and other villages around the Fontainebleau Forest were the earliest and most celebrated of these; but in the later part of the century, groups of painters congregated in the summer in many other villages: Grez-sur-Loing, on a river to the south of the Fontainebleau Forest; Cernay-la-Ville, beyond Versailles to the southwest of Paris (fig. 4.3); and Pont-Aven in Brittany, made famous by Paul Gauguin (plate 7) but a popular center for American artists twenty years before he went there.[33]

In such colonies painters could live cheaply and informally, and find a ready stock of subjects. The pattern of communal living—of transporting an artistic coterie from Paris for the summer—is closer to the "tourist" model than to the "traveler." As the many reminiscences of life in these colonies reveal, the artists formed self-contained communities, preoccupied by artistic affiliations and rivalries and, above all, by the effect that they would produce in Paris, through their paintings and the stories of their bohemian lifestyle.

The rival claims of solitude and communal discussion posed a real problem for the young landscapist seeking to establish his artistic identity. In December 1868 Monet wrote to Bazille from Etretat on the Normandy coast: "In Paris one is too preoccupied by what one sees and what one hears, however strong one is; what I am doing here has, I think, the merit of not resembling anyone, because it is simply the expression of what I myself have experienced."[34] Yet, as Monet well knew, it was in Paris that this artistic identity would make its mark.

The artist occupied a special place between the tourist and those who worked the land. Like the tourist, the artist was an outsider who saw the countryside as landscape; but he also had "inside knowledge," and his view of the landscape might be very different from that of the tourist. This emerges vividly in relation to Rousseau's vision of the Fontainebleau Forest (see fig. 2.1). While Rousseau was living there, Charles-François Denecourt was opening the forest to visitors, publishing guidebooks and creating walks that offered the visitor an easy path and interesting viewpoints. In a sense, this allowed the forest to be seen as "landscape"; but Rousseau and other painters opposed these developments, seeking to preserve its pristine wildness and to exclude the tourist hordes.[35]

As with the traveler and the tourist, the presence of the painter prospecting for sites in the countryside might be invasive, showing scant regard for property or local customs—as when the Orientalist painter Alexandre Lenoir hid behind a bush in Egypt to watch and sketch Muslim women bathing, and was stoned for

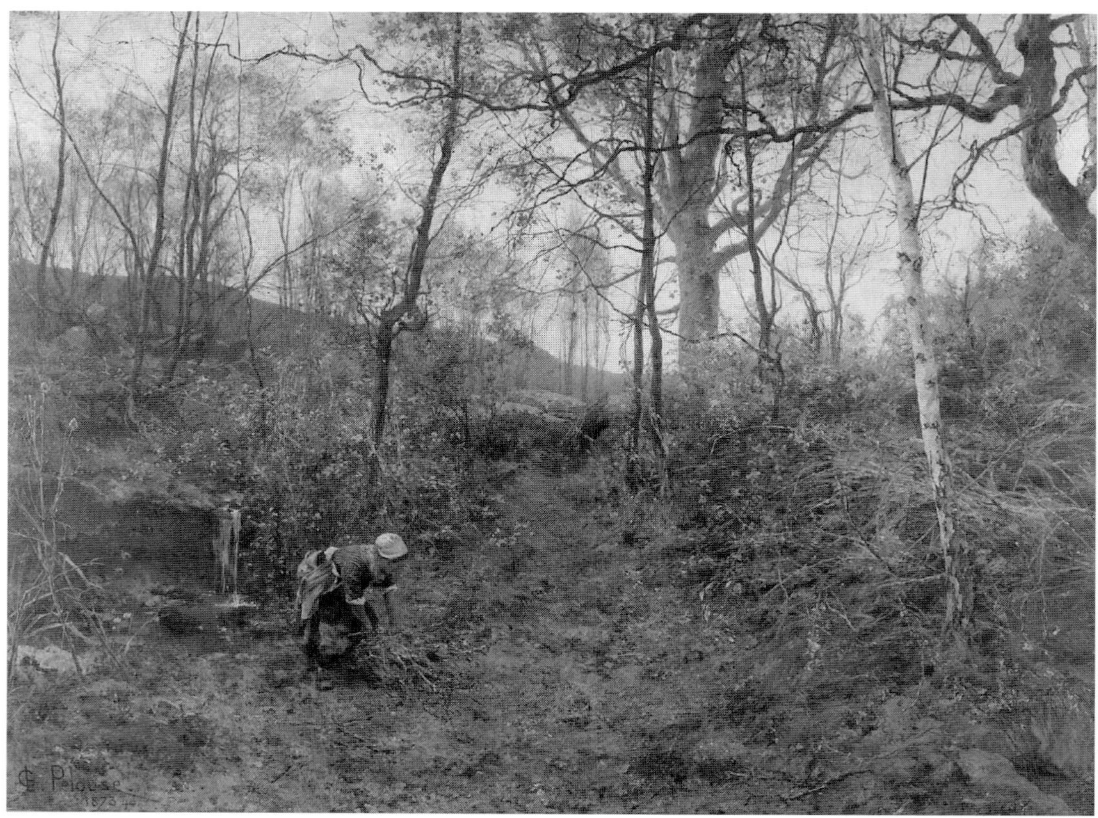

FIGURE 4.3. Léon Pelouse, *The Valley of Cernay (Seine-et-Oise)*, 1873. Musée des Beaux-Arts, Dunkerque. Photo: Musée des Beaux-Arts, Dunkerque.

his efforts.[36] But the landscapist's engagement with his subject was characterized in quite different terms in the nineteenth century. It was viewed as a solitary dialogue between painter and "nature," and the painter might even be presented as a passive receptor and translator of nature's voice. Of course the terms in which this "nature" and its "voice" were understood were a far cry from the lived countryside and its social networks; the landscapist's identity and the "nature" that spoke to him were an integral part of urban culture.

The Landscapist's Choices

When beginning a picture the landscapist had two important choices to make: his subject, and the way that subject should be presented on the canvas. The choice of subject may seem primary, but in practice it was the way in which it was structured that defined his position as an artist.

The Neoclassical landscape of the early nineteenth century, looking back to the Italianate landscapes of Claude Lorrain and Poussin, offered the principal model against which landscape paintings were judged. The landscapes of the "School of 1830," of artists such as Rousseau, Paul Huet, and Jules Dupré, provided an alternative paradigm and alternative artistic models: the landscapes of seventeenth-century Holland. Corot's early Salon paintings reveal how readily each of these models could be assimilated and then discarded: a Neoclassical Italian scene exhibited in 1827 was followed in 1833 by an em-

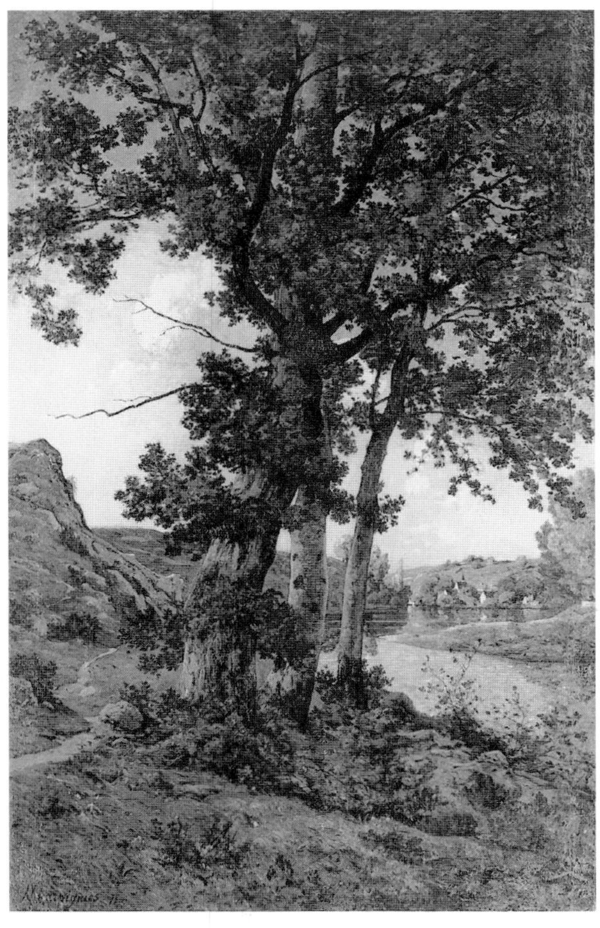

FIGURE 4.4. Henri Harpignies, *The Oaks of Château-Renard (Allier)*, 1875. Musée des Beaux-Arts d'Orléans. Photo: Musée des Beaux-Arts d'Orléans.

phatically Dutch view of the Forest of Fontainebleau.

Both models persisted throughout the century. The artifice of Neoclassical landscape enjoyed a brief revival in the mid-1870s when the French State again bought the paintings of Paul Flandrin, but echoes of the Neoclassical clarity of form and orderly spatial recession recur in works as dissimilar as Corot's late *souvenirs* and the landscapes of Henri Harpignies (fig. 4.4). Likewise the more informal Dutch mode, fundamental to the forest scenes of Rousseau (see fig. 2.1) and the river views of Daubigny (fig. 4.5), is echoed in the work of such painters as Léon Pelouse (see fig. 4.3) and Antoine Guillemet.

E. H. Gombrich has viewed the key developments in Western art in terms of schema and correction. While recognizing the artifice of every pictorial representation, he has described the development of naturalistic modes of representation as a succession of moments when artists looked afresh at the world around them and used the evidence of their eyes to correct the formulas or schemata that they had inherited.[37]

At first sight the history of French nineteenth-century landscape fits this pattern well. The Dutch mode was initially regarded as a "natural" corrective to the artifice of Neoclassicism, but by the 1860s it was widely seen as belonging to a particular moment in history and taste; the emergence of Impressionism in the late 1860s and 1870s is generally viewed as a further, decisive step toward a "natural" vision in art.

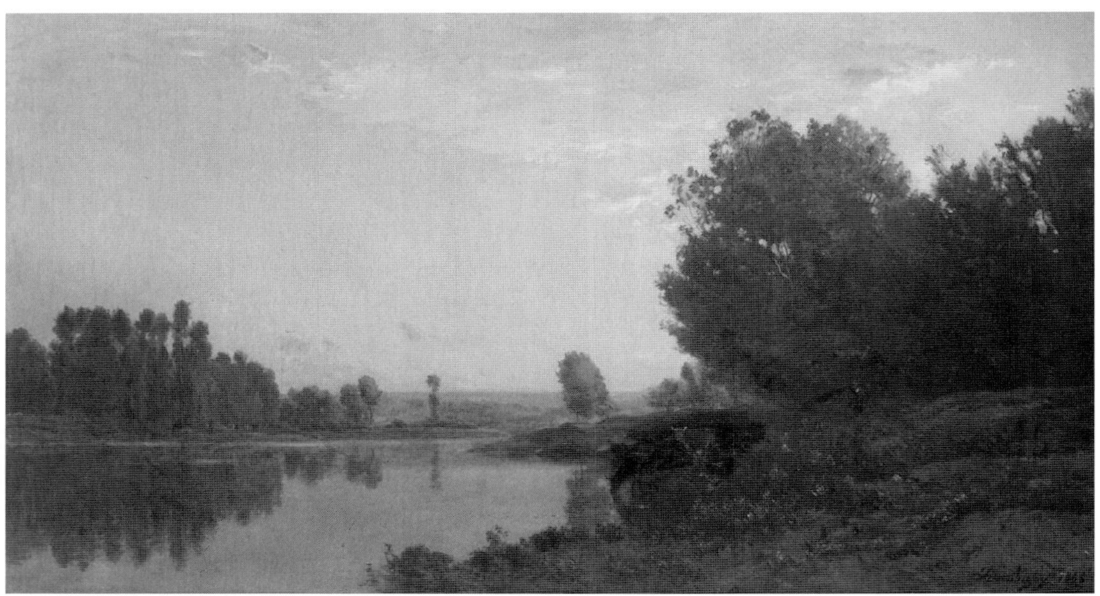

FIGURE 4.5. Charles François Daubigny, *Banks of the Oise River, Morning Effect*, 1866. Musée des Beaux-Arts, Rouen. Photo: Bridgeman-Giraudon/Art Resource, NY.

Any notion of naturalism, however, depends on cultural assumptions. There has never been a consensus about what constitutes naturalistic representation, even during the past two hundred years when something like our present-day notions of "nature" have been current.[38] This emerges clearly in the contrast between our own culture's assumption that the Impressionist landscape is a particularly "natural" form of painting and the responses of Impressionism's first viewers, most of whom saw it as a travesty of their idea of "nature" in art.

The issues of "realism" and the "natural" in painting were a central preoccupation in the 1860s and 1870s. The original critical responses to paintings reveal that many types of image could be regarded as natural or truthful in the later nineteenth century. Rather than seeing Impressionism as some sort of breakthrough, we find a range of competing conventions in landscape painting of the period, all vying with each other to be considered "natural."

Many different facets of a painting might make it appear "natural": the composition, the choice of subject, the way in which the elements in the scene were rendered, and the facture adopted. In compositional terms, the idea of the "natural" was best invoked by making the picture look as if it had not been "composed" at all. Yet the structure of the painting depended on the artist's choice of viewpoint and on the way in which he framed the scene; he might also modify the forms before him.

Seeking to rid themselves of both Neoclassical and Dutch conventions, many landscapists adopted deliberately simplified structures, even in landscapes exhibited at the Salon. A perspective might run straight into the picture. A scene might be viewed frontally, whether it was a slab of rocks or an open meadow; it might appear to continue uninterrupted beyond the frame of the picture; or it might be viewed from an unexpected angle.

The question of subject matter was central for the landscapist. The Prix de Rome for landscape painting, awarded at the Ecole des Beaux-Arts between 1817 and 1863, was explicitly for historic landscape—that is, for scenes including a historical or mythological scene.[39] Though painters such as François-Louis Français continued on occasion to treat such themes in their landscapes (see, for example, his *Daphnis and Chloe*, 1872; Musée des Beaux-Arts, Strasbourg), these requirements were widely seen as irrelevant to the types of landscape that developed after 1830.

However, the choice of subject remained crucial. The key question was the status of the *motif*. This was not simply a neutral designation of a picture's theme. A true motif was expected to be visually striking and to carry historical or poetic associations, and it needed to be presented in an ordered pictorial form. Views of historic sites or dramatic natural scenes most obviously fulfilled these prescriptions.

For conservative critics, the history of French nineteenth-century landscape was the story of the decline of the motif. In 1868 Edmond About contrasted past with current methods. Traditionally the artist had composed his subject from a repertory of elements:

> Forests, rocks, shorelines, valleys, flocks, palaces, ruins, cottages, costumes, types, these were the materials from which one composed a landscape. . . . When by chance one encountered a combination of beautiful things well grouped in nature, one said: "That's a picturesque site," that is to say a site worthy of being painted, comparable to those that true artists represent.

For contemporary artists, by contrast, "the slightest fragment of nature is material for a picture, provided one knows how to paint and how to render an impression."[40] For Georges Lafenestre, those who focused on mere impressions were "tourists of the brush" when compared with the few artists who still "raise themselves up to the poetic conception of the expressive landscape, to the pondered composition of their personal creation, where elements borrowed from living nature are grouped together and enhance and strengthen each other, so as to throw the individual sentiment of the artist into relief."[41]

The supporters of new developments saw these changes as positive gains in two ways: concentration on fleeting effects of atmosphere revealed the artist's sensitivity to nature itself; and this sensibility best expressed the emotion of the scene. The tensions between old and new notions of landscape emerge particularly clearly in Courbet's dealings with his patrons during the 1860s: collectors generally wanted paintings with recognizable features such as figures, boats, or deer, but Courbet sought to market his landscapes primarily as demonstrations of his mastery of the "*effet*."[42] However, the landscapes he showed at the Salon usually had more distinctive motifs.

The distinction between the emotional impact of the scene and the subjective response of the artist was consistently blurred in the writing of the period, in particular in the use of the terms *effet*, *sensation*, and *impression*. It was the artist's subjective engagement with nature's fleeting effects that was expressed by the picture and transmitted to the viewer.[43]

In the present context, *impression* is the most significant term. It referred initially to the impression made on the viewer by the experience of nature's most transitory effects and then, by extension, to paintings that recorded such impressions. In 1861 Théophile Gautier criticized Daubigny, "who has such a faithful and truthful feeling for nature," for "contenting himself with an *impression* and neglecting the details."[44] For Lagrange in 1865, Daubigny was the leader of the "school of the *impression*," and in the following year Charles Blanc criticized certain followers of Corot for being satisfied with "rendering the *impression*," commenting: "This is the big word in a certain camp."[45] In 1872 Jules Claretie lamented that landscapists were too readily satisfied "with an *impression*, with an *effet* for their pictures."[46]

To hostile critics all works by the new landscapists were mere *impressions*. Yet the artists themselves distinguished between their *impressions* and their more highly finished paintings. When Monet was asked why he had given the title *Impression, Sunrise* to his celebrated picture at the 1874 group exhibition (plate 1), he replied, "[because] it really couldn't pass as a view of Le Havre."[47] At the same exhibition he showed another, larger, and more finished picture of Le Havre, titled *Le Havre: Fishing Boats Leaving the Port*, which presumably could pass as a "view."[48]

After the naming of the group as "Impressionists" in 1874, the term was usually used to refer to their work. However, in 1876 Victor Cherbuliez contrasted the "formless, confused sketches" of these "intransigents" with "the reasonable and reasoned Impressionism" of paintings by Harpignies and Pelouse at the Salon (see figs. 4.3, 4.4).[49]

Notionally at least, the painting of *effets* and *impressions* was unconcerned with the actual site depicted. Yet discussion continued about the subject matter for landscape painting, in particular about the acceptability of overtly contemporary scenes. Henriet insisted that the true landscapist favored unspoiled sites and timeworn buildings, despite the incursions of "civilization": "Every conquest of industry, every material improvement involves some sacrifice of the poetry of memories or of picturesque beauties." For Charles Bigot, reviewing the third Impressionist group exhibition in 1877, their choice of subjects represented a wholesale misunderstanding not only of the art of landscape, but of "nature" itself:

> In the final analysis, it is not true nature that they have looked at and have tried to render, but rather the nature that one encounters on outings in the great city or its surroundings, where the harsh notes of the houses, with their white, red or yellow walls and their green shutters, clash with the vegetation of the trees and form violent contrasts with it. How much better have . . . our modern landscapists, the Rousseaus, the Corots and the Daubignys, understood how to express not only the poetry but also the truth of nature! How much better have they represented the countryside, with its waters, its woods, its fields and its meadows, with its distant and calm horizons![50]

The most positive endorsement of the potential of contemporary subjects came not from an artist or a critic, but in Amédée Guillemin's volume on *Les Chemins de fer* in the popular *Bibliothèque des merveilles:*

> The railways are not, as people keep repeating, the enemy of art and of the picturesque in landscape. These beautiful viaducts, with their long rows of white arches, masked in turn by rocks and clumps of greenery, have a decorative effect that is very simple and very satisfying.

The accompanying illustration, titled *The Viaducts and the Landscape*, juxtaposes the train on its viaduct with an archetypal ramshackle cottage.[51]

The problem was not simply the inclusion of the visible signs of modernization. The idea of "modernity" also involved a particular way of seeing the world. It was thus that Charles Baudelaire understood it in his essay on Constantin Guys, published in 1863: his *modernité* was based on the image of the man in the urban crowd, the *flâneur,* scrutinizing the figures around him but retaining his distance and anonymity. Baudelaire described this engagement with the world as *curiosité*—a type of indiscriminate looking that was fascinated by all sorts of visual stimuli but was unconcerned with the relative significance of the objects within a scene.[52] For contemporary moralists, such vision posed a real threat to social values and hierarchies.[53]

The Impressionists' landscapes of the 1870s explored this seemingly indiscriminate vision. In Alfred Sisley's *Boats on the Seine* (c. 1877; fig. 4.6), for instance, all the elements are equally trivial and none treated with special attention. Even where Sisley did choose a celebrated subject in *The Watering Place at Marly in Winter* (1875; National Gallery, London), he treated this remnant of one of Louis XIV's palaces as if it were no more important than the other elements in this mundane scene.

After the government changes of 1877–79 the new Republican authorities actively sponsored the painting of significant contemporary subjects.[54] In the 1880s the State purchased a number of pictures of such themes, among them Frank M. Boggs's *The Place de la Bastille in 1882* (Musée National de la Coopération Franco-Américaine, Blérancourt), a contemporary subject presented as a motif in the conventional sense. The Impressionists' paintings of Paris and its surroundings of the mid-1870s had been executed during the years when State policy was promoting a return to traditional academic values.[55] But

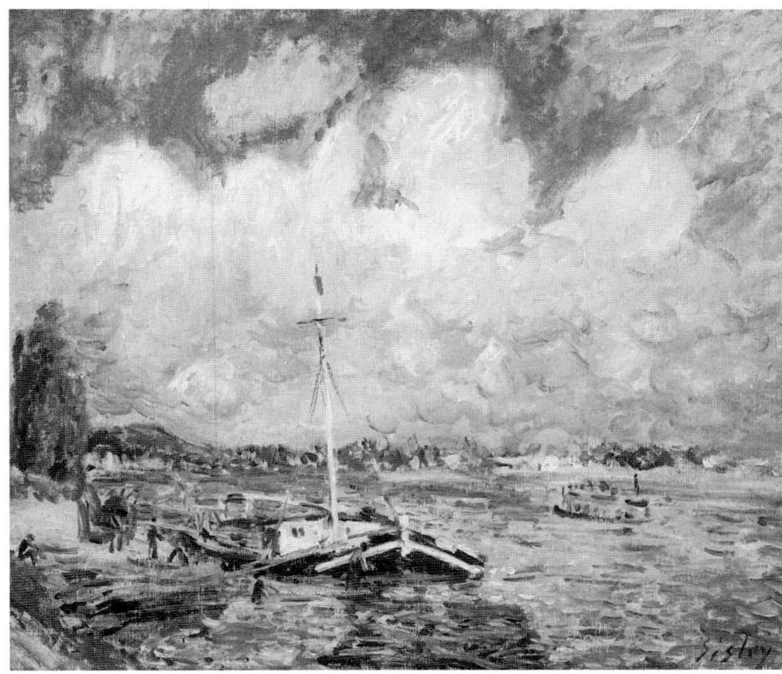

FIGURE 4.6. Alfred Sisley, *Boats on the Seine*, c. 1877. Courtauld Institute of Art Gallery, London. Photo: Bridgeman-Giraudon.

when the State began to encourage explicitly contemporary subjects, the members of the Impressionist group turned away from them. This shift coincided with their attempts to market their work through art dealers such as Paul Durand-Ruel; their pursuit of the bourgeois collector market probably led them toward more conventionally picturesque themes.

The question of painting technique was inseparable from the changing attitudes toward subject matter in landscape. Throughout these years the manual dexterity of French painters was much admired, but this was accompanied by fears that mere skill was replacing more serious, humanistic values. Landscape painting was a focus for these anxieties, because of the virtuoso sketch-like technique it often displayed, combined with the declining concern for the motif. Courbet's rejection of conventional drawing and his use of the palette knife were much debated; for Gautier, he was a master of *"peinture matérielle"* but lacked any higher values: "He will serve you up a fine morsel, just as a cook brings you a finely cooked steak."[56] Brushwork that treated every element in the scene as if it were equally significant was the visual equivalent of the unselective *curiosité* that so disconcerted the moralists (see plate 4).[57]

The concentration on color at the expense of modeling and drawing gave rise to related concerns. In academic theory the rendering of form relied on the intellect, whereas color belonged to the realm of the senses. A richly colored palette was acceptable if subordinated to clearly defined forms, as in Flandrin's Neoclassical landscapes (e.g., his *Souvenir de Provence*, 1875; Musée des Beaux-Arts, Dijon); but paintings dominated by color alone were seen as inadequate and superficial, or, worse, as subverting the supremacy of mind over matter. Such concerns lay behind the opposition to the luminous tonality and intense color of Impressionist landscape. However, for critics who supported a type of painting based on sensory experiences, the Impressionist palette marked the triumph of a spontaneous, "natural" form of painting over academic artifice.

Artistic theory of all types demanded a unity between the theme of the picture and its treatment. For most of their earliest critics in the 1870s, the Impressionists' landscapes lacked such unity: their subjects were trivial and fragmentary, their technique incomplete. However, one critic, Frédéric Chevalier, recognized in 1877 that even these discordant elements might be understood as a coherent worldview; together, their subjects and technique could stand for the idea of modernity:

> The characteristics that distinguish the Impressionists—the brutal handling of paint, their down-to-earth subjects, the appearance of spontaneity that they seek above all else, the deliberate incoherence, the bold coloring, the contempt for form, the childish naïveté that they mix heedlessly with exquisite refinements—this disconcerting mixture of contradictory qualities and defects is not without analogy to the chaos of opposing forces that trouble our era.[58]

Viewing the Painted Landscape

The Salon, held annually from 1863 onward, was the unequivocal focus of the Parisian art world. Its control was transferred from the State to the artists themselves in 1881, but it remained the single forum for displaying French art until 1890. In that year the Salon split in two, with the creation of the Société Nationale des Beaux-Arts (the Salon du Champ de Mars).

The position of the Salon was very problematic. It was widely felt that it served two irreconcilable interests: as a showcase for the best of contemporary French art, and as a shopwindow for artists to sell their wares. In principle it was felt that fine art and commerce belonged to two different worlds, but in practice this was unrealistic. The Paris Expositions Universelles that took place roughly every decade presented a considered retrospective of recent work, but a more frequent forum was needed to show the best current work. Plans were repeatedly mooted for the conversion of the Salon into a permanent exhibition focused solely on selling, and the institution of a more select temporary exhibition. The Exposition Nationale Triennale was launched in 1883, but it collapsed after one exhibition because of lack of public interest, and the Salon continued to serve both functions throughout the period.[59]

The position of landscape at the Salon, and in French art as a whole, was hotly debated. In the traditional hierarchy of the genres of painting it occupied a lowly place, below historical and religious painting.[60] The Prix de Rome for *paysage historique* gave it a certain recognition but at the same time implied that serious landscape painting should have a subject beyond the scene itself. From 1848 onward "pure" landscape was widely accepted at the Salon, but theorists and moralists repeatedly asked why it had become so popular.

Landscape was seen as the art of democracy and freedom, but this aroused mixed feelings. For the supporters of old hierarchies it represented decline and degeneration, and the loss of the heroic ideals of the past.[61] For others it represented liberation from the Academy and a renewal of both art and society. But even here opinions might vary: Alfred Sensier praised landscape as a mark of health, in contrast to the effects of urbanization and industrialization, while Jules Castagnary welcomed it, though only as one stage in the progression toward an art that would depict modern urban man, and thereby fulfill the Republican dream.[62]

The State played a complex and often ambiguous role as patron of art. The great majority of Salon landscapes were bought by the State, and their placement in provincial museums had a political as well as a cultural purpose.[63] Their purchase was central to the policy of Napoleon III in the 1860s, and again of the Third Republic from the late 1870s onward, of fostering a sense of national identity throughout France, but from 1875 to 1877 there was a sudden and marked decline in the number of landscapes purchased, coinciding with President MacMahon's "moral order" régime.[64] Regional differences were encouraged, provided they were subordinated to an overriding notion of nationhood. Many landscapes bought by the State were sent to museums in the provinces represented in the pictures;[65] but others were sent to regions of France far from their natural subjects (see fig. 4.3).

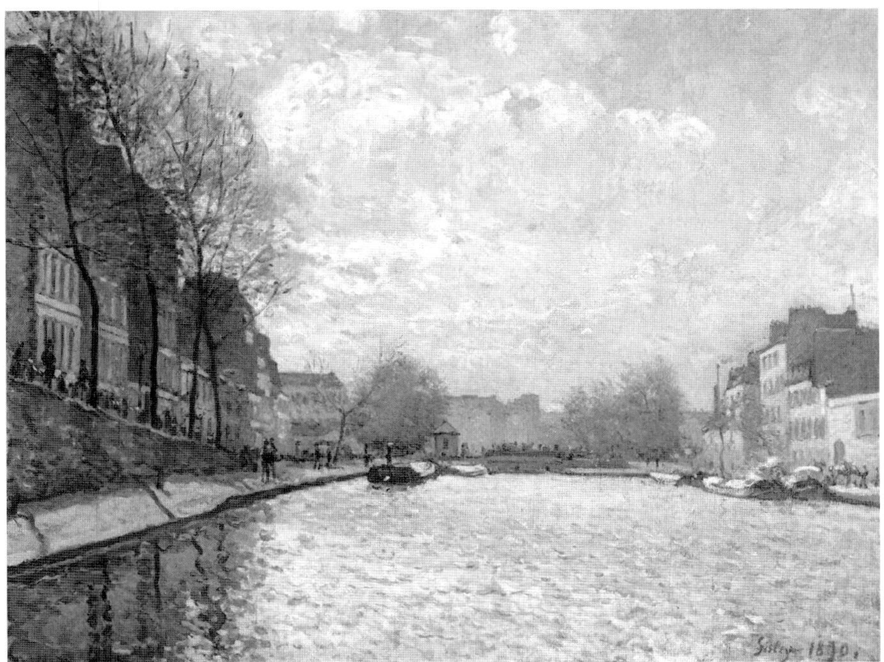

FIGURE 4.7. Alfred Sisley, *Le Canal Saint-Martin, Paris*, 1870. Musée d'Orsay, Paris. Photo: Erich Lessing/Art Resource, NY.

Major centers did own paintings of the local province, but they also displayed images of other and very different regions of France.

Under Napoleon III pictures were commissioned from some of the most controversial landscapists, notably Daubigny. In 1860–61, he painted decorative canvases for the Ministry of State in the Louvre Palace;[66] and in 1862–65 he executed another major State commission, *The Park of Saint-Cloud* (Musée de Châlons-sur-Marne),[67] a motif of a very conventional type, but with the fashionable figures in the foreground adding a note of modernity.

Many of the landscapes bought by the State in the 1860s and the 1880s did not represent motifs in the traditional sense; they were experimental in both composition and technique. Yet in one sense they did reflect a traditional approach to public painting: they were very large, on a scale to attract attention on the crowded walls of the Palais de l'Industrie, where the Salon was held.

This highlights a paradox in the position of landscape at the Salon. The developments in landscape all seemed to lead toward smaller pictures. Modest subjects suited smaller formats; the rapid technique needed to catch transitory effects also demanded portable canvases; and private collectors, often with modest-sized apartments, sought domestic-sized pictures. The large landscapes exhibited at the Salon, however informal their subjects, were only suitable for display in public buildings.

Small landscapes were exhibited at the Salon occasionally, and might attract critical notice if the painter was well known. Sisley's views of semi-industrial Parisian scenes (see fig. 4.7), that the Salon jury accepted in 1870, were, however, ignored. A comparably informal small landscape by Johan Barthold Jongkind (fig. 4.8) was rejected in 1863 and shown instead in that year's Salon des Refusés. The Salon was, on the whole, a most unsuitable site for bringing pictures like these before prospective buyers.

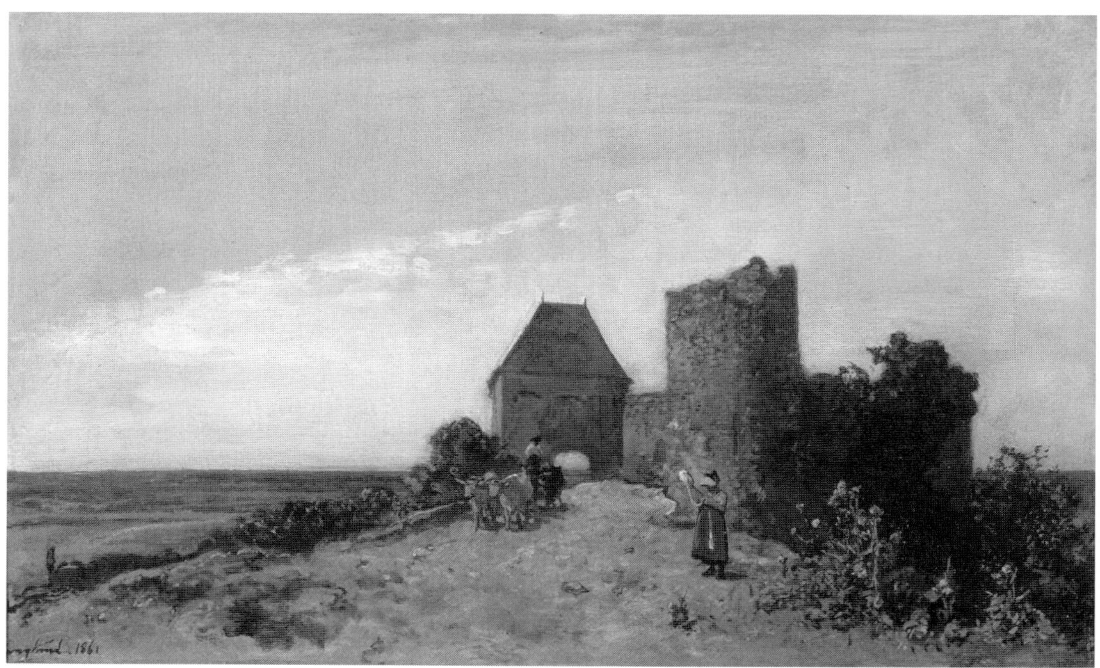

FIGURE 4.8. Johan Barthold Jongkind, *Ruins of the Château de Rosemont, Nievre,* 1861. Musée d'Orsay, Paris. Photo: Réunion des Musées Nationaux/Art Resource, NY.

The Impressionist group exhibitions of 1874–86 have generally been regarded as alternatives to the Salon, and as responses to the rejection of paintings by the Salon jury. However, there were other important outlets in these years: dealers' shops, exhibitions organized by *cercles* or other private bodies, and, probably most significant, auction sales.

The situation facing a little-known landscapist was summed up by the critic Théodore Duret, seeking to dissuade Camille Pissarro from joining the planned group exhibition in 1874:

> You have still one step to take: that is to succeed in becoming known to the public and accepted by all the dealers and art lovers. For this purpose there are only the auctions at the Hôtel Drouot and the big exhibition at the Palais de l'Industrie [the Salon]. . . . Your name is known to artists, critics, and to a special public. But you must make one more step and become widely known. You won't get there by exhibitions put on by private societies. The public doesn't go to such exhibitions, only the same nucleus of artists and patrons who already know you. The Hoschedé sale [at which Pissarro's work had recently fetched good prices] did you more good and advanced you further than all the private exhibitions imaginable. It brought you before a mixed and numerous public. . . . Among the 40,000 people who, I suppose, visit the Salon [figures of attendances at the Salon in the mid-1870s show annual totals of about 500,000], you'll be seen by fifty dealers, patrons, critics who would never otherwise look you up and discover you. [68]

Duret's letter indicates that, after the Salon, display at the Hôtel Drouot (the Paris auction rooms) was the next most important means of bringing works of art before the public. The landscapists Eugène Ciceri, Charles Hoguet, Narcisse Diaz, and Théodore Rousseau had pioneered the practice of artists organizing auctions of their own works in about 1850, and the practice spread in the 1860s.[69] In 1875 Amand Gautier, a painter of genre scenes and still lifes, mounted an auction of his own work. In the preface to the sale catalogue Philippe Burty explained Gautier's reasons:

> Unfortunately, no discreet, convenient location yet exists in Paris where one can, without pretension but also without reticence, display a few hundred studies or drawings—or even paintings—each of which is completed and explained by the others. The Hôtel Drouot alone has the advantage of attracting the mass public every day and thoroughly provoking the critics as a result.[70]

Just a week before the Gautier sale another auction had taken place at the Hôtel Drouot, with another preface by Burty: the auction of paintings by Monet, Morisot, Renoir, and Sisley that has played such a prominent part in histories of Impressionism.[71] Far from being an unusual experiment, these sales were more frequent than group exhibitions such as the one the artists had organized the previous year.

The *cercles,* the French equivalent of gentlemen's clubs, provided a forum very different from the auction house. Several of them organized regular exhibitions; in their relatively modest rooms smaller paintings could be displayed more sympathetically than at the Salon.[72] For Victor Champier they offered the ideal, elite alternative to the Salon:

> Amateurs, disheartened by the exhaustion of the Salon . . . prefer these intimate exhibitions that seem improvised. . . . Artists freely send to them the piece they have to hand: a successful sketch, a curious *pochade,* an indication of landscape, as well as a painting pushed to perfection.[73]

Others, though, felt that the *cercles* offered only second-choice works by the artists who showed at the Salon:

> At the Salon, they show the paintings which create their reputation, their most resolved and lasting works; at the *cercles,* portraits painted on commission or out of obligation, paintings quickly executed, successful sketches. . . . Also, newcomers never exhibit in them.[74]

Small, semi-private spaces also offered opportunities for exhibitions in these years, among them the offices of the fashionable periodical *La Vie moderne,* run by the publisher Georges Charpentier, which mounted small one-artist shows of Manet, Monet, and Sisley in 1880–81.

There were also the commercial galleries. In the 1860s it was unusual for art dealers to have a substantial gallery space.[75] They generally operated out of small shops; their primary display space was their shop window, in which they placed a limited and changing selection of their stock. It was the window displays that led Gautier in 1858 to describe rue Laffitte, the principal art dealers' street, as "a sort of permanent Salon."[76]

In 1854 Henriet welcomed the dealers' windows as legitimate contexts for the commercialism that worried the critics in the Salon, but he felt that the demands of dealers and collectors encouraged the taste for *petite peinture,* in contrast to the loftier ambitions that brought a painter real success.[77] However, he also pinpointed a particular type of painting that made a visit to rue Laffitte worthwhile: whereas Corot submitted his Italianate scenes to the Salon, "it is only in rue Laffitte that one can savor the intimate, domestic side of his talent, and learn to love the good, naïve Corot of Ville d' Avray, Bougival, and Bas-Meudon."[78]

This comment highlights the emergence of distinctive "dealer landscapes"—smaller and less formal than Salon paintings. They were the stock-in-trade of landscapists such as Boudin and Jongkind (see fig. 4.8) through the 1860s, and also formed the bulk of the production of painters like Daubigny, alongside the large pictures he showed at the Salon.

Such pictures played a key part in the production of the future Impressionists early in their careers, and it was this type of painting that Monet, Pissarro, and Sisley sold to the dealer Paul Durand-Ruel in the early 1870s, when he was trying to launch their careers outside the Salon (see fig. 4.9).[79] Although small and intended for a domestic setting, they are far more elaborately finished than the rapid sketches that contributed most to Impressionism's reputation (see plate 1).

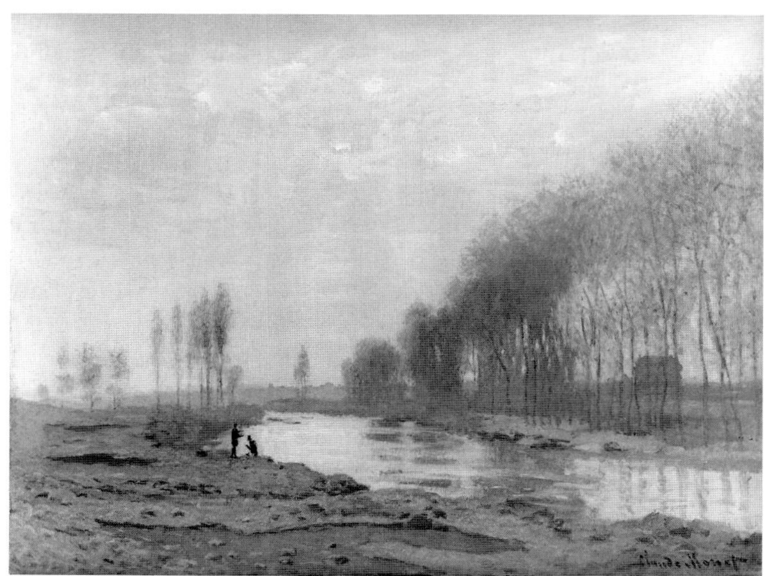

FIGURE 4.9. Claude Monet, *The Petit Bras of the Seine at Argenteuil*, 1872. National Gallery, London. Image © National Gallery, London.

Only in the 1880s did dealers, led by Georges Petit, begin to mount more ambitious exhibitions. Petit's Expositions Internationales, in which Monet, Renoir, Pissarro, and Sisley were included in the mid-1880s, offered a new model of display in lavish surroundings;[80] it was Petit's retrospective of Monet and Rodin in 1889 that established Monet's success. Durand-Ruel had tried to boost the reputation of the Impressionist landscapists in 1883 with one-artist shows of Boudin, Monet, Renoir, Pissarro, and Sisley (the first attempt anywhere to use a sequence of monographic shows as a marketing strategy). However, it was not until 1891 that Durand-Ruel began the long series of single-artist exhibitions that sealed the Impressionists' success. It is in the proliferation of alternative exhibiting groups and dealer exhibitions after 1890 that we find the real roots of the present-day structures of the art world, where dealers are the primary agents in establishing an artist's reputation.

The eight Impressionist group exhibitions of 1874–86 were presented as a single numbered sequence, but they did not reflect a single coherent strategy.[81] The initial abortive project for an exhibition in 1867 was directly triggered by the many rejections from that year's Salon.[82] The 1874 exhibition was discussed by most critics as an alternative to the Salon, but it was largely composed of smaller paintings. In part these were "dealer landscapes" of the sort that they had recently been selling to Durand-Ruel; the dealer's financial problems in 1874 must have been one of the catalysts that led them to mount their long-planned show. However, in this first show and the next two, in 1876 and 1877, several of the artists also included some of their most sketchy and improvisatory works, among them Monet's *Impression, Sunrise* (plate 1), shown in 1874. In the titles they gave their exhibition paintings, they made clear distinctions between these two types of picture, subtitling the sketch-like paintings *impression*, *esquisse* (sketch), or *étude* (study).[83]

In showing both sketches and "dealer landscapes," the painters brought together types of painting that normally belonged in different settings and addressed different publics. The primary audience for the "dealer landscape" was the stroller down the rue Laffitte, while the sketches were aimed toward a more elite and intimate viewership like that of the *cercles*. The appeal to a select, insider audience was central to

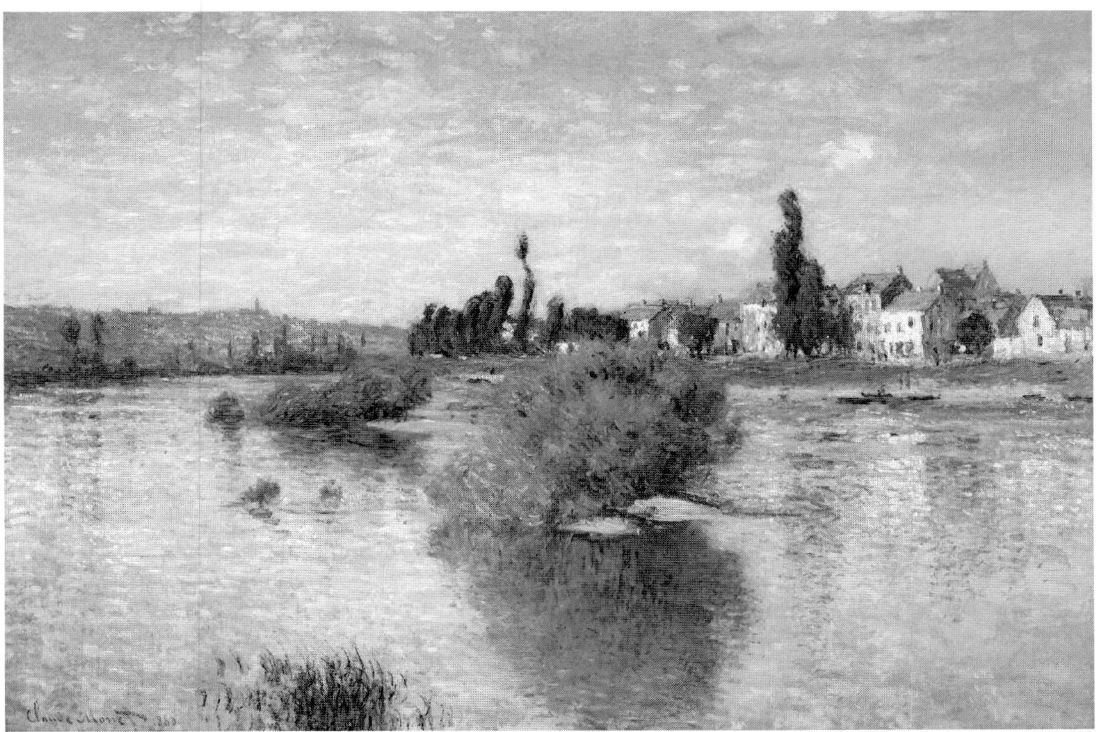

FIGURE 4.10. Claude Monet, *The Seine at Lavacourt*, 1880. Dallas Museum of Art, Munger Fund.

the propaganda surrounding the group's exhibitions. In 1876 their associate Duranty wrote of their work:

> The public wants finish above all. The artist, charmed by the delicacy or the boldness of a color effect, of a gesture, of a group, is much less concerned about finish and correctness, which are the only qualities appreciated by the inartistic. . . . It matters little that the public does not understand. It matters that artists should understand, and in front of them one can exhibit sketches, preparations, underpaintings where the thought, the intention and the draftsmanship of the artist are often expressed with more rapidity, more concentration.[84]

Both sketches and "dealer landscapes" were accommodated in the first three group shows. Thereafter, the conflicting interests of the artists pulled the group apart. First Renoir and then Monet withdrew, as their ambitions encouraged them to separate their reputation from the group's notoriety, and both submitted to the Salon again. Monet's one submission, in 1880 (fig. 4.10), followed the change in government and Jules Ferry's appeal, in his ministerial speech at the Salon prize-giving in 1879, to plein-airist landscapists to return to the Salon.[85]

When Durand-Ruel was able to resume buying their work early in 1881, Monet and Renoir realized that their future was not among the monumental public paintings of the Salon, but rather in the commercial space of the dealer.

At one extreme of the audience for art in Paris was the *grand public*, the half million who visited the annual Salon; at the other, the elite who attended the *cercles* or the Impressionist group shows. Notions of the "public" and of "popular" taste raise problems, for they are constructions made from an elite standpoint. Only a tiny proportion of nineteenth-century art viewers recorded their opinions. We have some informal comments, in letters and diaries, mostly written by one elite, the artists themselves. Otherwise, we have the printed accounts of art critics; and, whatever the critic's standpoint, he too represented an informed "insider" voice. In these writings the "public" puts in an appearance, but always set in contrast to the more enlightened views of the writer. Cast in this role, the "public" might have many contradictory views attributed to it; for defenders of academic ideals, public taste favored slapdash virtuosity, while supporters of the *impression* and the *effet* opposed their own taste to the idea of a public that favored anecdote and literal representation.

In nineteenth-century France there was no simple correlation between taste and social class. The notion of "bourgeois" taste was as much of a negative stereotype as that of the "public"; yet most art lovers and most artists, whatever their aesthetic position, were broadly members of the bourgeoisie. Any attempt to define taste in terms of birth or profession is contradicted by the evidence: the five key patrons of the Impressionists in the mid-to-late 1870s were a retired customs official (Victor Chocquet); an operatic baritone (Jean-Baptiste Faure); a pastry cook and restaurateur (Eugène Mürer); a homeopathic doctor (Georges de Bellio); and the spendthrift proprietor of a company that made fabrics for women's clothing (Ernest Hoschedé).

Taste needs to be discussed in terms of cultural constituencies or interest groups.[86] Personal preferences clearly played a part; but these gained their meanings and significance only in relation to the community who shared these interests, and by contrast with other communities with different tastes. Such groups might associate themselves with a particular institutional position (for instance the aesthetic of the Ecole des Beaux-Arts); or they might locate their own taste in relation to personal friendships, whether with critics, collectors, or artists.

The distinction between public and elite taste parallels the contrast between tourist and traveler. The tourist represents the "public" view of a place, while travelers define themselves by their distinctive responses or their specialized interests.

The landscapist was at the meeting point between art and travel. As a traveler, he was the ultimate antitourist, representing independent exploration and individual response; yet the sites he chose were defined and understood by reference to shared frameworks of knowledge about the French landscape. As a painter, he represented a personal sensitivity to his subjects and a privileged skill in transforming his experiences into "art." And yet the forms his paintings took—the subjects he chose and the schemata and techniques he adopted—inevitably located him within the framework of aesthetic debate. His uniqueness was defined in opposition to the public, but it was within that public that his art found its audience and its market.

Notes

Originally published in *Impressions of France: Monet, Renoir, Pissarro and Their Rivals*, exh. cat. (Boston: Museum of Fine Arts, 1995), 12–29.

1. P. Mantz, "Le Salon de 1863," *Gazette des beaux-arts* (1 July 1863): 36–37.
2. For instance H. Houssaye, "Le Salon de 1882—II," *Revue des deux mondes* (15 June 1882): 861.
3. L. Lagrange, "Le Salon de 1864," *Gazette des beaux-arts* (1 July 1864): 6, 9.
4. M. du Camp, *Le Salon de 1861* (Paris, 1861), 145–46.
5. W. J. T. Mitchell, *Landscape and Power* (Chicago, 1994), 14–15.
6. R. W. Emerson, "Nature," in *The Collected Works of Ralph Waldo Emerson, Vol. 1: Nature, Addresses, and Lectures* (Cambridge, Mass., 1971), 9, 39; quoted in ibid., 13–15.
7. For a key discussion of these issues, in the context of English literature, see R. Williams, *The Country and the City* (London, 1975).

8. The local lines were a central part of the Freycinet Plan, launched in 1878. François-Louis Français's *Valley of the Eaugronne* (collection of Walter Feilchenfeldt, Zurich) was a response to this process. On the Freycinet Plan, see E. Weber, *Peasants into Frenchmen: The Modernisation of Rural France, 1870–1914* (London, 1977), 209–11.
9. C. Nodier et al., *Voyages pittoresques et romantiques dans l'ancienne France*, vol. 1 (Paris, 1820), 1–5; on the *Voyages pittoresques* in relation to the development of the imagery of France in the nineteenth century, see especially B. L. Grad and T. A. Riggs, *Visions of City and Country: Prints and Photographs of Nineteenth-Century France* (Worcester, Mass., 1982).
10. Nodier et al., *Voyages pittoresques*, 7–8.
11. A. Hugo, *France pittoresque, ou Déscription pittoresque, topographique et statistique des départements et colonies de la France* (Paris, 1835), dedication to subscribers and p. 1. Abel Hugo was the brother of Victor.
12. N. Green, *The Spectacle of Nature: Landscape and Bourgeois Culture in Nineteenth-Century France* (Manchester, 1990), 80 ff.
13. See J. Buzard, *The Beaten Track: European Tourism, Literature, and the Ways to Culture, 1800–1918* (London, 1993), 3–10.
14. See R. L. Herbert, *Monet on the Normandy Coast: Tourism and Painting, 1867–1886* (New Haven, 1994), 2–4; J. Culler, "The Semiotics of Tourism," in *Framing the Sign: Criticism and Its Institutions* (Oxford, 1988), 156–59.
15. R. de Beauvoir, "Le Touriste," in *Les Français peints par eux-mêmes*, vol. 3 (Paris, 1841), 219; Hippolyte Taine presented a very similar account of the various types of tourists in *Voyage aux Pyrénées* (Paris, 1858; 1897 edition), 281–90.
16. On Trouville and Boudin, see V. Hamilton, *Boudin at Trouville* (Glasgow and London, 1992); for a description of Trouville and its tourist potential just before the arrival of the railways, see E. Chapus, *De Paris à Rouen et au Havre*, in series *Guides-Joanne* (Paris, 1862), 272–89.
17. Green, *Spectacle of Nature*, 84–89, 196 n. 71.
18. The urban fantasy of the *maison de campagne* was parodied by Frédéric Soulié in 1841 in *Les Français peints par eux-mêmes*, contrasting the dream of a rural idyll of cheap, healthy, natural living with the likely inconveniences and frustrations that such a house would bring (vol. 3, 25–32).
19. For example, the periodicals *L'Illustration* (1843+), *Le Monde illustré* (1857+), and *Le Tour du monde* (1860+).
20. J. Michelet, *La Mer* (Paris, 1861); J. Michelet, *La Montagne* (Paris, 1868).
21. For valuable discussions of these issues, see Mitchell, *Landscape and Power*, 16–18; and J. Urry, *The Tourist Gaze: Leisure and Travel in Contemporary Societies* (London, 1990), 7–14, 41–47. See also R. Barthes, "The *Blue Guide*," in *Mythologies* (London, 1972).
22. In this discussion I use the male personal pronoun; ambitious landscape painting in oils was overwhelmingly a male-dominated profession in these years. However, see Elodie La Villette (e.g., her *Chemin du Bas-Forte-Blanc, à marée basse, Dieppe*, 1886; Musée des Jacobins, Morlaix) and Berthe Morisot (plate 4).
23. T. Thoré, *Salons de W. Bürger, 1861 à 1868*, vol. 1 (Paris, 1870), 293, reviewing the London International Exhibition of 1862.
24. *Lettres de Degas*, ed. M. Guérin (Paris, 1945), 23.
25. A. Sensier, "Les Peintres de la nature," *Revue internationale de l'art et de la curiosité* (15 May 1870): 376.
26. On Sensier and Millet, see C. Parsons and N. McWilliam, "'Le Paysan de Paris': Alfred Sensier and the Myth of Rural France," *Oxford Art Journal* 6, no. 2 (1983).
27. Letter from Pissarro to Octave Mirbeau, 21 April 1892, in *Correspondance de Camille Pissarro*, ed. J. Bailly-Herzberg, vol. 3 (Valhermeil, 1988), 217.
28. See J. House, *Monet: Nature into Art* (New Haven, 1986), 137, 140–41.
29. On his working practices, see ibid., 135–56.
30. G. de Maupassant, "La Vie d'un paysagiste," *Gil blas*, 28 September 1886, reprinted in *Oeuvres complètes de Guy de Maupassant: Oeuvres posthumes*, vol. 2 (Paris, 1930); de Maupassant described watching Corot, Courbet, and, most recently, Monet painting at Etretat on the Normandy coast.
31. F. Henriet, *Le Paysagiste aux champs* (Paris, 1876), 19, 23, 25 ff., 48–49 (all reprinted from his 1867 essay, with an added section titled "Impressions et souvenirs").
32. Ibid., 105–7, from the section added in 1876.
33. For a useful anecdotal history of artists' colonies, see M. Jacobs, *The Good and Simple Life: Artist Colonies in Europe and America* (Oxford, 1985).
34. Letter from Monet to Bazille, December 1868, in D. Wildenstein, *Monet: Biographie et catalogue raisonné*, vol. 1 (Lausanne and Paris, 1974), 425–26.
35. Green, *Spectacle of Nature*, 167–81; on Rousseau's reaction, see 118–19, 179, 211 n. 8.
36. P. Lenoir, *Le Fayoum, le Sinai et Pétra* (Paris, 1872), 111–13.
37. See E. H. Gombrich, *Art and Illusion* (London, 1960).
38. For an important critique of Gombrich's position, see

W. J. T. Mitchell, *Iconology: Image, Text, Ideology* (Chicago, 1986), 75–94.

39. See A. Boime, *The Academy and French Painting in the Nineteenth Century* (London, 1971), 142–48.
40. Edmond About, "Le Salon de 1868," *Revue des deux mondes* (June 1868): 738–39; a very comparable account appears in A. de Montaiglon, "Salon de 1875 (2nd article)," *Gazette des beaux-arts* (July 1875): 20.
41. G. Lafenestre, "Le Salon de 1872," in Lafenestre, *L'Art vivant: La Peinture et la sculpture aux Salons de 1868 à 1877*, vol. 1 (Paris, 1881), 292.
42. See the fascinating discussion in A. M. Wagner, "Courbet's Landscapes and Their Market," *Art History* (December 1981).
43. See R. Shiff, *Cézanne and the End of Impressionism: A Study of the Theory, Technique, and Critical Evaluation of Modern Art* (Chicago, 1984), 3–54.
44. T. Gautier, *Abécédaire du Salon de 1861* (Paris, 1861), 119.
45. L. Lagrange, "Le Salon de 1865," *Le Correspondant* (May 1865): 152–53; C. Blanc, "Salon de 1866," *Gazette des beaux-arts* (1 June/1 July 1866): 40.
46. J. Claretie, "L'Art français en 1872," in *Peintres et sculpteurs contemporains* (Paris, 1874), 173; see also 231, 287.
47. M. Guillemot, "Claude Monet," *La Revue illustré* (15 March 1898): 1.
48. House, *Monet*, 158–64.
49. V. Cherbuliez, "Le Salon de 1876, I: Les Impressionnistes, les tableaux de genre et les portraits," *Revue de deux mondes* (1 June 1876): 515–18; on the use of the politically radical term "intransigent" to describe the "Impressionists," see S. Eisenman, "The Intransigent Artist *or* How the Impressionists Got Their Name," in C. S. Moffett, ed., *The New Painting: Impressionism, 1874–1886*, exh. cat. (San Francisco: Fine Arts Museums of San Francisco, 1986), 51–59 [reprinted as chapter 6 in this volume].
50. C. Bigot, "'Causerie artistique: l'exposition des Impressionnistes,'" *Revue politique et littéraire* (28 April 1877): 1046.
51. A. Guillemin, *Les Chemins de fer*, in *Bibliothèque des merveilles* (Paris, 1876), 104–5.
52. C. Baudelaire, "Le Peintre de la vie moderne," *Le Figaro*, 26 and 28 November, 3 December 1863, cited in Baudelaire, *The Painter of Modern Life and Other Essays*, trans. J. Mayne (London, 1964), 7–11.
53. For example, G. Merlet, *Causeries sur les femmes et sur les livres* (Paris, 1862), 263–64.
54. They were strongly advocated by Jules Ferry, the new Minister of Public Instruction and Fine Arts, at the Salon prize-giving in 1879; his speech is reprinted in the 1880 Salon catalogue, vi ff.
55. See J. M. Roos, "Herbivores versus Herbiphobes: Landscape Painting and the State," in *Impressions of France: Monet, Renoir, Pissarro, and Their Rivals*, exh. cat. (Boston: Museum of Fine Arts, 1995), 47–50.
56. T. Gautier, "Salon de 1857—XV," *L'Artiste* (20 September 1857): 34.
57. See Thoré's 1868 comments on Manet's brushwork: "His present vice is a sort of pantheism that places no higher value on a head than on a slipper" (Thoré, *Salons de W. Bürger*, vol. 2, 531–32).
58. F. Chevalier, "Les Impressionnistes," *L'Artiste* (May 1877): 331.
59. On the Salon and the Triennale in these years, see P. Mainardi, *Art and Politics of the Second Empire: The Universal Exhibitions of 1855 and 1867* (New Haven, 1993).
60. See Roos, "Herbivores versus Herbiphobes," 40–42; and R. Wrigley, *The Origins of French Art Criticism: From the Ancien Régime to the Restoration* (Oxford, 1993), 285 ff.
61. For example, M. du Camp, "Le Salon de 1864," *Revue des deux mondes* (1 June 1864): 685–86; T. Gautier, "Le Salon de 1866: IV and VIII," *Moniteur universel*, 4 and 26 July 1866; T. Couture, *Paysage: Entretiens d'atelier* (Paris, 1869), 136, 139, 223, 225 ff.
62. A. Sensier, "Le Paysage et le paysan," *Revue internationale de l'art et de la curiosité* (15 May 1869): 404; Sensier, "Les Peintres de la nature," 373–74; J. Castagnary, *Salons (1857–1879)*, vol. 1 (Paris, 1892), 203 ff. (on Salon of 1864), 235 (on Salon of 1866).
63. See D. J. Sherman, *Worthy Monuments: Art Museums and the Politics of Culture in Nineteenth-Century France* (Cambridge, Mass., 1989), especially chapter 1.
64. In 1866 there were 42 landscapes among 129 State purchases, from a total of 1,998 paintings at the Salon; in 1870, 48 landscapes among 126 purchases from 2,991; in 1872, 34 landscapes among 122 purchases from 1,536; in 1877, 3 landscapes among 37 purchases from 2,192; in 1878, 21 landscapes among 59 purchases from 2,330; in 1880, 20 landscapes among 108 purchases from 3,957. The figures for 1872 also include drawings. From 1864 to 1886, State purchases were photographed and published in folio volumes by Michelez; on State purchases in the 1850s, see P. Angrand, "L'Etat mécène: Période autoritaire du Second Empire (1851–1860)," *Gazette des beaux-arts* (June 1968); on the 1870s and 1880s, see P. Vaisse, "La Troisième République et les peintres: Recherches sur les rapports des pouvoirs publics et de la peinture en

France de 1870 à 1914" (thesis, L'Université de Paris IV, 1980), 396–444.

65. As noted by Sherman, *Worthy Monuments*, 35.
66. These rooms in the Louvre have recently been reopened to the public.
67. This was the only canvas Daubigny executed of a sequence that he proposed as a follow-up to Joseph Vernet's *Ports of France*; see Philadelphia Museum of Art, *The Second Empire: Art in France under Napoleon III* (Philadelphia, 1978), 284–85.
68. Letter from Duret to Pissarro, 15 February 1874, in L. R. Pissarro and L. Venturi, *Camille Pissarro: Sa vie, son oeuvre* (Paris, 1939), 1, 33–34; translation in J. Rewald, *The History of Impressionism* (New York, 1973), 310.
69. A. Sensier, *Souvenirs sur Th. Rousseau* (Paris, 1872), 204, 256–57, 273; Thoré, *Salons de W. Bürger*, vol. 1, 48–49; G. Jean-Aubry, *Eugène Boudin: La Vie et l'oeuvre* (Paris, 1922), 53–54, 66. On artists' sales, see Vaisse 1980, 300–301; there has been little research into the practice of artists sending their own work to auction sales and mounting whole sales of their work.
70. P. Burty, preface to sale catalogue, *Tableaux et dessins par M. Amand Gautier*, Hôtel Drouot, Paris (1 April 1875), 111.
71. On the auction, see Rewald, *History of Impressionism*, 351–54; and M. Bodelsen, "Early Impressionist Sales 1874–94 in the Light of Some Unpublished 'Procès-verbaux,'" *Burlington Magazine* (June 1968). Burty's preface, the nearest thing to a manifesto for the Impressionist group, is reprinted in D. Riout, ed., *Les Ecrivains devant l'impressionnisme* (Paris, 1989), 47–49.
72. On the exhibitions of the *cercles*, see M. Ward, "Impressionist Installations and Private Exhibitions," *Art Bulletin* (December 1991): 605–8 [reprinted as chapter 3 in this volume]; T. Garb, *Sisters of the Brush: Women's Artistic Culture in Late Nineteenth-Century Paris* (New Haven, 1994), 32–41.
73. V. Champier, *L'Année artistique, 1879* (Paris, 1880), 173–74; quoted by Ward, "Impressionist Installations," 607.
74. H. Houssaye, "Les petits expositions de peinture," *Revue des deux mondes* (1March 1880): 193–94.
75. An exception was the Goupil gallery; for an engraving of its display space in 1860, see Ward, "Impressionist Installations," 616 [fig. 3.3 in this volume]. On the development of the art dealer as a profession from the 1820s onward, see L. Whiteley, "Art et commerce d'art en France avant l'époque impressionniste," *Romantisme*, no. 40 (1983); N. Green, "Dealing in Temperaments: Economic Transformation of the Artistic Field in France during the Second Half of the Nineteenth Century," *Art History* (March 1987) [reprinted as chapter 2 in this volume]; Green, *Spectacle of Nature*, 25–28.
76. T. Gautier, "La Rue Lafitte," *L'Artiste* (3 January 1858): 10.
77. F. Henriet, "Le Musée des rues, I: Le Marchand de tableaux," *L'Artiste* (15 November and 1 December 1854): 113–14, 133–35; see also Gautier, "La Rue Lafitte," 12–13.
78. Henriet, "Le Musée des rues," 115.
79. From 1873 to 1875 Durand-Ruel published a series of three hundred etched reproductions of the paintings—mainly landscapes—in his stock, including three paintings by Monet, five by Pissarro, and three by Sisley, plus many by Corot, Millet, and Rousseau among others.
80. See Ward, "Impressionist Installations," 613–17.
81. On the group exhibitions, see Rewald, *History of Impressionism*, and Moffett, ed., *The New Painting*.
82. On the 1867 project, see Bazille's letters to his parents, April and May 1867, letters 91 and 93, in F. Bazille, *Correspondance*, ed. D. Vatuone (Montpellier, 1992), 137, 140.
83. On these terms, see House, *Monet*, 157–66.
84. E. Duranty, *La Nouvelle Peinture* (1876; reprinted in Moffett, ed., *The New Painting*), 483; and Riout, ed., *Les Ecrivains*, 130.
85. Reprinted in the 1880 Salon catalogue, vii.
86. See Green, *Spectacle of Nature*, 6–7, 139–40.

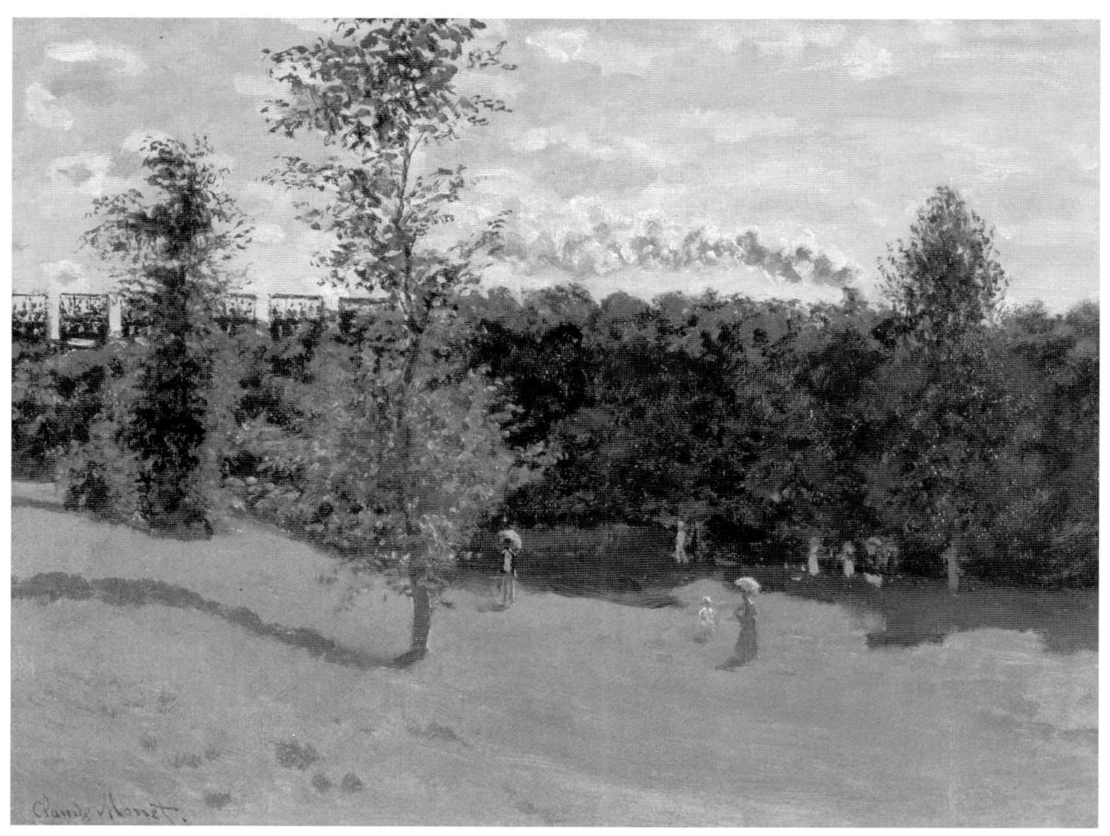

FIGURE 5.1. Claude Monet, *Train in the Country*, 1870. Musée d'Orsay, Paris. Photo: Réunion des Musées Nationaux/Art Resource, NY. Photographed by Hervé Lewandowski.

5

The Environs of Paris

T. J. CLARK

L'avenir est aux limonadiers. HONORÉ DE BALZAC

The Argument

That the environs of Paris from the 1860s on were recognized to be a special territory in which some aspects of modernity might be detected, at least by those who could stomach the company of the petite bourgeoisie. To use the word "suburban" to describe these stamping grounds—to apply it to resorts like Asnières or Chatou, Bougival, Bois-Colombes, or, preeminently, Argenteuil—was on the whole misleading, and remains so. It makes such places out to be the subordinates of some city, whereas in fact they were areas in which the opposite of the urban was being constructed, a way of living and working which in time would come to dominate the late capitalist world, providing as it did the appropriate forms of sociability for the new age. Where industry and recreation were casually established next to each other, in a landscape which assumed only as much form as the juxtaposition of production and distraction (factories and regattas) allowed, there modernity seemed vivid, and painters believed they might invent a new set of descriptions for it.

This chapter mostly looks for such descriptions, which occasionally do surface in modernist painting at this time. There are pictures by Manet and Seurat, for example, in which the environs of Paris are recognized to be a specific form of life: not the countryside, not the city, not a degenerated form of either. But the chapter also tries to explain why such descriptions were rare and for the most part metaphorical, the metaphors being those of dislocation and uncertainty, and the sense of the scene being suggested best by a kind of composition—perfected here—in which everything was left looking edgy, ill-fitting, or otherwise unfinished. These metaphors did not in the event turn out to be a way of storing knowledge: there was to be no sustained or cogent representation of suburbia in the twentieth century. Perhaps that had to do with the peculiar intractability—the foreignness of an unexotic kind—of the classes of people who came to occupy the new terrain. They were the petite bourgeoisie, but also the proletariat; and though each despised the other, they both existed, and still exist, at an equal distance from the realm of Art. Painting turned instead to other primitives, whose culture it could patronize more safely.

When painters went out to the countryside around Paris in the 1870s—in search of a landscape, say, or a modern *fête champêtre*—they would have known they were choosing, or accepting, a place it was easy (almost conventional) to find a bit absurd. The tone had been set as early as 1862 by the Goncourts in their journal, describing a day spent by the river at Bougival:

> We went to the country with Saint-Victor, like shop assistants. And we said to each other, as we went to look for a train, that really humanity—and all honor to it—is a great Don Quixote at heart. . . .
>
> We took a walk along the Seine at Bougival. In the long grass on the island people were reading aloud from *Le Figaro.* On the water, boaters in red jerseys sang songs by Nadaud. Saint-Victor came across an acquaintance of his among the willows: it was some stockjobber or other. Finally we found a corner where there was no landscape painter sitting at his easel and no slice of melon left behind.[1]

The terms that seem to me crucial in the Goncourts' entry are the first and last—the shop assistants and the landscape painter. It is they that dictate the Goncourts' peculiar tone—the comprehensive, slightly hectic irony that has to be applied, apparently, to every item of the scene. For how else could one deal—this is the text's essential burden—with the people now laying claim to landscape, painted or not; with their wish or pretense to be "by themselves," and with oneself as sharing that wish; or with those others who dispensed with the illusion of solitude and simply regarded the riverbank as backdrop for the songs they always sang, the same newspapers, the same slices of melon? And the great river itself, after these people were done with it!

The manner and imagery of this passage were much reproduced in the next twenty years or so, and frequently to great effect. It very often seemed that describing this landscape at all, in any detail, depended on finding it false—though false by what standard was never made clear. There was precious little clarity, we shall discover, in any of the writers' opinions in this area. They were in a cleft stick about the countryside, and trying for irony at their own indecision. They were part of the crowd at Bougival and Asnières, and almost willing to admit as much. In a sense they relished their fellow Parisians, or at least were ill-equipped to do without them; but they could not help wishing, at the same time, that the crowd would behave differently, put away *Le Figaro* and pick up the leftovers from the *Déjeuner sur l'herbe*.

Sometimes the sequence of their emotions was quite explicit in the text. Here, for example, is a writer called "Y" in *La Vie parisienne,* beginning an essay entitled "Un Dimanche d'été":

> I had been in the countryside for a week, and I was bored, tired of the silence, when at last the village bells announced the morning of the seventh day, the day of rest and rejoicing. And soon a shudder went through the woods, and the hills echoed with the sound of the day's first pun.
>
> —The Parisians are coming! I cried out in delight. Nature will leave off its role of mute and mysterious nymph, and become a barmaid to whom commercial travelers somewhat brutally pay court.
>
> Hour by hour the invasion mounted, taking possession of the countryside as of a *vast guinguette,* a café-concert even larger than those on the Champs-Elysées.
>
> These people came to handle the hillsides as if they were breasts, to look up the skirts of the forests, and disarrange the river's costume.
>
> The breeze began to murmur jokes and catcalls. The smell of fried fish and fricassee of rabbit rose in the air along the riverbanks and wafted across the fields. A concert of popping corks began, of knives clinking against glasses, and dirty songs; and it went on till nightfall, getting louder all the time. . . .
>
> When I had seen the countryside given over to those who alone understand and know how to enjoy it, when I had had my fill of the spectacle, I took the train and went back to Paris.[2]

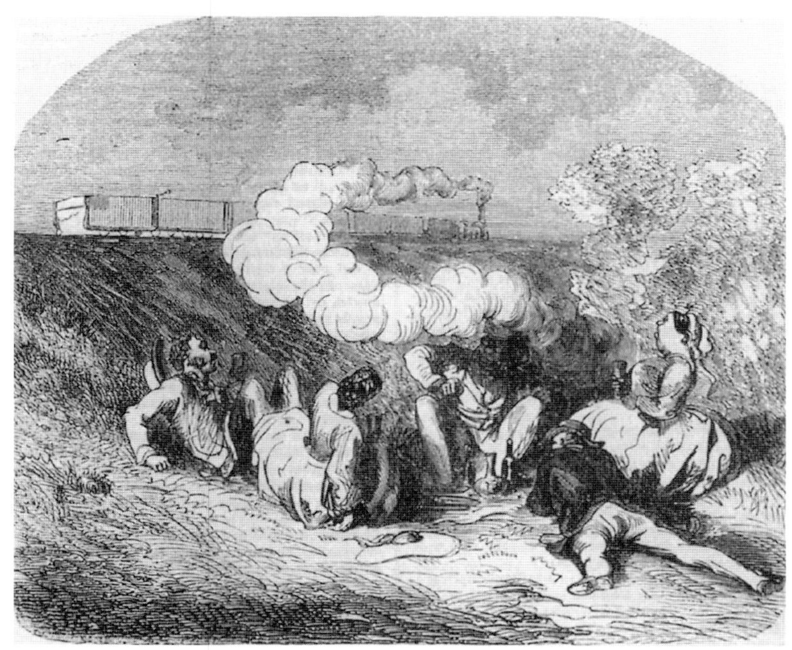

FIGURE 5.2. Gustave Doré, *Les Plaisirs champêtres du parc du Vésinet*. Engraving from Labédollière's *Histoire des environs du Nouveau Paris*, 1861. The British Library, London.

If any one thing was to blame for this state of affairs, it was the railway on which "Y" made his final escape. The lines laid down since 1850, especially those to the west of the city, had quite abruptly rendered the countryside available to Paris, as part of a weekend or even a workday. These facts became common knowledge in the 1860s and soon affected the critics' sense of how landscape painting was to be construed. The novelist Robert Caze, for example, writing a *Salon* [review] in 1885 and turning to a picture by Jacques-Emile Blanche—it seems to have had a lady sitting on a lawn as its central feature—was in no doubt as to what modern landscape amounted to:

> Oh! the poor little Parisienne, bewildered and bewildering in the midst of this imitation nature—the nature of Sèvres and Ville d'Avray. We should be grateful to Monsieur Blanche for having seen so well the odious turf of these villas extra muros, these lawns brought in from England on the Dover or Southampton boat, arriving each morning on the fish train. And look at the landscape in which this pasty-faced model tries to take her ease! I dare say there's a globe of silvered glass round the corner, and a little fountain pissing its monotonous song into a basin with three goldfish in it! And here is the bourgeois—the proprietor!—bringing in a bunch of flowers bought on the asphalt at the Madeleine after the stock exchange closed . . . bringing them back to his home *in the country*. Doubtless it is excellent to give us the sensation, or, rather, the smell, of Asnières and Bois-Colombes, without obliging us to take the tramway. If I were one for economies, I would buy Monsieur Blanche's Pivoines and be saved the trouble of visiting this landscape of boating parties and the humorous public of Sundays, these fields full of pianos and hunting horns, of factory chimneys and the perfume of manure.[3]

It was the railway that had made this landscape. It carried the bourgeois back from the Madeleine at five, it ushered in the shop assistants and commercial travelers, the blue songs, and the globes of silvered glass. It stood intrusive guard over the pleasures of Gustave Doré's picnickers in the *Parc du Vésinet* (fig. 5.2), and was pointed out by one bourgeois to another in a cartoon by Trock (fig. 5.3):

> —Really, living in Paris, on the Place de l'Europe, had become unbearable! . . . Nothing but the noise of the Western Railway all day . . .
>
> —And here, how do you entertain yourselves?
>
> We watch the trains go by.

Well might the "witty and benevolent" Monsieur Coindard, secretary of the same Western Railway, declare with satisfaction: "Les lignes de banlieue, c'est notre boulevard intérieur."[4] For he more than anyone stood to gain from the fact that Paris's outlines were changing; the city henceforth would have more than one thoroughfare, more than one scale, and no firm bounding lines between its various edges and interiors.

It was partly this last uncertainty that so provoked the critics of the Parisian countryside and had them lay on the irony with a trowel. The environs of Paris, they said, were neither town nor country anymore. Worse than that, these places failed to offer a visible—or even a symbolic—transition between one form of social existence and another, as the land outside the *barrière* had done for Hugo's philosophic stroller. At Sèvres or Le Vésinet, for example, there was nothing to be seen but countryside; it might be thick with the signs of Paris at the end of the line—with restaurants, watermelons, smoke from factory chimneys—but Paris itself had still not arrived. These were landscapes arranged for urban use, but part of their utility was the fiction, flimsy as it was, that city and citizens were far away.

The ironic commentator wished to make it clear that he for one was not deceived. There was no nature, he believed, where there were Parisians. The very sky over Bougival was pale and unhealthy, "the color of a Parisienne's skin."[5] The dust at Chatou was compounded with rice powder,[6] and "wherever there was a wretched square of grass with half a dozen rachitic trees, there the proprietor made haste to establish a ball or a café-restaurant."[7]

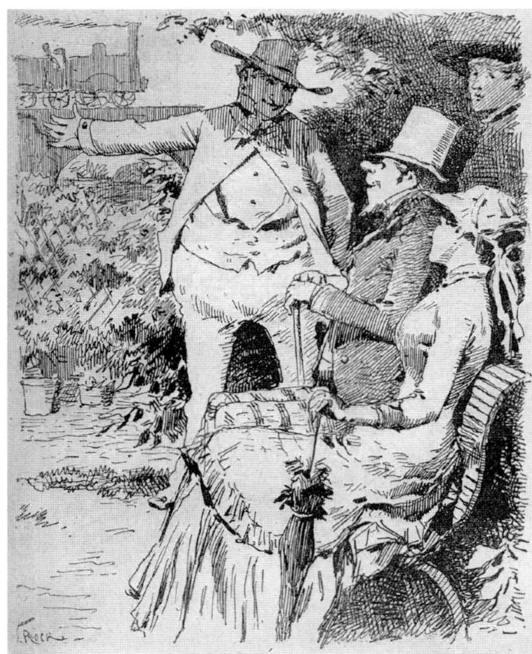

FIGURE 5.3. Trock, "Villégiature." Wood engraving in *La Caricature* 3, no. 133 (July 1882): 227. Photo: Archives and Special Collections at the Thomas J. Dodd Research Center, University of Connecticut Libraries.

No doubt the illusion was often perfunctory, but by and large it worked. The stockjobbers and landscape painters were in no doubt they had left the city behind. As they sat on the grass by the river, in another cartoon by Trock (fig. 5.4), their father opened his arms and said: "Ah! my children, how good it is to find a little solitude on Sundays!" For this was the way they wanted nature to be; this was the way it essentially *was*—a kind of demi-Paris whose trees were like those on the boulevards and whose restaurants resembled the best in the rue Montmartre.[8] Should not a village be equipped, to count as a village at all, with "sellers of *coco* and amusements, games of macaroon, shooting galleries, swings, and a motley crowd of people, swarming and rowdy, all using Parisian argot, and studded with *modistes*, drapers' assistants, students, and reporters"?[9]

It was possible, of course, for the illusion to be too threadbare and simply misfire. Monsieur Bartavel, for

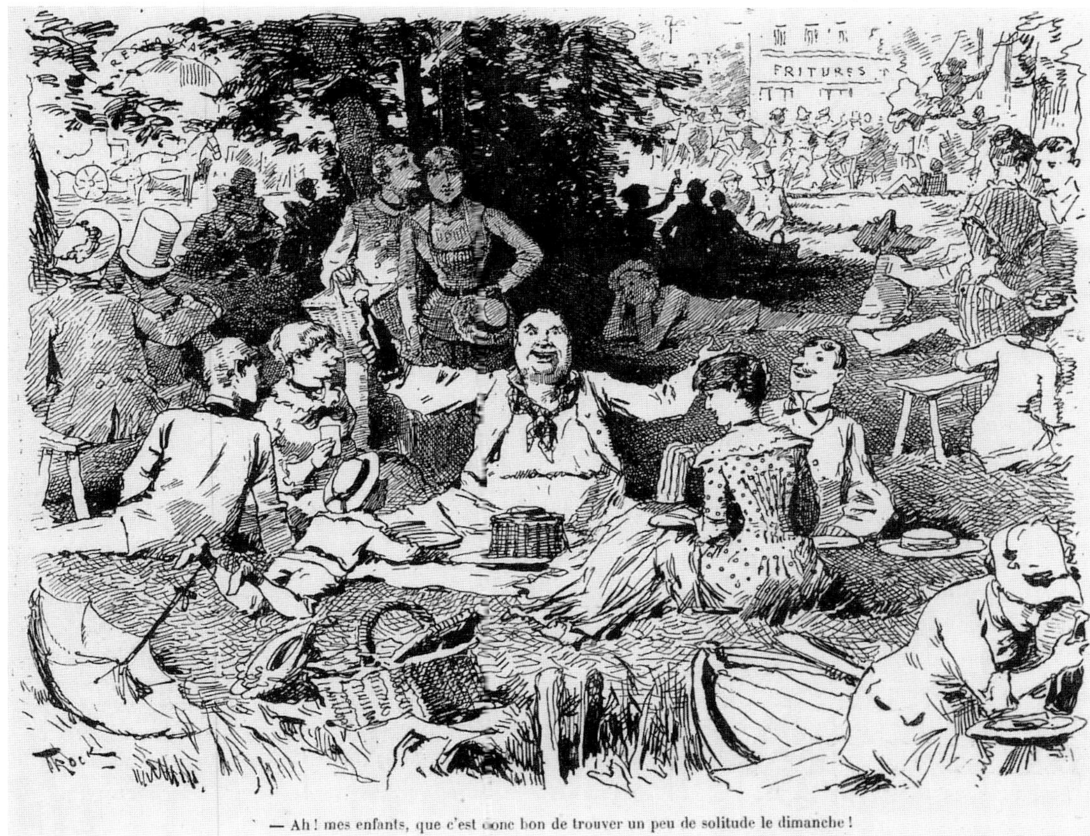

FIGURE 5.4. Trock, *Ces Bons Parisiens*. Wood engraving in *La Caricature* 3, no. 126 (May 27, 1882): 174. Bibliothèque nationale de France, Paris.

example, the amiable hero of an *opéra-bouffe* from 1875 entitled *Les Environs de Paris*, did not enjoy his trip to the suburbs. His top hat was crushed in a winepress at Argenteuil, he lost his companions, he was not impressed by the sights at Robinson and Montmorency. This is his verdict in the play's last act:

> BARTAVEL—Yes, my friend . . . apart from that everything has really been . . . disagreeable! . . . And behold before you a man who is completely disillusioned with the Environs of Paris!
>
> JOSEPH—Why is that? . . .
>
> BARTAVEL, *standing up*—Why is that? . . . Because I had a picture of the place which bore not the slightest resemblance to what I saw. When I set off I said to myself: And there, I shall have some air, some sun, and greenery! . . . Oh, yes, greenery! Instead of cornflowers and poppies, great prairies covered with old clothes and detachable collars . . . laundresses everywhere and not a single shepherdess . . . factories instead of cottages . . . too much sun . . . no shade . . . and to cap it all, great red brick chimneys giving out black smoke which poisons the lungs and makes you cough! . . . Coach drivers who jeer at you, restaurateurs who take you for all they can get . . . winepresses that flatten your hat . . . vinegrowers who spill white wine all over you . . . forests where you lose your daughter . . . hotels where you mislay your son-in-law! . . . And that, my dear Joseph . . . that is the faithful description of what are customarily called . . . the Environs of Paris![10]

There is a quality in these texts which may strike us now as little short of desperate. The writers are so anxious to outflank all the attitudes toward landscape they are describing, and they never explain what other attitudes they take to be less silly. *They* are all bourgeois, whereas *my* irony is not: that seems to be the writers' message, essentially, and the main reassurance they mean to offer their readers. Bartavel's disillusion may be safely comic, but his inventory of faults and blemishes would not inspire much disagreement in any of the writers quoted so far. For was it not true that the landscape consisted of rachitic trees and factory chimneys—or consisted too much of them? And which was more absurd, the good bourgeois who gave his blessing to the signs of industry in nature, or his partner who claimed not to notice them? "Come a little farther this way," says another Parisian, in *Le Nain jaune*, showing off his weekend villa to a guest:

> —You'll see a most delightful view. . . . Isn't it charming? . . . And you can make out part of the panorama from my house. . . . How do you find it?
>
> —I don't see anything very extraordinary . . . apart from those great chimneys and their black smoke, which for me rather spoil the landscape. . . .
>
> For me it's an added charm. . . . My dear fellow! It is industry which comes to add its note. . . . But here we are at the house. . . . Watch out for the puddle. . . . It never dries out, even in the height of summer.[11]

There was clearly some discord in the landscape, something which prevented nature from being seen in the proper way. It had to do with a fact as large as bourgeois society itself: not just the signs of its industry, but *other* bourgeois, too many of them, pretending not to be industrious. These were the people Bernadille described in an 1878 article entitled "Le Dimanche à Paris":

> On that day a whole new population takes possession of Paris, of its spectacles, its cafés, its promenades, its public gardens, its boulevards, its Palais-Royal, its railway stations, its *banlieue*. During the week, you could no doubt have seen them, mixed in with the ordinary public, but as it were effaced by it. Now they show themselves off in their pure state; they flood through the streets, they spread over Paris and overflow. The great city belongs to them all day long.
>
> Where do they come from? From behind the counters of humble shops and offices, from businesses and government departments. This is not precisely a "popular" public in the full force of that word, for the people of *L'Assommoir* celebrate Monday in preference to Sunday; it is a public of petits bourgeois, of small tradesmen, mixed up with real workers.[12]

Once a week, in other words, there was an excess of bourgeoisie in the spaces Haussmann had provided: it was this that upset the commentators and elicited their scorn. The excess was comprised of shop assistants and commercial travelers, readers of *Le Figaro*, clerks in detachable collars, the spawn of banks and bureaucracies—the new men.

These people's access to the public realm was a phenomenon of the 1870s, and much remarked on at the time. Politicians were fond of regarding them as a force to be reckoned with, and never tired of harking back to the radical leader Léon Gambetta's great verdict on the new republic—that it owed its existence to a great mass of men who had previously been excluded from the state, and would henceforth have to draw its strength directly from the "nouvelles couches sociales."[13] Those last three words were usefully vague, but what they pointed to essentially was a shift of power *within* the wider middle class. The regime of landowners and *notables*—those men whose influence at a local level had survived all previous changes in the form of government—was finally coming to an end; and in its place was a congeries of shopkeepers and small builders, schoolteachers and civil servants, "the party of pharmacists and vets."[14] Somewhere at the edge of that party—wanting a place in it, not sure of how to insist on one—was the odd new animal, the petit bourgeois.

The texts I have been quoting are ironical at the petit bourgeois's expense. What was held to be the most comical thing about him was his unpreparedness for the leisure he now enjoyed; he was a workaday creature, after all, who naturally clung to the society of his fellows and had need of fried food and regattas. He was naïve and tasteless; easily elated and easily duped; and he too mourned his own enfranchisement—there was always a time before trippers and tourists, when the spot was unspoiled and there wasn't a soul on the beach.

But it seems to me that more is at stake in the writers' irony than this. What they seem to find laughable in the "nouvelles couches sociales" is their *claim* to pleasure, the degree to which they asserted a right at all to solitude, to nature, to spontaneity. Various descriptions were offered of the absurdities that resulted, but these hardly account for the writers' acrid tone: they seem to be reasons, on the contrary, for finding the subject harmless and the claims quixotic. But the subject was not treated lightly; or, rather, the lightness was repeatedly tinged with a kind of hysterical loftiness. No doubt these people did not get what they asked for, and had only the faintest notion of what it would have been like to have had it. Yet the claim was enough; the claim was the threat, because it was their way of claiming to be part of the bourgeoisie.

There was a struggle being waged in these decades for the right to bourgeois identity. It was fought out quite largely in the forms the new city had brought to perfection: the squares, the streets, and the spectacles. The crowds on the riverbank on Sunday afternoon, all moving about in identical dresses, all eager to be seen, were engaged in a grand redefinition of what counted as middle class. And the redefinition was resisted: Gambetta, after all, was out of step with the general run of his class in the 1870s, and well aware that his slogans would be found provoking. One means of resistance was irony, and the ironists' message amounted to this: that the claim to pleasure was nothing if not an attempt to have access to Nature; that these people knew nothing but Paris and took Paris with them wherever they went; that that was the key to their vulgarity—and because they were vulgar, they could never be bourgeois.

To call someone vulgar is to say he insists on a status which is not yet proved or well understood by him, not yet possessed as a matter of form. It is a damaging charge, made by one bourgeois against another. To have access to Nature be the test of class is to shift the argument to usefully irrefutable ground: the bourgeoisie's Nature is not unlike the aristocracy's Blood: what the false bourgeois has is false nature, nature *en toc, la nature des environs de Paris;* and beyond or behind it there must be a real one, which remains in the hands of the real bourgeoisie.

> Cohue hebdomadaire à travers les banlieues!
> Parisiens! cherchant des fleurs sur les pavés!
> Ils se figurent être à des milliers de lieues . . .
> Parce qu'il est dimanche, et qu'ils se sont lavés.[15]

The reader could rest assured: the flowers in this landscape would wilt before evening, and the crowd would return to its counters and offices.

One of the great subjects of Impressionist painting was the landscape I have just been describing, and therefore it does not seem unreasonable to ask how far the painters' attitudes toward it resembled those of the journalists and poets. In particular we might want to know how they dealt with the signs that this landscape belonged to Paris—the traces of industry "adding its note" and the presence in nature of the "nouvelles couches sociales." There are certainly pictures where these are the characters round which the landscape is organized, and where the painter appears concerned to establish some kind of comic connection between them. Sometimes the comedy seems to me essentially the same as Trock's or Bartavel's, and at others it strikes a muted, almost respectful note, which is not quite ironical, at any rate not supercilious or unkind.

Compare, for example, Raffaëlli's depiction of middle-class pleasure in his *Promeneurs du dimanche* (fig. 5.5) with that of Seurat in the study for his *Baignade à Asnières* (fig. 5.6). There is no mistaking the coexistence of landscape, figure, and factory in both, or the fact that each one of the terms puts its neighbors in doubt. But the one picture surely invites its

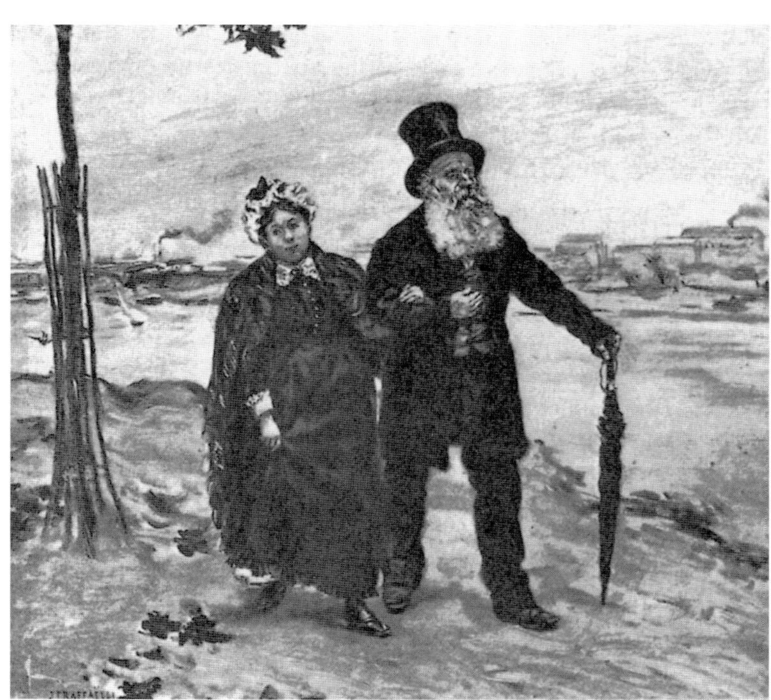

FIGURE 5.5. Jean-François Raffaëlli, *Promeneurs du dimanche*. From *Les Types de Paris*, 1889. The British Library, London.

viewers to recognize the easy contradiction and laugh (not too maliciously; this is Bartavel's comedy, not Robert Caze's); while the other seems still to be feeling for a way to characterize the same situation—as if the painter were not sure that it had taken on a character at all as yet. (It matters here that Raffaëlli's individuals are so much more securely established *as* middle class than Seurat's. There is a difference in kind between the solitary, slightly overdone respectability of Seurat's figure—his bowler hat immoveable against the sun—and that of Raffaëlli's patriarch.) Compare, in the same manner, Doré's *Plaisirs champêtres* (see fig. 5.2) with those portrayed in Monet's *Train dans la campagne* from 1870 (see fig. 5.1).

At this point an unsympathetic reader—one finding the victory of Seurat and Monet over Doré and Raffaëlli a trifle easy—might respond in the following way. Very well, she might say, I'm prepared to accept that the irony here is easy and condescending, but surely irony of any kind is preferable in such cases to outright complaisance? And is not Monet's picture merely accepting—of more or less anything, if seen in a good light? Do not such images put us back with the happy landscape painter at Bougival, sitting at his easel next to the melon segments? The objector might bring on hereabouts some depictions of Bougival by Monet or Sisley or Pissarro as circumstantial evidence. Isn't there a point, she might continue, at which we *know* that what we are dealing with is straightforward bad faith? . . .

The unsympathetic reader at least asks the right questions. It is presumably one thing to avoid irony and another to attain to blankness, and often in modernist painting it is not clear which description is the appropriate one. But let us put the same questions in a less aggressive form. Let us ask, for example, how Monet's depiction of the river bathing place called La Grenouillère might possibly stand in relation to an image of the same place taken from the weekly magazines—like the one I show by Jules Pelcoq (accepting straightaway that there is no question here of imitation or influence of a direct kind)? To what extent does Monet's oil painting (fig. 5.7) borrow its vitality from the illustration, or is its purpose somehow

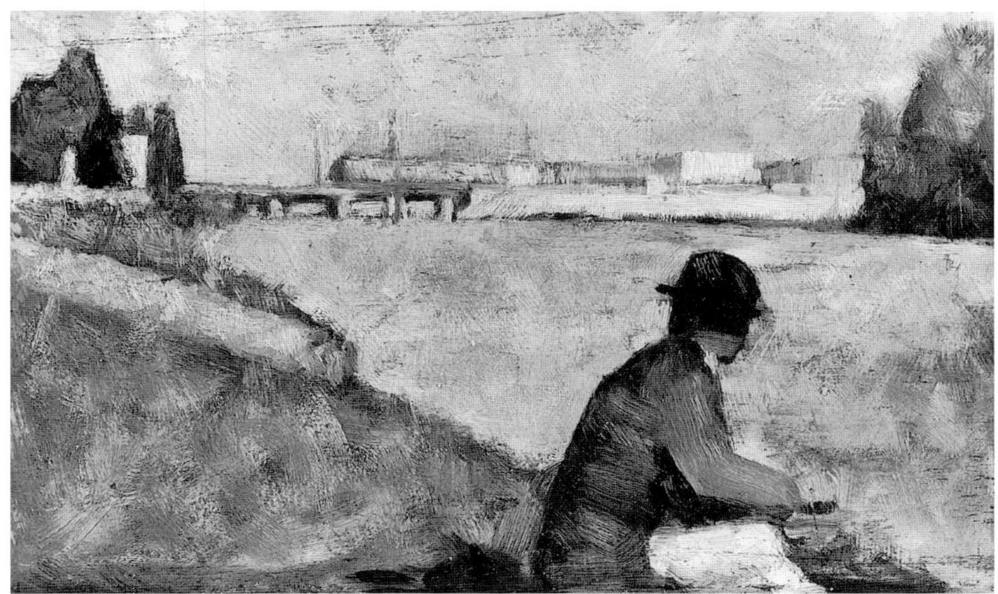

FIGURE 5.6. Georges Seurat, *Etude pour "Baignade à Asnières" (Study for "Bathers at Asnières")*, c. 1883–84, oil on panel. The Cleveland Museum of Art, Bequest of Leonard C. Hanna Jr., 1958.51. Photo © The Cleveland Museum of Art, 2003.

to contradict such a quality, or at least its generalizing force? The painting's composure, and the cool way it savors certain (rather simple) formal rhythms, in the pattern of boats or the punctuation of figures on the straight pontoon—are these meant, so to speak, as refutations of Pelcoq (fig. 5.8), as so many signs of the painter's way with things as opposed to the illustrator's? Does painting get done in spite of illustration—is that the proposal? Get done in spite of modernity, even, or because modernity does not amount to much? But then, why go to La Grenouillère in the first place? In search of the insignificant—is that it?

During the summer of 1875 Berthe Morisot did a number of paintings on the plain of Gennevilliers, a few miles east of Argenteuil. One of them, entitled *Un Percher de blanchisseuses* (plate 4), she chose to show the next year in the second Impressionist exhibition.[16] Is it in order for us to read her depiction of landscape with, say, Bartavel's monologue in mind? They are all there, the motifs of his disappointment: the laundresses instead of shepherdesses, the new villa, the horizon of chimneys and smoke. But are these the motifs that matter here? Does it affect our reading of the idyll to know that the very fields at Gennevilliers were irrigated with water from the great collector sewer, and that the local press resounded with rumors of bad-smelling eggplants and poisoned soil?[17]

Consider Jean Ajalbert's description—he is the poet whose lines on the weekend crowd in the *banlieue* I just quoted—in a poem entitled "Gennevilliers." It was part of a collection called *Sur le vif* published in 1886, with the subtitle *Vers impressionnistes:*

> Le soleil s'est lassé d'éclairer ce ciel, gris
> De la fumée opaque aux faîtes des fabriques,
> Qui bornent l'horizon du côté de Paris.
> Vers Argenteuil, pays des moulins minuscules,
> S'étagent des carrés de maigres échalas
> Condamnés, sous le poids d'éternels crépuscules,
> A fournir les marchés d'acides chasselas.
>
> Les récoltes ont là d'impossibles genèses;
> Les paysans sont plutôt des égoutiers,

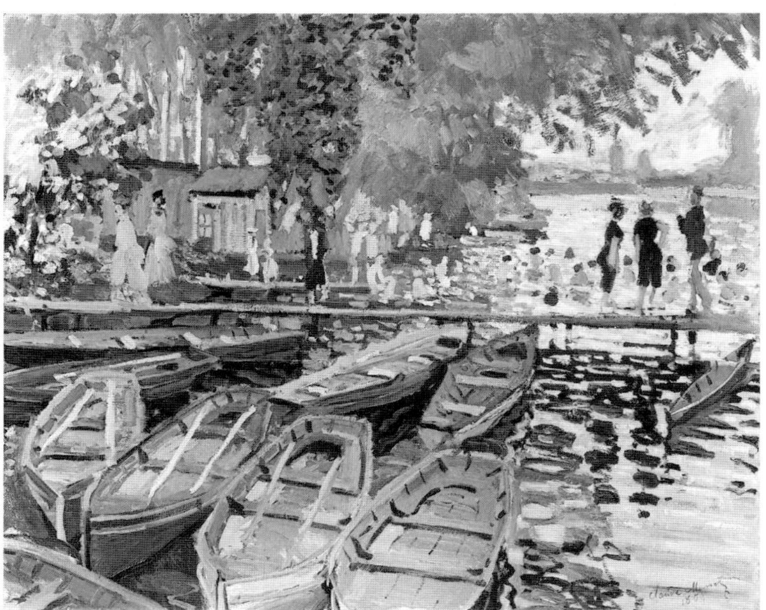

FIGURE 5.7. Claude Monet, *La Grenouillère*, 1869. National Gallery, London. Image © National Gallery, London.

Arrachant, par l'engrais, des légumes obèses
D'un sol à qui la Lune a caché ses quartiers,
Et pour qui le soleil n'a pas eu de lumière.

Sur les maisons, des toits de tuiles "vermillon" . . .

C'est la campagne, mais sans chaume et sans chaumière,
Sans la moindre alouette ou le moindre grillon.[18]

How much should it matter to us, this description? Or should we, rather, put our trust in the good humor of Morisot's husband, writing to her in 1882:

> I have come from the plain of Gennevilliers, which I went across on my way from Epinay. Everything is in blossom there and has the smell of spring. The plain looked pretty in every direction.[19]

The *Percher de blanchisseuses* does not seem quite so straightforwardly *delighted* with the landscape as this. The view it presents is not exactly "pretty in every direction," but it is not grim and lugubrious either. Morisot's peasants—they do occasionally appear in her pictures, standing in front of the waving grain (fig. 5.9)—are not like Ajalbert's "égoutiers." The sun evidently persists in illuminating the crude tiles on the weekend *lotissements;* the crudity and even the encroaching gray are given a place in the landscape and even some kind of weight; modernity is not overlooked, but the painter does not seem to find it in the least melancholy, or believe it should change her bright, bucolic handling of the things in front of her—those scraps of linen on the fence, that criss-cross of lines and figures against the grass.

And where—final question—are the lumpish boys supposed to be bathing in Seurat's *Baignade à Asnières* (fig. 5.10)? In what kind of landscape, in what kind of water? Opposite the mouth of the same *grand égout collecteur,* in fact; and this at a time—in the hot summers of the 1880s—when

> more than 120,000 cubic meters of solids have accumulated at the collector's mouth; several hundred square meters are covered with a bizarre vegetation, which gives off a disgusting smell. In the current heat wave, the town of Clichy [it is there in the background of Seurat's picture, its line of factories blocking the river] possesses a veritable Pontine Marshes of its own.[20]

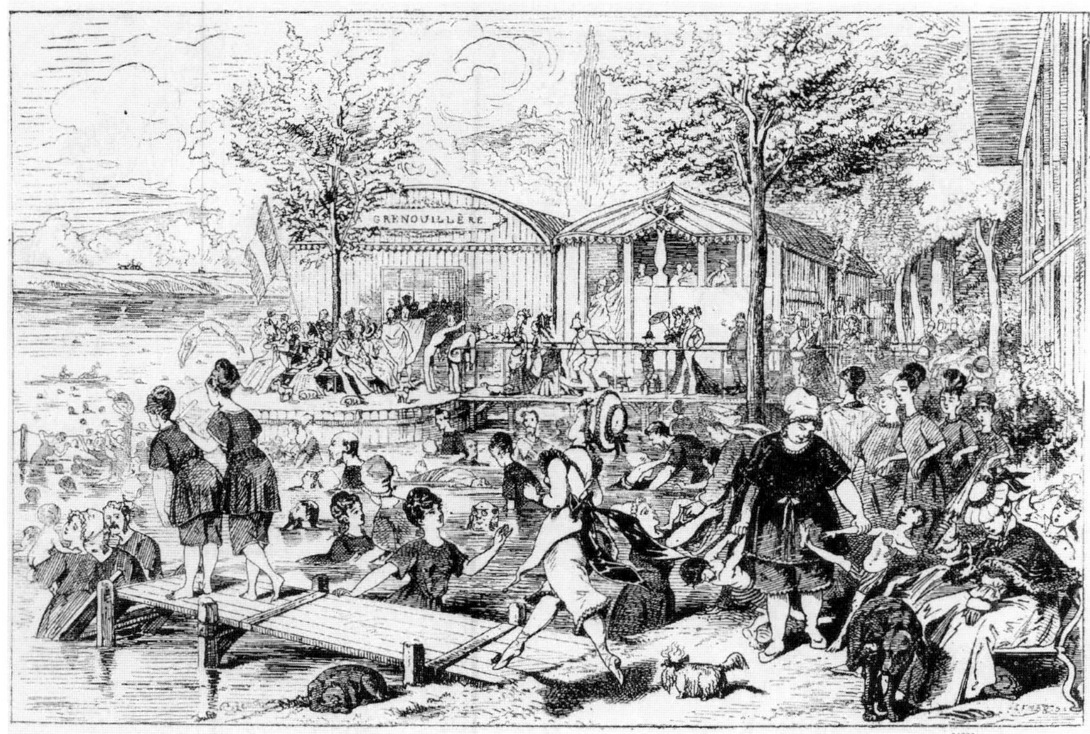

Un Eden où bêtes et gens se meuvent dans une douce confraternité; échange cordial de puces (de la part des individus de la race canine).

FIGURE 5.8. Jules Pelcoq, *A la Grenouillère*. Wood engraving in *Le Journal Amusant*, no. 991 (1875): 6. Bibliothèque nationale de France, Paris.

Pictures are being whisked in and out of the reader's field of vision, and questions multiplied, mainly because I do not have any very clear answers to most of them. Perhaps it would help if we focused on one picture, not noticeably less cryptic than the rest, Manet's *Argenteuil, les canotiers*, from 1874 (plate 3); for here, I believe, the main elements of the matter are assembled: the middle class and its pleasures, the countryside organized to attend to them, and the answering presence of industry. This is the picture, it seems to me, in which the most literal effort was made to put such things in order and insist they belonged together.

It is important that the picture is big. It is a picture for the Salon: a dominating image, four feet wide and nearly five feet high, whose message was meant to carry across a crowded room. And the first impression, as so often with Manet, is of a great, flat clarity of form—clearness of edge and plain abbreviation of surface within those edges. Of course the viewer soon sees that these qualities coexist with others: with an extraordinary, calculated fat richness of touch, a thick weave of individual brushstrokes, dab after dab in the woman's dress or the flowers she holds, in the distant boats or the great blue surface of water. The eye gets involved in the details: it makes out the fingers half lost in the flowers, or the stuff of the folded parasol on either side of the yachtsman's arm. But detail plays against plainness; an exuberant tissue of touches, worked over and into one another, mixed and remixed, hard-edged and soft-edged, and all of them quite safely *contained* in the end, made part of an order that is simplified and flat.

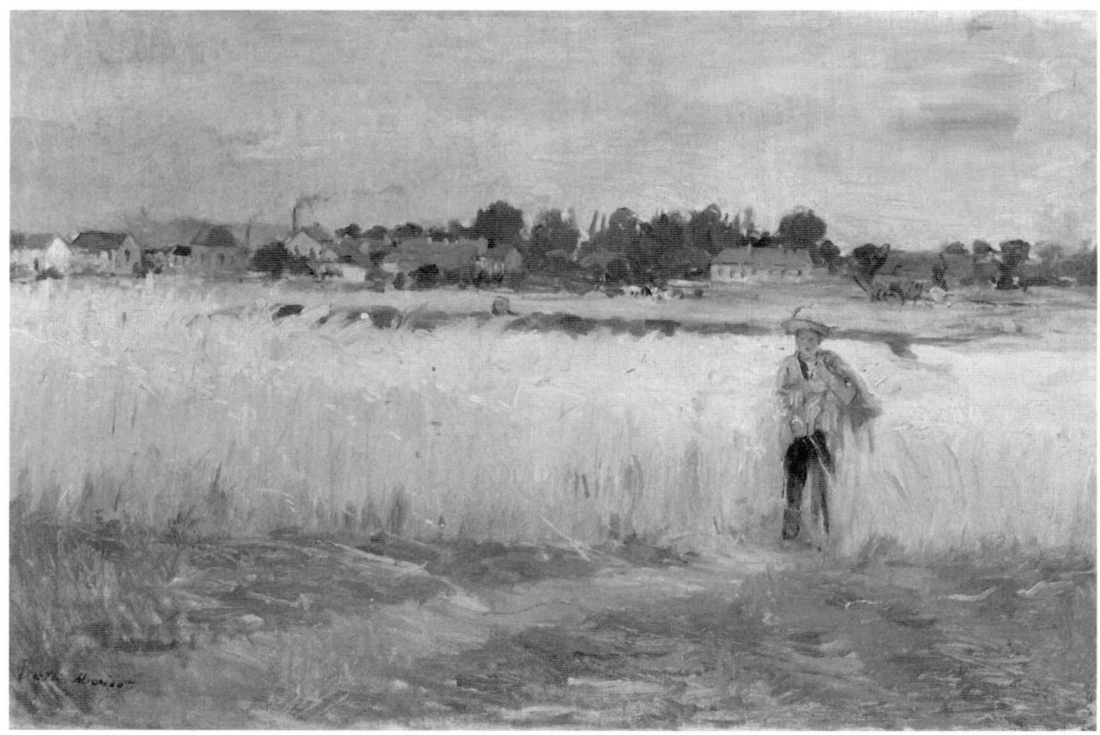

FIGURE 5.9. Berthe Morisot, *In the Wheatfields, Gennevilliers*, 1875. Musée d'Orsay, Paris. Photo: Erich Lessing/Art Resource, NY.

The examples are obvious. The man, for instance, is seemingly turned toward his inscrutable companion, no doubt in admiration; his body is swiveled in space, half leaning back from the picture's surface. And that obliqueness is half offered to the viewer and half refused: the tunic and torso are kept in touch with the surface, flattened out—by the curious line of light which runs from the neckline diagonally across the open chest; by the narrow, flat rainbow curve of lines on the man's far shoulder; by the ruck of brush marks where the tunic puckers; and by the shadowy flatness of the man's forearm, lined up as it is against the picture surface and touched with a couple of unattached, absolute dabs of color where the light outlines a knuckle and finger on the fist.

The picture offers these irresolutions to us: the flattened body; the mast which never quite manages to be modeled; the dense, opaque blue of the water and the floating, tilted, improbable woman's hat. The hat, I suppose, is the strongest sign of flatness in the picture. It is a black straw oval, hardly seeming to belong to the head underneath it. It is a simple surface; and onto the surface is spread that wild twist of tulle, piped onto the oval like cream on a cake, smeared on like a great flourishing brush mark, blown up to impossible size. It is a great metaphor, that tulle; and it is, yes, a metaphor of paint and painting. One of the things that the ornament does is put in doubt the picture's already fragile space; for it laps like a wave against the far white wall, the one across the river in front of the houses.

These are the things which are always said about Manet's painting; in his lifetime querulously, and later by critics and historians who were certain that here—in the oddities and flourishes—lay the point of the picture and the key to its classic appeal. They were not wholly wrong, it seems to me; but it has to be said—I shall say it again and again later, meaning

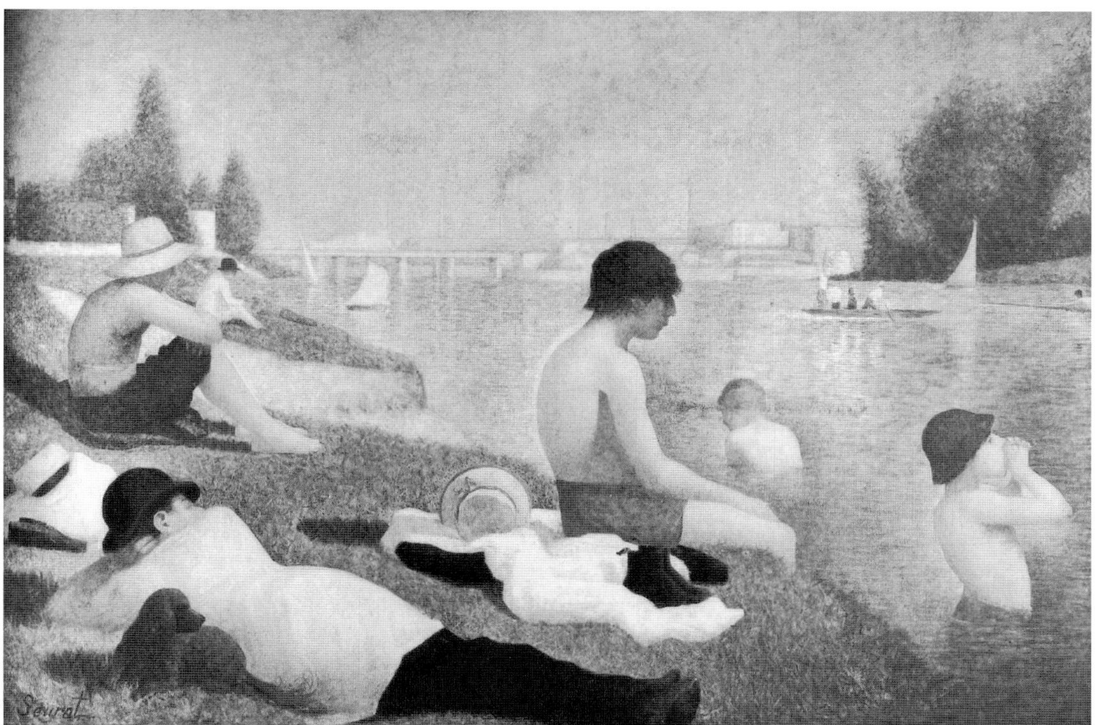

FIGURE 5.10. Georges Seurat, *Baignade à Asnières (Bathers at Asnières)*, 1883–84. National Gallery, London. Image © National Gallery, London.

it metaphorically—that Manet *found* flatness more than invented it; he saw it around him in the world he knew. I mean that literally here. If we look at one of the other pictures Manet did in Argenteuil [*Les Bords de la Seine à Argenteuil*, 1874; National Gallery, London], we can see, from the back, the unlikely construction of the black straw hat. For hats themselves were two-dimensional in 1874; they were tilted forward and tied up behind, real pieces of fashionable machinery. (That fact makes sense, incidentally, of a tiny fleck of black which can be seen, in *Argenteuil, les canotiers*, at the upper edge of the woman's ear: it must be the tip of the hidden bow, the clue to the whole outlandish construction.)

Nevertheless the later enthusiasts were right to single out the things they did. The more we look at the picture the more we come to dwell on its peculiarities, and see it as flaunting the facts of its own discrepancy. Signs, things, shapes, and modes of handling do not fit together here. Paint does not make continuities or engineer transitions for the eye; it enforces distinctions and disparities, changing completely across an edge, insisting on the stiffness of a pose or the bluntness of blue against yellow. This is the picture's overall language—this awkwardness of intersection, this dissonance of color. But once again the viewer is afforded a few special instances of the general lack of fit. For example, the hank of rope which hangs over the orange side of the boat toward the right. No doubt we decipher the flecked rope and the fluffy tassel without too much difficulty, and proceed to examine the more elusive trail of paint which starts down from the gunwale, bends, and seems to peter out into the orange—peter out for no good reason. And in due course the eye makes sense of the situation: we begin to see the wandering line as a shadow, and realize eventually that the orange surface is not—as it is first assumed to be—simply flat.

It is curved, it is concave; and the curve explains the peculiar shadow and is explained by it—or, rather, is half explained and half explaining: the broken triangle of brushstrokes is not mended quite so easily, and never entirely proves the illusion it plays with. It stays painted; it stays on the edge of a likeness.

And what are we supposed to make, finally, of the visual rhyme which Manet puts at the picture's center? In between the figures, outlined against the sky, is a distant factory chimney. Beneath it a reflection spreads out across the water, gray and white at first, opening slowly into the ripples of the river, then reappearing farther down, dispersed a bit more and touched with yellow, before the water surface finally breaks up. Now in fact these marks are *not* a reflection. They are a lineup of false equivalents—two pieces of rope hanging down from the end of a furled-up sail and four tiny yellow flowers straggling free from a band on the woman's hat brim. They are a kind of joke—the word comes awkwardly, but I cannot think of a better one—about false equivalence; about things appearing to connect and then being seen not to; about illusion, about the difference between illusion and untruth. These are the picture's main concerns, of course; and in general it is far from playful in its treatment of them.

It has the look of an icon, this picture, does it not?—an altarpiece with two great meek figures presented to us, dominant, the one half turning to the other, yielding, indicating, paying some kind of homage. And both of them closed in an arbor of boats, sitting on a plain horizontal throne, hemmed in by a patient system of straight lines—masts and chimneys, riverbank and far white wall. Yet it is no icon: it is too casual, too uncomposed, too untidy. The river is full of the signs of *canotage:* rigging and bits of boats and rolled-up canvas, the whole thing patchy and provisional. It is the lack of order which must have been striking in 1875, for here was a subject which lent itself normally to simple rhythms and sharp effects: sails bending in unison, rigging arranged in casual geometries, reflections laid out as counterpoint to the world above (see fig. 1.1). Manet's regatta was not like this: there was no single sail unfurled, and the whole of a boat was never shown. *Canotage* was a litter of ropes and masts and pennants, its casualness confirmed by the invading slab of blue which so perplexed the critics. The blue was the foil for this patchwork, this debris; it was the consistency of nature, they might have said, as opposed to the random signs of manufacture; it was what survived of landscape.

So what can we say of the objects and persons at Argenteuil? How are people depicted here, how do they present themselves, what kind of individuals are they? It would be nice to be as sure of the answer as the English critic in 1876 who called Manet's subject "these vulgar figures," this "couple of very ordinary-looking lovers sitting on the gunwale of a boat."[21] Or as certain as Maurice Chaumelin, writing a year earlier in *Le Bien Public:*

> Under the pretext of representing nature and society just as they present themselves, the realists dispense with balance in their pictures of both. But let that pass. There are at least, in this nature and this society, aspects which are more agreeable than others, and types which are more attractive. Monsieur Manet is deliberately out to choose the flattest sites, the grossest types. He shows us a butcher's boy, with ruddy arms and pug nose, out boating on a river of indigo, and turning with the air of an amorous marine toward a trollop seated by his side, decked out in horrible finery, and looking horribly sullen.[22]

We may prefer, however, the admission of uncertainty in Baron Shop's entry on the picture in *Le Petit National:*

> His *Canotiers d'Argenteuil* are two, one of them a lady. They are shown full face, sitting on a bench together, with the air of being tolerably bored, as far as the willful impasto on the faces allows one to judge.[23]

"L'air passablement ennuyé autant que permettent d'en juger les empâtements volontaires des figures"—at least this critic seems aware of the problem. The previous writers, one cannot help feeling, were wishing expressions and simplicities where the paint allowed them none. They were wanting the signs, the largely absent signs, of social inferiority: they would have their butcher's boy and brave "donzelle," they would have vulgarity and grossness; anything rather than the actual disguise they were offered, the deadpan, the uncertainty.

The people in the picture are *posing*, perhaps we could put it that way—posing not as artists' models do, but as people might for a photograph, as they might have done later in just such a place. Their faces go blank, their bodies turn awkward, they forget how to look happy or even serious. The woman's face, especially, is worked and reworked to the point of effacement; it is scarred and shadowed and abbreviated, hairless and doll-like, animate but opaque. The eyes look out levelly from underneath the hat brim, the mouth just opens, the earrings and necktie are neat as a pin. The woman resists the critics' descriptions: she is not quite vulgar, not quite "ennuyé," not quite even sullen.

This is a picture of pleasure, remember, of people taking their ease. We need a word to express their lack of assurance in doing so; or at least the curious, complex *qualification* of pleasure as these people seem to have it. Veblen talks of individuals—he has in mind considerably wealthier women than the one we are looking at—"performing" leisure, or "rendering" it.[24] The verbs are useful but a bit too strident. "Joylessness" would almost do—it has the advantage of defining the matter in negative terms—but in practice the word has lost its limitations and has too pejorative a ring. The best phrase, I believe, occurs in Norbert Elias's writings: he talks of the places allowed for excitement in our society—he thinks they are rather few—and points to "the cover of restraints" which spreads, more and more evenly, over action and affect in modern times.[25] The "cover of restraints" in the place of pleasure—that seems to me the great subject of Manet's art. But it should be said at once, by way of proviso, that in Manet's art the restraints are visible: they are not yet embedded in behavior; they still have the look of something made up or put on. Of course there is *fashion* already, and that is the strongest sign of the order to come; but it is important that fashions are still assumed a bit awkwardly and seem not to belong to their wearers. (Is that what Chaumelin meant by calling the woman "horriblement fagotée"?)

The part of the picture that has so far been left out of discussion is the landscape in the background. On the other side of the river is a town or a village—anyway, some kind of built-up area—in which the viewer can quite easily make out a mansarded villa, trees and houses, a white wall, and some factory chimneys—two of them idle, one producing smoke. These details were noticed in 1875. The cartoonist in *L'Eclipse*, Hadol, imagined the man's (now phallic) hat floating in the Seine beside its flowery partner, in front of a building labeled "Fabrique d'Indigo" (fig. 5.11). He added the caption, "The Seine at the Sewer of Saint-Denis." And thus the blue of the river was explained—by the great chemical-dye factories a few miles upstream from Argenteuil, pouring their indigo waste into the water.[26]

It is a pedestrian joke, of course, but its materials seem to me the right ones. The cartoonist's mistake, if I can put it this way, is to picture the landscape as literally *made* by industry, and therefore have the factories to blame for everything—the water, the people, the shape of the hats. That might prove to be true in the long run, but the point about Argenteuil and its neighbors was that the long run seemed such a long way off. This was not a terrain where industry was master, even picturesquely so. It was not like the hillside at Déville-lès-Rouen, for example, which Monet had painted a few years before: a forest of chimneys belching smoke, and the railway running past them like a river in spate—industry as landscape, certainly, with three small strollers in the foreground twirling parasols and taking in the sights (fig. 5.12). Nor was it the forge at Ivry, as Guillaumin showed it in 1873, blocking the river, backlit and melodramatic; nor the quiet enclosure of Monet's *Ruisseau de Robec;* nor the blunt shape of the starch works at Saint-Ouen, in the oil by Pissarro done in 1873 (fig. 5.13).

The presence of industry at Argenteuil is different from this. It lays claim to the landscape in rather the same way as the two people in the foreground—

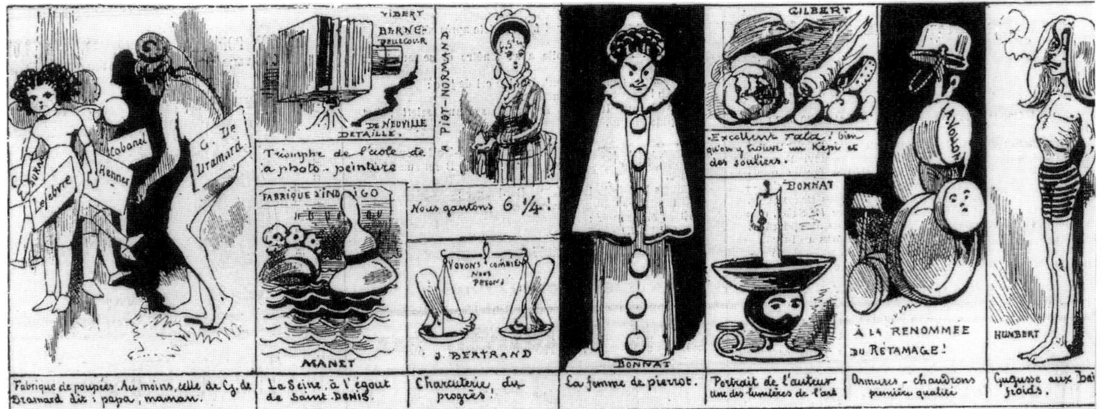

FIGURE 5.11. Hadol, *Le Salon comique*. Wood engraving in *L'Eclipse* (May 30, 1875): 4. Bibliothèque nationale de France, Paris.

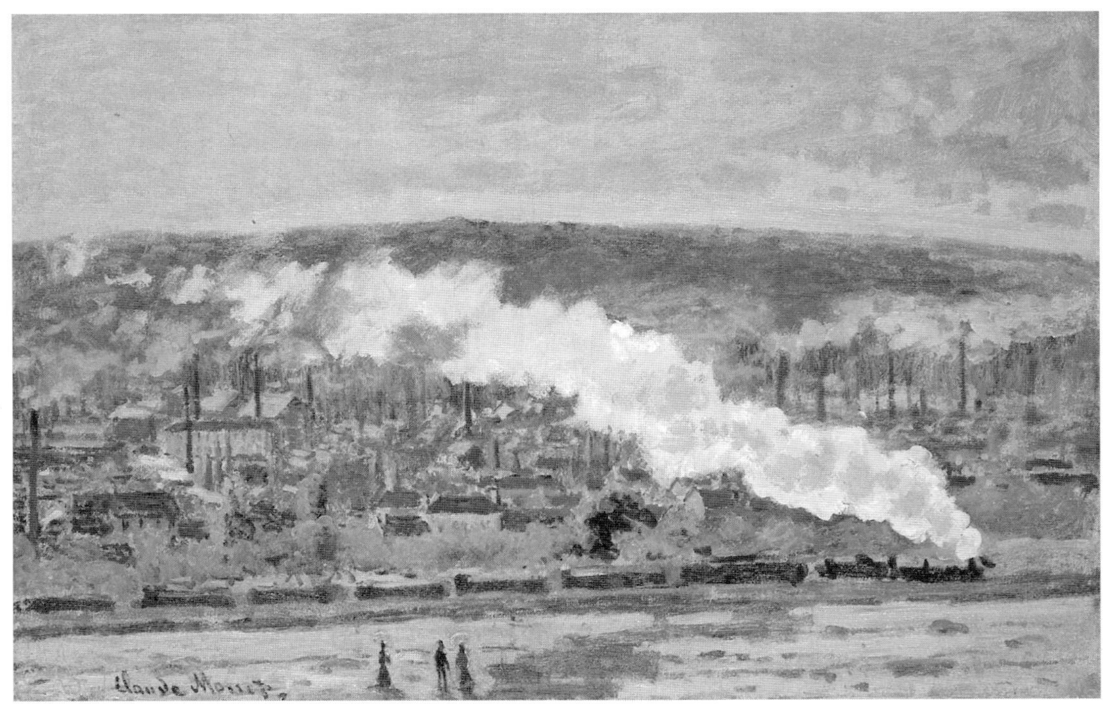

FIGURE 5.12. Claude Monet, *The Goods Train*, 1872. Pola Museum of Art, Japan.

a bit erratically, a bit naïvely, acre by acre, without much of a flourish. And this seems to me the ultimate point of the picture's formal language. It fits its figures and landscape together, it makes out relations between them—between shoulders and water, chimney and halyard, straw hat and white wall—but the edges and links are mostly implausible, and surely meant to be so. The forms are like cutouts against the bright blue ground; the outlines of everything are too sharp and simple.

This has to do, I think, with many things: with the look of objects close-up in sunlight, with the fact that

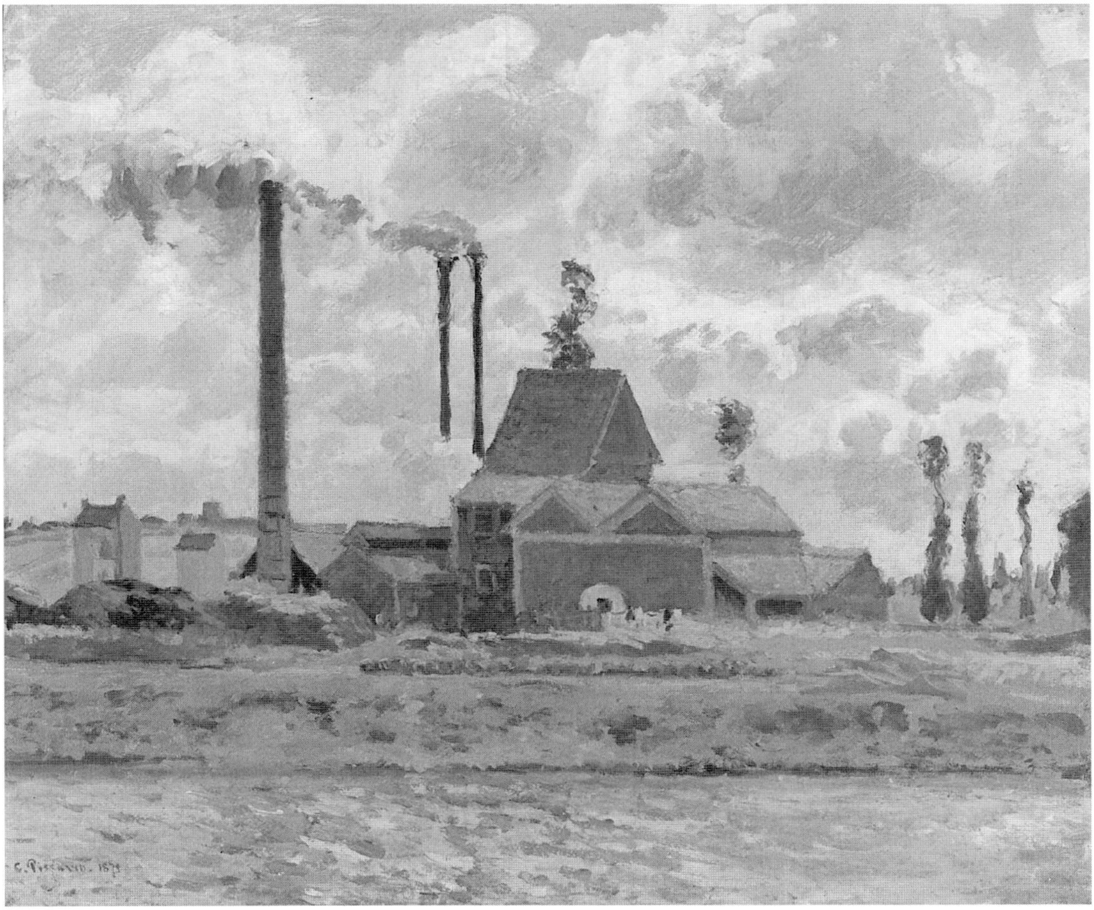

FIGURE 5.13. Camille Pissarro, *Factory near Pontoise*, 1873. Museum of Fine Arts, Springfield, Massachusetts, James Philip Gray Collection.

a picture is actually flat, and with the received wisdom in 1875 about such places as Argenteuil. It is not that Manet reproduced that wisdom in any simple form. His picture does not strike me as comic in the way of "Y" or Robert Caze; and irony is seemingly what he was working to avoid, above all in the woman's face. The best description is a limited one: the figures and landscape do not quite belong together yet; they are incomplete, they have the look of contingency. This does not mean they are shown as fugitive and impalpable, in the way of a sketch. On the contrary, the picture is massively *finished;* it is orderly and flawless, and the word "restrained" applies to it as much as the word "contingent." But whatever it is, it is not "natural": it is not offered to the viewer as something already made and self-evident, there to be looked at and not questioned (this is true of landscape and figures alike). What Manet was painting was the look of a new form of life—a placid form, a modest form, but one with a claim to pleasure. The careful self-consciousness of the woman, her guarded attention to us, the levelness of her gaze: these are the best metaphors of that moment. It is Olympia's gaze again, but lacking the fierce engagement with the viewer or the edge of insecurity. This woman looks out circumspectly from a place that belongs to people like her. How good it is, in these places, to find a little solitude on Sundays! How good, how modern, how right and proper.

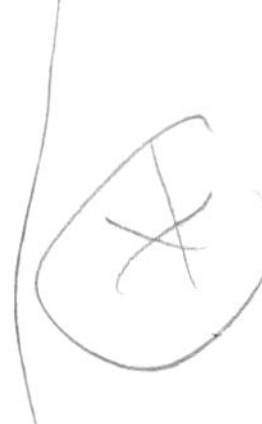

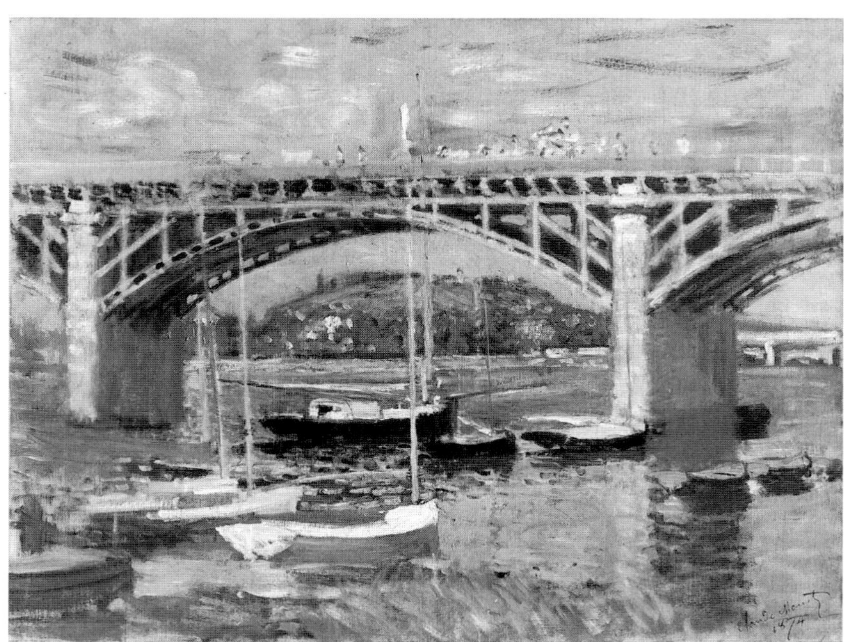

FIGURE 5.14. Claude Monet, *The Bridge at Argenteuil*, 1874. Bayerische Staatsgemäldesammlungen, Neue Pinakothek, Munich.

Argenteuil in the 1870s was modernizing fast.[27] It was still surrounded by vineyards, and one or two windmills looked down on it from the slopes of Orgemont and Sannois. The *petit bleu d'Argenteuil*—it had been the theme of many a joke at Manet's expense in 1875—was still just drinkable; and whatever the quality of the wine, people came out from Paris to watch the peasants get drunk at *vendange*.[28] The town was "famous for its plethoric asparagus"[29] and its figs: its agriculture was geared to the Parisian market, as it had been since the eighteenth century.[30]

In the 1870s Argenteuil grew: it had 8,000 people at the beginning of the decade and close to 12,000 in 1882.[31] Part of that increase was straightforwardly suburban: the town was a fifteen-minute ride from the Gare de l'Ouest, and many a stockjobber and commercial traveler decided that it was just the place for a house and garden. To the west of Argenteuil grew up what the locals called "la nouvelle cité," and to the east "la colonie parisienne."[32] Yet the majority of newcomers in the 1870s were most probably not bourgeois and no longer strictly Parisian: they were people who came in search of work to a town that was quietly making itself over to industry. Already in the 1860s it had boasted factories and plaster works. Five hundred men had made their living in the gypsum quarries;[33] three hundred or so had worked for Monsieur Joly in his iron foundry next to the railway bridge. They built the Palace of Industry for the Exposition Universelle of 1867 and the great iron canopies for Les Halles; they tried their hand at bicycles for a year or two, and of course they forged the parts for the new railway bridge itself when it was rebuilt in 1872.[34] The town had a sawmill and several distilleries, a tannery, a gasworks, an establishment which made mineral water, another producing cardboard boxes. There was lace making, fine crystal, and clocks. Bezons, to the south, had a rubber factory (by 1869 the waste from the plant had killed off the local fish).[35] In the 1870s more industry arrived: a new chemical works in 1872 and an albumin refinery two years later; another distillery, a second foundry with jobs for 170 men, and a third in 1876.

This list of premises and dates is all very well as

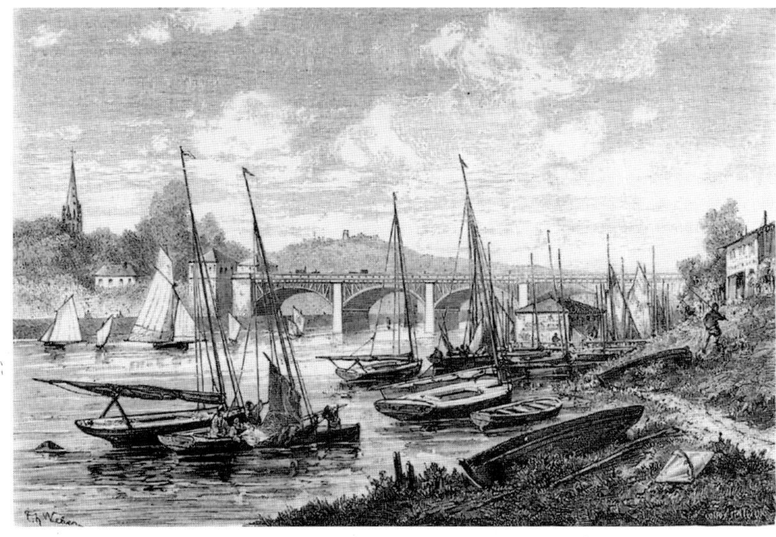

FIGURE 5.15. Charles Weber, *Environs de Paris—Argenteuil*, 1869. Wood engraving in *L'Illustration* 54 (September 25, 1869): 208. Bibliothèque nationale de France, Paris.

far as it goes, but it does not rule on most of the decisive questions. It does not permit us to say how much these new activities marked the landscape or transformed it, or whether the factories somehow stood in the interstices of the town, left out of sight between the vineyards and the river. Certainly the landscape had long since lost its claim on the attention of the traveler in search of the picturesque, and Louis Barron, on the Argenteuil road in the 1880s, "made haste to flee the monotonous spectacle of the quarries, marking the hillsides with yellow, and the plaster works which keep a whole population of poor workers tied to the region, and the vines, and the interminable squares of vegetables bordering the road."[36] But Barron's verdict does not really speak to the town and its immediate hinterland, and it is that area which concerns us most. What we need to know about Argenteuil is how large the twenty factories loomed, and whether the piles of coal and plaster on the towpath actually *showed*—whether they made the town look "industrial." (The force of that word is anyway not clear when applied to a place, as opposed to a way of working.)

The best evidence we have is Impressionist painting, but it too is ambiguous. Are we to trust the perspective it offers, for example, in Manet's *Bateau-atelier* (see fig. 5.17)—the river looking south and west, the atmosphere heavy with Ajalbert's twilight, the fields walled in with new buildings? Or should we prefer the hills upstream, in Sisley's hands (see fig. 8.2) or Renoir's, without a sign of industry to interfere? It is sleight of hand when Monet looks north through the toll bridge to the Côte de Sannois and has one pillar of the bridge block out the Joly ironworks to the right—sleight of hand or felicitous arrangement (fig. 5.14)? Might not the composition speak quite well, in fact, to the modest place of such things in the landscape, to the way they hardly interrupted vision?

One thing undoubtedly did mark the town, and that was the invasion of the pleasure seekers. The effects of that process on the riverside were unmistakable: they are there, innocently charted, in the engravings of the place published at the time in all the illustrated magazines. Argenteuil changes—from an open riverbank where clippers are drawn up casually for an afternoon, making use of a few slipways and a natural harbor; to a town still nestling deep in trees—the year is 1869—and a towpath still grassy and overgrown, but the river already thick with boats (fig. 5.15); to a bank which is crowded with shipyards, spectators, offices with boats-for-hire; to a suitable place for a steamboat race, or the launching of a new yacht (fig. 5.16), or the national rowing championships. Argenteuil was putting in its bid to be the capital of Parisian recreation—with what determination can be judged from this entry in *Le Petit-Journal* from May 1877, announcing the program for Trinity Sunday:

> *Argenteuil* (Gare Saint-Lazare)—Continuation of festivities. At 2:30, bicycle races organized by the Union Velocipédique with music provided by the municipality; costumes *de rigueur.*—At 9:00, grand torchlight procession with music and the fire brigade.[37]

It is by far the most flamboyant of the twenty-two local entertainments listed that weekend.

No wonder that by 1884 the town has taken its place in the ironic discourse which the reader now knows well. This is Louis Blairet, for example, in *L'Opinion,* describing Argenteuil in his series "Autour de Paris":

> Come Sunday, there is an invasion of the Gare Saint-Lazare, lady fruit-sellers from the rue Saint-Denis, cabinetmakers from the rue de Cléry, girls who make chocolate in the rue de Vivienne—there is not one of them who does not descend on the banks of the Seine, beneath the Moulin d'Orgemont or in the Auberge des Canotiers. And wherever there trots a Parisienne, a Parisien is sure to follow.
>
> . . . There is singing, shouting, dancing, running about, falling down, and going astray. It all begins with *entrecôtes au cresson* and ends with aching limbs. The banks of the Seine are full of mysteries that day, mysteries of the private and pastoral life.
>
> Here we serve lobster salad on the grass, messieurs![38]

The terms are the normal ones: grocers' wives and cabinetmakers have once again put paid to the genuine *fête champêtre* and established a counterfeit in its place. Argenteuil is part of the environs of Paris and can therefore be condescended to.

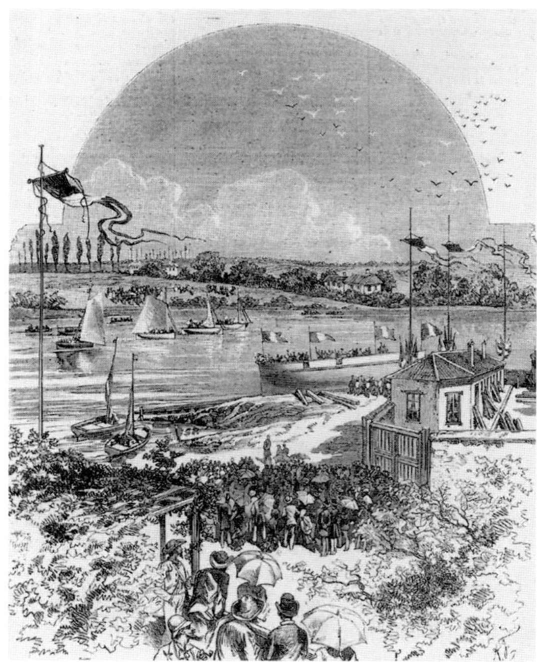

FIGURE 5.16. Ferdinandus, *Lancement d'un navire à Argenteuil,* 1877. Wood engraving. Bibliothèque nationale de France, Paris.

The other main picture Manet did at Argenteuil in 1874 was a portrait of his younger colleague Claude Monet at work in his houseboat studio (fig. 5.17). The scene is presented from roughly the same vantage point as that of *Argenteuil, les canotiers* (plate 3), though now the horizon is opened wide enough to give a glimpse of the Gennevilliers shore. The chimneys are all smoking fiercely, and the house with the mansard is no more than a smudge. To the left there is much the same debris of masts and furled sails as in *Argenteuil, les canotiers,* though one of the yachts is sailing now, or at least has its mainsail hoisted.

Monet, at any rate, is turned away from the evidence of industry: he seems to be looking toward the right, past a further crop of boats and rigging, whose forms are blocked out on the canvas on his easel. His manner of working is something Manet clearly admired and wanted his viewers to know about; he showed them Monet's way of painting in the way he

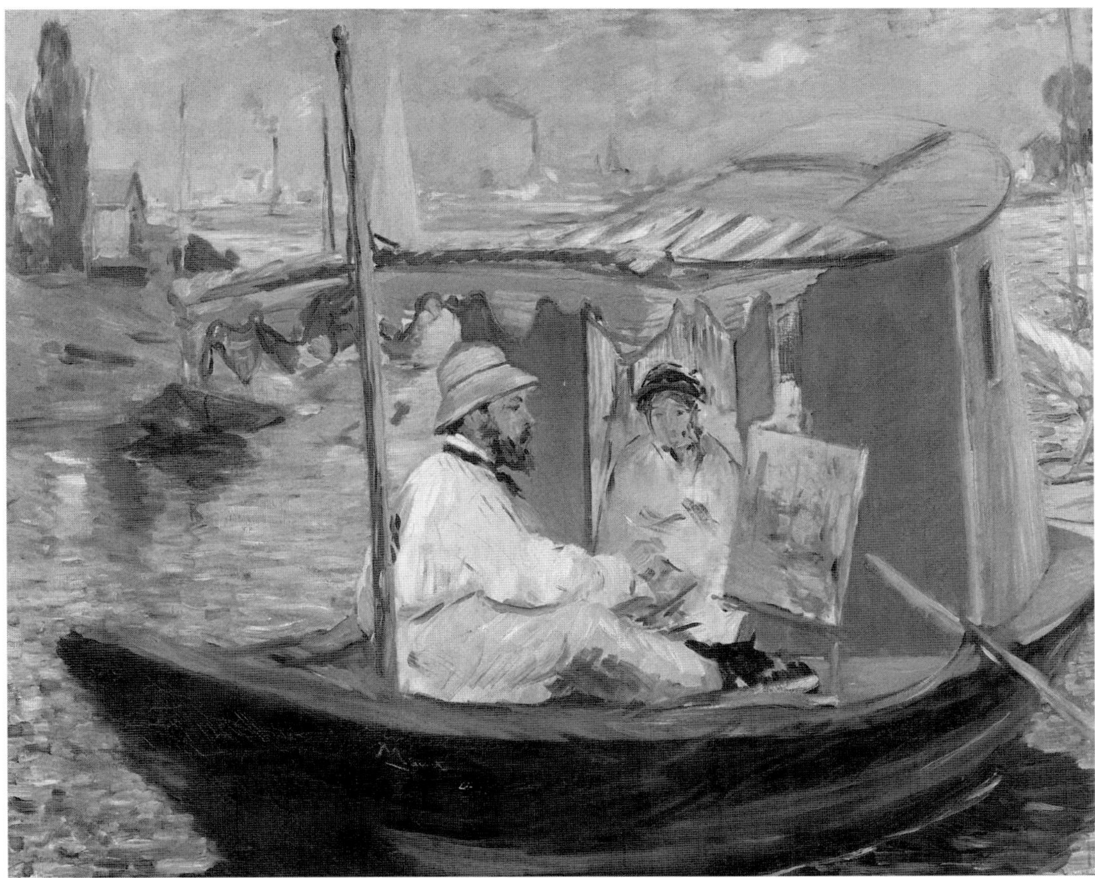

FIGURE 5.17. Edouard Manet, *Claude Monet with His Wife in His Floating Studio*, 1874. Neue Pinakothek, Munich. Photo: Scala/Art Resource, NY.

put on paint himself: it is looser and lighter than in *Les Canotiers*, with the edges of most things no longer so sharply outlined. The bow of the houseboat, for example, is splashed with a hatchwork of blue and gray strokes, and the water has lost its absolute color—it is gray, yellow, white, and green, mixed up with reflections and seeping into every solid it touches. The picture is surely concerned to associate these qualities with others the critics thought Monet deficient in: steadiness, for instance, patience, concentration, relentless detachment. The patience may strike us as belonging to the self-effacing wife as much as to her husband, but the relentlessness is all Monet's own. It is there in the profile he offers the viewer, sharp against a plain blue ground; and in the way his brush is held, tight in the fingers like a pen, ready for rapid and sure notation.

What Monet is insistent on is *landscape;* and Manet's depiction of him might be read as a kind of reflection on what it meant to keep hold of that category in a place like Argenteuil. It meant contriving to notice some things that loomed large in one's field of vision and to overlook others just as prominent; a picture depended on choosing and maintaining a certain point of view, doing so often with fastidious and, in its way, cynical care. No doubt painting landscape had always involved some such process of reading out and reading in; but what the painter excluded had rarely

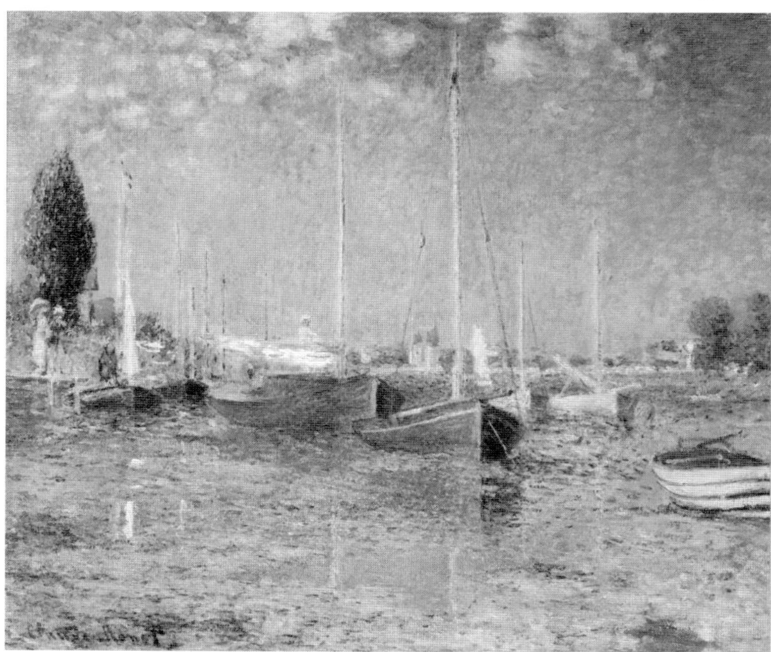

FIGURE 5.18. Claude Monet, *Les Bateaux rouges, Argenteuil*, 1875. Musée de l'Orangerie, Paris. Photo: Réunion des Musées Nationaux/Art Resource, NY. Photographed by J. G. Berizzi.

been there so emphatically, so much wrapped up with the matter in hand. Landscape is in doubt in Manet's picture: the sheer range of shapes and incidents which cry out for representation puts the whole business of landscape in question, and Monet has seemingly turned away from the untidiness, preferring to focus on what the scene still offers of pleasure or nature in undiluted form. Manet, by contrast, still looks to the south and west, as if resolved to show that the Bezons reach could be faced by painting—even painting of Monet's kind. There was a way to put down such matters in oils and have them be part of landscape quite strictly conceived. They would have to be sketched in lightly, almost carelessly, without much attention being paid to differences and identities, to the weight and substance of objects. The whole thing would necessarily be done with a great show of painterly wit, a flaunting of facility, as if daring the world to resist one's notation of it; and if the tour de force was successful, the play of paint would absorb the factories and weekend villas with scarcely a ripple. Surface would replace substance; paint would *perform* the consistency of landscape, in spite of everything a particular landscape might put in its way; there was nothing that could not be made part of a picture—of a picture's fragile unity—if the painter confined himself to appearances and put aside questions of meaning or use.

It may even be that one does Monet an injustice by having him disagree with that last verdict. If we look again at the picture on his easel and take notice of the tree at left, and the masts and water in roughly the right places, we may end by believing that Monet too is out to paint the view behind him—the one downriver, toward the smoke. Are we given enough on the slanting canvas to reconstruct a picture something like *Les Bateaux rouges, Argenteuil* (fig. 5.18) or *Au Petit Gennevilliers* (private collection)? (No particular surviving Monet seems quite to fit the vague clues on offer, but there are four or five which show the same slice of riverbank rendered from more or less the same spot.[39]) Pictures like the one I have chosen are in their way more absolute with industry than Manet could ever quite be. They look toward the industrial shore and do not seem for a moment to find the litter over there at odds with the water and masts in the middle ground; they have no high horizon with chimneys separate and clear; such things are incidental to the landscape, and if the painting stands to benefit, they can simply be left out. (That happens quite often and is done very matter-of-factly.) In any case, suppression is not usually necessary. The signs of industry can be included, in a picture like *Le Voilier au Petit Gennevilliers*, but in such a way that they hardly register as different from the signs of nature or recreation. A chimney is not so different from a tree or a mast; the shape and consistency of a trail of smoke can be taken up in other, stronger traces—the edge of a reflection or the body of a cloud. The factory is a minor note, and the smoke serves to provoke various analogies—between smoke and paint, smoke and cloud, cloud and water—all of them guaranteeing the scene's coherence.

The chimneys, in other words, are made part of landscape as Monet imagined it. And landscape, for Monet as for many other painters in the later nineteenth century, was the one genre left. They seemed to believe—the belief was not often stated explicitly, but the drift of practice is unmistakable—that nature possessed consistency now, in a way that nothing else did. It had a presence and a unity which agreed profoundly (this was the crucial point) with the act of painting. The flat unison of a picture like Monet's was *like* landscape, like the look of sky and water *en plein air;* and these were the things on which painting could thrive. No other subject proved to match so well with the actual material of oil and canvas; no other offered painting the right kind of resistance, the kind which had the medium seem more real the harder it was pressed in the service of an illusion.

This was a powerful belief and in some ways a merited one. The achievements of the previous generation, and above all the work of Courbet and the Barbizon school, could be taken to confirm it; though they also suggested—in Millet's art the suggestion was particularly strong—that the genre of landscape would have to be rephrased and extended if it were to go on providing matter for major art. The genre came down to the new group of painters in a necessarily complex form, with a special, and in many ways perplexing, history; and that history was not a dead past. It was supposedly part of the genre's appeal to practitioners that it seemed to offer them a wealth of examples which were still effective, still useable in detail. Landscape painters had access to a tradition, they believed; they were confident that there was almost as much still to be learned from Hobbema and Ruysdael, say, as from Daubigny and Jongkind; they might even go further and say that learning from the latter pair *was* learning from the former, and that a painter looked closely at Ruysdael precisely in order to understand better what Daubigny was doing.

The vividness of the tradition was exacting as well as helpful. The painter of landscape was notoriously engrossed in the natural world as it simply was, as it stood over there in front of his easel; and yet nature was nothing for painters if not encountered in other people's painting, and it existed there in not at all simple form. Nature had substance for Monet and his friends as a term in a tradition; they learnt it as part of their practice, by using and adapting what the Dutch had done, or Constable and Corot. The term in the hands of these older masters was specially protean: there *was* no nature, in the great tradition of landscape painting, except as part of a movement, an equivocation, in which Man and Nature (bravely capitalized) were seen to depend on each other for their sense. Landscape put together the man-made and the natural, the wild and the cultivated, the elements and man's attempts to defy them. Certainly it celebrated the limits of the human world, and often affirmed that people lived in a landscape that was not put there simply for their convenience—or not securely. There was the sea, the marshland, storms, waterfalls, wilderness, dark woods, ruins. But the wilderness could be charted, marshes drained, land pulled from the sea and found fertile; waterfalls could turn wheels, and ruins be restored and venerated.

These are the obvious examples, and no doubt they seem to be a little pat; but that is largely because they are the repeated conceits of the genre, by now a bit stale in the telling. Whether one looks at the painters of Rome and its *campagna*, or the Dutch, or the English in the eighteenth century, or Auvers and Barbizon, it is always the difficult, provisional relation of man to nature—the extent to which man makes the landscape or is made by it—that is the main motif. It is the stuff of landscape painting, this progress from barren waste to broken column to rude cot to decent farm to thriving village to nestling town with determinate edge; or from commons to enclosure and rapids to sluice. The modern artists of the 1870s inherited this idiom: they shared the older painters' assumption that nature could hardly be seen in the first place—or construed as an order apart from the human—unless as something mapped and tended, interfered with and not infrequently replaced by man. And how was man present in his landscape? What kind of mark did he make upon it, what kind of boundaries; how had his artifacts made peace with their surroundings, or had they made peace at all? (It was not necessarily the case that they should: a city wall and a windmill were equally part of a well-ordered province.) What forms of *visibility* were provided as part of this overall process of control and understanding? How was the countryside kept at a distance, brought into view, produced as a single human thing, a prospect or a panorama? Upon the answers to questions like these depended the artist's sense of a scene's amounting to landscape at all, and therefore being paintable.

These were practical matters, in other words, not just theoretical ones; from them derived the exercise of landscape as an art and the possession of its basic terms and skills. In the 1870s the questions recurred with a vengeance; they were not essentially different from the previous ones, but there was a feeling abroad that the answers this time might not prove particularly encouraging. Was there a way now for landscape to admit the new signs of man in the countryside—the chimneys, the villas, the apparatus of pleasure?* Could the factory be added to the series which went from wilderness to working river? (And if not, why not?) Was the city with determinate edge to be joined, in painting, by the city without one? How much of inconsistency and waste could the genre include and still keep its categories intact? So landscape was to be *modern;* but if it was—if the signs of modernity were agreed on and itemized—would the landscape not be robbed of what the painters valued most in it? Would it not lose its singular beauty, its coherence, the way it seemed to offer itself as an unbroken surface which paint could render well? For Monet and his colleagues, landscape was the guarantee of *painting* above all; it was the thing that justified their insistence on matter and making, on the artisanal facts of the art. Perhaps that guarantee would not hold, least of all in places like Argenteuil. But painting in a sense had nowhere else to go. It was here that the terms of the landscape tradition still seemed to present themselves with some kind of vividness. The roll call of edges and stages of civilization could still be taken at Argenteuil, as once it had been outside Rome or Haarlem. Without such a roll call, landscape painting was a poor thing.

Monet moved to Argenteuil just before Christmas 1871 and lived in the town for the next six years. Friends came to stay and paint—Sisley in 1872, Renoir on several occasions. Caillebotte's family had a summer place across the river at Petit Gennevilliers, and Manet lodged there while painting *Argenteuil, les canotiers*. Landscape painters came and went, but mostly the town and the river were Monet's property,

* The most interesting verbal evidence that questions of inclusion and exclusion—and questions of overall *attitude* toward landscape—were consciously raised at the time by painters of the group comes from Georges Rivière, the friend of Renoir and critical champion of the Impressionists in 1877. In his *Renoir et ses amis* ([Paris, 1921], 182), he discusses Renoir's sunny view of Bougival, Saint-Cloud, and Argenteuil, and adds: "This landscape which so delighted Renoir, other painters saw it in less cheerful colors. They noted only *terrains vagues* strewn with rubbish, scabby grass trodden by inhabitants in rags, miserable hovels and tumbledown cottages, a gray sky punctuated by tall factory chimneys belching thick black smoke. It is exactly the same place, but seen by men of different temperaments and interpreted in both cases with equal sincerity. I am thinking, in writing this, of Raffaëlli, who exhibited with the Impressionists.

"—In his pictures, Renoir said to me one day, looking at a picture by Raffaëlli, everything is poor, even the grass!"

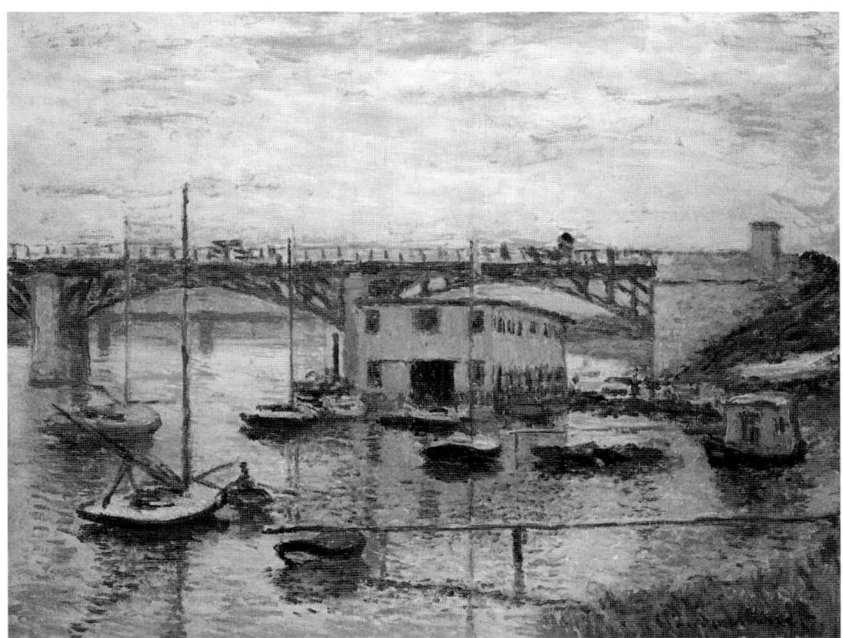

FIGURE 5.19. Claude Monet, *Bridge at Argenteuil on a Gray Day*, c. 1874. National Gallery of Art, Washington, Ailsa Mellon Bruce Collection. Image © 2007 Board of Trustees, National Gallery of Art, Washington.

and he charted them in picture after picture—over 150 by the time he left.

I do not intend to sum up the character of 150 canvases in a page or two, still less to endow them with an overall "attitude" to the landscapes they show. Their attitudes—and the very word had better be used sparingly, with the emphasis on the physical side of the underlying metaphor—are many; and from year to year Monet seems to have sought out quite different things in his surroundings, to have been seized with a sudden enthusiasm for a motif and given it up equally suddenly, made use of snowstorms or floods, painted reedy backwaters because at last he had a boat equipped to get him there, and so on. Yet something can be said about these pictures' specificity as landscapes: we can point to the ways they diverge from the genre's normal range of motifs. I believe that the paintings provide evidence that Monet was thoroughly alive, at least in his first three years at Argenteuil, to the kind of problem I outlined previously. In picture after picture—some of them frankly experimental and botched—he seems to be testing ways to extend landscape painting's range of reference and still have it serve his fierce, necessarily narrow conception of what painting was and ought to be.

About one of the new items in the landscape he never appears to have had much doubt. The boats on the river were there to be painted, even if, as happened on the Gennevilliers shore, they blocked out half the horizon and brought with them an accompaniment of floating offices, boatyards, boathouses, pontoons, and villas all bidding for their few yards of river frontage. The crush did not matter, or it did not seem offensive. The sails and masts were a useful middle ground; they added a touch of geometry, not too insistent, which the painter could edit or soften as he saw fit. Monet himself was part of the boating world; in one or two paintings from 1874 he found room for his own houseboat studio, tied up to a slipway next to the bureau where yachts could be rented (fig. 5.19).[40] The studio was part of the general litter, its outline more ungainly than most of its neighbors.

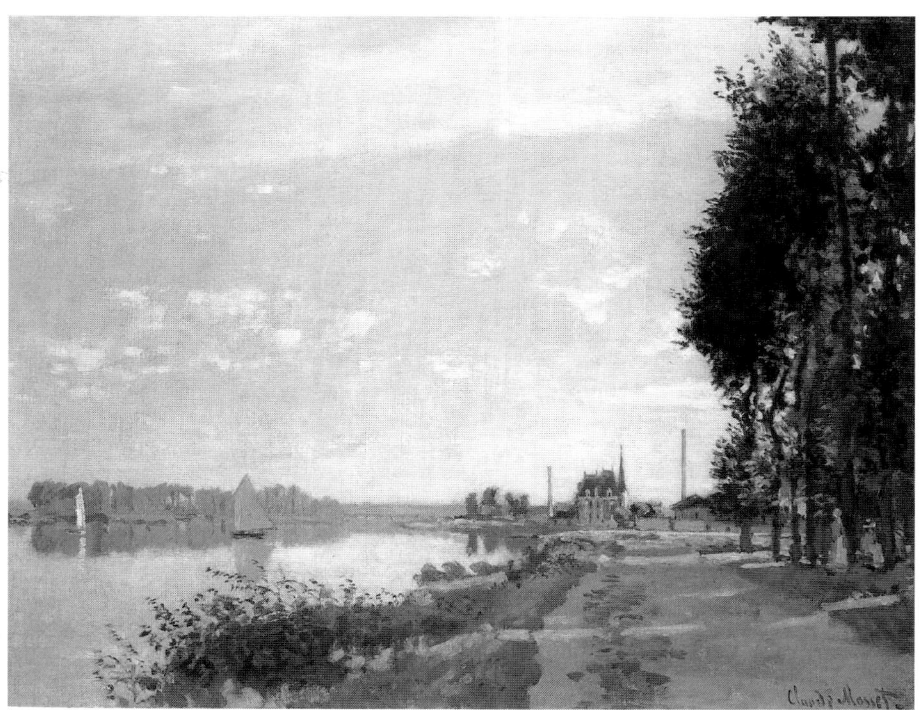

FIGURE 5.20. Claude Monet, *Argenteuil*, c. 1872. National Gallery of Art, Washington, Ailsa Mellon Bruce Collection. Image © 2007 Board of Trustees, National Gallery of Art, Washington.

There was an industry of pleasure taking its place in the landscape, making the river available to people who wished to go as far as Bezons, take a closer look at the false Louis XIII villa—the one with the mansard roof—and be back in time for the train. This industry could certainly be made part of landscape painting; Monet is often at his strongest when he spells out the encroachment of pleasure on the countryside, but insists, in the way he handles it, that the scene has lost none of its unity and charm. Pleasure of this kind is natural, these pictures seem to imply: it gives access to nature, whatever the ironists say. No doubt there was something abrupt and superficial about the boaters' encounter with the Bezons shore, but speed and superficiality were not qualities necessarily to be despised in one's dealings with nature. Did not Monet's own painting, in the 1870s, experiment with ways to make such qualities part of its repertoire (figs. 5.20 and 5.21)? Were not pictures required to be more casual and lighthearted now, less encumbered with grand forms and correct ideas? Did not Monet's painting make believe—the fiction was as crucial as it was peculiar—that its maker proceeded at breakneck speed and could hardly tell a hawk from a handsaw, let alone a chimney from a mast?[41] Perhaps it was true that Argenteuil was a factory, with nature produced as its best commodity; but Monet was seemingly prepared to accept the fact and take his place among the amorous marines.

Argenteuil, we have seen, had factories of the normal kind, more of them each year. The question therefore arose whether this industry would interfere with the other, and to that Monet's answer was less unequivocal. In due course he seems to have decided that it would and did, and that was presumably part of the reason for his moving from Argenteuil in 1878 and setting up house in an unspoiled spot. (Though it is a notorious fact that four trains a day passed along

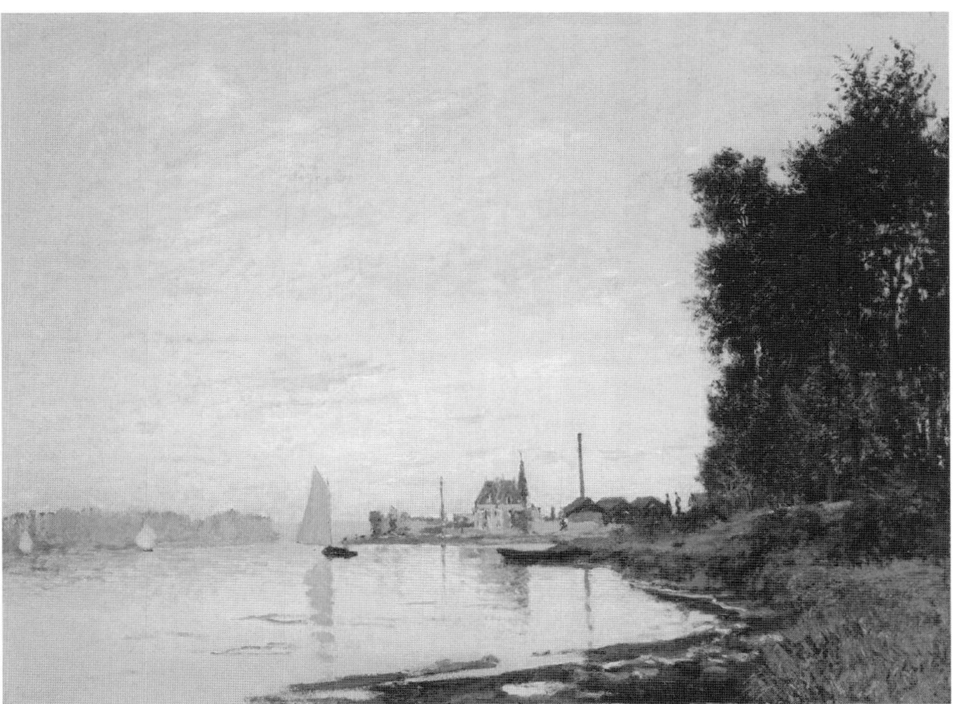

FIGURE 5.21. Claude Monet, *Argenteuil, fin de l'après-midi*, 1872. Private collection. Photo © 2007 Christie's Images, NY.

the railway line that cut off the artist's garden at Giverny from his precious lily ponds.) But again, in the first three years at Argenteuil his painting often seemed to dispute the very terms of the antithesis. What did it take, after all, to *spoil* a landscape? If one looked downriver on the Argenteuil side, did not the factory chimneys chime in with the villas and tree trunks, and was not the saw-toothed outline of the factory taken up in the mansard roofs and sails? Industry could surely be made part of the idyll if the painter tried hard enough; it could be precisely and firmly stated, but nonetheless balanced with landscape's other elements. We have seen Monet do it already in *Le Voilier au Petit Gennevilliers;* and in the four pictures he painted in 1872 on the promenade at Argenteuil he seems to be plotting the various means to put leisure and industry together.[42] Smoke drifts gently into a clouded sky in one; the blue roof of the villa is framed by trees in another, with the right-hand chimney half masked by leaves, and with smoke pouring from it like a pennant; people stroll on the footpath in black and gray, their shapes picked out against the water, played off against the white of the yachts. The chimneys catch the evening sun in another, and the shadows of trees establish distance on the promenade. In the largest picture of the four, the painter goes down to the water's edge and has the chimneys dark against the sky, with a sail put next to them in silhouette, and all three forms throwing long, clear reflections across the water; from this vantage point the whole shape of the factory is visible and plainly stated. Industry is masked or distanced or immobilized; it is part of the general well-being. (These pictures from 1872 take up a format Monet first devised two years earlier, in his great *Pont de Bougival* [fig. 5.22]: they imitate that painting's composition and also its basic tone. The landscape of the later nineteenth century is to be celebrated above all for its orderliness

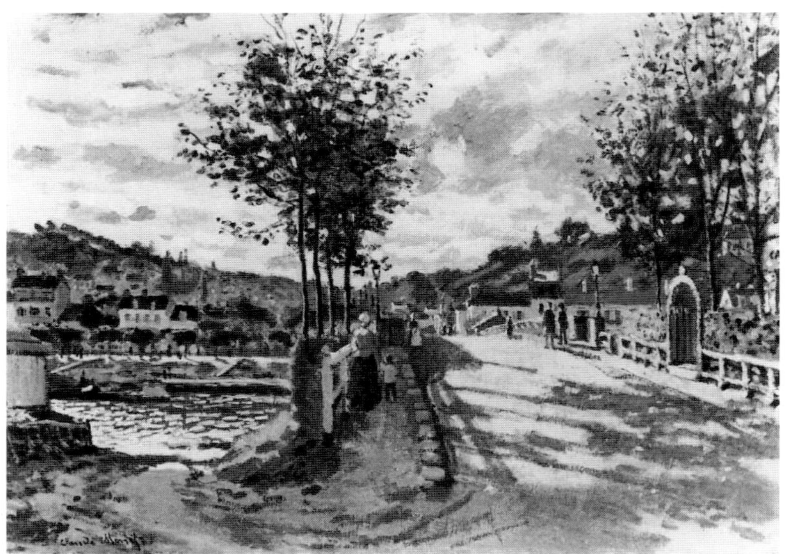

FIGURE 5.22. Claude Monet, *Le Pont de Bougival (The Seine at Bougival)*, 1870. Currier Museum of Art, Manchester, NH; Museum Purchase: Mabel Putney Folsom Fund, 1949.1.

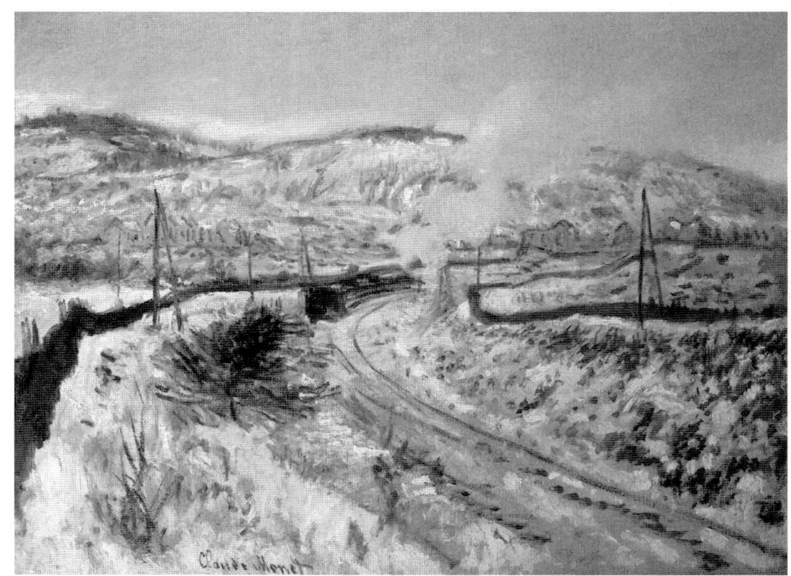

FIGURE 5.23. Claude Monet, *Train in the Snow at Argenteuil*, 1875. Collection of Mr. and Mrs. Stephen A. Schwarzman. Photo courtesy Richard L. Feigen and Co., New York.

and domesticity: it is all decent gas lamps and solid pedestrians, paved streets and convenient *terrasses de restaurant*. There is not a discarded melon in sight.)

There are other pictures of a similar kind from the first three years: chimneys appearing at the end of a path between the vineyards, aligned with Argenteuil's church steeple; chimneys in among reeds or almost lost in mist; smoke pouring from the funnel of a dredger or a barge, making freehand looped reflections in the water; floodwater or snow overtaking the promenade; flowers in the foreground of much the same scene, with the factories just above them in the distance, a vague gray against a pale yellow, smoke from the chimneys scrawled in lightly.[43]

There is a rule to these paintings, and it might be stated roughly as follows: Industry can be recognized

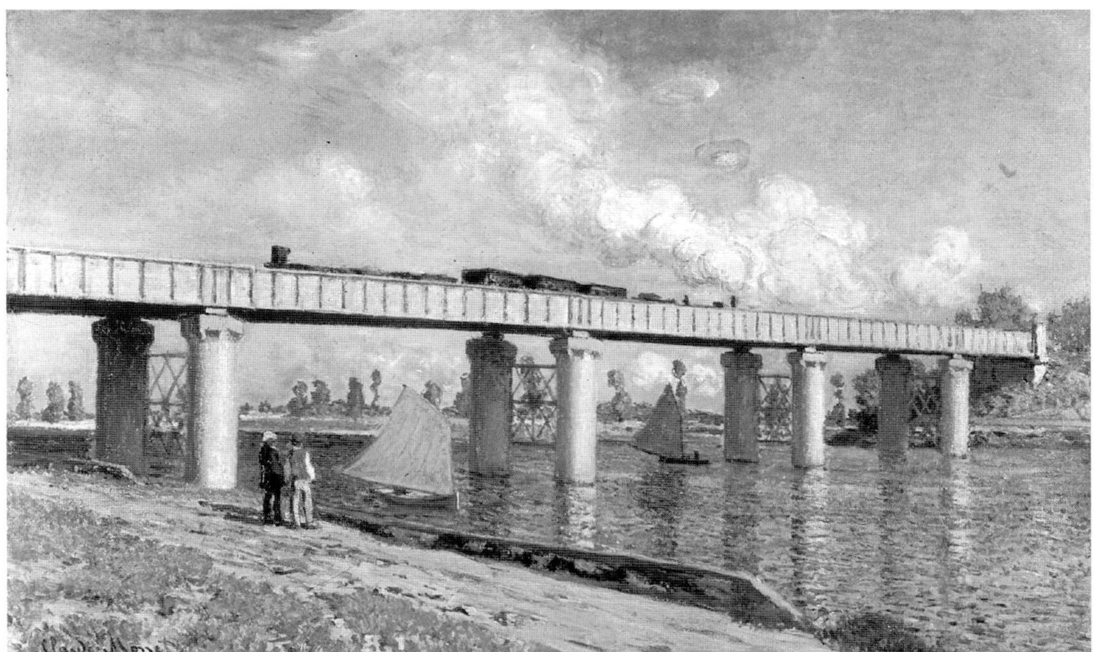

FIGURE 5.24. Claude Monet, *Le Pont du chemin de fer à Argenteuil*, 1873. Private collection. Photo © 2007 Christie's Images, NY.

and represented, but not labor; the factories have to be kept still, as if that were the guarantee of their belonging to the landscape—a strange guarantee in an art which pretended to relish the fugitive and ephemeral above all else. Industry must not mean *work;* as long as that fictitious distinction was in evidence, a painting could include as much of the nineteenth century as it liked. The railway, for instance, was an ideal subject because its artifacts could so easily be imagined as self-propelled or self-sufficient. The train went discreetly through the snow, in a landscape as wild as Monet ever found in the area (fig. 5.23); the station yard was full of machines and empty of people; the railway bridge was a fine, civic, obligatory sight, looking its best for the visitors (fig. 5.24).[44] (Train passing over, smoke becoming cloud; boat passing under, sail just entering the shade. If only modernity were always like this!)

Once, and only once, this general rule was apparently disobeyed. Some time in 1875 Monet painted a picture usually called *Les Déchargeurs de charbon* (fig. 5.25). At first glance it seems a close enough pendant to his other pictures of the bridge at Argenteuil, the ones with yachts and slipways and floating offices. Here instead is a line of barges drawn up by the riverbank, the nearest filled with coal, and a few dim figures inside it filling their baskets with the stuff or balancing the new load on the back of their necks. Out from the barges runs a pattern of planks with more men arranged along them in regular order, walking warily with their baskets full or coming back with the baskets upturned and empty, worn as hats. It seems to be the factual, repetitive rhythm of work that the painter is trying for: the scaffold of wavering lines and the rigid figures taking their small steps. In the indistinct background are more boats, a built-up riverside, and another range of chimneys in full spate.

But this is not a picture of Argenteuil. It is a scene by another bridge entirely, at Asnières, two or three miles down the railway line toward Paris. The rule is therefore followed after all: it seems that labor must always be absent from Argenteuil, and it is as if this

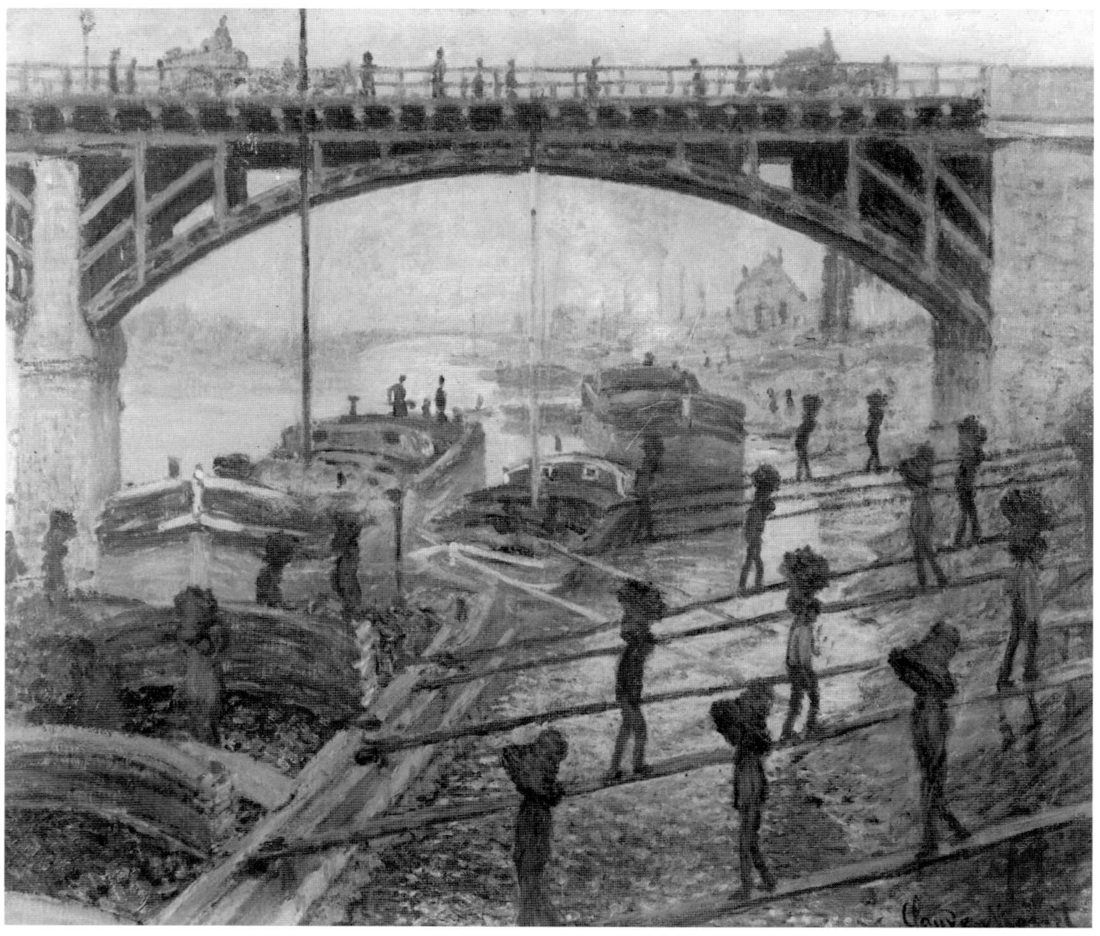

FIGURE 5.25. Claude Monet, *Les Déchargeurs de charbon (Unloading Coal)*, 1875. Private collection. Photo: Bridgeman-Giraudon/Art Resource, NY.

single unlikely picture—Monet himself called it *une note à part*—were done to confirm that fantasy and make it safe.[45] Labor would be imagined once, and the full range of qualities belonging to it be articulated—physical effort, caution, constraint, stiffness, monotony, even gloom. But it would be imagined somewhere else, as part of a landscape all its own. The qualities just listed are the strict opposites of those belonging to Argenteuil (or later to Giverny, and by implication to painting in general). Instead of effort there had to be an easy lucidity; openness, spontaneity, the taking of risks, and a willingness to improvise; above all there was not to be gloom. These were the characteristics of art itself and especially of landscape; they expressed the way that the one category informed the other now, and was its substance if the painter performed well. Such a picture of art necessarily depended on a strict system of exclusions.

It would be wrong to leave the impression, however, that Monet was systematic at Argenteuil. There is no single dominant sequence in the pictures he painted in the 1870s; there are many series, some echoing the others' strategies and some not; and there are single pictures, seemingly left behind from abandoned campaigns, pointing in all kinds of directions. It was true that labor could not be represented: the

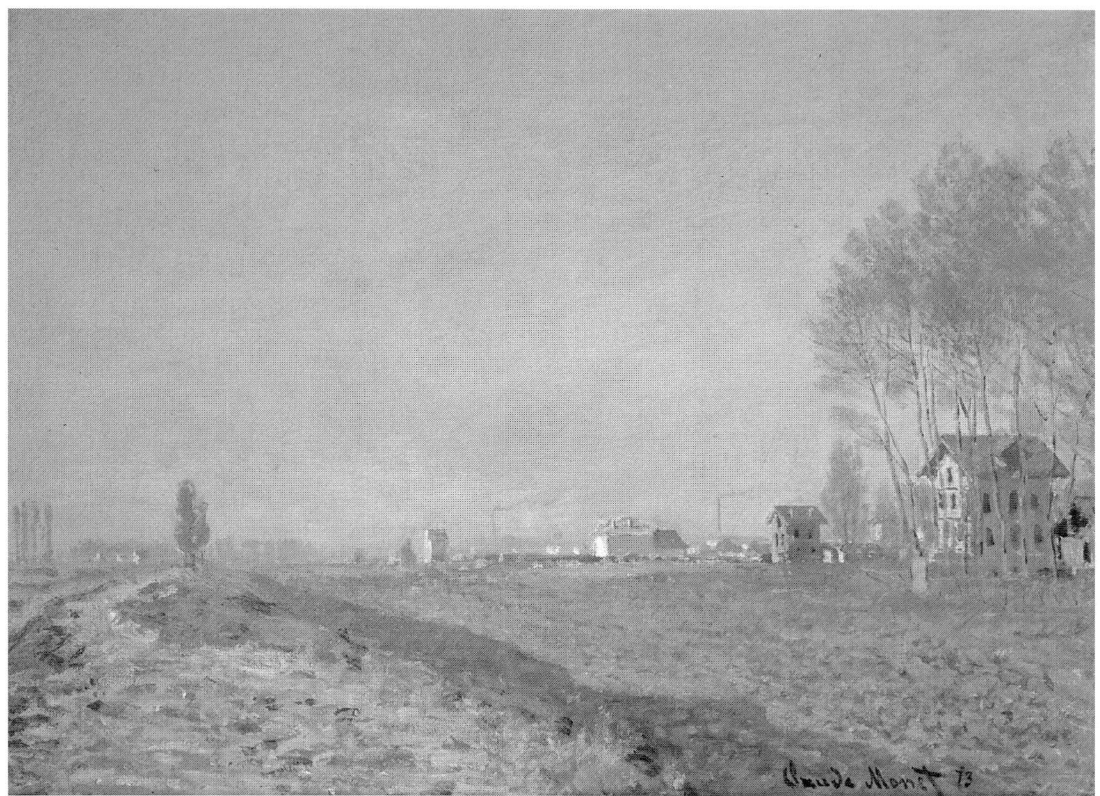

FIGURE 5.26. Claude Monet, *La Plaine de Colombes, gelée blanche*, 1873. The Niigata Prefectural Museum of Modern Art, Japan.

rule applied to agriculture as much as to industry, and the fields at Argenteuil are either empty or occupied by people with parasols.[46] But suburbia occasionally could be. There is a painting from 1873 which apparently represents the hinterland on the Gennevilliers side of the river, not far from where *les canotiers* must have been sitting (fig. 5.26); and it could almost be taken, compositionally speaking, as companion piece to Van Gogh's painting of the Plaine Saint-Denis thirteen years later.[47] The foreground of Monet's picture is the same disheveled waste of half-tilled, half-abandoned land, all frost and inconsequential furrows; and to the right, in the middle ground, are a few suitably rachitic trees concealing a villa, three stories high, complete with a roof of vermilion tiles. Farther back is another house, looking much the same as its neighbor, and then another and another; and so on down the riverbank toward Bezons. Bezons's chimneys are registered, lightly, with a couple of easy, unmistakable strokes; but what the eye is mainly directed to is the *terrain vague* in the foreground and the pungent red and yellow of the villas taking irregular possession of the plain.

This landscape cannot fairly be described as suburban, for there is too much space still remaining between the weekend retreats; but it can hardly be called countryside, in Monet's terms. It is too empty to deserve the name; too ragged and indiscriminate, lacking in incident and demarcation apart from that provided by the houses (which does not amount to much); too formless, too perfunctory and bleak. These negatives add up, it seems to me, to a specific kind of composition, one appropriate to the thing in hand: they are Monet's way of giving form to the

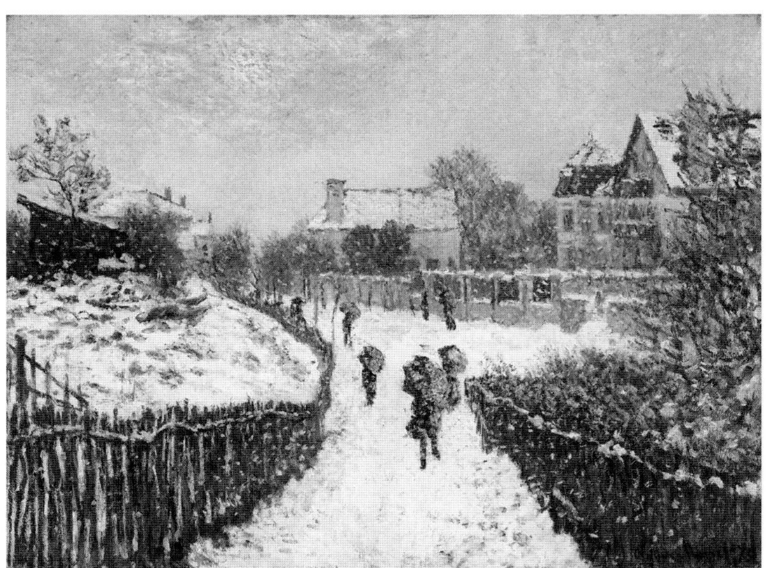

FIGURE 5.27. Claude Monet, *Boulevard Saint-Denis, Argenteuil, in Winter*, 1875. Museum of Fine Arts, Boston; Gift of Richard Saltonstall, 1978.633. Photo © 2007 Museum of Fine Arts, Boston.

elusiveness of Argenteuil's surroundings, their slow dissolution into something else. What had to be registered was the imperceptibility of the change; there had to be a sense of its almost not happening, and the factories and villas perhaps not posing a threat; the earth ought to be shown degenerating gradually in a fine light, and the viewer feel that the process was accidental, almost modest, a bit of a waste but not necessarily more than that. The tone and imagery are reminiscent of Van Gogh, but also of Ajalbert, with both picture and poem describing the landscape in an elliptical, half-cheerful deadpan. (Ajalbert was indebted to Jules Laforgue, and adapted for his purposes the younger poet's flatness of diction, his pretense of losing a train of thought between images, his dying fall, his apologetic dots at the end of a line.[48] Monet's picture secures its meaning through analogous devices: the looming redundancy of the earth in the painting's bottom third, the peculiar elusiveness of its horizon line, the tracks and furrows which lead off so boldly nowhere in particular, the general uncertainty of scale, and lack of relation between its main parts. Is the picture's immediate frosty foreground somehow raised higher than the ground to the right? How far away is the solitary left-hand tree, and where does it stand with respect to the houses? And so on . . .)

And then, finally, there was the inside of Argenteuil. During the years Monet lived there, the town was constantly changing shape, not just at the edges but internally as well. Wide new roads were built and old ones resurfaced, drains were laid, saplings planted à la Haussmann, land given over to *lotissements*, cafés opened, and remaining spaces fenced off in readiness for the developers. The process was most likely unspectacular and must have seemed rather a nuisance; Monet held back from painting the town until the first months of 1875, and what seems to have made the place paintable then—and discouraged him from going farther afield from his house—was a covering of snow. The weather gave Argenteuil the unity it lacked, taking the edges off most things. The signs of construction in *Effet d'hiver à Argenteuil* (National Museum of Western Art, Tokyo)—those haphazard piles of stones in the foreground—are naturalized, as it were, by the fall of snow. The new streets are similarly disguised, their surfaces enlivened by the erratic traces of cartwheels and a pattern of fresh-trod, improvised paths.

There were fifteen paintings done in early 1875,[49]

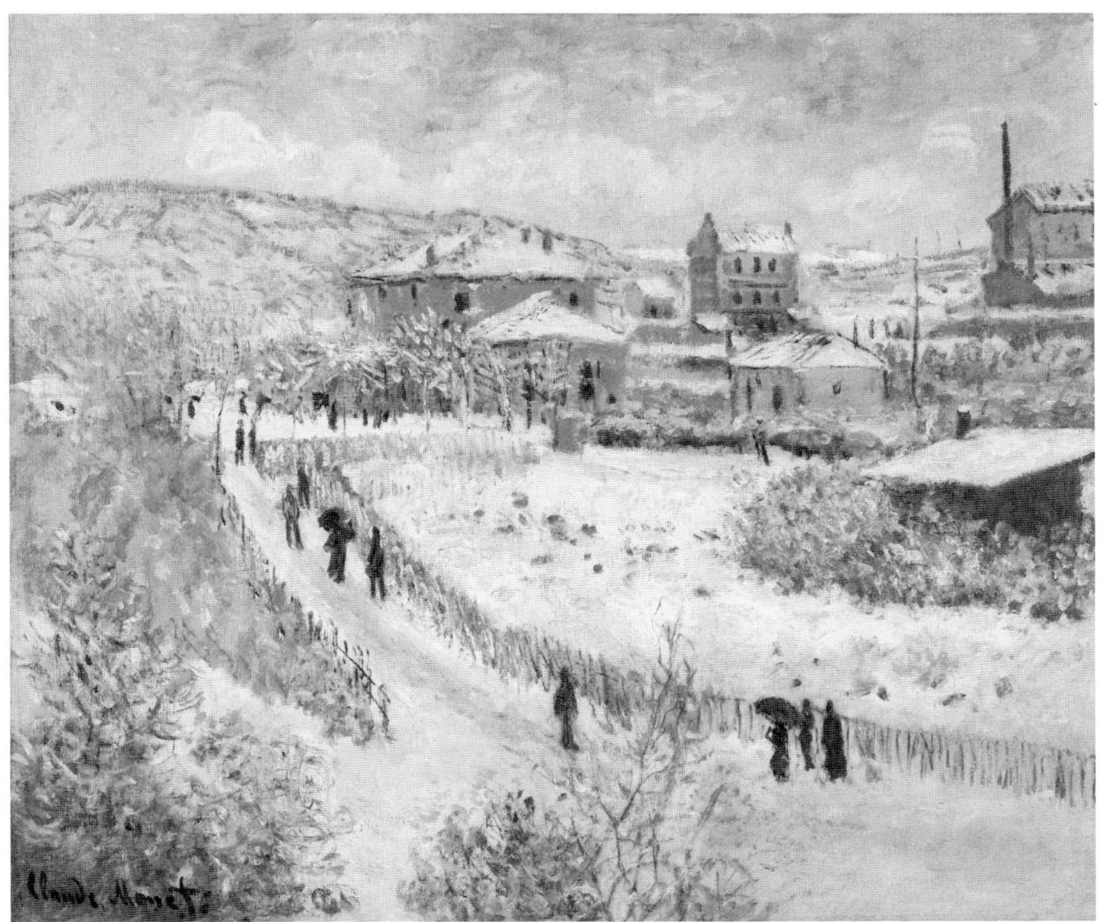

FIGURE 5.28. Claude Monet, *View of Argenteuil—Snow*, 1875. The Nelson-Atkins Museum of Art, Kansas City, Missouri; Gift of the Laura Nelson Kirkwood Residuary Trust, 44-41/3. Photographed by Jamison Miller.

and in spite of the snow the impression they end up giving of the town is of a place essentially lacking form, a territory of tracks, odd corners, abrupt coexistence of new streets and old waste land. Argenteuil was full of spaces where the town gave way to a stream, a marsh, and a few trees, and even its built-up areas often had the look of an overgrown village, all loose ends and lean-tos. The town was proud of its rural appearance and wanted it preserved; but it wished to be modern and have amenities, and it laid out new boulevards leading to the railway station.

There is a pair of pictures by Monet from 1875 which I take to be contrary views of much the same spot, across from Monet's house in the Boulevard Saint-Denis (figs. 5.27 and 5.28).[50] (The house was hard by the railway station—convenient for an afternoon trip to the dealer's.) In one, the painter is looking across the boulevard from a small path which leads to the station yard; an embankment goes up to the railway at the left, with some kind of shed at the top of the slope in an unprepossessing clump of bushes; snow is falling, a watery sun is struggling through the clouds, and people are pushing their way to the station, holding umbrellas. The house in the background to the right, with the steep roof and the two green balconies, is the one where Monet lived. It

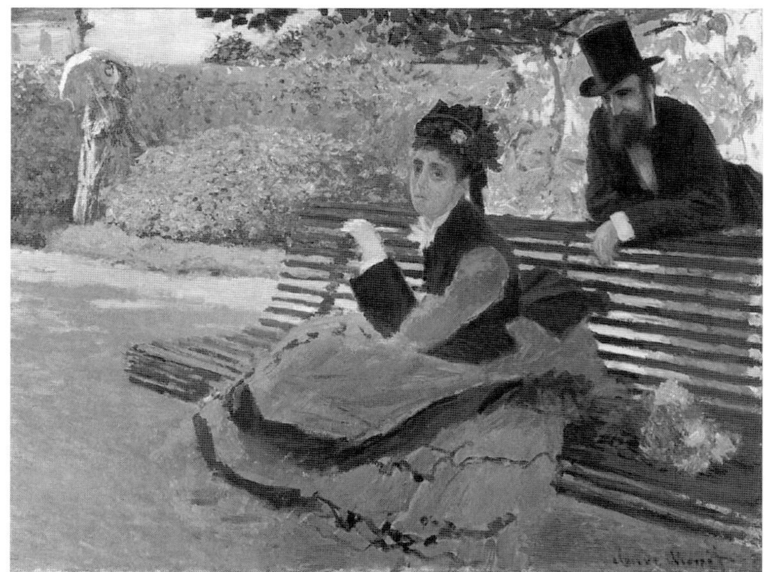

FIGURE 5.29. Claude Monet, *Camille Monet on a Garden Bench*, 1873. The Metropolitan Museum of Art, New York, NY; The Walter H. and Leonore Annenberg Collection, Gift of Walter H. and Leonore Annenberg, 2002, Bequest of Walter H. Annenberg, 2002 (2002.62.1). All rights reserved, The Metropolitan Museum of Art.

was as brand-new as the boulevard; Monet had moved in the previous October. The other painting is of the same scene, essentially, as it must have looked from one of those balconies or through the painter's studio window. It is certainly the view from Monet's new house: the boulevard, the path, the figures with umbrellas are the same, and the wicker fences and the railway shed. Beyond them is a little square in front of the station with regulation plane trees; the station itself, a factory or two, a smokestack, and the Côte de Sannois.

What we see is the artist's immediate world: his street, the way he went to Paris, his glimpse of open country. Is it any wonder that he chose to paint it only once? It stood too well for everything painting was supposed to ignore: the litter of fences and factories, the town seeping like a stain into the surrounding fields, the incoherence of everyday life. A painter in the nineteenth century very often believed he was faced with a choice because of such things, and here it appears with horrible vividness. Outside the window are the suburbs, and people determined to catch their train in spite of the weather. Inside the house is the world of landscape, preserved after all from the ironists' chatter. The house would have a garden, with high hedges and borders and permanent profusion. The painter would make his own landscape there, in a place he could fill with intimate things, hoops, hats, coffee, children, wives, maids. It would be an interior, a fiction, a *hortus conclusus*. There would be people in it, brought on to emphasize its artificiality: his wife, Camille, stiff-jointed on a garden bench, complete with smug proprietor (fig. 5.29); Camille holding the parasol, the maid holding the hoop and small boy; Camille putting up her hair among the dahlias, with the child like a broken toy on the grass; a great dim emptiness circulating round the table always laid for lunch; and, finally, the garden brought into the house—a watery, vegetable, uterine stillness, all polished floors and potted plants, with wife and child looking out of the orifice toward the daylight (fig. 5.30).[51] The painter is sitting on his balcony again, looking the other way.

This last series of pictures points forward to the work Monet did in the 1890s and later. The people gradually fall away, the garden grows larger, the studio is put out on a promontory next to the lily pond and the paintings are filled with weeds, water, flowers, and reflections of clouds. This chapter has tried to suggest

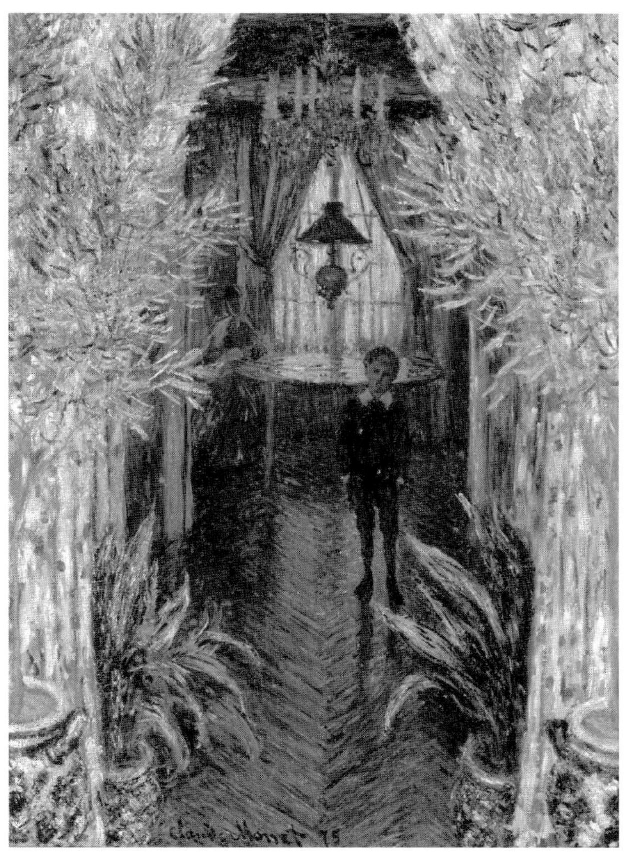

FIGURE 5.30. Claude Monet, *An Apartment Corner*, 1875. Musée d'Orsay, Paris. Photo: Réunion des Musées Nationaux/Art Resource, NY. Photographed by Hervé Lewandowski.

the circumstances of such a choice, and I want to end by listing again the things in the outside world that proved inimical to landscape, and eventually to art.

The countryside was being made part of the city; that was the first notorious claim. Several different things were meant by the formula. There was a sort of nature being built into the city's actual fabric: parks and squares and suchlike, homeopathic doses of air and greenery which were sure to do someone good. Yet no one pretended that this was a substitute for real fields and woods, and, after all, the genuine article could be had any time for the price of a round-trip ticket. It was the age of the "outing." The word itself, said the *Saturday Review* in 1861, "may not be found in Richardson or Webster or, indeed, anywhere within the pale of lexicon orthodoxy, but we are prepared to justify the use of it notwithstanding."[52] Of course they were: the word and the activity were suddenly indispensable.

Perhaps it is, strictly speaking, wrong to talk of the countryside's being *included* in Paris. For literally it was not: it was a kind of foil or frame for the city, and it took a little time to get out to it. There would have been no point to Argenteuil and Bougival if they had ceased altogether to be exotic. Parisians were looking for somewhere to act naturally, to relax and be spontaneous; people took pleasure in Argenteuil; they did what they wanted there, they left the city behind. That was the sense in which the environs belonged to Paris, or at least to its map of urbanity. The city had need of it, and certainly its citizens believed they had. They wanted the difference between town and country spelled out as part of their lives. Cities ought to have an ending, an outside, an elsewhere one could

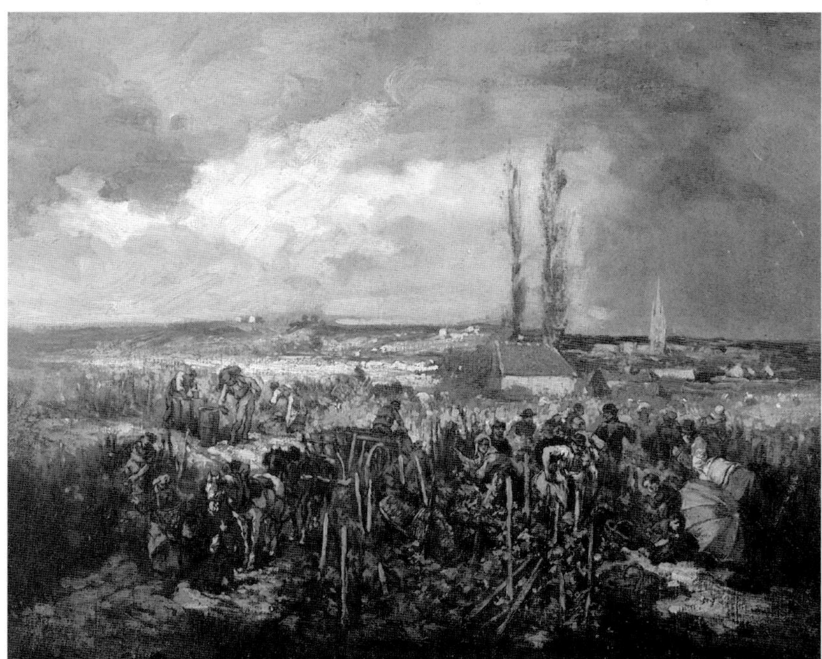

FIGURE 5.31. R. C. L. Debreaux, *Les Vendanges à Argenteuil (The Grape Harvest at Argenteuil)*, 1875. Musée de l'Ile-de-France, Sceaux. Photo: Lauros/Giraudon/The Bridgeman Art Library.

reach, as if in doing so one gave the city back a lost identity. Paris was a set of constraints and formalities, and thus the opposite of nature; from a distance it all seemed clear—what the city had to offer and why one had to get away from it; the exile was momentary and the crowds came home at evening re-created.

My tone has slipped too close to Ajalbert's. Irony at the expense of the new re-creation myth is prone to explode in the user's face, for the truth is that it proved entirely possible to imagine Argenteuil was the countryside. It was all the countryside one needed; nature was made up essentially of *vendanges* and regattas, and art lent support to the felicitous equation. If we put side by side two typical images from the 1870s, Roland Debreaux's *Vendanges à Argenteuil* of 1875 (fig. 5.31) and Paul Renouard's *Régates d'automne* (also at Argenteuil) of 1879 (fig. 5.32), we have the elements of the myth displayed and can appreciate its resilience. Such pictures in their innocence are foils to Impressionist painting; they help one understand why Manet's *Argenteuil* was unpopular, and perhaps why Monet's was not.

In this limited sense Manet may be said to belong to the ironists' camp. His picture is a kind of proof that what they have to say is potentially serious and ought to be included in a representation of the new class. Let me try to strip their case of its facetiousness and state it for the last time. They do not believe that the city has limits any more, and in particular they doubt it ends at Argenteuil and Asnières. The countryside provided there is false (if a true one still exists—and some of them are skeptical—it will be inaccessible to outings). The signs of its falsity are, first, the little Parisians themselves and their irredeemably urban manners and, second, the presence of industry in the landscape. It is especially this last that indicates what is bound to happen next: the factories will come out across the Plaine de Gennevilliers from Clichy, and Argenteuil will have no more *vendanges* and regattas.

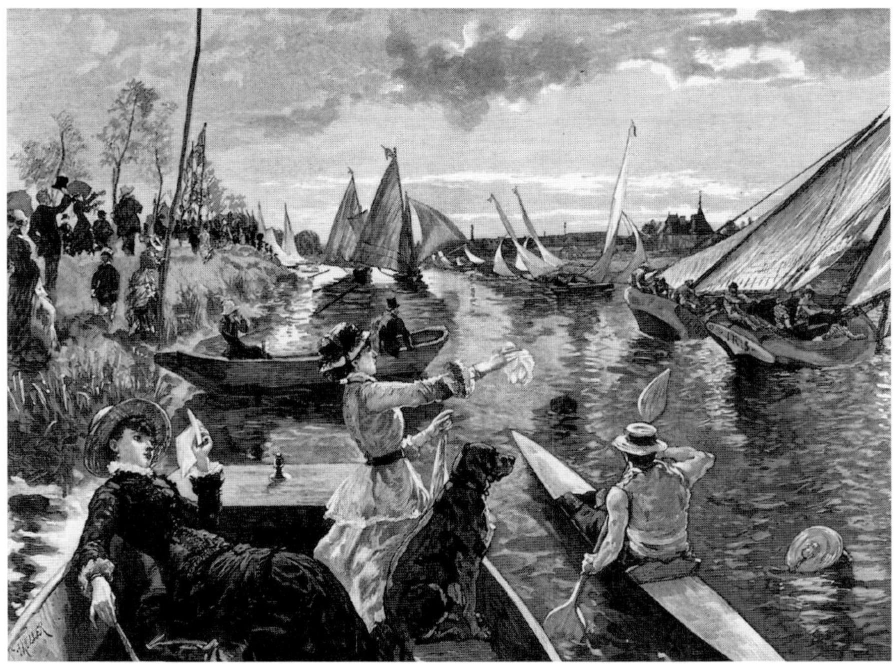

FIGURE 5.32. Paul Renouard, *Les Régates d'automne à Argenteuil.* Wood engraving by M. Moller, 1879. Bibliothèque nationale de France, Paris.

What one objects to in the ironists is not their diagnosis but their tone; and even here one's protest is not moral—not a request to the writers to be serious for once—but, rather, a suspicion that the tone reinstates the distinctions it claims to put in question. At one level the writers seem to be saying that town and country are hopelessly confused, and that this has to do with a blurring at the edges of the bourgeoisie. But the way that they say it enables them to insinuate, on no very good grounds, that somewhere the confusion stops and a real countryside remains, perhaps even a real bourgeoisie. They are constantly making fun of both concepts, and as constantly dependent on them for their comedy.

"Y," you will remember, admitted being bored with nature, but that was because he had actually had it: he had been in his village a full six days and could afford to escape to Paris on the seventh. Paris too belonged to him; he was a bourgeois, not a commercial traveler; he was one of "les riches," in a caricature by Alfred Grévin from 1875, where a peasant wife attempts to moderate her man's *ressentiment de classe.* "The rich!" she says, as the ladies and gentlemen walk past the potato field: "You'd never know it to look at them, but they work as hard as we do, my poor Baptiste—doing nothing, that's their job." They still existed, these fabulous creatures, and were not to be confused with their inferiors.

No doubt this landscape and its inhabitants would be difficult to portray in any other way than ironically, and the caricature is quite good about the reasons why. (It needs only a factory chimney or two—over Baptiste's left shoulder, perhaps—to satisfy the keenest wish for a comprehensive statement on the matter.) And yet serious depictions of it do exist: Manet's *Argenteuil, les canotiers* for one, and Seurat's *Une Baignade à Asnières* (fig. 5.10). Describing the landscape, these pictures suggest, depends on the painter's not avoiding the contact of industry and nature, and trying to show how the one term inflects the other. But

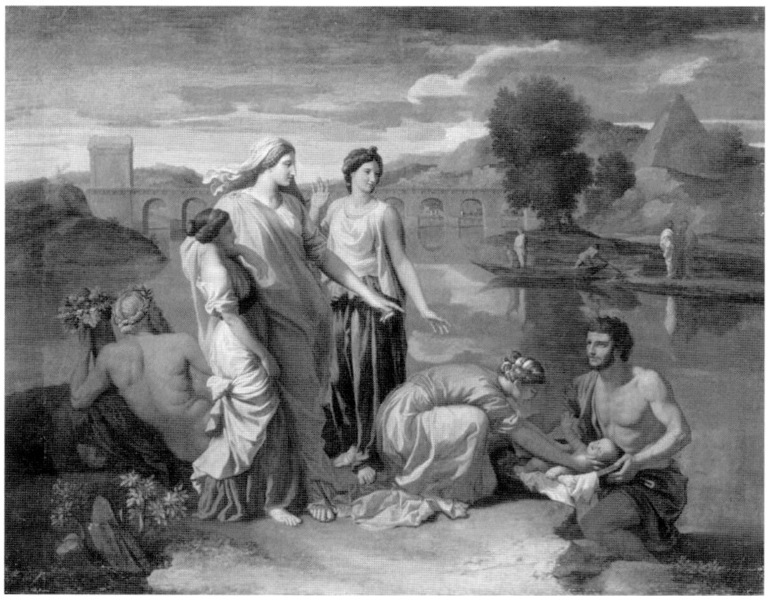

FIGURE 5.33. Nicolas Poussin, *Moïse sauvé des eaux (Moses Rescued from the Waters)*, 1638. Musée du Louvre, Paris. Photo: Réunion des Musées Nationaux/Art Resource, NY. Photographed by Arnaudet.

that in turn depends on describing how people behave in these new circumstances. A painting which did so would not lack comedy: it would inevitably have to do with the absurdities involved in performing idleness or not being used to it; but the painting would preeminently give form—at the risk of appearing a trifle stiff, a trifle wooden—to the dialectic within distraction: the play of ease and unease, restraint and spontaneity, pleasure and ennui, nature and artifice, fashion and recreation. It would try to make these moments articulate, and conceive them as part of the wider business of laying claim to bourgeoisie.

In Seurat's *Baignade*, for example, there are plenty of things to suggest that the idyll is awkward as well as dignified: the sheer unlikely neatness of the bathers' clothes, to start with, the boots and bowlers and concentric straw hats; the dim profile of the central boy (the "lout," as my mother insisted on calling him); the careful outlines of figures and grass; the doll's-house trees, the smokestacks and gasworks, the frantic rower going off frame. We would not need to know the unpleasant facts about the great collector sewer to realize that this was an unfashionable place to swim. The figures appear to be floating freely, self-absorbed and separate, each perfect in its artless way, sharp-edged and individual. They would not be here except for the landscape, by which is meant the factories as well as the river, the sewer as well as the grass. So the landscape has to be painted in a way which agrees with the figures: it has to be awkward and hieratic like them, but also lifelike and composed. The piles of clothes are put against the glittering water, smoke against sunlight, bland against pungent colors, the lout on the bank alongside the ephebe in the water shouting to the other shore.

I believe that Seurat's most important source for *Une Baignade à Asnières* was Poussin's *Moïse sauvé des eaux* (fig. 5.33), in the Louvre. It seems to lie behind some of the picture's details—the flat-bottomed boat on its way across the river, the backdrop of architecture, the tree put in place of the pyramid—and to be echoed in its overall format. Presumably the source was meant to be somehow appropriate as well as queer, as if the painter was arguing that there was order and calm at Asnières, and even the faint possibility a miracle might happen. There might be a Moses in the bulrushes yet, about to lead his people back from exile in the *banlieue!*

This chapter is essentially a study in the emergence of the lower middle class. That phenomenon seems to me one of the main circumstances of modernist art, though the connection between one thing and the other is by no means direct. Modernist art is characterized, indeed, by its desire to take its distance from the petite bourgeoisie and the world of entertainments it ushered in, but artists were paradoxically fascinated by those entertainments and made them the new art's central subject for a considerable time. It has sometimes seemed an intractable problem, this. Not so much that leisure and pleasure were chosen to be painted in the first place—their visual appeal is sufficiently obvious—but that they survived as the new art's favorite theme and underwent such a potent series of transformations: in the work of Seurat and his anarchizing followers; in the art of Toulouse-Lautrec and the Nabis; in Matisse's depictions of *Luxe, calme et volupté* or *Bonheur de vivre*, in the pictures of the other Fauves; within Cubism, even, in the images of *Aficionados* and *The Cardiff Team;* in the long procession of harlequins and picnickers, music halls and *jours de fête*, undressed natives and Englishmen in Moscow.

Historians talk about the rise of leisure in the later nineteenth century, by which they mean mainly its crystallization out from the rhythms and caesuras of work.[53] Something had certainly happened; leisure had become a mass phenomenon, a separately capitalized sector of social life in which great profits were to be had. Recreation took on increasingly spectacular forms: the park, the resort, the day at the river or the races, the café-concert, the football league, the Tour de France, and finally the Olympic Games. These various subcultures of leisure make more sense, I think, if they are put in relation to the history I sketched elsewhere.[54] From at least the start of the 1860s, there was felt to be some kind of threat to the moral economy of bourgeois society—the fine fabric of Parisian neighborhood trades and manufacture, the face-to-face, small-scale, master-and-man society of the metropolis in the earlier part of the century. Haussmannization was resisted as the visible form of that threat; it was held responsible for the dark deeds of the Pereire brothers and the owners of department stores.

The subcultures of leisure and their representations are part of Haussmannization understood in this light, part of a process of spectacular reorganization of the city which was in turn a reworking of the whole field of commodity production. Their role in the process was by no means trivial. It was not just that they were one main form in which everyday life was colonized in the later nineteenth century—given over to experts, addicts, entrepreneurs, consumers—but that there was such active disagreement over who had the right to plant the flag in the new territory. The colonies were claimed by various uneasy fractions of the middle class, by those who wished to reaffirm a status which had previously been made in the world of work but seemed no longer to be available there, and by those who believed they had a right to the same status, even if their conditions of employment still seemed menial in many ways. The world of leisure was thus a great symbolic field in which the battle for bourgeois identity was fought; the essential warring claims were to forms of freedom, accomplishment, naturalness, and individuality which were believed to be the keys to bourgeoisie; actions both rearguard and offensive were mounted; disinformation was much in evidence.

Leisure was a performance, Veblen said, and the thing performed was class; though what is interesting about the acting in the 1870s, say, is its relative incompetence, as in *Argenteuil, les canotiers*.

I think this implication of leisure in class struggle goes some way to explain the series of transformations undergone by the subject in painting from 1860 to 1914. In particular it seems to me to shed light on the painters' changes of mind about how leisure should be depicted: the way, for example, styles of spontaneity are repeatedly displaced by styles of analysis—grandly individualistic modes of handling, that is, abandoned in favor of ones claiming to be anonymous, scientific, and even collective. The classic instance is Neo-Impressionism: I do not believe that its vehemence (or its appeal to Pissarro) can be understood unless it is seen as deriving from an altered view of leisure, and of art as part of that leisure—which in turn derived from a new set of class allegiances. But just as interesting is the speed with which the Fauvist style—which had appeared for a moment to open nature again to the free play of fantasy—collapsed into its Cubist opposite. By the time of Fauvism, one could say, the myth of recreation could be stated only in overtly mythical terms: the dream of freedom and self-consciousness, of crepuscular boating and *Bonheur de vivre*, is adjourned to the golden age.

The reader should be warned, finally, that the notion of the "nouvelles couches sociales" being involved in any great revision of class society—any wholesale change in social structure—is controversial. Gambetta, for one, repudiated it. "I said *nouvelles couches* not *classes*," he said somewhat ruefully in a speech at Auxerre in 1874; "that last is a bad word I never use."[55]

Notes

Originally published in T. J. Clark, *The Painting of Modern Life: Paris in the Art of Manet and His Followers* (New York: Knopf, 1985; rev. ed. Princeton: Princeton University Press, 1999).

The epigraph is cited in Pierre Larousse's *Grand Dictionnaire universel du dix-neuvième siècle*, vol. 3 (Paris, 1865–90), 61 (in the entry "Café").

1. Edmond and Jules de Goncourt, *Mémoires de la vie littéraire*, vol. 1 (Paris, 1912), 1085 (8 June 1862).
2. "Y," "Un Dimanche d'été," *La Vie parisienne*, 3 July 1875, 375–76:

> "J'étais à la campagne depuis six jours, et je m'engourdissais, las de silence, lorsqu'enfin les cloches des villages annoncèrent le matin du septième jour, du jour de repos et de liesse. Puis bientôt un tressaillement se fit le long des bois et des prés, et l'écho des coteaux apporta un premier calembour.
>
> "—Voilà les Parisiens qui commencent! m'écriai-je avec transport. La nature va quitter son rôle de nymphe mystérieuse et muette, elle va devenir une fille d'auberge à qui des commis-voyageurs font une cour quelque peu brutale.
>
> "D'heure en heure l'invasion se répandit, prenant possession de la campagne comme d'une vaste guinguette, d'un café-concert plus grand que ceux des Champs-Elysées.
>
> "Tous ces gens-là venaient tâter les collines comme des gorges, trouser la forêt jusqu'au genou et chiffonner la rivière.
>
> "La brise se mit à souffler des *blagues* et des lazzis. Les odeurs de friture et de gibelotte s'élevèrent le long des berges et vinrent ramper sur les champs. Des bruits de bouchons qui sautent, de couteaux faisant tinter les verres, des chansons grivoises, ouvrirent le concert qui alla en grandissant jusqu'à la nuit. . . .
>
> "Quand je vis la campagne ainsi livrée à ceux-là seuls qui la comprennent et savent en jouir, et m'étant repu de ce spectacle, j'allai prendre le chemin de fer pour revenir à Paris." (Cited in part in Paul Tucker, *Monet and Argenteuil* [New Haven, 1982], 118.)

3. Robert Caze, *La Foire aux peintres: Extrait de Lutèce* (Paris, 1885), 15: "Oh! la pauvre petite Parisienne étonnante et étonnée au milieu de cette nature en toc de Sèvres ou de Ville d'Avray. Il faut être reconnaissant à M. Blanche d'avoir si bien vu les odieux gazons de villas hors murs, ces gazons que les paquebots de Douvres et de Southampton apportent d'Angleterre et qui doivent nous arriver tous les matins avec le train de marée. Dans le paysage où essaie de s'ébattre le souffreteux modèle du peintre, je devine une très prochaine boule en verre étamée, un petit jet d'eau qui pisse une chanson monotone dans une vasque où baignent trois poissons rouges et un bourgeois—le propriétaire!—rapportant, *à la campagne*, après la fermeture de la Bourse, des fleurs achetées sur l'asphalte du marché de la Madeleine. Et c'est excellent de nous donner ainsi la sensation ou plutôt la senteur d'Asnières et de Bois-Colombes sans nous obliger à prendre le tramway. Si j'avais des économies, j'acheterais les *Pivoines* de M. Blanche, pour me dispenser d'aller aux champs où poussent les canotiers, où court le spirituel public des dimanches, aux champs où il y a des pianos, des cords de chasse, des cheminées d'usines et des parfums de poudrette."
4. Cited in Manè, *Le Paris viveur* (Paris, 1862), 247; it is the climax of a facetious discussion of the high-priced *courtisane*'s need for several houses in which to carry on her several affairs: "Which increases the number of

these villas in miniature. . . . And thanks to all this, the trains to the *banlieue* are flourishing, particularly on the Western line, whose station is located in such a convenient spot, in the heart of the Chaussée-d'Antin" [i.e., next door to the rue de Bréda]. It was a stock maneuver of this kind of writing to picture the environs of Paris as overrun with prostitutes. Asnières was especially notorious, and the flavor of its reputation is well conveyed by a café-concert song from 1866, banned by the censor, entitled "Les Régates d'Asnières": "Je suis Cora, la canotière. . . . / Toujours Reine de la Régate, / Je trône encor', près de Vénus, / Et tour à tour l'gandin me flatte / Et l'Anglais m'offre des Ecus. . . . / Je suis canotière, ah! Oui Da! / Et tout aussi bien qu'la grand' Biche / J'me pay' du luxe et du fla-fla!" The cheerful consciousness of class conflict *within* prostitution here (the *canotière*'s *chic* is described as offending "Plus d'un p'tit Dam' du demi-ton") is interesting with reference to *Olympia*—as is the censor's sensitivity on the subject. (The song is preserved in the Archives Nationales, F18. 1860.)

5. "La Petite Marquise," "Salon de 1877," *Le Monde thermal*, 24 May 1877, on Jourdain's painting *Bougival:* "C'est bien là le ciel pâle des environs de Paris, ce ciel maladif, qui rappelle le teint des Parisiennes."
6. Victorien Sardou, "Louveciennes, Marly," in *Paris Guide, par les principaux écrivains et artistes de la France*, vol. 2 (Paris, 1867), 1455: "This is the real village! . . . Chatou is far away; and those little white flurries which the wind stirs up around you on the road, they are not rice powder . . . they are real dust."
7. Victor Fournel, "Etablissements de plaisir," in *Paris dans sa splendeur: Monuments, vues, scènes historiques, descriptions et histoire*, vol. 2 (Paris, 1861), 19: "De Sceaux à Romainville, et d'Auteuil à Meudon, dans ces villages où, chaque dimanche, les bourgeois parisiens s'engouffrent par torrents joyeux, partout où il y a un chétif carré d'herbe avec une demi-douzaine d'arbres rachitiques, le propriétaire se hâte d'établir un café-restaurant ou un bal." Victor Fournel can be relied on for the ultimate of scorn in such matters; an especially vitriolic picture of Asnières follows: "There are plenty of shopkeepers, *commis*, students, small investors, who would consider themselves disgraced if they spent a Sunday in summer without swallowing the dust of this appalling village" and so on. This list of actors will become familiar in the pages that follow.
8. Victor Fournel, *Paris nouveau et Paris future* (Paris, 1865), 91: "Ce qu'il trouve et ce qu'il lui plait, dans ces campagnes étiolées de la banlieue, c'est un demi-Paris, avec des ombres d'arbres qui lui rappellent ceux de ses boulevards, des restaurants qui ressemblent à ceux de la rue Montmartre."
9. Bernadille, "Le Parisien en villégiature," in *Esquisses et croquis parisiens: Petite Chronique du temps présent*, 1st ser. (Paris, 1876), 350: "Des marchands de coco et de plaisir, des jeux de macarons, des tirs, des balançoires, une population bariolée, grouillante et tapageuse, parlant l'argot parisien, émaillée de modistes, de commis en nouveautés, d'étudiants et de *reporters*." "Modistes" is meant to be read with a snigger. Always economical, Fournel ("Bernadille" is one of his pseudonyms) introduces this sentence with a repeat of the one from ten years earlier just quoted.
10. H. Blondeau and H. Monréal, *Les Environs de Paris: Voyages d'agrément en quatre acts et huit tableaux* (Paris, 1877), 26:

> "BARTAVEL—Oui, mon ami . . . à part ça tout a bien été . . . désagréable! . . . et tu me vois complètement désillusionné sur le compte des Environs de Paris! . . .
>
> "JOSEPH—Pourquoi ça? . . .
>
> "B. *se levant*—Pourquoi ça! . . . Parce que je m'en étais fait un tableau qui ne ressemble en rien à celui que j'ai vu. En partant je m'étais dit: Là, j'aurai de l'air, du soleil et de la verdure! . . . Ah! bien oui, de la verdure! Au lieu de bluets et de coquelicots, des prairies immenses toutes recouvertes de vieilles loques et de vieux faux-cols . . . des blanchisseuses partout et pas de bergères . . . des usines en guise de chalets . . . trop de soleil . . . pas d'ombre . . . et pour couronner le tout, des grandes cheminées en briques rouges d'où s'échappe une fumée noire qui empoisonne et qui vous fait tousser! . . . Des cochers qui vous gonaillent, des restaurateurs qui vous écorchent . . . des pressoirs qui vous aplatissent les chapeaux . . . des vignerons qui vous inondent de vin blanc . . . des forêts où l'on perd sa fille . . . des hotels où l'on égare son gendre! . . . Voilà, mon cher Joseph . . . voilà la description fidèle de ce qu'on est convenu d'appeler . . . les Environs de Paris!"

11. "Courrier de Paris," *Le Nain jaune*, 13 May 1877 (the "Courrier" is subtitled "Le Parisien à la campagne . . . Conversation du Parisien en allant à sa villa"): "Avance donc un peu par ici?—Pourquoi faire?—Tu verras la plus jolie vue. . . . N'est-ce pas que c'est charmant? . . . De chez moi on aperçoit une partie de ce panorama. . . . Comment le trouves-tu?—Je n'y vois rien d'extraordinaire . . . à part ces grands tuyaux avec cette fumée noire qui me gâtent le paysage. . . . —Pour moi c'est

une charme de plus. . . . Eh! mon cher, c'est l'industrie qui vient jeter sa note. . . . Mais nous voici arrivés. . . . Prends garde à ce trou. . . . Il ne sèche jamais, même au coeur de l'été."

12. Bernadille, *Esquisses et croquis parisiens,* 2nd ser. (Paris, 1879), 290:

> "Ce jour-là, c'est toute une population nouvelle qui prend possession de Paris, de ses spectacles, de ses cafés, de ses promenades, de ses jardins publics, de ses boulevards, de son Palais-Royal, de ses gares, de sa banlieue. Dans la semaine, vous aviez déjà pu l'apercevoir sans doute, mélangée au public ordinaire, mais en quelque sorte effacée par lui. Maintenant, elle s'étale sans alliage; elle coule à flots par les rues, elle déborde et recouvre Paris. La grande ville lui appartient pour tout le jour.
>
> "D'où sort-elle? Des comptoirs des humbles boutiques, des bureaux d'employés, des administrations, des ministères. Ce n'est pas précisément un public populaire dans toute la force du terme, car le people de l'*Assommoir* célèbre le lundi de préférence au dimanche; c'est un public de petits bourgeois, de petits commerçants, mêlé de vrais ouvriers."

13. Gambetta's first speech on this subject was made at Grenoble in September 1872. Though he was clear in the following year that the new republic rested "on a pact of indissoluble alliance between the proletariat and the bourgeoisie," he did not usually care to analyze where his "nouvelles couches" belonged in that essential class structure. Historical discussion of the same subject is still remarkably sparse and uncertain. There is some good general analysis by Adeline Daumard, "Progrès et prise de conscience des classes moyennes" and "Diversité des milieux supérieurs et dirigeants," in *Histoire économique et sociale de la France*, ed. F. Braudel and E. Labrousse, vol. 3 (Paris, 1976). She stresses the twofold aspect of the *moyenne* and petite bourgeoisie's "prise de conscience" in the 1870s: it was both a confident appropriation of new political and cultural places and a defense against those economic processes—concentration of capital, shifts in the division of labor and the organization of the firm—which profoundly threatened their security and their sense of themselves (see 929 ff.). There are interesting details on the *visibility* of the new *employée* in M.-H. Zylberberg-Hocquard's *Féminisme et syndicalisme en France* (Paris, 1978), 49–50. But here, as elsewhere, the most useful studies seemed to me of the lower-middle class in other countries. See especially G. Crossick, ed., *The Lower Middle Class in Britain 1870–1914* (London, 1977), in particular the essays by Crossick and R. Q. Gray (they both connect with a more obsessive debate within British historiography over the "labor aristocracy"). See also G. Stedman Jones, "Working-Class Culture and Working-Class Politics in London, 1870–1900: Notes on the Remaking of a Working Class," *Journal of Social History* (Summer 1974). For a more general discussion, see A. Mayer, "The Lower Middle Class: A Historical Problem," *Journal of Modern History* (September 1975).
14. Saint-Valry, *Souvenirs et Réflexions politiques,* cited in *Les Débuts de la troisième république*, by J.-M. Mayeur (Paris, 1973), 51.
15. Jean Ajalbert, "Chromolithographie," in *Sur le vif: Vers impressionnistes* (Paris, 1886), 108: "Once-a-week press of people across the suburbs! / Parisians! Looking for flowers between the paving stones! / They imagine they're thousands of miles away . . . / Because it's Sunday and they've had a wash."
16. There is some disagreement over whether the picture I show is the 1875 version. I see no reason that it should not be: the later date that is occasionally given it does not seem right.
17. The story is told in M. Phlipponneau's *La Vie rurale de la banlieue parisienne* (Paris, 1956), 484–92, 501–2. The years 1875–76 were a time of particularly bitter controversy, as the city proposed extending the *champs d'épandage* across to Argenteuil and downstream. In the end, opposition forced the abandonment of the scheme. For the effect on Argenteuil, see Tucker, *Monet and Argenteuil*, 149–53, 176–81.
18. Ajalbert, *Sur le vif*, 130–32: "The sun is weary of lighting this sky, gray / With the opaque smoke from factory chimneys, / Which line the horizon toward Paris. / Toward Argenteuil, land of minuscule windmills, / There are terraces of meager vinepoles, / Condemned, beneath the weight of the eternal twilight, / To furnish the market with acid white grapes. / Harvests have an impossible genesis here, / Peasants are more like sewer workers, / Putting on manure, and pulling obese vegetables / From a soil from which the Moon hides its phases, / And for which the sun has no light. / On the houses, roofs of 'vermilion' tiles . . . / It is the countryside, but without stubble fields or cottages, / Without a single swallow or a cricket."
19. *Correspondance de Berthe Morisot avec sa famille et ses amis*, ed. D. Rouart (Paris, 1950), 111.
20. "Clichy l'égout," *La Bataille*, 14 May 1884: "A l'heure actuelle, près de 120,000 mètres cubes sont accumulés à l'aval du collecteur; plusieurs centaines de mètres car-

rés sont couverts d'une vegetation bizarre, qui répand une odeur repoussante. Par les chaleurs actuelles, la ville de Clichy possède de véritables marais pontins." The issue was given added urgency in the mid-1880s by renewed debate over whether Paris should convert to the *tout-à-l'égout* system. Guidebooks and suchlike disagreed totally over the character of the *grand égout collecteur* at Asnières. Louis Barron, in *Les Environs de Paris* (Paris, 1886), 38, paints quite a sunny picture. Gigault de Labédollière, in *Histoire des environs du nouveau Paris* (Paris, 1861), 138, is already complaining of the effects of "cet exutoire." Most guidebooks were more anxious to warn visitors of the low company they risked keeping at the *bals publics*.

21. Anonymous, *The Art Journal* 38 (1876): 211 (on an exhibition of French painting at the Deschamps gallery): "The expounder of the new faith in the present exhibition is E. Manet, and the banner under which he and his fellow disciples propose marching to glory has inscribed on it the legend 'Impressionists.' 'Les Canotiers' . . . a couple of very ordinary-looking lovers sitting on the gunwale of a boat, with a piece of the most intensely-blue water we ever saw, is all the exposition we have of the school at present; and, consequently, we cannot speak judicially. But if these vulgar figures, this coarse brushwork, and this outrageously-crude colour, be the sort of 'impression' left on Monsieur Manet's mind, we would advise him to eschew impressions in future, and to sit down determinedly before concrete objective fact, and not leave it till he had mastered it."

22. My sampling of the critical reaction in 1875 was far from comprehensive but enough to show how thin and formulaic that reaction was, even in comparison to 1865. The following items contained something on Manet (entries of any substance are marked *):

*Anonymous, "Chronique du Jour," *La République française*, 1 May [strongly in favor of "le groupe dit des Intransigeants," for clearly political reasons]; E. Bergerat, *Le Journal officiel de la république française*, 1 June, 3902; Bertall, "Revue comique du Salon de 1875," *L'Illustration*, 22 May; A. Besnus, *Salon de 1875* (Paris 1875), 42–43; C. Bigot, *La Revue politique et littéraire*, 15 May, 1092; E. Blavet, *Le Gaulois*, 22 June; *J.-A. Castagnary, *Salons (1857–1879)*, vol. 2, 178–80; Cham, "Revue comique du Salon," *L'Univers illustré;* Cham, *Le Monde illustré*, 5 June, p. 357; Cham, *Le Charivari*, 9 May and 6 June [none of these four renditions is interesting]; *Maurice Chaumelin, *Le Bien Public*, 30 May; C. Darcours, *Le Journal illustré*, 9 May and 30 May; C. Desmarets, *Le Sifflet*, 16 May; Ernest Fillonneau, *Le Moniteur des arts*, 14 May ["un homme et une femme à ce qu'on dit; tous les deux aussi sales l'un que l'autre"]; Francion, *L'Illustration*, 29 May; "Une Inconnue," *L'Univers Illustré*, 3 July, p. 423; L. Leroy, *Le Charivari*, 5 May, etc.; G. Le Vavasseur, *Le Français*, 9 May; *J. de Marthold, *Le Monde thermal*, 27 May [a long general defense by one of the Nouvelle-Athènes circle; has little or nothing to say about *Les Canotiers* itself]; O. Merson, *Le Monde illustré*, 15 May, p. 306; *C. Pelletan, *Le Rappel*, 4th article of *Salon* [whole article in defense; not much to say of *Les Canotiers;* a Left-republican paper associated with Auguste Vacquerie]; Gonzague Privat, *L'Evénement*, 1 May [passing mention; Gonzague Privat had had a picture of his own rejected by the jury that year]; M. Proth, *Voyage au pays des peintres: Salon de 1875*, 11–12; Baron Shop, *Le Petit National*, 3 and 8 May; A. Silvestre, *L'Opinion nationale*, 7th article of "Salon"; P. Véron, *Le Journal amusant*, 8 May. Various other critics, including A. de la Fizelière, F. de Lagenevais, A. Duparc, J. Guillemot (in the radical paper *Le Journal de Paris*) and L. Enault (in *Le Constitutionnel*) ignored Manet altogether.

Chaumelin: "Sous prétexte de représenter la nature et la société telles qu'elles se présentent, les réalistes se dispensent d'équilibrer les tableaux qu'ils en font. Mais, passons. Il y a, du moins, dans cette nature et dans cette société, des aspects plus agréables, des types plus séduisants les uns que les autres. M. Manet s'en va justement choisir les sites les plus plats, les types les plus grossiers. Il nous montre un garçon boucher, aux bras rougeauds, au profil épaté, qui canote sur un fleuve d'indigo, et se retourne, de l'air d'un marsouin amoureux, vers une donzelle horriblement fagotée et horriblement maussade, assise à ses côtés."

23. Shop, 8 May: "Ses *Canotiers d'Argenteuil* sont deux, dont une canotière. Ils se présentent de face, assis sur le même banc, l'air passablement ennuyé autant que permettent d'en juger les empâtements volontaires des figures."

24. Thorstein Veblen, *The Theory of the Leisure Class* (New York, 1979; originally published 1899); see, e.g., 55 ff.

25. Norbert Elias and E. Dunning, "The Quest for Excitement in Leisure," *Society and Leisure: Bulletin of the European Centre for Leisure and Education* 2 (1969): 58–59 (the essay was first called "The Quest for Excitement in Unexciting Societies," which the authors subsequently thought too sardonic). Compare Norbert Elias and E. Dunning, "Leisure in the Sparetime Spectrum," in *Soziologie des Sports: Theoretische und methodische Grundlagen*, ed. R. Albonico and K. Pfister-Binz

(Basel, 1971). The basic concept is developed in Elias's *Über den Prozess der Zivilisation* (Basel, 1939), vol. 1 of which is now available in English as Norbert Elias, *The History of Manners: The Civilizing Process*, vol. 1 (New York, 1978).

26. On Saint-Denis and the arrival of *la grande industrie*, see J.-P. Brunet, "Aux origines de l'industrialisation de la region de Saint-Denis," in *Etudes de la région parisienne*, April, July, October 1969 and January, April 1970; and M. Fauque, *L'Evolution économique de la grande industrie chimique en France* (Paris, 1932), 119–21.
27. It was Robert Herbert who first suggested to me, in 1974, that the double aspect of Argenteuil would bear researching. I did some rather desultory work, and even some lectures on the subject, over the next few years. In the meantime, Herbert has published his own conclusions—R. L. Herbert, "Industry in the Changing Landscape from Daubigny to Monet," in *French Cities in the Nineteenth Century*, ed. J. Merriman (London, 1982)—and a solidly researched study of the whole subject has appeared by Paul Tucker, *Monet and Argenteuil*. The present chapter was drafted before Tucker's book appeared, though he kindly let me see part of his argument in article form. I have tried to avoid merely duplicating his insights, and anyway approach the subject with slightly different questions in mind.
28. The fourth tableau of Blondeau and Monréal's *opéra-bouffe (Les Environs de Paris)* was entitled *Les Vendanges d'Argenteuil* (Paris, 1877); see 14.
29. Anglo-Parisian (Walter Francis Lonnergan), *Paris by Day and Night: A Book for the Exhibition* (London, 1889), 84.
30. See discussion in Phlipponneau, *La Vie rurale*, 97–100, 503–5.
31. Tucker, *Monet and Argenteuil*, 15, gives 8,046 for 1871; J. Murray, ed., *A Handbook for Visitors to Paris; containing a description of the most remarkable objects . . .* (London, 1872 and later editions) gives 11,876 for 1882, which seems to tally with other evidence.
32. See Tucker, *Monet and Argenteuil*, 15–18, 35–42, and passim, for thorough detailing of industrial development and suburban building. Where not otherwise indicated, dates and figures are taken from him.
33. H. Lemoine, *Le Départment de Seine-et-Oise de l'an VII à 1871* (Largentière, Ardèche, 1943), 49.
34. See E. Réthoré, *Argenteuil et son passé*, vol. 3 (Paris, 1974), 243–47.
35. G. Poisson, *Evocation du grand Paris: La Banlieue nord-ouest* (Paris, 1960), 254. The first rubber works was built in 1863.
36. Barron, *Les Environs de Paris*, 72: "Par le chemin d'Argenteuil, on se hâte de fuir le spectacle monotone des carrières exploitées sur le flanc des collines aux larges sections jaunâtres, des plâtrières qui fixent dans la région toute une population d'ouvriers pauvres, des vignes, des interminables carrés de legumes dont la route est bordée." The Joanne guide *Environs de Paris* for 1878 describes the "carrières de plâtre" as employing 6,000 workers (p. 90), though this seems high. But given the itinerant character of this labor force, and of the pleasure seekers, population figures for Argenteuil do not give a good picture of the actual *occupation* of the land.
37. *Le Petit-Journal*, 27 May 1877: "*Argenteuil* (gare Saint-Lazare).—Continuation de la fête. A 2h.$^1/_2$, course de bicycles, organisée par l'Union vélocipédique avec la musique municipale; costume de rigueur—A neuf heures, grande retraite aux flambeaux avec la musique et les sapeurs-pompiers."
38. Louis Blairet, "Autour de Paris," *L'Opinion*, 8 June 1884: "Quand vient le dimanche, c'est une invasion à la gare Saint-Lazare; il n'y a pas une fruitière de la rue Saint-Denis, pas un ébéniste de la rue de Cléry, pas une chocolatière de la rue Vivienne, qui ne s'abatte sur le bord de la Seine, au pied du moulin d'Orgemont ou dans l'auberge des canotiers. Or, comme dit Amédée Achard, où trotte une Parisienne, passé un Parisien. Une femme représente toujours deux personnes. On chante, on crie, on danse, on court, on tombe, on s'égare. Tout commence par des entrecôtes au cresson et tout finit par des courbatures. Les bords de la Seine sont tout pleins de mystères ce jour-là, mystères de la vie intime et champêtre.

    "On mange des salads de homards sur l'herbe, messieurs!"
39. See D. Wildenstein, *Claude Monet: Biographie et catalogue raisonné*, vol. 1 (1840–81) (Paris, 1974), nos. 370 and 337; also nos. 334, 336, 338, 368–69. I notice since writing this that Herbert, "Industry in the Changing Landscape," 269, proposes Wildenstein no. 227 as the picture on the easel. The relation of the tree and rigging to the picture's upper edge is not quite right, but it does look closer than any other. (I have heard this picture's authenticity questioned, incidentally—even the suggestion made that it is a mock-up after the Manet!)
40. See Wildenstein, *Claude Monet*, nos. 316–17, 334–35.
41. See Robert L. Herbert, "Method and Meaning in

Monet," *Art in America* (September 1979), for extensive discussion of how little spontaneity Monet's technique actually had—which still leaves us with the question of what the *illusion* of spontaneity was for.

42. Wildenstein, *Claude Monet*, nos. 221–24.
43. Ibid., nos. 219; 327, 249; 314; 251, 354; 453.
44. Ibid., nos. 360; 242; 279.
45. See Monet's letter to Durand-Ruel, 15 February 1883, discussing a forthcoming exhibition: "If it's not too much trouble, try to see the picture of mine that Monsieur Hayem has, I have a good memory of it and it would strike a different note." In Wildenstein, *Claude Monet*, 447, supporting document 56. Compare Tucker's very similar discussion of this picture, in *Monet and Argenteuil*, 53–56, where the only point I cannot follow is the suggestion of catharsis in the final sentence.
46. See, for instance, Wildenstein, *Claude Monet*, nos. 271, 272, 201, or the distinctively unpicturesque *Moulin d'Orgemont, neige*, no. 254; the celebrated *Coqueliquots à Argenteuil*, no. 274; and nos. 220, 276, 341, 377, 379. The closest one comes to an exception is *La Plaine de Gennevilliers*, no. 437, looking back toward Argenteuil; in the foreground are piles of fresh-cut logs, and in the distance what appears to be a plow team. Compare my discussion of the related *Gelée blanche au Petit Gennevilliers*, no. 256 (here fig. 5.26), 191–93.
47. There is disagreement between Wildenstein and Tucker about the precise motif; Tucker's comparison to the houses in Wildenstein no. 278 is surely right.
48. There is (understandably) very little literature on Ajalbert. The most useful account is R. Bernier, "Un Poète impressionniste: Jean Ajalbert," *La Revue moderne* (Marseille), 20 January 1886.
49. Wildenstein, *Claude Monet*, nos. 348–62 (the most doubtful member of the series is the *Gelée blanche*, no. 361, though it seems thematically connected with the rest).
50. Tucker does not take them as a pair—he does not treat the Kansas City picture—but he and others provide the information which entitles one to do so. See *Monet and Argenteuil*, 42, 47 (on the new house near the station), 50–51 (on the proximity of the Joly ironworks), and 52 (on the Boston picture of the Boulevard Saint-Denis). For further information, and photographs of Monet's house, see R. Walter, "Les Maisons de Claude Monet à Argenteuil," *La Gazette des beaux-arts* (December 1966), and the expanded version of this essay in Wildenstein, *Claude Monet*, 58 ff. There is brief mention of the Kansas City picture in Herbert, "Industry in the Changing Landscape," 155, again on its own.
51. Wildenstein, *Claude Monet*, nos. 281; 280; 282 (cf. the connected series nos. 383–86, 406, 411, 414, 415—the last two the dahlia pictures!); 285; 365. Tucker, *Monet and Argenteuil*, chap. 5, has much fuller discussion, though somewhat different emphases.
52. See Compact Edition of Oxford English Dictionary, 1971, 1:2023, "outing."
53. See, e.g., M. Marrus, ed., *The Emergence of Leisure* (New York, 1974), for a representative selection of articles. E. P. Thompson's "Time, Work-Discipline, and Industrial Capitalism," *Past and Present*, no. 38 (1967), is the fundamental discussion of the changes brought by capitalism into the ordering of the work day and week and the separation of activities—kinds of work and recreation—once bound up with each other. There is a growing literature on the organization of leisure in the new cities or the new edges of old ones; see, e.g., P. Bailey, *Leisure and Class in Victorian England: Rational Recreation and the Contest for Control, 1830–1885* (London, 1978); H. Meller, *Leisure and the Changing City, 1870–1914* (London, 1976); H. McLeod, *Class and Religion in the Late Victorian City* (London, 1974); R. Q. Gray, *The Labour Aristocracy in Victorian Edinburgh* (London, 1974).
54. See chapter 1 of Clark, *Painting of Modern Life*.
55. Léon Gambetta, *Discours et plaidoyers politiques*, vol. 4 (speech at Auxerre, 1 June 1874), 155. "Messieurs, j'ai dit les nouvelles couches, non pas les classes: c'est un mauvais mot que je n'emploie jamais."

PART THREE

The Critical Climate

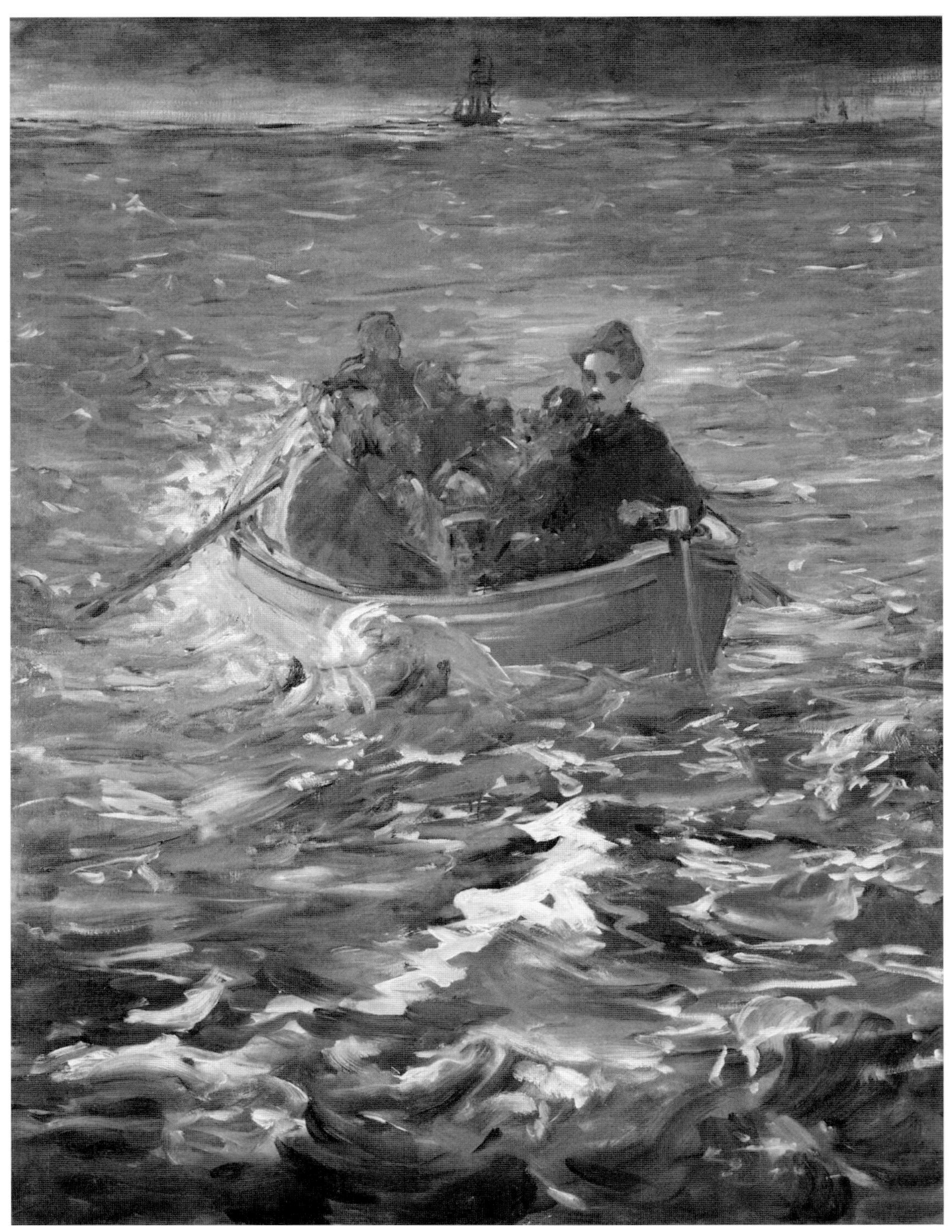

FIGURE 6.1. Edouard Manet, *The Escape of Henri de Rochefort*, 1874. Kunsthaus Zurich. Photo: The Bridgeman Art Library.

6

The Intransigent Artist *or* How the Impressionists Got Their Name

STEPHEN F. EISENMAN

MOST HISTORIES of Impressionism provide an account of how the movement got its name; the formula is as follows.[1] On April 15, 1874, there opened at the Paris studios of the photographer Nadar an exhibition billed as the "*Première exposition*" of the Société anonyme des artistes peintres, sculpteurs, graveurs, etc.[2] Thirty artists participated, including Claude Monet, who submitted a painting entitled *Impression, soleil levant*.[3] Within a week, the terms "impression," "effect of an impression," and "quality of impressions" were employed in press accounts of the exhibition, in particular referring to the paintings of Monet, Renoir, Sisley, Degas, Pissarro, and Cézanne.[4] Louis Leroy was apparently the first to speak of a school of "Impressionists," in his now famous satirical dialogue published in *Le Charivari* on April 25, while it was Jules Castagnary who described "Impressionism" for readers of *Le Siècle* on April 29.[5] The name apparently stuck, and three years later, in February 1877, the Société itself accepted the sobriquet, voting to call its imminent third exhibition the "Exhibition of Impressionists."[6] The organization went on to have five more exhibitions (the last in 1886), and its members would remain in loving art historical memory simply as the Impressionists.

Two aspects of this story of origins concern me. First, the basic accuracy of the account—how common was the term "Impressionism" in the period between April 1874 and February 1877, and why did the Société anonyme adopt a name that apparently had been used in derision? Second, what was at stake in naming the new art? Why did the artists and their critics attach such importance to the matter? My answer to these questions is intended as a contribution both to the history of an art movement narrowly conceived and to the ongoing debate over Modernism itself, of which Impressionism constitutes a signal moment.

The term "Impressionism" derives from "impression," a word of considerable antiquity denoting a physical mark upon a surface or the immediate effect of an experience or perception upon the mind. This latter definition underlay a school of British epistemology, sometimes called "Impressionism," of which David Hume was the spokesman. In his *Essay on Human Understanding* of 1742 he wrote,

By the term impression, I mean all our more lively perceptions, when we hear, or see, or feel, or love or hate, or desire, or will. . . . Impressions are distinguished from ideas, which are the less lively perceptions of which we are conscious, when we reflect on any of those sensations or movements above mentioned.[7]

Hume's description of the sensual immediacy of impressions was echoed by the French physiopsychologists of the mid-nineteenth century, Hippolyte Taine, Théodule Ribot, and Emile Littré, who understood impressions as the middle term between subject and object or the self and non-self.[8] In his great *Dictionnaire* of 1866, Littré explicitly severed any ties between perception and cognition by defining impression as "the more or less pronounced effect which exterior objects make upon the sense organs."[9]

The word "impression" entered the vocabulary of art criticism at about the same time that the French positivists were undertaking their studies of perception. Charles Baudelaire, for example, in 1863 described the "impression produced by things on the spirit of M.G. [Constantin Guys]."[10] Other texts could be cited, but the recent studies of Richard Shiff and Charles Stuckey permit a generalization to be made at once. By 1870 it had become clear that any art based upon impressions, that is, upon unmediated sensory experience, must resemble the colored patchwork that it was believed constituted unreflective vision, what Ruskin had earlier called "the innocence of the eye."[11] In that year Théodore Duret said of Manet,

He brings back from the vision he casts on things an impression truly his own. . . . Everything is summed up, in his eyes, in a variant of coloration; each nuance or distinct color becomes a definite tone, a particular note of the palette.[12]

Duret thus detected two aspects in Manet's Impression(ism): first, its utter individuality, and second, its structure of discrete color "notes" juxtaposed against, but not blended with, their adjacent tone. The dual nature of Impressionism also underlay Castagnary's celebrated usage of 1874, cited above in part. "They are *Impressionists* in the sense that they render not the landscape but the sensation produced by the landscape. . . . [The Impressionists] leave reality and enter into full idealism."[13] By "idealism," as Shiff has shown, Castagnary meant to signify the individualism of the artists, an individualism that corresponded to their technique of laying down a mosaic of colors and forms, which was determined by the impression of the exterior world upon their sense organs.[14]

Impressionism in 1874 thus connoted a vaguely defined *technique* of painting and an *attitude* of individualism shared by an assortment of young and middle-aged artists unofficially led by Manet. Yet if the word "Impressionism" offered only the merest coherence to the exhibition at Nadar's, it had one significant advantage over any other. Serving as a description of unbridled individualism, Impressionism assured politically moderate critics that the new art had both broken with increasingly discredited Salon conventions and remained unsullied by any troubling radical affiliations. "Does it constitute a revolution?" asked Castagnary of Impressionism. "No . . . it is a manner. And manners in art remain the property of the man who invented them."[15] To such supporters of the Third Republic as Castagnary, individualism was deemed an essential instrument for the emancipation of citizens from debilitating ties to former political, economic, or religious dogma. Individualism would be necessary in the massive work of reconstructing France after the disasters of the Franco-Prussian War and Commune.[16] We may conclude that the combination of painterly daring and political discretion suggested by the word "Impressionism" helps account for the surprisingly positive reception given the new art by many critics.

Not all critics, however, were sanguine about the political moderation of the new art. Indeed, "Impressionist" was not the only name given to the artists who exhibited at Nadar's studio in April 1874. The word "Intransigent" also appeared, and continued to gain in popularity until the Impressionists' self-naming in 1877. A critic for *Le Figaro*, writing two weeks after Leroy, described the "brutality of the Intransigents."[17] Jules Claretie commented that "the skill of these Intransigents is nil," while Ernest Chesneau noted that "this school has been baptized in a very curious fashion with the name of the group of Intransigents."[18] Before citing other critical articulations, it is necessary to outline the derivation and meaning of this curious word "Intransigent."

The French word *intransigeant*, like the English "intransigent," is derived from the Spanish neologism *los intransigents*, the designation for the anarchist wing of the Spanish Federalist Party of 1872.[19] The Intransigents were opposed to the compromises offered by the Federalist *Benevolos* (Benevolents), led by Pi y Margal, believing instead that the Spanish constitutional monarchy led by the Savoy Prince Amadeo could best be toppled by mass armed resistance and a general strike.[20] When in fact Amadeo's fragile coalition finally collapsed in February 1873, the Intransigents pressed their claims for Cantonal independence against the newly empowered Benevolent Republicans. The dispute soon would escalate into civil war.

The French government led by President Thiers had in the meanwhile been watching the events in Spain with concern. The perception was widespread that the newly hatched Spanish Republic might degenerate into a radical Commune. Indeed the links between the two were direct, as it had been the Commune that helped inspire the Federalist challenge in Spain.[21] In addition, many Communards had found refuge there (including Karl Marx's son-in-law Paul Lafargue), precipitating the belief in France that Communard agitators were responsible for destabilizing the Spanish executive. In late February 1873 the correspondent for *Le Temps* sought to quash rumors that a contingent of Communards had arrived in Spain. "As for those Communards who would come to Madrid seeking an audience for their new exploits, let them not doubt that they will receive here the welcome they deserve."[22] The ex-Orleanist minister Marquis de Bouillé refused to recognize the new Benevolent Republic, and amid reports that the French might militarily intervene if the Intransigents gained control, the correspondent for *Le Temps* assured his readers that Spain remained stable. An attempted Intransigent coup in July 1873 ignited civil war, but without support of the International, the major Spanish cities, or France (its conservatism strengthened by the May election of Marshal MacMahon), the rebels were routed. The last Intransigent stronghold, Cartagena, submitted to the increasingly conservative Republic in January 1874. By the end of the year the Republic itself had been defeated and the Spanish Bourbons restored to power.

With the destruction of Intransigentism in Spain, the word "Intransigent" entered the political and cultural vocabulary of France. In the March 1875 preface to a catalogue for an auction of Impressionist paintings, Philippe Burty described the landscapes of the new group, "who are here called the Impressionists, elsewhere the Intransigents."[23] By 1876 the name Intransigent had grown considerably in popularity. In his April 3 review of the Second Impressionist Exhibition, Albert Wolff wrote, "These self-proclaimed artists call themselves the Intransigents, the Impressionists. . . . They barricade themselves behind their own inadequacy."[24] At the same time Armand Silvestre spoke of Manet and "the little school of Intransigents among whom he is considered the leader," while the Impressionist painter and patron Gustave Caillebotte composed a last will and testament that stipulated, "I wish that upon my death the necessary sum be taken to organize, in 1878, under the best conditions possible, an exhibition of works by the painters called Intransigents or Impressionists."[25] A more ominous note was sounded in *Le Moniteur universel*. Responding to a favorable review by Emile Blémont in the radical *Le Rappel*, an anonymous critic wrote,

> Let us profit from this circumstance to understand that the "Impressionists" have found a complacent judge in *Le Rappel*. The Intransigents in art holding hands with the Intransigents in politics, nothing could be more natural.[26]

The assertion that the Impressionists had joined hands with the Intransigents in politics was given further support by Louis Enault in *Le Constitutionnel*. In his review of the second "Exposition des Intransigeants," he recalled the origins of the word "Intransigent":

> If our memory is faithful, it is to Spain that we owe this new word whose importation is more recent than *mantilles* and less agreeable than *castagnettes*. It was, I believe, the Republicans from the southern peninsula who for the first time employed this expression whose meaning was not perfectly understood at the beginning. . . . The political Intransigents admit no compromises, make no concession, accept no constitution. . . . The terrain on which they intend to build their edifice must be a blank slate.[27]

The Intransigents of paint, Enault proceeded, similarly wished to begin with a clean slate, unburdened by the lines that the great draftsmen used to mark the contours of figures or by the harmonious colors that offered such "delicacies to the eyes of dilettantes."

A critic for *La Gazette [des étrangers]*, Marius Chaumelin, was more precise about the politics of Intransigent art and the appropriateness of its name:

> At first they were called "the painters of open air," indicating so well their horror of obscurity. They were then given a generous name, "Impressionists," which no doubt brought pleasure to Mlle Berthe Morisot and to the other young lady painters who have embraced these doctrines. But there is a title which describes them much better, that is, the *Intransigents*. . . . They have a hatred for classical traditions and an ambition to reform the laws of drawing and color. They preach the separation of Academy and State. They demand an amnesty for the "school of the daubs *[taches]*," of whom M. Manet was the founder and to whom they are all indebted.[28]

Chaumelin claimed that the principles of the new art—reform of the laws of color and design, "separation of Academy and State," and amnesty for daubers—were derived from the principles of the political Intransigents, that is, the radicals who had gained some thirty seats in the March 1876 elections to the Chamber of Deputies. Among the radical leaders was Georges Clemenceau representing Montmartre, whose campaign platform included reform of electoral laws, separation of church and state, and amnesty for imprisoned or exiled Communards.[29] This latter issue of giving amnesty, highlighted by Chaumelin, was particularly controversial as it implied that the 1871 Commune had been a legitimate political contest between classes and not, as conservatives or moderate Republicans claimed, a criminal insurrection whose brutal suppression was deserved. Chaumelin offered his readers little help, however, in determining just how political turned into artistic Intransigence, preferring like Enault to treat them both as largely nugatory affairs.

Not all the evaluations of the new art as Intransigent came from the political right, however. Indeed, it was no less a critic than Stéphane Mallarmé who described with the greatest clarity as well as the greatest subtlety the link between radical, or Intransigent, art and politics. Mallarmé perceived the new art as an expression of working-class vision and ideology. His essay, long forgotten but now justly celebrated, was published in English in an issue of the *Art Monthly Review* of September 1876. Toward the end of the essay, Mallarmé wrote,

> At a time when the romantic tradition of the first half of the century only lingers among a few surviving masters of that time, the transition from the old imaginative artist and dreamer to the energetic modern worker is found in Impressionism.
>
> The participation of a hitherto ignored people in the political life of France is a social fact that will honor the whole of the close of the nineteenth century. A parallel is found in artistic matters, the way being prepared by an evolution which the public with rare prescience dubbed, from its first appearance, Intransigent, which in political language means radical and democratic.[30]

Mallarmé argued that, as Romantic fantasy and imagination characterized the art of the first half of the century, the new Impressionist art marked a significant new stage in social evolution. The Impressionist artist became the eyes of the "energetic modern worker" and assisted him in his drive for a radical republic. Thus the individualism that some critics perceived in Impressionism may have been valuable to Mallarmé, but a collectivist impulse too was celebrated. He wrote:

> Rarely have three workers [Manet, Sisley, and Pissarro] wrought so much alike and the reason of the similitude is simple enough, for they each endeavor to suppress individuality for the benefit of nature. Nevertheless the visitor would proceed from this first impression . . . to perceiving that each artist has some favorite piece of execution analogous to the subject accepted rather than chosen by him.[31]

Impressionism was a movement with a radical cooperative program, Mallarmé believed, and the currency of the name Intransigent signaled to him the widespread perception of that fact.

Mallarmé offered a set of homologies between Impressionist art and working-class, or radical, vision. As did Enault and Chaumelin, Mallarmé began by noting that Intransigent art or politics stripped away outmoded principles, seeking a blank slate upon which to write a new cultural or political agenda. Yet, unlike these critics, Mallarmé suggested that this radical erasure was itself a positive style, akin to the popular art commonly supposed indigenous to the working classes. The key term in Mallarmé's dialectic was "the theory of the open air," by which academic formulas were jettisoned in favor of a greater truth. He noted that "contours, consumed by the sun and wasted by space, tremble, melt and evaporate into the surrounding atmosphere, which plunders reality from the figures, yet seems to do so in order to preserve their truthful aspect." Mallarmé continued,

> Open air:—that is the beginning and end of the question we are now studying. Aesthetically it is answered by the simple fact that there in open air alone can the flesh tints of a model keep their true qualities, being nearly equally lighted on all sides. On the other hand if one paints in the real or artificial half-light in use in the schools, it is this feature or that feature on which the light strikes and forces into undue relief, affording an easy means for a painter to dispose a face to suit his own fancy and return to bygone styles.[32]

Open-air painting thus provides an objective justification for the discarding of academic traditions or individualist caprice. Yet Mallarmé further claims that the Impressionists' stripping away results in a pictorial clarity and flatness that mimics the look of the simple, popular art forms favored by the rising class of workers and petit bourgeois: "But today the multitude demands to see with its own eyes; and if our latter-day art is less glorious, intense and rich, it is not without the compensation of truth, simplicity and child-like charm."[33] The poet's analysis of Manet's sea pictures illuminates this vaunted simplicity, revealing how the artist's technique of cropping reiterates pictorial flatness. Mallarmé most likely referred to Manet's *Alabama and Kearsarge* (John F. Johnson Collection, Philadelphia), but *The Escape of Henri de Rochefort* (fig. 6.1) serves as well. By placing the boat containing Rochefort and his comrades in the center of a vertical sea, Manet denies the traditional and essential metonymy that prevails between horizontal sea pictures and horizontal seas. Nor has Manet compensated for this elimination of lateral extension by providing a deep space. The even tonal value between fore-, middle-, and background and the numbing repetition of comma-shaped brushstrokes preclude extending the vision along the line of sight. Indeed, the juxtaposition of Rochefort's boat to the tiny ship at the top (no doubt inspired by the relationship between the two vessels in Géricault's *Raft of the Medusa*) merely caricatures the convention that diminution in size indicates flight into pictorial space. Similarly, Mallarmé wrote that "the function of the frame is to isolate [the picture]," thereby excluding from its concerns all that is nonpictorial.[34] One is reminded here of Renoir's remarks to Ambroise Vollard concerning Manet's simplicity:

> He was the first to establish a simple formula, such as we were all trying to find until we could discover a better. . . . Nothing is so distracting as simplicity. . . .

> You can imagine how those [Barbizon "dreamers" and "thinkers"] scorned us, because we were getting paint on our canvases, and because, like the old masters, we were trying to paint in joyous tones and carefully eliminate all "literature" from our pictures.[35]

Both Mallarmé and Renoir assert that the Impressionist followers of Manet remained loyal to the simple or popular character of his art. Indeed, Renoir's own *Etude* [*Torso, Sunlight Effect;* plate 2], reviled by Albert Wolff in 1876 as a "mass of decomposing flesh," perfectly exemplifies the "theory of the open air." The anatomy of the figure is dissolved by the dappled light produced by irregular brushwork, oddly shaped and ordered patches of pink, and shadows composed of the collision between warm and cool tones of yellow, orange, or purple, and green, gray, or blue. The face of Renoir's nude does not permit the imputation of character, or "literature." Eyes are unfocused, lips are unresolved, and the nose is articulated solely by rough daubs of green at the nostrils and bridge. Nevertheless, simple contours are created through the conformity of hair to shoulders and the vertical scumblings bordering the figure. To borrow the language of 1960s Modernism, the torso "stamps itself out" as a simple shape set amid a shallow pictorial space.[36] Indeed, this clarity, simplicity, and formal self-regard are the positive features that Mallarmé perceived in the Impressionist art of erasure. Mallarmé's ideal Impressionist painter proclaims in conclusion, "I have taken from [nature] only that which properly belongs to my art, an original and exact perception which distinguishes for itself the things it perceives with the steadfast gaze of a vision restored to its simplest perfection."[37] Here Mallarmé anticipates the late Modernist credo of medium purity. Clement Greenberg has written that

> Manet's paintings became the first Modernist ones by virtue of the frankness with which they declared the surfaces on which they were painted. The Impressionists, in Manet's wake, abjured underpainting and glazing, to leave the eye under no doubt as to the fact that the colors used were made of real paint that came from pots or tubes. Cézanne sacrificed verisimilitude, or correctness, in order to fit drawing and design more explicitly to the rectangular shape of the canvas.[38]

To both Mallarmé and Greenberg, Impressionism was a method of dispensing with all the artistic conventions fatally compromised by academicism. Mallarmé, however, believed that the Modernist art that resulted would be favored by a working class whose own visual culture it resembled. He could not have foreseen what Greenberg brilliantly described, that is, the growth of mass culture or kitsch. In the decades after 1870, the European and American working classes were provided with an administered culture which did indeed borrow the superficial forms that became characteristic of Modernism but now turned them into shallow receptacles for fashion, entertainment, and economic consumption. Far from becoming an instrument of working-class ideology, Modernism would narrow its audience and its range of expression nearly into extinction.

Faced with the conflicting interpretations of such formidable writers as Castagnary and Mallarmé, the reader must by now be wondering whether the new art, between 1874 and 1877, was in fact Impressionist or Intransigent, that is, affirmative and individualist, or radical and democratic. The answer must be that it was neither and both. The essence of the new art was its insistent indeterminacy, or, put another way, its determined position between those polarities Impressionist/Intransigent. As such, the new art must be understood as a signal instance of Modernist dialectics. On the one hand, works that primarily explore their own physical origins or constituents (Renoir's "simple formula," Mallarmé's "simplest perfection," or Greenberg's "frankness") are Intransigent rebukes to a society that seeks to tailor all culture to its own interests. On the other hand, the apolitical self-regard of Modernist art creates an environment favorable to the eventual industrial appropriation of the works. The "free space" desired by Modernism also is valuable to a culture industry that relies for its vitality upon the public generation of new desires. Yet there have been times when this process of appropriation has been sufficiently slowed that a semblance of autonomy (what Adorno has called "the duty and liberty of [the mind's] own pure objectification") has been achieved.[39] Such was the case between 1874 and 1877 when the new art was definable only by the uncertainties in critical language.

The opposition between Impressionist and Intransigent art is unresolved in the criticism of Claretie, Chesneau, Burty, Wolff, Silvestre, Blémont, Enault, Chaumelin, and Mallarmé. Indeed, even those critics who worked hardest to claim Impressionism for the moderate Republic were strangely compelled to call attention to its Intransigent alter-ego. Thus Emile Blavet wrote in the conservative *Le Gaulois* of March 31, 1876,

> Let us consider the artists who for the second time are calling on the public directly; are they rebels as some are pleased to call them when they are not stupidly called Communards? Certainly not. A few dissidents have simply come together to show to the public the several styles and varieties of their work in finer exhibition conditions than the Salon can offer.[40]

Blavet went still further in his effort to rescue Impressionism from the left, claiming that the new art represented "the fruitful renovation of the French School, the affirmation, in a word, of a principle of art whose results may be considerable." But once again the critic resurrects the radical bogey by suggesting that the new art offered the young Republic a chance to demonstrate its magnanimity, just as Courbet offered a chance to an earlier republic: "When the *Burial at Ornans* appeared it was in fact [the academician] Flandrin who was the first to exclaim: 'What beauty! What grandeur! What truth!' . . . In a Republic there are no pariahs." If the new art, as we have seen, embodied a "theory of the open air," so too did its criticism, often seeming to "tremble, melt and evaporate" into ideological unease, the critics on the left proving no more confident than those on the right. This uncertain art criticism was thus wholly appropriate to the ambiguities of the new art. May we suppose that the artists took *deliberate* steps to cultivate a zone of aesthetic autonomy that could remain free from the political polarizations disfiguring the art of the previous decades? The selection of the group's name in 1874 as the neutral Société anonyme suggests a high degree of premeditation. Renoir later explained,

> The title failed to indicate the tendencies of the exhibitors; but I was the one who objected to using a title with more precise meaning. I was afraid that if it were called the "Somebodies," or "The So-and-Sos," or even "The Thirty-Nine," the critics would immediately start talking of a "new school," when all that we were really after, within the limits of our abilities, was to try to induce painters in general to get in line and follow the Masters, if they did not wish to see painting definitely go by the board. . . . For in the last analysis, everything that was being painted was merely rule of thumb or cheap tinsel—it was considered frightfully daring to take figures from David and dress them up in modern clothes. Therefore it was inevitable that the younger generation should go back to simple things. How could it have been otherwise? It cannot be said too often that to practice an art, you must begin with the ABCs of that art.[41]

Indeed, Renoir's rejection of a name encouraged critical uncertainty over the new art, thereby prolonging the period during which it remained between ideological antinomies. Such a stance was considered by Renoir as part of the tradition of "the Masters," essential if painting was not to "definitely go by the board," that is, be absorbed into the "cheap tinsel" or academicism that predominated in the Salon.

The success of the new art in evading either academicism or political tendentiousness is thus attributable both to the refusal of a proper name and the articulation of a new style; it was apparently Renoir who was responsible for the former and Manet who, despite his refusal to join the Société, set the standard for the latter. If Romanticism had vested artists with the power symbolically to breach the Enlightenment fissure between subject and object or word and thing,

Manet instead chose to expose these scissions through an art that called attention to its status as fiction; the refusal of tonal modeling and perspective, the purposeful cultivation of visual ambiguity, and the disrespectful highlighting of revered art historical sources are all the well-known devices by which Manet refused academic closure. Yet it is equally well known that in rejecting Romantic symbolism, Manet did not adopt what may be called the Jacobin tradition—art as the purposely tendentious iteration of a predetermined political position. On the contrary, as T. J. Clark has shown in his study of Manet's *Argenteuil, les canotiers* [see plate 3 and chapter 5], what we most often find in Manet's work is an avoidance of the explicit signs of politics or class achieved through blankness of human expression and an odd unreadability of gesture, posture, and physical place. Yet Manet has not thereby given in to abstraction, to the willful effacement of the norms of anatomy and composition, but instead offers a different kind of rationality based upon the consonance between the flatness of the canvas, the flatness of those vertical and horizontal stripes of paint that comprise a woman's dress or a man's *chemise*, and a flatness actually perceived in the world—in the peculiar mass-produced costumes and places of urban entertainment or suburban leisure. Clark claims that *Argenteuil, les canotiers*

> is massively finished; it is orderly and flawless, and the word "restrained" applies to it as much as the word "natural": it is not offered to the viewer as something already made and self-evident, there to be looked at and not questioned (this is true of landscape and figures alike). What Manet was painting was the new look of a new form of life—a placid form, a modest form, but one with a claim to pleasure. . . . This woman looks out circumspectly from a place that belongs to people like her. How good it is, in these places, to find a little solitude on Sundays! How good, how modern, how right and proper.[42]

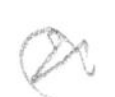

Manet's art, it may generally be said, elided the oppositions that comprised contemporary ideology: work/leisure, city/country, artifice/authenticity, public/private—in short a whole rhetoric of binaries that seemed to assure political and class stability. Manet questioned this stability and did so with a Modernist style that compelled conviction. His painting revealed an undeniable finish, solidity, composure, and simple rationality *that signaled a real knowledge*, a knowledge that could not be overlooked by a people who took so seriously their own reasonableness. Now it seems to me that the Impressionist followers of Manet similarly succeeded in eliding ideological oppositions while still offering something that could approach knowledge. The evidence of that knowledge is in the pictures, for example, in the decomposition of figures and their resurrection as shapes; the evidence of the new painters' success in eliding comforting social oppositions provide the aporias that dominated criticism of the new art, that is, the free space between Impressionist and Intransigent.

What I have described as the evasive posture of the new art began to erode after 1876. The polarization in that year, between radicals such as Clemenceau and so-called Opportunists (who sought a more opportune time for the granting of amnesty) such as Léon Gambetta, made it difficult for artists to find any ideological free space to cultivate for themselves. Merely to seek such a posture was to be Intransigent. Was the Société anonyme attempting to discourage Intransigent interpretations of its art when in early 1877 they decided to designate their upcoming group show an Exhibition of Impressionists? Charles Bigot, writing on April 28, 1877, in *La Revue politique et littéraire* believed so:

> The public baptized them the "Intransigents," and the name did not appear to be repugnant to them: they have undoubtedly discovered, however, that recent political events have rendered this name compromising; they have definitively adopted the name "Impressionists."[43]

Indeed, it was only in 1877 that the Impressionists pushed forward with their plan, originally announced in 1874, of publishing a journal through which their

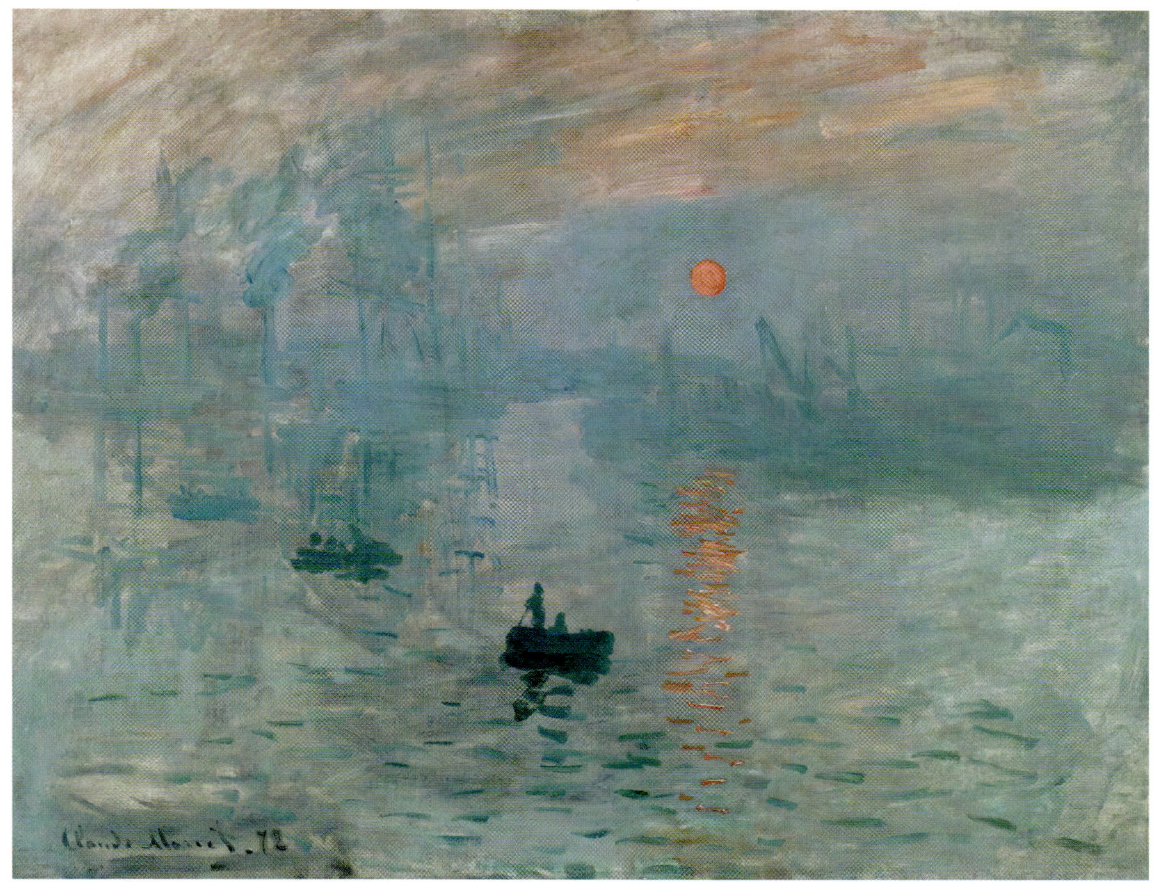

PLATE 1. Claude Monet, *Impression, Sunrise*, 1872. Musée Marmottan–Claude Monet, Paris. Photo: Erich Lessing/Art Resource, NY.

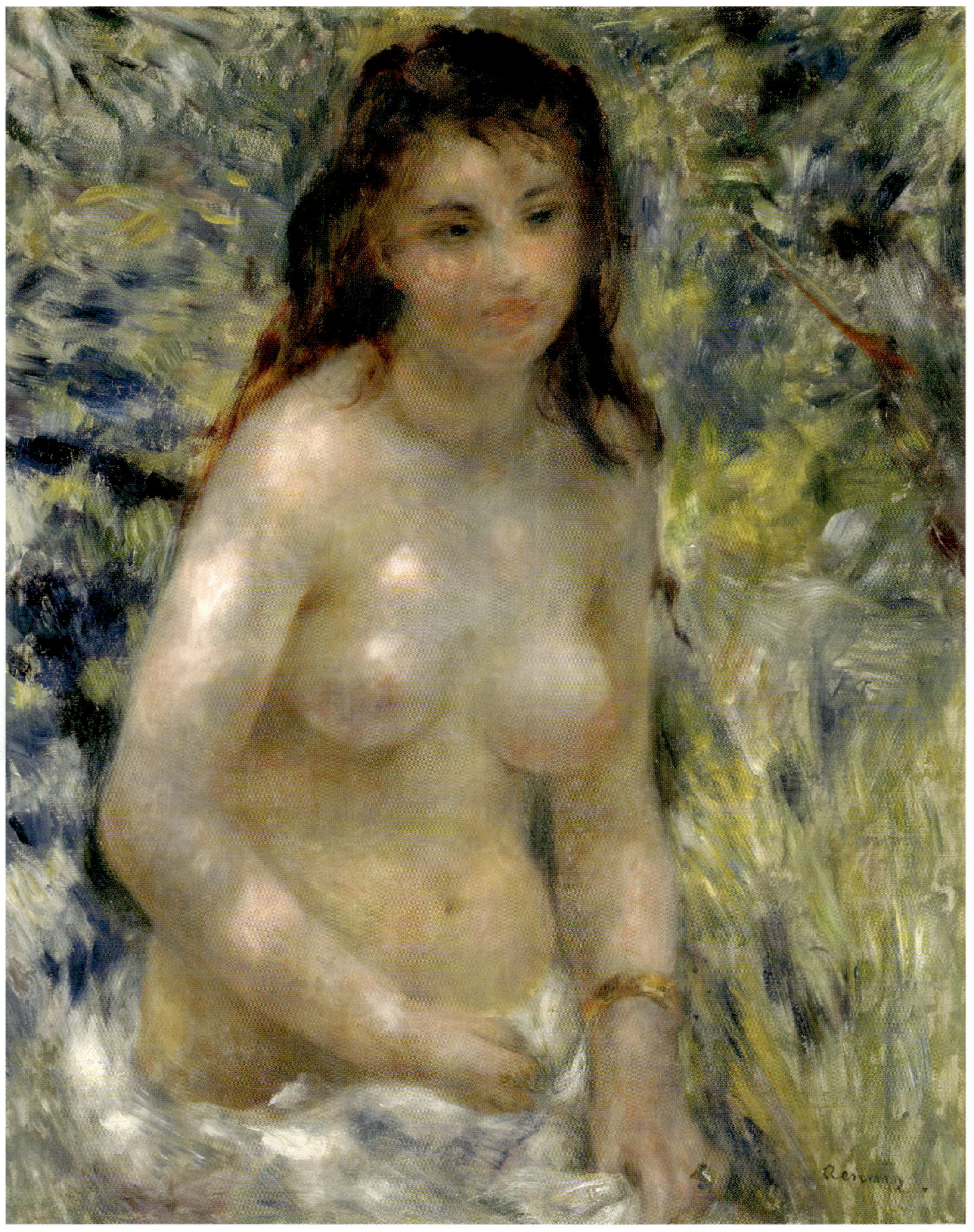

PLATE 2. Pierre-Auguste Renoir, *Torso, Sunlight Effect*, c. 1875–76. Musée d'Orsay, Paris. Photo: Réunion des Musées Nationaux/Art Resource, NY. Photographed by Hervé Lewandowski.

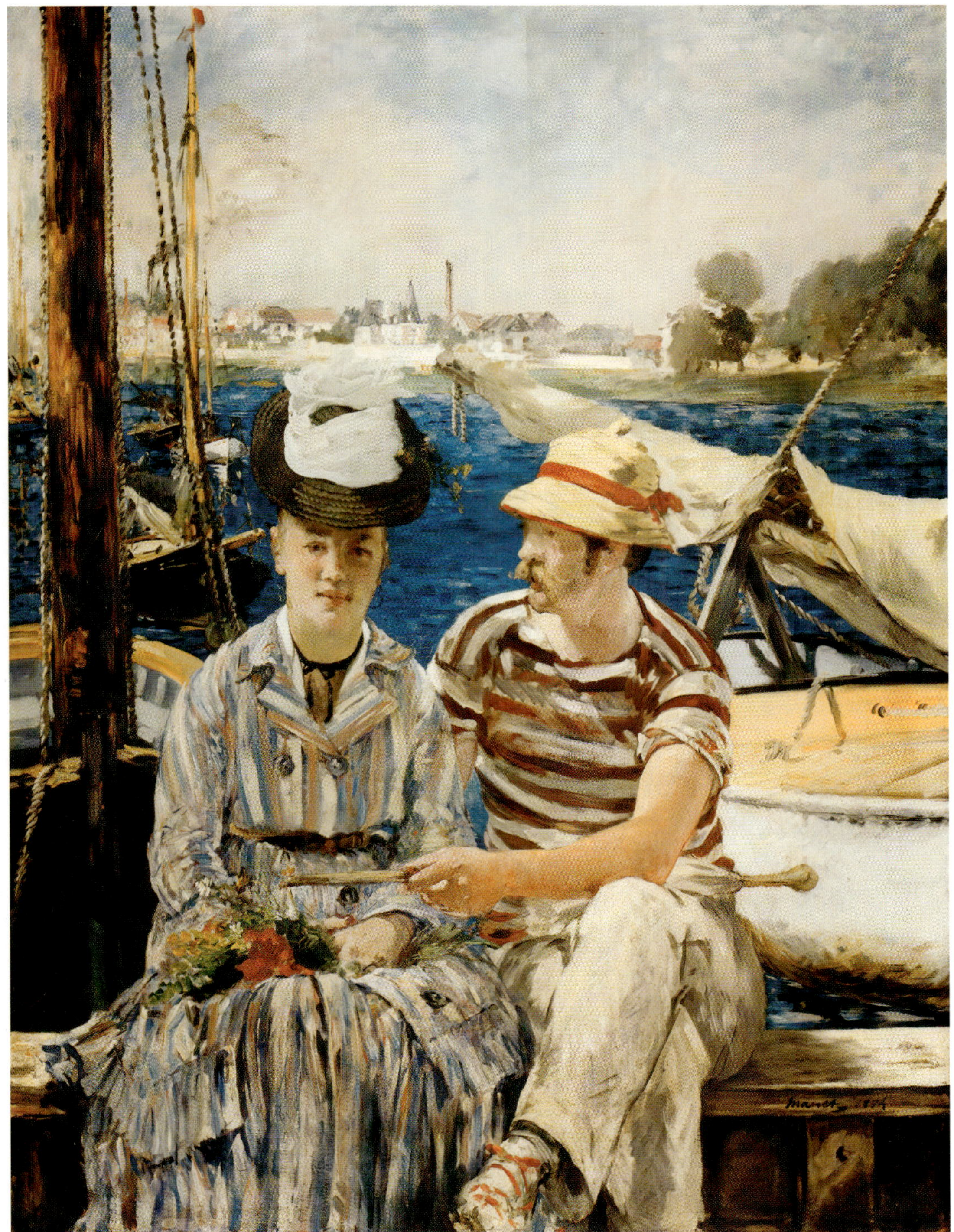

PLATE 3. Edouard Manet, *Argenteuil, les canotiers*, 1874. Musée des Beaux-Arts, Tournai, Belgium. Photo: Scala/Art Resource, NY.

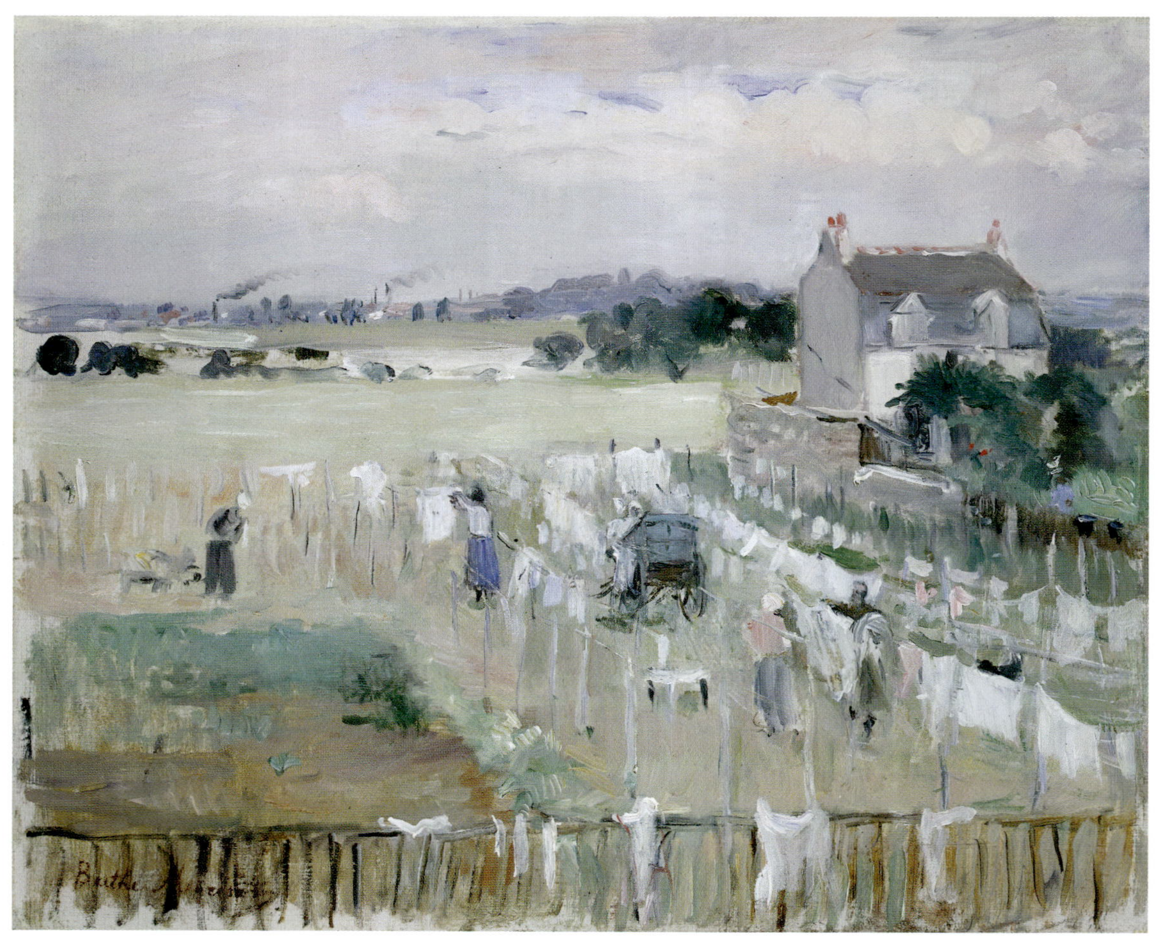

PLATE 4. Berthe Morisot, *Un Percher de blanchisseuses (Hanging Out the Wash)*, 1875. National Gallery of Art, Washington; collection of Mr. and Mrs. Paul Mellon. Image © 2007 Board of Trustees, National Gallery of Art, Washington.

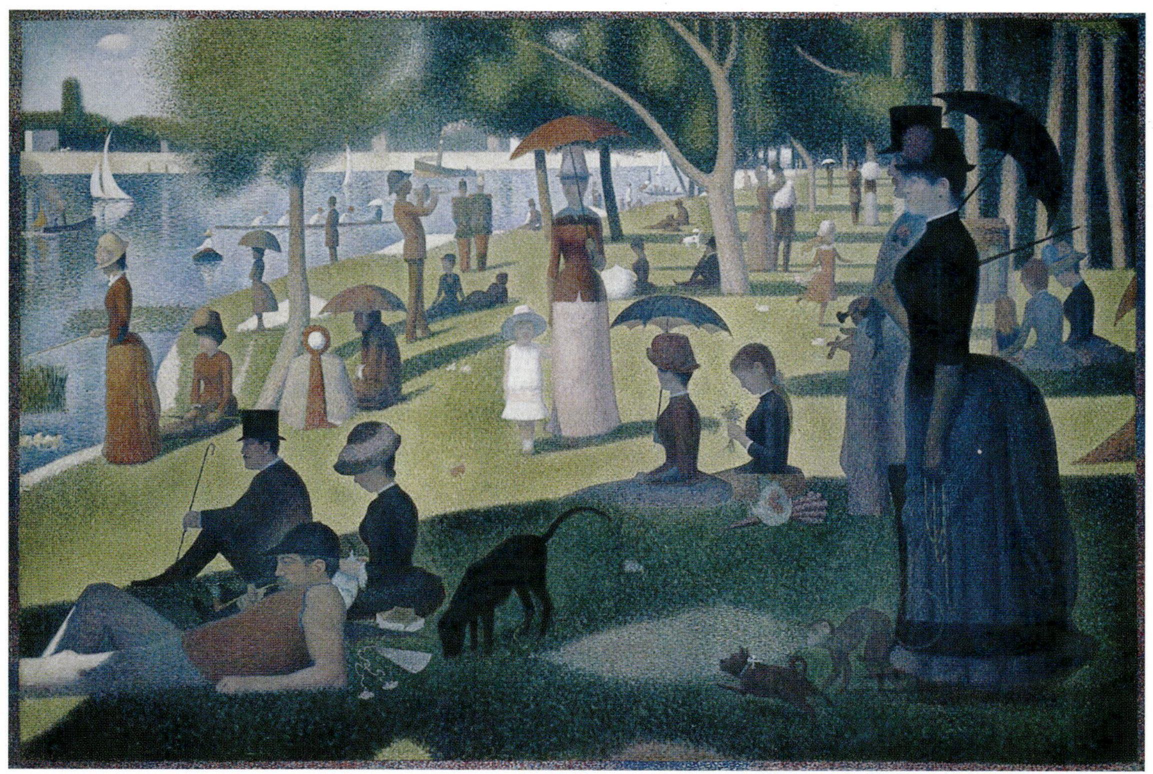

PLATE 5. Georges Seurat, *A Sunday on La Grande Jatte*, 1884–86. The Art Institute of Chicago; Helen Birch Bartlett Memorial Collection, 1926.224. Photo © The Art Institute of Chicago.

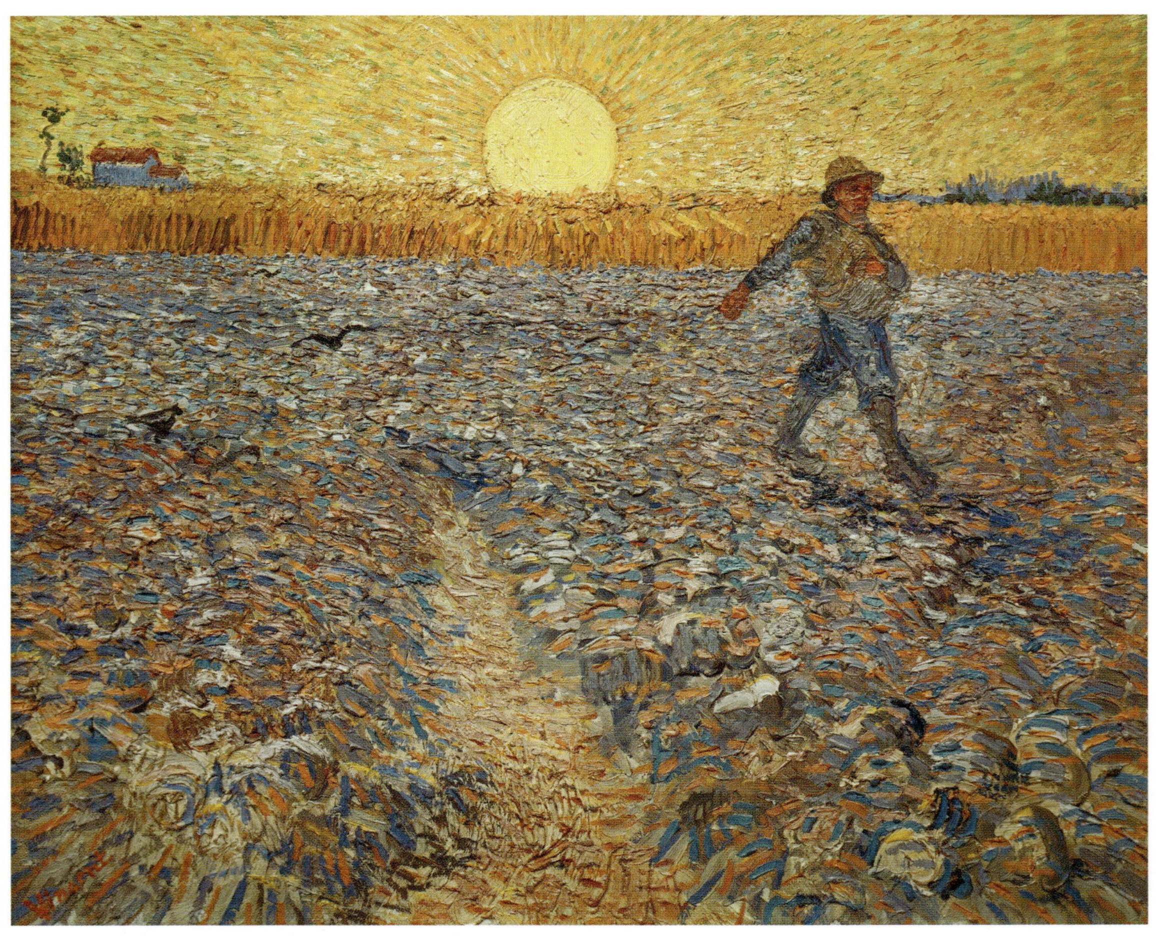

PLATE 6. Vincent van Gogh, *The Sower*, 1888. Rijksmuseum Kroeller-Mueller, Otterlo, The Netherlands. Photo: Erich Lessing/Art Resource, NY.

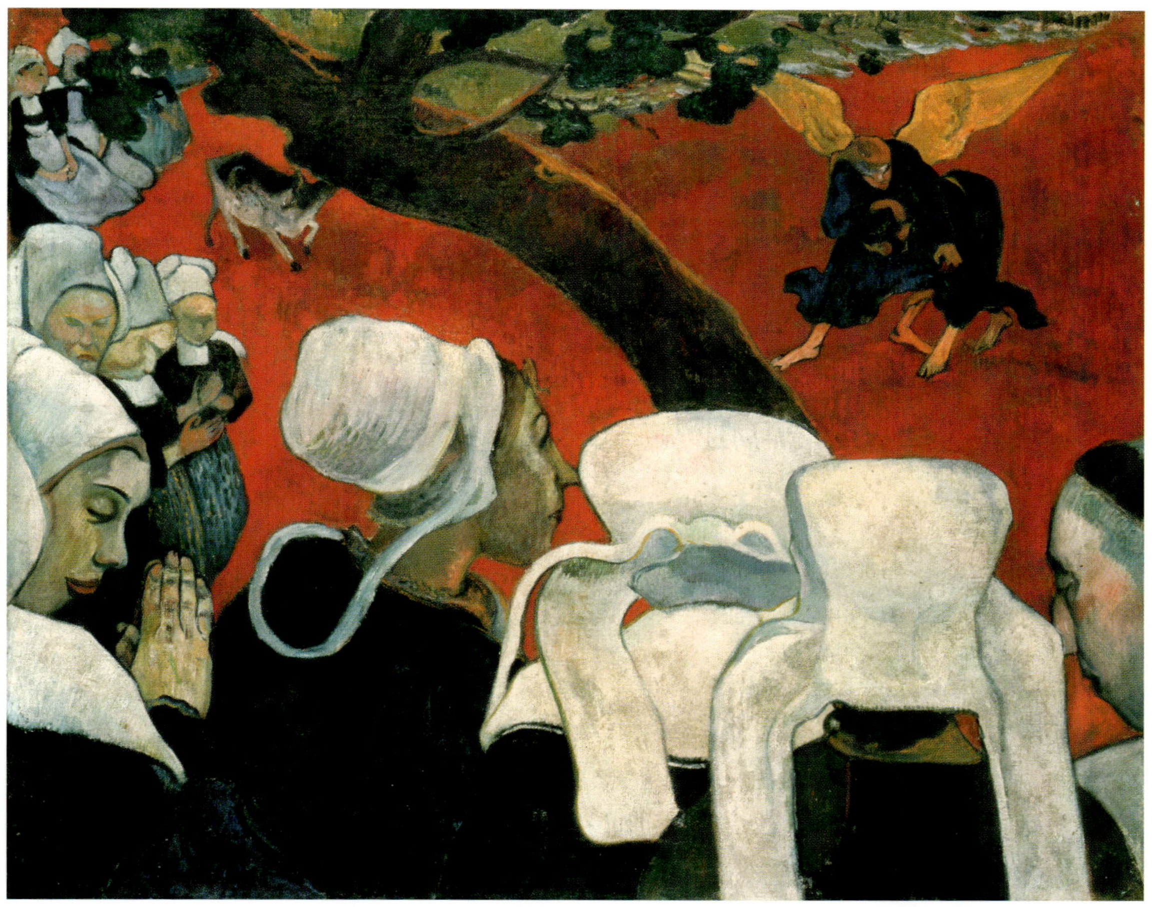

PLATE 7. Paul Gauguin, *The Vision after the Sermon: Jacob Wrestling with the Angel*, 1888. National Gallery of Scotland, Edinburgh. Photo: Art Resource, NY.

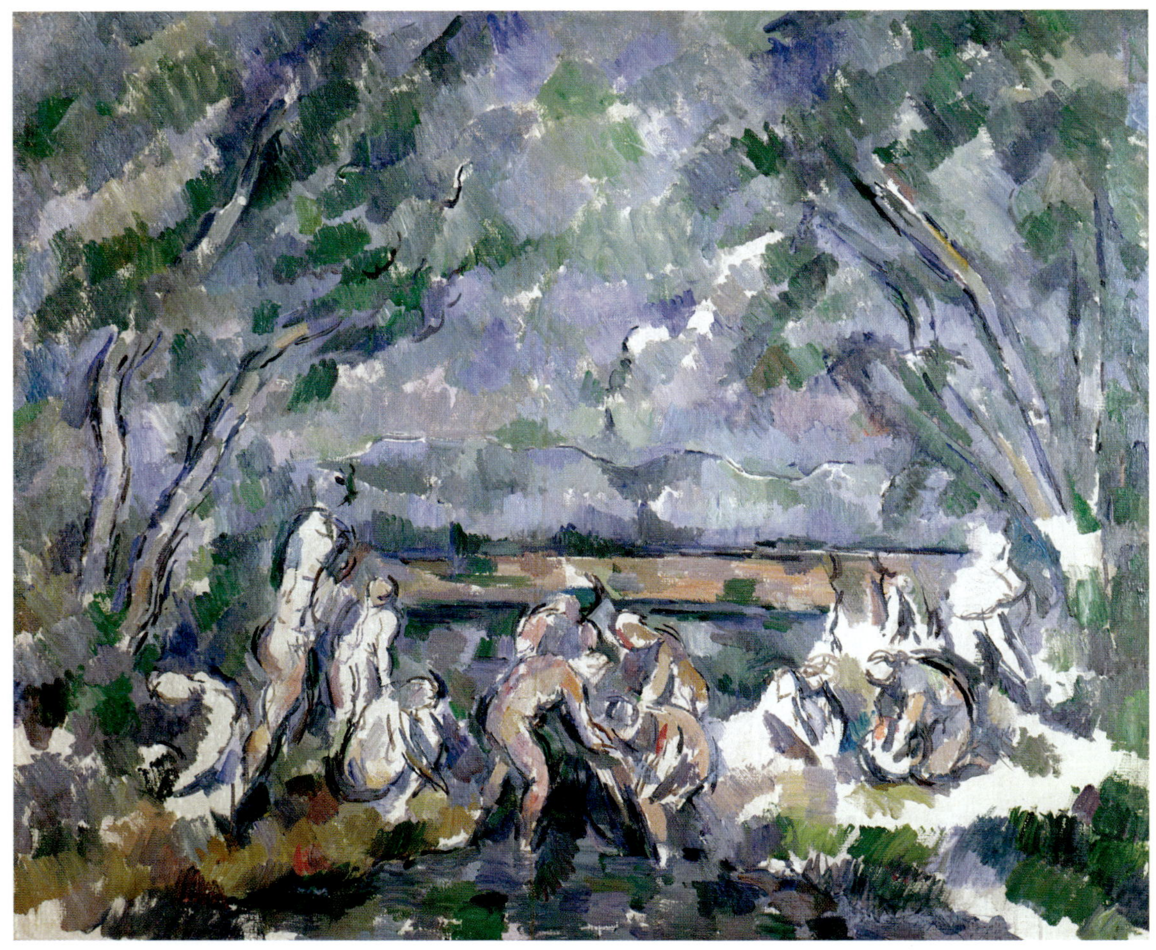

PLATE 8. Paul Cézanne, *Bathers*, 1902–6. Private collection. Photo: Lauros/Giraudon/The Bridgeman Art Library.

art would be publicized and their views articulated. Renoir's friend Georges Rivière was entrusted with the task of writing and editing *L'Impressionniste*. It was the third number of this journal, dated 21 April, that contained the Impressionists' own account of their choice of a name, the account from which all others derive:

> Some journalists . . . have been asking for fifteen days why the artists showing on the rue le Peletier have taken the name Impressionists. It is very simple. They have finally put the word Impressionist over the entrance door to their exhibition in order to avoid being confused with any other group and because the word clearly and forcefully represents them before the public. . . . This name reassures the public because the "Impressionists" are sufficiently well known so that no one will be fooled about the manner of works on display. . . . All these artists, I assure you, are sincere; if what they create is bad, it is not their fault because they could not make it either better or different. "Impressionists" they are, and their works are the result of sensations they have experienced. I can hardly understand it when artists can doubt, even for an instant, the sincerity of the works shown on the rue le Peletier.[44]

Rivière's explanation of the naming of the Impressionists was an effort to protect the group from academic imitators by claiming that their style was the ineluctable result of individual sensations, and at the same time to shield them from charges of political subversion. In the same issue of *L'Impressionniste*, Rivière directed remarks "Aux Femmes":

> But you have a husband. . . . Your husband, who is perhaps a Republican, enters into a rage against those revolutionaries who sow discord in the camp of the artist. . . . He rails against political routine and against administrative routine . . . but he looks at painting through the prejudicial routine of old canvases.[45]

Rivière and Renoir apparently had it in their minds to direct their words and pictures at a very particular Republican audience. In early 1877, Renoir made a pilgrimage to the offices of *La République française*, the Opportunist journal edited by Léon Gambetta, in order to plead for the insertion of a notice favorable to the group. Rivière later recounted how Renoir, unable to find Gambetta in his office, made his request to Challemel-Lacour, cofounder of the journal, who answered by exclaiming, "What! You ask me to speak about some Impressionists in our journal! That's impossible, it would be scandalous! Do you forget, you are revolutionaries?" Renoir was apparently discomfited by this response and left without saying another word. Immediately, however, he ran into Gambetta, who asked him the reason for his visit. Rivière wrote, "When Renoir repeated to him the remarks of Challemel-Lacour, Gambetta laughed and said, 'You, one of the revolutionaries. Ah, well, and us, what then are we?' "[46] Renoir's appeal and Gambetta's mocking response suggest that Renoir had largely succeeded in putting distance between himself and Intransigent politics, and that Gambetta was ready to accept the artist into the camp of Opportunism. Gambetta was no longer a radical and neither then was Renoir. The ground was being prepared for the assimilation of Impressionism into the mainstream of French culture.

The subsequent critical fortunes of Impressionism fall beyond the limits of this essay, but a kind of epilogue is in order. In January 1882 President Gambetta's minister of art, Antonin Proust, awarded Edouard Manet the Legion of Honor. Shortly thereafter, a columnist for the popular *L'Illustration* wondered at the effect the election would have upon the "irreconcilables of the brush" and the "Bellevillois of the canvas." The author continued,

> It is the triumph of the *Nouvelle-Athènes* over the School of Rome. The Intransigents of painting have triumphed. Ah, but not quite! They have knitted their brows, passed their fingers through their beards. Manet decorated is no longer Manet . . . The painter Degas one day remarked, "He is better known than Garibaldi." "Manet," exclaimed a *nouvel athénien* who was not the young Forain, "Oh well, may he rest in peace! He is only an Opportunist with color!"[47]

Here indeed was Gambetta's and Proust's triumph. Manet the Intransigent, Manet the Communard, was now Manet the Opportunist. The award to Manet was followed up by other liberal initiatives, including the acquisition of five paintings from the estate of Courbet, and a plan by Proust to "democratize" the Ecole des Beaux-Arts by eliminating the Rome prize and replacing the "autocratic" heads of the three painting ateliers, Gérôme, Cabanel, and Lehmann, with a rotating group of ten or twelve instructors, among them Manet.[48] The Impressionists had by now adopted the name Independents, perhaps, as Joel Isaacson suggests, to paper over serious personal and political divisions within the group, but also to promote a stance of artistic purity.[49] This combination of political retreat and aestheticist celebration is revealed most clearly in a letter of early 1882 from Renoir to Durand-Ruel concerning plans for a new group exhibition:

> To exhibit with Pissarro, Gauguin and Guillaumin would be the same as exhibiting with a Socialist. What is more, Pissarro would probably invite the Russian Lavroff, or some other revolutionary. The public does not like what it feels is political, and I do not want, at my age, to be a revolutionary. . . . Free yourself from such people and show me artists such as Manet, Sisley, Morisot, etc., and then I will be yours because then there will no longer be politics, only pure art.[50]

What had once been an art whose simultaneous reductiveness and rationality signified the elision of aesthetic traditions, now embraced *l'art pour l'art*. What had once been an art that explored a dynamic free space between conflicting ideologies now sought an apoliticism that was in fact deeply political. The autonomy of 1874 became by 1882 the aestheticism that affirmed an Opportunist status quo. The pattern of this transformation—from autonomy to affirmation—is by now a familiar part of twentieth-century art history, but its origins may be traced to the burial of the Intransigent and the birth of the Impressionist.

Notes

Originally published in *The New Painting: Impressionism, 1874–1886*, exh. cat. (San Francisco: The Fine Arts Museums of San Francisco, 1986), 51–59.

For their insightful criticisms and generous suggestions, my sincerest thanks extend to David James, Occidental Colleges; Richard R. Brettell, the Art Institute of Chicago; Fronia E. Wissman, the Fine Arts Museums of San Francisco; John H. Smith, University of California, Irvine; Thomas Crow, Princeton University; and M. Lee Hendrix, the J. Paul Getty Museum.

All translations are the author's except where otherwise indicated.

1. Three examples: Théodore Duret, *Histoire des peintres impressionnistes* (Paris, 1939), 20; Lionello Venturi, *Les Archives de l'impressionnisme*, vol. 1 (Paris and New York, 1939), 22; John Rewald, *The History of Impressionism*, 4th rev. ed. (New York, 1973), 336–38.
2. Paul Tucker has recently recounted the facts of the first Impressionist exhibition and the implicit nationalism of Monet's *Impression, soleil levant* in "The First Impressionist Exhibition and Monet's *Impression, Sunrise:* A Tale of Timing, Commerce and Patriotism," *Art History* 7, no. 4 (December 1984): 465–76. See also Anne Dayez et al., *Centenaire de l'impressionnisme*, exh. cat. (Paris: Grand Palais, 1974).
3. The identity of this painting remains in doubt. See Tucker, "First Impressionist Exhibition," 470–71, and Rewald, *History of Impressionism*, 339 n. 23.
4. Cited by Jacques Lethève, *Impressionnistes et symbolistes devant la presse* (Paris, 1959), 64–69.
5. These reviews are reprinted in Dayez et al., *Centenaire*, 259–61, 264–65. Tucker cites nineteen reviews of the exhibition: "Six were very positive; three were mixed, but generally positive; one was mixed but generally negative; four were negative; five were notices or announcements" ("First Impressionist Exhibition," 469, 475–76 n. 20).
6. Rewald, *History of Impressionism*, 390. The author does not document his suggestion that the name was definitively adopted in February. See also Barbara Erlich

White, *Renoir, His Life, Art, and Letters* (New York, 1984), 74. The phrase "Exposition des impressionnistes" does not appear on the title page of the accompanying catalogue but was placed above the door of the entrance to the galleries on the rue le Peletier. See G. Rivière, "Explications," *L'Impressionniste* (21 April 1877): 3; cited in Venturi, *Archives*, vol. 2, 322.

7. David Hume, *Essay Concerning Human Understanding, Original Ideas*, vol. 2 (1817), 16; cited in *The Oxford English Dictionary*, ed. James A. H. Murray, vol. 5 (Oxford, 1978), 110.
8. Richard Shiff, *Cézanne and the End of Impressionism* (Chicago, 1984), 19, 239 n. 24.
9. Emile Littré, *Dictionnaire de la langue française*, vol. 2 (Paris, 1866), 36; cited in Charles F. Stuckey, "Monet's Art and the Act of Vision," *Aspects of Monet*, ed. John Rewald and Frances Weitzenhoffer (New York, 1984), 120; also cited in Shiff, *Cézanne*, 18.
10. Charles Baudelaire, *Oeuvres complètes*, ed. Claude Pichois, vol. 2 (Paris, 1976), 698.
11. John Ruskin, *The Complete Works*, ed. E. T. Cook and Alexander Wedderburn, vol. 15 (London, 1904), 27; cited in Stuckey, 108.
12. Théodore Duret, "Salon de 1870," *Critique d'avant-garde* (Paris, 1885), 8; cited in Shiff, *Cézanne*, 22.
13. Dayez et al., *Centenaire*, 265.
14. Shiff, *Cézanne*, 4.
15. Dayez et al., *Centenaire*, 265.
16. Tucker, "First Impressionist Exhibition," 474.
17. Lethève, *Impressionnistes et symbolistes*, 72.
18. Jules Claretie, "Salon de 1874 à Paris," *L'Art les artistes français contemporains* (Paris, 1876), 260; Ernest Chesneau, "Le plein air, Exposition du boulevard des Capucines," *Paris-Journal*, 7 May 1874; cited in Dayez et al., *Centenaire*, 268.
19. E. Littré, *Dictionnaire de la langue française: Supplement* (Paris, 1897), 204; Centre National de la Recherche Scientifique, *Trésor de la langue française: Dictionnaire de la langue de XIXe et XXe siècle, 1789–1960*, vol. 10 (Paris, 1983), 490; *The Oxford English Dictionary*, vol. 5, 435. The following account of Intransigentism is largely based on C. A. M. Hennessy, *The Federal Republic in Spain: Pi y Margal and the Federal Republican Movement, 1868–74* (Oxford, 1962). See also Friedrich Engels, "The Bakunists at Work: Notes on the Spanish Uprising in the Summer of 1873," in *Marx, Engels, Lenin: Anarchism and Anarcho-Syndicalism* (New York, 1978), 128–46.
20. The Intransigents' platform was never very clear, although it may generally be said to have been based upon a separation of church and state, land reform, direct democracy, price controls, nationalization of banks, and Cantonal independence. The Benevolents, however, were equally unable to draft a precise social program (much to the chagrin of their supporters in the International, Marx, Engels, and Lafargue), with the result that neither faction was able to claim leadership of the growing revolutionary movement. Hennessy asserts that the bulk of Intransigent support came from the proletariat of Madrid and Cartagena but that its leadership was mixed in its class and political backgrounds, including the moderate general Contreras, the socialists Córdoba y López and Luis Blanc, and the antisocialist Roque Barcia (*Federal Republic in Spain*, 152).
21. "The Commune's aim is not an unrealizable utopia, but simply the autonomy of the Commune," *La Redención social* (9 April 1871); cited in ibid., 149.
22. *Le Temps*, 23 February 1873. See the subsequent report (24 February) that ex-Communards were reported to be arriving in Spain in the guise of journalists. See also Hennessy, *Federal Republic in Spain*, 181.
23. Cited in Venturi, *Archives*, vol. 2, 290.
24. Albert Wolff, "Le Calendrier parisien," *Le Figaro*, 3 April 1876.
25. Armand Silvestre, "Les Deux Tableaux de Monsieur Manet," *L'Opinion nationale*, 23 April 1876; cited in Françoise Cachin et al., *Manet*, exh. cat. (New York: Metropolitan Museum of Art, 1983), 32; Marie Berhaut, *Caillebotte, sa vie et son oeuvre* (Paris, 1978), 251.
26. *Le Moniteur universel*, 8 April 1876; cited in Lethève, *Impressionnistes et symbolistes*, 79.
27. Louis Enault, "Mouvement artistique: L'exposition des intransigeants dans la galerie de Durand-Ruelle *[sic]*," *Le Constitutionnel*, 10 April 1876. "Si nos souvenirs sont fidèles, c'est à l'Espagne que nous devons ce vocable nouveau, dont l'importation est plus récente que celles des mantilles, et moins agréable que celle des castagnettes. Ce sont, je crois, les républicains du midi de la péninsule qui employèrent pour la première fois, cette expression, dont on ne comprit pas parfaitement la valeur tout d'abord. . . . Les intransigeants politiques n'admettent aucun compromis, ne font aucune concession, n'acceptent aucun tempérament. . . . Le terrain sur lequel ils entendent élever leur monument doit leur offrir l'image d'une table rase."
28. Marius Chaumelin, "Actualités: L'Exposition des intransigeants," *La Gazette [des étrangers]*, 8 April 1876. "On les a d'aborde appelés 'les peintres du plein air,' ce qui indique assez bien qu'ils ont horreur de l'obscurité. On les a décorés du doux nom 'd'impressionnistes,' pour faire plaisir, sans doute, à Mlle Berthe

Morisot et aux autres jeunes peintresses qui ont embrassé leurs doctrines. Mais il y a un titre qui leur convient beaucoup mieux: celui d'*intransigeants*. . . . Ils ont en haine les traditions classiques et ambitionnent de reformer les lois du dessin et de la couleur. Ils prêchent la séparation de l'Académie et de l'Etat. Ils réclament l'amnistie pour 'l'école des taches' dont M. Manet fut le fondateur et d'où ils sont tous sortis."

29. Jack D. Ellis, *The Early Life of Georges Clemenceau* (Lawrence, Kansas, 1980), 64. Clemenceau's Radical program, fully articulated during his election campaign of 1881, was an expansion of the celebrated "Belleville Program" of Léon Gambetta from 1869. Clemenceau's text is translated and reproduced in Leslie Derfler, *The Third French Republic, 1870–1940* (Princeton, 1966), 121–23. See also R. D. Anderson, *France, 1870–1914: Politics and Society* (London, 1977), 88–99, as well as his extensive bibliography, 187–208. The internecine Republican struggles of 1876 are described in J. P. T. Bury, *Gambetta and the Making of the Third Republic* (London, 1973), 263–327.
30. Stéphane Mallarmé, "The Impressionists and Édouard Manet," *Documents Stéphane Mallarmé*, ed. C. P. Barbier (Paris, 1968), 84.
31. Ibid., 79–80.
32. Ibid., 74–75.
33. Ibid., 84. See also the remarks of Renoir to Ambroise Vollard, *Renoir: An Intimate Record* (New York, 1934), 47. "You realize then that for us the great task has been to paint as simple as possible; but you also realize how much the inheritors of tradition—from such men as Abel de Pujol, Gérôme, Cabanel, etc., with whom these traditions, which they did not comprehend, were lost in the commonplace and the vulgar, up to painters like Courbet, Delacroix, Ingres—were bewildered by what seemed to them merely the naive efforts of an *imagier d'Epinal*. Daumier is said to have remarked at the Manet exhibition, "I'm not a very great admirer of Manet's work, but I find it has this important quality: it is helping to bring art back to the simplicity of playing cards." On the continuing affinity between Modernist art and popular culture see Thomas Crow, "Modernism and Mass Culture in the Visual Arts," in *Modernism and Modernity*, ed. S. Guilbaut and D. Solkin (Halifax, 1983). See also T. J. Clark, *The Painting of Modern Life: Paris in the Art of Manet and His Followers* (New York, 1984), 205–58.
34. Mallarmé, "Impressionists," 77.
35. Vollard, *Renoir*, 66.
36. Michael Fried, "Shape as Form: Frank Stella's New Paintings," in *New York Painting and Sculpture: 1940–1970*, ed. Henry Geldzahler (New York, 1969), 403.
37. Mallarmé, "Impressionists," 86.
38. Clement Greenberg, "Modernist Painting," in *Modern Art and Modernism: A Critical Anthology*, ed. Francis Frascina and Charles Harrison (New York, 1982), 6.
39. Theodor Adorno, "Commitment," in *Aesthetics and Politics*, ed. Ronald Taylor (London, 1980), 177.
40. Emile Blavet, "Avant le Salon: L'Exposition des realists," *Le Gaulois*, 31 March 1876. "Les artistes qui, pour la seconde fois, en appellent directement au public, sont-ils des révoltés, comme on se plait à le dire, quand on ne les traite pas idiotement de communards? Non, certes. Des dissidents, tout au plus, groupés, associés afin de montrer au public l'ensemble de leurs tendances et la variété de leur oeuvre dans d'excellentes conditions de place et de lumière que le Salon ne saurait leur offrir."
41. Vollard, *Renoir*, 62–63.
42. Clark, *Painting of Modern Life*, 172–73.
43. Charles Bigot, "Causerie artistique: L'Exposition des 'impressionnistes,'" *La Revue politique et littéraire* (28 April 1877): 1045. "Le public les avait baptisés les 'intransigeants,' et le nom ne paraissait pas leur répugner: ils auront trouvé, sans doute, que les derniers incidents de la politique en avaient rendu la qualification compromettante; ils ont définitivement adopté le nom 'd'impressionnistes.'"
44. Venturi, *Archives*, vol. 2, 322–24. "Des journalistes . . . demandent depuis quinze jours pourquoi les artistes qui exposent rue Le Peletier ont pris le titre d'impressionnistes. C'est bien simple. Ils ont mis à la porte de leur exposition le mot impressionniste afin de ne pas être confondus avec d'autres et parce que ce mot les désignait d'une façon fort claire pour le public. . . . Ce titre rassure le public, les 'impressionnistes' sont suffisamment connus pour que personne ne soit trompé sur la qualité des oeuvres exposées. . . . Tous les artistes, je le soutiens, sont sincères; ils donnent toujours dans leurs oeuvres leur valeur exacte; si ce qu'ils produisent est mauvais, il n'y a pas de leur faute, ils ne sauraient ni faire mieux, ni faire autrement. Les 'impressionnistes' sont ainsi, leurs oeuvres sont le résultat des sensations qu'ils ont éprouvées, et je conçois peu que des artistes puissant mettre en doute un seul instant la sincerité des oeuvres exposées rue le Peletier."
45. Venturi, *Archives*, vol. 2, 322. "Mais vous avez un mari. . . . Votre mari, qui est peut-être républicain, en-

tre en fureur contre un révolutionnaire qui sème la discorde dans le camp artistique. . . . Il crie contre la routine politique, contre la routine administrative . . . mais il regarde la peinture à travers les vieux tableaux."

46. G. Rivière, *Renoir et ses amis* (Paris, 1921), 89–90. On Challemel-Lacour, see M. Prevost and Roman D'Amat, *Dictionnaire de biographie française*, vol. 8 (Paris, 1959), 210–211.

47. Perdican, "Courrier de Paris," *L'Illustration*, 7 January 1882. "C'est le triomphe de la *Nouvelle Athènes* sur l'Ecole de Rome. Les *intransigeants* de la peinture devraient triompher. Eh! bien, non, pas du tout. Ils ont froncé le sourcil, passé leurs doigts dans leur barbe. Manet décoré n'est plus Manet . . . disait, un jour, le peintre Degas: 'Il est plus connu que Garibaldi!'—'Manet,' s'est ecrié un *nouvel athénien* qui n'est pas le jeune Forain, 'Alloas! *Requiscat!* Ce n'est qu'un opportuniste de la couleur!'" Degas's sarcastic comparison between Manet and Garibaldi also is reported by Jacques-Emile Blanche, *Manet* (Paris, 1924), 37; cited in Clark, *Painting of Modern Life*, 82.

48. Henry Houssaye, "Le Ministère des Arts," *Revue des deux mondes* 49 (1 February 1882): 619–20.

49. Joel Isaacson, *The Crisis of Impressionism: 1878–1882*, exh. cat. (Ann Arbor: University of Michigan, Museum of Art, 1980), 18.

50. Venturi, *Archives*, vol. 1, 122. "Exposer avec Pissarro, Gauguin et Guillaumin, c'est comme si j'exposais avec une sociale quelconque. Un peu plus, Pissarro inviterait le Russe Lavroff ou autre révolutionnaire. Le public n'aime pas ce qui sent la politique et je ne veux pas, moi, à mon âge, être révolutionnaire. . . . Débarassez-vous de ces gens-là et présentez-moi des artistes tels que Monet, Sisley, Morisot, etc., et je suis à vous, car ce n'est plus de la politique, c'est de l'art pur." The anarchist Lavroff had been deported to London on 10 February 1882 on the order of Prime Minister Charles Freycinet.

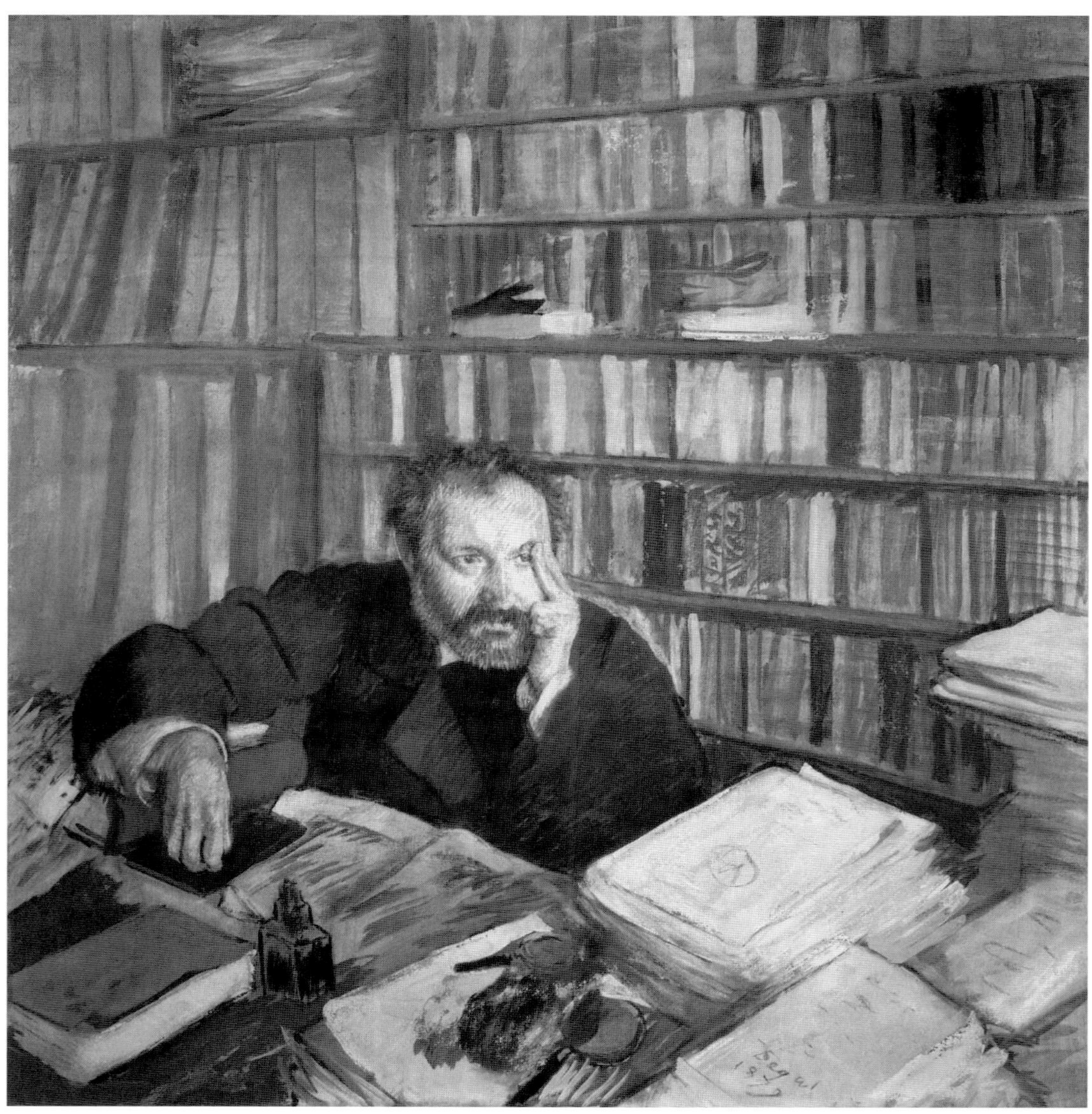

FIGURE 7.1. Edgar Degas, *Portrait of Edmond Duranty*, 1879, tempera, watercolor, and pastel on linen. Burrell Collection, Glasgow. Photo: The Bridgeman Art Library.

7

Duranty on Degas

A Theory of Modern Painting

CAROL ARMSTRONG

THE BEST-KNOWN and most extensive of the discussions of Degas's work of the 1870s was Edmond Duranty's *La Nouvelle Peinture,* which was supposed to have served as the introduction to the catalogue for the Impressionist exhibition of 1876 (when the *Cotton Office* [see fig. 7.2] was shown).[1] Like many other critics, Duranty seems to have thought of Degas's pictures of that year as a group of undifferentiated images—he did not refer to them individually. In Duranty's case, the explanation for this lies in the fact that his was more a theory meant to match a body of work than a review of the pictures in a show—"Therefore it's more the cause and the idea than the present show that I mean to consider" ("J'ai donc moins en vue l'exposition actuelle que la cause et l'idée").[2] Indeed, it is because of this that Duranty's essay is important to us: because his was an attempt to articulate a theory about the works; and because it was a piece of engaged critical discourse in a way that the reviews of the other critics were not; and also because in it Duranty addresses issues of realism and realist legibility more directly and in greater detail than any of the other critics. His is the most sustained example of the realist interpretation of Degas's oeuvre, matching Degas's attempt to neutralize and privatize the realist project more thoroughly and programmatically than the other critics' short remarks on the artist's works. In spite of the fact that Duranty did not name Degas directly or address individual pictures by Degas, his essay was also alone among the reviews of the Impressionist shows in its stress upon Degas's oeuvre.

So Duranty's essay provides us with a theory of realism against which Degas's realist practice can be measured. That his essay about the Impressionists was primarily about Degas was a fact well known to Duranty's contemporaries. It is equally well known to any present-day student of Impressionism.[3] Alike in personality, Duranty (fig. 7.1) and Degas were friends and cohorts. Together they played active roles in the discussions that went on at the Café Guerbois and the Nouvelle Athènes—Duranty was known as the "docteur du cénacle." They were both more articulate and theoretical than the others; in fact, they shared a sense of their difference from the Impressionist group, and were equally unimpressed with the aesthetics of the Impressionist sketch. They were both confirmed Parisians[4] with equal commitments to the human, social scene. As such they both disparaged the predominant concern for landscape painting and shared a preoccupation with an art of physiognomic perception and social observation.

The fact that *La Nouvelle Peinture* is about Degas's oeuvre is obvious from the text itself. It is true that superficially Duranty's essay was designed to elucidate the aims of the Impressionist group in its entirety—"these artists exhibiting in Durand-Ruel's gallery" ("ces artistes qui exposent dans les galeries Durand-Ruel")[5]— in the broadest of terms, "La nouvelle peinture" equals "Impressionism." Like other critics of Impressionism, Duranty opens with a lengthy disparagement of academic painting, and traces the history of the nineteenth-century avant-garde from Courbet and the Barbizon school through Jongkind, Boudin, and Manet. He does pay repeated homage to the notion of plein air painting. And he does include a lengthy discussion of color, light, and prismatic decomposition, as well as of Japanese influence. All of these are familiar issues of Impressionist criticism.

Yet Duranty never once calls the "new" painters "Impressionists," nor does he use the word "impression"—he is careful not to do so. Like many other critics disposed to be friendly to the Impressionist group and the exhibiting option which it provided, he was critical of the Impressionist preoccupation with landscape, and of the rendering of the retinal impression rather than the material qualities of the land.[6] He goes so far as to distinguish drawing from color and to come out on the side of the former. Degas was the *dessinateur* in this group of colorists, according to Duranty.

Duranty launches his discussion of the "new" painting with an oblique reference to Degas himself, "your guide, the honorable and able painter-writer, so courteous, so ironic and so disenchanted in his sayings" ("votre guide, l'honorable et habile peintre-écrivain, si courtois, si ironique et si désenchanté dans ses dires").[7] He mentions, as other critics had, the wit and erudition, the visual and verbal acuity—the *esprit*—for which Degas was famed. He even quotes one of Degas's letters, in which the image of a snub-nosed demimonde woman is used as a symbol for modern art, a passage typical of Degas's *dires* in its ambiguous inversion of traditional symbols, its deliberate mixing of realist and classical imagery:

> A sculptor, a painter have for a wife or mistress a woman with a pug nose and little eyes, who is thin, light, and lively. They love this woman in all her faults. Perhaps they risked everything to have her. Now, this woman who is the ideal of their heart and mind, who awoke and brought alive the truth of their taste, their sensibility, and their *invention*, because they discovered and chose her, is absolutely the contrary of the *feminine* which they so stubbornly articulate in their canvases and statues. There they return to Greece, to dark, severe women with the strength of horses. The pug nose which delights them during the evening, they betray in the morning by straightening it out; they die of boredom or else they bring to their work the gaiety and effort of *thought* of a box maker who knows his job very well, and who thinks about where he will be going to find his *pleasure* after the day is done.
>
> Un sculpteur, un peintre ont pour femme, pour maîtresse, une femme qui a un nez retroussé, de petits yeux, qui est mince, légère, vive. Ils aiment dans cette femme jusqu'à ses défauts. Ils se sont peut-être jetés en plein drame pour qu'elle fût à eux! Or, cette femme qui est l'idéal de leur coeur, et de leur esprit, qui a éveillé et fait jouer la vérité de leur goût, de leur sensibilité et de leur *invention*, puisqu'ils l'ont trouvée et élue, est absolument le contraire du *féminin* qu'ils s'obstinent à mettre dans leurs tableaux et leurs statues. Ils s'en retournent en Grèce, aux femmes sombres, sévères, fortes comme des chevaux. Le nez retroussé qui les délecte le soir, ils le trahissent le matin et le font droit; ils s'en meurent d'ennui ou bien ils apportent à leur ouvrage la gaieté et l'effort de *pensée* d'un cartonnier qui sait bien coller, et qui se demande où il ira rigoler, après sa journée faite.[8]

This modern, urban physiognomy becomes the symbol for the "new painting," and from here on it seems clear that Duranty could be talking of no one

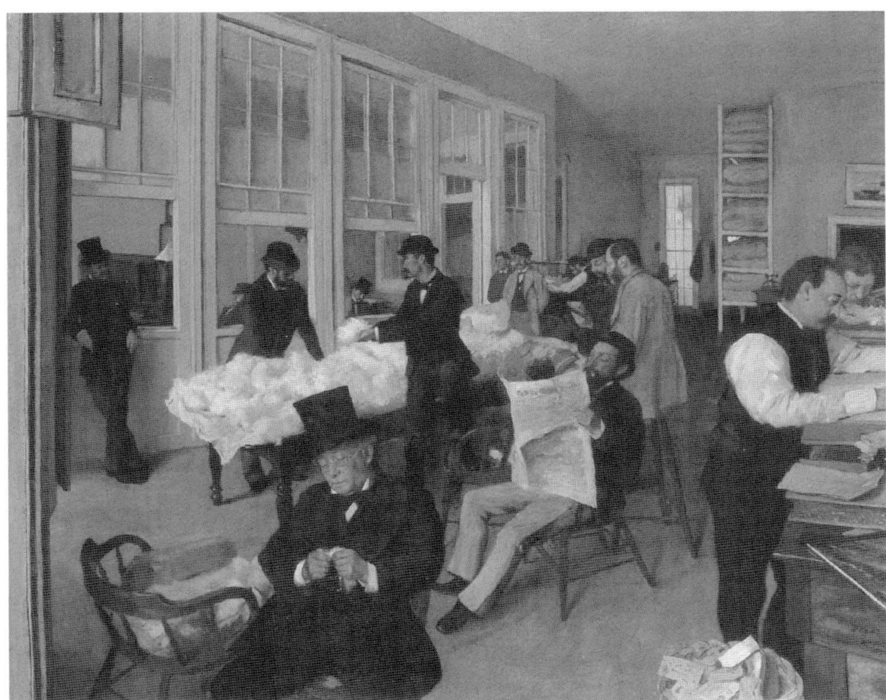

FIGURE 7.2. Edgar Degas, *Interior of a Cotton Buyer's Office in New Orleans*, 1873. Musée des Beaux-Arts, Pau, France. Photo: Réunion des Musées Nationaux/Art Resource, NY.

else but Degas. Only Degas did the kind of modern-life painting that went with that epigram. And only Degas painted subjects like the following: "He will be at his piano, or he will examine his cotton sample in his business office, or he will await the moment of stage entrance behind the wings, or he will apply the iron to the trestle table, or he will avoid vehicles while traversing the street, or he will look at his watch for the time while hurrying through the public square" ("Il sera à son piano, ou il examinera son échantillon de coton dans son bureau commercial, ou il attendra derrière le décor le moment d'entrée en scène, ou il appliquera le fer à repasser sur le table à trétaux ou il évitera des voitures en traversant la rue, ou il regardera l'heure à sa montre en pressant le pas sur la place publique").[9] This is the only time that Duranty makes reference to specific subjects, indicating some of the pictures by Degas that the other critics had mentioned: the laundresses, the dancers, and the *Cotton Office* (fig. 7.2), as well as other images not shown or mentioned, such as what sounds like the [once] lost *Place de la Concorde*.[10]

Having introduced Degas as a "dessinateur," "peintre-écrivain," and man of *esprit*—he makes Degas over into a mixture of Diderotian observer and Balzacian Virgil, a kind of street guide to the *comédie humaine* of the 1870s—Duranty turns to the kind of imagery that would best fit his theory. His general remarks about Impressionism sharpen into a discussion of an acute, radically framed and fragmented, physiognomic mode of vision:

> Farewell to the human body, treated as a vase, from the point of view of the decorative curve . . . what we need is the *special detail* of the modern individual, in his clothes, in the midst of his social habits, at home or in the street. *The datum becomes singularly acute* . . . it is . . . the observation . . . of *the special feature* which

inscribes in him his profession, gestures which it leads him to make, *partial aspects*. . . . With *one back*, we desire that a temperament should be revealed, the age, the social class; with *a pair of hands*, we must *express* a magistrate or a merchant; with *one gesture, a whole series of sentiments*. . . . *Hands sunk in pockets could be eloquent*. . . .

If one takes a person either in a room or in the street, he is not always at an equal distance from two parallel objects, . . . *he is never at the center of the canvas or at the center of his setting. He does not constantly appear complete—so that sometimes he appears cut off at mid-leg, at mid-body, or sliced longitudinally*. . . . The details of all these cuts would be infinite, just as the indication of all the settings would be. [Italics are mine.]

Adieu le corps humain, traité comme un vase, au point de vue du galbe décoratif . . . ce qu'il nous faut, c'est la note spéciale de l'individu moderne, dans son vêtement, au milieu de ses habitudes sociales, chez lui ou dans la rue. La donnée devient singulièrement aiguë . . . c'est l'observation . . . du trait spécial que lui imprime sa profession, des gestes qu'elle entraîne à faire, des coupes d'aspect. . . . Avec un dos, nous voulons que se révèle un tempérament, un âge, un état social; par une paire de mains, nous devons exprimer un magistrat ou un commerçant; par un geste, toute une suite de sentiments. . . . Des mains qu'on tient dans les poches pourront être éloquentes. . . .

Si l'on prend à son tour le personnage soit dans la chambre soit dans la rue, il n'est pas toujours à l'égale distance de deux objets parallèles, en ligne droite . . . il n'est jamais au centre de la toile, au centre du décor. Il ne se montre pas constamment entier, tantôt il apparaît coupé à mi-jambe, à mi-corps, tranché longitudinalement. . . . Le détail de toutes ces coupes serait infini, comme serait infinie l'indication de tous les décors.[11]

These are the passages most clearly about Degas's art. They do not exactly fit the rhetoric surrounding Impressionism, with its emphasis upon landscape, optical and surface effects, "violetomania" and slapdash execution, light, color, and diffuse vision. Rather than diffuse, the world which Duranty describes in these passages is sharp, focused, and exclusive: the field of vision is narrowed to isolated, singular details, a back and a pair of hands. Rather than surface, it is all edge, a pictorial world without a center, in which both bodies and spaces are radically partialized. And finally, it is a world made up not so much of paint, color, and optical sensation, but of human gestures, bodies, and spaces. No matter how rebelliously fragmented and out of kilter, it still has the traditional arts of drawing, physiognomic expression, and perspective as its fundamental concerns.

Duranty's vocabulary, then, is like the language that many other critics would use when they wrote about Degas's pictures, that of dislocation and dismemberment. Duranty pays attention to a vision which slices through the world, uproots and unbalances it, and dismantles the human bodies which people it. It was this world of corporeal incoherence that Degas's hostile critics would equate with pictorial illegibility—while his friendly critics would match it with a discussion of realist textuality.

Duranty's essay was the most striking example of the latter type of criticism. For, more insistently than the others, he defines Degas's pictorial world as a profoundly legible one. In writing about Degas's fragmented pictures, he sets out, point by point, the different readable elements, movements, and accoutrements of the human body: faces, hands, backs, a way of leaning against a door, a manner of wearing a suit. He alludes to the information that those details should provide: age, profession, class, sex, personal character, and life history. And he implies that Degas's realist images are ones that narrate as they describe: "with one gesture, a whole series of sentiments." In short, the "coupes d'aspect" and "mi-corps," the fragments and details so characteristic of Degas's art, are, according to Duranty, quite literally eloquent: they *speak* of contexts and histories.

Duranty had opened his essay by citing Eugène Fromentin's "Les Maîtres d'autrefois," which had appeared earlier that year in several installments of the *Revue des deux mondes:* "You will remark that the goal of the most recent painting is to confront the eyes of the crowd with striking, *textuelle*[12] images, easily recognized for their truth, stripped of artifice" ("Vous remarquez que la peinture la plus récente a pour but de frapper les yeux des foules par des images saillantes, textuelles, aisément reconnaissables en leur vérité, dénuées d'artifices").[13] Duranty took issue with this passage, objecting to Fromentin's bias against the "new" school. Yet the passage also provided him with an appropriate introduction to "la nouvelle peinture." For Fromentin's phrase "images textuelles" served as a kind of motto for Duranty, condensing the realist criteria that he applied to Degas's painting: those of striking accuracy, readability, and textuality. The "image textuelle," the image as a literal text of modern life, this in a nutshell was Duranty's theory of the "new" realist painting—i.e., of Degas's physiognomic drawing-painting.

Duranty's theory of the "image textuelle" was simply a more extended version of the assertions of critics like Burty who were concerned more with realism than with Impressionism. (The rhetoric of Impressionism with which we are now familiar was by and large a creation of the flippant, negative critics—the dominant mode of the serious critics was that of realism and had very little to do with what we now think of as the dominant aesthetics of the period.) But Duranty's theory of realist legibility is of particular importance because of his direct connection to the Realism of the 1850s and 1860s, and because of the way his essay engages certain critical traditions. His essay is the best exemplar of the Third Republic theory of realism—the best theoretical counterpart to Degas's own neutralization of the earlier Realist project. For Duranty's is an opinion about Degas's work which more or less reconstitutes it in terms of mid-century Realism, of which Duranty had been one of the foremost champions in the early years of the Second Empire. We will come back to the "textuality" of the "new painting"; let us first explore its relation to the older Realism.

In 1856 Duranty, Jules Assézat, and Henri Thulié began a short-lived journal called *Réalisme;* only six issues were published, between July of 1856 and May of 1857. After its demise there were a few vague plans to revive it in a new form—in the end, *La Nouvelle Peinture,* itself a kind of resuscitation of the 1850s pamphlet, was all that remained of those plans.[14] *Réalisme* had been devoted to the defense and propagation of the ideas born of the 1840s and 1850s—those of Courbet, Proudhon, Baudelaire, and Champfleury—and to the program of the encyclopedic representation of the "social spectacle." Indeed, the series of articles contained in the pages of *Réalisme* constituted the main theoretical writing about Realism in the 1850s, much more extensive than the more famous pamphlet by the same name by Champfleury.

In 1857 Duranty undertook to devote himself to the writing of Realist fiction—at the instigation of Champfleury. Champfleury helped him enter into and make his way in the world of Realist writing—it was Champfleury who pushed to get Duranty's stories published, and who, as a critic, stood up for him in the face of a critical press that was largely hostile. According to his biographer, Crouzet, Duranty was a confirmed Champfleuryste—Champfleury's style, subjects, and concerns were consistently at the root of his own.[15]

In the 1870s, Duranty was still following in Champfleury's footsteps, still echoing his concerns and taking up his genres of criticism. In 1872, he wrote about caricature, taking up a genre of criticism that Champfleury had initiated. Just as Champfleury before him had done, and would continue to do, Duranty tied his discussion of the caricatural medium to a particular context and specific historical moment, in this case to the Franco-Prussian War.[16] In 1878, at the time of Daumier's first retrospective, both he and Champfleury wrote about that artist.[17] Duranty's late 1870s series of articles on the collections of the Louvre, called "Promenades au Louvre," also echoes Champfleury's criticism.[18]

At the same time Duranty began to take up the critical themes of the new generation, specifically those of his more recent supporter, Emile Zola; in the late sixties and early seventies, he began writing about Manet and the Impressionists in a manner that recalls

Zola's criticism.[19] And he became an intimate of the circle of naturalist writers that surrounded Zola. But Duranty continued to call himself a Realist. In 1867 he said, "Oh! the new philosophy, the positivist, materialist philosophy. . . . Go on, do not count only on your adversaries to keep you on the proper road: that of Realism!" (Eh! la nouvelle philosophie, la philosophie positiviste et matérialiste. . . . Allez donc, et qu'on ne compte pas seulement sur vos adversaires pour vous maintenir dans la voie du salut: le Réalisme!").[20] This was a motto for 1876 as well.

But if Duranty's attachment seemed to be the avant-garde ideologies of the Second Republic and Second Empire, nevertheless, he, like Champfleury and other "Courbetistes," attempted to disassociate himself from the 1848 beginnings of those ideologies, to sever Realism from its particular political moment and rid it of the resonances that identified it with 1848 and made it a radical matter.[21] He made the realism of the Second Republic, Realism with a capital R, over into the realism of the Third, realism with a little r. In this, Duranty's theory was like the strange little Biedermeyer picture by Degas which critics noticed in the 1876 exhibition, the *Cotton Office*. It was also a bit like Degas's own claim that "realism need no longer fight."

One way that Duranty depoliticized the concept of realism was by citing Courbet's painting as the *prehistory* of the new realism.[22] Another way was by quoting Diderot's "Essai sur la peinture":

> I have never heard a figure accused of being badly drawn as long as its exterior organization clearly manifested its age and its habits and its ability to fulfill daily tasks. These tasks determine both the overall size of a figure and the true proportions of each of his limbs—and of the relationship between them: it is out of that that I see the child, the adult, and the old man emerge; as well as the wild and the civilized man, the magistrate, the soldier, and the porter alike. If there is a figure difficult to find, it is that of a twenty-five-year-old man who has suddenly been born out of the clay of the earth and who has so far done nothing—but that man is a chimera.

> Je n'ai jamais entendu accuser une figure d'être mal dessiné lorsqu'elle montrait bien dans son organisation extérieure l'âge et l'habitude ou la faculté de remplir ses fonctions journalières. Ce sont ces fonctions que déterminent et la grandeur entière de la figure, et la vraie proportion de chaque membre et leur ensemble: c'est de là que je vois sortir et l'enfant et l'homme adulte, et le vieillard, et l'homme sauvage, et l'homme policé, et le magistrat, et le militaire, et le porte-faix. S'il y a une figure difficile à trouver, ce serait celle d'un homme de vingt-cinq ans, qui serait né subitement du limon de la terre, et qui n'aurait encore rien fait; mais cet homme est une chimère.[23]

This quote helped to substantiate Duranty's contrast between the realist physiognomy, "the modern individual, in his clothes, in the midst of his social habits, at home or in the street," and the academic "corps," "the human body, treated like a vase, from the point of view of the decorative curve." (Diderot had done the same, opposing "the figure [whose] exterior organization clearly manifests its age and its habits and its ability to fulfill daily tasks" to "a twenty-five-year-old man who has suddenly been born out of the clay of the earth and who has so far done nothing.") Duranty also echoed Diderot's contrast between "l'école" and "mon carrefour" and emphasis on direct, modern-life observation[24] when he demanded that the studio be opened up to the light of day and that the painter descend into the street to observe the contemporary human scene.[25] In short, Duranty claimed Diderot as an eighteenth-century progenitor of nineteenth-century realism. He says, "This extraordinary man is at the back of all that the art of the nineteenth century shall have realized" ("Cet homme extraordinaire est au seuil de tout ce que l'art du dixneuvième siècle aura réalisé").[26]

Duranty claimed Diderot's text as a model for his own anti-academic stance. Earlier in *La Nouvelle Peinture* he had echoed Diderot's language in another way, mocking the poses and masquerades of academic models, characterizing them as cosmetics and fancy-dress costume rather than "habits" and "habitudes," as masks rather than physiognomies: "They have done better than the teacher, demanding that actors teach them theatrical grimaces to put on the face, always the same face, of their little *marquis* and *incroyables*. . . . They have dressed up, made up, and trussed up nature, they have covered it in curl papers. They have dressed its hair, and prepared it for an operetta" ("Ils ont renchéri sur le maître, demandé aux comédiens de leur enseigner quelques grimaces de théâtre à mettre sur la face, invariablement la même, de leurs petits marquis, de leurs incroyables. . . . Ils ont chiffonné, maquillé, troussé la nature, l'ont couverte de papillotes. Ils la traitent en coiffeurs, et la préparent pour une opérette").[27]

Duranty ends his essay with a passage that reads as if there too he were harking back to Diderot's "Essai sur la peinture." Diderot had finished his essay on painting with a discussion of the genre of history painting: "Oh! if only a sacrifice, a battle, a triumph, a public scene could be rendered with the same truth in all its details as a domestic scene by Greuze or Chardin" ("Ah! si un sacrifice, une bataille, un triomphe, une scène publique pouvoit être rendue avec la même verité dans tous les détails qu'une scène domestique de Greuze ou Chardin!").[28] (That passage was the beginning of Diderot's famous lament about the state of eighteenth-century history painting, and his commentary on the relationship between genre pictures and history paintings.) The terms are not the same, but in his summation Duranty addresses the issue of genre painting raised to the level of history painting just as Diderot had done:

> I envisioned a painting that would undertake vast series of men of the world, priests, soldiers, peasants, workers, merchants, series in which the characters would be varied in their own tasks, and related in scenes common to all: marriages, baptisms, births, successions, parties, familial interiors—above all scenes which take place frequently and which, consequently, express the general life of a country . . . a generosity of views which perhaps does not obtain in any of the present painters.
>
> J'entrevoyais la peinture abordant de vastes séries sur les gens du monde, les prêtres, les soldats, les paysans, les ouvriers, les marchands, séries où les personnages se varieraient dans leurs fonctions propres et se rapprocherait dans des scènes communes à tous: les mariages, les baptêmes, les naissances, les successions, les fêtes, les intérieurs de familles; surtout des scènes se passant souvent et exprimant bien, par conséquent, la vie générale d'un pays . . . une largeur de vues qui n'appartient peut-être à aucun des hommes d'à present.[29]

The comments that follow this passage expand on the vision of large-scale, significant modern painting, with some remarks about the uncertainty of the future of the "new painting." Like Diderot, Duranty complains that good modern, properly ambitious painting done on a properly grandiose scale, in other words, serious modern history painting, was lacking. It is possible that Duranty was thinking of Diderot's summation when he wrote his own. Certainly he established an equivalence between the pre- and post-1789 programs of physiognomic expression, modern-life observation, and pictorial legibility. Certainly his new realism, a renewed, renamed, and reapplied version of the old, paralleled Diderot's anti-Rococo argumentation of the 1760s. Perhaps, by recalling the summation to Diderot's essay, he also equated his own nineteenth-century demands for seriousness, significance, and renewed vigor in painting with the demands of the eighteenth century. Since the "big paintings" which he desired can also be taken as a reference to Courbet's large Second Republic works, perhaps he even meant to rid them of their attachment to 1848 by attaching them instead to the older demands of the eighteenth century. In any event, Duranty matched *La Nouvelle Peinture* to a diachronic rather than a synchronic history of realism, and attempted to give it something of a pre-1789 sound—by connecting it up to a piece of prerevolutionary art theory, and identifying it with the observations and argumentation of a *philosophe*.

Other Realist writers and critics, among them Balzac, Champfleury, Baudelaire, and Proudhon, had discovered in Diderot's writing a precedent for their own attitudes; Diderot makes his appearance in the writing of nineteenth-century Realists as a kind of eighteenth-century *eminence grise*. Like Duranty, other Realists seem to have thought of him as a progenitor of nineteenth-century avant-gardism in many of its aspects: in his stance of opposition, criticism, and skepticism; his apparently unstructured style; his language of sarcasm; even his themes and subjects. Certainly it is true that Diderot's works gained public recognition as realism gained acceptance.[30] His complete works were published between 1875 and 1877 (contemporaneous to *La Nouvelle Peinture*) by Duranty's old friend and realist cohort Jules Assézat, who planned to write a study of Diderot and the Enlightenment as a follow-up on his publication of the *Oeuvres complètes*. (Assézat died before this project came to fruition. Duranty, who had apparently read the proofs for volumes fourteen and fifteen of the *Oeuvres complètes* for Assézat, was to have written one of a series of essays that was supposed to take the place of Assézat's general study on Diderot. Duranty's essay, which never saw the light of day, was to have been about Diderot and the fine arts.)[31]

Assézat's interest in Diderot fits with the concerns of the circle of people to which he, Duranty, and Thulié were connected. To these men, a group of anticlericals, educational reformers, positivists, and republicans—they were known as "freethinkers"[32]—the eighteenth century was extremely important; they quoted it, wrote about it, published its works, and based their ideas upon it.[33] Theirs was a different eighteenth century from that of the Rococo revivalists, like the Goncourts, for example—theirs was the anti-Rococo eighteenth century, the "siècle des lumières." Diderot, Voltaire, and Rousseau were, for them, the first anticlericals, the first educational and social reformers, the first modern natural and social scientists: the first encyclopedists and the first positivists, in other words. Duranty's cohorts thought of the *philosophes* as the original exemplars of their own *libre-penseur* philosophies.

And so did Duranty. This is the context of friends and associates, persuasions and preoccupations into which his use of Diderot's "Essai sur la peinture" properly fits. His claiming of Diderot as the progenitor of his own theory of realism defined Duranty as a man of the Third Republic, rather than of the Second, aligned his realist aesthetics with those of bourgeois positivism rather than those of radicalism, and defined his "avant-garde" criticism as a piece of liberal discourse with a prerevolutionary tradition to back it up. The reference to Diderot served, ultimately, to disconnect Duranty's "new" realism from the resonances of 1848.

Duranty depoliticized and neutralized realism in other ways as well. As Crouzet has pointed out, *La Nouvelle Peinture* was written only shortly after Quinet's *L'Esprit nouveau* was published (in 1874); Crouzet suggests that Duranty was aware of that late text by the follower of Michelet and the historian of the Restoration and the Second Empire when he wrote *La Nouvelle Peinture*.[34] *La Nouvelle Peinture* undoubtedly echoes Quinet's concerns in its preoccupation with the liberalization of French institutions (i.e., the Ecole des Beaux Arts), its proclamation of contemporaneity and its critique of academicism, its interest in physiognomics as a semiotics of human history and society, and in its task of discovering and defining a new, vital French art form to match the new French age.[35] Certainly it is true that *La Nouvelle Peinture* is predicated on newness: it posits a new beginning—an "esprit nouveau"—and identifies itself with a new era. It compares the new school to the old one, explicitly in its contrast between "la nouvelle peinture" and academic painting; implicitly, in its reference to Fromentin's "Les Maîtres d'autrefois" as a kind of companion text.

Duranty's reference to Fromentin's article also helps to detach the new realism from 1848—by attaching it to a growing genre of criticism which emphasized national culture as the basis for style. The writings of Fromentin,[36] along with those of Thoré-Bürger, Taine, and Charles Blanc, constitute an early social art history defined by nationalism and racialism.[37] They posited the encyclopedic, contextual, proto-anthropological approach as a model for art criticism, establishing historical description and narration, rather than aesthetic judgment, as the proper critical model. Most obviously, they also attached realism to nationalism and national culture—one of their principal preoccupations was the contrast between realism and classicism, the Northern and Italianate schools;[38] another was the issue of where the French school fit.

In *La Nouvelle Peinture,* Duranty engages every one of these aspects of the new art history of realism. First, there is a narrative strain to his tracing of the history of Impressionism. It is his stated task to consider the "new painting" as French, contemporary, and socially representative. His essay is entirely given over to the contrast between a bastard classicism and a new realism—his quote of Fromentin's "Les Maîtres d'autrefois" serves to highlight that contrast. Finally, Duranty was very much concerned with what to do with the French school, where to locate it, how to define the Frenchness of the new French painting—it was the passages on French painting in Fromentin's articles on Dutch art that he cited. Put these aspects of *La Nouvelle Peinture* together with Duranty's later "Promenades au Louvre," in which Dutch and Italian, classical and realist paintings are explicitly compared, and it is clear that Duranty was thoroughly engaged in the new nationalist art history.

By citing Fromentin, Duranty attempted to lend some measure of respectability to his own argument. By citing Diderot, he tried to give a history—a French history—to the French practice of and discourse on realism. That Duranty conflated Fromentin's and Diderot's, as well as Champfleury's, genres of criticism underscores the fact that *La Nouvelle Peinture* was about realism as subsumed within a larger, less charged debate—made over into a part of national "art history," and thereby separated from recent period-specific sociopolitical history. *La Nouvelle Peinture* is a good example of the degree to which the old 1848 Realism had been transformed into the "new" French realism, and of the degree to which the social issues engaged in the painting of Courbet had been neutralized,[39] converted into questions about how French art was French, how it represented the French social scene, and how it was to be read. So, though written by a man with rather different political opinions from those of Degas, *La Nouvelle Peinture* was consistent with Degas's own attempt to deradicalize the business of realism.

Duranty's *libre-penseur,* positivist affiliations were also the basis for his notion of the "image textuelle." Let us take a look, now, at his account of realist readability. Though Duranty uses the language of optical sensation belonging to Impressionism, his is always a language of language as well. For even the luminous, prismatic instants of Impressionism are also flashes of instantaneous textuality, according to him: the Impressionist's "laws of light" are also laws of "expression." For Duranty, the Impressionist "hour of the day" is a human and social hour, rather than merely an optical one—it is identical to a "moment of public life":

> Our existence takes place in rooms or in the street, and . . . the rooms, the street have their *special laws of light and expression* [my italics]. . . . With us, the tonal values of our interiors change with infinite variety, depending whether one is on the first floor or the fourth, whether the lodging is extremely furnished, papered, and carpeted, or meagerly embellished; thus an atmosphere is created in every interior as well as a sense of family between all the furnishings and objects which fill them. . . .
>
> . . . we will no longer separate the individual from the background of his apartment or the street. Never in our existence does he appear to us against a neutral, empty, vague background. Instead there are furnishings, chimneys, wall hangings around him, *an interior which expresses his fortune, his class, his métier* [my italics] . . . [40]
>
> *The language of the empty apartment will be precise enough so that one may deduce from it the character and the habits of him who inhabits it, and the street, by its passersby, will tell us what hour of the day it is; what moment of public life is represented.* [My italics.]
>
> Notre existence se passe dans des chambers ou dans la rue, et . . . les chambers, la rue, ont leurs lois spéciales de lumière et d'expression. . . . Chez nous,

les valeurs des tons dans les intérieurs jouent avec d'infinies variétés, selon qu'on est au premier étage ou au quatrième, que le logis est très meublé et très tapissé, ou qu'il est maigrement garni; une atmosphère se crée ainsi dans chaque intérieur de même qu'un air de famille entre tous les meubles et les objets qui les remplissent. . . .

. . . nous ne séparerons plus le personnage du fond d'appartement ni du fond de rue. Il ne nous apparaît jamais dans l'existence sur des fonds neutres, vides et vagues. Mais autour de lui sont des meubles, des cheminées, des tentures de murailles, une paroi qui exprime sa fortune, sa classe, son métier . . .

Le langage de l'appartement vide devra être assez net pour qu'on puisse en déduire le caractère et les habitudes de celui qui l'habite et la rue dira par ses passants quelle heure de la journée il est, quel moment de la vie publique est figuré.[41]

Duranty joins the "impression" to "expression," thoroughly conflating visibility and textuality, insisting on the legibility of every visual aspect of the world, reading the discursive imperatives of the French tradition,[42] its privileging of language and literature, rhetoric and exegesis, right into his discussion of Impressionism, and thus refusing to recognize any essential difference between Impressionism and a realism strongly inflected by literary expectations. Impressionism was simply a new realism—and Duranty's combination of the visual and the discursive was absolutely central to his "new painting."

This is not altogether surprising. Duranty was a story writer first and foremost, trained in the literary practice as well as the criticism of the 1850s.[43] His new realism was based not only on an older pictorial realism but also on an older literary school of realism. His "image textuelle," including not only human features, gestures, and accoutrements but also human spaces and settings, was derived from the descriptive practices of realist writers such as Balzac. In a series of pieces in *Réalisme* about the different aspects of a literary work—plot, characterization, description, and so on—Duranty's cohort, Henri Thulié, had cited Balzac, criticizing him for the surfeit of description in his writing, yet implicitly referring to him as the grand old man of the realist tradition in literature.[44] Although Duranty was also critical of Balzac's novels,[45] it is obvious as well that Balzac was his model—he says as much when, in *La Nouvelle Peinture,* he cites Courbet and Balzac as the twin fathers of realism. By the 1850s most critics concurred with the view of Balzac as the *paterfamilias* of realism; by the 1870s Balzac was considered a realist classic, and his notions of description, observation, and encyclopedic social classification formed a standard, popularly accessible part of the French literary tradition.[46] In a general way, Duranty too thought of Balzac as the exemplar of realist observation. He thought that paintings should be readable in the same way that the verbal pictures in Balzac's novels were. In any event, it is clear that Duranty's theory of the readability of the visual data of realist depictions, in particular his codification of the expressiveness of inhabited places and owned inanimate objects, was founded on the example set by Balzac's fiction.

Duranty's emphasis on the narratability of the striking descriptive image, and his sense of the textuality of immediate visibility, owe more to Thulié's essays on literature in *Réalisme* than to his own earlier writing on painting in that journal. In his article on novelistic description, which was obviously indebted to Balzac's writing, Thulié had written explicitly about the way that description should do the work of narration:

The interior is the intimate part of life; there one deposits all one's hypocrisies; like clothing, little by little it takes on the inflections of the body, it betrays all its habits, one can guess at a man by seeing his rooms. The choice of furniture, colors, of a thousand little nothings spread all about are traitors which recount tendencies, meannesses, and secret vices. Frequently, in describing an interior, one recounts the private life of an individual or of a family.

L'intérieur c'est l'intimité de la vie; on dépose chez soi toutes ses hypocrisies; comme le costume il prend peu à peu toutes les inflexions de corps, trahit toutes ses habitudes, on peut deviner un homme en voyant sa chamber. Le choix des meubles, des couleurs, des mille petits riens qui traînent partout sont des traîtres qui racontent les tendances, les mesquineries, les vices secrets. En décrivant un intérieur, on raconte souvent la vie privée d'un individu ou d'une famille.[47]

In *Réalisme,* Duranty had been careful to keep painting and literature distinct, farming the latter out to Thulié, while he focused on the former. He was aware that painting and writing operated on different principles. But he and Thulié shared the feeling that literature functioned best through descriptive imagery—through verbal pictorializations (even plot and action were nothing more than a succession of images: Duranty's own novels were composed that way)—and that painting should be a kind of pictorial literature. Indeed they shared the belief that painting was a more powerful kind of literature than literature itself. Thulié's remarks about Balzac's tendency to drown his stories in detail indicated that the advantage of a picture was its directness, its obviation of the need to explicate and interpret a description (the way Balzac had to explain the import of his descriptions), its immediate readability and self-exegesis.

In *Réalisme,* Thulié had used the word "impression" in a physiognomic way: "To understand a physiognomy well, one must render the *impression* that one has when one sees it. There are always *conspicuous features* in a face or a costume that are immediately *striking* [my italics]" ("Pour bien comprendre une physionomie, il faut rendre l'impression qu'on a éprouvé en la voyant. Il y a toujours des traits saillants dans le visage et dans le costume qui frappent de primes abords").[48] In *Réalisme* and elsewhere, Duranty spoke of the "trait saillant" as Thulié had done, referring to the *impressive,* immediately significant visual detail, the one that made an image more immediately readable than an equivalent descriptive passage in a novel by Balzac.[49] In *La Nouvelle Peinture,* Duranty uses similar terms—not "impression" or the "trait saillant," but the "trait spécial" and the "images saillantes, textuelles" in the quote from Fromentin. Terms like these betray the older, novelistic basis of Duranty's theory of the "new painting"—appropriately, they also refer to the "science" of physiognomics. For that is the positivist semiotics which lies at the back of Duranty's conception of the readable realist image, his joining of the concept of modern life to the concern with legibility, and his union of "impression" and "expression," visibility and textuality. The science of physiognomics permeates both *Réalisme* and *La Nouvelle Peinture,* as well as all the rest of Duranty's writings, both fictional and critical. It had informed Thulié's interest in Realism, providing the link between his brief venture as a critic and theorist of Realist literature and his vocation as doctor and anthropologist.[50] It was central to the Realist movement in both painting and literature, the subject of Balzac's *Comédie humaine,* and the basis on which Courbet's paintings were received. Most in vogue at the beginning of the nineteenth century, it remained popular until the end of the century—Duranty's 1867 essay on it in *La Revue libérale,*[51] and Degas's own interest in it in the late 1860s, 1870s, and early 1880s,[52] were not exceptional.[53] It had also become a matter of scientific and pseudoscientific debate, informing the work of physicians, criminologists, sociologists (like those concerned with prostitution), and social reformers. It was very much a part of the encyclopedic-positivist concerns of Duranty's circle—Duranty himself wrote it into *La Nouvelle Peinture* in many ways: not only in his Balzacian discussion of readable figures, features, and interior settings, but also in his citation from Diderot and his quote of Fromentin.

Physiognomics meant many things in the later nineteenth century. Essentially, it was an eclectic semiotics, founded on the theory of expressions and based on a reading of the human form, but applied to all the objects and spaces of the world, cultural, natural, animate, and inanimate. A mixture of contradictory discourses and epistemologies, it was a system on the basis of which everything visible could be a text, every surface and exterior could be read.[54] The particular brand of physiognomic "science" that informed Duranty's and Thulié's theory of realism was a semiotics of costume and setting, accoutrement and context familiar from the writing of Balzac and the days of Courbet, a system of social signs which placed special emphasis on those of profession: "It is that conspicuous physiognomy produced by the costume and the way of life that each profession demands which strikes the public more readily" (C'est cette physionomie saillante produite par la costume et le genre de vie qu'exige chaque profession qui frappe plus vivement le public").[55]

Above all, Duranty's was a physiognomics of exteriority—"the science of exterior observation" ("la science de l'observation extérieur")[56]—rather than one of interiority; of social signs and unambiguous visibility rather than elusive personality and private psychological quirks:

> [T]he investigation of little interior movements, infinitely finicky sensations, troubles, and aspirations, which are not directed toward a clear, definite end, straightforward in a word, are imperceptible and consequently not very interesting for the large majority of readers, in whom they awake no important idea. . . . It is for that reason that the public prefers a badly written book which paints the life of a soldier or a bourgeois—i.e., a social man—to the well-written book full of elusive, irritating psychological details . . . [which] paint a being who is too individual for the public.
>
> [L]es recherches sur les petits mouvements intérieurs, sur les finesses infinies des sensations, sur les troubles et les aspirations qui ne sont pas dirigés vers un but clair, défini, carré, en un mot, sont imperceptibles et par conséquent peu intéressantes pour la presque totalité des lecteurs chez qui elles ne réveillent aucune idée importante. . . . Voilà pourquoi le public préférera le livre mal fait qui lui peint la vie du soldat, ou du bourgeois, homme social, au livre bien fait . . . plein de détails psychologiques insaisissables et ennuyeux . . . ils lui peignent un être trop individuel.[57]

This notion of physiognomics was the basis of Duranty's concept of pictorial legibility—it lay at the root of his conception of the "new painting" and of its basis in earlier, novelistic versions of realism. It also lay at the root of the other critics' readings of Degas's works, and of their perception of him as a realist painter concerned with the gestures of profession and the textuality of modern urban life.

Though Degas's works were supposed to exemplify Duranty's theory of the "trait saillant" and the "image textuelle," Duranty did not attempt to test his theory against Degas's images by reading them—he simply listed a series of such "traits": a back and a pair of hands, etc., and left it at that. A year later, however, in an article about gesture in painting that showed how much Duranty was engaged in the new realist-nationalist art history of his period, he did attempt to apply his theory of realist physiognomics. In his first "Promenades au Louvre," he addressed a series of seventeenth-century Dutch pictures and tried to read them, with a thoroughness that is remarkable and a fascination for subtle, conflicted gestures and enigmatic expressions, for physiognomies hovering at the very edge of illegibility, that are worth our extended attention:

> But sometimes, because of their subtlety, sometimes because [these pictures] localize the truth too much, they become veritable enigmas. But these enigmas are amusing to decipher. . . .
>
> M. Villot is mistaken, I think, vis-à-vis an enigma by the adorable Metsu, which, in his catalogue, he entitles: *A Soldier Receiving a Young Woman* (no. 293). Metsu wanted to present us with a scene that was a little more difficult to interpret. One thing is sure, the soldier does not receive—he is received; his attitude is that of a man who is on the point of bowing and taking his leave. The expression of the exchanged glances, the glass that is just about to be offered to him, indicate that he is being detained and that he will stay. This picture is prodigious in spirit—in it, Mersu has succeeded in rendering intentions, contained sentiments, and movements which are about to take place. But is a very knowledgeable and very intelligent catalogue-writer condemned to remain in front of this composition for ten minutes, in order to read it as one reads a book?

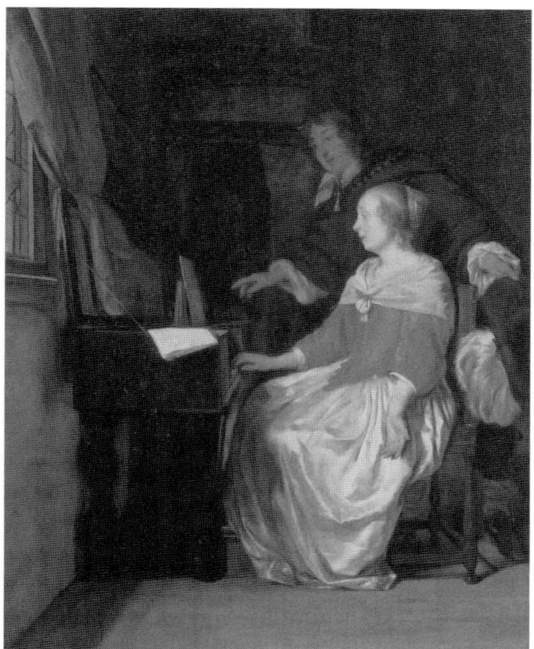

FIGURE 7.3. Gabriel Metsu, *The Music Lesson [Lesson at the Virginal]*, 1660s, oil on wood. Musée du Louvre, Paris. Photo: Réunion des Musées Nationaux/Art Resource, NY. Photographed by Gerard Blot.

I stand charmed in front of his ravishing *Music Lesson* (no. 294 [fig. 7.3]), which is truly a moving, speaking picture—in the serious sense of those two words. "I don't see how this can be played otherwise," says the woman with some resentment, letting her hand fall open—protesting the impossibility of playing the clavichord in another manner besides her own. "But yes, yes, it goes like this!" responds the teacher, and he gives her the bar, he gives her the pitch, and the accent—and we are within the scene, we follow it, we hear it! That is the height of expressiveness and all because of the simplicity of his means. But whereas here the natural gesture gives clarity to the incident, an equally natural expression leads to a kind of uncertainty in another picture by Metsu. That is, in this other picture, the *Vegetable Market,* reality has been too localized, as I said before. I'm referring to the man dressed in red who laughingly addresses the townswoman with her white iron bucket. This man has positioned his right arm on his left in such a way that its meaning is not easy to analyze—even though there is nothing unexpected or forced about it. Is he hamming it up and pretending to beg? Is he pretending to salute her with good manners? Is he proposing to carry the bucket, which must, he says, tire her arm? Is he prodding at his arm with a kind of lust—as if he were groping that of the woman? Is he feeling somewhat embarrassed because he risked some familiarity or some pleasantry that might be poorly received?—his gesture approximating that of scratching one's ear? The woman evidently wears a surprised look: "That," she thinks, "is an impudent, gay rascal"—but it is clear that she is about to smile. Nevertheless, she could become angry, one senses that. Might she have already slapped him? In contrast, one cannot mistake the argumentative marketwoman with her hands planted on her hips. What a singular gesture that popular gesture is—and how complex! It indicates many things at once: that she restrains her hands temporarily, with great disdain, itching to lash out and hit; that she wishes to give herself a majestic air appropriate to assuring and affirming her superiority over her opponent, and finally, that she dreads the other so little that she walks toward him, leaving her weapons sheathed, that's to say with her fists reposing and hanging from her belt. Two fists on the hips: low gesture, or at least vulgar—one fist alone on the hip: noble, royal gesture. It is interesting to compare Charles I by Van Dyck to Metsu's fishwife.

Mais parfois à force de subtilité, et quelquefois en localisant trop la vérité, ils en arrivent à des véritables énigmas. Ces énigmas sont d'ailleurs amusantes à déchiffrer. . . .

M. Villot s'est donc trompé, je crois, en face d'une énigme de l'adorable Metsu, que, dans son catalogue, il intitule: *Un Militaire recevant une jeune dame* (no. 293). Metsu a voulu donner à deviner une scène un peu plus compliquée. A coup sûr, le militaire ne reçoit pas, mais il est reçu; son attitude marque un homme qui s'apprète à saluer pour prendre congé; l'expression des regards échangés, le verre qu'on est près de lui tendre, indiquent qu'on le tient et qu'il va rester. Ce tableau est d'un esprit prodigieux; Metsu est parvenu à y rendre des intentions, des sentiments contenus, des mouvements qui vont avoir lieu. Mais un très savant et très intelligent redacteur de catalogue était-il condamné à rester dix minutes devant cette composition, pour la lire comme on lit un livre?

Je reste donc charmé devant cette ravissante *Leçon de musique* (no. 294) qui est un véritable tableau mouvant et parlant, dans le sens sérieux de ces deux mots. "Je ne vois pas que cela puisse se jouer autrement que je ne fais," dit avec quelque dépit la dame, en laissant tomber sa main ouverte qui proteste de son impuissance à attaquer le clavecin d'une autre manière qu'elle n'en a l'habitude. "Mais si, mais si, c'est comme ceci!" répond le maître, et il bat la mésure, et il donne le ton, et il scande; on est dans la scène, on la suit, on l'entend! C'est le maximum de l'expressif, à cause de la simplicité des moyens. Mais tandis que le naturel du geste donne ici une parfaite clarté à l'incident, un naturel égal laissera une espèce d'incertitude dans un autre tableau du même Metsu. C'est que, dans cet autre tableau, le *Marché aux herbes,* la vérité a été trop localisée, comme je l'ai dit plus haut. Je veux parler de l'homme vêtu de rouge qui s'adresse en riant à la bourgeoise au seau de fer blanc. Cet homme a une façon de poser son bras droit sur son bras gauche dont le sens n'est pas facile à analyser, quoiqu'elle n'ait rien d'inattendu ni de forcé. Feint-il de mendier avec bouffonnerie? feint-il de faire un salut à belles manières? propose-t-il de porter le seau qui doit fatiguer, dit-il, le bras de la personne? tâte-t-il le bras avec une sorte de convoitise comme s'il tâtait celui de cette bourgeoise? éprouve-t-il un certain embarrass parce qu'il a risqué quelque amabilité ou quelque plaisanterie qui peut être mal accueillie, son geste équivalent alors presque à celui de se gratter l'oreille? La dame a évidemment l'air surpris: "Voilà, pense-t-elle, un hardi et gai polisson," mais il est clair qu'elle va sourire. Cependant elle pourrait se fâcher, on le sent. Lui aurait-elle déjà donné une tape? En revanche, il n'y a pas à se méprendre sur la marchande en dispute, les mains campées sur les hanches. Singulier geste que ce geste populaire, et très complexe! Il indique beaucoup de choses à la fois: que l'on retient dédaigneusement et provisoirement ses mains désireuses de frapper, qu'on veut se donner une contenance majestueuse proper à assurer et affirmer la supériorité qu'on se croit sur l'adversaire, qu'enfin on redoute si peu celui-ci qu'on marche sur lui en laissant les armes au fourreau, c'est-à-dire les poings au repos et comme accrochés à la ceinture. Les deux poings aux hanches, geste "canaille" ou au moins vulgaire; un seul poing sur la hanche, geste noble et royal: Il est intéressant de comparer le Charles Ier de Van Dyck à cette harengère de Metsu.[58]

And Duranty goes on in the same vein, musing about the thin line between popular and aristocratic gestures, debating Darwinian notions of the evolution of gestures and expressions, wondering, but unable to decide, whether or not certain gestures were particularly Dutch, or seventeenth century, or whether they could be traced back to Spain or Sicily, and so on.

Duranty's "Promenades au Louvre" brings together the new art history of the Dutch school with the realist engagement in physiognomics. It shows what he might have done had he chosen to read Degas's pictures. But it also bears witness to a curious contradiction in Duranty's sense of what picture-reading and physiognomic perception were about. For one thing, the "Promenades" betrays its involvement in a paradox that informed all of Duranty's writing about physiognomics. This was the paradox of positivist "objectivity": the presumption of the possibility of objectivity without subjectivity, empirical induction without deduction from a system, together with the reliance upon, indeed the celebration of, subjective sensation. According to Duranty's system, physiognomic information was to be arrived at through direct sensation. A physiognomic feature was readable because it was literally *striking*, because it s*truck* and *impressed* itself upon the viewer: "a *striking* individuality, the contemplation of which was brimming with ideas and *sensations* [my italics]" ("une individualité saisissante, dont la contemplation était grosse d'idées et de sensations").[59]That was what Thulié had meant by "impression" and the "trait saillant," and what Duranty meant by the "trait spécial"—that was how he could conflate the vocabularies of "impression" and "expression," arriving at a "science" of sensation which symbiotically joined "objectivity" to the subjective responses of the viewer, the exteriority of the physiognomic object to the interiority of the physiognomist. The "Promenades," with its first-person account of Duranty's interpretations, and his disagreements with other critics' readings, demonstrates just how subjective this supposedly objective physiognomic system was and always had been.[60]

The "Promenades" also conflicts with Duranty's stated theory to an extent, succumbing to a certain slippage between the system and its application. For as much as Duranty may have wished for a physiognomics of exteriority, contextuality, and plain social fact, of clarity, classifiability, and immediate readability, that is not what he finds when he starts looking for it; it is not what fascinates him most. When he sets out to read, he writes about *not being able* to read, about an *inability* to classify or deduce historic moment from the physiognomic image, or context from the gestural text before him.

It was not the clearly readable that caught Duranty's attention at all. In "Promenades au Louvre," his readings are uncertain ones; more often about the ins and outs and indeterminacies of pictured psychologies than about plain social facts, they all involve multiple choices and many possibilities. Almost every time Duranty begins to interpret a physiognomy as a straightforward social sign, he ends by asserting the impossibility of doing so. Instead, he constantly attempts to hunt down the subtlest, minutest, most individual physiognomic twitches to their source. Indeed, rather than simply exposing manifest social meaning, Duranty seems to have desired to plumb the psychological depths of social surfaces, *to make them surface:* to make the most private pantomime a matter of public meaning, and the most public gesture a matter of private convolution. In short, in "Promenades au Louvre," the social and the psychological, the clear and the convoluted, the readable and the unreadable, are all confounded.

Nevertheless, though Duranty's actual picture-reading is somewhat at odds with his theory, in its first-person subjectivity the "Promenades au Louvre" underscores his obsession with the activity of physiognomic reading. His sense of the impossibility of clear social readings, his uncertainty, his listing of many possible interpretations, his insistence on tracking and pinning down the most inconsequential, fleeting, and ambiguous of gestures, all bear witness to this obsession. His insistence on *difficult* readings demonstrates that he was fascinated with the act of reading itself, more than with what it turned up: Duranty plays with several different manners of reading, ranging from debate with another critic and explication of artists' intentions to mesmerization before and entrance into pictures, animation of pictorial characters, eavesdropping on conversations between them, queries about them, and so on.[61] The activity of paying attention to pictures was his concern; physiognomic acuity and the process by which a physiognomy *impressed* itself on the consciousness of the viewer were what preoccupied him. Indeed, his reduction of the grand program of the representation of the "Spectacle social" in *Réalisme* to that of the "trait saillant" in *La Nouvelle Peinture,* to the narrowest, the most "aigu," the sharpest, most striking of details—in short, to Degas's imagery as opposed to Courbet's—shows that there too Duranty was more interested in the act of physiognomic observation itself than in the social significance of realist physiognomics or the realist program per se. In this respect as well, *La Nouvelle Peinture* matches Degas's concerns: not only the partial, fragmentary look of his images, and his obsession with repetition, but also his privatization of realism and modern-life imagery, his engagement in innuendo and his interest in the process, rather than the products, of physiognomic readability.

There is one picture by Degas which provides a modern, French counterpart to Duranty's reading of private relationships in Dutch pictures in "Promenades au Louvre." This is *The Interior* of 1868 (fig. 7.4), the most obviously relatable of Degas's images to the discourse on realism, the "new" art history, and the engagement in seventeenth-century Dutch

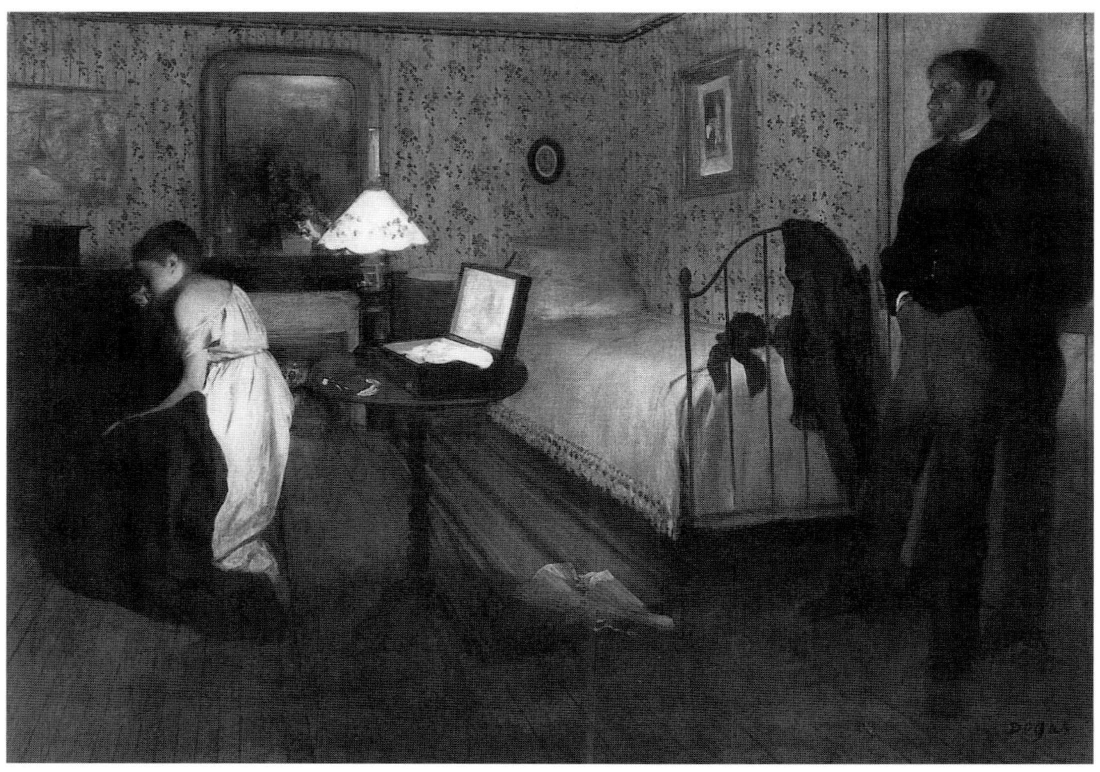

FIGURE 7.4. Edgar Degas, *The Interior*, 1868. The Philadelphia Museum of Art, The Henry P. McIlhenny Collection in memory of Frances P. McIlhenny, 1986. Photo: The Philadelphia Museum of Art/Art Resource, NY.

genre-painting. Duranty might even have indicated this picture specifically in *La Nouvelle Peinture*, with his mention of those speaking "hands sunk in pockets," possibly referring to the man standing by the doorway at the right-hand side of *The Interior*.

Even more than the *Cotton Office*, and unlike Degas's other, serial images of the seventies, *The Interior* is full of the kind of genre detail found in Dutch seventeenth-century pictures. It includes, as few of Degas's other works do, a world of information such as would meet Duranty's requirements for the readable realist image. It is an interior that can be described in detail: an inventory of its contents reveals a carpet, wallpaper, a bed, lamp, and table, a door and a mirror, and dim lamp lighting which bespeaks a particular time of day—if not Duranty's "moment of public life," at least a moment of private life. It contains a man and a woman, the one in street clothes, the other in her chemise, with her corset cast off on the floor. The two figures are manifestly young, it is clear that the male at least belongs to the middle class—his clothes and the accoutrements of the room connote a certain comfortable economic position in life. The stances of the two figures, aggressive and vulnerable, as well as their coloring and costume, dark as opposed to light, dressed versus undressed, clearly speak of a gender opposition between the two. As well as the "hands sunk in pockets," *The Interior* contains another one of Duranty's speaking elements, the back of the woman. Seen together with that vulnerable female back and the man's feral gaze, the gesture of "hands sunk in pockets" seems to solicit from the viewer an interpretive response much like those that the gestures in Metsu's pictures in the Louvre received—a wish to know what emotion it betrays, what event lies behind it.

Indeed, *The Interior* has acquired exaggerated narrative significance in the eyes of later critics. It has been taken to be an illustration of an event in one of Duranty's novels, *Les Combats du François Duquesnoy.*[62] It has also, variously, been seen as an illustration of very specific events in two of Zola's novels, *Madeleine Férat* and *Thérèse Raquin*, published serially as newspaper *feuilletons* in the 1860s.[63] Moreover, it has been used, in a rather extreme way, as a piece of pseudopsychoanalytic evidence for an interpretation of the personality of the artist.[64] The narrational, or at least anecdotal, dimension of the image was one which Degas himself seemed to suggest—though he reportedly did *not* give the painting the title *The Rape* that it has since acquired, he did call it "my genre painting,"[65] as if to stress the anecdotal content and possible readability of *The Interior*, as well as its connection to the tradition deriving from Dutch seventeenth-century imagery.

Yet, as fully descriptive as *The Interior* is, its "meaning" is at least as ambiguous, if not more so, as the "meanings" that Duranty discovered in Metsu's genre pictures. While denotation is plentiful, the most straightforward kinds of physiognomic connotation yield themselves up with some difficulty. The profession of the male figure is not clear. Neither, because she is unclothed, is the class or status of the young woman—she could be a servant, a mistress, or a wife; it is not evident whether she is working class, demimonde, or bourgeois. And it is not clear what the relationship between the two characters is. The setting in which they find themselves could be the interior of a house, a hotel chamber, or a furnished apartment room. The stances of the figures are as connotatively multivalent as the Dutch pictures interpreted by Duranty seemed to be: on the one hand, aggression, anger, lust, seen in the brooding gaze, the dark, vaguely rodent-like facial features, and the splayed legs of the male figure; on the other hand, vulnerability, victimization, dejection, rejection, seen in the turned back, the nape of the neck, and the listless, drooping arms of the female figure. Has the youngish man just come in, or is he about to leave? (That was Duranty's question in front of Metsu's picture.) Is the youngish woman undressing, has the man raped her, has the couple failed to consummate their marriage or their liaison? Is it before or after such an event? Is the nature of the violence and distance between the two of them pre- or post-coital, that of frustration, general unhappiness, or specific violation? What kind of couple are they—if they *are* a couple? The questions multiply, as did Duranty's questions in front of Dutch genre paintings—indeed, these are the kinds of questions that have been asked of *The Interior* in trying to ascertain the moment that is depicted in it and to pin down the narrative that it illustrates.[66] Ultimately, however, all that one may be sure of is the latent violence and the probably sexual nature of the relationship between the two figures; beyond that, it is a picture which requires a caption in order to be read. The stances and poses of the two figures resonate with questions, but not with answers—like the pictorial equivalent of a detective novel without a solution, yet replete with its repertoire of clues: the corset on the floor, the valise on the table, for example. Theirs is a body language and a set of accoutrements full of resonances but possessing no clearly pictorialized text. *The Interior* speaks of the difference between the textuality of genre painting and that of history painting: for its language of gestures and accoutrements is of a reserved rather than a rhetorical nature, which is to say that here those gestures and accoutrements work by holding information back and in reserve, rather than by displaying conventional, and thus clearly and publicly readable body language. It is also to say that the prior text, whatever speculations there are about it, is not known—and is not clearly recognizable in the picture. While Henri Thulié may have suggested, in contrast to the literary example of Balzac, that descriptive pictures contain their own exegesis, and, following the example of Balzac, that settings betray their owners' characters and stories—their "vices"—and while Duranty echoed him on both counts with his discussion of "traits saillants," informative interiors, and expressive luminous instants and impressions, this picture provides evidence that contradicts those claims: all by itself, pictorial description does *not* yield narration,

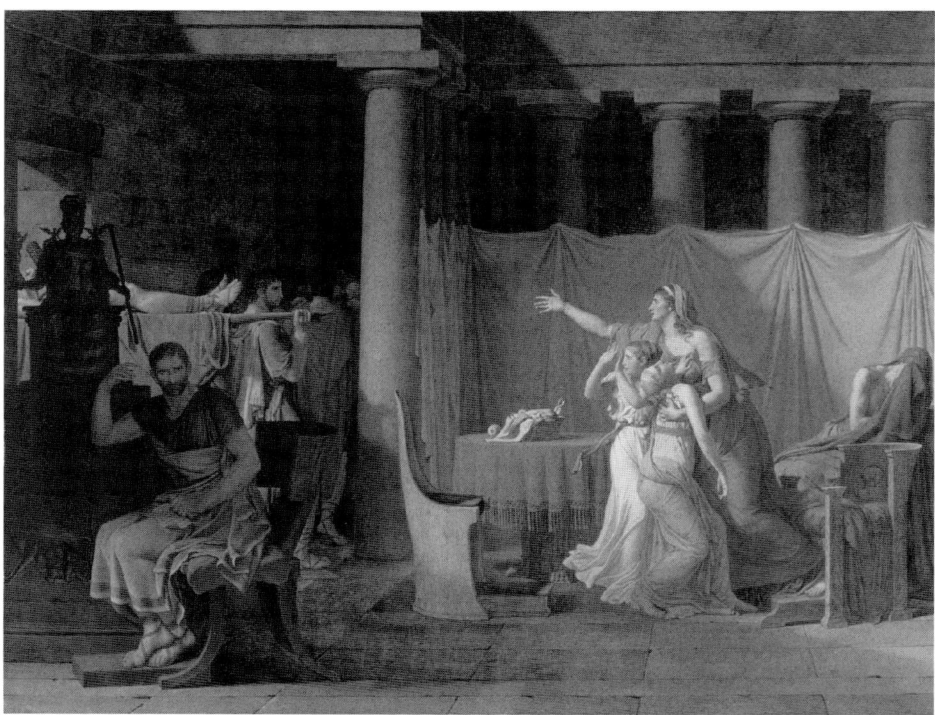

FIGURE 7.5. Jacques-Louis David, *The Lictors Returning to Brutus the Bodies of His Sons*, 1789. Musée du Louvre, Paris. Photo: Réunion des Musées Nationaux/Art Resource, NY. Photographed by G. Blot/C. Jean.

unless it is supported by a known text and a familiarity with characters and actions shared by painter and viewers.

Interpreters of this picture have looked upon it as an unprecedented image. Quentin Bell, in particular, implied that its polarization of male and female was one of the original elements of the picture. This is not precisely true. Degas was drawing on an established tradition of internally bifurcated, sexually split imagery, i.e., the Neoclassical history paintings of David, and in so doing, he was subtly Frenchifying, as well as both updating and backdating, his Dutch-inspired, modern genre picture, and at the same time privatizing narrative painting. Organized around the Davidian lacuna, *The Interior* seems to draw directly on David's *Oath of the Horatii*, and even more on his *Lictors Returning to Brutus the Bodies of His Sons* (fig. 7.5), replacing the seated stance of Brutus with a female back and maintaining his brooding Roman glare in the face of the modern male figure. Those "sources" are both split between male and female poles, and both are based on texts similar to those suggested for *The Interior* (in the cases of the Neoclassical pictures, those texts are known and given in their titles)—narratives of conflict and desire, dramatized through radical, black-and-white oppositions between passive and active figures. In *The Interior*—illustrating as it does an unknown text, given a neutral, uninformative title that critics have attempted to replace with a luridly expressive one, and marked by a resonating, twilit space rather than by an event or an action—those oppositions have been undercut. The expressive, rhetorical gestures of Neoclassical history painting (whose connotations are fully denoted) have been deleted, and the left-to-right, passive-to-active, empty-to-full, dark-to-light reading interrupted by the weirdly lit and furnished orthogonals of the room: the bodily rhetoric of traditional history painting has been interrupted and quite literally replaced by the mutely descriptive surfaces and spaces of genre painting.

One of the key elements of the *Brutus* that Degas may be said to maintain in *The Interior* is the still life in the center of the image. In the *Brutus* the still life serves as the displacement of the violence of the narrative: the decapitation of the sons of Brutus onto the domestic image of shears and pins stuck into balls of thread and yarn.[67] In *The Interior*, such displacement may also be said to occur, but in a more generalized fashion. The latent violence and sexuality of the relationship between the two figures also seem to be displaced onto a still life—the exposed, luridly pink interior of the valise open on the little table between the figures in the center of the room, which might be read as an instance of discreetly erotic display, as an image of an inside opened out and offered up, as one of secret contents exposed and divulged, which the rest of the clue-laden room, as long as it remains without caption, utterly refuses. (Unlike the still life in the *Brutus*, however, this is not a narrative displacement; it does not, as far as we know, implicate any part of a narrative which occurs offstage.)

In calling *The Interior* a genre painting, Degas surely meant to distinguish it from the history painting with which he was still somewhat preoccupied. In drawing on history painting as a compositional source for his own image of male-female conflict and desire (one of the mainstays of the tradition of history painting), and in transforming the rhetorical devices of history painting into his own antirhetorical structure of pictorial reserve, Degas seems to have underlined the essential antitextuality of the modern-life genre image—its *difference* from the tradition of textual painting. He seems to have pointed to the fact that the requirements of history paintings could *not* be applied to modern-life imagery, nor could the same demands of readability and textuality be met by it, or the physiognomics of modernity and modern painting ever really be a physiognomics of direct, single-meaning readability. *The Interior* continues, even now, to ask to be read, but it fails to provide its own reading. Thus, rather than illustrating a story by Duranty, it illustrates the problems inherent in reading genre imagery that Duranty would expose and explore in "Promenades au Louvre."

The Interior is a good counterpart to both *La Nouvelle Peinture* and the "Promenades au Louvre." In look and theme it is a "new painting" variation on the art history of the "maîtres d'autrefois": a modern realist response, not only to the French tradition of history painting, but also to seventeenth-century Dutch genre painting (its ambiguous subject is even rather similar to the frequent ambivalence found in Dutch pictures combining domesticity with allusions to sexual transactions and prostitution).[68] The ambiguity of its social signs, the tense muteness of its interpretation-soliciting collection of clues, its transformation of the public into the private *histoire* and of narrative forms into descriptive ones, its separation of the connotational and the denotational, and the association of its descriptive contents with sexual resonances rather than social meanings: all of these aspects of *The Interior* make it a good counterpart to Duranty's peculiar, subjective/objective positivism, his new-realist physiognomics. It is also the counterpart to Duranty's updating (and backdating) of realism: his detachment of it from 1848 through his attachment of it to the eighteenth century and the "maîtres d'autrefois," his modernization and depoliticization of the old republican Realism by Frenchifying, and even, however reluctantly, by privatizing it.

Certainly known to friends of his, a source of curiosity and puzzlement to them, *The Interior* was just as certainly important to Degas. Though he executed it early in his career it continued to preoccupy him—he worked it over later in the 1890s.[69] It sat in the back of his mind and his studio through much of his working life—possibly as an illustration of how the "trait saillant" of realist physiognomics actually worked and didn't work. Meanwhile Degas isolated the "trait saillant" as his peculiar specialty—rehearsing it repeatedly throughout his series, studying its condensation and materialization of positivist physiognomics over and over again, obsessed with the process by which it collapsed the objective into the subjective and rolled the public text over into the private.

Indeed, all the elements of readability that Duranty listed in *La Nouvelle Peinture*—physiognomies and gestures, glances and stances, pieces of costume and context—are present in Degas's other, later images, as the critics noticed. Body parts, bits of accoutrement, human features and spaces are so obviously and exclusively concerns in Degas's 1870s imagery, yet so radically fragmented and juxtaposed, scattered and shuffled, lined up feature to isolated feature, that they do at least seem to thematize Duranty's preoccupations. Certainly Degas's are images in which acuity is the issue; attention and inattention, sharpness and diffusion, precision of detail, absence and elision, are played out throughout them. Individually and as a body of work, they come together as a collection of physiognomic *sensations*. Many of their viewers seemed to understand them this way: as a series of "traits saillants," strangely repetitive, marginal and self-interrupting, insistently physiognomic, insistent in their demand to be read for some critics and in their refusal to be read for others. Across his various specialties, before and after *La Nouvelle Peinture*, Degas began to remove the "trait saillant" from the context of *The Interior*'s genre-picture space and its narrative pretensions, to give it over to caricature, and to further introvert and invert the nature of its readability, always, however, making physiognomic picture-reading the problem, just as Duranty did both in *La Nouvelle Peinture* and in "Promenades au Louvre."

Notes

Originally published in Carol Armstrong, *Odd Man Out: Readings of the Work and Reputation of Edgar Degas* (Chicago and London: The University of Chicago Press, 1991), 73–100.

1. Oscar Reütersward, "An Unintentional Exegete of Impressionism: Some Observations on Edmond Duranty and His *La Nouvelle Peinture*," *Konsthistorik Tidskrift* (Stockholm), vol. 4 (1949): 111–16, suggests that it was not meant as a catalogue at all and that in fact Duranty was writing about an altogether different group of painters who were also showing in the Durand-Ruel galleries. As evidence for this he refers to a letter by Duranty written to Diego Martelli and to a copy of *La Nouvelle Peinture* with names of the artists to whom Duranty was referring written in the margins (p. 112). That this list of names does not include any of the bona fide Impressionists is no argument against the pamphlet's being dedicated to Degas's group, however—it coincides with other histories of Impressionism, such as that of Duret ("Salon de 1870," *L'Electeur libre* [May–June 1870], reprinted in *Critique d'avant-garde par Th. Duret* [Paris, 1885], 3–53), in its stress on academic painters and in its mention of Jongkind, Boudin, Manet, and others—and it clearly singles out Degas's faction within the group: Bracquemond, de Nittis, Desboutin, Lepic, and Degas himself. Reütersward himself suggests that Degas's work was the basis for Duranty's argument (114). See also Hollis Clayson, "A Failed Attempt," in Charles Moffett, ed., *The New Painting: Impressionism, 1874–1886*, exh. cat. (San Francisco: Fine Arts Museums of San Francisco, 1986), 145–59.
2. Louis Emile Edmond Duranty, *La Nouvelle Peinture: A Propos du groupe d'artistes qui exposent dans les galeries Durand-Ruel* (1876; Paris, 1946). Reprinted and translated in Moffett, ed., *New Painting*, 37–47; this quotation from 38.
3. See John Rewald, *The History of Impressionism*, 4th ed. (New York, 1973), 376–78; and Linda Nochlin, *Impressionism and Post-Impressionism, 1874–1904* (Sources and Documents in the History of Art Series) (Englewood Cliffs, N.J., 1966), 3; and Venturi, *Les Archives de l'impressionnisme*, vol. 1, 50. Rewald denies the allegation made by many of Degas's contemporaries, and by Georges Rivière, in *M. Degas, bourgeois de Paris* ([Paris, 1935], p. 81), that Degas had actually coauthored, or indeed entirely dictated, Duranty's essay. It is much more likely that, as Marcel Crouzet, in *Un Méconnu de Réalisme: Duranty* (Paris, 1964), 337, suggests, Duranty's ideas may have influenced Degas's conception

of what he was about. See also Marianne Marcussen, "Duranty et les impressionnistes," *Hafnia: Copenhagen Papers in the History of Art*, vol. 5 (1978): 24–42; vol. 6 (1979): 27–49.

4. Duranty was reputed to be the illegitimate son of Emilie Lacoste and Louis-Edmond Anthoine. His mother's and father's people were Bonapartists, liberal financiers, and government officials opposed to the Restoration regime. On his father's side, he appears to have been partly aristocratic. Duranty grew up to be remote and reserved, taciturn and protective about his beginnings and his private life, and combative about his place in the world. At his death, his friends remarked on how difficult he had been to know. In this, he was strikingly like Degas, although for rather different reasons. (Crouzet, *Un Méconnu de Réalisme*, 10–26.) Duranty was educated at the Ecole François 1er, a municipal school which, unlike the Lycée Louis le Grand, which Degas attended, was conducted on the basis of the educational theories deriving from the revolution. The sciences and modern European arts and letters were stressed there, as opposed to Latin and Greek; thus it became an important breeding ground for the school of realism. Duranty's friends at the Ecole François 1er were of mixed background. It was there, for example, that he met Jules Assézat, son of a typesetter, who was later to be an important realist cohort of Duranty's. (Ibid., 26–32.)
5. Duranty, *La Nouvelle Peinture*, 38.
6. In the only other article (after the beginning of the Impressionist shows) in which he included remarks on Degas, Duranty was careful to downplay Impressionism: "Pour en revenir aux indépendents, impressionnistes, réalistes ou autres sans étiquette," and to distinguish Degas from those of the group who might be termed Impressionists—Degas was one of the "autres sans étiquette," an "homme à part."—Duranty, *La Chronique des arts et de la curiosité*, 1879. Moreover, Duranty's only direct commentary on the Impressionists is extremely cool: he doesn't like Renoir, he says Sisley's work is but a pale copy of Jongkind's, and Pissarro's pictures he finds good, but restricted—Edmond Duranty, "Les Irréguliers et les naïfs ou le clan des horreurs," *Paris-Journal*, 19 May 1870.
7. Duranty, *La Nouvelle Peinture*, 28.
8. Ibid., 29. Also cited in Rivière, *M. Degas, bourgeois de Paris*, 323.
9. Duranty, *La Nouvelle Peinture*, 45.
10. It is possible that Duranty might also be referring to one of Caillebotte's works with his reference to a man crossing a public square, as well as his mention of a person playing piano (Caillebotte's *Young Man Playing Piano*, 1876). See Clayson, "A Failed Attempt," in Moffett, ed., *New Painting*, 148–49.
11. Duranty, *La Nouvelle Peinture*, 42–43, 45–47.
12. "Textuelle," like "littérale," means "literal" in English, as in a word-for-word quotation or translation—but, particularly in the context of the rest of Duranty's essay, I believe its resonances for him are also textual, whereas for Fromentin it probably only meant "literal."
13. Duranty, *La Nouvelle Peinture*, 22; Eugène Fromentin, "Les Maîtres d'autrefois, IV: Ecole hollandaise-Ruysdael-Cuyp," *La Revue des deux mondes*, vol. 13, 15 February 1876, 796.
14. Crouzet, *Un Méconnu du Réalisme*, 190–91, 372.
15. Ibid., 43–48, 167–95.
16. Edmond Duranty, "La Caricature et l'imagerie pendant la guerre de 1870–71, en Allemagne, en France, en Belgique, en Italie et en Angleterre," *Gazette des beaux-arts* 5 (1 February and 1 April 1872): 155–72, 322–43; 6 (1 November 1872): 393–408. See Champfleury's series on caricature, for example: *Histoire de la caricature moderne* (Paris, 1865); *Histoire de la caricature sous la République, l'Empire et la Restauration* (Paris, 1874).
17. Duranty, "Daumier," *Gazette des beaux-arts* 27 (1 May and 1 June 1878): 429–43, 528–44; Champfleury, "Notice biographique sur Honoré Daumier," in *Exposition de peinture et dessins de H. Daumier. Galeries Durand-Ruel* (Paris, 1878).
18. See Champfleury, "Une visite au Louvre," *L'Artiste*, 1 December 1844: 212.
19. Edmond Duranty, "Ceux qui seront les peintres," *Almanach parisien*, 1867: 13–18; "M. Manet et l'imagerie" *Paris-Journal*, 5 May 1870, and "Le Salon de 1872," *Paris-Journal*, 30 May 1872. Duranty's guarded enthusiasm vis-à-vis Manet and the Impressionists resembles Zola's own mixture of admiration and disappointment.
20. Duranty, "Ceux qui seront les peintres."
21. Meyer Schapiro, in "Courbet and Popular Imagery, an Essay on Realism and Naivété," *Journal of the Warburg and Courtauld Institutes*, vol. 4, 1941: 164–91 (reprinted in Schapiro, *Modern Art, Nineteenth and Twentieth Centuries*, 67–71), shows how Champfleury modified his "avant-garde" tone during the Second Empire, disassociated himself from the worker-peasant ethos that Courbet had adopted, and gradually erased the 1848 overtones from his Second Empire writings on caricature and popular imagery. And T. J. Clark, in *The Absolute Bourgeois: Artists and Politics in France, 1848–1851* (London, 1973), 141–77, traces Baudelaire's gradual alienation from the cause

of 1848. (I should add that when I claim that Duranty set out to detach the "new" realism from "ideology," and that he aimed to "depoliticize" it, I do *not* mean to imply that Duranty's move was not political or ideological: in fact, the depoliticizing, de-ideologizing aspect of *La Nouvelle Peinture* is precisely what makes it political, and what makes it conform to bourgeois or positivist ideology.)

22. Duranty, *La Nouvelle Peinture,* 30. Over and over again, in his articles of the late sixties and early seventies Duranty had cited Courbet as the example to follow: "Nous n'insisterons pas non plus, à leur propos, sur M. Courbet, le robuste initiateur de ces tentatives. M. Courbet parait avoir imprimé personellement tout le mouvement qu'il pouvait donner"—Duranty, "Ceux qui seront les peintres," 13 ff.; see also Duranty, "M. Manet et l'imagerie" and "Où est donc la vérité?" *Paris-Journal,* 8 May 1870.
23. Duranty, *La Nouvelle Peinture,* 41; Denis Diderot, "Essai sur la peinture," in *Oeuvres complètes de Diderot,* Jules Assézat, ed. (Paris, 1876), 463.
24. Diderot, "Essai sur la peinture," 464, 466.
25. Duranty, *La Nouvelle Peinture,* 32.
26. Ibid., 41.
27. Ibid., 31. The following were Diderot's words in the section of the "Essai sur la peinture" that Duranty cited: "Toujours le même pauvre diable, gagé pour venir trios fois la semaine se déshabiller et se faire mannequiner par un professeur, . . . J'aimerais autant qu'au sortir de là, pour compléter l'absurdité, on envoyât les élèves apprendre la grâce chez Marcel ou Dupré, ou tel autre maître à danser qu'on voudra." Diderot, "Essai sur la peinture," 464.
28. Diderot, "Essai sur la peinture," 505 ff.
29. Duranty, *La Nouvelle Peinture,* 49. This complaint echoes those repeated by Duranty himself in the criticism that intervened between *Réalisme* and *La Nouvelle Peinture:* "Il faut arriver à l'imagerie transcendante, l'imagerie admirablement faite, admirablement dessinée, d'une puissance complète. Sauf M. Courbet, nos peintres actuels manquent de puissance" (Duranty, "M Manet et l'imagerie"); "Cependant, les peintres dont nous venons d'indiquer [Fantin, Whistler, Manet, Legros, among others] petite succession historique, ne sont pas arrivés à la plénitude de leur talent, et il faut que de nombreux travaux leur apportent de plus décisifs résultats" (Duranty, "Ceux qui seront les peintres").
30. See Schapiro, "Courbet and Popular Imagery": 66; Mary Lane Charles, *The Growth of Diderot's Fame in France from 1784 to 1875,* Bryn Mawr, 1942: 76–78, 91–93, 96–97; Gita May, *Diderot et Baudelaire,* Paris, 1957: 1–16.
31. Crouzet, *Un Méconnu du Réalisme*, 347–51.
32. Duranty and Assézat were associated with a group of "libre-penseurs," including Henri Thulié, Louis Asséline, and André Lefevre (the latter two also worked on the *Oeuvres complètes*), who collaborated on the positivist, "libre-penseur" publications *La Libre Pensée, La Pensée nouvelle, L'Encyclopédie générale*, and the *Revue d'anthropologie,* and after the war, worked together on the *Bibliothèque des sciences contemporaines* editions. These men, including Thulié, were important members of the Société d'Anthropologie, instructors at the Ecole d'Anthropologie, and dignitaries of the Conseil Municipal. Thulié, for one, was also a freemason. (Besides his principal involvement in the study of madness, Thulié was concerned with questions of hygiene, public works, and education. He was also a confirmed anticlerical.) See Crouzet, *Un Méconnu du Réalisme*, 63, 272–73, 453–54, 952. The ideas of these men were close to those of historians like Quinet. They were preoccupied with pedagogy, history, and the sciences; with the history of science; and with the relationship between the natural and social sciences. They were ardent evolutionists, though theirs was a modified, humanized version of Darwinian theory.
33. Assézat saw himself as editor and publisher of the eighteenth century. In his biographical and critical notices to his three-volume collection of Restif de la Bretonne's works (*Restif de la Bretonne—Les Contemparaines, ou les aventures des plus jolies femmes de l'âge présent*, Paris, 1875–76), he showed that he considered that author to be a father of the nineteenth-century "science de l'homme"—vol. 2, xxxvi. He also connected his work on that eighteenth-century author with his earlier contribution to *Réalisme*—vol. 2, v. Asséline wrote *Diderot et le dix-neuvième siècle* (1865), and, with Lefevre, edited and published the *Chefs-d'oeuvres de Diderot* (1879–80), *Jacques le Fataliste* (1885), and *La Religieuse* (1886). It is clear that others saw their preoccupation with the eighteenth century as part and parcel of their "libre-penseur" philosophies and scientific interests, and that they themselves understood their collaboration on the *Revue encyclopédique* and the *Bibliothèque des sciences contemporaines*, for which Duranty was to have written a "history of art," as continuations of the eighteenth-century *Encyclopédie*. (Larousse's *Grand Dictionnaire universel du dix-neuvième siècle* was probably conceived in the same

way.) Thulié, for his part, made it quite clear that he saw his own medical and scientific work as thoroughly in the spirit of the eighteenth century (Crouzet, *Un Méconnu du Réalisme*, 75, 348–55). In a more general way, Charles shows us the extent to which Diderot, both as encyclopedist and as novelist, was thought of as the parent of nineteenth-century positivism, social thought, and style (Charles, *Growth of Diderot's Fame*, 96–101).

34. Crouzet, *Un Méconnu du Réalisme*, 340.
35. See Edgar Quinet, *L'Esprit nouveau*, in *Oeuvres complètes*, 5th ed. (Paris, 1895), 11–15, 36–42, 45–50, 97, 329 ff.
36. Fromentin's articles on Dutch and Flemish painting are a little different from those of Thoré-Bürger, Taine, and Blanc. His writing tends to be much more vividly descriptive of individual paintings, and much more devoted to evocations of the individuality and personal genius of particular painters—such as Rubens and Rembrandt. But his remarks on the Dutch school, as opposed to the Flemish one, do concentrate on the national character of the Dutch to a certain extent. Whereas he opens his account of Belgian art (where he focuses on the work of one individual, Rubens) with a discussion of the museum in Brussels and of artistic tradition, by contrast, his opening remarks on the Dutch school have to do with Dutch culture and character, Dutch "egalitarianism," even the particular qualities of Dutch nature—its landscape. See Eugène Fromentin, *Les Maîtres d'autrefois*, in *Oeuvres complètes* (Paris, 1984), *Belgique I*, 571–81, and *Hollande I* and *II*, 649–66.
37. Duranty was aware of the works of Thoré-Bürger and Taine. He was personally acquainted with Thoré-Bürger and in *La Nouvelle Peinture* explicitly echoed Thoré-Bürger's "Nouvelles tendances de l'art," written the same year as *Trésors d'art en Angleterre (Trésors d'art exposés à Manchester en 1857, et provenant des collections royales, des collections publiques et des collections particulières de la Grande Brétagne)* (Paris, 1857)—see Crouzet, *Un Méconnu du Réalisme*, 190–91; Théophile Thoré-Bürger, "Nouvelles tendances de l'art," in introduction to *Salons de Théophile Thoré* (Paris, 1868). He was, moreover, openly competitive vis-à-vis Taine's standing as a critic and historian (Crouzet, *Un Méconnu du Réalisme*, 467), and he must have been aware of Charles Blanc's extremely well-known works. His "Promenades au Louvre: Remarques sur le geste dans quelques tableaux," *Gazette des beaux-arts* 15 (1 January 1877), clearly shows his engagement with the current discussion of Dutch seventeenth-century painting—there certainly, he followed in Fromentin's footsteps, analyzing the same group of pictures in the Louvre that Fromentin had described the year before. That he saw himself as a contributor to the discussion of Dutch and Flemish painting is clear in an article of two years later: Edmond Duranty, "Bibliographie de l'art et les artistes hollandais, par Henry Havard," *Gazette des beaux-arts* 20 (1 August 1879): 169–72. Furthermore, he wrote his "Promenades au Louvre" in the context of an encyclopedic discussion, of which the writings on Dutch art were a part, about the schools of art of the world, considered nation by nation. He wrote four more "Promenades," all about the Louvre's Egyptian collection: "Promenades au Louvre. Remarques à propos de l'art egyptien," *Gazette des beaux-arts* 17 (1 March 1878): 221–33; 19 (1 March 1879): 209–24; 20 (1 August 1879): 135–45; and 20 (1 October 1879): 132–36. At the same time, he was writing articles—also for the *Gazette des beaux-arts*—about various national schools of art represented at the Universal Exhibition and in other shows: "L'Exposition Universelle: Les Ecoles étrangères de peinture," *Gazette des beaux-arts* 18 (1 July 1878): 50–62, and 18 (1 August 1878): 147–68; "L'Extrême Orient. Revue d'ensemble des arts asiatiques à l'Exposition Universelle," *Gazette des beaux-arts* 18 (1 December 1878): 101–48; "L'Exposition de la Royal Academy et de la Grosvenor Gallery à Londres," *Gazette des beaux-arts* 20 (1 October 1879): 366–76; "Munich et l'exposition allemande," *Gazette des beaux-arts* 20 (1 November 1879): 454–61. In this respect, he obviously echoed Thoré-Bürger, Taine, and Blanc.
38. Thoré-Bürger's *Trésors d'art exposés à Manchester*, later known simply as *Trésors d'art en Angleterre*, was an overview not only of Dutch painting but of most of the national schools of Europe. In it, the Dutch and Italian schools are seen as the two principal, contrasting schools of Europe. See Frances Suzman Jowell, *Thoré-Bürger and the Art of the Past* (Harvard Ph.D., 1971), New York, 1977. Taine's *Philosophie de l'art dans les Pays Bas* of 1869 was a companion work and follow-up on, and in explicit contrast to, his *Philosophie de l'art en Italie* of 1866 (Hippolyte Taine, *Philosophie de l'art*, in *Miroir de l'art* series, Paris, 1964), while Fromentin's "Les Maîtres d'autrefois" of 1876 was, according to Gonse, originally intended to be part of a much larger history of world art (Louis Gonse, *Eugène Fromentin, peintre et écrivain* [Paris, 1881], 173–74).

Similarly, Charles Blanc's *Ecole hollandaise* was part of his larger *Histoire des peintres de toutes les écoles,* which was also published in 1876. In his introduction to it, written in 1860, he quite explicitly distinguished the Italian tradition from the northern one.

39. For a discussion of the depoliticization of Courbet's reputation, see Linda Nochlin, "The De-Politicization of Gustave Courbet: Transformation and Rehabilitation under the Third Republic," *October,* no. 22 (Fall 1982).
40. This presents quite a striking contrast to Duranty's description of Manet's "fond gris somber" and Manet's protest against bric-à-brac settings and the too detailed rendering of costumes and materials—Duranty, "M. Manet et l'imagerie." It also contrasts with Duranty's only extended description of an individual work by Degas, the latter's so-called "*Dame au clair-obscur social (Mme Camus),*" of which, in "Où est donc la vérité?" he says that he finds it lacking in "l'accord, auquel il tient d'ordinaire, entre le personnage et l'intérieur" and also lacking in "sa compréhension si particulier de la physionomie."
41. Duranty, *La Nouvelle Peinture,* 44–46.
42. Theodore Zeldin, in *France 1848–1945: Intellect and Pride* (Oxford, 1980), 205–42, gives a good account of the stress on "verbalism" in French nineteenth- and twentieth-century culture, as inculcated in its citizens in the classroom.
43. A complete list of his novels, novelettes, short newspaper stories, and works of criticism is available at the end of Crouzet, *Un Méconnu du Réalisme,* 735–45.
44. Henri Thulié, "Du Roman: La Description," *Réalisme,* no. 4 (15 January 1857): 38; and "Du roman: L'Action," ibid., no. 5 (15 March 1857): 701.
45. Duranty echoed another criticism of Balzac's oeuvre that was very common: that Balzac's writing was overwrought, baroque, and exaggerated, and therefore more romantic than realist—Bernard Weinberg, *French Realism: The Critical Reaction, 1830–70* (London, 1937), 33–81.
46. Ibid., 73–81.
47. Thulié, "Du roman," 38.
48. Ibid.
49. Louis Emile Edmond Duranty, "Le Spectacle social," *Réalisme,* no. 2 (15 November 1856): 4.
50. Henri Thulié was a medical man, a psychologist, sociologist, and anthropologist, and a "libre-penseur." In the 1850s he was part of Champfleury's circle, where he met Duranty (Crouzet, *Un Méconnu du Réalisme,* 62–63). He shared with Duranty an interest in mental disease and aberration and in the social conditioning, physiological aspects, and bodily appearance of extreme psychological states. His foray into literary criticism was of very brief duration—it lasted only as long as the journal *Réalisme* (ibid., 75)—but his involvement in Realism was clearly part and parcel of his lifelong professional commitment to the positivist linkages between medicine, psychology, and social science. This is evident in his works of the 1860s—*Etude sur le délire aigu sans lésions* (Paris, 1865), and *La Folie et la loi* (Paris, 1866), and in his "avant-propos" to his *La femme, essai de sociologie physiologique* (Paris, 1885). See also his history of the Paris School of Anthropology—Henri Thulié, *L'Ecole d'Anthropologie de Paris depuis sa fondation, 1876–1906* (Paris, 1907). Duranty's "La Liberté et la folie," in *Paris-Journal,* 21 February 1870, closely echoes Thulié's writings—indeed, he mentions "Dr. Thulié" several times, referring to the pro-institutional, pro-control attitude toward the mad evidenced in Thulié's *La Folie et la loi.* So Thulié's interest in Realism is very much in the tradition of the earlier nineteenth-century use of realist observation as a tool of physiognomic investigation and medical-psychological diagnosis.
51. Louis Emile Edmond Duranty, "Sur la physionomie," *La Revue libérale* 2 (25 July 1867): 499–523.
52. There is this remark in one of Degas's notebooks from the late 1860s: "Make of the *tête d'expression* a study of modern feeling—it's like Lavater, but a more relative Lavater in a way. Study Delsarte's observations on those movements of the eye inspired by feeling—Its beauty must be nothing more than a specific physiognomy. . . . Make portraits of people in typical, familiar poses, being sure above all to give their faces the same kind of expression as their body. Thus if laughter typifies the individual—make her laugh!"—quoted in Kendall, *Degas by Himself,* 37. See also Ian Dunlop, *Degas* (London, 1979), 63; Theodore Reff, *Degas: The Artist's Mind* (New York, 1976), 216–19.
53. Although the heyday of physiognomic studies, "phrenology," and the "physiologies" was between the 1830s and 1850s, as Judith Wechsler points out in *A Human Comedy: Physiognomy and Caricature in Nineteenth-Century Paris* (Chicago, 1982), 32, treatises and essays continued to appear through the seventies, eighties, and nineties, as Graeme Tytler, in *Physiognomy in the European Novel: Faces and Fortunes* (Princeton, 1982), 116–18, demonstrates. Physiognomy continued to be the subject of a variety of discourses, ranging from treatises for artists to books of mime, dancing, and comportment; pseudoscientific works of anthropology, sociology, criminology, psychology,

and physiology; and popular typologies and parlor-game hermeneutics in the manner of Jean Gaspard Lavater, whose works were extremely well known and widely read in France throughout the century: *Essai sur la physionomie, destiné à faire connoitre l'homme et à le faire aimer* (Paris, 1781–1803) (this, or versions of this, were published throughout the first and second decades of the nineteenth century and in 1826, 1835, 1841, 1845, as well as in 1909. Lavater's work and Charles Le Brun's *Expression des passions de l'âme* (Paris, 1727) were still the standard physiognomic texts in the nineteenth century (Jurgis Baltrusaitis, "Physiognomie animale," *Abérrations: Quatre Essays sur la légende des formes* [Paris, 1957], 43; and Tytler, *Physiognomy in the European Novel*, 82–84). Duranty himself mentions Lavater as standing for the notion of physiognomy, in "Les Irréguliers et les naïfs ou le clan des horreurs." Other important texts were those of Descartes, Gall, and Darwin: René Descartes, *Les Passions de l'âme* (Amsterdam, 1650); Franz Gall and G. Spurzheim, *Anatomie et physiologie du système nerveux en général, et du cerveau en particulier, avec des observations sur la possibilité de reconnoitre plusieurs dispositions intellectuelles et morales de l'homme et des animaux, par la configuration de leurs têtes* (Paris, 1810–19); Charles Darwin, *L'Expression des émotions chez l'homme et les animaux*, trans. Samuel Pozzi and René Benoit (Paris, 1874). These were the sources for later nineteenth-century writers on physiognomy, the most important of which was Dr. Pierre Gratiolet (*De la physionomie et des mouvements d'expression* [Paris, 1865], based on lectures given at the Sorbonne), who trained in the Academy of Medicine and worked in the Museum of the Jardin des Plantes and then in the Faculté des Sciences de Paris (Gratiolet, pp. 389 ff.), and whose works Duranty was aware of—Duranty, "Sur la physionomie," 508. Degas, who had read Lavater's work, also demonstrated an interest in the widely read works of the criminologist-anthropologists Bordier and Lombroso—Reff, *Degas: The Artist's Mind*, 220. See Arthur Bordier, *Etude anthropologique sur une série de crânes d'assassins* (Paris, 1881) and *Pathologie comparée de l'homme et des êtres organisés* (Paris, 1889); Cesare Lombroso, *L'uomo bianco e l'uomo di colore: letture sull'origine e le varietá delle razze umane* (Padova, 1871), *L'Homme de génie* (Paris, 1889); *Le Crime politique et les révolutions par rapport au droit, à l'anthropologie criminelle et à la science du gouvernement* (Paris, 1892), *L'Homme criminel, criminel, criminel né, épileptique, criminel fou, criminel d'occasion, criminel par passion* (trans. from 5th Ital. ed.—the first one was 1876) (Paris, 1895), *La Femme criminelle et la prostituée* (Paris, 1896), and *Etudes de sociologie, les anarchistes* (Paris, 1897).

54. Eugène Mouton's *La Physionomie comparée, traité de l'expression dans l'homme, dans la nature et dans l'art* (Paris, 1885), one of the most interesting and extensive of the late nineteenth-century texts on physiognomy, bears witness to this eclecticism. At the beginning (p. 4), he speaks of the "langage universel de la nature," and then he ends his treatise with a series of chapters on the physiognomics of the animal and vegetal kingdom and even that of the inorganic world. He also refers to the notion of man as the microcosm of the world, and to the Renaissance theory of resemblances (p. 34), to physiognomics as a "grammar" and as an "anthropology" (p. 50). He speaks of laws of proportion, of Le Brun-like temperaments and laws of expression, and of "les influences de milieu," in a manner akin to Diderot, Darwin, Balzac, and the Realists. And he returns repeatedly to aberrational and marginal physiognomies, very much in line with the interests of Bordier and Lombroso. Thus, Mouton collapses together ideas deriving from completely different eras and pertaining to epistemologies widely at variance with one another—it is as if he had taken the epistemological structures of the sixteenth, seventeenth, eighteenth, and nineteenth centuries as described in Michel Foucault's *Les Mots et les choses* (Paris, 1966) and blithely elided them. As Baltrusaitis shows, his text was typical of the physiognomic tradition in general and particularly of the nineteenth-century French obsession with it (Baltrusaitis, "Physiognomie animale," 42–43).
55. Duranty, "Le Spectacle social," 4.
56. Louis Emile Edmond Duranty, "Notes sur l'art," *Réalisme*, no. 1 (10 July 1856): 2.
57. Duranty, "Le Spectacle social," 4.
58. Louis Emile Edmond Duranty, "Promenades au Louvre," 20–22.
59. Duranty, "Notes sur l'art," 2.
60. The most often cited physiognomist of them all, Lavater, was certainly subjectivist in his method, and indeed he celebrated the subjectivity of the physiognomist, whom he termed an "artist"—Jean Gaspard Lavater, *Essai sur la physionomie destiné à faire connoitre l'homme et à le faire aimer* (La Haye, 1781).
61. Michael Fried, in *Absorption and Theatricality: Painting and Beholder in the Age of Diderot* (Berkeley, 1980), sees these modes of criticism as the inventions of Diderot: see 55, 58–59, 122–30. Indeed, in the nineteenth century Diderot's writings on art were widely

adopted as models not only for realism writing but also for art criticism—by conservative and avant-garde critics alike. See Charles, *Growth of Diderot's Fame*, 90–96. Charles Blanc, for example, paid homage to him in the *Grammaire des arts du dessin*, 5th ed. (Paris, 1883; 1st ed., 1867), by structuring his book like the "Essai sur la peinture"—according to the categories of judgment. It would appear, however, that Duranty and other nineteenth-century critics looked to Diderot's writing as a model—*not* for a system of judgment categories, but for what it also provided: an anticategorical, unsystematic style of critical prose and critical attention. From mid-century on, when his art criticism became known, critics increasingly aped the Diderotian style: the breeziness, the playful dialogues and arguments, the mixed modes, the sarcasm, the epigrams, the contradictions, and the carelessnesses—Diderot's critical whimsy, in other words, rather than his theoretical structure. Diderot's was a language which sounded like casual talk; as such it became associated with wit, rapid judgment, and lack of structure—Frenchness, flair, and facility—with eighteenth-century *esprit*, in short, rather than with seventeenth-century rigor. Nineteenth-century critics appropriated this eighteenth-century critical style and made it over into a rhetorical mode of their own, marked by flippancy and impudence—a rhetorical mode derived from critical, journalistic precedents rather than from careful theoretical models. In their hands, the chatty style of writing initiated by Diderot became a mode of inattention. Though Duranty was interested in processes of attention and acuity, he often seemed to adopt this style himself. In "Promenades au Louvre," he used a variety of critical modes: from dialogue with another critic to absorption within, eavesdropping upon, and direct questioning of images. The abrupt shifting from one mode to another characteristic of "Promenades" was itself a thoroughly Diderotian strategy. On a broader level, Duranty's lightly sarcastic tone, his casual, conversational style, his summary treatment of some issues and lengthy treatment of others, his sometimes contradictory didacticism—in short, his combining of theoretical aspirations with antitheoretical modes—is reminiscent of Diderot's style of criticism. In other words, he too used the *disorder*, rather than the order, of Diderot's critical style for his own purposes. (It is interesting, in this respect, that in one of his Salon reviews, "Réflexions d'un bourgeois sur le Salon de peinture"—*Gazette des beaux-arts* 15 (1 June 1877): 547–81, 16 (1 July 1877): 48–82, and 16 (1 October 1877): 355–67—Duranty expressly addresses the issue of "disorganized" criticism, saying in his first installment [p. 581] that in judging the pictures at the Salon he had followed the path of his personal whim rather than respected the hierarchy of genres.)

62. Rivière, *M. Degas, bourgeois de Paris*, 97–98; Reff, *Degas: The Artist's Mind*, 202. Quentin Bell, *Degas: Le Viol: Charlton Lectures on Art* (Newcastle-upon-Tyne, 1965), cites Duranty's novel, but denies that it is the story represented. That the story, in its original serial form, "Les Combats de François d'Hésclieu," published in *L'Evénement illustré* between April and July of 1868, could have inspired the picture generally is possible because of its date (the picture has been redated several times) and because this newspaper was much read by Degas and his circle—see Hélène and Jean Adhémar, "Zola et la peinture," *Arts*, no. 389 (12–18 December 1952).
63. Reff, *Degas: The Artist's Mind:* 202 ff.
64. Bell centers his whole argument around the question of exactly which of the above texts was illustrated in *The Interior*, finding that none of them exactly match the image. Finally, he places *The Interior* within a whole series of images by Degas which he terms "private fantasies" of "murder, torture and rape," and which he explains as deriving from Degas's familial relationships and his obsession with blindness, etc. It is, I think, a picture which solicits such interpretation—but into which the failure of such interpretation is also built.
65. P. A. Lemoisne, *Degas et son oeuvre*, vol. 1 (Paris, 1946), 61–62; Paul Lafond, *Degas*, vol. 2 (Paris, 1918–19), 4; and Georges P. F. Grappe, *Edgar Degas* (Paris, 1908), 50, all assert that Degas called the picture *The Rape*, but Jeanniot and Henri Rouart said he called it simply *The Interior*, and "my genre painting," while Paul Poujaud angrily denies that the artist himself ever conceived of the image as *The Rape:* G. Jeanniot, "Souvenirs sur Degas," *Revue universelle*, no. 55 (1933): 29; letter of 11 July 1936 (written by Paul Poujaud), in *Lettres de Degas*, ed. Marcel Guérin (Paris, 1945), 255. See Reff, *Degas: The Artist's Mind*, 201–2: "My Genre Painting." Apparently the image was of such significance to Degas that he was at work restoring it in 1903 (E. Rouart, "Degas," *Le Point* 2, no. 1 [February 1937]: 21).
66. See Bell, *Degas: Le Viol;* Camille Mauclair, *Degas* (Paris, 1937), 14; Reff, *Degas: The Artist's Mind*, 200 ff.
67. Suggested to me in lectures on David's painting by Thomas Crow at Princeton University.
68. Ambiguous subject matter with sexual references is indicated by Fromentin, for example, in his description

of Terborch's *Militaire et la jeune femme:* "ce gros homme en harnais queue, avec sa cuirasse, son pourpoint de buffle, sa grande épée, ses bottes à entonnoir, son futre posé par terre, sa grosse face enluminée, mal rasée, un peu suante, avec ses cheveux gras, ses petits yeux humides et sa large main, potélée et sensuelle, dans la-quelle il offre des pièces d'or et dont le geste nous èclaire assez sur les sentiments du personnage et sur l'object de sa viste"—*Les Maîtres d'autrefois (Oeuvres complètes)*, 686 (this after he had earlier announced that Dutch painting in general was characterized by "l'absence totale de ce que nous appelons aujourd'hui *un suget*," 669).

69. E. Rouart, "Degas."

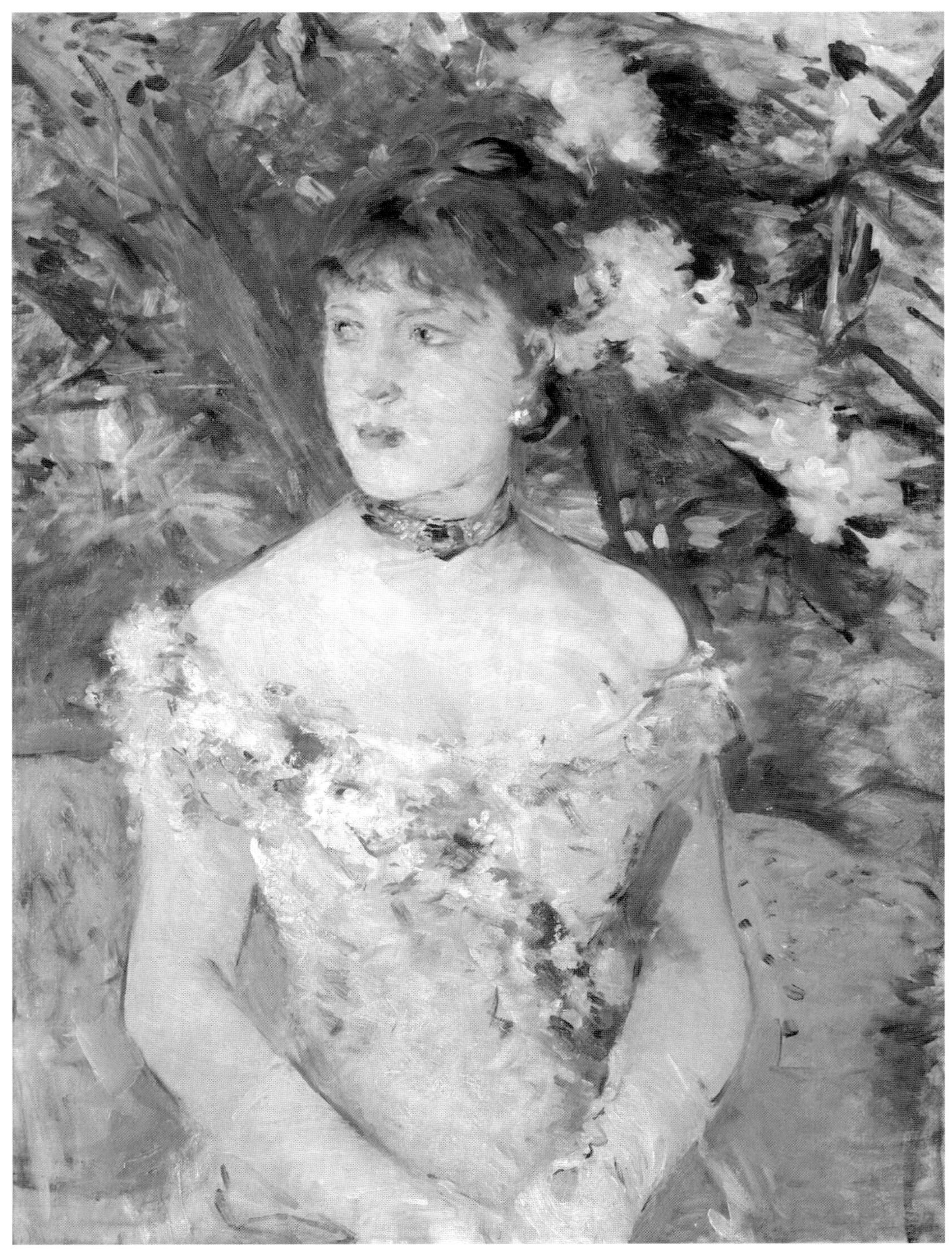

FIGURE 8.1. Berthe Morisot, *Young Woman in a Ball Gown*, 1879. Musée d'Orsay, Paris. Photo: Réunion des Musées Nationaux/Art Resource, NY. Photographed by Hervé Lewandowski.

8

Berthe Morisot and the Feminizing of Impressionism

TAMAR GARB

> Dispersing, piercing those metaphors—particularly the photological ones—which have constituted truth by the premises of Western philosophy: virgin, dumb, and veiled in her nakedness, her vision still naively "natural," her viewpoint still resolutely blind and unsuspecting of what may lie beneath the blindness. LUCE IRIGARAY, 1974

IN AN ARTICLE PUBLISHED in *La Nouvelle Revue* in the spring of 1896, the year of the posthumous retrospective of Berthe Morisot's work, the prominent critic Camille Mauclair announced that Impressionism was dead.[1] It had become history. It was an art form that had lived off its own sensuality, and it had died of it. It was possible, now, in the 1890s, to detect the unsatisfactory and illusory principle on which it had been founded. For Mauclair, Impressionism was a style based on the misguided aim of restricting itself to the seizing of visceral sensation alone. It rejected all general and underlying truths in favor of the appearance of the moment. Its meager resources were the hand and the eye. Like many of the supporters of Symbolism in the 1890s, Mauclair approved of the Impressionists' assertion of "subjectivity" ("nature seen through a temperament," in Emile Zola's words) and their rejection of old-fashioned beliefs in academic beauty, but he objected to their reliance on what he called "realism." By precluding from its orbit anything that was not to be found in the world of immediate experience, he claimed, Impressionism had destroyed itself. While understandably avoiding the excesses of idealism, it had lapsed into crass materialism.[2]

Although this view of Impressionism became prevalent in the 1890s, Impressionism had for some time been regarded as an art form of spontaneous expression, as a means of finding the self in the execution of a painting whose very technique came to represent a direct and naïve vision, however hard won. For its supporters it could be defended in terms of its "sincere" and "truthful" revelation of the temperament of the artist, who filtered the world of visual sensation through the physical acts of making marks on a surface, approximating those sensations by inventing an appropriate technical language and thereby presenting a just and personal vision of the outside world. For many of its detractors, though, Impressionist painting could be construed as a thoughtless, mechanical activity, which required no exercise of the intellect, no regard to time-worn laws of pictorial construction, and involved simply the unmediated reflex recordings of sensory impulses, a practice that smacked of both decadence and superficiality.

It was, however, Impressionism's alleged attachment to surface, its very celebration of sensory experience born of the rapid perception and notation of fleeting impressions, that was to make it regarded in the 1890s as a practice most suited to women's temperament and character.[3] Indeed, Mauclair himself, while denigrating Impressionism at large, called it a "feminine art" and proclaimed its relevance for the one artist whom he saw as having been its legitimate protagonist—a woman, Berthe Morisot. In turn, Impressionism's demise is traced to its allegedly "feminine" characteristics: its sensuality, its dependence on sensation and superficial appearance, its physicality, and its capriciousness.[4]

While the discourse that produced this apparently seamless fit between Impressionist superficiality and women's nature attained the level of a commonplace in avant-garde circles in the 1890s, those critics who read the art press had long heard Morisot's works discussed in terms that inscribed them as quintessentially "feminine."[5] In 1877 Georges Rivière had commented on her "charming pictures, so refined and above all so feminine."[6] When *Laundresses Hanging Out the Wash* (plate 4) was exhibited in 1876 and *Young Woman in a Ball Gown* (fig. 8.1) in 1880, the works were praised for their delicate use of brushwork, their subtlety and clarity of color, their refinement, grace, and elegance, their delightfully light touch.[7] Her paintings were repeatedly praised for what was described as their "feminine" charm. Although many critics lamented the lack of finish in her work, some could still observe as Albert Wolff did that: "Her feminine grace lives amid the excesses of a frenzied mind."[8] She was seen, at worst, as the "victim of the system of painting that she has adopted."[9] On one occasion her lack of "finish" was attributed to a primordial feminine weakness. Paul de Charry, writing in *Le Pays*, asked, "With this talent, why does she not take the trouble to finish?" and answered himself, "Morisot is a woman, and therefore capricious. Unfortunately, she is like Eve who bites the apple and then gives up on it too soon. Too bad, since she bites so well."[10]

It is true that the qualities of "grace" and "delicacy" were on some occasions used to describe the techniques of the male Impressionists. Alfred Sisley was even credited with a "charming talent," and his *The Bridge at Argenteuil* (1872; fig. 8.2) was said to show his "taste, delicacy and tranquility."[11] Camille Pissarro on the occasion of showing his *Path through the Woods* (1877; Musée d'Orsay) was said to be gifted with a fine sensibility and great "delicacy."[12] But the analyses of work by men in these terms alone were few and far between. What is more interesting than such occasional applications of traditionally "feminine" attributes to individual male artists is the "feminizing of Impressionism" as a whole.[13]

The first critic to develop a sustained argument seeking to prove that Impressionism was an innately "feminine" style was the Symbolist sympathizer Théodor de Wyzewa, who, in an article written in March 1891, claimed that the marks made by Impressionist painters were expressive of the qualities intrinsic to women.[14] For example, the use of bright and clear tones paralleled what he called the lightness, the fresh clarity, and the superficial elegance that make up a woman's vision. It was, he wrote, appropriate that women should not be concerned with the deep and intimate relationships of things, that they should see the "universe like a gracious, mobile surface, infinitely nuanced. . . . Only a woman has the right to rigorously practice the Impressionist system, she alone can limit her effort to the translation of impressions." In his preface to the catalogue for her first solo exhibition, in 1892, Gustave Geffroy had called Morisot's a "painting of a lived and observed reality, a delicate painting . . . which is a feminine painting."[15] In the same year Georges Lecomte had claimed that Impressionism, with its "sincerity" and "immediacy," was more suited than any other mode of expression to allow "this delicate female temperament which no external influence alters or corrupts, to develop."[16] Writing in the *Revue encyclopédique* in 1896, Claude Roger-Marx felt able to assert that "the term Impressionism itself announces a manner of ob-

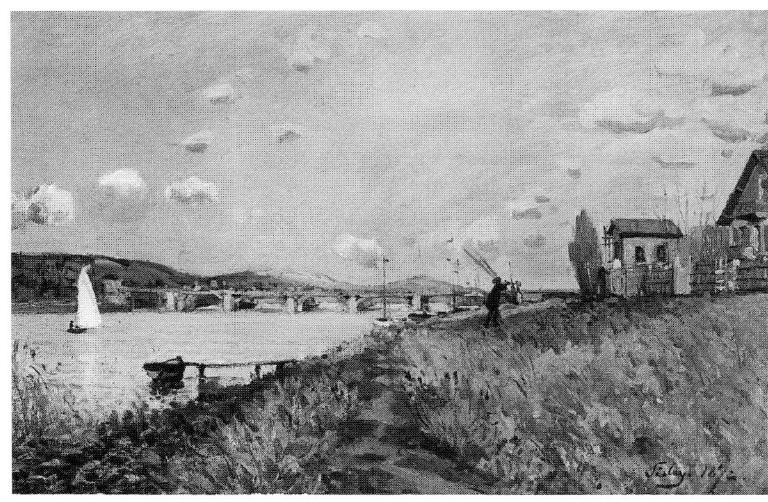

FIGURE 8.2. Alfred Sisley, *Le Pont d'Argenteuil (The Bridge at Argenteuil)*, 1872. Memphis Brooks Museum of Art, Memphis, Tennessee; Gift of Mr. and Mrs. Hugo Dixon, 54.64.

servation and notation which is well suited to the hypersensitivity and nervousness of women."[17]

These sentiments were echoed in a review of the work of women artists in Boston by the Parisian critic S. C. de Soissons, who stressed that the superficiality that attended woman's fitting restriction of her sensibility to the mimetic function central to Impressionism would be recompensed by her "incomparable charm, her fine grace and sweetness."[18] Arguing for the suitability of Impressionists' technique to women's manner of perception, de Soissons wrote:

> One can understand that women have no originality of thought, and that literature and music have no feminine character; but surely women know how to observe, and what they see is quite different from that which men see, and the art which they put in their gestures, in their toilet, in the decoration of their environment is sufficient to give us the idea of an instinctive, of a peculiar genius which resides in each one of them.[19]

Women artists, according to de Soissons and his colleagues, could give expression to their intrinsic natures by being Impressionists. What was peculiar to women were the sensitivity of their sensory perceptions and the lack of development of their powers of abstraction. What was peculiar to Impressionism was its insistence on the recording of surface appearance alone. As such they were made for each other. A particular construction of "Woman" and "Impressionism," which becomes operative and meaningful within the political and aesthetic climate of the 1890s (although its formation can be traced back for decades and its influence can still be seen today), is at stake here. In the context of the Symbolist valorization of the imagination on the one hand and the resurgence of various forms of idealism on the other, Impressionism came to connote a relatively inadequate aesthetic model based on the filtering and recording of impressions, hastily perceived, of the outside world. "Woman" was the graceful, delicate, charming creature, nervous in temperament, superficial in her understanding of the world, dexterous with her hands, sensitive to sensory stimuli and subjective in her responses, who could most legitimately make use of this mode of expression. Berthe Morisot came to represent the happy fusion of these two constructions.

In order for the myth of Morisot's well-adjusted femininity to function as naturalized speech, however, her artistic practice had to be seen as the result of an unmediated outpouring. The condition of myth according to Roland Barthes is that it emerge "without any trace of the history which has caused it."[20]

Implicit in much of the Morisot criticism during this period is the assumption that her painting was achieved without effort. Gustave Geffroy compared her hands to those of a magician. Her paintings were the result of "delicious hallucinations" that allowed her quite naturally to transport her "love of things" to an intrinsic gift for painting.[21] Moreover, her strength was said to reside in her feminine powers of observation that allowed for an intuitive filtering of the outside world, uncorrupted, in Georges Lecomte's words, by any learned system of rules.[22]

Morisot's success, the critic George Moore wrote, lay in her investing "her art with all her femininity," thereby creating a "style" that is "no dull parody of ours" (men's); her art is "all womanhood—sweet and gracious, tender and wistful womanhood."[23] But such gifts, necessarily, set her apart from other women artists. She had since the 1880s been compared with her female contemporaries whom she was said to outstrip in "femininity." The most famous casualties in such comparisons were Rosa Bonheur, Marie Bashkirtseff, and even Morisot's fellow Impressionist Mary Cassatt, described by Roger-Marx as "that masculine American."[24] None of these artists eschewed linearity, precision of execution, or contrived compositional arrangements. None of them was prepared to concentrate on color at the expense of line. All of them were accomplished at drawing. As such they were often seen to be reneging on their natural feminine attributes. The general mass of women artists were regularly described as imitative, sterile, and unconsciously derivative. They had, in the words of de Soissons, "a hatred for feminine visions; they make every effort to efface that from their eyes." They wished to usurp a masculine mode of seeing. Writing to his assumed male audience, he claimed:

> Many even succeed in assimilating happily our habits of vision; they know marvelously well the secrets of design and of colors, and one could consider them as artists, if it were not for the artificial impression which we receive in regarding their pictures. One feels that it is not natural that they should see the world in the way in which they paint, and that while they execute pictures with clever hands they should see with masculine eyes.[25]

The slippage between seeing and representing is easily achieved. While vision is fleetingly acknowledged to be habitual and in that sense cultural, de Soissons quickly moves on to the conflation, common among his peers, of seeing with rendering. If women are constitutionally different from men, it follows that they should see differently. Art, in this discourse, is produced as the extension of a manner of seeing and is, in that sense, an extension of a process that is by nature sexually differentiated. Where Morisot's talent allegedly triumphed over her misguided female contemporaries was in her intuitive translation of perception through a natural ability to draw and harmonize color. Her work seemed, to her critics, to be untainted by any intellectual system of drawing or composition. She was praised, therefore, for not reneging on the characteristics intrinsic to her sex. As the *Journal des artistes* critic put it in 1892, she was praiseworthy for the appropriateness of her ambition, which, unlike that of other women would-be painters, propelled her toward an art "entirely imbued with the essential virtues of her sex," an art that was devoted to the idea of a "*peinture feminine*."[26] Her work managed, according to Théodore Duret, to escape "falling into that dryness and affectation which usually characterises a woman's workmanship."[27] Lecomte praised her for resisting the temptation of creating "an artificial nature, a man's vision." She managed to ignore the sentimentality and gratuitous prettiness to which most women artists fell prey.[28] According to Roger-Marx, she "escaped the law which pushes women towards a sterility of invention, passivity and pastiche."[29] By being an Impressionist, Morisot was being, truly, herself.

If such claims are to make sense at all, it is crucial to appreciate the context within which these comparative assessments were made. Morisot, exemplary *haute bourgeoise*, a "*figure de race*," as Mallarmé called her, came to represent for her admirers the acceptable female artist.[30] In her refined person and her secluded domestic lifestyle, she was seen to embody the dignity, grace, and charm regarded as the mark of a peculiarly French femininity. In comparison with the deviant women who threatened to disturb traditional social and moral values, the *femmes nouvelles,* focus of anxiety for numerous French commentators in 1896, the year of the large International Feminist Congress in Paris, Berthe Morisot, wife, mother, and elegant hostess, could be acclaimed as a suitably womanly woman. What was more, her wholehearted adoption of Impressionist techniques could express an intrinsically feminine vision at the very moment women were being accused of denying their unique qualities and adopting the perverse posture of the *hommesse.* Paris of the 1890s, characterized by fear of depopulation and a suspicion of the recently proven German military strength and growing industrial prowess, saw the collaboration of scientific populists, politicians, and social theorists to create a xenophobic defense of the notion of a "racial" Frenchness, centering on the traumatic Dreyfus affair at home and the attempts of the assimilationists in the colonies. It was to women that many of the commentators turned for salvation. If women did not renege on their natural duties, France's future would be assured.[31] Berthe Morisot's work and person came to symbolize for her supporters, therefore, the essence of a Frenchness under threat and of a femininity at risk.[32] It is not surprising that her paintings were embraced by many of her defenders as, in the words of the avid Francophile George Moore, "the only pictures painted by a woman that could not be destroyed without creating a blank, a hiatus in the history of art."[33]

The discourse on art and femininity that produced Berthe Morisot as its heroine must also be situated within the more specific debates on women's potential and actual contribution to art at their height in Paris in the late 1880s and 1890s. The mobilization of women in organizations to represent their own interests had resulted in the foundation and growth of the Union des femmes peintres et sculpteurs, formed in 1881, which by the 1890s offered a venue for the display of some one thousand works by women at its annual exhibitions.[34] This decade witnessed concerted campaigns for women's professional rights. Attention was focused on the protracted struggle of women artists, led by the leaders of the Union des femmes peintres et sculpteurs, to open tuition at the Ecole des Beaux-Arts to women, to end the male monopoly on the competition for the Prix de Rome, and to elect women to Salon juries and to the Académie française. Such initiatives and the Union leadership's policy to encourage the press to review the women's exhibitions catalyzed a public debate on women's relationship to artistic practice.

Discussion of women's art at the Union exhibitions was permeated with the same concerns evident in the Morisot criticism. But whereas many critics felt satisfied that Morisot's oeuvre in the 1890s adequately and appropriately expressed the femininity of its creator, such was not the case at the Union. Many of the critics were disappointed at the neutrality of the work, at its apparent sexual indifference. Besides the abundance of flower paintings that the critics expected from an exhibition of women's work, there was little in the art itself to prove it had been created by the hands of women. In a culture that constructed masculine and feminine subjects as intrinsically different, critics wanted art to provide a concrete instance, a visible manifestation, of difference. When that did not occur, women were accused of masculinization. Critics complained that women mimicked the work of their male teachers. Some, like Charles Dargenty of the *Courrier de l'art,* even contended that the overeducation of women was to blame. If only women would remain untutored and natural, their work would express their innate characters and not the lessons absorbed from their male mentors.[35]

Against such a background Morisot's apparent ability to harness the art of her time into a practice that expressed her femininity deserved the highest praise. While many critics commented on her indebtedness to Manet, most praised her for successfully transforming his art into one of grace and charm befitting a lady of her class and background. She translated his lessons into "a language which is very much her own."[36] And it was not, as we have suggested, primarily in the subject matter of her paintings that Morisot's femininity was seen to be most evident. Although critics commented on the woman's world she pictured, her true femininity was seen to lie in her manner of perceiving and recording that world: "Close the catalogue and look at the work full of freshness and delicacy, executed with a lightness of brush, a finesse which flows from a grace which is entirely feminine . . . : It is the poem of the modern woman, imagined and dreamed by a woman," wrote one enthusiast.[37] Femininity in painting, according to these critics, was a question of technique, although to name it thus would have brought it into the realm of conscious choice rather than unmediated expression. To function ideologically, Morisot's adherence to a particular set of pictorial practices had to be viewed as an unconscious and happy expression of self and sex.

That certain kinds of mark making were regarded as masculine and others as feminine was by no means accidental. The debates on the relative merits of *dessin* and *couleur* had been couched in gendered terms since at least the seventeenth century. In the seventeenth and eighteenth centuries, however, sexual difference provided one of many ways of conceptualizing the relative merits of the terms of this binary opposition and seems to have operated more on the level of metaphor than as a framework for the assessment of the pictorial practices suited to men and women. By the mid-nineteenth century, drawing, *dessin,* with its connotations of linearity and reason, and the closely associated design, *dessein,* with its connotations of rational planning and cerebral organization of the elements on the surface, were firmly gendered in the masculine. They were not only descriptive terms but indicators of a manner of perceiving exclusively suited to the male of the species. Color, on the other hand, with its associations with contingency, flux, change, and surface appearance, was firmly grounded in the sphere of the feminine.[38]

For late nineteenth-century students the gendering of formal language was most clearly expressed in Charles Blanc's widely used textbook *Grammaire historique des arts du dessin* (1867), with which most fin-de-siècle artists and critics were familiar. Blanc proclaimed the dominance of line over color, taking issue with the relative importance that thinkers like Diderot had attributed to color. "Drawing," he stated, "is the masculine sex in art, color is its feminine sex."[39] Drawing's importance lay in the fact that it was the basis of all three *grands arts:* architecture, sculpture, and painting, whereas color was essential only to the third. But the relationship between color and drawing within painting itself, Blanc wrote, was like the relationship between women and men: "The union of drawing and color is necessary for the engendering of painting, just as is the union between man and woman for engendering humanity, but it is necessary that drawing retains a dominance over color. If it were otherwise, painting would court its own ruin; it would be lost by color as humanity was lost by Eve."[40]

Color plays the feminine role in art, "the role of sentiment; submissive to drawing as sentiment should be submissive to reason, it adds charm, expression and grace."[41] What is more, it must submit to the discipline of line if it is not to become out of control. A formal hierarchy is framed within an accepted hierarchy of gender that functions as its defense. The language of form and the language of sexual difference mutually inflect one another, creating a naturalized metaphoric discourse that operates on the level of common sense in late nineteenth-century parlance.

Such claims would not have made sense had they not drawn upon assumptions deeply embedded in nineteenth-century culture and legitimated across a number of discourses. Aesthetic theory was not alone in representing the world to itself in gendered terms. Indeed it provided only one site among many for the articulation of sexual difference. Where the nineteenth century's approach differed from previous centuries' was in its attempts to understand these differences scientifically, to prove them empirically and thus use them as the basis for social theory. What had been the stuff of religion, philosophy, and common sense became increasingly a matter for medicine, the new discipline of psychology, and social policy. Where the theologians and artists had used faith and metaphor to support these contentions, now the scientists offered "facts" and "evidence."

In the face of nineteenth-century feminist agitation, the conservative medical and anthropological establishments used science to corroborate the belief in the natural hierarchy of the sexes.[42] Scientists' overriding conclusion was that women were not equipped to deal with the superior mental functions, especially those for abstract thought. In organizing thoughts, synthesizing material, and making judgments based on evidence, women and people from so-called inferior races were stunted. Such inferiority was physically determined and depended on differences in the structure, size, and weight of the human brain. Although the relevance of these factors in determining mental capacities was disputed and the findings of experiments often hotly contested, the discoveries of craniology, as the pseudo-science of comparative brain measurement came to be called, generally endorsed the contemporary view of men and women. What was controversial was not the belief in the superiority of European males itself but the craniologists' conviction that it could be proven through measurement and quantification. As each form of comparative analysis was shown to be inadequate because it failed to prove the known "facts," new and more complicated instruments and procedures were developed. There were, of course, social theorists who thought the scientists had got it all wrong, but they produced their own evidence based on evolutionary theory, social conditioning, or simple observation to support essentialist theories of sexual difference.[43] While not all spoke of women's inferiority to men, all were convinced of their difference. The manner of describing this difference and the values placed on it were what varied.

Science's findings by no means remained the preserve of the experts. Robert Nye has shown that medical theories pervaded everyday life in late nineteenth-century France and that doctors became credible mediators between laboratory experiments and society's problems.[44] Research findings were widely disseminated in popular scientific and general journals, the finer points of dispute and doubt often eradicated. A general reference book like the *Grande Encyclopédie,* for example, drew heavily on current scientific knowledge in its entry for *femme*. Henri de Varigny, the author of the article, wrote that the differences between men and women could be explained through anatomical and physiological factors. The origin of woman's mental weakness was found in the structure of her brain, which de Varigny described as "less wrinkled, its convolutions . . . less beautiful, less ample" than the masculine brain. In men, he asserted, "the frontal lobes, in which it is agreed that the organ for intellectual operations and superior psychic functions are placed, are preponderant; they are also much more beautiful and voluminous when it is a question of the more civilised races."[45] Men also, he added, were endowed with greater blood irrigation to the brain than women, which was presumed to help their capacity for thought. Theorists like Alfred Fouillée, favorite of Republican politicians, who were skeptical of such forms of explanation, nevertheless endorsed the belief in men's superior capacities for rational and abstract thought. Although he distanced himself from the evidence used by the well-known defenders of masculine superiority Gustave Le Bon and Cesare Lombroso, who were widely quoted during the period, Fouillée endorsed the universally held belief in women's intellectual inferiority. The cause of this he attributed to women's social role: "Woman's brain is now less capable of prolonged and intense intellectual efforts, but the reason is entirely creditable to her: her rôle in the family involves a development of heart-life and moral force rather than of brain force and intellectual life."[46]

The idea that women's mental capacities were necessarily stunted so that they could fulfill their maternal role was widespread. Pregnancy and menstruation were widely thought to lead to mental regression, and women's generative capacities were regarded as responsible for their innate nervousness and irritability. The development of women's intellectual capacities, it was feared, would result in the deterioration of their capacity to breed and to mother effectively. Women were thought, therefore, to stop developing intellectually at the onset of puberty when their constitutions became consumed with their reproductive functions.[47]

Women's intellectual deficiencies were compensated by capacities that were more highly developed in them than in men. According to de Varigny, in women it "was the occipital lobes [of the brain] which were the most developed . . . and it is here that physiology locates the emotional and sensitive centers." Although women were intellectually weak, they possessed greater *sensibilité* than men.[48] And together with their heightened capacities for feeling, they were believed to possess a "more irritable nervous system than men," hence the claims, across a number of discourses, for women's "nervousness" and "excitability."[49] Some commentators believed women had a larger visceral nerve expansion and hence were endowed with greater visceral feeling than men. Women thus experienced the world more directly through their senses, acting upon the impulse of the moment. Whereas European men's responses to sensory impulses were delayed, complex, and deliberate, the result of cerebral reflection, those of women, children, and "uncivilized races" were direct and immediate. Peripheral stimuli, in these groups, produced unmediated reactions. These groups shared a similar psychological makeup: they had short concentration spans; they were attracted indiscriminately by passing impressions; they were essentially imitative, their mental actions dependent on external stimuli; and they were highly emotional and impulsive. Their strengths lay in their highly developed powers of observation and perception.[50]

One hears echoes of the art critics here. Theirs was obviously not a discourse that was elaborated in isolation. Popular scientific theory of the late nineteenth century projected Woman as a person who was not quite in control. Hysteria was the extreme expression of the characteristics intrinsic to all women (and certain men). Prey to her sensory impulses, Woman could become excessive, dangerous. Like color, she threatened to overspill her boundaries, to corrupt the rational order of *dessin/dessein*. She needed to be disciplined, controlled by rational forces.[51] But she could not usurp that world of reason and make it her own. To do so would be to step outside the natural boundaries on which order and civilization were based, to destroy sexual difference—that is, the fundamental binary opposition, masculine/feminine, self/other, on which culture is founded. In the sphere of art practice and criticism, it follows that it would be laughable, even unnatural, for women to absorb academic art theory, to aspire to *la grande peinture* or to ambitious imaginative work. Such work called upon capacities that women did not possess. Their attempts could only amount to, at worst, crude pastiche, at best, skillful copying. Science had proved this and morality and social order demanded that it remain so.

Berthe Morisot's position within this nexus of anxieties is fascinating. A woman, lauded for demonstrating women's most appreciable qualities in her art: "sparkling coquetries, gracious charm, and above all tender emotion," she was also widely praised for the dignity of her person, her elegance, and her high breeding.[52] A delicate balance is struck. In Morisot, women's innate qualities are turned to the good. They are harnessed to a project that is seen as the fulfillment of her sex and as unthreatening to the social order. Her life, with its necessary domesticity, and her art, content to sing the praises of the surface, are exemplary. Only occasionally do we sense the fear that she will go over the edge, that she will live out her femininity too fully and become ill. One such instance was in 1883 when Joris-Karl Huysmans described Morisot's work as possessing "a turbulence of agitated and tense nerves," suggesting that her sketches could perhaps be described as *hysterisées*.[53]

But for the most part critics in the 1890s saw in Morisot's work the realization of a well-adjusted femininity. Her painting gave stature and dignity to a way of perceiving different from men's. For a man to be an Impressionist in the 1890s would have been to relinquish his powers of reason, of abstraction, and of deliberate thought and planning. It would have led to an art that was weak, an "effeminate" art. But for a woman to be an Impressionist made sense. It was tantamount to a realization of self. In the words of Roger-Marx, Morisot's practice proceeded "according to the logic of sex, of temperament and of social class." Hers was "a precious art, . . . which successfully employed the most vibrant and impressionable apparatuses of the organism, and a refined almost sickly sensibility, [which was] the hereditary privilege of the eternal feminine."[54]

Notes

Originally published in *Perspectives on Morisot*, ed. T. J. Edelstein (New York: Hudson Hills Press, 1990), 57–66.

I am grateful to Kathleen Adler, Briony Fer, Rasaad Jamie, and Paul Smith for their invaluable comments on an earlier draft of this article. The first art historians to comment critically on the conflation of Morisot's "femininity" with "Impressionism" were Rozsika Parker and Griselda Pollock in *Old Mistresses, Women, Art, and Ideology* (London, 1981), 41–42. It was this work that first stimulated my interest in the issue, and I gratefully acknowledge it.

1. Camille Mauclair, "Le Salon de 1896," *La Nouvelle Revue* 1 (May–June 1896): 342.
2. Mauclair supported a return to "abstract principles" so that "realism" would be tempered by "idealism." For a discussion of these debates, see Richard Shiff, *Cézanne and the End of Impressionism* (Chicago, 1984), 70–98.
3. Of course, this construction of Impressionist technique took no account of the efforts artists made to affect the appearance of spontaneity and immediacy in their works. The aesthetics of the *non fini*, the sketchiness of the surfaces of so many Impressionist paintings, and the apparent informality of their compositional structures allowed them to be read as unmediated records of visual appearance. A study of the technique of an artist like Claude Monet reveals how inadequate such an understanding of Impressionism is. For such a discussion, see John House, *Monet: Nature into Art* (New Haven, 1986).
4. Camille Mauclair, "Le Salon de 1896," 342.
5. Many articles on Morisot's retrospective exhibition held in March 1896 at Durand-Ruel mentioned the fact that her work was little known at this time. See, for example, "L'Oeuvre de Berthe Morisot," *Moniteur des arts*, no. 2227 (20 March 1896): 125. Mallarmé also made this point in his preface to the catalogue: "Paris knew her little." Stéphane Mallarmé, *Berthe Morisot (Mme Eugène Manet):1841–1895*, exh. cat., Durand-Ruel (Paris, 1896), 5. "Poor Madame Morisot, the public hardly knows her!" wrote Camille Pissarro to his son Lucien on the eve of her funeral on 6 March 1895. See *Camille Pissarro: Lettres à son fils Lucien*, ed. John Rewald (Paris, 1950), 371.
6. Georges Rivière, "L'Exposition des impressionnistes," *L'Impressionniste*, no. 1 (6 April 1877), reprinted in Lionello Venturi, *Les Archives de l'impressionnisme* (Paris, 1939), 308.
7. Charles Moffett, ed., *The New Painting: Impressionism, 1874–1886*, exh. cat. (San Francisco: Fine Arts Museums of San Francisco, 1986), 182, 328.
8. Albert Wolff, *Le Figaro* (3 April 1876), quoted in Monique Angoulvent, *Berthe Morisot* (Paris, 1933), 54.
9. Charles Bigot, *La Revue politique et littéraire* (8 April 1876), quoted in Moffett, ed., *New Painting*, 182.
10. Paul de Charry, *Le Pays* (10 April 1880), quoted in Moffett, ed., *New Painting*, 326.
11. Georges Rivière, *L'Impressionniste* (10 April 1877), quoted in Moffett, ed., *New Painting*, 240.
12. Edmond Duranty, *La Chronique des arts et de la curiosité* (19 April 1879), quoted in Moffett, ed., *New Painting*, 288.
13. In 1877 Paul Mantz had already claimed that there was only one "real Impressionist" in the group, Berthe Morisot: "Her painting has all the frankness of an improvisation: it does truly give the idea of an 'impression' registered by a sincere eye and rendered again by a hand completely without trickery." *Le Temps* (21 April 1877), quoted in Angoulvent, *Berthe Morisot*, 56. At the same time Philippe Burty wrote of her "double privilege of being both a woman and an artist," invoking the eighteenth-century pastelist Rosalba Carriera as her predecessor in "liberty and charm." *La République française* (25 April 1877), reprinted in Venturi, *Archives de l'impressionnisme*, 291–92.
14. Théodor de Wyzewa, "Berthe Morisot," in *Peintres de jadis et d'aujourd'hui* (Paris, 1891), 215–16.
15. Gustave Geffroy, *Berthe Morisot*, exh. cat., Boussod and Valadon (Paris, 1892), 12–13.
16. Georges Lecomte, *Les Peintres impressionnistes* (Paris, 1892), 105.
17. Claude Roger-Marx, "Berthe Morisot," *Revue encyclopédique* (Paris, 1896), 250. This thesis was later

expanded in his "Les Femme peintres et l'impressionnisme," *Gazette des beaux-arts* 38 (1907): 491–507. In keeping with the construction of Morisot as "intuitive Impressionist" who does not self-consciously adopt a style or working method, contemporary critics rarely, if ever, allude to changes or developments in her working practice. So, for example, the stylistic changes in her work in the early 1890s, such as her increased linearity, are not the subject of much discussion by her contemporaries.

18. S. C. de Soissons [Charles Emmanuel de Savoie, comte de Carignan], *Boston Artists: A Parisian Critic's Notes* (Boston, 1894), 75–78.
19. Ibid., 76.
20. Roland Barthes, "Myth Today" (1972), reprinted in Susan Sontag, ed., *Barthes* (Oxford, 1982), 111.
21. For an appreciation of Morisot's works in these terms, see Geffroy, *Berthe Morisot*, 6, 10. Geffroy's comments paradoxically inscribe Morisot as attentive to Edouard Manet's lessons and as an intuitive, untutored painter: "Mme Berthe Morisot, who heard and understood the good lesson in painting given during this period by Edouard Manet, has arrived totally naturally, by her love of things, to the development of the gift which is within her." Ibid., 10. The construction of Morisot as the intuitive painter has been perpetuated in the Morisot literature, most notably in the writings of Denis Rouart, who in 1950 declaimed: "It is essential to her nature to be a painter and everything is a pretext for painting. . . . She could not stop painting the people and the things she loved for with her to love was to paint. The way in which 'she lives her painting and paints her life' gives her work a special quality which Paul Valéry has rightly compared 'to the diary of a woman who expresses herself by colour and drawing.'" Denis Rouart, in Arts Council of Great Britain, *Berthe Morisot*, exh. cat. (London, 1950), 5. Even a cursory reading of her letters compiled by Rouart himself, which indicate both Morisot's struggle as an artist and her conscious identification with certain painters and practices, undermines the reading of her work as an intuitive outpouring. See Denis Rouart, ed., *The Correspondence of Berthe Morisot*, trans. Betty W. Hubbard, introduction and notes by Kathleen Adler and Tamar Garb (London, 1986).
22. Lecomte, *Peintres impressionnistes*, 105.
23. George Moore, "Sex in Art," *Modern Painting* (London, 1898), 235.
24. Claude Roger-Marx, *Les Impressionnistes* (Paris, 1956), 39. Indeed, the comparison of Morisot's and Cassatt's styles in terms of what were thought of as intrinsic French and American characteristics had been around for some time. Not only were ostensible national character traits brought into play here, but an idea of a national construction of "femininity" had great currency at this time. For a comparison of Morisot's and Cassatt's work in these terms, see C. E., "Exposition des peintres indépendants," *La Chronique des arts*, no. 17 (23 April 1881): 134. For a discussion of the peculiarities of French women as opposed to their Anglo-Saxon sisters who are described as excessively masculine, see Gustave Le Bon, "La Psychologie des femmes et les effets de leur éducation actuelle," *Revue scientifique* 46 (11 October 1890): 451.
25. De Soissons, *Boston Artists*, 77–78.
26. Raoul Sertat, "Berthe Morisot," *Journal des artistes*, no. 23 (13 June 1892): 173.
27. Théodore Duret, *Manet and the Impressionists*, trans. J. E. Crawford Flitch (Philadelphia, 1910), 173.
28. Lecomte, *Peintres impressionnistes*, 105.
29. Roger-Marx, *Revue encyclopédique*, 250.
30. Mallarmé, *Berthe Morisot*, 5.
31. For a discussion on the fear provoked by the *femme nouvelle*, see Debora Leah Silverman, *Nature, Nobility, and Neurology: The Ideological Origins of "Art Nouveau" in France, 1889–1900* (Ph.D. diss., Princeton University, 1983).
32. For a general discussion on the atmosphere of gloom and the fear of degeneration that obsessed intellectuals in this period, see Eugen Weber, *France: Fin de Siècle* (Cambridge, Mass., 1986).
33. Moore, "Sex in Art," 234. For another statement proclaiming Morisot the only woman to prove women's capacities in painting in the nineteenth century, see H. N., "Berthe Morisot," *Journal des artistes*, no. 10 (10 March 1895): 955.
34. For a broad overview of feminist campaigns and personalities in this period, see Jean Rabaut, *Féministes à la belle-époque* (Paris, 1985). For a discussion of the formation of the Union, see Charlotte Yeldham, *Women Artists in Nineteenth-Century France and England*, vol. 1 (New York, 1984), 98–105. For a contextual analysis of the formation of the Union, see Tamar Garb, "Revising the Revisionists: The Formation of the Union des femmes peintres et sculpteurs," *Art Journal* 48 (Spring 1989): 63–70.
35. For a discussion of the criticism of the exhibitions, see Tamar Garb, "'L'Art Féminin': The Formation of a Critical Category in Late Nineteenth-Century France," *Art History* 12 (March 1989): 39–65.
36. The critic for the *Moniteur des arts* put it as follows: "Sister-in-law to Manet, it was under his direction that she

made her first essays in painting, penetrating his ideas but not submitting to his influence and rendering her impressions in a language which is very much her own: modest, without working for a public but for herself, for the satisfaction of her artist's dreams, without care for fashion, without desire for fame." "L'Oeuvre de Berthe Morisot," *Moniteur des arts,* no. 2227 (30 March 1896): 125. For a representative example, see also Raoul Sertat, "Mme Berthe Morisot," *Journal des artistes,* no. 11 (15 March 1896): 1381. Morisot's femininity is seen to reside in her indifference to a public and the sale of her works; she is, therefore, suitably modest and withdrawn from the public sphere. Even the most cursory glance at her correspondence with its many allusions to sales, dealers, and public exhibitions exposes the myth of such a construction. The allusions are too numerous to itemize. See Rouart, *Correspondence,* passim.

37. "L'Oeuvre de Berthe Morisot," 125.
38. The link with makeup was already made in the seventeenth century by Roger de Piles. I am grateful to Katy Scott for her helpful comments in relation to the gendering of pre-nineteenth-century academic theory.
39. Charles Blanc, *Grammaire historique des arts du dessin* (Paris, 1867), 22. I am grateful to Jennifer Shaw for her discussions with me on this book. It is not surprising that Blanc became hostile to Impressionism, regarding its realist enterprise as trivial. For his views on Impressionism, see Charles Blanc, *Les Beaux-arts à l'exposition universelle de 1878* (Paris, 1878).
40. Blanc, *Grammaire historique,* 23.
41. Ibid., 24.
42. For a discussion of the links between the discoveries of science and an antagonism toward feminism, see Elizabeth Fee, "Nineteenth-Century Craniology: The Study of the Female Skull," *Bulletin of the History of Medicine* 53 (Fall 1979): 415–33.
43. For a representative account of this type, see Alfred Fouillée, *Woman: A Scientific Study and Defense,* trans. Rev. T. A. Seed (London, 1900), based on Fouillée's *Temperament et caractère selon les individus, les sexes et les races* (Paris, 1895).
44. Robert A. Nye, *Crime, Madness, and Politics in Modern France: The Medical Concept of National Decline* (Princeton, 1984).
45. Henri de Varigny, "Femme," in *La Grande Encyclopédie,* vol. 17 (Paris, 1892–93), 143. For a critical analysis of de Varigny's theories in the context of late nineteenth-century medical and psychological studies on women's intellectual capacities, see Jacques Lourbet, *Le Problème des sexes* (Paris, 1900), 63–72.
46. Fouillée, *Woman,* 48.
47. For a representative argument of this type, see Gaston Richard's review of Jacques Lourbet, *La Femme devant la science contemporaine* (Paris, 1896), in *Revue philosophique* 43 (1897): 435. See also Charles Turgeon, *Le Féminisme français* (Paris, 1907), 315.
48. De Varigny, "Femme," 145. There were theorists who were reluctant to grant women a greater sensibility than men. Lombroso, for example, distinguished between *irritabilité* and *sensibilité,* according the former to women, the latter to men.
49. Prof. M. Benedict, "La Question féminine," *Revue des revues* (August 1895): 182.
50. The most extreme proponent of such views in France was the scientific populist Gustave Le Bon, who likened women's psychological makeup to the uncontrollability of a crowd. The qualities shared were: "impulsiveness, irritability, incapacity to reason, the absences of judgment and of the critical spirit, the exaggeration of the sentiments." Quoted in Susanna Barrows, *Distorting Mirrors: Visions of the Crowd in Late Nineteenth-Century France* (New Haven, 1981), 47. For a detailed discussion of his beliefs regarding the qualities intrinsic to women and their concomitant social roles, see Le Bon, "La Psychologie des femmes," 449–60. For a discussion of women's and men's capacities in these terms, see the much-quoted H. Campbell, *Differences in the Nervous Organisation of Men and Women* (London, 1891).
51. In 1887 George J. Romanes compared women's emotions with men's, describing the former as "almost always less under control of the will—more apt to break away, as it were, from the restraint of reason, and to overwhelm the mental chariot in disaster." "Mental Differences Between Men and Women," *Nineteenth Century* 21 (May 1887): 657.
52. These are the qualities identified by Gustave Le Bon as women's great strengths. They are also the ones that frequently recur in the Morisot criticism. See Le Bon, "La Psychologie des femmes," 451.
53. Quoted in Roger-Marx, "Les Femmes peintres," 499.
54. Ibid., 508.

PART FOUR

Impressionism, Politics, and Nationalism

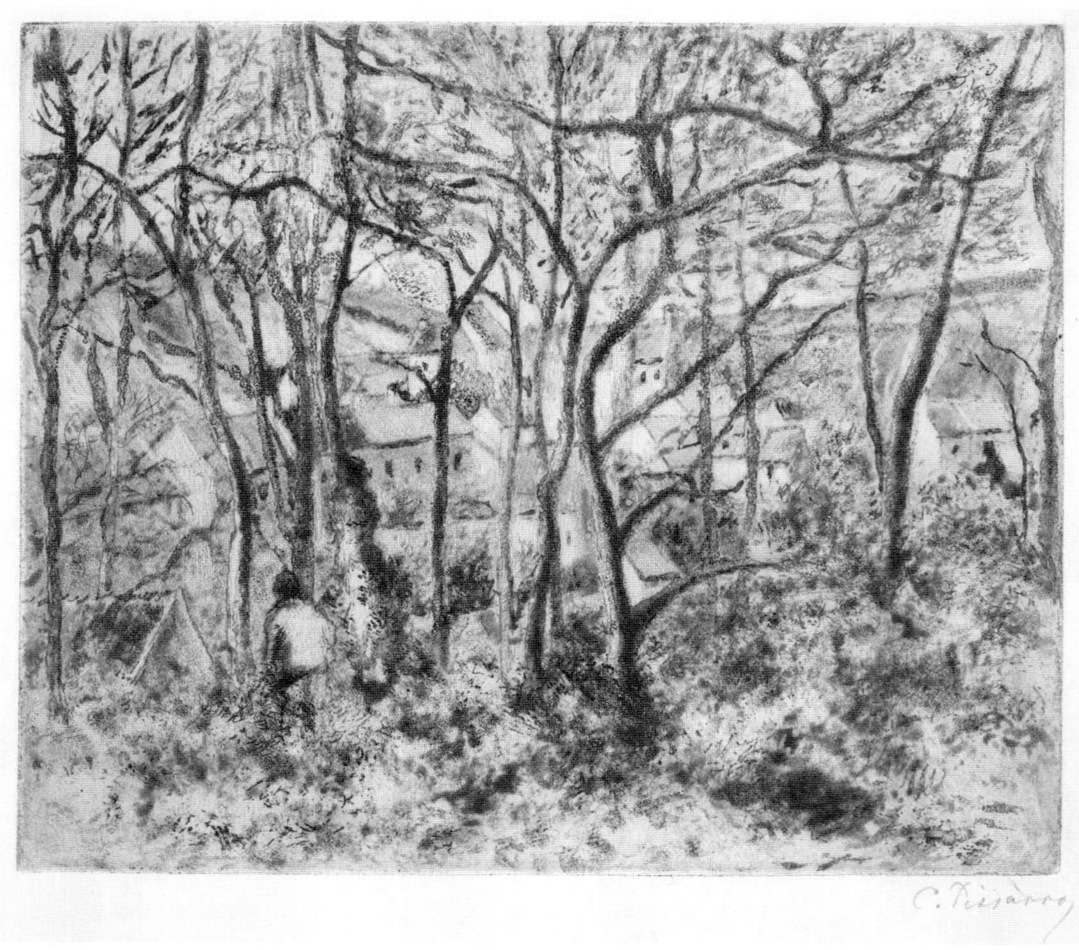

FIGURE 9.1. Camille Pissarro, *Undergrowth at the Hermitage*, 1879; etching. The New York Public Library. Photo: The New York Public Library/Art Resource, NY.

9

Camille Pissarro in 1880

An Anarchistic Artist in Bourgeois Society

MICHEL MELOT

IN THE LATE 1870s the Impressionist painter Camille Pissarro became significantly engaged in printmaking. In 1879–80 he executed his first uniform series of etchings—about 200 in all—pulled from a group of twenty-odd plates.[1] He made these prints during a period of economic depression and had no hope of selling them. Degas, better off than Pissarro and the owner of a press, made the series possible and even printed some of them himself.[2] Today the prints are well known.

Pissarro's practice as a printmaker in 1880 fully illuminates a complex historical moment. The prints he made with Degas express values that were becoming dominant, although the artists themselves could only partly acknowledge them. These etchings were among the first to be signed and numbered—a practice that has since become the rule for prints that aspire to the official title "art." These marks of authenticity, which today excite connoisseurs at least as much as the prints themselves, provide a clue to the ideological use of such works.

The Immediacy of Visual Experience

Unlike Degas, Pissarro was not an experienced printmaker in 1879. During the previous five years he had experimented with etching techniques and had developed a personal style: *The Chestnut Seller*, an etching of 1878, is loaded with technical and graphic innovations. The etchings of 1879–80 mark the high point of the Impressionist style. With the greatest clarity they reveal a new way of drawing and printing and, above all, a new concept of reality.

No artist more strongly opposed lines, contours, and clear boundaries. As both painter and etcher, Pissarro was preoccupied with eliminating pictorial hierarchies. In *Undergrowth at the Hermitage* (fig. 9.1), for example, everything—figures, trees, the house behind the trees—appears to be on the same plane. The effect is like that of a telephoto lens. The intention is not so much to destroy perspective overtly, but to ignore it as a working device. Pissarro builds his composition from purely visual data, painting what

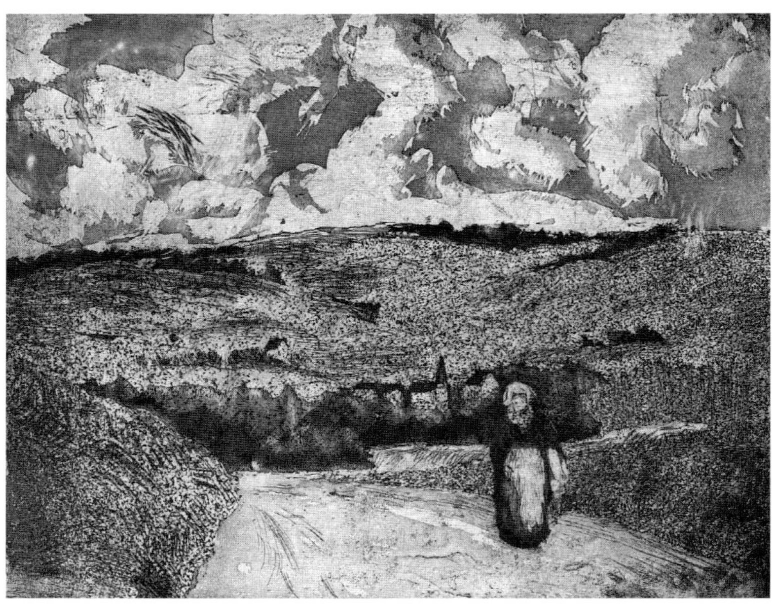

FIGURE 9.2. Camille Pissarro, *Woman on the Road*, 1879; aquatint. Photo: Michel Melot.

is seen even before identifying it. The Impressionist vision takes reality *en bloc*, isolates one piece of it for a composition, and gives everything within that piece equal importance. In *Undergrowth at the Hermitage*, as in *Woman on the Road* (fig. 9.2), the intermixing of figures and trees is highly unconventional. An older landscapist—Corot, for example—highlighted his figures or set them apart spatially or with color, making the figures more important than anything else. The Impressionists rejected the tradition of giving certain things a privileged place in a painting because they are thought to have it elsewhere. Instead, they took reality as a more or less undifferentiated totality and poured it onto the canvas the way a liquid is poured into a mold.

Thus, in the first state of *The Cottage*, everything appears fluid, without lines or clear details. The entire scene becomes a uniform, shadowy mass. From the moment Pissarro begins to lay in his composition, he mixes everything together on one plane. Objects quite distinct from one another in reality melt into a single substance. In *Lacroix Island at Rouen*, his technique is even more telling. There, the water of the river reflects a landscape with a smoking factory chimney, with the smoke treated in exactly the same manner as the more solid objects. In *Haystacks*, shadows and haystacks are given equal pictorial weight. An Impressionist makes no representational distinctions between shadows and material reality, nor even between reality and its reflection—the apparent and the real. Pissarro puts down areas of dark and light without thinking about representing distinct objects in space. Then he adds details but avoids sharp contours, letting the surroundings penetrate them. Traditional painters described solidity and weight, using transparent glazes, opaque impastos, and colors of different intensity and value. Impressionism breaks with this method. In *Setting Sun*, the sky is as solid as the earth. In *Sunset with Haystacks* (fig. 9.3), the resin of the aquatint is as thick for the trees as for the clouds.

Pissarro used other graphic techniques to "homogenize" the motif. Just as he juxtaposed small touches of different colors in his paintings, so in his etchings he interspersed white flecks among other marks in order to blend one area with another. The most startling of these innovative techniques is the use of abrasives—sandpaper, emery-cloth, or metal brushes. Pissarro referred to this technique as "the

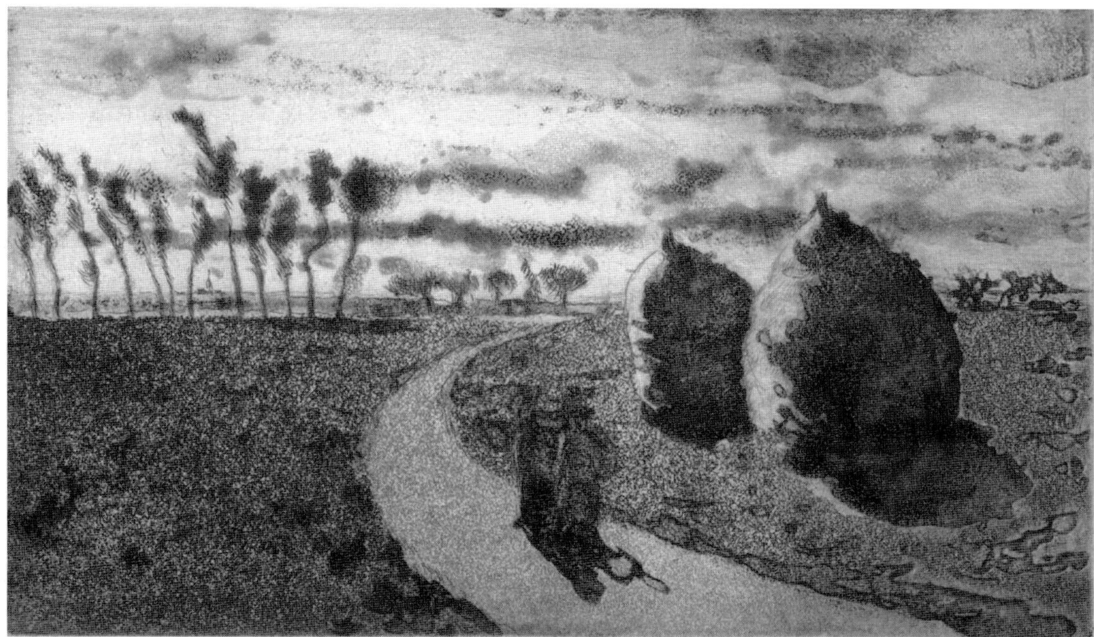

FIGURE 9.3. Camille Pissarro, *Sunset with Haystacks*, 1879; etching. The New York Public Library. Photo: The New York Public Library/Art Resource, NY.

gray style" and even used the term as a subtitle for certain prints.[3] Abrasives rubbed on the plate produced a hazy gray mass, which might be left by itself or superimposed over objects that threatened to stand out too much *(Undergrowth at the Hermitage)*. It could also suggest rain, as in *Effect of Rain* or *Saint Martin's Fair*. Impressionists also liked the light scratches and fuzzy line of drypoint. Whatever technique they used, they avoided definite, stable lines precisely located in space.[4]

Printing, as a method of turning out reproductions, was of no "economic" interest to Pissarro and Degas, but printmaking offered something of great aesthetic interest to them. The term *impression* signifies both a generalized and an immediate way of seeing things—the immediate impact of raw reality on the viewer's retina. The viewer does not have to analyze things intellectually and perceives on the canvas a system of equivalent touches and colors clearly differentiated from the objective motif. In making prints, the "impression" can be repeated and varied. The method of reproduction is of no great importance—what is important is that each printed "impression" please the artist. The Impressionist print is no longer a reproduction. This conception of the print gives birth to the "monotype"—a technique that produces only one-of-a-kind prints.

Before reaching that extreme deviation from the essence of printmaking, both Pissarro and Degas revealed a predilection for the sort of distinctive inking and printing that characterizes monotype. Their friend, the Impressionist Lepic, called the process "changeable etching" and claimed to have invented it. The process was, in effect, all of printmaking for the Impressionists. The artist had to become a printer. Indeed, their favorite printer, Delâtre, considered himself a "printer-artist" since it seemed absolutely necessary to think of the *impression* as the most important part of the creation reciprocally. Reproduction was not the point. It is impossible to reproduce Impressionist plates without the artist since the inking, done specifically for each print, determines the character of the work. No doubt, Pissarro's *Haystacks* is the most astonishing example. Several proofs, each different, are signed by Pissarro with the notation "printed by Degas." One cannot help thinking that if they were hung together in a series they would be the equivalent of Claude Monet's *Haystacks*, painted at different times of the day.

Here we see clearly how much these works differ from the identical reproductions that today are called "original" prints. The Goncourts spontaneously hit upon the same idea:

> If I were an artist, I would make an etching plate of the section of Paris that can be seen from the top of the Pont Royal. From this plate I would pull a hundred prints on sized paper, and I would amuse myself painting in watercolor all the different hazy colors that rise up from the Seine, all the magic colors of our autumns and winters, which turn the sky the color of gray plaster and rusty stone.[5]

Thus, a new sense of time appears as an element in Impressionist representation. As Manet once said, "This isn't a landscape, it's an hour." The term "changeable etching" expresses the same thing. Just as the Goncourts conceived of it, Manet and later Pissarro enhanced their prints with watercolor or pastel—*Le Père Melon* is a print enhanced with pastel.[6] The same effect could be achieved by varying the paper from print to print or, if not the paper, the color of the ink: There are versions of *Haystacks* printed in bister, blue, green. For this plate no two prints are alike.

Not only can different inkings be used to vary the motif, the plate can be modified between printings. Up to then, the technique of making different states of a print allowed the engraver to follow the progress of his work. It was also used to increase the value of the very few prints deliberately made for collectors—especially at the beginning of the eighteenth century—as opposed to the undifferentiated proofs made for a broader public. In both cases the various states of the print were thought of in relation to the "definitive proof" that was the only version the artist considered worthy of his name. The traditional states were incomplete works sold as curiosities but without the initials that signified they were finished. Pissarro and Degas had a very different conception of "states." At the exhibition of 1880 Pissarro exhibited states as such. Both Pissarro and Degas carefully signed and numbered their prints contrary to the practice that prevailed before 1880.

Placed side by side, the different states of a print have yet another meaning. The work consists of all its states. Taken together, they form a series of different *impressions* of the same motif—a series that implies neither direction nor ending. They emphasize the difference between the painter's experience and objective reality—an idea unacceptable to the academic mind in search of an absolute ideal. The artist no longer believed in a unique, permanent, and authoritative view of reality but in an infinity of successive views, all equivalent to one another. This interest in relativity also permeated the sciences before being formulated into a theory between 1890 and 1900. Before long, mathematicians would introduce this new idea of time into their calculations, and the Bergsonian philosophers would eventually refute determinism and invent, in theory, individual liberty.

In a similar vein Henri Bergson, in *Time and Free Will* (1889), argued that movement cannot be understood as superimposed upon a preexisting objective reality. Reality *is* movement. So, too, for the Impressionists. Drawing was no longer a question of representing the world according to what we know from our understanding but according to what we perceive instantaneously, and what is, instantaneously, recreated in front of us. In effect, it would be necessary to make a new image every second, as is the case with film. This desire for instantaneousness was first satisfied with the repetition of the same image in different media (oil painting, drawing, lithography, printing) and, in prints, with different states and printings. To show movement requires a style of spontaneous drawing that captures close and direct observation. Academic doctrine conceived of a world of inert objects. The object was a totality placed within a momentary situation. Movement was thought of as a quality that could be applied to the object, much as an adjective qualifies a noun. However, for the observer who refuses to accept the primacy of the object's existence—whether he is a philosopher or painter—truth is the motion *of* something, not something *in* motion. Movement must be shown in itself, at the risk of the observer no longer being able to identify the object in motion.

The main criticism lodged against Impressionism was that it was "unfinished." To be considered a thing of value, a painting had to resemble a finished product, reproducing clearly discernible objects. The intrusion of time into representation is incompatible with this taste. A print that is made from a succession of states is never demonstrably finished; rather, each state is related to a moment of work.

The Impressionist's interest in light and color results from an underlying commitment to capturing immediate experience. For the Impressionist artist color is not a quality that can be separated from the object to which it adheres. Color exists *with* its object. Indeed, for the painter who does not think about what he is painting, color alone is the only object of perception. As psychologists know, color is form and not something that fills up a form. Thus, Pissarro paints the gray he sees. It remains for the public to say whether it is the gray of the sky or of the ground or of a mist. The painter knows only the gray his eye sees and is indifferent to anything else.

In printmaking light and dark values become primary for recording immediate experience. In *Path under the Trees at Pontoise*, an abruptly foreshortened path leads to a more distant area, also visible through the many openings among the trees. But this distant area, since it is rendered in the same values as the trees, appears to be on an almost identical plane. Traditional perspective has not been used to structure the composition since it is not a given of immediate visual experience. It is something that the eye—and the intellect—must learn. Indeed, the viewer who looks for a permanent world of recognizable and distinct objects will be confused by this print. The delicate drypoint scratches weave into a single fabric things that I know must be different. Is the vertical line in the foreground a twig or the spire of a distant church? And this clear area that stands out sharply in the center of the composition—is it simply an area of light or is there some object there? The drawing does nothing to make the human figure more noticeable. It remains immersed in the moving yet immobile mass of clouds, lights, and mists. Nothing detaches itself from the ever-fluctuating stillness.[7]

What is striking is an overall rejection of rationalized, traditional systems of visual description. The authority of established empirical practice has been eroded by the pressures of modern life. Impressionism rejects the visual language of the Renaissance—with its inherent concerns for volume, space, and weight—and, in so doing, it rejects the materialist view of the world that Renaissance art embodied. Wölfflin had described this aesthetic to perfection, but it was Frederick Antal who explained it in relation to the beginnings of capitalism. As Antal and others have argued, the Renaissance concept of the world as a permanent, material realm served the intellectual and ideological needs of a new merchant class.[8] This assumption of permanence, visible in the art of both Florence and Flanders, corresponds to the invention of clock time—the arbitrary division of time into hours. (The new public clocks take timekeeping out of the hands of the clergy.) In the late nineteenth and early twentieth century, clock time—originally a convention, a tool created to regulate the new social relations of production and the market—is called into question in different ways by Proust, Bergson, and Einstein. New social-economic conditions thus give rise to a new philosophy, the essence of which, significantly, is a revision of the notion of time. Indeed, modern social relations change the meaning of time. Making money is more and more removed from its real source in production, and more and more associated with the value and movement of time.

The New Art and the Emergence of Banking Capital

What connections can be drawn between the Impressionists' altered vision of the world and the new capitalist structures that had recently begun to dominate society? The golden affluence of the 1850s and the development of an all-powerful financial base for industry and commerce created a new type of capitalism that had a completely different appearance from older capitalist forms. The merchant capital of the *ancien régime* idealized the Object (land, gold, commodities) as the foundation of all wealth and abstracted from that ideal an aesthetic of clearly defined and stable forms—the aesthetic of Renaissance art. Second Empire society knew, or rather thought it knew, other sources of wealth. Increasingly, money became an abstraction, its material origin increasingly invisible to those who were accumulating it. The use of bank notes and checks was becoming widespread. A few examples will show that the accumulation of wealth no longer could be measured by the accumulation of durable goods but rather seemed to come out of thin air, or rather out of time, with no real base.

Speculation tended to become the rule—a normal law of finance rather than a perversion of the system. Increasingly, transactions involved fictitious capital—futures, stock schemes, credit. Profits extracted from colonies strengthened the illusion that wealth no longer had a material base. The trader no longer had any contact with the source of his wealth. Money appeared as if by magic. We also see the birth of the art of advertising which appears capable of creating money without work. P. T. Barnum's book, *Humbugs of the World*, dates from 1865. He taught how to get rich without possessing anything at the outset except ingenuity.

With the rapid and easy circulation of money, capitalist philosophy underwent a profound change. The belief in the value of lasting equilibrium and the well-defined object gave way to such values as mobility, flexibility, and a capacity to invent and adapt. By the end of the century fixed revenues no longer accounted for the greatest fortunes. The future belonged to finance capital even if a large part of French society remained conservative and petty bourgeois and continued to prefer rent and fixed incomes. By 1890—if we consider the total capital of the French bourgeoisie—speculators had become more important than landowners and holders of fixed obligations.[9]

These new values became artistic values in Impressionism. The audience for this new art was the advanced bourgeoisie—what might be logically called an economic avant-garde made up of liberal members of the petty bourgeoisie and the upper middle class. In the very beginning the experience of reality that Impressionism embodied was too radical to please—let alone be understood by—this ascendant class. Yet, this class, for the moment absorbed in enriching itself, was destined to become the patron class of avant-garde art. From the start Impressionists found some support there—the collectors Hoschedé, Charpentier, and more modest types like Murer.[10] The values celebrated in avant-garde art would remain far removed from the preoccupations of the masses and the majority of the petty bourgeoisie. This larger public would remain indifferent to or actually irritated by the new art, reproaching it for renouncing the traditional values by which most people are constrained to live.

What was the relationship between the new art and the old art institutions—the state-controlled Academy and its Salon, which still dominated the market? As individuals the Impressionists were often ambivalent, but as a group they banded together against the Salon. Beginning in 1874, they organized their own group exhibitions, which continued until 1886. By then the Academy's domination of the art market had been effectively broken. What emerged in the interval was a new system of dealers, the modern art market, in which free competition has reigned.

The need for the new has been written into the new social contract of the free, modern artist. Freedom has been guaranteed to him as the precondition for his production. The artist must produce unique objects and endlessly renew them. He must do so within the framework of a mode of production that remains intangible: His is the exuberant freedom of a moth circling a flame. The avant-garde endlessly runs up against the limits of the economic and social system. In a society that claims to be free, limits are not placed on the form of the product but on its function. The avant-garde, with all its insecurity and risk-taking, consists of volunteers whose function is to act out Freedom, with all its ambiguities.

The flag of freedom is broad. Certainly, freedom is a widely held belief, and the evolution of artistic styles from at least the middle of the eighteenth century is there to prove it. Félix Ponteil writes of the Constitution of 1875 ("this sheaf of texts voted one after the other"):

> Each period has, so to speak, its signature. During the parliamentary monarchy and the Second Empire, the magic word freedom, never evoked in vain, was claimed by all parties, adapted to all doctrines, allowing the politician to get elected and the poor naive devil, who believed in the meaning of words, to get himself killed.[11]

This passage is useful in demonstrating the mythical side of Freedom and in explaining the ideological role played by art in its diffusion. Freedom can be read in the very form of modern art as well as in the artist's struggle against the Salon's almost absolute control over distribution.

What is usually called an avant-garde in art really exists only in a liberal economy. There, different forces confront each other and translate different interests, which do not exactly correspond either to social classes defined by economic relations or to ideologies in the form of consciously formulated doctrines. This competitive system presupposes a victor retrospectively recognized as avant-garde. The outcome of the competition is, of necessity, uncertain. But it would not always be as difficult as it was for the Impressionists.[12]

The fate of Impressionism in the terrible and unprecedented economic crisis of 1877 reveals the relationship between the new art and the liberal middle class that had just begun to support it. When the crash comes, the avant-garde loses what support it has and is among the first to fall.

In 1878 Pissarro wrote to his friend Murer, "I am at the end of my rope." For the first and only time in his life, Pissarro, like Cézanne, considered giving up art as a profession. "I do my studies without joy, knowing that I have to abandon art and find something else to do—if I can apprentice myself again. Too bad."[13] And there is even a revolt against art and the artist in himself: "I've had enough of this depressing art, this exacting, stupid painting which takes so much attention and reflection. It's too serious. By now, seeing and feeling should be easy and enjoyable. Besides, what good is art? Can it be eaten? No. Oh well."

The years 1878–80 were undoubtedly Pissarro's darkest. They were for all the Impressionists. The group exhibitions, begun in 1874, continued, but with more difficulties than usual. The Impressionists had originally banded together against the Salons—the annual Academy exhibitions that were still, in 1880, the most important place an artist could exhibit. Although united in their opposition to the Salon, the Impressionists came from different backgrounds and worked in different styles. Fiercely individualistic, they continually argued with each other about who should be admitted to the group shows. Degas above all proposed artists whose art struck the others as too academic. The arguments created serious rifts and even desertions from the group. Pissarro's opinions were as different as possible from Degas's, but he remained the most faithful member of the group, no doubt because he wanted to keep it going.[14] These tensions, together with financial pressures, made the Salon of 1880 a great temptation. Monet and Renoir could not resist. Even Zola encouraged them: The battle, he said, must be fought "on the inside"[15]—a typically reformist position radically opposed to Pissarro's.

After 1880 things began to ease a little. Pissarro's dealer, Durand-Ruel, started selling a small but steady number of Impressionist canvases and could assure Pissarro a fixed income. "I am not rolling in gold," Pissarro wrote, "but I am enjoying the fruits of moderate but constant sales. I dread only a return to the past."[16] Critics were becoming more favorable to Impressionism. The conservative Ephrussi was positively benevolent in the *Gazette des beaux-arts*, and Albert Wolff, once a virulent enemy of Impressionism, began to change his mind. Durand-Ruel could now establish new premises on the boulevard de la Madeleine, while his main competitor, Georges Petit, opened "L'Exposition internationale," a sumptuous gallery in which De Nittis was one of the best sellers. De Nittis, whose work typifies a watered-down modern style, flirted with Impressionism without much compromising himself. His sugary, refined realism pleased a large clientele.

In 1882–83 the depression began again, this time worse than ever. Now Durand-Ruel was directly affected. He had borrowed from Feder, a director of the Union General Bank—a completely modern and catholic bank, and dynamic—perhaps too much so. The Union General's crash and Feder's arrest jeopardized Durand-Ruel's whole business. From 1883 on, the Impressionists had no regular income; unable to afford Paris, they dispersed. Cézanne returned to Aix, Sisley went to Saint-Mammès, Monet to Giverny. Pissarro left Pontoise for the more rural Osny, and Gauguin, who had picked exactly the wrong moment to try his hand at speculation, went with him.

The economic crisis was also an aesthetic crisis. The insolvent artists began to feel they had reached the end of their artistic adventure. The pressures of the 1880s affected even Renoir, the only Impressionist to have enjoyed a public success, albeit at the price of compromise. He now became restless, began to travel, announced that he had "come to the end of Impressionism," and completely changed his style. Pissarro soon converted to Pointillism, joining the group around Seurat. By the early 1880s, as John Rewald observes, "Zola was right in stating that the Impressionist group no longer existed."[17]

An Anarchistic Artist in Bourgeois Society

Concerned with immediate sensations and purely visual impressions, Impressionism affirmed personal and intuitive experience in opposition to socially conditioned knowledge and shared beliefs. This issue—the conflict between the individual and society—often lies at the center of artistic activity: With the new capitalism it became more pressing than ever.

Let us look again at the work. In an Impressionist composition, the point of view appears to have been chosen arbitrarily. The artist seizes a fragment with no regard for the conventional social meaning that the "whole" scene would carry. In *The Chestnut Seller,* the human figure is cut in two by the frame. *Saint-Martin's Fair* (figs. 9.4 and 9.5) prominently features empty space. In selecting and framing subjects in this way, Impressionist iconography refuses to reproduce the world in terms of a hierarchical order. The relative importance of things, as designated by social usage, is ignored. Thus, in Degas's ballet scenes the scenery upstages the spectacle; dancers are tying their shoes instead of dancing; and the bassoonist Dehau is in the spotlight. This odd selection of subjects characterizes realism in general—it is even better seen in Manet. But Pissarro's subjects in 1879 realize this general realist vision in a very particular way.

In the 1879 series all except one of the prints are landscapes: This is exceptional for Impressionist printmakers. Art historians have argued that Impressionists were indifferent to their subject matter. This outworn cliché—that they sacrificed the subject to form—is an evasion of the problem. Pissarro's realism is not shocking, but it does have its subversive side. Like Millet's, Pissarro's peasant women are working women and not picturesque, rustic subjects. Nothing is further from the traditional shepherdess theme (including the Barbizon School's) than *Woman in a Cabbage Field.* So, too, Degas's dancers are unlike conventional images of pretty ballerinas. They, too, are working women, and Degas depicts them in the same spirit as he depicts his *Laundresses.* This kind of realism is awkward and less easily idealized in the way chromolithographs of the *Angelus* idealized Millet's peasants.

The comparison between Millet and Pissarro was a commonplace even in Pissarro's time, and it irritated him. Pissarro clearly felt and expressed the difference between them: "I'm Jewish, he's biblical." And Degas: "Millet's *Sower* is sowing for eternity;

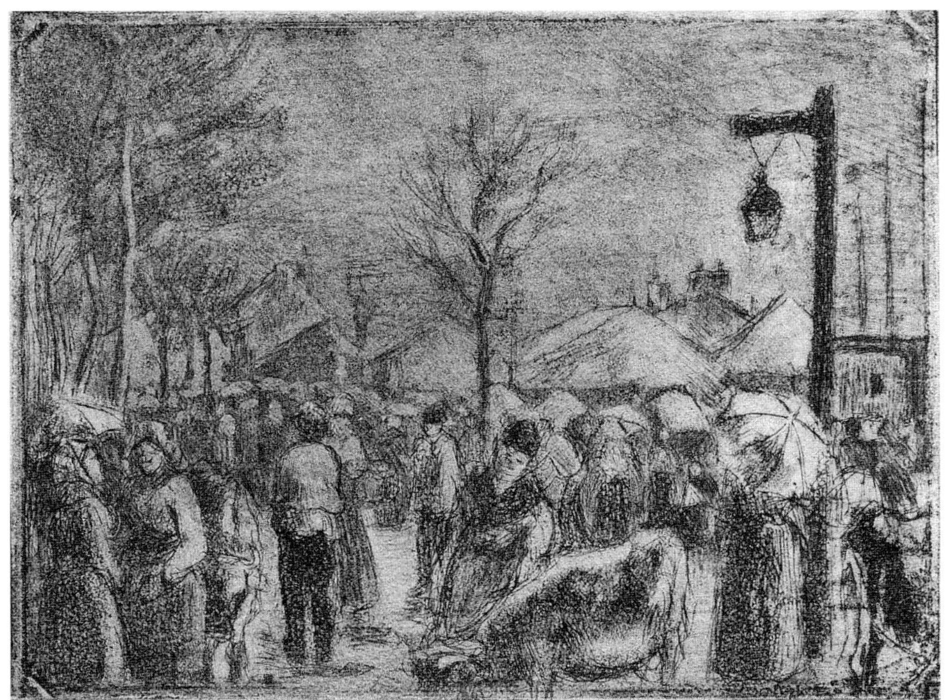

FIGURE 9.4. Camille Pissarro, *Saint-Martin's Fair,* 1879; first state etching. Photo: Michel Melot.

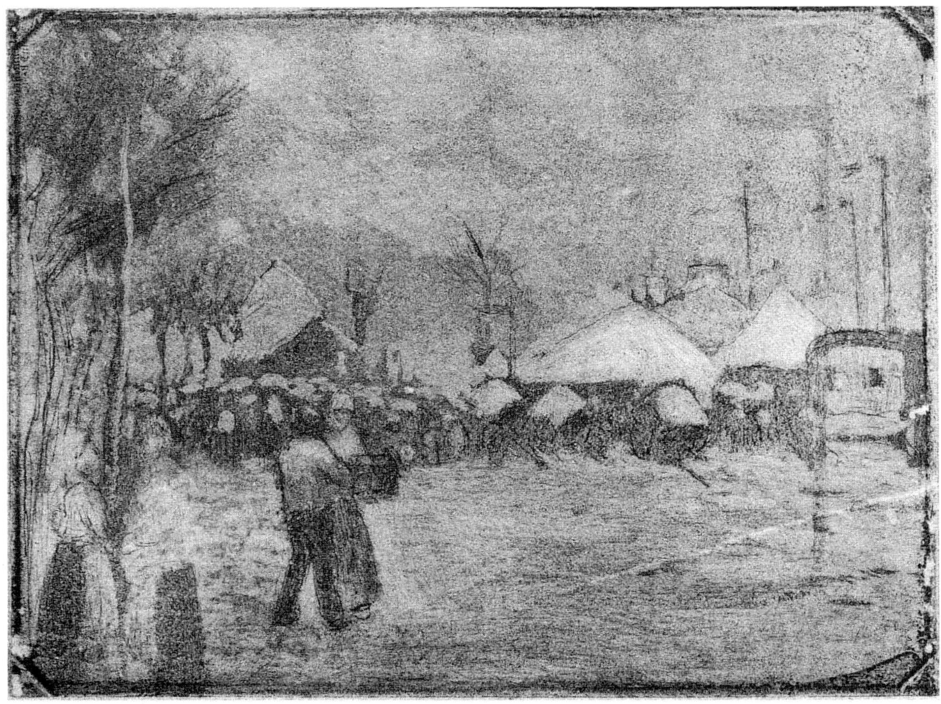

FIGURE 9.5. Camille Pissarro, *Saint-Martin's Fair,* 1879; third state etching. Photo: Michel Melot.

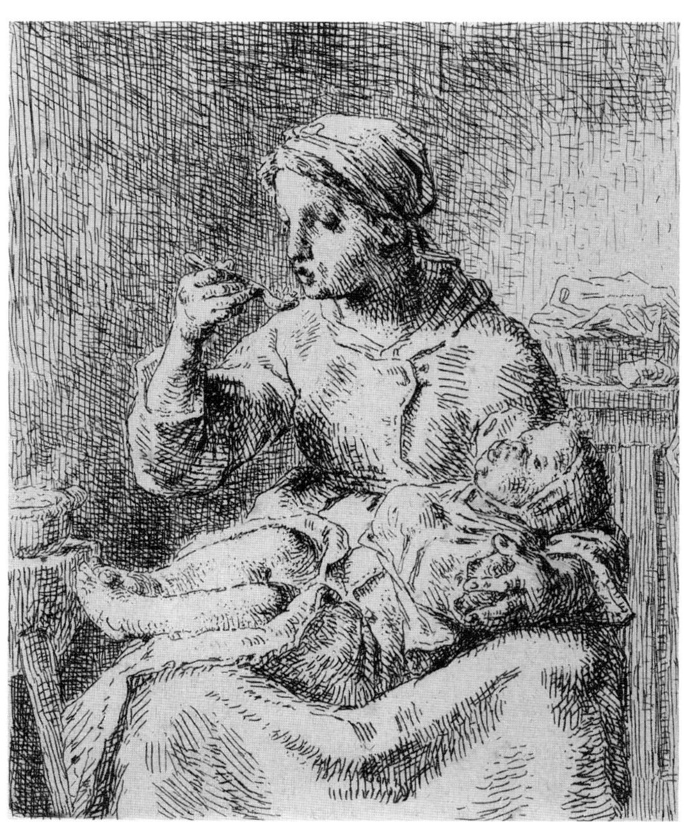

FIGURE 9.6. Jean François Millet, *Porridge*, 1861; etching. The New York Public Library. Photo: The New York Public Library/Art Resource, NY.

Pissarro's works for his bread." Thus the progress of realism. There is nothing romantic in Pissarro's figures, although the iconography is often identical to Millet's. For the most part, Pissarro's early prints belong to the generation of 1848. His first etching is virtually a Corot. Later prints bring him closer to Daubigny—apple trees replace weeping willows, and peasants replace the type of innocuous figures with which Corot, in the tradition of Watteau, populated his landscapes. After Daubigny comes the powerful influence of Millet, with his laborers and earthy scenes of family life: *Porridge*, *Churning*, *A Woman Carrying Buckets*, *The Sower*—these are some of the themes Millet and Pissarro share. In Millet the crude becomes an exaltation of work, even though the public might have seen it as a prophecy, threat, or mockery. The sense of exaltation disappeared with Pissarro, whose field hands blend into nature in a kind of degrading harmony. The exaltation of backbreaking work was evidently an important part of Republican ideology at this time. Liberals and progressive industrialists, unlike conservatives, could accept and even collect images of hard work—so long as only peasants were depicted. The posthumous history of Millet's work completely bears this out. At his death in 1875 the prices of his paintings fell. The contents of his studio were put up for sale, glutting the market. The depression was not the best time to sell art. Significantly, the best Millet collections were in America, where the ideology of hard work, far from disturbing anyone, benefited the wealthy. After the economic recovery, however, when the Third Republic was more solidly established than it had been in 1875—that is, by 1885–90—*The Gleaners* and *The Angelus* became symbols for a whole class. No school, Republican city hall, or petty-bourgeois interior was

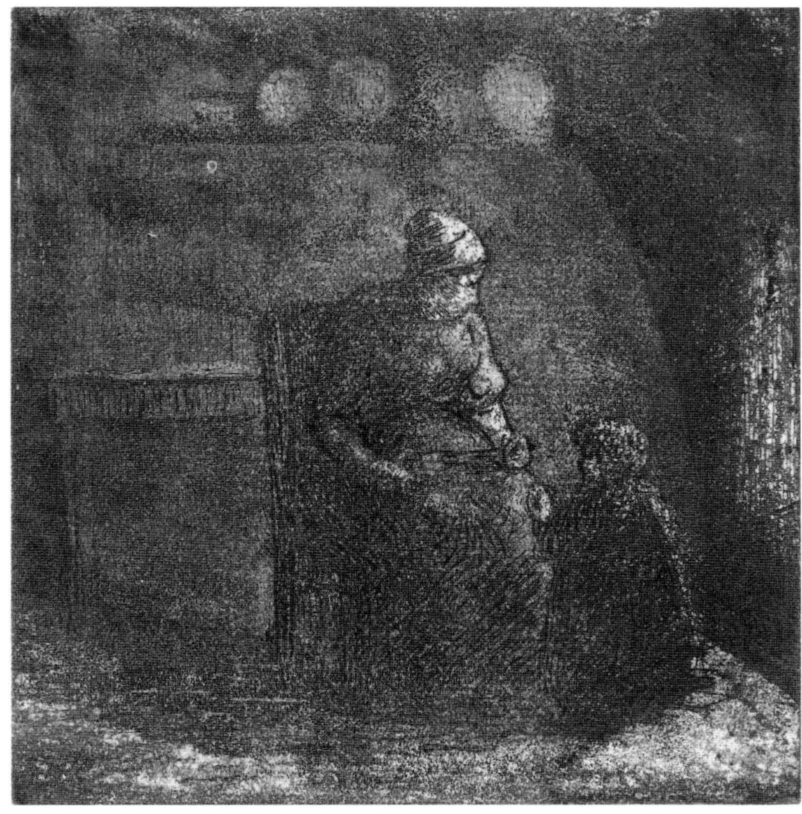

FIGURE 9.7. Camille Pissarro, *Woman Feeding Her Child*, 1889 (reworking 1874 plate); etching and aquatint. Museum of Fine Arts, Boston; Gift of Mr. and Mrs. Adolph Weil Jr. in memory of Adolph and Rossie Schoenhof Weil, 1977.740. Photo © 2007 Museum of Fine Arts, Boston.

complete without a Millet. He was now as popular in France as he was in America.

It is necessary to recall these well-known facts in order to understand better why Pissarro's situation is more complex and ambiguous than Millet's and why his images of peasants—close as they are to Millet's—could never become national symbols. Pissarro did not share Millet's conception of labor nor the social relations it implied. Compare, for example, Millet's *Porridge* (fig. 9.6) with Pissarro's treatment of the same theme, *Woman Feeding Her Child* (fig. 9.7). Despite her simple task, the mother in Millet's painting, with her proud bearing and broad gesture, is reminiscent of the allegorical figure of *La République* as she appears in official art. Pissarro's figure is no *Alma Mater*. The artist no longer believes in the Republic, nor does he believe in redemption through work. In 1875, when Millet was still avant-garde, who could understand such a radical statement? Who could appreciate Pissarro's prosaic style and disillusioned attitude? A few intellectuals, no doubt, but certainly not the rich bourgeois, however advanced his ideas.

After 1870 the political climate became especially hostile to modern art. This is the period of MacMahon and his Republican regime, the post-Commune trauma, and the penitential building of Sacre Coeur. This reactionary Republic had no use for realism and the program of social and economic redress it implied. In 1877, at the Salon, critics expressed an unbounded loathing for all modern art. Not only Manet, but also Delacroix, Decamps, Troyon, and Barye were excluded from this Salon. The exclusion was clearly political. The avant-garde of the bourgeoisie was identified with social danger. All of modern art was associated with progressive positions. Pissarro's realism was even more profound in meaning, even if less explicit.

The figures in his landscapes fade into a general impression. They are often seen from the back *(In the Fields at Ennery, Undergrowth at the Hermitage)*, or in the distance *(Haystacks, Woman on the Road)*, or they melt into mist *(Effect of Rain)*. Nature is not wild, but the product of human labor (haystacks, villages, paths). Pissarro rarely depicts labor as Millet did. However, as labor disappears as a theme in his work, another theme appears with even greater frequency—the road. Most of his figures are en route. Even seated figures (*Père Melon, Effect of Rain*) seem to be at roadside. The road becomes more important than labor. A decade later, the road will be a favorite theme for anarchistic writers and illustrators. They will portray marginal types per se—immigrants, vagabonds, and other homeless persons. In the context of the anarchist movement the full meaning of these images will become clear, and during the 1890s the theme of the road will often attain the level of allegory. In a modest way Pissarro's etchings of 1880 initiate this iconography.

Pissarro's proto-anarchist iconography can be seen as romantic—lone figures lost in nature. The road disappears over the horizon or into the forest. The figure in *Undergrowth at the Hermitage* is lost in the brushwood. But at the same time, Pissarro takes up another, very different, theme—the market *(Chestnut Seller, Saint-Martin's Fair)*. He was very much attached to this theme and even talked about turning it into a "series." The market is also a rustic theme, like almost all his subjects at this time. Pissarro lived in the country because he could not afford the city, but he also liked it there and wanted to stay. He was not a peasant—his origins were petty bourgeois—but he had the taste of a peasant. He saw the countryside as city people have often seen it—as a pure, harmonious world that contrasted with industrial society.

This world corresponds to the rather naive idea he had of anarchy—that "sweet" anarchy where everyone would live in peace and develop according to his potential. Pissarro has been justly called a "sweet" anarchist. He had a taste for simplicity and the natural—for example, his well-known obsession with health. He shared with the Pre-Raphaelites a predilection for manual arts and old-fashioned technology and encouraged his sons in the same direction. This predilection, among other things, led him to traditional printmaking, which he contrasted to modern, industrial image-making processes. There was little Pissarro could do to stop the development of modern society, but if he dreamed, it was surely of a simpler, more direct economy—of the kind he found at country fairs and markets. His iconography seems simple, but it embodies a complex ideology and projects the social reality he longed for.

L'Isolement, the Wandering Man, the Road, the Village, the Market: In the Paris of 1880 these images resonated with ideas and feelings that would be even more meaningful in the future. In 1880 France was still mainly rural, and the rural economy still genuinely preindustrial. The contrast between country and city was far greater than it is today. And Pissarro's position was at once much more subtle and more coherent than twentieth-century versions of back-to-rural-life. Pissarro did not naively idealize his subjects.

Pissarro's realism in 1880, then, differed significantly from that of Manet, Millet, or Courbet. It belongs to a different set of historical circumstances. The Republic, which was still shaky, both blocked and provoked revolutionary activity. These circumstances gave rise to the anarchist movement of which Pissarro later became a militant adherent. Between 1878 and 1888 the discouraged artist became more interested than ever in printmaking. The first anarchist assassination attempts took place in 1878: Nobiling's attack on Kaiser Wilhelm I, Moncasi's on King Alphonse XII of Spain, and Passamenti's on King Umberto I of Italy.

Pissarro's convictions can be easily understood. A Jew born in the Antilles, half French and half Portuguese, he was—officially—Danish. An artificial political entity like the Antilles could hardly make a patriot of him. He studied in Venezuela and in France and nourished a predilection for England, where part of his family had settled and where he advised his children to go live. During the Commune this man of the far left emigrated to London. Nothing suggests that he thought of himself as a Frenchman. But he was sure about his identity as an artist. Since 1830 this state, art, had claimed many young petty bourgeois—Pissarro's parents were grocers. After the Commune Pissarro's generation, born of Romanticism and now about forty, knew that its heyday had ended at the Wall of the Fédérés. After some schooling in Caracas, in 1855, he had gone to Paris, where he lived on the fringes of the art world. As an artist he was essentially self-taught. He was an exceptional case at a time when tradition was revered even by the boldest. Evidently, he started out without the usual biases and was more open to the influence of the modern painters he liked—Daubigny, Daumier, Delacroix, Corot, and above all Millet. He named Corot his teacher, a respectful if superficial gesture. But he did not revere any particular artist. He knew the old masters only vaguely: He compared Legros to Rembrandt and never cited a classical name. Without attachment to a traditional, conventional "culture," he was freer to find his own way.

But what do these biographical facts tell us about his work? The art historical literature stresses their importance, but in fact it is impossible to deduce Pissarro's convictions simply by looking at his paintings. From the visual evidence alone, one could easily conclude that his work has no relation to society and has even less to do with politics. In Pissarro's case there is even some evidence that might support just that conclusion. The particular etchings we are considering are signed by Pissarro and printed by Degas. The letters of these two artists reveal their profound agreement about the practice of art and even its contents. They pursued the same ends, fought the same enemies. Degas's reactionary opinions are well known—he shouted them loudly enough. This banker's son, an anti-Semite, misogynist, upholder of tradition, admired the old masters; and, if he had a preference among modern artists, it was for the conservative academic painter Bouguereau and not Millet. Yet the etchings we are studying, made between 1879 and 1880, can be considered the product of their close collaboration. In October 1891 Pissarro again assured a surprised Mirbeau, "Those are the years that we remained good friends."

In fact, the biographical approach tells us almost nothing about this art. We also get nowhere by trying to explain it with Pissarro's explicit political opinions. If Degas and Pissarro created an art in common, it is because they had a common practice, and that is what we must analyze if we are to discover political meaning. Art historians normally cite their opinions as evidence of how different the two artists were in their outlook. But beneath their different political stances we discover a common ideology expressed in a common art practice.

Whether or not they were aware of it, Degas and Pissarro fought for the same cause. In the context of the avant-garde, both opposed the traditional system of art but not to the point of deliberately breaking with the social practice that determined it. Thus, a man of the far left and a man of the far right made common cause in the same studio. Neither denied that, as artists, they were condemned to make art for the bourgeoisie and that their particular work could appeal only to a small segment of it. Degas was less troubled by the narrowness of the situation within which he chose to work. He rejected the bourgeoisie less vehemently than Pissarro. In contrast, Pissarro suffered acute pangs of conscience. His relations with his clients were like forced marriages, filled with terrible quarrels and humiliations. He was never comfortable with the bourgeois mask he had to wear, and he knew it: "It's terrible to be a penniless bourgeois." How many intellectuals lived—still live—this duplicity! Expensive lunches, dinner on credit. Myths about "the artist" piously justify this poverty and attribute it to the supposed "nature" of the artist. The poverty of the artist is thus idealized and becomes a symbol of freedom in general. What is not mentioned is that society needs that "nature" to perpetuate its ideal of freedom.

Pissarro had to live in the country. But at least once a month he also had to go to Paris—forced labor for him—in order to make the rounds of the dealers. There he would stay in a hotel, like a bourgeois. In Eragny he was in debt to all the tradesmen. In Paris he flattered buyers who talked about the nuances of his colors. His neighbors at Eragny could not have cared less about the difference between an original print and a chromolithograph. Whom did he feel closer to? Where were his loyalties? He asked himself this question and answered it: Remain an artist.

The solution he opted for condemned society but not the kind of individual artist Pissarro was determined to remain. In other words, he embraced an anarchist position. Anarchism solved his problems in principle if not in practice by affirming above all else the value of his individual freedom as well as the work created through the exercise of that freedom. But at the same time it radically opposed any institution that would restrict the freedom to create. Because it emphasizes the struggle for individual freedom, anarchist thought can easily sidestep the question of class struggle. Particularly in the case of artists, it evades the thorny problem of their social status. The artist is given leave to continue working for the privileged class without modifying his practice, at least for the time being. In demonstrating his own ideal freedom, he does exactly what the bourgeoisie asks of artists—but only of artists: Represent ideal freedom in general. This libertarian ideal, which portrays the practice of art as the perfect flowering of all individuals, accords with the liberal conception of art as a symbolic activity reserved for a chosen few. Not all anarchists fell for this ideal. The anarchist press itself attacked artists who served power and the powerful. An article in *La Révolte* in 1891, in which artists are called "a pack of thieves," made this point with particular violence.

It is hard to say if Pissarro's opinions are representative of anarchism in general. Anarchism was no one thing, and, especially where art was concerned, it assimilated both intellectual and proletarian currents of thought. It would certainly be interesting to know whether this collusion between two ideologies is the work of a few intellectuals in an ambiguous situation or whether it reflects a larger constituency, including, for example, working-class avant-gardes. (Here we would have to make allowance for bourgeois intellectualism, either imported into or imposed upon the taste of those avant-gardes.) The notion of "handicrafts," for example, preached by Pissarro, was a value shared by many bourgeois and workers at the same time. It was not simply a proletarian value, nor did it necessarily mean something different to these two publics. We have yet to explore the whole domain of how workers expressed through their taste their relationship to the machine and to industrialization. For now we can only point out that Pissarro's views might well be symptomatic of currents that art historians have hardly begun to analyze.

Pissarro's art in no way contradicted his anarchist opinions, contrary to what critics have observed. They have been surprised not to find an art explicitly directed at the masses, in which coded messages do not take precedence over the meaning latent in the form. We need only recall the essentials of the anarchist aesthetic: It is undidactic, in the name of creative liberty; and it stresses formal qualities, out of respect for the individual who should not be given a vulgarized or "low quality" art.[18] Within the framework of anarchist thinking, these positions are logical and coherent since the free development of the individual is the anarchists' ideal. This free development is to be realized from now on by a type of individual and by artistic creativity. The anarchists believed that if the artist were free of economic constraints (the Salon or the art market) he would fully live up to this ideal. No one thought that these constraints in fact determined the artist's identity.

Yet, if the conditions of liberation coexist with conditions of servitude, then it is impossible simply to suppress one of the terms of the equation without falling into an idealistic assumption: Artistic identity is "natural" and exists outside the given historical situation. The idea of "the artist" in 1880 embodied two fiercely opposed identities—the prototype for the ideal man liberated by anarchism, and the privileged individual, symbol of the bourgeoisie. This ambivalence masked Pissarro's dilemma. Thus, he consciously assumed the role of bourgeois to the extent it contained his longings for universality.

This ambiguity still blinds criticism to the anarchist character of Pissarro's works. But it is precisely this character that explains his artistic practice. An ill will occasionally led to an outright refusal of clients and dealers. Pissarro often refused to sell his prints despite the demand for them, just as he had always refused to submit works to the Salon jury. He was the only member of the Impressionist group to have maintained such a radical position. But he also refused to abandon the artistic profession, and in the end he had to sell his prints—but with "death in his soul." He made rare, delicate, recherché works; in other words, he worked in the same vein as the most elite of the aesthetes. His justification: fear of vulgarizing art, of the "massification" of art. His solution: Everyone should become an artist. The artist does not need much of a public. There is no need for stars or authorities, in art or anywhere else. He displayed an almost maniacal attachment to formal quality without questioning its criteria. Pissarro chose to get by with quality "in itself," as if the idea of quality were universal. And he employed archaic techniques and even occasionally took up archaic themes.

As in Pissarro's iconography, the notion of individual freedom was accompanied by an anti-industrialism that led many anarchist artists to outmoded artisanal practices. Anarchist art and certain types of bourgeois art shared the taste for manual work and preindustrial processes. Finally, all these principles apply equally well to the art advocated and appreciated by a section of the liberal bourgeoisie, whose slogan, "art for art's sake," approximates the anarchist aesthetic of "art for myself" (Proudhon).

Degas's situation thus appears more logical than Pissarro's. Pissarro's anarchist convictions respect the formal values that collectors use to judge the "quality" of a work. Would not the print medium furnish a means perfectly adapted to reproducing great numbers of prints without vulgarizing or diluting them? But Pissarro would not and could not create a print of that sort; to do so would violate his most fundamental principles.

The Original Print as Social Practice

Pissarro and Degas, making prints together in 1879–80, often improvised materials. The copper plates, now in the Bibliothèque Nationale, were acquired in different places. Some are reused photographic plates: Degas often salvaged materials from print shops. Since the prints were not being published, little paper was needed, and anything at hand could be used—a proof of *Sunset* could just as well be made on the back of an invitation to the wedding of Louis Gonse, director of the *Gazette des beaux-arts*.[19] These prints remained within the artist's family until dispersed by the Degas and Pissarro sales.[20] Many of them were found in Degas's studio—evidence that the few prints that were pulled had never been used and had been left in boxes. Forgotten, too, were the original plates. Pissarro wrote Lucien in 1891, "I have rediscovered my lost plates. *The Tumbledown Cottage*, *Le Père Melon*, a whole package at Degas's. Degas found them while reorganizing his studio and passed them on to me. I don't know how many there are."[21] Hence, no published editions, and printing only for the enjoyment of family and friends.

Did Pissarro ever try to sell them? That was out of the question in 1880. Cadart was the only publisher who would have accepted a bit of modernism and defended the idea of the original print, but the depression had bankrupted him. When Pissarro made them, he knew he could not sell them. He made them anyway, even though, as he said, "I have no intention of selling them." But what bothered him when he was without money was the idea of "sacrificing" them—that is, selling cheap. He did not make them to sell: hence, the small number he printed. Consequently, he looked upon them as rarities and held onto them. It was a vicious circle. And he had no press; to print them he had to go to a printer who could not be paid.

Thus, the eventual buyer had to pay a high price for these modest, reproducible objects.

> I have decided to sacrifice these watercolors. . . . I hope I won't have to sacrifice these etchings in order to keep the wolf from the door. . . . I haven't yet finished printing. I've had enough trouble getting good proofs. It takes a long time, a very long time. Will I have the same luck with my watercolors? The publishers aren't used to paying high prices, they like to wait for sales; the collectors here are even more patient. For them, the greatest thing is to find miracles, rare proofs for three or four francs and even less (February 20, 1889).[22]

In 1889, when sales were more likely, Pissarro had not changed his practice and continued to hold out for high prices for rare works. He was irritated by Burty's haggling when he bought two of Pissarro's etchings for the state from Durand-Ruel for 50 francs. His prices, nonetheless, seemed astonishingly changeable. In 1888 he agreed to send an entire lot of etchings to a "print museum in the United States" for 100 francs—apparently the Avery collection, which contains suites of signed and numbered etchings. This attitude toward prices is underscored by the anecdote told by Jean Grave in his memoirs, *Forty Years of Anarchist Propaganda:*

> X said he was a collector of paintings. He asked me to introduce him to Pissarro. I was somewhat reluctant to do so since I didn't yet know Pissarro very well. This man made a profit selling a painting which Pissarro, because of the ideas he proclaimed in our propaganda, had sold to him at a low price for the sake of friendship. Afterwards, Pissarro had to buy it back at a sale in order to prevent his prices from falling.[23]

It is hard to date this episode, but Pissarro does not seem to have changed his attitude about selling prints even in the worst of circumstances. It would always have been painful for him to sell his prints at bargain prices, even though he made them only as a "pastime." After 1888 and Avery's purchase, the situation clearly opened up. From then on, his prints frequently appeared in exhibitions, and sales increased.[24]

Pissarro's artistic practice resulted directly from his artistic theories. The same is true for Degas, whose theory was radically different. But the two theories—the anarchist and the bourgeois—here led to the same practice, which, for different reasons, reserved art for a small number of privileged people.

Is there really any contradiction in Pissarro's choice not to distribute his prints at a time when he could not have done so even had he wanted to? The socioeconomic conditions that prevented him from distributing his prints were the same conditions that created him as an artist who did not want to distribute his work. The notion of a work of art defined by the needs of society implied this limit. In other words, Pissarro's real choice was between acting in the way he did and not being an artist. How was this choice posed in terms of the practice of printmaking?

First, by the choice of techniques. Artists like Manet, who, in the middle of the nineteenth century confronted new forms of social distribution, ignored the question of the role art would play, the public it would have to address, even whether or not it would survive. Manet made original etchings, but he also worked in media that could be mass-produced. It was not clear yet what the future would recognize as a work of art or what class would dominate. In 1880 the chips were down. With the industrialization of printed images, the original print took shape in both theory and practice. It was distinguished from the industrial image by its manual or archaic artisanal technique, by its being a unique work, by its rarity.

Pissarro accepted and even embraced these conditions. No difference between his attitude and that of the bourgeoisie of his time on that point. This new attitude meant a break with the general practice of regarding prints as reproductions.[25] Thus, when Charpentier's illustrated paper, *La Vie moderne*, asked him for drawings, he refused. "I declined because of fear of *guillotage*. From a financial viewpoint it's not worth the trouble. I believe that only renowned illustrators get paid!!! We could always make a stab at it" (February 10, 1884).[26] Pissarro thus did not see the advantage of disseminating his drawings. There were no financial benefits, but the first reason for refusing was a "fear of *guillotage*," or, more precisely, *gillotage*—a lithographic process considered artistically mediocre but with possibilities for large-scale reproduction. Elsewhere, he repeated that "*gillotage* and *goupillage*" (Goupil's reproduction process) were twin disasters. The argument about technical quality took precedence. Then too, he had as little as possible to do with illustrations for the anarchist press, although he offered generous financial support to Jean Grave's anarchist newspaper *La Révolte* and sold paintings in order to raise money for the anarchist cause.

Following his social theories, he placed a great deal of emphasis on the quality of his work, which he apparently judged according to the dominant criteria then in force: handmade, individual, unique. In March 1891 he wrote, "You know these prints are rare, I have only eight and even these aren't very good, it's a difficult plate to print." And elsewhere he said, "The woman with a wheelbarrow is rare. Remember that there are only two prints and only one is good, the one I'm sending you. It's in the gray manner." And again, "There are only three of this type, the steel facing has destroyed the subtlety of the background."

Pissarro's position on the industrial process of steel facing copper plates is especially significant. Today, few printmakers think that steel facing noticeably alters the quality of a print. Even connoisseurs who know about the process are incapable of seeing the difference with the naked eye if not forewarned. In fact, steel facing offers the possibility of larger printings with no loss of quality. Thus, it is above all the awareness of rarity that informs the refusal to steel face rather than quasi-imperceptible qualities in the print.

What is quality in a print? Every amateur knows the answer. But as soon as the answer goes beyond the subjective, technique must be invoked. The problem, then, is to know how techniques are valued.

Connoisseurs have a definite hierarchy of techniques. Those techniques which result in the fewest and most individualized prints are the most favored. (Prints that Pissarro made from nonsteel-faced plates are judged superior to prints pulled from steel-faced plates.) Mass production techniques, whether or not used to produce large quantities of prints, are suspect. Certain techniques are thought incapable of producing true works of art. (Catalogues of Renoir's prints never mention the illustrations he made for *La Vie moderne*.) Thus, in this hierarchy of techniques, "aesthetic quality" is really a code name for another quality—rarity, the necessary condition for a true work of art. All the talk about the relation between quality and technique in effect masks another discourse about the ideological value of rarity. The technique an artist chooses must agree with the values he chooses to express—the values Pissarro objectified by using the "gray manner" and by varied inkings cannot be achieved by using steel-faced plates—but the social conditions that determine artistic choices also determine their social function.

Pissarro chose to express himself through a process of reproduction, but one that made reproduction as difficult as possible. The conditions that led to his choice were the same as those that required works of art with finely ranked differences in quality. To put it bluntly, Pissarro chose the "gray manner," zinc, and nonsteel-faced plates because the society he addressed needed rarified and differentiated works of art. The differences in quality between prints made from steel-faced and nonsteel-faced plates can be verified objectively, even if they are minute. Collectors glory in being the only ones able to detect them.

The practice of signing prints did not begin with Pissarro and Degas. As early as the eighteenth century, some printmakers who, unlike Pissarro and Degas, worked for a flourishing market signed each print by hand in order to "authenticate" their reproductions and thus prevent counterfeiting and bad printings. They did so at a time when publishers generally owned the plates and determined their use. The prints were not made rare deliberately; just the opposite. The artists attempted to exercise some control over their products in order to prevent them from being "botched." In the mid-nineteenth century the same desire to control the quality of the print is exemplified by Meyron, who protested against the reuse of his plates. But when Degas, beginning in 1856, Whistler, and Pissarro signed their prints by hand, they did so not as a protest against the commercial abuse of their work. There had been no abuse. Their practice of signing by hand can be attributed precisely to the absence of commercial use, which led them to regard their prints as drawings.

But this practice would soon lead to the development of a new type of art market, reserved for an elite, which, reacting to the popularization and mass production of undifferentiated images, cultivated a taste for original and unique images. Connoisseurs claimed that the new mass taste for images resulted in a general lowering of aesthetic quality. In the liberal version of this explanation the public's "bad taste" resulted from bad education. This explanation has some truth if "good taste" is identified with the taste of the bourgeoisie, or rather with the bourgeoisie's need for rarity. The new trade in art prints claimed to sell artistic images that could be distinguished from mass-produced images by external factors: the artist's handwritten signature and a deliberately limited number of prints. What is important about Pissarro's artistic practice is not so much what it meant to him in 1880 but what it became ten years later and what it remains today. Today, the traditional print is sold as a work of art by dealers who also sell paintings and drawings. It is no longer a part of the general traffic in images.

So, at the very moment when images began to be mass-produced, Pissarro created unique handmade prints, signed and numbered. And this practice, begun in isolation and inspired by anarchist ideals, ended by satisfying the bourgeois need for original art prints. The co-optation was entirely logical since the anarchist and the bourgeois agree that art must be individualistic and differentiated. Its very essence as art depends upon these criteria, which, between 1880 and 1890, were gradually applied to reproductions. Two watertight categories and two distinct markets developed. The mass-produced image, a utilitarian object, was separated from the unique print—a product of pure ideological use that sells at prices with no relation to the amount of immediate labor in its production. A signed and numbered poster and a mass-produced one, to the naked eye identical to the "original," can sell at prices that vary enormously.

The high exchange value of rarity and differentiation testifies to the value society places on them. For one thing, they reinforce class distinctions. We are not saying that one class buys mass-produced objects while another buys works of art, although generally that is what happens. We are saying that the distinction between owners and nonowners of artworks is itself based on the idea of class or at least justifies it. Certainly, this is not what Pissarro had in mind in 1880 when he varied his prints. He was concerned with individuality. When the market commercialized his values, he saw—as a rationale for selling—only the buyers' interest in individuality: a preference for original prints as opposed to industrial products. Thus, Pissarro's anarchist rationale for rarefaction limited his prints to one class. Outside of this class these values had no meaning.

Rarity and differentiation also play an important role within the privileged class. Through them, members of the class distinguish themselves from each other as individuals and determine the limits of the class as a whole. These social needs translate into aesthetic demands for rarity (limited editions) and differentiation (numbered prints) that are viable only in the context of a privileged class that needs to recognize itself and affirm its individuality. How can an art object assure people that they are distinctly individual members of the privileged class? Art is a luxury, a pleasure—but a pleasure that has a social function and is socially located within a class structure.

Aesthetic pleasure is a mark of privilege. To repeat a famous formula, the work of art "treats the individual as a subject." But which individual is important? Only the individual who accepts the value-system of the dominant class. For the two conditions—rarefaction (limitation to the class of owners) and differentiation (the individuality of the owner)—

correspond to the two ideological needs of the bourgeoisie. They justify and provide a symbolic foundation for the idea of individual appropriation of capital and its limitation to the dominant class. Thus, the work of art is a constant stake in the game between possessors and would-be possessors, and the game is deliberately if not exclusively bourgeois.

The contradictions in Pissarro's position shed light on the situation, for he stood at a point at which liberalism and anarchism met. Liberalism claims that educating the masses will resolve the conflict between the individual and society—everyone can have a crack at social power and property. The working-class position would destroy social distinctions but at the same time preserve the cultural heritage of class society. Pissarro's position—anarchist and bourgeois—does not entirely correspond to any single theoretical position but rather situates itself at the most disputed point within the class struggle. The modernist bourgeois effaces the idea of social differences between classes—modern publishers of prints seek a larger public, enlarged editions, lower prices—without affecting individual distinctions.

An anarchist who makes the flowering of individualism a precondition for the disappearance of classes would logically engage in a similar practice. These two positions, each reflecting the other, express the opposition between the individual and society—an opposition that finally cannot be resolved. For, on the contrary, it is based on and justified by a social practice in which the art object functions as an instrument of preference and selection.

Notes

Originally published in *Marxist Perspectives* 2 (Winter 1979–80): 22–54. Translated from the French by Carol Duncan and Alan Wallach. An earlier version of this essay appeared as "La Practique d'un artiste: Pissarro graveur en 1880" in *Histoire et critique des arts* 2 (June 1977): 14–38.

1. Loys Delteil, *Le Peintre graveur illustré* (Paris, 1923), vol. 17, nos. 15–33 and 39. The grouping is confirmed by the sales catalogue of the contents of Degas's studio. Degas kept a complete set there—sometimes several states. See also Jean Cailac, "The Prints of Camille Pissarro, A Supplement to the Catalogue by Loys Delteil," *Print Collector's Quarterly* 19 (1932): 75–86.
2. Delteil, *Le Peintre graveur illustré*, nos. 15–20, 23, 25, 31. Degas also left written instructions for two others, nos. 29 and 30.
3. He explained this technique to Fénéon, whose article contains a detailed description of it. See Félix Fénéon, "Exposition de la Revue Indépendante," *La Revue indépendante* (January 1888), republished in Joan V. Halperin, ed., *Félix Fénéon, Oeuvres plus que complètes*, vol. 1 (Geneva, 1970), 92.
4. Pissarro explored other print techniques to realize his artistic vision. Besides the "gray manner," he also tried a little-known technique called soft-ground etching. Pissarro had Degas explain this delicate process after having tried it unsuccessfully in *The Cabbage Field*. In a long, often-published letter—in J. Adhémar and F. Cachin, *Degas, gravures et monotypes* (Paris, 1973), xiii—Degas described how the technique worked, and his advice seems to have been taken in *The Cabbage Field*. The velvety, fluid line of soft-ground etching was well suited to the Impressionist graphic style.
5. Edmond de Goncourt and Jules de Goncourt, *Journal: Mémories de la vie littéraire*, ed. Robert Ricatte, 3 vols. (Paris, 1989), February 24, 1874.
6. Ludovic-Rodo Pissarro and Lionello Venturi, *Camille Pissarro, son art, son oeuvre* (Paris, 1949), no. 1542.
7. Since the beginning of the nineteenth century, avant-garde artists claimed that a human figure is simply another spot of color. This new way of representing the figure, first seen in the contorted poses of Goya, Delacroix, and Manet and ending in figures like Pissarro's, was criticized as grotesque or ridiculous caricature. Pissarro's figures were seen as remarkably awkward attempts at conventional figure drawing rather than what they were: seen human movement described without reference to conventional concepts of anatomy. This new way of seeing movement and the critical reception of it is a subject that is better pursued in the art of Degas, whose figures are more interesting in this regard than Pissarro's.
8. Frederick Antal, *Florentine Painting and Its Social Background* (New York, n.d.; originally published 1948).

9. For recent studies of the period, see Jean Marie Mayeur, *Les Débuts de la IIIe République, 1871–1898, Nouvelle Histoire de la France Contemporaine*, X (Paris, 1973); Pierre Solin, *La Société française, 1860–1914* (Paris, 1969); J. Bouvier, F. Furet, M. Gillet, *Le Mouvement du profit en France au XIXe siècle* (Paris, 1965); J. Bouvier, *Etudes sur le krach de l'Union Générale* (Paris, 1950); See also Emile Zola, *L'Argent*, which was inspired by the same bankruptcy; Y. Gonjo, "Le Plan Freycinet, 1878–1882, un aspect de la 'grande dépression économique' en France," in *Revue historique* (July–September 1972): 49–72.

10. Hoschedé, the director of large department stores, championed modern art and owned a significant collection. He defended Manet with an argument typical of the idealist eclecticism of the progressive bourgeois. Art, he said, in his *Promenade au Salon de 1882*, is neither modern nor academic, but belongs to all times. Hoschedé was one of those wealthy bourgeois who aspired to be avant-garde in his taste. He bought and then resold Impressionist canvases like the modern speculator collector, who seems to run his avant-garde collection in the same way he runs his business—the same principle of risk and the same propensity to switch loyalties. In a boom period a dozen Hoschedés could have handsomely supported fifty Impressionist artists. Now, in 1878, what does Hoschedé do? Like many of his peers, he goes bankrupt and puts his art up for sale. But no one buys it. See John Rewald, *History of Impressionism*, 2nd ed. (New York, 1946), 331.

    Besides Hoschedé, there was Charpentier, another wealthy and progressive bourgeois, the publisher of Zola, Daudet, and the celebrated "Petite bibliothèque Charpentier." But he already belongs to the category of intellectuals, and Impressionism had no lack of such defenders. Thanks to such men as Duret, Duranty, and Huysmans, the Impressionists were never entirely neglected.

    Another type of collector had also been buying Impressionist works on a regular basis: the petty bourgeois with a varied but sure income. Like his wealthier counterpart, this modest collector type can be counted on the fingers of one hand: two doctors, Gachet and de Bellio, a civil servant, Choquet, a restaurateur and amateur painter, Murer. Murer was the one Pissarro turned to for help when he was most desperate, and it was Murer to whom he confided his worst troubles. The letters to him are moving. They have been used mostly to fuel sentimental accounts of the suffering of the Impressionists. Tabarant, Pissarro's first and, for a long time, only biographer, had to base almost the whole of his monograph on these letters, the only letters available to him. See A. Tabarant, *Pissarro* (Paris, 1924).

    The depression of the late 1870s and early 1880s would end the support of almost all these collectors.

11. Félix Ponteil, *Les Classes bourgeoises et l'avénement dela démocratie* (Paris, 1968), 382.

12. The preceding generation recognized its avant-garde. In 1878 one could see that that generation had come to an end; Millet and Corot died in 1875, both having been decorated with the Legion of Honor; Diaz died in 1876; Courbet in 1877. In 1878, 1500 people walked in Daubigny's funeral cortege.

13. Tabarant, *Pissarro*, 40–41.

14. In fact, Pissarro found it difficult to accept as fellow realists a number of Degas's friends—Forain, Raffaëlli, Rouart, and Zandomeneghi. Some of Pissarro's own recruits—Guillaumin, Berthe Morisot, Gauguin, and Cézanne—added to the dissension within the group as did Manet's charge that it was accepting mediocre painters (Vidal, Lepic). See Rewald, *Impressionism*, passim.

15. Ibid., 344.

16. Pissarro to Duret, Feb. 24, 1882, in Tabarant, *Pissarro*, 46.

17. Rewald, *Impressionism*, 352.

18. For anarchist aesthetics see Pierre Joseph Proudhon, *Du Principe de l'art et de sa destination sociale* (Paris, 1865); Eugenia and Robert Herbert, *The Artist and Social Reform: France and Belgium, 1885–1898* (New Haven, 1961); André Reszler, *l'Esthetique anarchiste* (Paris, 1973).

19. Only in a few instances did Pissarro make as many as two prints from a particular state. See Cailac, *Print Collector's Quarterly* 19 (1932): 75–86. He probably considered them the most successful since these were the prints he circulated and later exhibited at the Painters-Printmakers exhibitions in 1889–90 and at Durand-Ruel in 1890–91. Previously, he had made some prints for a publication that never came off—Caillebotte was going to finance a series of booklets of prints. Pissarro made a large plate for this project and pulled fifty prints at Salmon's—a printer more closely tied to commercial printing than the "artist-printer" Delâtre, who varied his prints through different inkings. When Pissarro considered a publication that required a faithful reproduction, he changed printers.

20. Pissarro sent his prints to his son Lucien who circulated them in England in the hope of exhibition. In making his catalogue of Pissarro prints, Loys Delteil depended mainly on the collections of Lucien Pissarro,

Pissarro's notary, Teissier, and for the late lithographs, Taillardat, Pissarro's printer, as well as several American collectors. Pissarro usually gave a proof to the Luxembourg Museum, whose curator, Léonce Bénédite, was open to innovation and defended new techniques in debates about original prints.

21. Camille Pissarro, *Lettres à son fils Lucien*, ed. John Rewald with Ludovico Pissarro (Paris, 1950), 230.
22. Ibid., 180.
23. Jean Grave, *Quarante ans de propogande anarchiste* (Paris, 1973), 392.
24. After the Avery purchase Pissarro sold prints to two other large American dealers, Kennedy and Keppel. About the same time he began to exhibit prints in 1889 and 1890 at the Société des Peintres-Graveurs, and in 1890 and 1891 at Durand-Ruel. There were also exhibitions in Amsterdam, Dresden, and England. In 1893 he recorded as collectors the singer Faure and the jeweler Vever, "a big speculator in the School of 1830." Prices increased. In 1896 he sold Gutbier (from the Arnold Gallery, Dresden) *The Tumbledown Cottage* for 100 francs and *The Stone Bridge* for 75 francs. Finally, in 1903, the year of his death, he received a visit in the countryside from the great Berlin dealer Cassirer.
25. Although the print as a drawing had always attracted some painters, this practice was barely evident in the nineteenth century, when the demand for images for an enlarged public increased the number of reproductions and made the solitary work of the artist-printer exceptional and risky.
26. Pissarro, *Lettres*, 78.

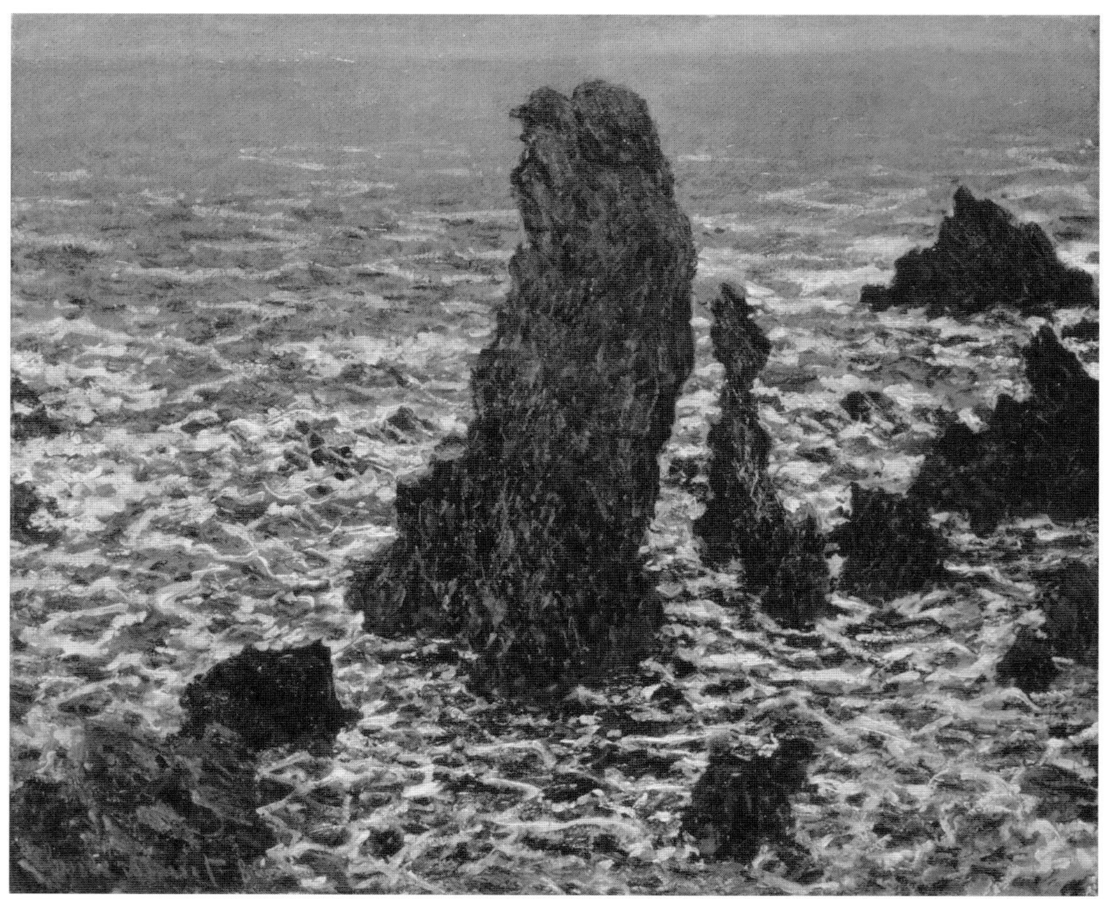

FIGURE 10.1. Claude Monet, *The "Pyramids" of Port-Coton, Belle-Ile-en-Mer,* 1886. Ny Carlsberg Glyptotek, Copenhagen.

10

Monet and the Challenges to Impressionism in the 1880s

PAUL TUCKER

OF ALL THE ISSUES pertaining to the *Grainstack* [or *Haystack*] paintings that Monet so eloquently discussed in his letter to Gustave Geffroy of October 1890, none perhaps are more important—and more overlooked—than the following: first, that Monet began a group of them two years earlier; and second, that he was forty-eight years old at the time, and thus not a young man.[1] The importance of these facts cannot be underestimated. For if we are to find explanations for Monet's serial efforts of the 1890s, we must first examine his work of the previous decade, a time in which serious questions about narrative and continuity, tradition and contemporaneity were being asked generally of avant-garde painting. If we pose these questions anew, we find that certain notions about the avant-garde tradition, as represented by Impressionism, need to be revised. Equally significant and equally problematic is the realization that Monet had been on the Paris scene for more than twenty years. He had earned an international reputation, as well as a great deal of money, and had rightfully been singled out as the leader of the Impressionists. Thus, to understand the *Grainstack* series fully, we would want to know what it meant for an artist of his age and stature to embark on such a novel path and what it says about the pressures of cultural production at the time.

The issue of pressure in this regard is extremely important. In most writings on Impressionism, the notion of pressure is understood as self-generated—that is, the product either of each artist's creative urge or of the shared desire to combat the status quo as represented by the Academy and the state-run Salon. But in the 1880s, as Impressionism and its practitioners matured, there were other external factors that developed, market factors in particular, that may be the key to understanding what really happened to the movement in that decade. They may also help to explain why Monet began painting *Grainstack* pictures in 1888.

To frame this issue, we should recall that the history of Impressionism in the 1880s has long been understood as a history of crisis.[2] After forging a novel alliance in the previous decade and making enormous strides toward establishing an alternative to the official Salon, the Impressionists essentially scattered, each artist going his separate way in search of himself, it is said, and of new forms of personal expression. Whether this constituted a crisis or not is open to debate. What is certain is the fact that the group became even more fractured than it had been previously and that fewer of the original members participated in the so-called Impressionist exhibitions, which continued to be staged until 1886. What is also true is the fact that each member's style underwent some form of change, and that by the middle of the 1880s the movement, as represented by its original practitioners, no longer occupied such a unique position in the Parisian art world. The divisive formal strategies, which had stood out so boldly against the hegemony of contemporaneous Salon art, had become familiar; the feared renegades were now widely recognized names; and the group's claims to the leadership of French painting, formerly understood as vile threats, were now tolerated (though not widely accepted) notions. Impressionism had not completely lost its capacity to irritate conservative critics, but its edge had been blunted by time, exposure, and historical circumstances.[3]

What placed the whole situation in vivid perspective was the emergence in the middle of the decade of the young Georges Seurat. At the age of twenty-seven, Seurat stunned the Parisian art world when he exhibited his monumental *A Sunday on La Grande Jatte* (1884–86; plate 5), at the eighth and last Impressionist exhibition held in Paris in May and June of 1886. Executed by juxtaposing hundreds of small touches of paint in a broad range of complementary colors that attempted to describe the essential components of perceived color-light in a "scientific" way, Seurat's huge canvas challenged the basic premises of the Impressionists' style and orientation and was immediately recognized as a new direction for avant-garde painting.[4]

No one made this challenge clearer than contemporary reviewers, particularly Félix Fénéon, who was beginning his career as an art critic with his writings on Seurat. In his groundbreaking pamphlet *Les Impressionnistes en 1886*, Fénéon drew the battle lines from which the Neo-Impressionists and their supporters would wage their attack on the older leaders of advanced French art, specifically Monet.[5]

Fénéon declared that Seurat's divisionist art relied on structure and science, not intuition and chance; that it resonated with references to history and past art, not the immediate and the mundane; and that it laid claims to higher realms and principles, to museums and the eternal, not to bourgeois drawing rooms and fleeting moments in time. It was therefore superior to Impressionism and deserved to be recognized as the most innovative and up-to-date style of the day.

Such claims had not been lost on Pissarro. The oldest member of the Impressionist group had met Seurat in 1885 and had enthusiastically adopted the younger artist's pointillist technique. Calling Monet's brushwork "rancid" and Impressionism "romantic," Pissarro abandoned his former colleagues and began painting pictures that clearly placed him in an opposing camp (fig. 10.2). However, Pissarro went one step further. He insisted that Seurat and his principal follower, Paul Signac, be included in the eighth Impressionist show, something that contributed to the decision by the leading Impressionist landscape painters—Monet, Renoir, and Sisley—to abstain.[6]

Monet's abstention was particularly understandable. Unlike Renoir, he had not left France to study ancient and Renaissance art in Italy. Neither had he sequestered himself and become endlessly repetitive as the forlorn Sisley had; in fact, he had been enormously productive during the decade. Although plagued by self-doubts, he had worked at a prodigious pace, producing almost twice as many paintings in the first six years of the 1880s, when he supposedly was "in crisis," as he had during the same period in the '70s, when in theory he had not been hampered by such serious personal and aesthetic questions.[7]

Aloof and self-absorbed, he never gave up on Impressionism. In 1880 he had become disillusioned with the exhibition practices of the group and had returned to the Salon. Motivated in part by a desire to broaden his market, particularly through private dealers, Monet took this step back into the traditional arena because he also felt "our little temple has become a dull schoolroom whose doors are open to any

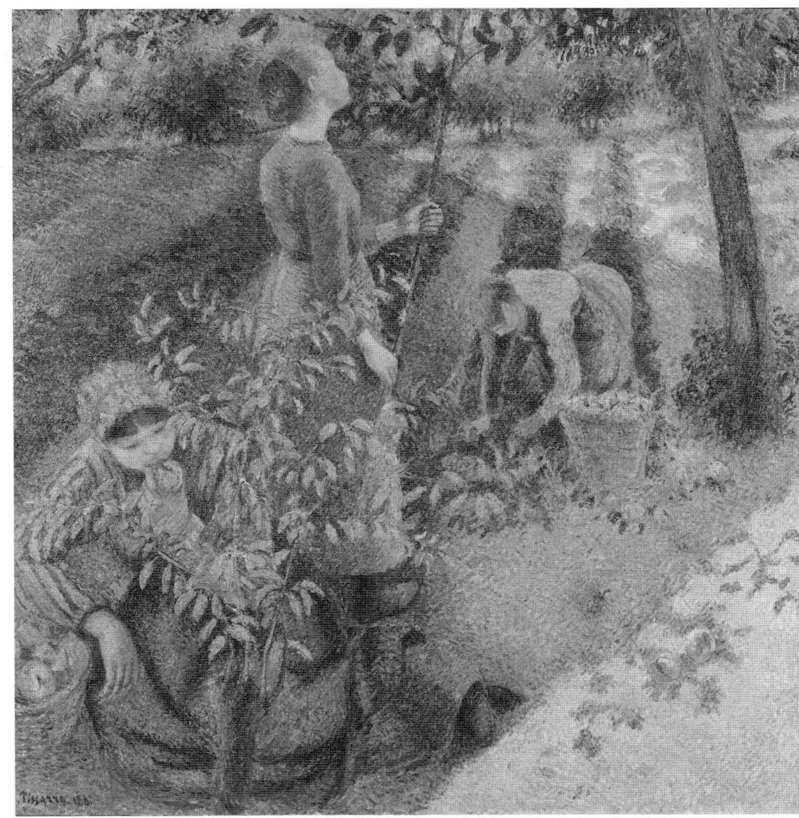

FIGURE 10.2. Camille Pissarro, *The Apple Pickers*, 1886. Ohara Museum of Art, Kurashiki, Japan. Photo: Bridgeman Lauros/Giraudon.

dauber," a barb that was directed at Degas and Pissarro, who had invited artists like Raffaelli and Gauguin to participate in the fourth Impressionist exhibition in 1879. Egotistical as usual, Monet nonetheless felt that the Impressionists should present a united front. When queried in 1880 about his defection, he asserted, "I am still an Impressionist and will always remain one."[8]

Unlike his former colleagues, Monet staunchly maintained that belief. Indeed, he put it into practice in an unprecedented way, traveling extensively during the decade to paint some of the most spectacular and varied sites in all of France, from the black, ocean-pounded coast of Belle Isle in the Atlantic south of Brittany to the lush, sun-drenched shores of Antibes on the Mediterranean (figs. 10.1 and 10.3). The places he chose had dramatically different geological formations, weather conditions, lighting effects, and temperature ranges. They also possessed strikingly different moods, mythologies, associations, and appeals. Little wonder that Monet could write about his difficulties so frequently during the decade. "It is so difficult, so delicate, so tender [in Antibes]," he told Berthe Morisot in 1888, "particularly for someone like me who is inclined toward tougher subjects."[9] He clearly had set a taxing agenda for himself.

This agenda developed for a number of reasons. Having abandoned the challenges of painting contemporary subjects in the late 1870s, Monet was attempting to find appropriate replacements, diverse locales that would similarly tax his imagination and energy. He was also trying to widen his audience; not everyone was as attracted to the ruggedness of Belle Isle as he was. In addition, he was perhaps attempting to satisfy a wanderlust that had built up over the

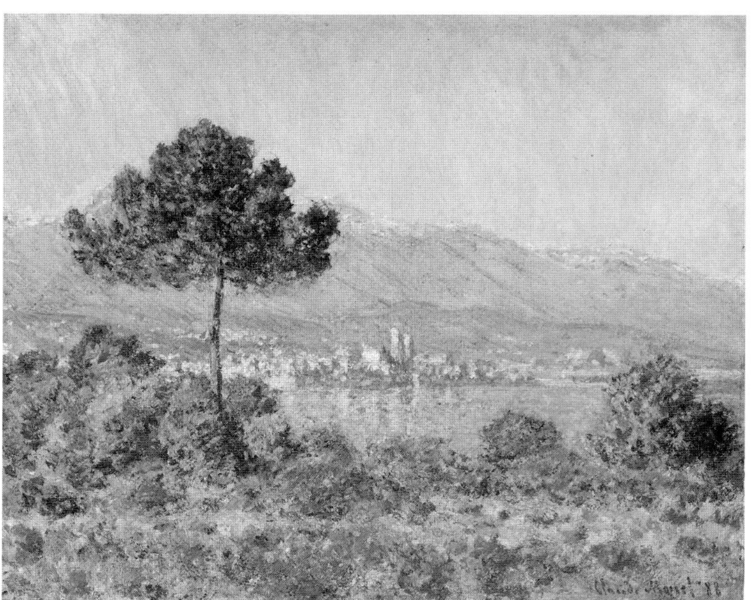

FIGURE 10.3. Claude Monet, *Antibes Seen from the Plateau Notre-Dame*, 1888. Museum of Fine Arts, Boston; Juliana Cheney Edwards Collection, 39.672. Photo © 2007 Museum of Fine Arts, Boston.

previous ten years, during which he had done very little traveling.

There were larger motivations operating here as well. He seems, for example, to have been attempting to decentralize Impressionism. In the 1860s and '70s, the movement had gained its impetus and following from the cauldron of Paris. Its practitioners and patrons were for the most part residents of that city or the surrounding suburbs, its subjects Parisian-related, its style a means of describing modern metropolitan and suburban life.[10] When Monet abandoned the capital region and contemporary subjects, he set out to remove Impressionism's strong ties to Paris and the Ile de France. He wanted to make it a style that would be responsive to the country as a whole. Thus, he chose sites that covered France from the north to the south. Furthermore, Monet participated in many more provincial exhibitions than he had joined in the 1870s, including ones held in such unlikely places as Grenoble, Limoges, and Nancy (which afforded him the opportunity to increase his income as well). Finally, he concentrated almost exclusively on French sites, suggesting his desire to assert Impressionism's continued association with the nation. By painting such varied and demanding subjects, Monet could also assert his powers as an artist and demonstrate the range and versatility of Impressionism as a style. Thus, just as one location differed from another, so each group of paintings that Monet produced at these sites contrasted in palette, touch, and composition.

To realize these imperatives—to gain prominence for himself and his decentralized style, to underscore Impressionism's ties to the French countryside, and to broaden his market while satisfying his urge to paint new sites—to do all of this in the most profound and professional manner was Monet's primary goal in the 1880s. And in the competitive art world of late nineteenth-century Paris, having such a goal was absolutely essential, especially if one wanted to live well, as Monet did.

The competitiveness of that world and the importance of Monet's objectives were dramatically increased, of course, when the Impressionists broke up and Seurat laid claim to the leadership of contemporary French painting, luring Pissarro and many others into his camp. Monet responded at once. Not only did he refuse to join the eighth Impressionist exhibition;

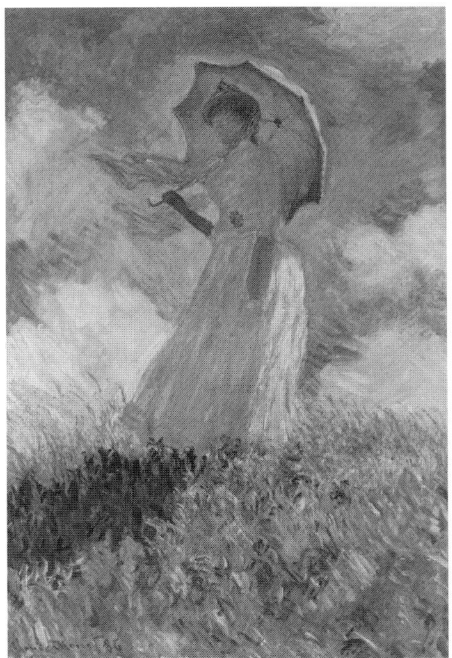

FIGURE 10.4. Claude Monet, *Study of a Figure Outside: Woman with a Parasol Turned to the Left*, 1886. Musée d'Orsay, Paris; Gift of Michel Monet, son of the artist. Photo: Réunion des Musées Nationaux/Art Resource, NY. Photographed by Hervé Lewandowski.

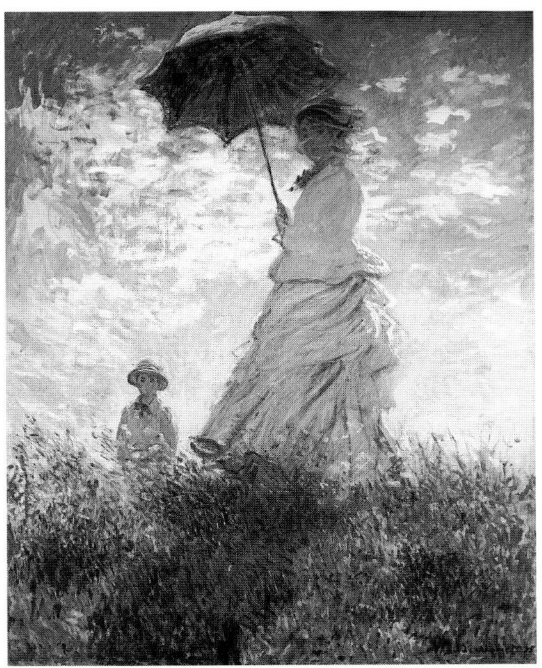

FIGURE 10.5. Claude Monet, *Woman with a Parasol: Madame Monet and Her Son*, 1875. National Gallery of Art, Washington; Collection of Mr. and Mrs. Paul Mellon. Image © 2007 Board of Trustees, National Gallery of Art, Washington.

he immediately painted two very large decorative canvases of a woman with a parasol *en plein air* (fig. 10.4). Not having done a figure painting in more than a decade, Monet was taking up the challenge posed by Seurat's *Grande Jatte* and Pissarro's pointillist paintings, as well as Renoir's classicized figure pictures of the time. And he was doing so in strictly Impressionist terms. His two paintings are filled with the soft winds and strong light of a balmy summer's day. They are rendered with a wide range of heightened colors and remarkably discrete but energized brushstrokes. The foregrounds in both pictures are textbook demonstrations of painterly bravura. As pendants, the paintings reiterate Monet's interests and represent an Impressionist's alternative to Seurat's more hierarchical notion of repetition, which had so seduced Pissarro. Significantly, the figures in Monet's pictures strongly recall the various standing female figures in Seurat's huge canvas. They even have the anonymity that the latter all possess.

But Monet's women are far more animated than Seurat's or Pissarro's and more natural than Renoir's, thus making them seem more a part of their environment. In addition, Monet's painted surface appears more varied, implying his greater involvement with his subject and medium. Appropriately, perhaps, Monet's figures stand on much higher ground than Seurat's and tower over the viewer in an imposing, almost condescending way, enforcing their own authority and that of the artist. Not surprisingly, the pendants strongly recall Monet's own *Woman with a Parasol: Madame Monet and Her Son* of 1875 (fig. 10.5). With its equally striking juxtapositions and loose brushwork, *Woman with a Parasol* was not only

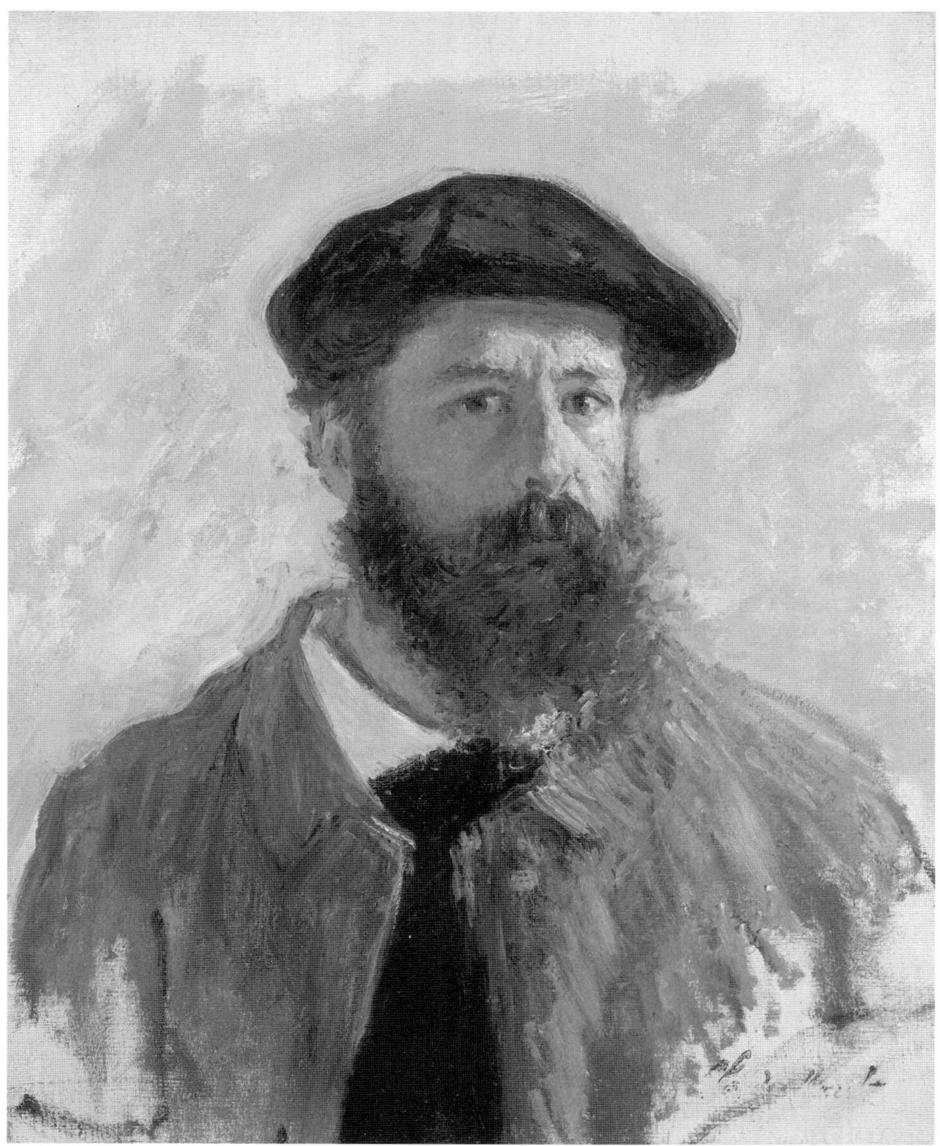

FIGURE 10.6. Claude Monet, *Self-Portrait*, 1886. Private collection. Photo: Archives du Wildenstein Institute, Paris.

one of Monet's most dramatic outdoor figure paintings of the 1870s; it was also his largest and most imposing such work of the decade. This battle would be waged on issues of size as well as style.

It was also a battle that would encourage Monet to take stock of himself and paint the first self-portrait of his career (fig. 10.6). This haunting, deeply introspective picture, which Monet executed at the same time as his paintings of the woman with a parasol (and which he kept until his death in 1926), is a study of competing forces held together by Monet's unrelenting gaze and his expressive, non-reductive style.

As in similar paintings by Cézanne, one cannot escape the artist's piercing stare. It is emphasized by the strongest contrast of light and dark in the picture, Monet's furrowed brow, and the frame created by his beret and beard. But, as with Cézanne's self-portraits, there is much to be found in other areas of this picture. The head, for example, is set precariously on a pyramidal base of extraordinary contrasts. Monet's jacket on the left is rendered with long, thin strokes of purple and blue. It rises assuredly and, in the case of the shoulder, almost lyrically to the generally defined lapel and the harsh angles of the white collar and blue sweater. Forms become clearer and more competitive as they approach the head. They are even rendered with greater amounts of paint. On the right, everything is exactly the opposite. Frenzied brushwork defines no clear elements anywhere. Even the shoulder is a Matisse-like series of painted strokes. This splay of paint not only contrasts with the more controlled handling on the left; it literally overwhelms the lapel on the right and then makes forays into the neck and beard. Similar, though opposite, events occur in the background. On the left, the paint is applied with bolder, more independent touches than on the right. This makes the left side press up against Monet's figure and occasionally invade it, as along the shoulder. The paint then sweeps up and around the beret, descends along the edge of his face like a soft cloud, and dissipates into the background on the right. All of this makes Monet's head appear to push out from the darker, more solid left side into the lighter, more ethereal right side, a transition that seems appropriate. For a primary issue here is the question of how Monet—or Seurat—understood that light. Even more important is the question of how either artist rendered the world illuminated by that light. These questions, of course, had long been fundamental to Impressionism. But when they were posed anew by Seurat and his followers, particularly Pissarro, they clearly caused Monet to test his former answers and to see how many new ones his Impressionist style might offer.

After completing these canvases, Monet traveled to Belle Isle to paint the most dramatic of all of his 1880s sites (fig. 10.7). Nothing could have been further from the gentility of the figures bathed in summer sunlight or the introspection of his self-portrait. And no site could have been further from Grandcamp and its tranquil *Bec du Hoc* (fig. 10.8), which Seurat painted the previous year and exhibited at the eighth Impressionist show. But that was precisely the point. Monet was out to prove his worth as the leading exponent of modernism and to claim for Impressionism its proper place as the leading avant-garde style. Even the fact that he had to extend his stay because of unaccommodating weather conditions (he arrived on the island in the beginning of September and did not leave until the end of November) was a way of testing his own stature and asserting the vital character of his art, something critics emphasized when the canvases were exhibited the following year.[11]

These were not the only paintings Monet did with the competition in mind. Another is *Bend in the Epte River near Giverny*, 1888 (fig. 10.9). With its remarkable facture and immensely rich surface, its daunting color combinations and startling light effects, this painting is fitting testimony to Monet's sensitivity to nature and his evident abilities as an artist. But the picture is virtually inconceivable without Seurat's dot as a reference point and Pissarro's conversion to this "mechanical" style.[12] Monet's dashes are quite different, however, from Seurat's or Pissarro's touch. Although their independence and highly regimented order smack of the divisionist dot, they have a different shape and orientation. They are larger than those dots, they are oriented along diagonal axes, and they do not appear to have been set down with the same sense of exquisite deliberation. There seems to be greater emotion behind them and greater spontaneity, as if we are seeing the results of an individual reacting to the changing scene in front of him in an immediate and heartfelt way. This is not completely true, of course, for Monet undoubtedly worked on the painting in the studio. It is, however, one of the effects that Monet wanted to achieve.[13]

In the same year, Monet painted another picture, *Five Figures in a Field* (fig. 10.10), which is perhaps one of the most telling of the more than fifteen figure

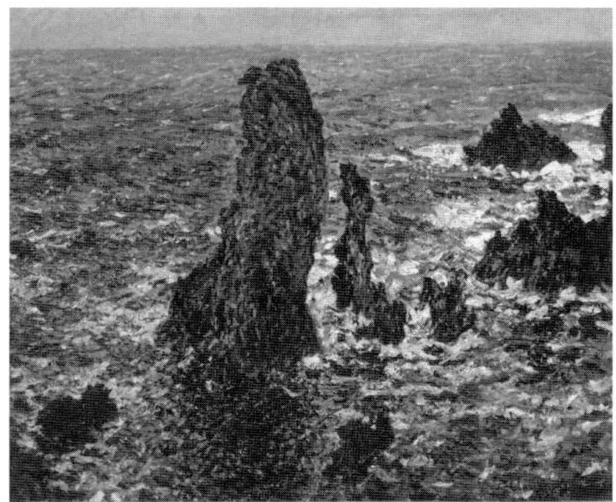

FIGURE 10.7. Claude Monet, *Rocks at Belle Isle*, 1886. Pushkin Museum of Fine Arts, Moscow. Photo: Scala/Art Resource, NY.

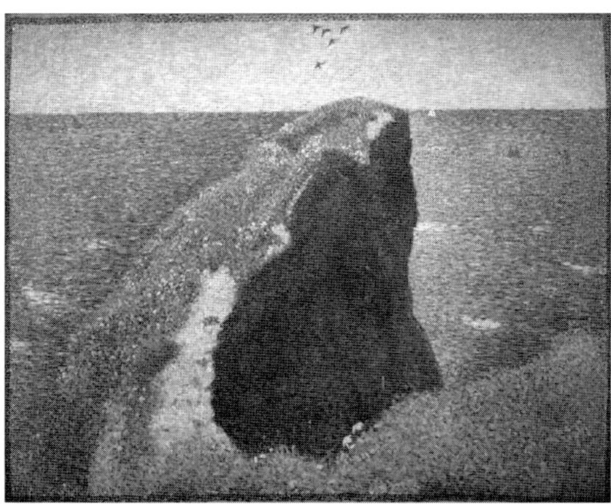

FIGURE 10.8. Georges Seurat, *Le Bec du Hoc, Grandcamp*, 1885. Tate Gallery, London. Photo: Tate Gallery, London/Art Resource, NY.

paintings he did after Seurat so consciously set out to update that characteristic Impressionist genre. This is a curious work, but much that is odd or atypical about it—the hierarchical figures and dramatic spatial qualities, the strong color contrasts and extraordinary stillness—seems to derive not only from Renoir's turn to classicism and Pissarro's Neo-Impressionist figure paintings but also from Seurat and the *Grande Jatte*. Again, Monet has artfully rephrased these challenges in strictly Impressionist terms, employing dazzling, almost blinding light, a remarkably intense palette, and large, varied touches of rich impasto. Monet's scene is also distinctly rural, in keeping with his rejection in the late 1870s of urban and suburban settings. And it is more casual. None of the figures exhibit the kind of rigidity, for example, that paralyzes those in Seurat's picture. The two boys in the foreground have their hands in their pockets or behind their backs, while they bear their weight on opposite legs as if in contrasting contrapposto. Behind them, the older man assumes an equally unrestrained pose, while the woman to his left tilts her head to one side, slumps her shoulders, and places one hand by her hip and the other slightly behind her. There are tensions in Monet's scene created particularly by the distance between the children and the adults, and by the immediacy of the former in the foreground, but they are vastly reduced from those that permeate Seurat's, just as the number of figures have been radically diminished.

What Monet seems to be asserting in all of these paintings is his ability to outdo Seurat, Pissarro, and Renoir—to prove Impressionism's superior capacity to exploit color, describe particular climatic conditions, use paint in novel ways, and reveal fundamental truths about art and the world. For the latter, what Monet insists upon is the importance of nature. According to these pictures, nature should not be submitted to harsh, premeditated analysis, as in the *Grand Jatte* or contemporary works by Pissarro. On the contrary, it should be allowed to reign in the painting as it does in the world—resplendent in all its nuances, variants, subtleties, and surprises. The real artist, therefore, should not impose himself upon nature but attempt to be fully attuned to its rhythms and powers in order to become one with it.

These premises are central to *Five Figures in a Field*. Unlike the isolated and interchangeable mannequins in Seurat's *Grande Jatte*, for instance, who have no interaction and no real relationship with their environment, Monet's five figures are bathed in

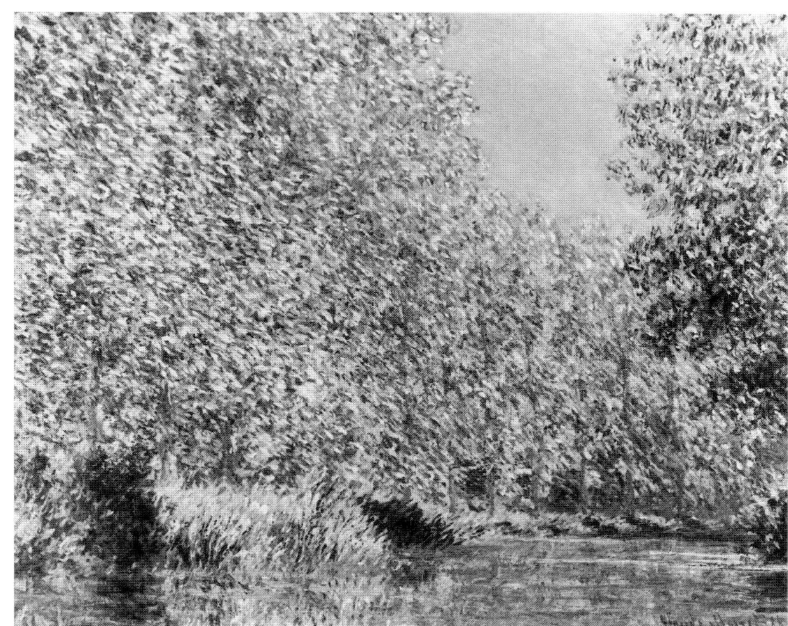

FIGURE 10.9. Claude Monet, *The Bend in the Epte River near Giverny*, 1888. The Philadelphia Museum of Art, The William L. Elkins Collection. Photo: The Philadelphia Museum of Art/ Art Resource, NY.

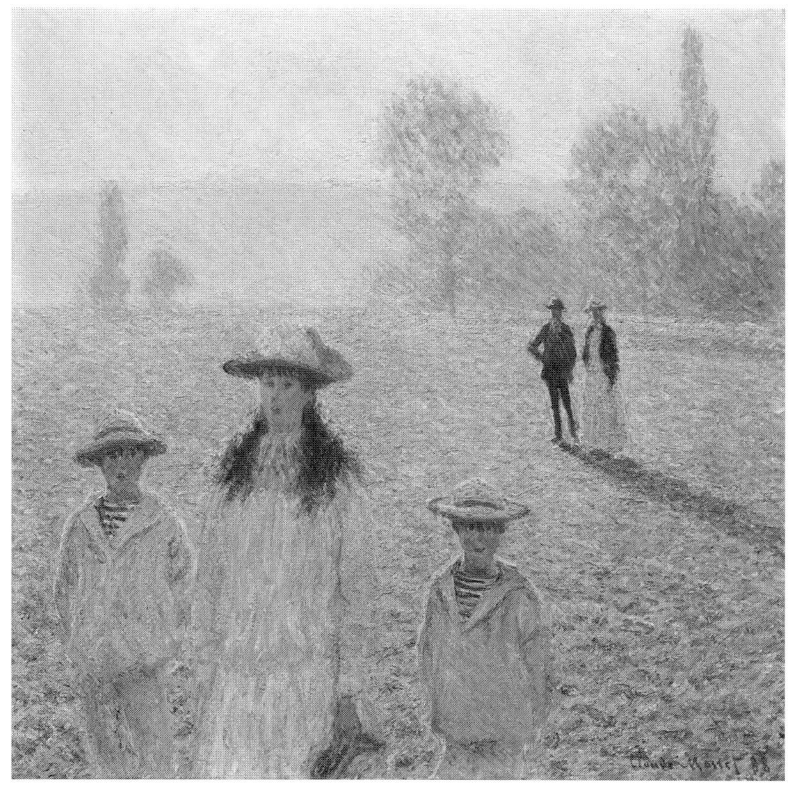

FIGURE 10.10. Claude Monet, *Five Figures in a Field*, 1888. The Art Institute of Chicago, Anonymous Loan. Photo © The Art Institute of Chicago.

extraordinary light and are actually identifiable. The adults in the background are Monet's son Jean and Alice Hoschedé's daughter Suzanne and in the foreground are their younger siblings Michel Monet and Germaine and Jean-Pierre Hoschedé. The older children appropriately stand behind the younger ones and are paired with the larger, more substantial grove of trees in the background. The younger ones, unlike their older counterparts, stand in more vulnerable positions against more open fields, the edge of which they do not break. Jean and Suzanne are not self-absorbed, as is the case with every figure in Seurat's scene. Instead, they appear to be watching their younger siblings, who have stopped on their way out of the picture. Though youthful, the children assume adult postures, as if preparing for their exit by cleverly imitating the poses of their elders. The two groups are also united by their similar diagonal arrangements, by the long shadow that the adults cast, and by subtle details, such as Germaine's dark hair, which echoes Suzanne's jacket, the boys' V-neck openings, which are humorous variations on Michel's beard, and the fact that they all wear similar, though individualized, hats. Unlike all of Seurat's figures, the younger children have recognizable personalities; they even exhibit combinations of uneasiness and naiveté befitting their age.

Combined, these factors suggest that Monet is advancing rather traditional ideas about innocence and maturity, sentimentality and sharing, dedication and persistence, all of which seem to be the result of the fact that these figures are not in a city or suburb but are intimate parts of a more natural environment. Imagine Seurat's compendium of modern Parisians in Monet's country setting! The values Monet asserts in his picture have little place in Seurat's more critical view of contemporary life. And rightfully so, as they are not essential to the industrial society Seurat is describing, driven as that society is by profit margins and technical developments, cheap labor and mass production. Little wonder, therefore, that when Monet was working on *Five Figures in a Field* he told the critic Théodore Duret that he had begun "some new things, figures *en plein air,* as I understand them, done like landscapes," a veiled reference perhaps to his differences with his contemporaries.[14]

What Monet also seems to insist upon in all of these post-Seurat paintings is the superiority of a style that could assert these multiple values about art and life while preserving the individuality of the artist and the integrity of his personal vision—concerns that, on the surface at least, Seurat and Pissarro as well as Renoir seemed to have abandoned. These concerns, of course, had been central to Impressionism and had derived in large part from the Impressionists' battle to break with the hegemonic practices of mainstream artistic production. Like laissez-faire capitalists, the Impressionists had claimed the right to devise their own methods and to market their own results.[15] It was precisely because the results challenged accepted canons and so threatened the closed, hierarchical system in France that the Impressionists had been the target of persistent criticism. Unsympathetic critics in the 1860s and '70s had frequently claimed that Monet and his colleagues were untutored individuals who dashed off childlike splatterings without study or care. This point of view appeared to be confirmed when the Impressionists were compared with Seurat. Trading individuality for strict methods based on the latest aesthetics and technical ideas, Seurat and his followers automatically engendered in many younger critics a reassuring sense of seriousness, intelligence, and academic training. This naturally raised their work above the seemingly more spontaneous efforts of the older Impressionists. The *Bend in the Epte* and Monet's return to large figure paintings after Seurat's emergence were clear attempts to refute that notion.

Monet had been trying to combat the prejudice against Impressionism since the beginning of the decade in other ways as well. In 1880, for example, in his first publicized interview, with Emile Taboureaux (the art critic for *La Vie moderne*), he laid out what soon would become the essential components of his personal legend.[16] It is the now familiar tale of the fiercely independent artist who was "systematically rejected by [Salon] judges" and "energetically booed by all the critics of the time." It is also the story of the natural artist. Monet admitted to attending

Gleyre's atelier as a student, but only for "three months" and only "to please my family." Nature was his teacher. When Taboureaux asked to see his studio, "Sparks flew from Monet's eyes. 'My studio! But I have never had one, and personally I don't understand why anybody would want to shut themselves up in some room. Maybe for drawing, sure; but not for painting.'"

Sympathetic critics took up these points. By mid-decade, when the Impressionists went their separate ways and Seurat assumed his position of prominence, such writers began to emphasize these biographical "facts," underscoring not only Monet's seriousness but also his heartfelt commitment to his art and the extent to which he would go to achieve his ends. Thus, they often repeated stories of the wind and rain that Monet would brave or the ice that would form on his white beard as he stood steadfast in front of his motif, all of which increased the legitimacy of his work as well as the viewer's sense of Monet's deep, personal involvement with nature.[17] Although these stories were for the most part true, no one ever disclosed their real ending—that Monet was finishing his pictures not under the difficult conditions of the particular location but in the calm of his Giverny studio.

These critics also gradually recognized, and from mid-decade onward tended to stress, another of Monet's tactics—his increased concentration on individual sites and his efforts to capture particularly complex effects. By the end of the decade, Geffroy would even go so far as to claim that "if Monet were forced to stay in one place, in front of one motif for the rest of his life, he would not waste a moment; he would find a different aspect to paint every minute of every hour of every day."[18] By narrowing his focus but at the same time expanding the number of paintings he could make from a single place, Monet once more could assert his personal powers and those of his Impressionist style. Understandably, this aspect of his agenda likewise became increasingly important after the dissolution of his group and the rise of Neo-Impressionism. It was another way to claim supremacy.

Nowhere is this narrowing of focus more apparent than in Monet's campaign on Belle Isle where, with a limited number of motifs, he produced some thirty-eight paintings. Monet, of course, had painted various sites more than once prior to this campaign. There are dozens of canvases from the 1870s, for example, that show the Seine at Argenteuil from certain set locations. Monet seems to have conceived of some of these as pairs or ensembles, continuing a practice that he had begun in the previous decade with his views from the Louvre of 1867 or those of the beach at Saint-Adresse from the same year.[19] The most notable group of pictures of a single motif prior to Belle Isle, however, was Monet's twelve views of the Gare Saint-Lazare of 1877 (figs. 10.11 and 10.12). These canvases have often been cited as the first series paintings, or at least as the most significant precedent for Monet's later efforts in this format.[20] And not without reason. Monet had never focused so extensively on one motif as he had with these paintings. In addition to their shared locale, the group was produced in a concentrated period of time—between January and April of 1877 when seven of them were exhibited, together with twenty-two of Monet's other canvases, at the third Impressionist exhibition. Monet appears to have worked on nothing else during those four months.

For all of their shared concerns, however, the *Gare Saint-Lazare* paintings are only tangentially related to the *Belle Isle* or later series paintings of the 1890s. First, they do not maintain a consistent point of view. Some paintings are set inside the huge iron-and-glass shed, some outside. Even within those two areas, there are significant differences, as Monet shifted positions for almost every canvas (the Musée d'Orsay's picture and the one in the Fogg Art Museum being the closest pair). Thus, they do not possess the rigor of the Brittany canvases or those from the 1890s. Second, while they capture particular events and specific atmospheric conditions, they do not form an integrated ensemble of sequential moments charted with a keen eye for nuances and variations. Third, they vary greatly in format, some being considerably larger than others. They also differ formally. Some

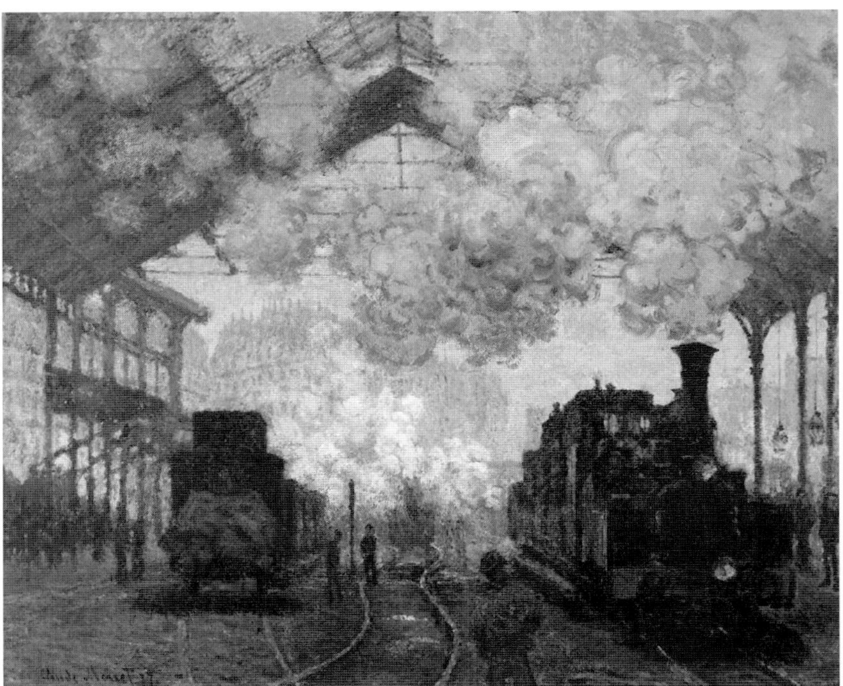

FIGURE 10.11. Claude Monet, *The Gare Saint-Lazare: Arrival of a Train*, 1877. Fogg Art Museum, Cambridge, Massachusetts. Courtesy of the Fogg Art Museum, Harvard University Art Museums, Bequest from the Collection of Maurice Wertheim, Class of 1906. Photographed by David Mathews, © 2007 President and Fellows of Harvard College.

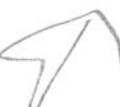

have complicated compositions, others quite simple ones. There are no evident color relationships that would unite some of the more disparate works. And the way that paint is applied is dramatically different in many of the canvases. Thus, in the end, the *Gare Saint-Lazare* paintings are more an exploration of the bustling railroad station than a methodical examination of it, more of an ensemble than a series per se. To relate these paintings too closely to Monet's later serial efforts, therefore, is misleading.

To separate them even more, we should recall that Monet did not pursue the idea of interrelated pictures that, in hindsight, writers have asserted the station paintings suggest. He did complete dozens of canvases in the first half of the 1880s that he considered as going together; indeed, there are very few pictures from those years that are unrelated in some way to at least one other work of the time. Monet also produced two sizable groups of paintings of various motifs in Varengeville and Etretat between 1882 and 1885, his efforts in the former town resulting in nearly forty pictures. But he never attempted anything that approached the classic series works of the 1890s in focus and comprehensiveness, at least not in the first part of the decade.

His campaign in Brittany, however, begun in September 1886 shortly after the eighth Impressionist exhibition and Seurat's apparent triumph, marked a subtle change in Monet's orientation. Of the thirty-eight views of Belle Isle that he produced, for example, thirty-five include no reference to humankind. There are no people in those pictures, no houses, no boats, or other traces of civilization. There are only earth, sea, and sky (fig. 10.1). In addition, the formats of these works are fairly regularized; most are standard-size canvases of 65 × 80 centimeters (25½ × 31½

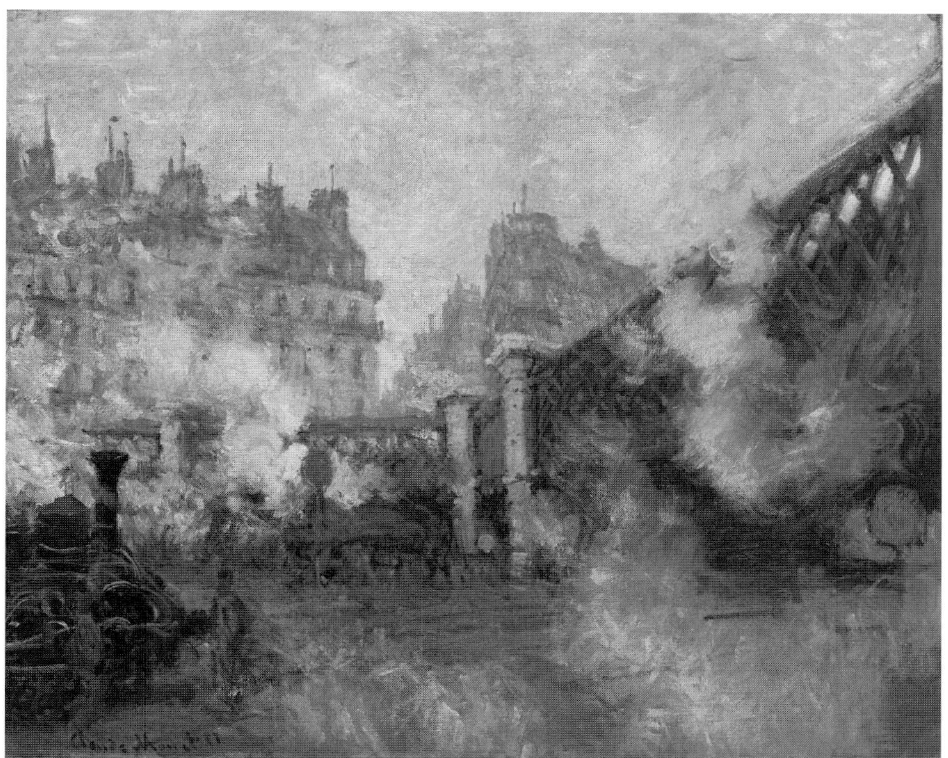

FIGURE 10.12. Claude Monet, *Le Pont de l'Europe, Gare Saint-Lazare*, 1877. Musée Marmottan–Claude Monet, Paris. Photo: Erich Lessing/Art Resource, NY.

inches). The paintings also explore a relatively limited number of motifs and do so with an equally restricted number of compositional options. While these limitations resulted in pictures that are near replicas (Monet did six paintings of the needle rocks, for example), they also appear to have forced him to be even more exacting in his description of natural phenomena—the action of the sea, the way the light danced upon the water, or the interplay of shadows and reflections cast by the craggy black rocks—subtle differences that can be seen in fig. 10.1 and fig. 10.7. Most telling, perhaps, unlike his handling of previous groups of pictures, Monet felt no qualms about exhibiting eight of these *Belle Isle* canvases together at the Sixth International Exhibition held at Georges Petit's in the spring of Monet's return, and then showing twelve of them in his huge retrospective with Rodin two years later in 1889, also at Georges Petit's. He was obviously more confident about them as a group than any other suite of paintings from the 1880s, despite, if not because of, their proximity to each other.

Critics who reviewed the 1887 exhibition recognized the importance of these pictures. Joris-Karl Huysmans, for example, was ecstatic about them and called Monet "the most significant landscape painter of modern times," while Alfred de Lostalot felt they possessed "the power to silence the critics."[21] Both writers were struck by the forcefulness of Monet's efforts. De Lostalot, for example, saw Monet as being "more violent and excessive than ever before in his application of paint and his choice of color," but that such "coarseness" was countered by extraordinary control. "You have to admire these feverish canvases, for despite their intense color and rough touch, they are so perfectly disciplined that they easily emit a feeling for nature in an impression filled with grandeur." Huysmans sensed connections between the pictures, and described the group as "a series of tumultuous landscapes, of crashing, violent seas, with wild tones—harsh blues, garish purples, acrid greens—jarring waves with stiff crests, under raging skies." That he should have called them a "series" is understandable. The term was commonly used throughout the nineteenth century to describe a group of paintings; Monet himself used it many times in the 1870s and early '80s.[22] It had appeared at least twice before in the critical literature on Monet, first with Emile Zola, who used it when referring to Monet's garden subjects of the 1860s, and second with the critic for *La Presse*, who employed it to characterize Monet's submissions to the second Impressionist exhibition in 1876.[23] While somewhat fortuitous, therefore, Huysmans's use of the term for these *Belle Isle* paintings nonetheless suggests that they came across as a group, something that Gustave Geffroy made even clearer in his review of the show.

Geffroy claimed that Monet's paintings revealed inherent interrelationships, that they were "views of an ensemble." "All of these forms and these glimmers of light speak to one another, collide with each other, influence one another, saturate each other with color and reflections."[24] In his opinion, these paintings were the product of "a rustic alchemist, always living out of doors, . . . [who is] active enough to be able to begin several studies of the same motif under different lighting conditions in the same afternoon [and who] had acquired a singular ability to see the disposition and influence of tones immediately." To support his contention, Geffroy provided a sketch of Monet's working method. "Quickly, he covers his canvas with the dominant values, studying their gradations, contrasting [and] harmonizing them. Then, [he works toward] the unity of these paintings, which, with the form of the coast and the movement of the sea, establishes the hour of the day by the colors of night and the disposition of the clouds. Look at these thin bands of clouds, these limpid, gloomy effects, these fading suns, these copper horizons, the violet, green, and blue seas, all these states so far from a singularly defined nature, and you will see mornings dawn before you, middays brighten and nights fall." It was this kind of interpretation, even this kind of language, that would be repeated over and over again about Monet's later work, particularly his series paintings from the 1890s. That the *Belle Isle* pictures could suggest this "critical paradigm" to Geffroy once again underscores the significance of Monet's campaign on the island while indicating the subtle shift that was taking place in his art.[25]

That shift is evident not only in the number and the focus of the *Belle Isle* paintings and the critical reaction they provoked but also in the fact that just prior to this campaign, Monet had selected ten quite different works to show in the Fifth International Exhibition at Georges Petit's. Following past practice, he had wanted to affirm his ability to cover a wide range of subjects. Thus, he chose a view of Menton, one of Cap Martin, a Giverny landscape with haystacks and children, three diverse views of Etretat, a snow scene, a springtime picture, and two different paintings of tulip fields in different parts of Holland.[26] To have opted the following year for eight *Belle Isle* pictures out of the seventeen works that he exhibited in the Sixth International emphasizes once more the emergence of a new orientation, something collectors may have sensed, as nearly every one of his paintings in that show was sold on the spot.

The strong focus of Monet's work on Belle Isle perhaps could be explained by the constraints of the place; the island was not very large. It may also have had something to do with the fact that Monet had blocked out only a few weeks to spend there. However, neither of these reasons is satisfactory. Monet could easily have found many more motifs, if that had been part of his plan; he was too driven and imaginative to have been limited by a site as dramatic as Belle Isle's *côte sauvage*. In addition, despite his best intentions, he extended his stay no less than half a dozen times, remaining eight weeks longer than he had originally intended. The focus appears instead to have been the result of other factors—perhaps his own urge to confront new and challenging pictorial problems, or his desire to capitalize on the increased interest in his work. “This trip must be very good to me,” he told Alice Hoschedé, “it is very useful after my success at Petit’s.”[27] It might also have been the result of Monet’s desire to know a place so intimately that he could feel a certain mastery over it. After being on the island for approximately a month, Monet actually admitted that the latter was an issue. “I well realize that in order really to paint the sea, one must view it every day, at every time of day and in the same place in order to get to know its life at that particular place; so I am redoing the same motifs as many as four or even six times.”[28] This important admission makes a good deal of sense in light of the pressures Monet was experiencing. For although always uneasy about his work, he now was more concerned than he had ever been in the past. That he reached such a level after the eighth Impressionist exhibition and Seurat’s veritable triumph was surely no coincidence. The stakes for avant-garde painting had risen in like measure.

Even if Monet had wanted to escape those pressures by going to the wilds of Belle Isle, they would have pursued him. For within a week of his arrival, he had received letters from Renoir and the critic Octave Mirbeau, he was corresponding with Durand-Ruel and Georges Petit, and he was spending a fair amount of time with the Australian painter John Russell, who owned a house on the island and had recognized “the prince of the Impressionists,” to Monet’s pride and amusement.[29] More significant than these continued connections to the capital and the world of contemporary painting was the chance arrival on the island of Gustave Geffroy. Monet was both surprised and pleased upon his return to his hotel one evening to find the art critic for *La Justice* seated at the table that he generally occupied. “It’s funny to be so far away and to have these meetings,” Monet told Alice when describing this fortuitous encounter.[30] Geffroy had come to Belle Isle to do research for a book on the anarchist Blanqui. He had had no idea that Monet had made the long voyage there as well. Indeed, the artist and the critic had never met before, although Geffroy had written an appreciative article on him in 1883, to which Monet had responded with a letter of thanks.[31] The two got along very well right from the beginning. Like most artists of the period, Monet was happy to be able to establish good relations with empathetic people in positions to assist him. It was a mutually beneficial meeting, however, as Geffroy was able to watch Monet paint. He thus left the island with firsthand information about the artist and his practices, which he clearly tapped for his 1887 review and many others thereafter.

This chance occurrence gave rise to a friendship that would last for forty years. It also led to discussions about Monet’s position and his particular inclinations, as Geffroy’s review suggests. Those topics were the subject of various letters that Monet wrote from Belle Isle to Durand-Ruel, Alice, and Geffroy himself. In a letter that apparently no longer survives, for example, Durand-Ruel told Monet that he was out of his element on Belle Isle, that he should come home and spend the winter in the Midi “because,” as Monet described it to Madame Hoschedé, “my business is the sun.”[32] This did not sit well with Monet. “Hey,” he griped to his future wife, “they will end by drowning me with the sun! One has to do everything,” he declared, “and it’s precisely because of that that I congratulate myself for doing what I’m doing.” The desire to do it all had never been so strong, but, of course, neither had the contemporary scene been so competitive—which is undoubtedly one reason why, after admitting to Durand-Ruel that the sinister qualities of the island were forcing him out of what he was used to painting, Monet insisted that “it is not necessary to specialize in a single theme.”[33]

It was this same desire to be seen as all-encompassing and yet focused that perhaps led Monet to follow his dealer’s suggestion and go to Antibes, the antithesis of the “somber and terrible” Belle Isle (fig. 10.3). The ultimate for an avowed painter of sunlight, Antibes more importantly afforded Monet the opportunity to expand his repertoire and paint the physical extremes of the nation from the north to the south, thus laying claim once again to the capacities of Impressionism to represent the country. And as in Brittany, Monet produced an astonishing number of pictures (close to forty) of a relatively limited number of motifs. Unlike his immediate enthusiasm for Belle Isle, Monet was initially concerned about the area. He expressed his admiration for it when he first arrived, but he felt that parts of it were also "not very diverse." "I should guard against repeating myself," he cautioned. "That's why before retracing my steps, I take a good look; maybe I will even go tomorrow to Beaulieu and Eze [which lay about twenty kilometers to the east]. That will cause me to lose time, but I think it would be prudent; I will work with greater confidence afterward."[34]

Monet's fears about repeating himself proved partially founded, as the paintings that he brought back from Antibes were less varied within individual groups than those from Brittany. His lapse might have had something to do with the greater consistency of the light in the south or with Monet's assumption that people simply would have been attracted to the picturesque sites that he had chosen and that he did not have to vary his effects as much. Perhaps it was also due to the fact that he felt even more out of his element than he had been at Belle Isle, something he had admitted to Berthe Morisot (as quoted above). He repeated this fear to Alice and to Geffroy. "I definitely see that this area is not for me," he told Alice when he first arrived, "Tomorrow, I am going to see if I can find lodging elsewhere, possibly in Agay."[35] A month later he told Geffroy, "I am very worried about what I am doing. It is so beautiful here, so clear and luminous! You are bathed in blue air, it's frightening."[36] His repetitions might therefore have been the result of his need to come to grips with this less familiar area and its climate.

Whatever the reason, he felt confident enough about his efforts upon his return to Giverny to create a whole exhibition from ten of the works. The show opened at Boussod and Valadon's in June 1888, barely a month after he had left the south. That Monet would have staged such a show again is significant. For the second time in less than a year, he was staking his claim on a very closely related group of pictures of a single locale, a fact that did not go unnoticed in the press. Geffroy once again made it a central part of his review, feeling that Monet had been able to capture in these works "all that was characteristic about the area and all the deliciousness of the season."[37]

However, neither these Antibes paintings nor those from Belle Isle nor the many others that he did between and after these campaigns approached Monet's initiative of late 1888. At the end of the summer or early in the fall, after having completed *Five Figures in a Field* and *Bend in the Epte*—his most conscious responses to the challenges of Neo-Impressionism—Monet turned to his surroundings at Giverny and began at least three and perhaps as many as five views of grainstacks (fig. 10.13). They would prove to be the most propitious group of paintings of the decade.[38] For more than Monet's *Antibes* ensembles or his six paintings of the needle rocks at Belle Isle, these *Grainstack* pictures focused on a known landscape and a familiar motif and were clearly conceived of as a suite. In three of them, Monet stood in exactly the same position and rendered two stacks under three distinct lighting conditions. In the others, which show a single stack, he likewise assumed a consistent position and similarly developed quite different effects—one of late fall (which he left unfinished), the other of winter fog.

Begun long before the famous letter to Geffroy, these paintings should be seen as the apogee of Monet's agenda for the 1880s. They are the culmination, for example, of Monet's efforts to decentralize Impressionism, as their generic qualities of site and subject make them, in the end, representations of the French countryside as a whole. Even more than the *Belle Isle* or *Antibes* pictures, these paintings also reveal Monet's intense scrutiny of a single subject *en plein air* and his evident desire to extract highly refined variations from that one motif. No one could say that these canvases were dashed off or that Monet lacked discipline, seriousness, or skill. Indeed, his palette appears expansive in these works, his brushwork a brilliant combination of description and independence, his composition both classical and novel, his sensitivity to light astonishingly artful yet strikingly believable. Reaffirming de Lostalot's contention that Monet had the ability to silence the critics

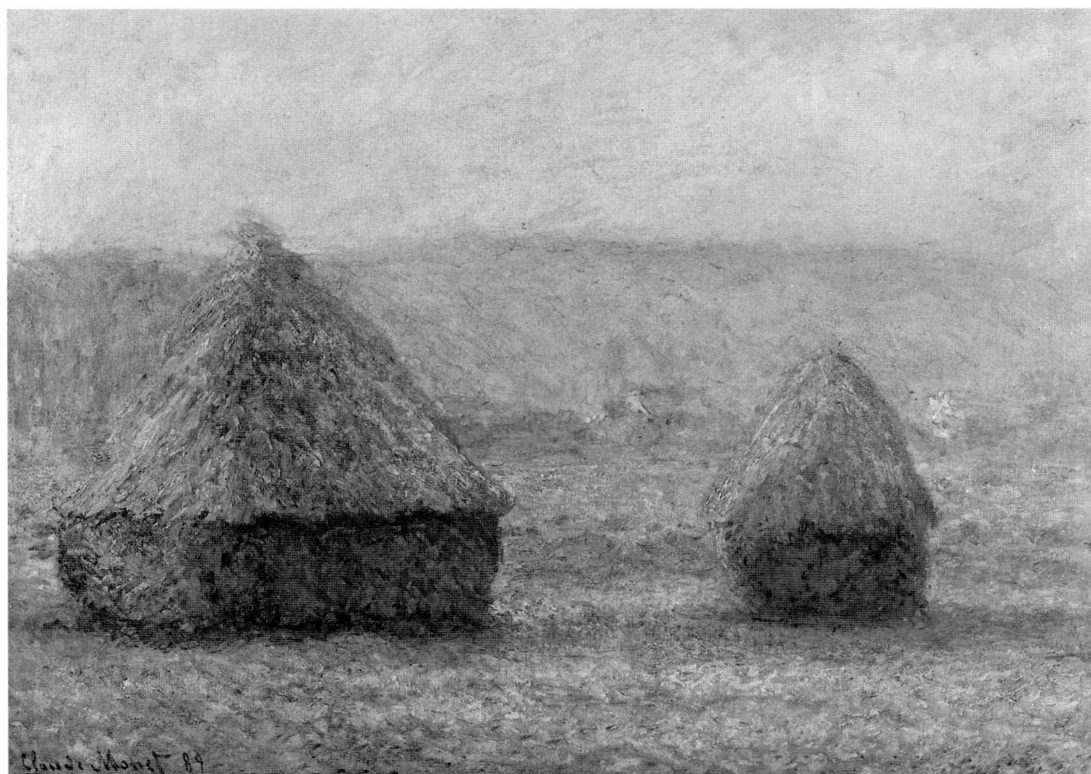

FIGURE 10.13. Claude Monet, *Grainstacks, White Frost, Sunrise,* 1888–89. Hill-Stead Museum, Farmington, Connecticut; Alfred Atmore Pope Collection.

once and for all, these paintings and the series that they prompted in 1890 would earn Monet his long-sought place in the hierarchy of contemporary art.

With these paintings, as with *Five Figures in a Field* and *Bend in the Epte,* Monet was going to advance his reputation on the basis of his craftsmanship, persistence, imagination, and eye. But even more important, he was going to attain the stature he desired because he invested in these canvases values that were dear to himself and his native culture, values that had always been a part of his work but now were stated with eloquent simplicity. They were values that were not readily apparent in Neo-Impressionism. First among these was a love of the French countryside, something sympathetic critics had always pointed to in Monet's work but which in these canvases was now evident for all to see. Second was a deep admiration for nature, again a point that had been made often in the past but which had gained greater credence from the *Belle Isle* pictures onward. With the sublime pictorial effects that Monet was able to achieve in these *Grainstack* paintings, he reaffirmed that admiration in a way that was now both uncompromising and all-inclusive. Nature in these pictures becomes magisterial, a source of wonder and fulfillment, a power that is at once elusive and omnipresent, chilling and restorative. Although essential to any landscape painter, such feelings about the natural world did not seem central to Seurat and his followers, as various negative critics at the time were quick to point out. Third among these values was the element of individualism. Critics of all persuasions had recognized this distinct characteristic in Monet's work. Indeed, it had been the primary cause of the negative criticism that he and his Impressionist colleagues had received in the 1870s. In the 1880s, Monet and supportive writers emphasized this quality, beginning with Taboureaux's interview at the outset of the decade. By 1889, the outspoken novelist, anarchist, and cultural critic Octave Mirbeau, who was also one of Monet's most ardent supporters, would go so far as to assert that Monet had purged himself of all past influences and had developed revolutionary work "due to [his] moral isolation, self-focus, [and] immersion in nature."[39] Mirbeau asserted that Monet did not go about this in a haphazard fashion. He did it "according to a methodical, rational plan, of inflexible rigor, in some ways, mathematical," a not-so-veiled attempt to claim some of the science from Seurat.

Monet's independence was evident not only in how he conducted his life and practiced his craft; it was also apparent in his choice of subjects. Monet himself attested to the importance of his selection process when he expressed his concern about repeating himself in Antibes. He even blasted all of the painters there, labeling them "idiots" because they had indicated to him, "from their stupid point of view, the less interesting spots to paint." The next day, "listening only to my instincts, I discovered superb things."[40] No one made the significance of selecting appropriate subjects more apparent than Geffroy. "To believe that these thoughtful, liberated artists [the Impressionists] did not choose their subjects is one of the numerous fantasies born by accident from the practice of Impressionism. On the contrary, their choice was always their profound and important preoccupation. But legends are made of this kind of stuff. We have grown used to characterizing these artists as indifferent cameras focusing on all spectacles and the error is going to be repeated, even by those who are capable of knowing better."[41] Mirbeau took the whole issue one step further. In remarks directed precisely at the Neo-Impressionists and their supporters, he asserted that Monet's entire art was the product "of reflective thought, of comparison, analysis, [and] a knowing will."[42]

These assertions should cause us to consider Monet's choice of subjects in the 1880s more carefully. For example, during all of his travels in the decade Monet painted non-French sites only twice, once in 1884 when he spent two months in Bordighera on the Italian Riviera, and again in 1886 when he went to Holland for a fortnight during tulip season. Speaking no foreign languages and being particular about what he ate (Monet even found the food in Antibes "vile"), Monet undoubtedly wanted the security of the French tongue and his native cuisine. Returning to France from Bordighera in 1884 gave him "the greatest pleasure."[43] The fact that he concentrated so heavily on sites in his own country, and was truly excited by each one, bespeaks his deep-rooted feelings for his homeland.

However, Monet was not an ardent patriot, as is evident from his many disparaging remarks about the government when negotiating the donation of Manet's *Olympia* in 1889. When the Franco-Prussian War broke out, it was Monet who fled the country to avoid military duty (unlike Manet, for example, who volunteered for the National Guard). But Monet had a deep affection for the land and for the beauties of *la France*, as he revealed to Pissarro in 1871 during his self-imposed exile from his war-torn country. Monet told Pissarro to cheer up because when he got back home he would find "beautiful things to paint in France; the country's not lacking in that regard."[44] In the 1880s, he confirmed that over and over again.

Although always influenced by economic concerns, his affection for his country came to the fore when he learned that Durand-Ruel was planning to sell his paintings outside of France. Initially, he seemed to support the idea. "Your son told me about your hopes for (future) *[sic]* business in America and Belgium," he informed the dealer in June of 1885. "I hope to hear good reports."[45] However, barely a month later, he wrote Durand-Ruel again to express his misgivings. "I recognize that certain canvases regretfully are leaving the country for the land of the Yankees and I would like to reserve a selection of

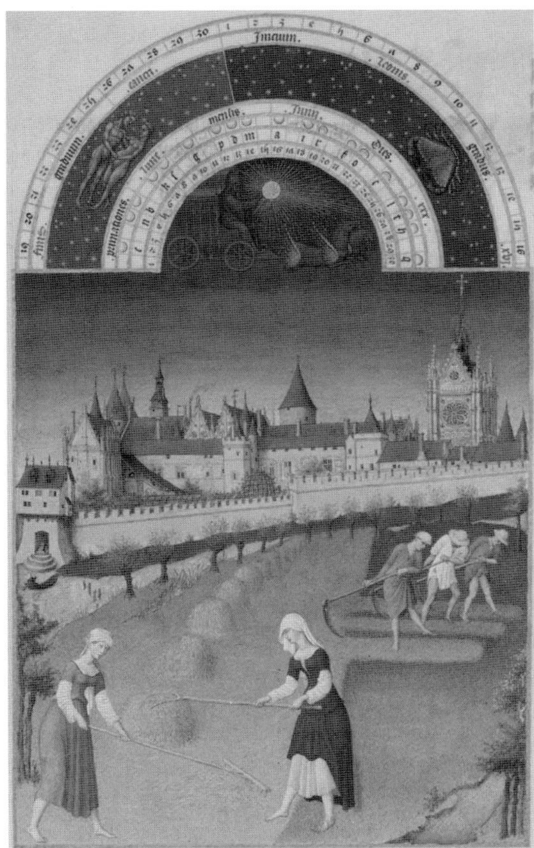

FIGURE 10.14. Limbourg Brothers, *June* (Haymaking; in the background: the Palace and Sainte-Chapelle, Paris). Calendar miniature from *Les Très Riches Heures du Duc de Berry*, 1416. Musée Condé, Chantilly. Photo: Réunion des Musées Nationaux/Art Resource, NY. Photographed by R. G. Ojeda.

them for Paris, for [Paris] is above all and [maybe] the only place where there is still a little taste."[46] Six months later he was quite upset about the whole situation. "After all that you have sent to America, what remains in France? I would very much like to believe in your hopes for America, but I would chiefly want my paintings to be made known and sold here. All of that is difficult, I understand, but [the other] is worrisome."[47] Two years later while in Antibes, he raised this complaint to Durand-Ruel again.[48] Ironically, soon after he returned from the south, the government offered him the Cross of the Legion of Honor, one of the most prestigious awards a Frenchman could earn. Monet refused it—an example of his disdain for authority and its accolades—but the government's gesture underscores the recognition he was receiving and the fact that he was touching responsive chords.[49] He undoubtedly understood this, for shortly afterward he began his *Grainstack* paintings.

These paintings are as replete with associations as they are rich in visual incident. In *White Frost, Sunrise* (1888–89; fig. 10.13), the early morning light glistens on the frozen earth, filling the scene with the aura of potential. The grainstacks stand in the cold, waiting to be warmed by the rays of the rising sun. Though isolated and erect like weighty monuments, the stacks are literal extensions of the town.[50] They are the farmer's source of income and the town's most substantial product. They are also the tangible evidence of the prosperity of the place and of the countryside's fertile soil and benevolent climate. As they rise from the earth, their conical tops receive the largest amount of morning light. Those tops also imitate the houses that Monet includes deep in the distance. Like the roofs of those structures, the stacks are built out of sheaves of individually bound stalks that were then thatched, the result of the farmers' long hours in the fields. Labor is totally absent from these views, unlike so many late nineteenth-century depictions of the fields of France. There are no sweating peasants here and no indication of the difficulties entailed in producing those stacks.[51] There is also no sense of the poverty that existed in rural areas or the routine of rural life that artists such as [Jules] Breton tended to stress. Instead, Monet's pictures breathe the air of contentment. For this is the countryside that fulfills all promises, the rural France that is wholesome and fecund, reassuring and continuous.

It is also the rural France that had been represented by French artists for centuries—in the labors of the months from Romanesque churches and medieval manuscripts (fig. 10.14); in the paintings of Claude Lorraine or Nicolas Poussin; in the fêtes of Watteau, Monet's favorite painter, and the canvases of his followers. It is also the rural France that had so preoccupied dozens and dozens of nineteenth-century French artists, particularly Barbizon painters such as Millet, in addition to the hundreds of anonymous French artists who produced innumerable images over the centuries that serve as popular precedents for Monet's later efforts. Even Pissarro had done several paintings of stacks in the 1870s and '80s as well as a series of prints of the subject (see fig. 9.3).[52] Anyone who took up the motif, therefore, automatically took his place in this heralded lineage.

Monet would not have wanted it any other way, for his pictures affirm not only the essential values of the French countryside but also the fecundity of the nation's artistic past, something once again that Seurat and his followers seemed to criticize or ignore. In addition, they lay claim to certain principles, such as order and permanence, seriousness and harmony, that Fénéon felt belonged to the Neo-Impressionists. Monet seems to have arrived at a new understanding of these principles, not only from his knowledge of past art, but also from his involvement with nature. For it was the partnership between humanity and the natural world, artist and visual phenomena, that produced the best art, according to Monet, not preordained notions of artistic practice scientifically applied to a canvas in the isolation of the studio. It was precisely on this partnership that Monet had been staking his claim for the hegemony of Impressionism. It was why he could stand out in the rain to paint the stormy sea at Belle Isle, bemoan the passing of an effect at Antibes, or fulfill his "wish to prove that I can do something else" and paint a picture such as *Five Figures in a Field* (fig. 10.10).[53]

In fact, the grainstacks themselves in many ways are analogous to the figures in that earlier picture. Like the figures, they too are products of nature and are clearly understood as part of the landscape. They also are similarly shaped by man and the environment. In addition, they are at once vulnerable and hardy, potential victims in their splendid isolation and stalwart constructions made to endure. Like the family members, the stacks too are sources of pride and concern and stand as the tangible evidence of natural continuities. Formally, they assert themselves as individual entities, although at the same time they are one with the enveloping atmosphere, just like the figures. They even have a kind of aura around them, like their human counterparts. And just as the children in the foreground of *Five Figures in a Field* recall their older siblings behind them in pose and overall shape, so the larger stacks echo the smaller ones while recalling the shapes of the houses in the distance.

These *Grainstack* pictures, therefore, are not only about light and color, instantaneity, and agrarian phenomena. They are also about nurturing and growth, commitment and community, concerns that Monet believes can be found in the countryside and that, rightly or wrongly, once again seem alien to Seurat's enterprise on his overcrowded suburban island. They were concerns that had particular relevance to France in the later 1880s and the decade of the '90s, and that contributed substantially to Monet's success during those years. They were also concerns that the artist did not abandon. In 1896 Monet offered the American painter Lilla Cabot Perry an unqualified opinion. "Nature does not have 'points,'" he told her when painting his *Mornings on the Seine*. Seurat and his followers had clearly challenged that belief, but they had been unable to overcome it. Even Pissarro soon began professing it again. After four years of Neo-Impressionism and many verbal jabs at Monet, he abandoned the dot and returned in 1890 to what he described as "the fullness, suppleness, liberty, spontaneity, and freshness of sensation postulated by our Impressionist art."[54]

Notes

Originally published in *Monet in the '90s: The Series Paintings*, exh. cat. (Boston: Museum of Fine Arts, 1989), 15–37.

1. The group of earlier *Grainstacks* are W.1213–17 in D. Wildenstein, *Claude Monet: Biographie et catalogue raisonné*, vols. 1–4 (Lausanne, 1974–85).
2. See, for example, John Rewald, *The History of Impressionism*, 4th ed. (New York, 1973), 439–45; K. Berger, "Monet's Crisis," *Register of the Museum of Art* (University of Kansas) 2, nos. 9/10 (May 1963): 17–21; J. Isaacson, *The Crisis of Impressionism: 1878–1882*, exh. cat. (Ann Arbor: University of Michigan Museum of Art, 1980); and Cecil Gould, *Seurat's "Bathers, Asnières" and the Crisis of Impressionism* (London, 1976). John House, *Monet: Nature into Art* (London, 1986), 2, treats the issue in a more sensible way, noting that "there was no single moment when . . . questions simultaneously came to a head and more significantly, the debates about these issues were essentially continuous involving constant discussion and disagreement."
3. Why all of this occurred might have had something to do with a number of considerations—with the inherent qualities of Impressionism as a style, for example; with how adequately it could claim to describe the visual world and be the bearer of meaning; with the personalities of specific individuals and with developments in their lives; with the nature of the subjects that the group chose to paint in the 1860s and '70s and those that they focused upon in the 1880s, a change that suggests a different concept of modernism; with developments in the art market; and with the changing relationships between Impressionism and mainstream artistic production. In any case, it certainly merits further study. On the eighth Impressionist exhibition, see Ward, "The Rhetoric of Independence and Innovation," in Charles Moffett, ed., *The New Painting: Impressionism, 1874–1886*, exh. cat. (San Francisco: Fine Arts Museums of San Francisco, 1986), 421–42.
4. On Seurat and the *Grande Jatte*, see ibid.; T. J. Clark, *The Painting of Modern Life: Paris in the Art of Manet and His Followers* (New York, 1984), 259–68; Richard Thompson, *Seurat* (Oxford, 1985), 97–126; and John House, "Meaning in Seurat's Figure Paintings," *Art History* 3, no. 3 (September 1980): 345–56. The most complete collection of contemporary reactions to Seurat's work in 1886 is found in Henri Dorra and John Rewald, *Seurat: L'Oeuvre peint; biographie et catalogue critique* (Paris, 1959), 292–93.
5. *Félix Fénéon: Oeuvres plus que complètes*, ed. J. Halperin (Geneva, 1970), 29–38. This is a slightly revised version of his original review of the eighth Impressionist exhibition, "Les Impressionnistes en 1886 (VIIIe Exposition impressionniste)," *La Vogue* (13–20 June 1886): 261–75. The standard work on Seurat's methods is William Innes Homer, *Seurat and the Science of Painting* (Cambridge, 1964). Many of Homer's basic premises have recently been challenged. See, for example, John Gage, "The Technique of Seurat: A Reappraisal," *Art History* 10, no. 3 (September 1987): 448–54; and Alan Less, "Seurat and Science," *Art History* 10, no. 2 (June 1987): 203–26. Although both of these articles rightfully debunk the idea of Seurat's "science," they do not alter the argument presented here, which is based on the perception of Seurat's public in the 1880s.
6. See J. Rewald, *Post-Impressionism: From Van Gogh to Gauguin*, 3rd rev. ed. (New York, 1978), 83–84. Monet and Renoir had been seeking other markets prior to this show and had declined to participate in the Impressionists' exhibitions as early as 1880. In 1886 Monet had also committed his work to Georges Petit's 5th International Exhibition, which meant he could not show elsewhere; see w.616 [in Wildenstein, *Claude Monet*] to Pissarro, 9 November 1885. On Pissarro's acrid comments about Impressionism see, for example, letters of 7 and 9 January and March 1886, *Camille Pissarro: Letters to His Son Lucien*, ed. John Rewald (London, 1980), 71–72, 89–92.
7. According to Wildenstein, *Claude Monet*, vols. 1–2, Monet produced approximately 480 paintings between 1880 and 1885 (W.557–1040) and only about 240 between 1870 and 1875 (W.146–389).
8. See Emile Taboureux, "Claude Monet," *La Vie moderne* (12 June 1880), in C. Stuckey, *Monet: A Retrospective* (New York, 1985), 89–93. On Monet's interest in expanding his market, see w.173 to Duret 8 March 1880.
9. w.852 to BM 10 March 1888.
10. On the ties between Impressionism and Paris, see R. Herbert, *Impressionism: Art, Leisure, and Parisian Society* (London, 1988); Clark, *The Painting of Modern Life;* and Tom Crow, "Modernism and Mass Culture in the Visual Arts," in *Modernism and Modernity*, ed. Benjamin H. D. Buchloh et al. (Halifax, 1983). On Monet in particular, see P. Tucker, *Monet at Argenteuil* (London, 1982). On Monet's participation in provincial exhibitions, see G. Seiberling, *Monet's Series* (New York, 1981), 307. For Grenoble, see Nemo, "Exposi-

tion de Grenoble," *Moniteur des arts* (13 August 1886): 272–73; for Limoges, see Jean Limousin, "Exposition de Limoges: Partie moderne," *Moniteur des arts* (29 November 1888): 110. According to Raymond Moulin, "Les Expositions des Beaux-Arts en Province, 1885–87" (thèse, Faculté des letters, Paris, 1967), 174–75, Monet also exhibited in Le Havre and Rouen in the 1880s.

11. On Monet's Belle Isle campaign, see Wildenstein, *Claude Monet,* vol. 2, 50–58; D. Delouche, "Monet et Belle-Ile en 1886," *Bulletin des Amis du Musée de Rennes,* no. 4 (1980); and House, *Monet,* 150, 195–96.
12. Herbert noted this more than twenty years ago in *Neo-Impressionism,* exh. cat. (New York, 1968), 157.
13. On Monet's brushwork and his apparent spontaneity, see R. Herbert, "Method and Meaning in Monet," *Art in America* 67, no. 5 (September 1979): 90–108; House, *Monet,* 75–108, 162–65; and Ronald R. Bernier, "The Subject and Painting: Monet's 'Language of the Sketch,'" *Art History* 12, no. 3 (September 1989): 298–321.
14. w.794 to Théodore Duret 13 August 1887.
15. See R. Herbert, "Impressionism, Originality, and Laissez-Faire," *Radical History Review* 38 (Spring 1987): 7–15 [reprinted as chapter 1 in this volume].
16. Taboureux, 1880.
17. The most quoted of these is Guy de Maupassant's "The Life of a Landscapist," *Gil Blas,* 28 September 1886, as cited and translated in Stuckey, *Monet,* 121–24. See also Georges Jeanniot, "Notes sur l'art: Claude Monet," *La Cravache parisienne,* 23 June 1888, in Stuckey, *Monet,* 129.
18. GG [Gustave Geffroy], "La Chronique: Paysages et figures," *La Justice,* 26 February 1889.
19. On Monet's pairs, see S. Levine, "Monet's Pairs," *Arts Magazine* 49, no. 10 (June 1975): 72–75.
20. See Lionello Venturi, *Impressionists and Symbolists* (New York, 1950), 61; and John Coplans, *Serial Imagery,* exh. cat. (Pasadena, 1968), 21.
21. Alfred de Lostalot, "Exposition Internationale de peinture et de sculpture (Galerie Georges Petit)," *Gazette des beaux-arts,* 2nd ser., vol. 35 (June 1887): 522–27; and Joris-Karl Huysmans, "L'Exposition Internationale de la rue de Sèze," *La Revue indépendante de littérature et d'art,* n.s. (3 June 1887): 345–55; cited in S. Levine, *Monet and His Critics* (New York, 1976), 84–85.
22. On Monet's use of the term "series," see, for example, w.90 to de Bellio 20 June 1876, w.200 to Duret 3 Oct. 1880, w.388 to DR 12 January 1884, w.405 to AH 4 February 1884, w.543 to DR 20 January 1885, w.563 to DR ca. 25 April 1885.
23. Emile Zola, *Mon Salon, Manet: Ecrits sur l'art,* ed. A. Ehrard (Paris, 1970), 154; *La Presse,* 31 March 1876, reprinted in Gustave Geffroy, *Claude Monet: Sa Vie, son temps, son oeuvre,* vol. 1 (Paris, 1924), 80. See also House, *Monet,* 193–94.
24. GG [Gustave Geffroy], "Salon de 1887, Hors du Salon," *Le Journal,* 2 June 1887, cited in J. Paradise, *Gustave Geffroy and the Criticism of Painting* (New York, 1985), 269. Paradise provides a very sensitive analysis of Geffroy's art criticism.
25. Levine, *Monet and His Critics,* 88, calls it a "critical paradigm"; see also Paradise, *Gustave Geffroy,* 269.
26. Wildenstein tentatively identified seven of them as W.1084, W.1093, W.1096, W.1097, W.1101, W.1106, W.1114. See Wildenstein, *Claude Monet,* vol. 3, 2. Monet showed ten Belle Isle canvases in his retrospective with Rodin in 1889. See Wildenstein, *Claude Monet,* vol. 2, 21.
27. w.705 to AH 5 October 1886.
28. w.730 to AH 30 October 1886; also w.701 to DR 1 October 1886.
29. On being called "the prince of the Impressionists," see w.688 to AH 18 September 1886. On his correspondence, see w.701, w.726, w.727, w.728.
30. w.702 to AH 2 October 1886.
31. GG [Gustave Geffroy], "La Chronique: Claude Monet," *La Justice,* 15 March 1883.
32. w.712 to AH 14 October 1886.
33. w.727 to DR 28 October 1886.
34. w.808 to AH 17 January 1888.
35. w.807 to AH 15 January 1888.
36. w.836 to GG 12 February 1888.
37. GG [Gustave Geffroy], "Dix tableaux de Claude Monet," *La Justice,* 17 June 1888; reprinted in Gustave Geffroy, *La Vie artistique,* vol. 3 (Paris, 1894), 77–81.
38. For the most provocative discussion of the *Grainstack* series, see Herbert, "Method and Meaning in Monet"; and R. Brettell, "Monet's Haystacks Reconsidered," *The Art Institute of Chicago Museum Studies* 11, no.1 (Fall 1984): 4–21. For differing views, see C. Moffett, "Monet's Haystacks," in J. Rewald and F. Weitzenhoffer, eds., *Aspects of Monet: A Symposium on the Artist's Life and Times* (New York, 1984), 140–59; J. House, "The Origins of Monet's Series Paintings," *Claude Monet, Painter of Light,* exh. cat. (Auckland, 1985), 19–23; and House, *Monet,* 28–32, 193–204.
39. Octave Mirbeau, *Exposition Claude Monet–Auguste Rodin: Galerie Georges Petit,* exh. cat. (Paris, 1889), 10–11, cited in Levine, *Monet and His Critics,* 104.
40. w.810 to AH 14 January 1888.

41. GG [Gustave Geffroy], "Claude Monet," *Le Journal*, 7 June 1898.
42. Mirbeau, *Exposition Claude Monet . . .*, 16, cited in Levine, *Monet and His Critics*, 107.
43. On returning to France, see w.409 and w.446 to AH 6 February and 14 March 1884; on the vile food, see w.879 to AH 24 April 1888.
44. w.427 to Pissarro 2 June 1871; on Monet's disparaging remarks about the government during the *Olympia* subscription, see chapter 3 in Paul H. Tucker, *Monet in the '90s*, exh. cat. (Boston: Museum of Fine Arts, 1989).
45. w.573 to DR 27 June 1885.
46. w.578 to DR 28 July 1885.
47. w.651 to DR 23 January 1886.
48. "I would always be happy to do business with you again, although I am brokenhearted to see all of my paintings leave for America." w.868 to DR 11 April 1888.
49. Unfortunately, there is no record of Monet being offered the Cross and no letter indicating his refusal. However, we can surmise that he was in fact in line for this national honor from Mirbeau's correspondence in which the idea of turning the offer down is discussed. See Octave Mirbeau, "Lettres à Claude Monet," *Cahiers d'aujourd'hui*, no. 5 (29 November 1922): 165; and Wildenstein, *Claude Monet*, vol. 3, 11 n. 724. Monet raised the issue obliquely two years later in a letter to Geffroy when he claimed that he did not need government officials such as Antonin Proust or their crosses; see w.1023 to GG 21 January 1890. Refusing the Cross would have been in keeping with Monet's disdain of such awards, particularly those given by the government, something he made clear more than a decade later when he criticized Renoir for being inducted into the Legion in 1900; see w.1566 to Renoir end of August 1900. He expressed his regrets to Geffroy as well. "Isn't it sad to see a man of his talent accept the decoration at the age of 60, after having fought for so many years and having been so valiant when he emerged from the struggle despite the administration?"; see w.1565 to GG 23 August 1900.
50. This reading of the *Grainstacks* was first offered by Herbert, "Method and Meaning in Monet." I am much indebted to his interpretations.
51. For a description of the difficulties of constructing these stacks, see Emile Zola, *The Earth* (Harmondsworth, 1980), 237–41.
52. On Pissarro's treatment of this subject, see, for example, Sotheby's London, 30 April 1969, no. 24 of 1878, and Ludovico Pissarro and Lionello Venturi, *Camille Pissarro: Son art—son oeuvre* (Paris, 1939), no. 589 of 1883, as well as his series of prints of grainstacks, which are discussed by M. Melot, *L'Estampe impressionniste*, exh. cat. (Paris, 1974), 16, and his "La Practique d'un artiste: Pissarro graveur en 1880," *Histoire et critique des arts* 2 (June 1977): 16 [an earlier version of chapter 9 in this volume].
53. On Monet wanting to do something else, see w.1425 to GG 20 June 1888.
54. See Pissarro letter of 6 September 1888, *Camille Pissarro: Letters to His Son Lucien*, 130–32. Also see letter of 20 February 1889, ibid., 134–35, for complaints about the "dot." For Pissarro's first *plein-air* painting since 1889, see letter of 21 July 1891 to Monet in *Correspondance de Camille Pissarro*, ed. Jaime Bailly-Herzberg (Paris, 1988), 111. For Monet's quip to Perry, see Cecilia Beaux, *Background with Figures* (Boston, 1930), 201, as cited in David Sellin, *Americans in Brittany and Normandy, 1860–1910*, exh. cat. (Phoenix: Phoenix Art Museum, 1982). Like Pissarro, Renoir recognized the value of Monet's allegiance to Impressionism. In 1891, after eight years of studio painting, he confessed to Durand-Ruel, "I have lost a lot of time by working within the four square meters of my studio. I would have gained ten years by doing a little of what Monet has done." See Pissarro and Venturi, *Camille Pissarro*, vol. 1, 130.

PART FIVE

Recent Studies in Post-Impressionist Painting

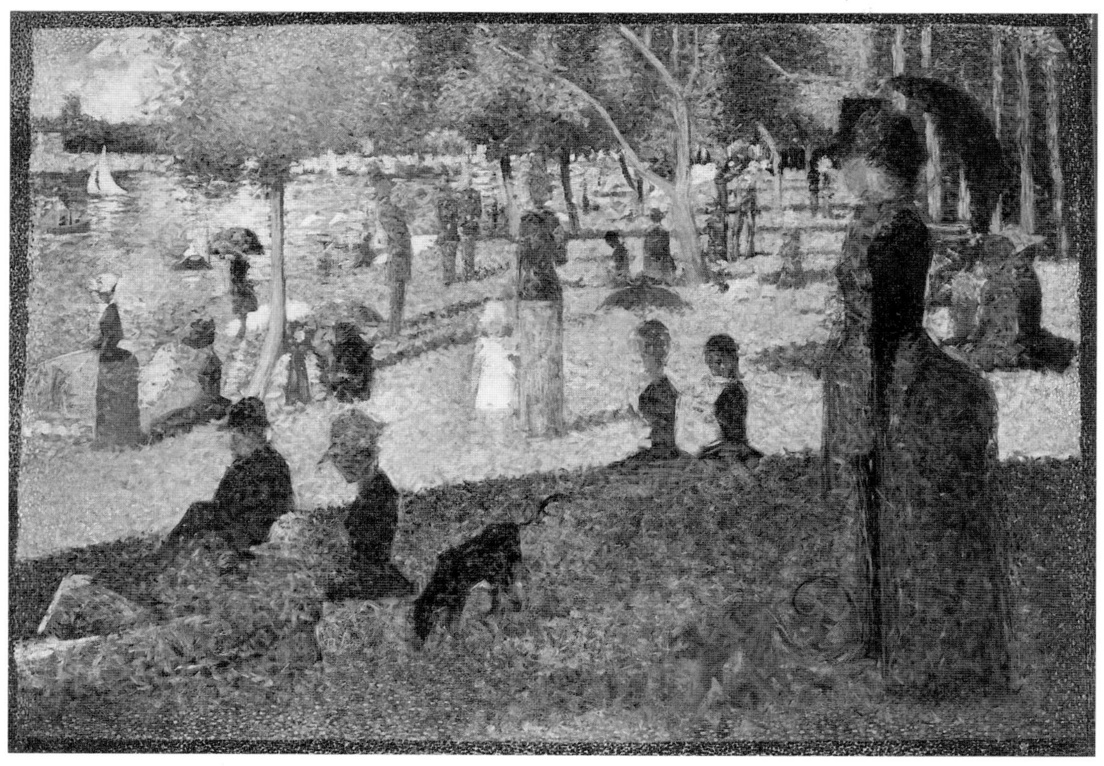

FIGURE 11.1. Georges Seurat, *Study for "A Sunday on La Grande Jatte,"* 1884–85. The Metropolitan Museum of Art, New York; Bequest of Sam A. Lewisohn, 1951 (51.112.6). Photo: The Metropolitan Museum of Art, all rights reserved.

11

Seurat's *Grande Jatte*

An Anti-Utopian Allegory

LINDA NOCHLIN

THE IDEA THAT Georges Seurat's masterpiece, *A Sunday on La Grande Jatte* (1884–86; plate 5), was in some sense anti-utopian came to me when reading a chapter entitled "The Wishful Landscape Portrayed in Painting, Opera, Literature" in *The Principle of Hope*, the *magnum opus* of the German Marxist historian and philosopher Ernst Bloch. Here is what Bloch, writing in the first half of the twentieth century, had to say:

> The negative foil to Manet's *Déjeuner sur l'herbe*, or rather its mood of gaiety gone sour, is embodied in Seurat's promenade piece: *Un Dimanche à la Grande-Jatte*. This picture is one single mosaic of boredom, a masterful rendering of the disappointed longing and the incongruities of a *dolce far niente*. The painting depicts a middle-class Sunday morning *[sic]* on an island in the Seine near Paris; and that is just the point: it depicts this merely with scorn. Empty-faced people rest in the foreground; most of the others have been grouped into wooden verticals like dolls from the toy box, intensely involved in a stiff little walk. Behind them is the pale river with sailboats, a sculling match, sightseeing boats—a background that, despite the recreation going on there, seems to belong more to Hades than to a Sunday. A great load of joyless leisure is in the image, in the bright matte glare of its atmosphere and in the expressionless water of the Sunday Seine, the object of an equally expressionless contemplation. . . . As the workaday world recedes, so does every other world, everything, recede into watery torpidness. The result is endless boredom, the little man's hellish utopia of skirting the Sabbath and holding onto it too; his Sunday succeeds only as a bothersome must, not as a brief taste of the Promised Land. Middle-class Sunday afternoons like these are landscapes of painted suicide which does not come off [even at that] because it lacks resolve. In short, this *dolce far niente*, if it is conscious at all, has the consciousness of an absolute non-Sunday in what remains of a Sunday utopia.[1]

The anti-utopian signification about which Bloch wrote is not merely a matter of iconography, subject matter, or social history transcribed to canvas. Seurat's painting should not be seen as merely passively reflecting the new urban realities of the 1880s or the most advanced stages of the alienation associated with capitalism's radical revision of urban spatial divisions and social hierarchies of his time. Rather, the *Grande Jatte* must be seen as actively producing cultural meanings through the invention of visual codes for the modern experience of the city. This explains the inclusion of the word "allegory" in the title of this article. It is through the pictorial construction of the work—its formal strategies—that the anti-utopian is allegorized in the *Grande Jatte*. This is what makes Seurat's production—and the *Grande Jatte*—unique. Of all the Post-Impressionists, he is the only one to have inscribed the modern condition—with its alienation and anomie, the experience of living in the society of the spectacle,[2] of making a living in a market economy in which exchange value took the place of use value and mass production that of artisanal production—in the very fabric and structure of his pictorial production.

If Seurat, rather than Paul Cézanne, had been positioned as the paradigmatic Modernist painter, the face of modern art would have been vastly different. But such a statement is of course itself utopian, or, at the very least, insufficiently historical. It was part of advanced art's historical destiny in the later nineteenth and early twentieth centuries to retreat from the worldly, the social, and above all from the negative and objectively critical position iterated in Seurat's art and establish the realm of the atemporal, the nonsocial, the subjective, and the phenomenological—in other words, a "pure" painting—as synonymous with Modernism. This paradoxical instating of pure visibility and the flat surface of the canvas as synonymous with the modern is, as we shall see, at the polar opposite of Seurat's project in the *Grande Jatte* and in his other works as well.

It has been the aim of ambitious Western art from the High Renaissance onward to establish a pictorial structure that suggests a rational narrative and, above all, an expressive coherence relating part and part, and part and whole, at the same time that it establishes a meaningful relationship with the spectator. A painting is understood to "express," to externalize by means of its structural coherence, some inner meaning, to function as the visible manifestation of a core or a depth of which the representational fabric constitutes but a surface appearance, albeit an all-important one. In a Renaissance work like Raphael's *School of Athens* [1510–11; Stanza della Segnatura, Vatican], the figures are constructed to react and interact, thereby suggesting, indeed determining, a meaning beyond the mere surface of the painting, to create an expression of complex signification that is at once comprehensible yet, at the same time, transcends the historical circumstances that produced it. In a sense, Edouard Manet's *Luncheon on the Grass* [*Déjeuner sur l'herbe*, 1863; Musée d'Orsay] constitutes the end of that Western tradition of high art as expressive narrative: the shadow begins to thicken up, the priority accorded to the surface denies the implication of transcendence, the gestures fail of their usual dialogic mission. But even here, as Bloch pointed out in the same chapter in which he discussed the *Grande Jatte*, there remain utopian emanations. Indeed he read the *Luncheon* as a counterfoil to the *Grande Jatte*, interpreting it as a "wishful scene of epicurean happiness," and describing it in the most lyrical of terms: "Soft light, as only Impressionism could create, flows through the trees, surrounds the two couples, the naked woman and the one undressing to bathe, the dark male figures. What is portrayed is an extraordinarily French, extraordinarily lingering situation, full of innocence, supreme ease, unobtrusive enjoyment of life, and carefree seriousness." Bloch assigned the *Luncheon* to the same category as the *Grande Jatte*'s, that of the Sunday picture. "Its subject is: an immediate other world, beyond hardship. Though this subject could no longer be easily painted in the nineteenth century, Manet's *Luncheon on the Grass* constitutes an exception precisely because of its naïveté and presence. Its wholesome Sunday would hardly be possible [in 1863, when it was painted] with the petit-bourgeois; thus it could not exist without artists and their models." Bloch then moved on to the negative description of the *Grande Jatte* cited above: "The real bourgeois Sunday, even a painted one, thus looks even less desirable or varied. The *negative* foil to Manet's *Luncheon on the Grass*, in other words, the *merriness that has become powerless,* is presented in *Seurat's* promenade piece. . . ."[3] Not until the 1880s, it would seem, was it possible to produce a work that so completely, so brilliantly and convincingly inscribed the condition of modernity itself.

In Seurat's painting, there is almost no interaction between the figures, no sense of them as articulate, unique, and full human presences. The Western tradition of representation has been undermined, if not nullified, here by a dominant language that is resolutely anti-expressive, rejecting the notion of a hidden inner meaning to be externalized by the artist. Rather, in these machine-turned profiles, defined by regularized dots, we may discover coded references to modern science, to modern industry with its mass production, to the department store with its cheap and multiple copies, to the mass press with its endless pictorial reproductions. In short there is here a critical sense of modernity embodied in sardonic, decorative invention and in the emphatic, even overemphatic, contemporaneity of costumes and accouterments.[4] For the *Grande Jatte*—and this too constitutes its anti-utopianism—is resolutely located in history rather than being atemporal and universalizing. This objective historical presence of the painting is above all embodied in the notorious dotted brushstroke—the *petit point*—which is and was of course the first thing everyone noticed about the work—and which in fact constitutes the irreducible atomic particle of the new vision. For Seurat, with the dot, resolutely and consciously removed himself as a unique being projected by a personal handwriting. He himself is absent from his stroke: there is no sense of the existential choice implied by Cézanne's constructive brushwork; of the deep, personal *angst* implied by Van Gogh's; nor of the decorative, mystical dematerialization of form of Gauguin.[5] The paint application is matter-of-fact, a near- or would-be mechanical reiteration of the functional "dot" of pigment. Meyer Schapiro, in what is perhaps the most perceptive single article ever written about the *Grande Jatte*, referred to Seurat as a "humble, laborious, intelligent technician," coming from the "sober lower middle class of Paris from which issue the engineers, the technicians, and the clerks of industrial society," and pointed out that Seurat "derived from the more advanced industrial development of his time a profound respect for rationalized work, scientific technique and progress through invention."[6] But before examining the *Grande Jatte* in detail to see how the anti-utopian message is inscribed in every aspect of the painting's stylistic structure, we must examine what counted for "utopian" in the visual production of the nineteenth century. It is only by contextualizing the *Grande Jatte* within that which was seen by Seurat and his contemporaries as utopian that the oppositional character of his creation can be fully understood.

There is of course the classical utopia of the flesh established by J. A. D. Ingres in his *Golden Age* (Fogg Art Museum). Harmonious line, smooth and ageless bodies, a pleasing symmetry of composition, a frictionless grouping of inoffensively nude or classically draped figures in a landscape of Poussinesque unspecificity—this is not so much a representation of utopia as it is nostalgia for a distant past that never was and never can be recaptured—not so much utopia (meaning no or beyond place) as u-chronia (meaning no or beyond time). Completely lacking is the social message we usually associate with utopian discourse. This is rather a utopia of (idealized) desire.

The same incidentally might be said of Gauguin's much later renditions of tropical paradise: there, it is not distance in time but geographic distance that functions as the utopian catalyst. But, as in Ingres's version, it is the naked or lightly veiled human body, female above all, in noncontemporary costume, that constitutes the utopian signifier; still, as in the work by Ingres, this is manifestly an apolitical utopia, whose reference point is male desire and whose signifier is female flesh.

Far more apposite in constructing a context of utopian representation to serve as a foil to Seurat's anti-utopian allegory is a work like Dominique Papety's *Dream of Happiness* (fig. 11.2), shown in the Salon of 1843. Utopian in form and content, this work is explicitly Fourierist in its iconographic intentions and classically idealizing in its style, which is not very

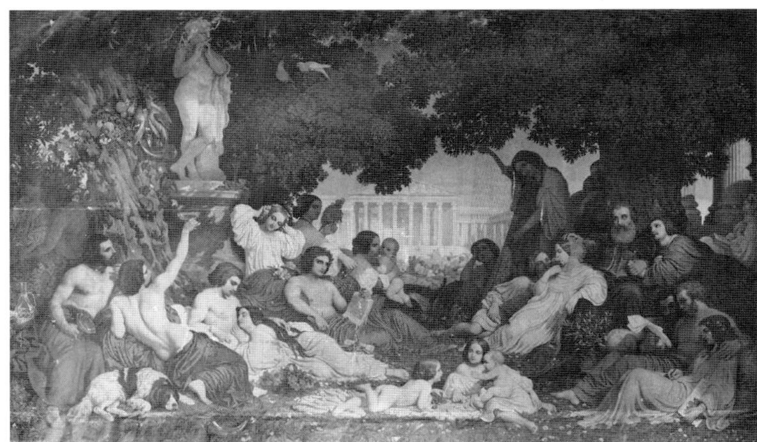

FIGURE 11.2. Dominique Papety, *Un Rêve de bonheur (A Dream of Happiness)*, 1843. Musée Vivenel, Compiègne, France. Photo: Réunion des Musées Nationaux/Art Resource, NY.

different from that of Ingres, Papety's master at the Académie française in Rome.[7] Yet there is a significant difference between Papety's and Ingres's utopian conceptions: although the Fourierists considered the present—the so-called realm of civilization—depraved and unnatural, the past for them was little better. The true golden age lay not in the past, but in the future. The explicitly Fourierist content of this utopian allegory is corroborated by the inscription "Harmonie" on the base of the statue to the left, which refers "both to the Fourierist state and to the music of the satyr," and a second inscription, "Unité universelle," on the book studied by the youthful scholars, a direct allusion to Fourierist doctrine and the name of one of Fourier's theoretical treatises.[8] Indeed it is possible to read certain aspects of the *Grande Jatte* as an explicit refutation of Fourierist utopianism, or more accurately of utopianism, *tout court*. In Papety's painting, this was allegorized by the inclusion of figures personifying the poet "singing harmony"; a group embodying "maternal tenderness," another referring to friendship under the graces of childhood, and, at the sides, various aspects of love between the sexes. All are conspicuous by their omission in the *Grande Jatte*. Other embodiments of virtuous satisfaction are the "working thinkers" (*laborieux penseurs*) engaged in studies, a beautiful woman asleep on the chest of her husband, and a noble, old man stretching his hand out in blessing over the head of his daughter and her fiancé. The architecture is resolutely classical, although the painting at one time suggested the futurity of this utopian vision by the inclusion of a steamboat and an electric telegraph, later removed by the artist.[9] The figures are smooth and harmonious, classical or neoclassical in their poses; the paint is conventionally applied; the signs of modernity, at least in this version, erased in favor of a utopian dream which, however Fourierist, is firmly rooted in references to a long-vanished past and an extremely traditional, not to say conservative, mode of representation.

Far more apposite to Seurat's anti-utopian project is the work of his older contemporary Pierre Puvis de Chavannes. Indeed one might say that, without the precedent provided by Puvis, in works such as his huge canvas *The Sacred Grove* (Art Institute of Chicago), exhibited at the Salon of 1884, the very year that Seurat began work on the *Grande Jatte*, the latter might never have come into being, or might have been different. From a certain standpoint, the *Grande Jatte* may be considered a giant parody of Puvis's *Sacred Grove*, calling into question the validity of such a painting and its relevance to modern times—in both its form and content. For Puvis's timeless muses and universalized classical setting and drapery, Seurat substituted the most contemporary fashions, the most up-to-date settings and accessories. Seurat's women wear bustles and modish hats rather than classical

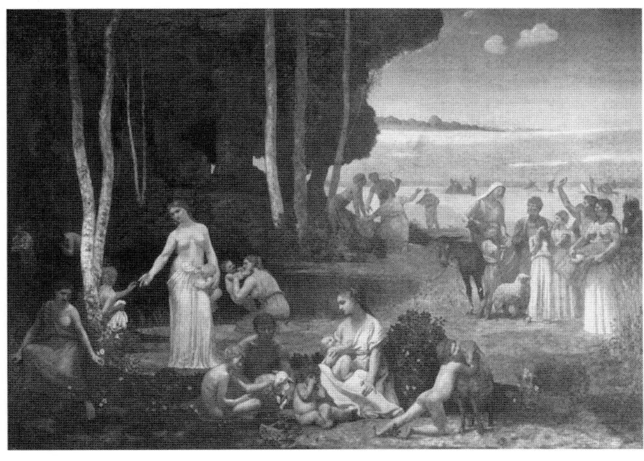

FIGURE 11.3. Pierre Puvis de Chavannes, *Eté (Summer)*, 1873. Musée des Beaux-Arts, Chartres. Photo: The Bridgeman Art Library.

drapery; his most prominent male figure holds a coarse cigar and a cane rather than the pipes of Pan; the architectural background is in the mode of modern urbanity rather than that of pastoral antiquity.

A work such as *Summer* (fig. 11.3), painted by Puvis in 1873, two years after the defeat of France in the Franco-Prussian war and the terrible, socially divisive events of the Commune and its aftermath, represents the utopian vision at its purest. Although the recognizable depiction of a distant past, the imagery of *Summer* suggests, as Claudine Mitchell has pointed out, a more general, even a universal time scale, the representation of what is true of human society generally. To quote the critic Théophile Gautier, who pondered Puvis and his works deeply: "Puvis seeks the ideal beyond time, space, costumes, or particular details. He likes to paint primitive humanity, as they *[sic]* perform one of those functions that we could call sacred, so close to Nature they are." He praised Puvis for avoiding the contingent and the accidental, pointing out that his compositions always have an abstract and general title: Peace, War, Repose, Work, Sleep, or, in this case, Summer. Gautier suggested that for Puvis the signifiers of a distant, primitive, purer past serve to define a more universal order, the order of Nature itself.[10]

This then is the nineteenth century's prototypical pictorial version of classical utopia. If Puvis's world is beyond time and space, Seurat's *Grande Jatte* is definitely and even aggressively of his. Indeed one wonders whether the mundane specificity of Seurat's original title—*A Sunday on La Grande Jatte (1884)*, in its chronological and geographical exactitude, does not constitute an anti-utopian critique of Puvis's and other allegorical classicists' vague and idealized names for paintings.

It is perhaps above all the utopian harmoniousness of Puvis's construction that Seurat most forcefully challenged in his canvas. Although Puvis may have deployed his figures in separate groups, this in no sense implies social fragmentation or psychic alienation. Rather the painting serves to idealize the value of the family and that of communal productivity, in which each trade, each age, and above all each gender serves its allotted task. In effect Puvis's works function ideologically to produce an aesthetic harmony out of what in contemporary society is a source of disharmony, conflict, and contradiction: issues like the position of the worker, class struggle, or the status of women. Thus, for example, in the formal structure of his art, the moral value of maternity for women and that of work for men are represented as inscribed in, and indistinguishable from, the order of Nature rather than figured as highly volatile, contentious issues. This is the crux of Puvis's utopian vision. In Seurat's work, as we shall see, the classical elements are deliberately disharmonized, exaggerated into self-revealing artifice or deliberately frozen and

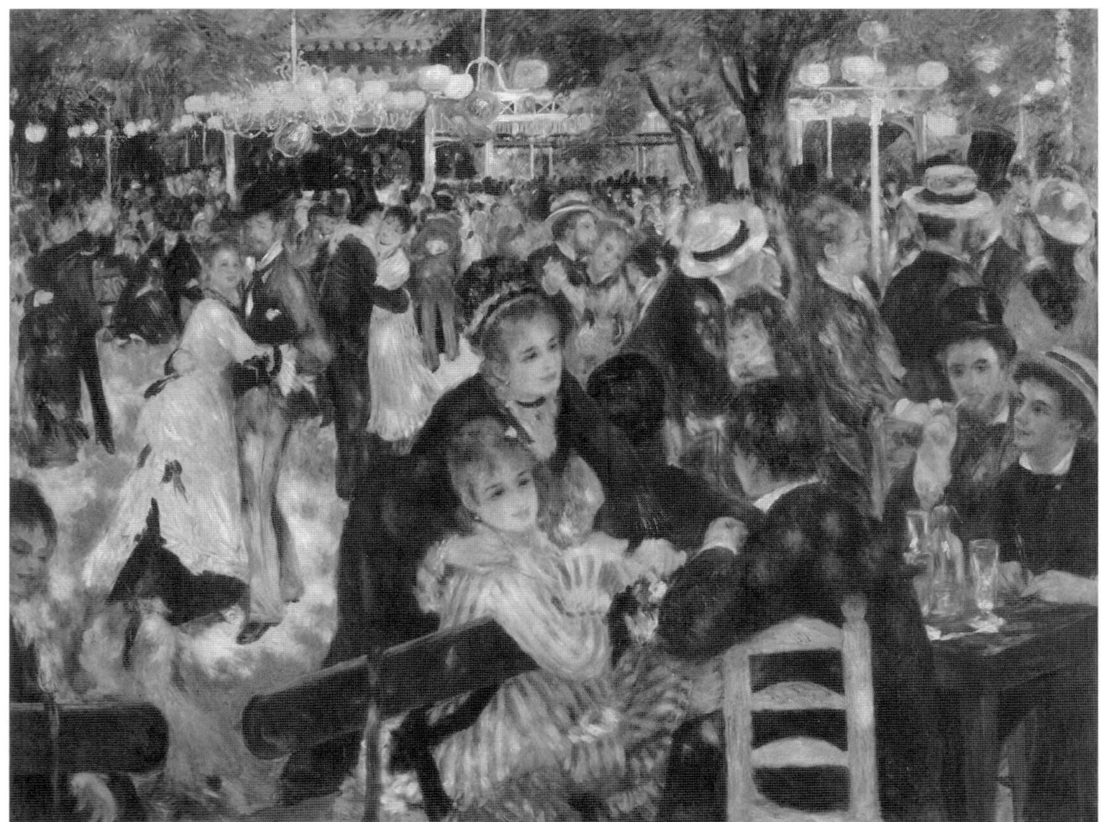

FIGURE 11.4. Pierre-Auguste Renoir, *Ball at the Moulin de la Galette*, 1876. Musée d'Orsay, Paris. Photo: Réunion des Musées Nationaux/Art Resource, NY. Photographed by J. G. Berizzi.

isolated. This is part of its anti-utopian strategy, its bringing of contradictions into focus.

But it is not only the classical and more traditional work of Puvis that offers a startling contrast with Seurat's anti-utopianism. More advanced painters, like Auguste Renoir, had created semi-utopian visions based on contemporary reality, images of the joys of ordinary urban existence posited on the pleasures of healthy sensuality and youthful joie de vivre in a work such as the *Ball at the Moulin de la Galette* of 1876 (fig. 11.4). Here the melting colors, broken brushwork, and swirling, dynamic rhythms play out in formal terms, in their joyous intermingling, the eradication of class and gender divisions in a context of idealized recreation in contemporary Paris. As such Renoir's work offers the most pointed opposition to Seurat's sardonic view of the New Leisure. Renoir naturalized daily life in the great modern city; Seurat, on the other hand, made it strange.

But perhaps it is the work of Seurat's disciple and fellow Neo-Impressionist Paul Signac that is most apposite in establishing the context of utopian imagery against which the *Grande Jatte* stands out most forcefully. Signac was fully aware of the social import of his friend's oeuvre. In an article of June 1891, which appeared in the anarchist publication *La Révolte*, he declared that, by painting scenes of working-class life, "or, better still, the pleasures of decadence . . . as the painter Seurat did, who had such a vivid perception of the degeneration of our transitional era—they will bear witness to the great social trial that is taking place between workers and Capital."[11]

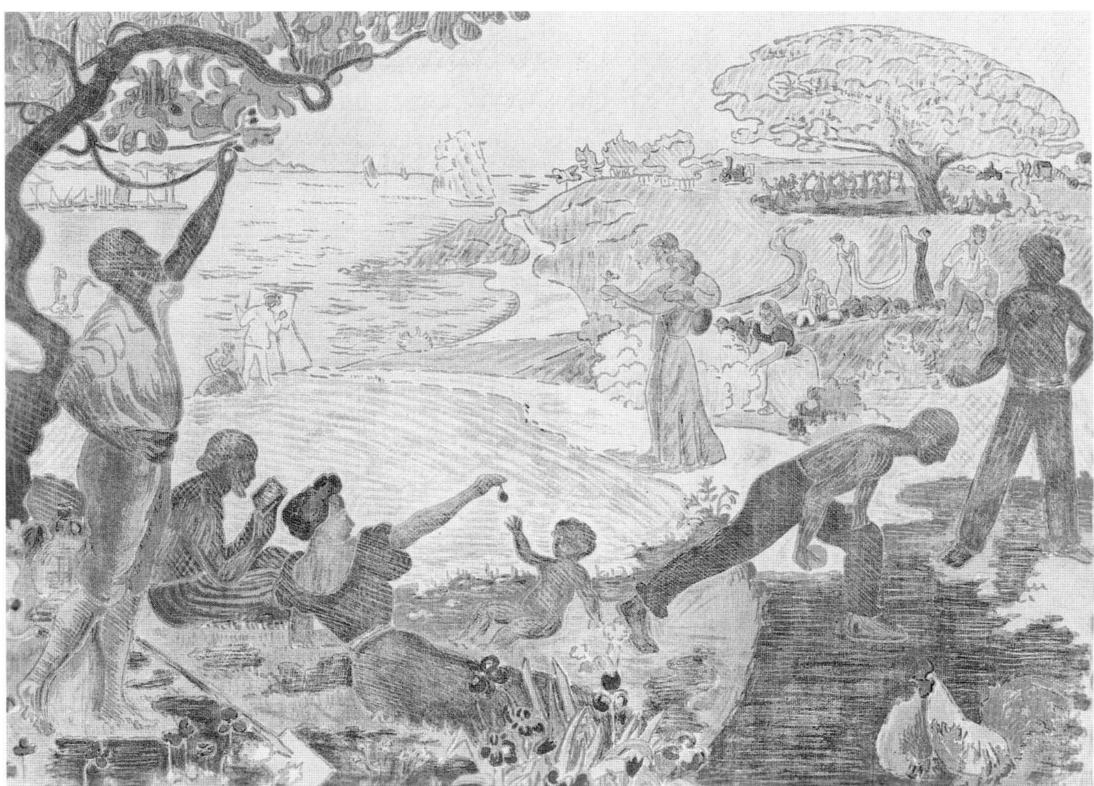

FIGURE 11.5. Paul Signac, *Harmonious Times (The Pleasures of Summer)*, 1895–96, color lithograph. The Cleveland Museum of Art, Dudley P. Allen Fund, 1925.1053. © 2007 Artists Rights Society (ARS), New York/ADAGP, Paris. Photo © The Cleveland Museum of Art, 2002.

Signac, in *In the Time of Harmony*, an oil sketch for a mural created in about 1893–95 for the town hall of Montreuil, seems to have been constructing a response to the specifically capitalist conditions of anomie and absurdity—in other words, the "Time of Disharmony"—represented by his late friend's most famous painting. The very use of the term "harmony" in the title refers to the specifically Fourierist and later, more generally socialist and anarchist designations of social utopia. (The Fourierist colony established in the United States was called New Harmony.) In a lithographed version (fig. 11.5) of his mural entitled *The Pleasures of Summer*, intended for Jean Grave's *Les Temps nouveaux*, Signac created his anarchist-socialist version of a classless utopia, substituting wholesome recreation and human interaction for the stasis and figural isolation of the *Grande Jatte*, emphasizing the joys of the family in place of Seurat's relative muting of them, and replacing the suburban setting of the Art Institute's painting with a more pastoral, rural setting in keeping with the utopian project as a whole. Clearly the style of the figures, despite the more or less contemporary clothing they wear, owes more to Puvis in its flowing idealization than to Seurat's stylishness. The flowing, curvilinear composition and its decorative iterations suavely emphasize the theme of togetherness—of the couple or the community as a whole—in some utopian future, a Never-Never land. Even the hen and the rooster in the foreground play out the theme of mutual aid and interaction spelled out by the work as a whole, and so deliberately excluded by Seurat's vision.

But it is not merely through contrasting Seurat's *Grande Jatte* with appropriate utopian imagery of his time that one can come to an anti-utopian interpretation of the work. This is corroborated in the viewer reaction of the time, as can be seen in the critical reactions of Seurat's contemporaries who established a negative critique of the modern condition as embodied in the painting.[12] "Reviewers," to borrow the words of Martha Ward in a catalogue essay, "interpreted the expressionless faces, isolated stances, and rigid postures to be a more or less subtle parody of the *banality and pretensions of contemporary leisure* [emphasis mine]."[13] For example one critic, Henry Fèvre, remarked that after looking at the image for a while, "then one understands the stiltedness of the Parisian promenade, stiff and distorted; even its recreation is affected."[14] Another critic, Paul Adam, equated the stiff outlines and attitudinizing postures of the figures with the modern condition itself: "Even the stiffness of the figures and their punched-out forms contribute to the note of modernity, reminding us of our badly cut clothes which cling to our bodies and our reserved gestures, the British cant imitated everywhere. We strike poses like those of the figures of Memling."[15] And still another critic, Alfred Paulet, maintained that "the artist has given his figures the automatic gestures of lead soldiers, moving about on regimented squares. Maids, clerks, soldiers all move around with a similar slow, banal, identical step, which captures the character of the scene exactly"[16]

This notion of the monotony, the dehumanizing rigidity of modern urban existence as the founding trope of the *Grande Jatte* inscribes itself even in the relentlessly formal analysis of the most important of the *Grande Jatte*'s critics, Félix Fénéon, when he described the uniformity of the technique as "a monotonous and patient tapestry"—the pathetic fallacy with a vengeance.[17] In Fénéon's memorable figure of speech, the monotony and patience of the technique of Pointillism allegorize not merely an artistic practice, but rather the dominant quality of modern urban life itself.

And what of Seurat's formal language in the *Grande Jatte?* How does it mediate and construct and, in some sense, allegorize the social malaise of its time? Daniel Catton Rich was absolutely correct when, in his seminal book on the painting of 1935, he stressed the primacy of Seurat's formal innovations in what he termed the "transcendent" achievement of the *Grande Jatte*,[18] using reductive diagrams so typical of that moment of formalist, "scientific" art analysis, to reduce further Seurat's already diagrammatic compositional structure.[19] But as Schapiro pointed out, in his brilliant rebuttal to this study, Rich was wrong to eliminate on the basis of the precedence of formal concerns, the all-important social and critical implications of Seurat's practice.[20] Equally misguided, in Schapiro's view, was Rich's correlative attempt to impose a spurious classicizing, traditionalist, and harmonizing reading on the work, thereby, in the best art historical fashion, assimilating Seurat's provocative innovations into the peaceful and law-abiding mainstream of pictorial tradition.

The peculiarly modern idea of "system" must be dealt with in separating Seurat from that mainstream of tradition and in approaching his formal innovations. The notion should be understood under at least two modalities: 1) the systematic application of a certain color theory, scientific or would-be scientific, according to the authority one reads, in his Chromoluminarist method;[21] or 2) the related Pointillist system of paint application in small, regularized dots. As Norma Broude has pointed out, Seurat may actually have borrowed his systematic paint application from one of the most recent techniques of mass diffusion in the visual communication industry of his time, so-called *chromotypogravure*. The choice of this "mechanical" technique served to critique the objectified spectacle of modern life and thereby, as Broude stated, "proved understandably offensive not only to the public at large but also to many artists of the Impressionist and Post-Impressionist generation, artists whose attachment to a romantic conception of originality and spontaneous self-expression in painting was threatened by the apparently impersonal attitude of Seurat and his followers." "It was, in fact," as Broude pointed out, "precisely the 'mechanical' aspect of the technique, so foreign to contemporary notions of fine taste and 'high art,' that, in these terms, may ultimately have proved attractive to Seurat, whose radical political leanings and 'democratic' predilection for popular art forms had already become important formative factors in the evolution of his attitudes toward his own art." One might go even further and say that, in some sense, all of the systematizing factors in Seurat's project—from his pseudo-scientific color theory and his "mechanized" technique to his later adaption of Charles Henry's scientifically legitimated aesthetic protractor to achieve fool-proof equilibration of compositional factors and expressive effects—all could ultimately serve a democratizing purpose. He sought a method—a fool-proof method—of creating successful art available to everyone, a sort of democratically oriented, high-type painting by dots that would totally wipe out the role of genius, the exceptional creative figure, in the making of art, even "great art" (although the very term might become superfluous). This indeed is a utopian project from a radical standpoint, although a totally banalizing and anti-utopian one from a more elitist one.[22]

Nothing could be more revealing of Seurat's deliberate rejection of charming spontaneity in favor of incisive distancing than to compare elements from the large final sketch for the *Grande Jatte* (fig. 11.1) with those of the final version (plate 5). Can anything be further from the generalizing tendencies of classicism than the diagrammatic concision and up-to-date stylishness of Seurat's construction here, as potent in nailing down a concrete referent as any advertising logo? Or can any image be further from the bland idealizations of a later Neoclassicist like Puvis than the sharp, critical detailing of the motif of a hand holding a cigar and the mechanical roundness of the head of a cane, both forms aggressively signifying the class-coded masculinity of the male "diagram" as opposed to the systematically circular shapes iterated by the clothing, almost topiary in its relentless shearing down of the living raw material, of his equally socially specific female companion? Gender difference too is objectified and systematized by means of obvious artifice.

I would like to demonstrate with one figure, that of the wet nurse, the way Seurat worked on one character in his sardonic pageant of frozen recreation, honing the image down to its signifying minimum, reducing the vital and charming irregularity of the original painted sketch to a visual hieroglyph. Ward, in a word picture as beautifully concise as the image itself, has described the final version as "a faceless configuration: an irregular quadrangle bisected by a triangular wedge and capped with circumscribed circles."[23] The *nourrice*, more familiarly known as "Nounou," had become a stock character in the proliferation of visual typologies disseminated by the popular press during the second half of the nineteenth century. Seurat of course avoided this sort of vulgar caricaturing, as he did the naturalistic representation of the wet-nursing profession as a social practice, a relatively popular theme in the Salon art of the time.

Then there is Berthe Morisot, whose representation of her daughter Julie being fed by a wet nurse, in a painting of 1879 [private collection; Washington, D.C.], presents us with the activity of nursing itself. The nurse is frontal, exposed, spontaneously painted and, despite the diffusion of her form through the brushwork, evokes a vivid sort of biological immediacy. In contrast, by choosing a back view, Seurat erased all concrete evidence of the wet nurse's professional activity and her relation to a suckling infant, leaving us with a minimal sign—her long-ribboned hat and cloak—not a human process.[24] Seurat really worked at this figure; we can see the process of reduction in a series of conté crayon drawings, ranging from a relatively descriptive and empathetic one (now in the Goodyear collection) to a monumental back view (fig. 11.6). Despite the fact that the body in *Nurse with a Child's Carriage* is constructed of a few black-and-white curves and rectangles, joined by the most subtle nuances of tone marking the wet nurse's identifying ribbon (doubling as a kind of tonal spinal column), the wet nurse is nevertheless represented as connected to her charge, pushing a pram. In another version, the baby has become a faceless echo of the nurse's circular cap; her body, though still standing,

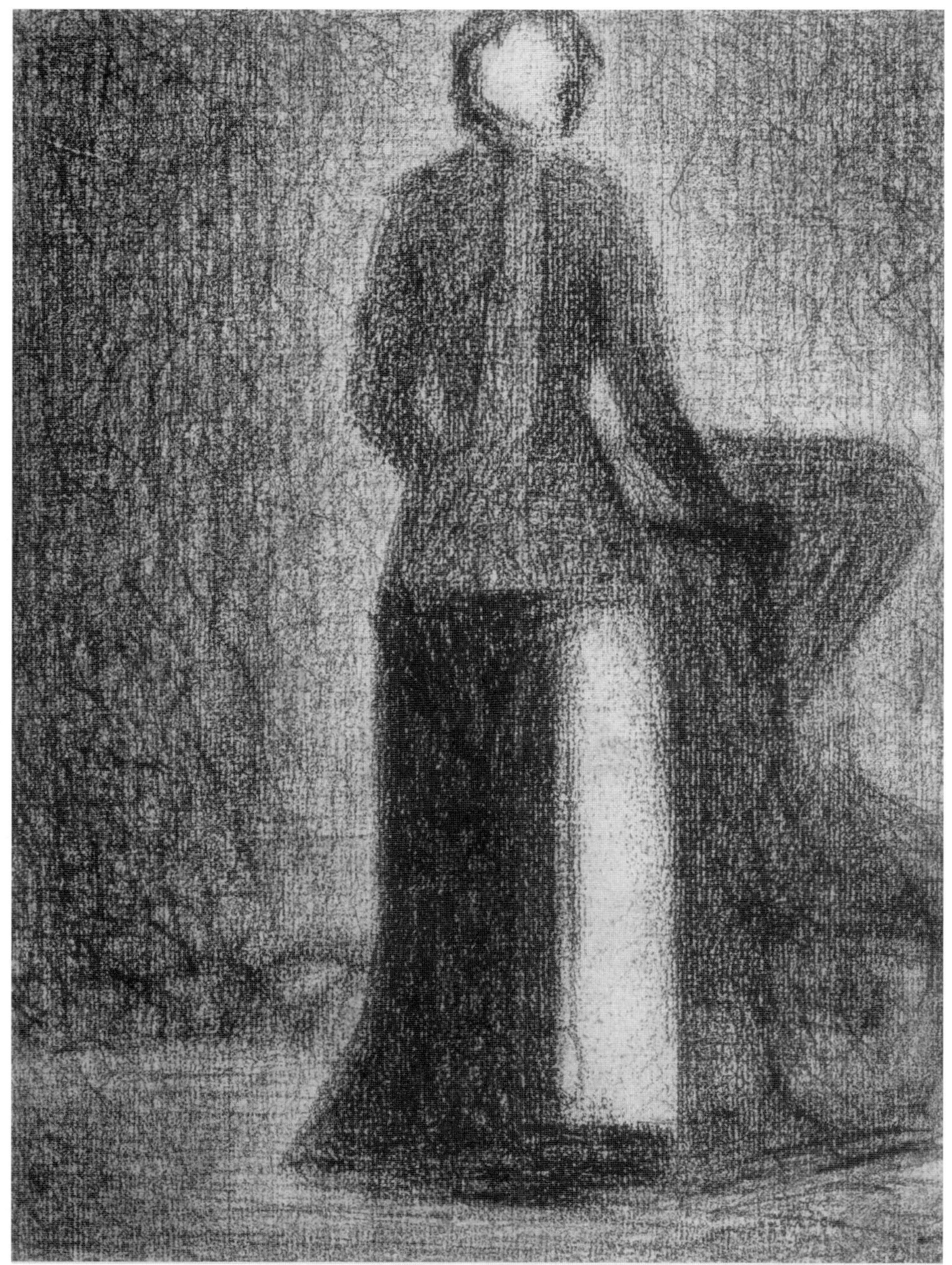

FIGURE 11.6. Georges Seurat, *Nurse with a Child's Carriage,* c. 1884, conté crayon on Ingres paper. The Pierpont Morgan Library, New York, NY; Gift of the Eugene Victor Thaw Art Foundation. Photo: The Pierpont Morgan Library/Art Resource, NY.

begins to assume the symmetrical, wedge-shaped form of the wet nurse in the final version of the *Grande Jatte*.

The series ends with a drawing (now in the Albright-Knox Gallery) specifically related to the wet nurse group in the *Grande Jatte*. Of this drawing Robert Herbert remarked: "The nurse, seen from behind, is as chunky as a boulder. Only her cap and ribbon, flattened into the vertical plane, make us sure she is indeed a seated woman."[25] Seurat in short reduced the wet nurse to a minimal function. There is no question, in the final version, of her role as a nurturer, of a tender relation between suckling infant and "second mother," as the wet nurse was known. Here we do not witness her nurturant action. The signs of her trade—cap, ribbon, cloak—*are* her reality: it is as though no others exist to represent the individual in mass society. Seurat then may be said to have reduced, not to classicize or generalize, as Rich believed, but to dehumanize, to transform human individuality into a critical index of social malaise. Types are no longer figured as picturesquely irregular, as in the old codes of caricature, but flattened into sardonically eloquent logos of their trades—a process akin to the workings of capitalism itself, as Signac might have said.

I must then end as I began, reading the *Grande Jatte* darkly, seeing in its compositional stasis and formal reduction an allegorical negation of the promise of modernity—in short, an anti-utopian allegory. To me the *Grande Jatte* would seem, as it did to Roger Fry in 1926, to represent "a world from which life and movement are banished and all is fixed forever in the rigid frame of its geometry."[26] And yet there is a detail that contradicts this reading—small but inflecting its meaning with a dialectical complexity and lying at the very heart of the *Grande Jatte:* the little girl with the hoop. This figure was hardly conceived in its present form in the large, final sketch (fig. 11.1). In the earlier version, it is hard to tell she is running at all. The figure is less diagonal, more merged with surrounding strokes; she seems connected to a brown-and-white dog, which is missing or displaced in the final version. The little girl is unique in that she is dynamic, her dynamism emphasized by her diagonal pose, her flowing hair, and her fluttering sash. She exists in total contrast with the other child contained under a geometric umbrella, passive, dependent, almost a clone of her mother. The running child is free, mobile, and goal-directed, chasing after something we cannot see. She also forms the apex of a triangle formed by the prancing dog in the foreground and a soaring, reddish butterfly to the left. Indeed the pose of the pug (like the running child, added late in the process of composition) seems to have been made in response to the dynamic contour of the running child.[27] She signifies Hope, in Bloch's terms, the utopian impulse buried in the heart of its dialectical opposite, the antithesis of the thesis of the painting.[28]

How different is Seurat's dynamic figuration of Hope—not really an allegorical figure but one that can allegorize—from Puvis's stiff and conventional post-Franco-Prussian war and Commune version [1872; Walters Art Gallery]. Puvis's images of hope, one might say, are hopeless, if we conceive of hope as the possibility of change, of an unknown but optimistic futurity rather than a rigid, permanent essence, couched in a classical language of embarrassed nudity or chaste drapery.

Seurat's figuring of the child-as-hope, active in the midst of a sea of frozen passivity, brings to mind a similar figuration—the child artist busily at work hidden away in Courbet's *Painter's Studio* of 1854–55 (fig. 11.7), subtitled "a real allegory." Unlike the *Grande Jatte* though it may be in many other ways, it is the nineteenth-century work that comes closest to Seurat's in the way it envisions utopia as a problem rather than a ready-made solution, as well as in its resolutely contemporary setting, and paradoxically in its static, frozen composition. Like the *Grande Jatte*, the *Painter's Studio* is a work of great power and complexity in its inextricable blending of utopian and non- or anti-utopian elements, indeed its representation of the utopian and anti-utopian as dialectically implicated in each other. In the gloomy cavern of the studio, the child artist, half hidden on the floor to the right, is the only active figure aside from the working artist himself. His alter ego, the little boy

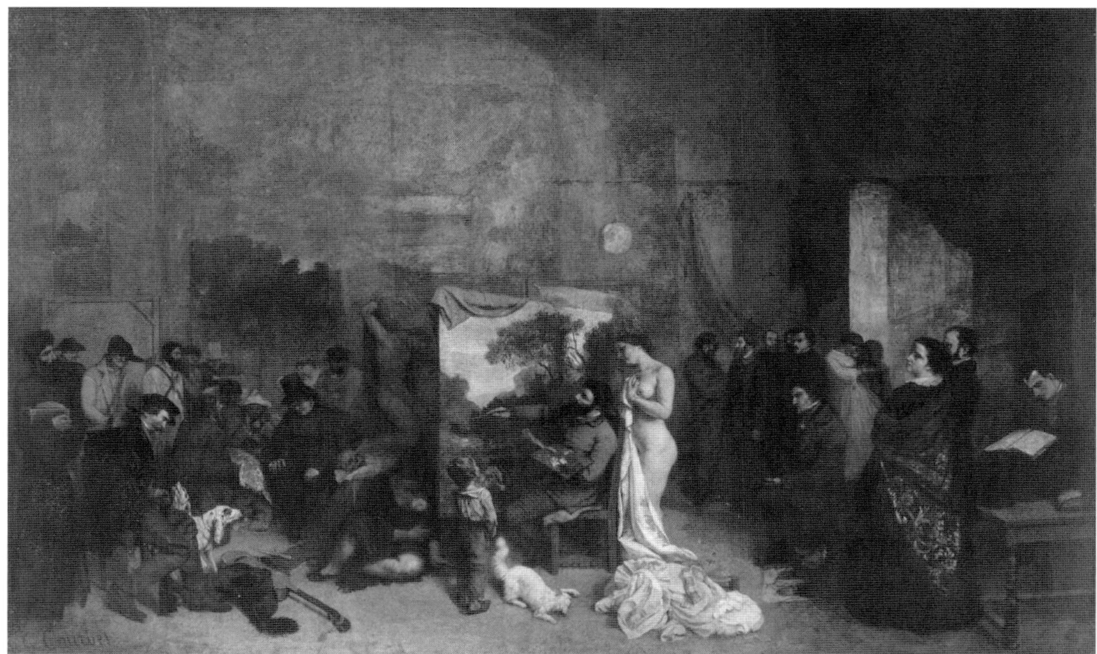

FIGURE 11.7. Gustave Courbet, *The Painter's Studio: An Allegory*, 1854–55. Musée d'Orsay, Paris. Photo: Réunion des Musées Nationaux/Art Resource, NY. Photographed by Hervé Lewandowski.

admiring Courbet's handiwork and occupying center stage, according to the artist himself, stands for the admiration of future generations; like Seurat's little girl, this child can also be read as a figuration of hope—hope as embodied in an unknown future.[29]

Yet the negative vision of modernity, specifically urban modernity, predominates in Seurat's oeuvre. His project of social critique through the construction of a new, partly mass-based, scientific formal language continued throughout his short but impressive career: in *The Models* (1887–88; Barnes Foundation), a sardonically humorous statement of the contradictions involved in modern society in the relationship between life and art, contemporary models peel off their clothes in the artist's studio, baring their reality in the presence of an artwork, a portion of the *Grande Jatte*, which is more contemporary, more socially circumstantial than they are. Which element stands for art? The traditional nudity of the "three graces," systematically presented as frontal, profile, and back view, or the grand painting of modern life that foils them? In *Le Chahut* of 1889–90 (Kröller-Müller Museum), commodified entertainment, the coarse product of the mass-culture industry adopted by the cosmopolitan and less-sophisticated middle classes alike, is pictorially constructed as hollowness and artifice, rather than as spontaneous pleasure, as Renoir might have figured it, or even as spontaneous sexual energy, in the manner of Henri de Toulouse-Lautrec. The transformation of the nose of the man on the right into a piglike snout overtly emphasizes the greedy consumption of pleasure. The dancers are types, decorative diagrams, high-class advertisements for slightly dangerous recreation.

In *The Circus* of 1891 (fig. 11.8), it is the modern phenomenon of spectacle and its concomitant, passive spectatorship, that are at issue. The picture parodies the production of art, allegorized as a kind of public performance, dazzling in its technique, turning somersaults to gratify an immobilized audience.

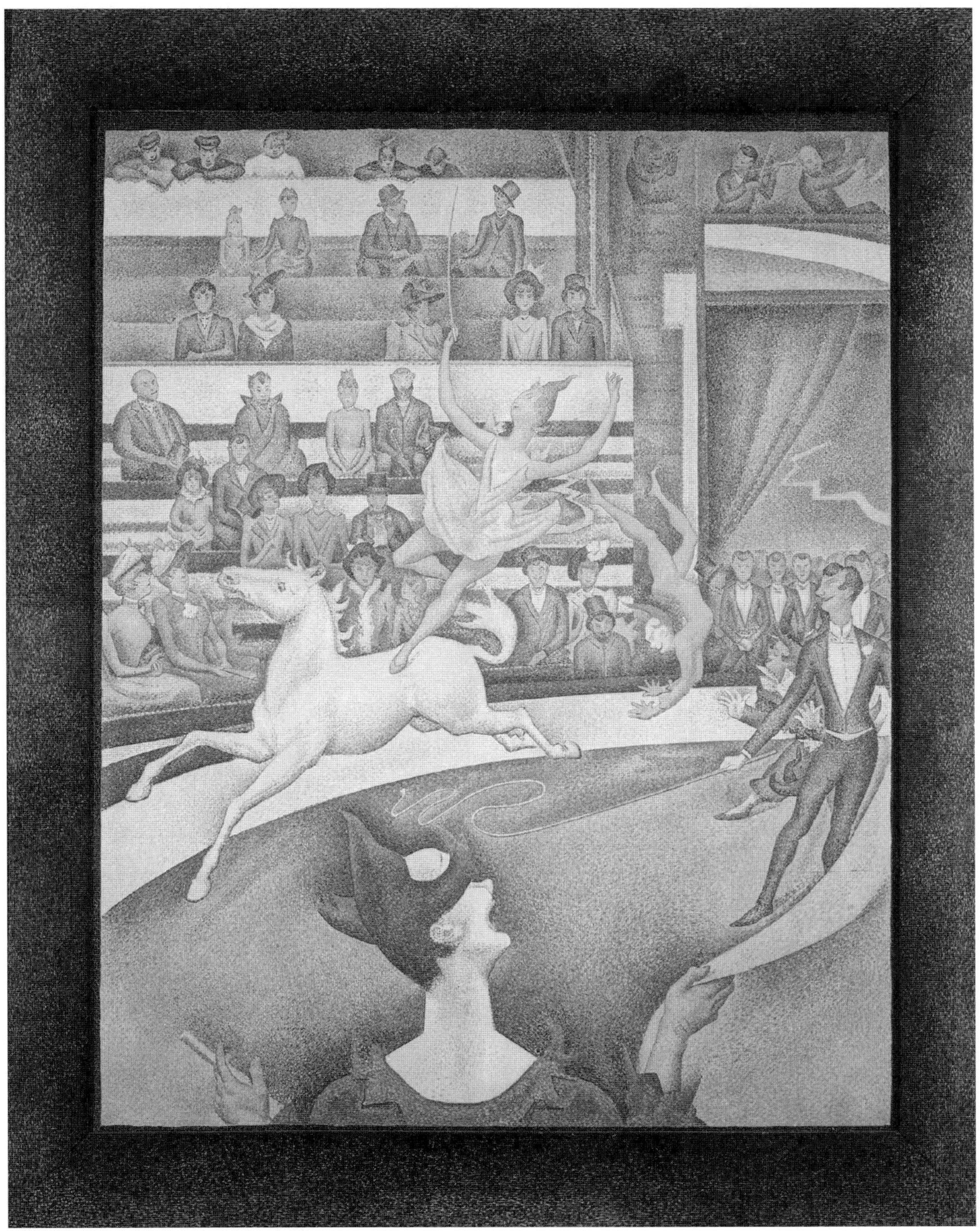

FIGURE 11.8. Georges Seurat, *The Circus*, 1891. Musée d'Orsay, Paris. Photo: Réunion des Musées Nationaux/Art Resource, NY. Photographed by Hervé Lewandowski.

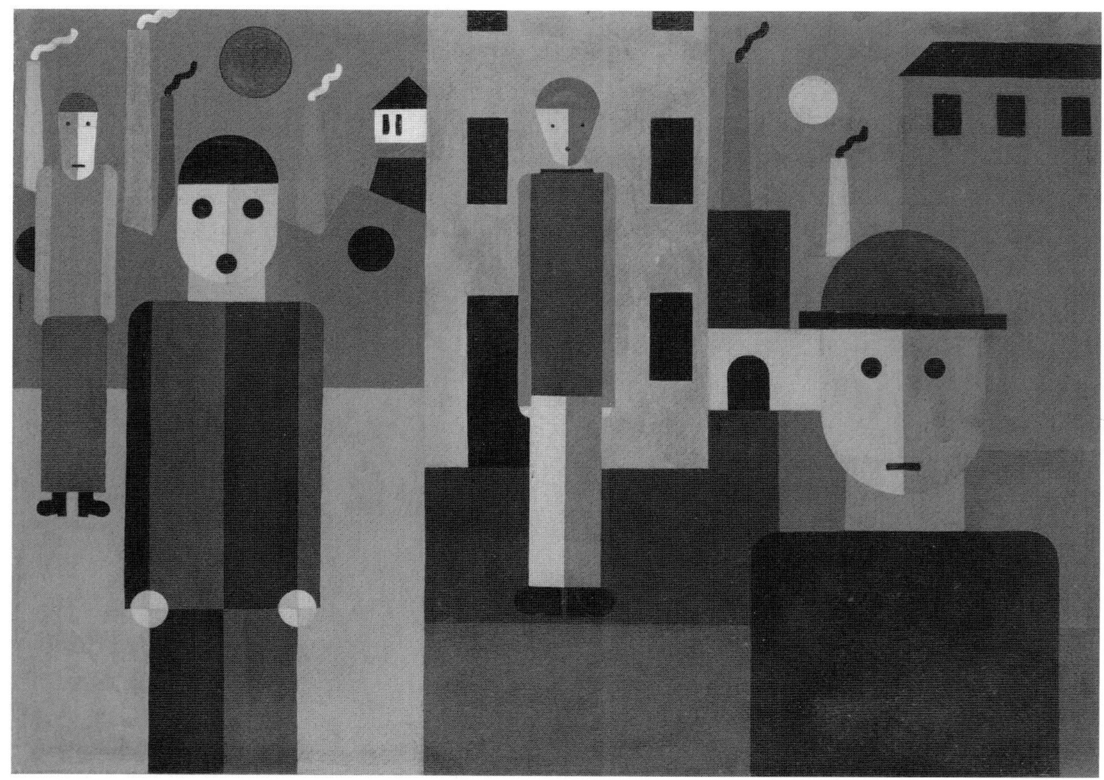

FIGURE 11.9. Franz W. Seiwert, *Factories*, 1926, oil on card. Hamburger Kunsthalle, Hamburg, Germany. Photo: The Bridgeman Art Library.

Even the performers seem frozen in poses of dynamism, coerced into standardized arcs, disembodied diagrams of movement. There are even more sinister interpretations of the relation of spectators to spectacle in *The Circus*. As well as standing for the public of art consumers, that audience, fixed in a state approaching hypnotic trance, may be read as indicating the manipulation of the masses. In this regard, Thomas Mann's sinister *Mario and the Magician* comes to mind, or Hitler and the crowd at Nuremberg, or more recently the American electorate and the performer-candidates who mouthed slogans and gesticulated with practiced artistry on television. Thus the meanings of the *Circus*, as an anti-utopian allegory, extend into time beyond inscribing the social problematic of its day.

If the *Grande Jatte* and Seurat's work in general have too often been enlisted in the "Great Tradition" of Western art, force-marched from Piero to Poussin to Puvis, they have all too little been related to some of the more critical strategies characteristic of the avant-garde art of the future. For example, in the work of an obscure group of political radicals working in Germany in the 1920s and early 1930s—the so-called Cologne Progressiven—Seurat's radical formulation of modern experience finds its inheritance—not its influence or continuation—in the twentieth century, although the Progressiven went much further in their anti-utopianism than Seurat did himself. Political activists, they were equally against art for art's sake and the contemporaneous Expressionist inscription of social malaise in agitated paint surfaces or expressive distortions, which they felt to be simply individualist hyperbole. The group, including Franz Wilhelm Seiwert (see fig. 11.9), Heinrich Hoerle, Gerd Arntz, Peter Alma, and the photographer August Sander, turned to the dispassionate diagramming of social iniquity and class oppression in a style appropriated from the flowcharts used by capitalists themselves, as a weapon of revolutionary consciousness raising. Anti-utopians par excellence, they like Seurat used the codes of modernity to question the legitimacy of the contemporary social order. Unlike Seurat, they called the legitimacy of high art itself into question; yet one might say that this too is inherent in certain aspects of the artist's practice. With his emphasis on the antiheroic rather than the gestural; on the "patient tapestry," with its implications of machinelike repetitiveness rather than the impatient slash and scumble of what Fénéon denominated as "virtuoso painting";[30] and on his insistence on social critique rather than transcendent individualism, Seurat may be seen as the ancestor of all those who rejected the heroic, and apolitical, sublimity of modernist art in favor of a critical practice of the visual. The photomontages of Berlin Dada or the collaged constructions of Barbara Kruger are, from this vantage point, more in the line of Neo-Impressionist descent than the innocuous oil paintings of those who happened to use little dots of paint to construct otherwise conventional landscapes or sea scenes and called themselves Seurat's followers. The anti-utopian impulse lies at the heart of Seurat's achievement, in, as Bloch saw it, the "single mosaic of boredom," the "empty-faced . . . dolls," the "expressionless water of the Sunday Seine"—in short, the landscape "of painted suicide which does not come off because it lacks resolve." It is this legacy that Seurat left to his contemporaries and to those who came after him.

Notes

Originally published in *Art Institute of Chicago Museum Studies* 14, no. 2 (1989), 133–53.

This essay is derived from a lecture delivered at The Art Institute of Chicago on October 5, 1988, initiating the Norma U. Lifton Memorial Lecture Series for the School of the Art Institute. A member of the art history faculty at the school, Norma Lifton died in January 1988. I prefaced my talk as follows: "I would like to think of this lecture as a kind of homage to Norma Lifton, a woman I never actually knew but somehow feel as though I had known, thanks to the words of her friends and admirers. One of them described her as having 'a sharp mind, a good ear, and a wonderful instinct for quality in all she saw and did'; I cannot think of higher or more honest praise."

1. The standard translation is Ernst Bloch, *The Principle of Hope*, trans. Neville Plaice, Stephen Plaice, and Paul Knight, vol. 2 (Cambridge, Mass., 1986), 814. Used here is the translation in Erich Franz and Bernd Growe, eds., *Georges Seurat: Drawings*, exh. cat. (Kunsthalle Bielefeld and Staatliche Kunsthalle Baden-Baden, 1983–84; trans. John William Gabriel, Boston, 1984), 82–83. Bloch was associated with the Frankfurt School, an influential group of Marxist theoreticians of social and aesthetic issues in Germany before World War II and, after the war, in the United States.
2. The concepts of "spectacle" and "spectacular society" were developed in the 1960s as part of the theoretical work of a group in France called the Situationist International and especially by Guy Debord. For further information, see T. J. Clark, *The Painting of Modern Life: Paris in the Art of Manet and His Followers* (New York, 1984), 9–10.
3. Bloch, *Principle of Hope*, 813–14. The translation here is by Plaice, Plaice, and Knight.
4. The satiric exaggeration of structure itself constitutes an anti-utopian strategy, allegorizing the failure of formal harmony in more traditional paintings of the time and calling into question, like the so-called social harmony it refers to, the whole idea of a "paradise on earth."
5. Seurat did not simply remove the process of pictorial construction from painting, neutralizing handiwork into nonexistent smoothness and universality, as did a Neoclassical artist such as J. A. D. Ingres. The facture is unremittingly present. It has simply been mechanized, positively depersonalized, and made antiexpressive.
6. Meyer Schapiro, "Seurat and 'La Grande Jatte,'" *Columbia Review* 17, no. 1 (November 1935): 14–15.

7. Fourierism was an influential utopian socialist movement founded by Charles Fourier (1772–1837). On Papety, see Nancy Finlay, "Fourierist Art Criticism and the *Rève de Bonheur* of Dominique Papety," *Art History* 2, no. 3 (September 1979): 327–38. Finlay referred to the *Dream of Happiness* as having "its message of Fourierist utopia conveyed by standard classical formulas in a classicizing style" (330).
8. Ibid., 331.
9. Ibid., 334.
10. Théophile Gautier, in *Moniteur universel*, June 3, 1867, cited in Claudine Mitchell, "Time and the Ideal of Patriarchy in the Pastorals of Puvis de Chavannes," *Art History* 10, no. 2 (June 1987): 189.
11. [Paul Signac], "Impressionistes et revolutionnaires," *La Révolte* 4, no. 40 (13–19 June 1891): 4; cited in R. Thomson, *Seurat* (Oxford, 1985), 207, 233 n. 82.
12. Indeed, looking at the criticism of the time, it becomes clear that it is the expressive formal structure of the whole rather than the social differences marking the picture's cast of characters—or more exactly the unprecedented juxtaposition of working- and middle-class figures so emphasized by T. J. Clark in his account of the work (*The Painting of Modern Life*, 265–67)—that made the most forceful impression on articulate viewers of the 1880s and made them read the *Grande Jatte* as pointed social critique. As Martha Ward pointed out ("The Eighth Exhibition 1886: The Rhetoric of Independence and Innovation," in Charles Moffett, ed., *The New Painting: Impressionism, 1874–1886*, exh. cat. [San Francisco: Fine Arts Museums of San Francisco, 1986], 420–42), contemporary critics "acknowledged diversity but did not attend to its implications. Most were far more concerned to explain why all of the figures appeared to be rigid, stiff, expressionless, and posed" (435).
13. Ward, "The Eighth Exhibition," 435.
14. H. Fèvre, "L'Exposition des impressionnistes," *La Revue de demain* (May–June 1886), 149; cited in ibid., 435, 442 n. 80.
15. Paul Adam, "Les Peintres impressionnistes," *La Revue contemporaine, littéraire, politique et philosophique* 4, no. 4 (April–May 1886), 550; cited in Ward, "The Eighth Exhibition," 435, 442 n. 81.
16. Alfred Paulet, "Les Impressionnistes," *Paris*, 5 June 1886; cited in Thomson, *Seurat*, 115 n. 31, 229, 230 n. 33.
17. Félix Fénéon, "Les Impressionnistes en 1886 (VIIIe exposition impressioniste)," *La Vogue*, 13–20 June 1886, 261–75; trans. in L. Nochlin, *Impressionism and Post-Impressionism, 1874–1904: Sources and Documents* (Englewood Cliffs, N.J., 1966), 110.
18. Daniel Catton Rich, *Seurat and the Evolution of "La Grande Jatte"* (Chicago, 1935), 2.
19. One need only think of the famous diagrams of Cézanne's paintings in Erle Loran, *Cézanne's Compositions* (Berkeley, 1943), which were recycled by Pop artist Roy Lichtenstein in such works as *Portrait of Madame Cézanne* of 1962 (see John Coplans, *Roy Lichtenstein*, exh. cat. [Pasadena: Pasadena Art Museum, 1967], fig. 11).
20. Schapiro 1935, 11–13.
21. On Seurat's "scientific" color theories, see A. Lee, "Seurat and Science," *Art History* 10, no. 2 (1987): 203–26. Lee concluded unequivocally, "Far from being scientifically well founded, his 'chromo-luminarist' method was pseudo-science: it was specious in its theoretical formulation, and was applied with an indifference to any critical appraisal of its empirical validity" (203).
22. N. Broude, ed., *Seurat in Perspective* (Englewood Cliffs, N.J., 1978), 173.
23. Ward, "The Eighth Exhibition," 434–35.
24. From the front, a wet nurse can be understood to be any nursing woman; from the rear, because of the presence of the circular cap and the signifying ribbon and cloak, the figure can only be seen as a wet nurse. Thus the back view reduces ambiguity of signification along with human relationship. For a full-scale analysis of Morisot's *Nursing*, see Linda Nochlin, "Morisot's *Wet Nurse:* The Construction of Work and Leisure in Impressionist Painting," in idem, *Women, Art, and Power and Other Essays* (New York, 1988), 37–56. For a differing interpretation of the nurse, see Mary Gedo, "The *Grande Jatte* as an Icon of a New Religion: A Psycho-Iconographic Interpretation," *Art Institute of Chicago Museum Studies* 14, no. 2 (1989): 236–37, 251 n. 47.
25. Robert L. Herbert, *Seurat's Drawings* (London, 1962); cited in Broude, *Seurat in Perspective*, 129.
26. Roger Fry, "Seurat," in *Transformations* (London, 1926); cited in John Russell, *Seurat* (New York: 1965), 157.
27. The animal freedom of the dog, a chattel by definition, cannot signify social freedom the way the girl does. And indeed his position, a parodic version of the capriole, one of the advanced positions of equestrian dressage, signifies artificed constriction itself.
28. For this notion, as well as the relation of the transient and fragmentary to the utopian function of art, see Ernst Bloch, "The Conscious and Known Activity Within the Not-Yet-Conscious, the Utopian Function," in *The Utopian Function of Art and Literature*,

trans. J. Zipes and F. Mecklenburg (Cambridge, Mass., 1988), 103–40, especially 139.

29. For the negative contradiction of Courbet's figuration of hope in the *Studio,* in the form of the Irish beggar woman, see Linda Nochlin, "Courbet's Real Allegory: Rereading 'The Painter's Studio,'" in Sarah Faunce and Linda Nochlin, *Courbet Reconsidered,* exh. cat. (Brooklyn: Brooklyn Museum, 1988), 26–29.

30. Fénéon, "Les Impressionistes en 1886"; cited in J. Halperin, *Félix Fénéon: Aesthete and Anarchist in Fin-de-Siècle Paris* (New Haven, 1988), 83.

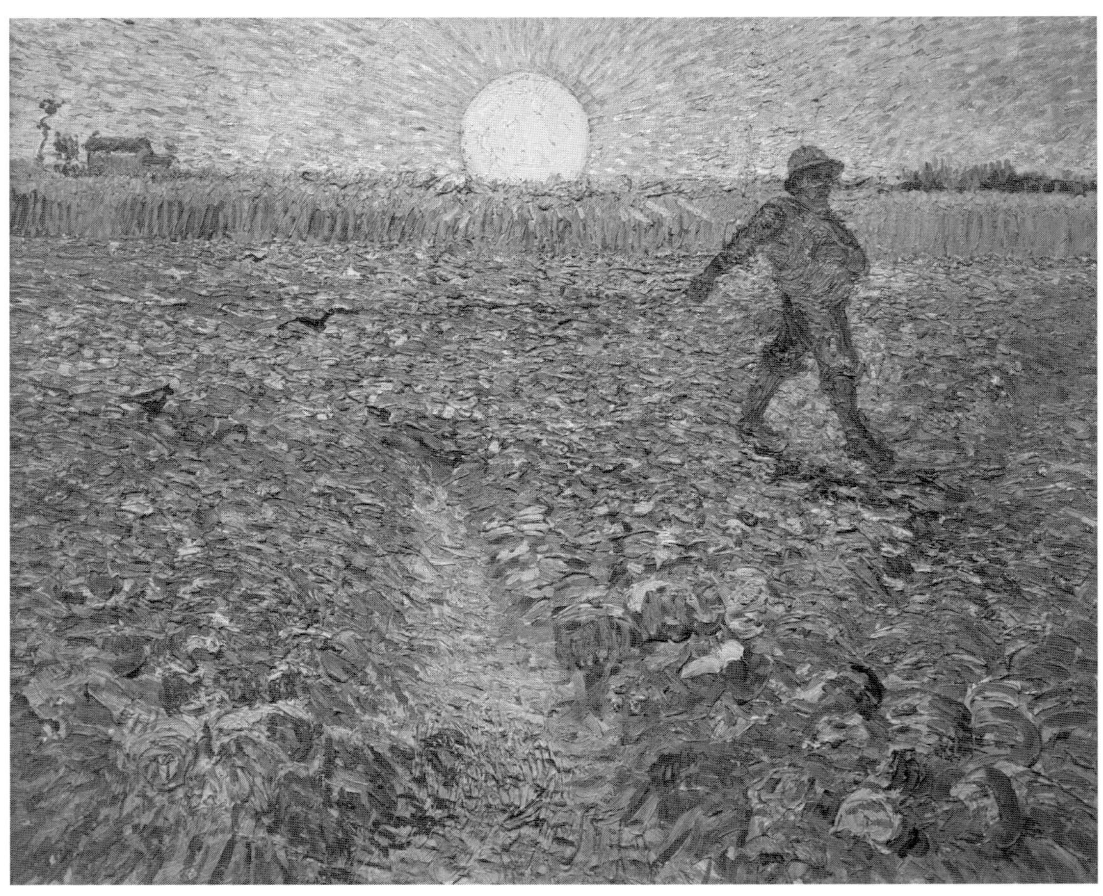

FIGURE 12.1. Vincent van Gogh, *The Sower*, 1888. Rijksmuseum Kroeller-Mueller, Otterlo, The Netherlands. Photo: Erich Lessing/Art Resource, NY.

12

At the Threshold of Symbolism

Van Gogh's Sower *and Gauguin's* Vision after the Sermon

DEBORA SILVERMAN

Art is an abstraction; derive this abstraction from nature while dreaming before it.

PAUL GAUGUIN

My attention is so fixed on what is possible and really exists that I hardly have the desire or the courage to strive for the ideal as it might result from my abstract studies . . .

I do not invent the whole picture; on the contrary, I find it all ready in nature, only it must be disentangled.

VINCENT VAN GOGH

IN THE SUMMER of 1888 Vincent van Gogh and Paul Gauguin—in close contact through correspondence and deliberating the final arrangements for their impending collaboration in Arles—each undertook a distinct pictorial experiment. Both regarded their experiments as particularly challenging, emphatically modern, and singularly "symbolist," a term they first attached to specific paintings made between that July and November. Van Gogh's inaugural "symbolist" venture produced *The Sower* (plate 6 and fig. 12.1), a laborer striding through a sun-saturated landscape as he tosses seeds from his bag into a plowed field. Gauguin charted out his "path of symbolism" in a "religious painting," *The Vision after the Sermon: Jacob Wrestling with the Angel* (plate 7). Similar to Van Gogh's *Sower* in size, but radically different in form, meaning, and function, Gauguin's *Vision* captures Breton peasant women transfixed in prayer. Heads bowed, eyes closed, and hands clasped, they project their inner vision onto a dream landscape, rendered, Gauguin explained in a letter to Van Gogh, as a "non-natural" field of "pure vermilion."[1] The broad mass of bright red, enveloping the static figures as it signifies the externalization of their inner vision, provides a formal medium for Gauguin's goal of depicting the crossing of the divide between material reality and the realm of the supernatural.

Underlying the divergent "symbolist" agendas of Van Gogh's *Sower* and Gauguin's *Vision after the Sermon* are a number of points in common. Both painters set their artistic experiments in preindustrial peasant communities. Both employed formal innovations, particularly the evocative power of color, as vehicles for what Robert Goldwater has described as a distinguishing feature of Symbolist art: to move painting beyond anecdotal realism toward a more direct, and more universal, mode of discourse.[2] And both painters pressed their art into the service of a sacred, eternal, and invisible world beyond the self and the senses.

While neither Van Gogh nor Gauguin adhered to an institutional religion, each transposed to his painting career the indelible stamp of his religious formation. Van Gogh, a Dutch Reformed minister's son, and Gauguin, schooled in a French Jesuit seminary, inextricably linked their art and their identities to a larger, purposive and transcendent order, and each gave symbolist painting a role hitherto located in their respective religious doctrines: that of mediator of divinity.

The differing forms of that mediation of divinity expressed in Van Gogh's *Sower* and Gauguin's *Vision after the Sermon* reveal the disparities between the two painters' symbolist projects, and the divergent religious legacies that shaped them. While both artists linked their paintings to an "aspiration for the infinite," the 1888 canvases show they were ready to proceed on "the path of symbolism" in different directions: Gauguin by dematerializing nature in a flight to metaphysical mystery; Van Gogh by naturalizing divinity, in the service of a "perfection" that "renders the infinite tangible to us."[3]

Van Gogh's and Gauguin's divergent conceptions of art—as sacred embodiment and as transcendent idealism—were set in cognitive styles forged early in their particular religious and educational formations, which have received scant attention from scholars. These discordant formations provided each artist with different sets of culturally transmitted resources and constraints, which structured their radically different attitudes toward reality. From his Jesuit training, Gauguin assimilated a profound receptivity to idealism, a presumption of man's supernatural destiny and of material reality as a spurious way station to divinity, and a fluency with visual memory and interior visualization. Van Gogh, by contrast, absorbed from his Dutch Reformed Calvinism a number of powerful cultural barriers to idealism and consolidated, long before he chose the vocation of art, historically specific values of enacted faith, the primacy of sight, and a receptivity to nature as a source of immanent divinity.[4] *The Sower* and *The Vision* set the stage for a collaboration that would be strained not simply by personal and temperamental incompatibilities, but by more profoundly irreconcilable mental frameworks that implied different conceptions of the status of the self, the value of the image, and the meaning of the visible world.

In part, the dissimilar symbolist agendas of the two canvases expose the different artistic ideals and practices each painter had established before their affiliation. *The Sower* expressed powerful continuities with three unifying concerns that had guided Van Gogh's stylistic development since his apprenticeship in the Netherlands. First, the choice of subject, inspired by Millet's *Sower* of 1850, reaffirmed Van Gogh's commitment to depict the strain of human labor and the integrity of humble people. From the diggers of The Hague and Etten to the weavers of Nuenen, the Arles *Sower* extended Van Gogh's attempt to realize what he defined as "the very core of modern art": "*a peasant's figure in action*."[5] Accordingly, Van Gogh reworked the painting to emphasize the sower's moving stride across the field.[6]

Second, *The Sower* reaffirmed Van Gogh's persistent expressions of personal identification with laborers, derived partly from his Calvinist belief that active work was the source of grace and partly from his Evangelical ideal of the sanctity of humble labor. Convinced that he looked "more or less like a peasant," "only peasants are of more use in the world," Van Gogh set out on daily treks to the Arles fields, where he engaged in long hours of "hard, close work" in "the full sun."[7] In describing his work on *The Sower* to his brother Theo and Émile Bernard, he recounted the exhaustion he surmounted, painting under the glaring sun with the "mistral raging."[8] To withstand the mistral's gusts, Van Gogh demonstrated his artisanal ingenuity as he devised a mechanism for anchoring his easel: he proudly explained to Bernard that he was able to complete *The Sower* only because he had staked his easel down by ramming the legs into the ground and then tying them to adjacent iron pegs driven deep into the soil.[9]

And third, the Arles *Sower* reaffirmed Van Gogh's pattern of regarding the act of painting as visually equivalent to the labor and preindustrial methods he

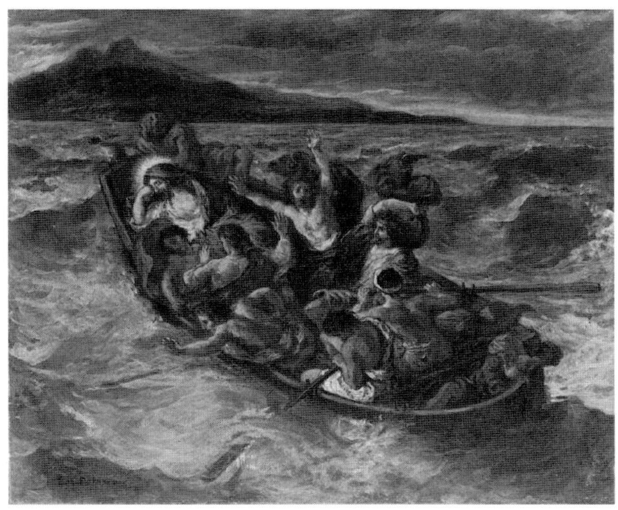

FIGURE 12.2. Eugène Delacroix, *Christ Asleep during the Tempest,* 1853. The Metropolitan Museum of Art, New York; H.O. Havemeyer Collection, Bequest of Mrs. H.O. Havemeyer, 1929 (29.100.131). Photo: The Metropolitan Museum of Art, all rights reserved.

so deeply admired.[10] He worked and reworked the image to give his brushwork "firmness" and wrestled to build up a coloristic field of "heightened structural density."[11] The bristling textural quality of the flecks of broken color, applied in multiple layers, gave the canvas its palpable roughness and animation. The physical exertion expended on the canvas surface grew more intense in the furrow cut through the field in the center of the picture, and in fact, some months later Van Gogh commented, "I am plowing on my canvases as they do on their fields."[12] The separate paint strokes, thickly applied to the stubble, ripe stalks, flying seeds, and sun's rays, unite in Van Gogh's aspiration that a painting of a rural subject should "have a rustic quality" and "smell of the earth" and "hard and coarse reality."[13]

While extending earlier ideals and practices, *The Sower* also marked a point of departure, for the composition coheres not only through its rough textrous physicality but through the blazing sunlight that seems to saturate every pore of the canvas. In this combination of grounded peasant work and immaterial irradiation, Van Gogh located a new theory of art and an attitude toward reality that he assigned to "symbolism."

The letters about *The Sower* register Van Gogh's definition of its "symbolist" features. To Bernard, he noted how, at work in the fields, he was beset by "memories of the past" and "a longing for the infinite, of which the sower, the sheaf are the symbols."[14] Rather than ascribing *The Sower* a literary meaning derived from Christ's parable, Van Gogh interpreted the symbolic quality of the subject in the more inclusive terms of "longing for the infinite," the aspiration toward an eternal order beneath surface appearances.[15] What visual techniques were appropriate to convey this "symbol" of the infinite lodged in a peasant figure? Not the subject alone, Van Gogh claimed, but the linkage of the subject to a theory and practice of expressive color promised *The Sower's* new symbolic stature. He called Millet's *Sower* "a colorless *gray*"; "what remained to be done" was the large-scale striding figure "in color."[16] Paradoxically, in his ambition to "modernize Millet," Van Gogh turned to Millet's predecessor, Delacroix, whose expressive complementary color laws he had studied but not systematically applied to a major canvas.[17] The way Van Gogh invoked Delacroix's colorism is significant: he turned to the evocative forms of a religious painting for the revitalizing color scheme of his *Sower.* Writing to Theo as he worked on the picture, Van Gogh juxtaposed Delacroix's *Christ Asleep during the Tempest* (fig. 12.2) and Millet's *Sower* as "absolutely different in execution." He went on,

"Christ Asleep in the Tempest—I am speaking of the sketch in blue and green with touches of violet, red, and a little citron-yellow for the nimbus, the halo—speaks a symbolic language through color alone."[18]

In planning *The Sower,* Van Gogh would apply what he considered Delacroix's "suggestive color"[19] to a Millet-inspired peasant subject by composing the painting in two interlinked contrasting color zones, the "upper half predominantly yellow and the lower part in complementary violet";[20] by continuing the juxtaposition of colors along a slender painted yellow and violet frame;[21] and by transferring the luminous citron yellow of Christ's nimbus to the sun.[22]

Van Gogh experimented with this "symbolist" melding of peasant activity and transfigurative light even as he resisted the pull toward idealism and the revival of religious art. During the months he worked on *The Sower,* he clarified some of the differences that would deepen during his collaboration with Gauguin. Writing to Bernard in late July 1888, Van Gogh urged his friend to forgo the fantasy and aestheticism of Baudelaire for what he considered a perfection and completeness that render "the infinite tangible."[23] The examples he cited of this "infinite tangible"—Millet, Courbet, and the Dutch school—departed resolutely from the unreal realm he ascribed to religious painting. He made exception for Rembrandt and Delacroix, whose work may have encompassed occasional religious subjects but differed absolutely from "all the rest of religious painting." When Rembrandt painted angels, Van Gogh asserted, he painted his self-portrait in a mirror, a humanized supernatural figure he "knew" and "felt." For Delacroix, the choice of a Christ figure was subordinate to the evocative form devised to represent him in a bright yellow and "luminous" radiance.[24]

This critique of religious art, in conjunction with the conception and stylistic framework of *The Sower,* captures the essence of Van Gogh's emergent symbolism in a theory and practice of embodiment and emanation. *The Sower* exemplifies Van Gogh's ideal of an art rooted in the indivisible union of tangibility and the infinite in its depiction of redemptive production physically enacted by its peasant subject, technically emulated by the painter's course and effortful brush, and transcendently charged by its blasting illumination. The canvas's horizontal and vertical zones yoke the realms of human action and celestial power: as the sower casts seed into the bare earth split open in the center foreground, the erect stalks at the back of the field, drenched by vitalizing sun, signal the end of the cycle yielding the fruits of labor. The painter, through his interlocking design and matched yellow dabs for seeds and shafts of sunlight, ties the two realms together and absorbs the power of each, the agent of irradiation and germination. Van Gogh's artist, like the sower, embodies matter; his was a nature not to be overcome, but poised to be "disentangled" and realized. And his artist, like the sower's sun, activates emanation of the eternal in the tangible; he floods a dense, materialized light that penetrates every ground and grain of the picture plane. *The Sower*'s paradigmatic status was recapitulated in the very process of preparing the ground of artistic production in the sower's fields. Resisting the blast of mistral by ramming, clamping, and tying his easel down with rope, stakes, and iron pegs, Van Gogh applied his sparkling streaks of color to a canvas anchored from flight, embedded deep in the soil.

At the same time Van Gogh was striving to render the tangibility of the infinite, Gauguin pressed his art into the service of visionary incorporeality. Pictorial, personal, and ontological factors, which combined to endow *The Sower* as a symbolist image weighted down from flight, made of Gauguin's *Vision after the Sermon: Jacob Wrestling with the Angel* a symbolist image released into the weightlessness of the dream, what Gauguin called "freeing painting from its chains"—"the shackles of verisimilitude" and materialism.[25]

Gauguin's symbolist experiment, like Van Gogh's, was related to preexisting ideals and practices. The appeal of the subject of *The Vision,* which Gauguin said represented the scene enacted within the praying women's imaginations, had precedents in his work. In 1881, for example, while exhibiting with the Impressionists and training alongside Camille Pissarro, Gauguin presented a distinctly anti-Impressionist motif in a large oil named *La Petite Rêve* (Ordrupgaard-samlingen, Copenhagen), a depiction of his daughter Aline asleep, prefiguring his "later preoccupations with the world of the unconscious" and the "interior life of human beings."[26] And in letters of January 1885 and August 1888 to his friend Emile Schuffenecker, he registered artistic attitudes and an epistemology that set the framework for the exploration of the different levels of reality given form in *The Vision after the Sermon*. The 1885 letter proposed an art directed toward the mediation of a mystical reality beneath appearances, capable of conveying what he called "phenomena which appear to us supernatural, and of which, however, we have the *sensation*."[27] In August 1888, Gauguin goaded Schuffenecker to subordinate nature to the imperatives of the artist's dream, as he edged toward the primacy of a subjectivist antinaturalism as the core of modern art and the equivalent of divinity: "Art is an abstraction; derive this abstraction from nature while dreaming before it. . . . This is the only way of rising toward God—doing as our Divine Master does, create."[28]

Gauguin's *Vision after the Sermon*, a religious painting in a dream landscape, thus extends attitudes already consolidated in his evolving aesthetic. Yet, it also represents a self-conscious break with his previous style, training, and subject matter, which he characterized as a turning point in his development.[29] *The Vision* deploys a new arsenal of visual forms designed to "offer salvation from the ontologically wanting world of appearances" in order to mediate a realm beyond perceptual experience.[30] The Impressionists, Gauguin later explained, "heed only the eye and neglect the mysterious centers of thought."[31] Abandoning his Impressionist canon, Gauguin celebrated his *Vision* as a first step along "the path of symbolism," a path ascending toward a dematerialized purity he now proclaimed as "fundamental to my nature."[32]

In mid-August 1888, then, while Van Gogh was mired in "clods of earth" and "hard, close work" in the fields, an imperturbable Gauguin began composing *The Vision after the Sermon* in the hush of religious meditation: his subject was a group of Breton women withdrawn into an interior vision inspired by a sermon. While the kneeling figures at the left look down, eyes closed and hands clasped in prayer, the central figure looks up and across a diagonal tree to where the vision of Jacob wrestling with the Angel is projected, as if it were really taking place in the distance. As Gauguin explained in a letter to Van Gogh, "The landscape and the fight exist only in the imagination of the people praying after the sermon, which is why there is a contrast between the people, who are natural, and the struggle going on in a landscape which is non-natural and out of proportion."[33] Gauguin constructed his *Vision* as a mystical encounter between the natural and the supernatural, the conduit between them being the fusion of the artist's dream and the peasant's visionary faith.

Like Van Gogh, Gauguin elaborated new visual techniques to convey the form and meaning of his inaugural symbolist venture. Composed of two overlapping zones of pictorial space, the vividly colored *Vision* is devoid of a middle ground, thus confounding traditional perspective. The praying women are assembled in the foreground along the edges of the canvas; the central figure focuses on the two biblical characters behind a tree that cuts across the canvas at a diagonal. Gauguin's use of the tree as an asymmetrical flattening device was inspired by Japanese prints; its use as a boundary separating the two levels of reality in the picture is his invention.[34] The treatment of the tree exposes it as a permeable border, befitting the theme of the interpenetration of reality and apparition. Distending upward and lacking a visible base, the tree appears to float; its one point of fixity is formed not by an anchoring middle ground but by the white bonnet of the figure in the foreground, to which it appears to be stuck, further compressing the picture space.

A second element of Gauguin's antiperspectivism formalizes the drift of the natural into the supernatural. In setting the scale and proportions of the figures, Gauguin scrambles the logic of illusionism to bring the distant realm closer, creating a picture space that tilts up and presses forward. This breach of traditional adjustments of scale is particularly apparent in the triad of the women in front, the cow at the left, and the Angel and Jacob beyond the tree. The three women in front are rendered in large dimensions; the Angel and Jacob, in the distance, do not diminish proportionally. While closer to the women in space, the cow appears much smaller in scale than Jacob and the Angel; its placement recapitulates the weightlessness configured elsewhere in the painting.[35] Although visually the animal's body shares the women's "natural" space, the rearing head, blocked from view by the tree, has migrated to the spiritual realm occupied by Jacob and the Angel. Like the tree, which hovers as if unrooted, the cow floats into the ethereal spheres. Gauguin's transformation of a lumbering creature into an airy messenger of incorporeality offers one of the clearest signs of *The Vision*'s thematics of supernaturalism.

Gauguin's most conspicuous innovation in *The Vision after the Sermon* is the antinaturalist palette, applied in unbroken color masses outlined in black, resembling medieval enameling or stained glass. The outlines intensify the bright colors as well as flatten the painting's surface.[36] Like the spatial zones, the color range conforms to Gauguin's poles of "natural" and "non-natural," with black and white chosen for the "natural" elements and multicolored tones for the "non-natural" ones. The Breton women, Gauguin explained in a letter to Van Gogh, wore "very intense black clothes" and "yellow-white bonnets, very luminous." The tree, rendered in dark hue, ascends to brighter colors: as its foliage spills into the area near the Angel and Jacob, Gauguin introduces a sparkling green, converting the density of leaves into the ethereality of what he called "greenish emerald *clouds*."[37] Gauguin adds another color sign of the tree's dual position in the natural and non-natural realms of experience: while the edge of the tree trunk toward the women is outlined in black, the edge nearer Jacob and the Angel glows orange. But the most startling aspect of *The Vision* is the dazzling expanse of unreal red—"*pure vermilion*"—that renders the heavenly ground permeating the picture plane as it fills the consciousness of the praying women. The red spreads in a broad field of largely unmodulated color, thinly and evenly applied with a fluid brush that rarely breaks the canvas's uniform surface. The picture's highest point of luminousness as well as the most saturated coloristic hub lie in the Angel and Jacob characters. Gauguin described Jacob's robe as "bottle green" and the Angel as dressed in "violent ultramarine blue." The eye quickly settles on the Angel's wings, painted with "pure number 1 chrome yellow"; the Angel's hair modulates to "number 2 chrome," and the feet are "flesh orange."[38] These gradations of intense yellow to orange, reinforced by the flashing orange edge of the tree and the brilliant red of the surround, make the Angel radiate light and heat from an invisible source, a flushed treatment that contrasts sharply with the faces of the praying women: drained of flesh color and highlighted with frosty white, the women appear as dissipated "masks of meditation" riveted to a blazing site of heated light.[39]

A religious painting born in repudiation of Impressionist facticity, *The Vision after the Sermon* captures the essence of Gauguin's emergent symbolism in a theory and practice of dematerialization. Indeed, *The Vision*'s subject and form are a pictorial realization of Gauguin's clarion call in August 1888 for art as an abstraction derived "from nature while dreaming before it": taking the raw material of the sermon they have heard and the natural scene before them, transforming it and projecting it outward, the praying women enact Gauguin's charge. The resulting vision places the women in the position of the artist that Gauguin asserted arises from this exercise of the primacy of creative abstraction over nature—this "way of mounting toward God"—and the women are physically and spiritually poised in the picture plane to fulfill this act of ascent.

Van Gogh's and Gauguin's symbolist projects of 1888 display striking contrasts. Although both artists used the peasant figure and initiated their experiments in preindustrial rural communities, they construed peasants, and incorporated them into their innovative art, in dissimilar ways. *The Sower* expressed Van Gogh's abiding definition of modern art as linked to the exertion of peasant laborers. In depicting lowly labor, Van Gogh attached himself to those he considered the true servants of God, whose worthiness surpassed a self-taught painter struggling with inner and outer pressures for justification.

Gauguin, by contrast, approached the peasant not as a vehicle for self-justification, but as a means of metaphysical and metapsychical extension. His peasants do not work—they dream; they do not expend bodily action, but compress mental space. And even when they were engaged in physical work, Breton peasants appeared to Gauguin as vessels of pious resignation, unmarked by signs of outdoor exposure:

> There is something medieval looking about the peasants here in Brittany. . . . Their apparel, too, is little short of symbolic. . . . Look how the bodice forms a cross in back, how they wrap their heads in headscarves, like nuns. . . . Still fearful of the Lord and of the parish priest, Bretons hold their hats and tools as though they were in church.[40]

If Van Gogh maximized both his labor and that of the subject depicted in *The Sower,* Gauguin, ever on the alert for a "glimpse of the dream," promoted *The Vision* as an effortless transcription of the dissolving powers of mind over matter: "Go on working, *freely and furiously,* you will make progress. . . . Above all, don't perspire over a picture. A strong emotion can be translated immediately; dream on it and seek its simplest form."[41]

Formally, *The Sower* exemplifies Van Gogh's expressive imperative of marking the canvas with tangible signs of a labor equivalent to that of his subject. The physicality of his loaded brush unifies the painting in intersecting units of horizontal ground and vertical crops drenched with radiant flecks of light. The spatial organization and format emphasize a visual interaction of density and the movement enacted by the subject, reproduced by the painter's animated brush. The furrow unfolding kinetically from the picture's front edge to the middle ground already traversed by the striding sower immediately opens up the space and forcefully pulls the viewer in.

Where Van Gogh reworked his sower to render the stride more convincing, Gauguin's pursuit of translating "strong emotion" and the lineaments of the dream yielded figures in trance-like stillness. The large heads and truncated bodies of the Breton women splayed out against the front edges of the canvas accord with their dissociated state of pure consciousness, split off from anchorage in corporeal reality. The two women on the right with their backs to the viewer are faceless, and their enormous white bonnets appear improbably anchored to them, like giant wings at rest. The other earthly components of *The Vision,* like the floating tree with its vaporous leaves and the dainty cow, enhance the panoply of figuration as an experiment in abstracted antinaturalism.

It is in the handling and application of the brush that Van Gogh's and Gauguin's emergent symbolisms diverge most tangibly. Van Gogh's sculptural brush yielded a thick sediment of color by building up individual sticks of paint in the foreground field, and bristling, abraded bars of ripe crop in the background. He reworked the canvas to reinforce it as a surface of "heightened structural density"; the application of paint in sticks and fibrous blocks exemplifies how Van Gogh realized in his symbol of "longing for the infinite" a record of his "hand-to-hand struggle with nature,"[42] a nature wrestled, penetrated and "disentangled."

By contrast, Gauguin's smooth, attenuated brush, aspiring to the fluidity of the dream projected from his subjects' inner consciousness, glided across *The Vision* in an unbroken surface of rhythmic linear banding and broad masses of color. Pigment melts into the canvas rather than augmenting it by amassing a second layer, as on the coarse canvas of *The Sower.* The areas of white defining the Breton women's headgear spread with the delicacy of chalk rather than oil. The daring red of the dreamscape appears not molded but aqueous, level as a sheet of ice.

Gauguin achieved his flattened, lissome surface as deliberately as Van Gogh had calibrated his brushwork for maximum density. By 1888 Gauguin had devised a number of techniques to "mute the surface" and "enhance the flatness" of the image: his own formula for a matte, white primer; thinned oil paint; and a wax finish instead of varnish.[43] The primer created "a highly absorbent, chalklike surface" that registered the thinned paint in a distinctive manner. As Reinhold Heller has put it, "no trace of a sculptured surface texture appears, and instead a very thin matte finish is made, its sheen diminished even more by the fusion of the paint substance with the absorbing, chalky primer. . . . With its colors melting into the canvas itself, moreover, the physicality of the image disappears."[44]

"Sculptured surface texture" and "physicality" are precisely the formal vehicles the brushwork of *The Sower* exploits to "render the infinite tangible"; Gauguin's strategies to attenuate and suppress these potentials of oil paint brushed onto canvas exemplify his ambition to weaken materiality's hold on consciousness, to invert outer and inner reality, and to repudiate the "disentangling" encounter with the stuff of nature in favor of a transcendent abstraction.

The artists' choice and application of color also accord with their respective materialist and idealist orientations to the sacred. Van Gogh, seeking to modernize Millet, turned to the evocative colorism of Delacroix's laws of simultaneous contrast, which as Van Gogh knew, had a scientific foundation posited by the chemist Michel Chevreul, director of the Gobelins Tapestry Works, who urged painters to approximate the operation of colored light in nature by juxtaposing complementary hues. While conceding some departures from these laws, Van Gogh's attempt to render *The Sower* in interlocking zones of violet and yellow complementaries, including their rearticulation along the painting's frame, indicates his interest in an optically based formula for heightened luminosity. This naturalistic element of his symbolist colorism is analogous to his other inspiration from Delacroix for *The Sower:* the transfer of the radiant yellow halo from the *Christ Asleep during the Tempest* to the glowing disk of his *Sower*'s sun, a secularized source of sacred light.

Gauguin's palette in *The Vision* moved away from natural optical laws to a supernatural effulgence. Rather than trying to match the interaction of colored light he had assimilated from Impressionism and Chevreul's model, Gauguin invented a chromatic key modulated to the contours of inner vision, which led to an inversion of Van Gogh's color choices. Van Gogh, redirecting the intensity of Christ's nimbus to the sower's domain, reserved the brightest color and fullest light for the sun saturating the fields, which he painted in high-keyed "chrome yellow, number I." Gauguin employed exactly the same color for his Angel's wings, reserving the radiant high point of his *Vision* for the supernatural realm. The surreal red of the dreamscape serves to further diminish the color of the human figures in the foreground; the women's black and white costume and faces rendered in low flesh tones covered over with pasty white pale in comparison with their Technicolor vision.[45]

Yet another formal feature reveals the disparity between Van Gogh's and Gauguin's symbolist orientations. Compositionally, both paintings cohere in two main spatial zones. In *The Sower,* the horizontal plowed field in front interlocks with the vertical crops and sun at the back, mediated by the figure of the sower, who moves toward the viewer in a diagonal swath. As Van Gogh lures the eye to retrace the sower's forward steps, he also impels the eye into a corridor that shoots dramatically into the distance: the furrow at the extreme front edge of the canvas creates a recessional thrust that immediately embeds the viewer in clods of earth, as it directs the eye further into depth toward the distant, blazing sun. The sun's position at the recessional center of the horizon suggests that Van Gogh may have situated it with the aid of his perspective frame. Further evidence for this perspectivally correct impulse is provided by the trees originally flanking the sun but eventually painted over.[46] Van Gogh's spatial organization constitutes a three-tiered play on perspectival dynamics, summoning viewers into the picture plane and inserting them into all levels of the animated, worked space: he coaxes the eye to follow the path of the sower, to propel down the runner of the furrow and to alight unavoidably on the pivoted center of the sun at the exact horizon point at the back. Back to front, front to back, and diagonally across, Van Gogh incorporates viewers into *The Sower* canvas, enlisting them as active participants in his artistic practice of sacred embodiment.

If Van Gogh arrayed *The Sower* with perspectival signposts, Gauguin's *Vision after the Sermon* dramatizes a spatiality of obstruction. *The Vision*'s two zones, conveying Gauguin's conception of different levels of reality, are bisected by the tree, which acts not as a passageway into the distance but as a hurdle. Where Van Gogh's figure of the sower moves toward the viewer, whose eyes are simultaneously riveted in the open furrow, Gauguin's women visionaries—backs towards the beholder and flat against the edges of the canvas—impede the viewer from entering their mesmeric, spiritual field. The women's meditative isolation from one another is restated in their positioning as stalwart gatekeepers of the recessional space the beholder desires to penetrate. Where Van Gogh's *Sower* could serve as a primer on the workings of orthogonals and converging horizon lines, Gauguin's *Vision* shatters the rules of perspectival illusionism. The weightless cow, rootless tree and floating women at the left upper edges break with the conventions of pictorial organization. The biblical figures at the back appear to tilt up and out from their shallow space. And rather than pulling the viewer in towards a target, as Van Gogh moves the beholder through the worked field to a stasis on the sun, Gauguin catapults the background forward, suppressing perceptual exertion for a sudden dissolution of material reality by the imperious permeation of the dream.

Gauguin and Van Gogh conceived of different settings for these paintings. Gauguin wished to see his in a Breton church, returning his depiction of popular piety to the place where his subjects worshipped. "I wanted to give it to the Church of Pont-Aven," he wrote to Van Gogh in September 1888. It "would be all right in surroundings of bare stone and stained glass," he noted, and indeed a pair of stained glass windows in the apse of the Pont-Aven chapel portray angels whose unscrolling wings and radiant color scheme harmonize with *The Vision*'s.[47] One can imagine how Gauguin's painting might have functioned as part of a mutually reinforcing and interdependent field of religious experience, much like that analyzed by Michael Baxandall for an earlier period, where sermon, gesture, and painting operated as indivisible and interacting steps in a communal choreography of worship.[48] While the curés in Pont-Aven and the neighboring village of Nizon refused the offer to hang *The Vision* in their chapels, Gauguin's conception of its religious role highlights his determination to link his artistic vision to the elemental visual faith he imputed to Breton peasants.[49]

Van Gogh's comments on *The Sower* also suggest his interest in a reciprocal connection with his peasant subjects, but unlike Gauguin, in construing a function for his symbolist experiment, he focused not on worship but on work. In describing *The Sower* to Bernard, he related it to traditional popular prints that combine prototypes of reverent toil with information on farming: "I would much rather make naïve pictures out of old almanachs, those old 'farmer's almanachs' in which hail, snow, rain, fair weather are depicted in a wholly primitive manner."[50] In seeking to hang *The Vision* in a village church, Gauguin hoped to commune with what he called the "very rustic, very *superstitious*" simplicity of Breton peasant faith.[51] Van Gogh's discussion of *The Sower*'s function pointed to another kind of word-image interaction: a community storehouse of pictorial and verbal information to aid farmers' proficiency at cultivation.

When Van Gogh and Gauguin began working together in Arles in the fall of 1888, their incompatible conceptions quickly surfaced. "In general, Vincent and I agree on very few topics, especially not on painting," Gauguin wrote to Bernard in November.[52] Yet, the two artists did engage in a short and intense, if strained, period of reciprocal influence. Gauguin urged Van Gogh to relinquish the model and paint from imagination. Van Gogh produced only one such painting, the *Memory of the Garden at Etten* (fig. 12.3). Gauguin executed a companion scene, *Old Women of Arles [The Arlésiennes]* (fig.12.4). Gauguin's motif is from "one of the gardens opposite the Yellow House."[53] The garden's bench, pond, and path are depicted but barely recognizable in an arbitrary, unmodeled rendering. The women's procession moves from the distant path to a foreground bush, shaped like

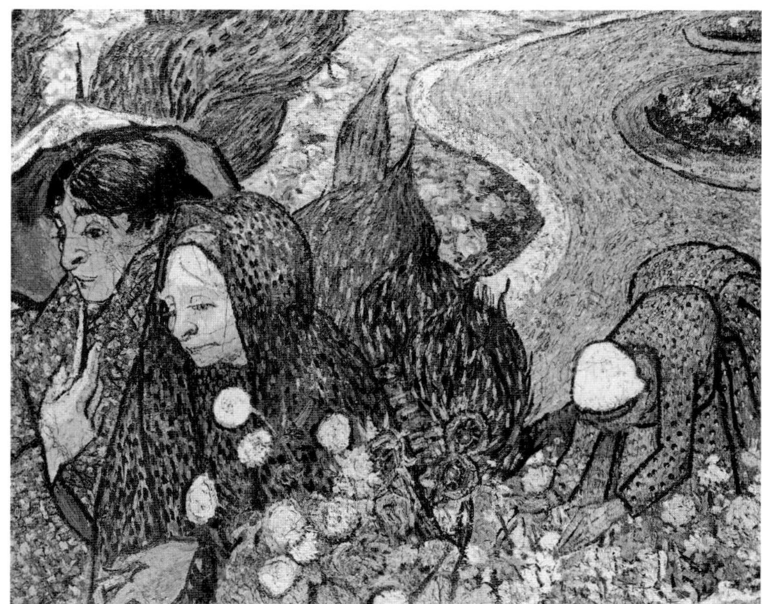

FIGURE 12.3. Vincent van Gogh, *Two Women Taking a Walk in a Park (Memory of the Garden at Etten)*, 1888. The State Hermitage Museum, St. Petersburg, Russia. Photo: Scala/Art Resource, NY.

the artist's profile and with a definable eye at its right.[54] In the back left, a trunkless, rootless tree is intimated by gossamer branches. The delicate leaves melt into a green bench below, which, cut off at the top of the painting, tilts up and hangs, its wispy legs as weightless and insubstantial as the feathery cow at the upper left of *The Vision after the Sermon*. Gauguin applied the paint in thin layers and light strokes in the *Old Women of Arles*. Its strong canvas was from a twenty-meter roll he purchased in Arles, coarse burlap of "heavy, textured weave."[55] Before painting on it, Gauguin primed the surface to disguise its rugged texture. When the thinned oil paint was applied, it "was permitted to seep into the fabric" and produce a filmy matte effect, like a fresco, which diminished the "physicality of the image" and enabled it to "relate more to the non-corporeal realm of ideas . . . as the true subject matter of painting."[56] The dissimulation of the graininess of the canvas is particularly striking in Gauguin's rendering of the women's shawls, which presumably protect them against the harsh mistral winds. Yet, like the immaterial "cloak for the idea," Gauguin treated the women's shawls not as textiles of some consistency, but as wispy coverings for a realm of irreducible essences. The second woman in the procession wears a shawl whose thinness is emphasized by an almost transparent brushwork that lets the matte canvas underneath show through—a double layer of pictorial dematerialization.

While *Memory of the Garden* amplified Van Gogh's symbolist conception of evocative form, it also demonstrates the obstacles to his embrace of the incorporeal idealism that came so easily to Gauguin. "Gauguin gives me the courage to imagine things, and certainly things from the imagination take on a more mysterious character," Van Gogh wrote to Theo, describing his work on this painting.[57] Yet, his venture into the realm of mystery and imagination quickly alighted on memories of real things and people that could be rearticulated by internal scrutiny even when no external models were present. Van Gogh wrote that the painting was "a memory of our garden at Etten, with cabbages, cypresses, dahlias, and figures."[58] The figures of the old woman and the younger lady in colored shawls were suggested by his mother and sister Wil, although he himself said they

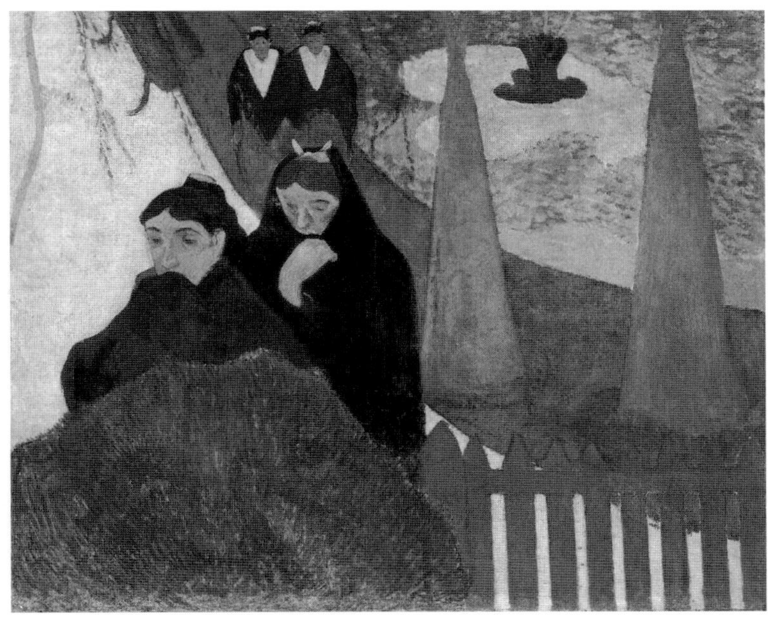

FIGURE 12.4. Paul Gauguin, *Les Arlésiennes (Old Women of Arles)*, 1888. The Art Institute of Chicago; Mr. and Mrs. Lewis Larned Coburn Memorial Collection, 1934.391. Photo © The Art Institute of Chicago.

were more impressions than exact likenesses and that the juxtapositions of meandering lines and bright color contrasts may "fail to give the garden a vulgar resemblance, but may present it to our minds as seen in a dream, depicting its character, and at the same time stranger than it is in reality."[59] To be sure, the *Memory of the Garden* went beyond the limits of a specific site and memory. As scholars have noted, the image is a composite, "in which the physical features of the gardens of Arles pure are blended with memories of the gardens at Nuenen and Etten that Van Gogh had known in his youth."[60]

One of Van Gogh's most "abstract" compositions, the *Memory* nonetheless reaffirms the core principles of his sacred realism. While the painting essayed a Gauguinesque tactic of obstructed horizon and obliterated recessionals, the dense, textrous paint application and fascination with the fibrous quality of canvas expose the distance between the *Memory of the Garden* and Gauguin's *Old Women of Arles*. Gauguin invented procedures to smooth down his abraded burlap surface, which enabled the thin colors to melt away into the chalky ground. Van Gogh, by contrast, executed the *Memory of the Garden* by building up a thick patterned deposit of laced color strokes.

While the shawls draped on the figures in Gauguin's female procession in the Arles garden are thinned pretexts for the incorporeal, the shawls in Van Gogh's *Memory* reconstitute the physicality of his paintings emulating weaving. Preoccupied from his earliest apprenticeship with woven subjects, Van Gogh packed the shawls not only with reminiscences of those in his Hague drawings, but with the lessons of the Nuenen hand-loom weavers. When he described the younger woman as wearing a "Scottish shawl" of "green and orange checks," he recalled the plaid cloth he had watched being woven in Nuenen.[61] The *Memory of the Garden at Etten* also returned to the visual techniques that had accompanied Van Gogh's persistent presentation of woven objects: the articulation of texturally heightened paint surfaces as pictorial equivalents to the woven cloth represented. The entire surface of the *Memory* bears a thick, raised, grainy deposit replicating the woven qualities of the shawls depicted and reemphasizing in its coarse facture the woven surface to which it was applied.

The formal coherence of the *Memory* points to Van Gogh's resistance to freeing painting from the penetrative encounter with matter and suggests he recorporealized in paint sediment the missing presence of the model, "the possible and the true." The differences between Van Gogh's and Gauguin's paintings of 1888 are rooted in the cultures that formed them and offer two historically specific responses to the paradox at the heart of all Symbolist painting: how to link the seen and the unseen, the visible image to an invisible domain inaccessible to artist and spectator.

Notes

Originally published in *Lost Paradise: Symbolist Europe*, exh. cat. (Montreal: Musée des Beaux-Arts, 1995), 104–15.

The epigraphs are from Paul Gauguin, letter to Emile Schuffenecker, 1888, quoted in Robert Goldwater, *Gauguin* (New York: Abrams, 1983), 26; Vincent van Gogh, letter to Emile Bernard, late October 1888, in Vincent van Gogh, *The Complete Letters of Vincent van Gogh*, 2nd ed., vol. 3 (Boston: New York Graphic Society, 1978), 518.

1. Quoted in Richard Brettell, Françoise Cachin, Claire Frèches-Thory, and Charles Stuckey, *The Art of Paul Gauguin*, exh. cat. (Washington, D.C.: National Gallery of Art, 1988), 103; 104 for "the path of symbolism."
2. Robert Goldwater, "Symbolic Form–Symbolic Content," in *Acts of the XXth International Congress of the History of Art*, vol. 4 (Princeton, 1963), 91–133. See also *Art Journal* 45, no. 2 (Summer 1985), special issue on "Symbolist Art and Literature," ed. Sharon Hirsh.
3. Letter to Bernard, late July 1888, in Van Gogh, *Letters*, vol. 3, 503.
4. Gauguin was a boarding student at the Petit séminaire de la Sainte-Chapelle in Orléans from 1859 to 1862, where he was taught by the bishop of Orléans himself, Monsignor Dupanloup. A national Catholic educational reformer, Bishop Dupanloup devised a new curriculum and catechism at the Petit séminaire, which I believe had a profound impact on Gauguin's receptivity to subjectivist, idealist, and antirational definitions of reality and self-expression. Van Gogh, by contrast, was raised in his parents' version of Dutch Reformed Calvinism, the Groningen School Theology, also known as the Evangelicals, which stressed the humanist imitation of Christ through enacted faith, service, and the sanctification of labor. Van Gogh studied in the Tilburg state high school under C. C. Huysmans, a painter and Arts and Crafts reformer who, like a William Morris of Holland, encouraged his pupils to "learn how to see" and to integrate beauty into everyday objects. These anti-idealist tendencies were amplified by Van Gogh's exposure as a theology student to a religious reform movement within Dutch Calvinism called "modernism," which prompted antisupernaturalism and a belief system based in nature, emanation, and human expressive consciousness. For a detailed discussion, see Debora Silverman, *Weaving the Picture: A Life of Vincent van Gogh* (in progress), chap. 8 [see also Silverman, *Van Gogh and Gauguin: The Search for Sacred Art* (New York: Farrar, Straus and Giroux, 2000)].
5. Letter to Theo, summer 1885, in Van Gogh, *Letters*, vol. 2, 402 (emphasis his). The Arles *Sower* of 1888 returned to the Millet subject Van Gogh had attempted numerous times between 1881 and 1884. For discussion and illustration, see Louis van Tilborgh, "The Sower," in *Van Gogh and Millet* (Zwolle: Waanders, 1989), 156–77.
6. For discussion of the alterations between the two states of the *Sower* painting, see Ronald Pickvance, *Van Gogh in Arles* (New York: Metropolitan Museum of Art, 1984), 102–3; and Evert van Uitert, Louis van Tilborgh, and Sjaar van Heugten, *Van Gogh: Paintings* (Milan: Arnoldo Mondadori Arte, 1990), 128–29.
7. Van Gogh, *Letters*, vol. 3, 226; vol. 2, 591. The religious sources underpinning Van Gogh's identification with labor are complex, deriving not from a unitary Calvinism but from a number of competing sources within Calvinism that Van Gogh absorbed in the Netherlands and Great Britain. The importance of these religious legacies has been reemphasized in Tsukasa Kōdera, *Vincent van Gogh: Christianity versus Nature* (Amsterdam and Philadelphia: John Benjamins, 1990), especially chap. 1. On the centrality of Van Gogh's parents' Groningen Theology of service, as well as the pre- and post-Arles patterns of association with weavers and peasants, see Debora Silverman, "Weaving Paintings: Religious and Social Origins of Vincent van Gogh's Pictorial Labor," in Michael S. Roth, ed., *Rediscovering History: Culture, Politics, and the Psyche* (Stanford: Stanford University Press, 1994), 137–68; and Silverman, *Weaving the Picture*. For an analysis of the significance

of the populist religious tradition of John Bunyan that Van Gogh assimilated during his English period, see Debora Silverman, "Pilgrim's Progress and Vincent van Gogh's *Metier*," in *Van Gogh in England: A Portrait of the Artist as a Young Man*, exh. cat. (London: Barbican Art Gallery, 1992), 98–115.

8. Van Gogh, *Letters*, vol. 3, 493.
9. Ibid. The ingenuity and flexibility of this system recalls Van Gogh's other craft tool, the perspective frame, built in collaboration with a carpenter and blacksmith in The Hague in 1882. The frame was adjustable and operated outside by being staked into the ground and secured on its frame with adjustable iron pegs, illustrated and described by Van Gogh in *Letters*, vol. 1, 383, 431–33. Van Gogh was still using the perspective frame in Arles, and during the time he was working on *The Sower*, he was giving a new friend, Paul Milliet, art lessons and training in perspective with the frame. This is also discussed in Van Gogh, *Letters*, vol. 3, 493.
10. By 1885 Van Gogh had begun loading the pigment in rough-hewn, bricklike applications, choosing deep earth tones and mudlike coloring, and applying colors as fibers and paint strokes as threads to the canvas so as to intersect like the woof and weft of weaving a coarse fabric. The emergence of this form of pictorial labor is discussed in Silverman, "Weaving Paintings" and *Weaving the Picture*.
11. "This blasted mistral makes it very hard to get one's brushwork firm"; Van Gogh to Theo, in *Letters*, vol. 3, 57; the compositional alterations on *The Sower* toward heightened density are discussed in Pickvance, *Van Gogh in Arles*, 102–3.
12. Van Gogh, *Letters*, vol. 3, 226.
13. Ibid., 233.
14. Ibid., 492.
15. Van Gogh was certainly familiar with the parable of the sower (Matthew 13:2–9, 18–23; Luke 8:4–15; and Mark 4:13–20), and it is significant that he does not invoke the biblical precedent explicitly. See Van Tilborgh, "The Sower," 156. For accounts of the "religious overtones" of the image, see Evert van Uitert, "Van Gogh's Concept of his *Oeuvre*," *Simiolus* 12 (1981–82): 239; and Judy Sund, "The Sower and the Sheaf: Biblical Metaphor in the Art of Vincent van Gogh," *Art Bulletin* 70 (1988): 660–76.
16. Van Gogh, *Letters*, vol. 2, 597, 591 (emphasis his).
17. Van Tilborgh, "The Sower," 177.
18. Van Gogh, *Letters*, vol. 2, 597.
19. Ibid., vol. 3, 44.
20. Van Uitert et al., *Van Gogh: Paintings*, 128.
21. Pickvance, *Van Gogh in Arles*, 103.
22. In another version of *The Sower* painted in November 1888 (F450, in J. B. de la Faille, *The Works of Vincent van Gogh: His Paintings and Drawings* [Amsterdam: Meulenhoff, 1970]), Van Gogh used the disk of the sun as a halo for the sowing figure, placing it directly behind him. According to Kōdera, this sun-as-halo may have originated in Van Gogh's exposure to images of the sower and the sun and to depictions of solar festivals in the illustrated magazine *Le Courrier français* of 1886. However, Van Gogh's earlier invocation of Delacroix's exemplary "symbolic color" in Christ's aureole as a model for the evocative colorism of the July 1888 *Sower* suggests a more obvious and fundamental transposition of religious precedent to a rural form and content. For Kōdera's argument, see his *Vincent van Gogh: Christianity versus Nature*, 27–39, especially 30–33.
23. Van Gogh, *Letters*, vol. 3, 503.
24. Ibid., 504.
25. Quoted in Mark A. Cheetham, *The Rhetoric of Purity: Essentialist Theory and the Advent of Abstract Painting* (New York: Cambridge University Press, 1991), 4; see also 7.
26. Belinda Thomson, *Gauguin* (London: Thames and Hudson, 1987), 25; Charles Morice, cited in Georges Hamilton, *Painting and Sculpture in Europe, 1880–1940* (Harmondsworth, England: Penguin, 1967), 80.
27. Quoted in Linda Nochlin, ed., *Impressionism and Post-Impressionism, 1874–1904: Sources and Documents* (Englewood Cliffs, N.J.: Prentice-Hall, 1966), 158 (emphasis his).
28. Quoted in Goldwater, *Gauguin*, 58.
29. On completing the painting, Gauguin explained that "this year I have sacrificed everything—execution, color—for style, because I wished to force myself into doing something other than what I know how to do." Quoted in Brettell et al., *Art of Paul Gauguin*, 103.
30. Cheetham, *Rhetoric of Purity*, 17, recovering Gauguin's intellectual debt to Neoplatonist philosophy. Cheetham's effort to take Gauguin seriously as a thinker is important, though I believe he oversecularizes Gauguin's modernism and ignores the preexisting religious mentality that facilitated Gauguin's receptivity to Neoplatonism in the 1880s.
31. Quoted in ibid., 4.
32. Letter of October 16, 1888, to Schuffenecker, quoted in Brettell et al., *Art of Paul Gauguin*, 104.
33. Quoted in ibid., 103.
34. Ibid., 104; Hamilton, *Painting and Sculpture in Europe*, 84. To be sure, Van Gogh and Gauguin shared this ad-

miration for Japanese prints, and indeed, Gauguin may have seen Van Gogh's adaptation of Hiroshige's *Plum Trees—Japonaiserie: The Tree* (1887)—before beginning work on *The Vision after the Sermon.* Yet, Van Gogh and Gauguin translated their common interest in Japanese prints into their own idioms. Unlike the diagonal slicing of Gauguin's tree in the *Vision,* Van Gogh's *Japonaiserie* was an exercise in viewing juxtapositions of near and far, and looking through keyholes in the branches or flanked branch frames. This type of viewing accorded well with Van Gogh's preexisting interest in such juxtapositions in seventeenth- and nineteenth-century Dutch painting, as well as with the framed and telescoped viewing structured by his own perspective frame. More generally, Van Gogh assimilated Japanese prints to enhance his paintings' surface textures; in Paris he attempted to emulate the rough fabric surfaces of the Japanese crepons with his brushstroke. Rather than texture, Gauguin celebrated the flatness and unmodulated color areas of wood-block prints. On the multiple possibilities of the Japanese model, especially the juxtaposition of near and far, see Kirk Varnedoe, *A Fine Disregard: What Makes Modern Art Modern* (New York: Abrams, 1990), 55–78. On Van Gogh's emphasis on Japonism as texture, see Silverman, "Weaving Paintings" and *Weaving the Picture.*

35. As Gauguin commented, "The cow under the tree is tiny in comparison with reality, and is rearing up." Quoted in Brettell et al., *Art of Paul Gauguin,* 103.
36. See ibid., 104. The critic Edouard Dujardin characterized Gauguin's *Vision after the Sermon* as the emblem of a new style he dubbed "cloisonnism," resembling the cloisonné technique in enameling "whereby metal partitions or *cloisons* are used to divide one area of brightly colored enamel from another." Thomson, *Gauguin,* 67. Gauguin's experiments with thirteenth- and fourteenth-century glass design and its translation into oil are noted by his contemporary the painter A. S. Hartrick, in *A Painter's Pilgrimage through Fifty Years* (Cambridge: Cambridge University Press, 1939), 34. On cloisonnism, see the discussion of Gauguin in Bogomila Welsh-Ovcharov, *Vincent van Gogh and the Birth of Cloisonism,* exh. cat. (Toronto: Art Gallery of Ontario, 1981), 168–226; and Henri Dorra, *Symbolist Art Theories: A Critical Anthology* (Berkeley: University of California Press, 1994), 102.
37. Gauguin, quoted in Brettell et al., *Art of Paul Gauguin,* 103.
38. Ibid.
39. The term of Brettell, ibid., 104, who does not, however, discuss the contrasting color ranges between the women and the supernatural figures and terrain.
40. Letter to Van Gogh, Le Pouldu, October 20, 1889, quoted in Françoise Cachin, *Gauguin: The Quest for Paradise* (New York: Abrams, 1992), 142.
41. Gauguin, letter to Schuffenecker, 1885 (emphasis his), quoted in Nochlin, ed., *Impressionism and Post-Impressionism,* 159. Gauguin's phrase "glimpse of the dream" is quoted in Cachin, *Gauguin: Quest for Paradise,* 144.
42. Letter to Bernard, 1889, in Van Gogh, *Letters,* vol. 3, 522.
43. This analysis is drawn from an extremely interesting article on Symbolist surfaces by Reinhold Heller, "Concerning Symbolism and the Structure of the Surface," 148–49, in the special issue of *Art Journal* cited in note 2 above. It is one of few articles that explore the formal mechanisms of 1880s Symbolist pictorial innovation within a comparative context.
44. Ibid., 148–49.
45. For Van Gogh's choice of colors, see Van Gogh, *Letters,* vol. 3, 492; for Gauguin's, see Brettell et al., *Art of Paul Gauguin,* 104.
46. Van Gogh often relied on anchoring trees or posts to flank objects depicted in the picture plane during his Hague period, in reference to his own framed view through the posts of his perspective frame. On the melding of Van Gogh's staked perspective tool and flanking compositional format, see Silverman, "Weaving Paintings" and *Weaving the Picture.*
47. Gauguin's proposal of the chapel site is in Brettell et al., *Art of Paul Gauguin,* 103; a description of the church windows and their possible harmonization with *The Vision* is suggested by Ziva Amishai-Michels, *Gauguin's Religious Themes* (New York: Garland 1985), 28–29.
48. See Michael Baxandall, *Painting and Experience in Fifteenth-Century Italy* (London: Oxford University Press, 1972).
49. The episodes of the offers and explanations to the curés, and their perplexed and diffident reactions, are noted in Brettell et al., *Art of Paul Gauguin,* based on Bernard's rendering, which can be found in his "L'Aventure de ma vie," introduction to *Lettres de Paul Gauguin à Emile Bernard, 1888–1891* (Geneva: Callier, 1954).
50. Letter to Bernard, June 1888, in Van Gogh, *Letters,* vol. 3, 492.
51. Quoted in Brettell et al., *Art of Paul Gauguin,* 103 (emphasis Gauguin's).
52. Quoted in ibid., 113.

53. Pickvance, *Van Gogh in Arles*, 217.

54. Pickvance, ibid., disagrees with the writers who have interpreted the bush as bearing the features of Gauguin's profile. Whether the bush precisely resembles Gauguin or not, it does configure an eye on its right side. Gauguin thereby invests a natural form with an animate quality, another indication of his conviction that there are "supernatural phenomena" of which we nevertheless "have the *sensation*."

55. Gauguin, quoted in Brettell et al., *Art of Paul Gauguin*, 112; see also Heller, "Concerning Symbolism," 148.

56. This discussion of the primer, the fusion of medium and support, and the dissimulation of paint structure relies on Heller, "Concerning Symbolism," 148–49.

57. Quoted in Pickvance, *Van Gogh in Arles*, 214; see the letter to Theo, about November 1888, in Van Gogh, *Letters*, vol. 3, 105.

58. Van Gogh, *Letters*, vol. 3, 104.

59. Letter to Wil, ibid., 447–48.

60. Brettell et al., *Art of Paul Gauguin*, 117. See also Pickvance, *Van Gogh in Arles*, 216, who notes that the "memory" of the family gardens is "evidently a conflation of those at Etten and Nuenen."

61. The description of the checkered "Scottish shawl" in the *Memory* is in the letter to Wil, in Van Gogh, *Letters*, vol. 3, 447. For the Hague shawls, see, for example, the 1882–83 pencil and lithographic chalk drawing of *Girl with a Shawl, Half Figure* (F1008); and the 1882 pencil, ink, and watercolor *Old Woman with Walking Stick and Shawl* (F913). On the selection of woven objects during the Hague period, and the persistent reliance on woven color schemes, brushwork, and compositional formats in Van Gogh's later periods, see Silverman, "Weaving Paintings" and *Weaving the Picture*.

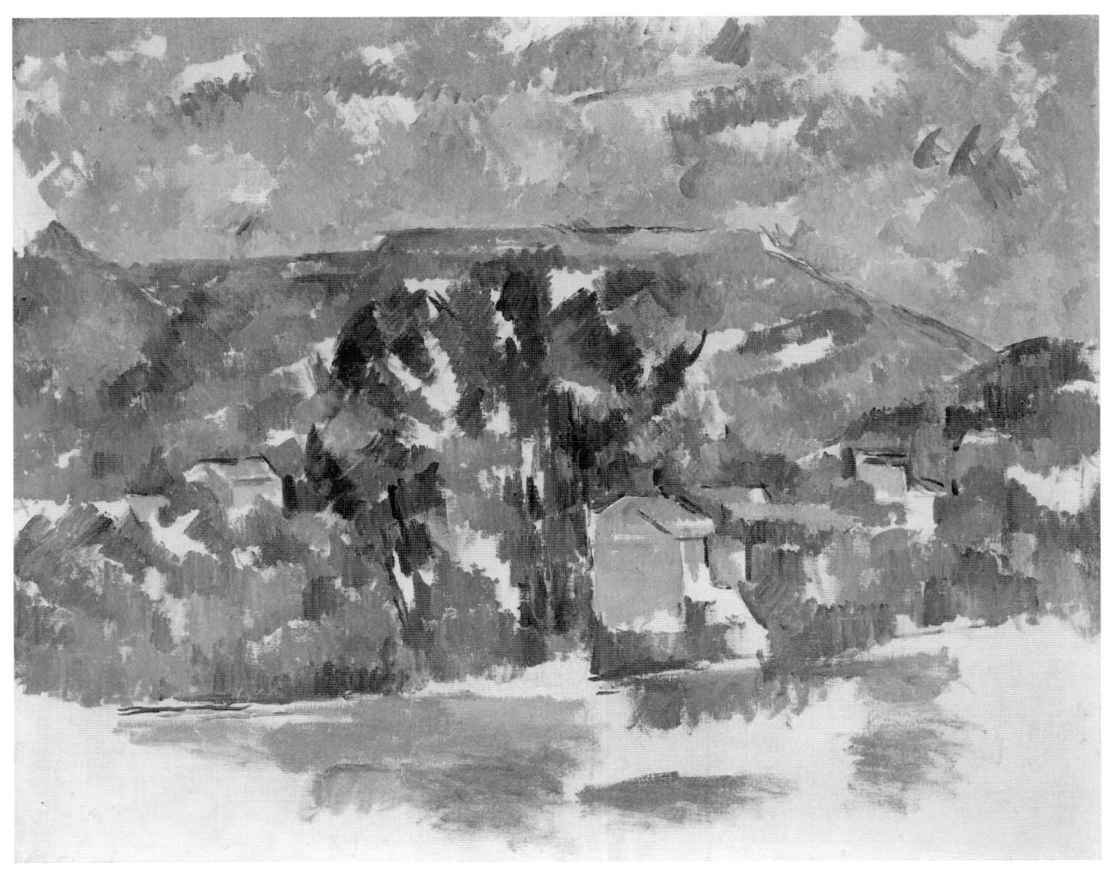

FIGURE 13.1. Paul Cézanne, *Le Mont de Cengle*, c. 1904–6. Foundation E.G. Bührle Collection, Zurich.

13

Mark, Motif, Materiality

The Cézanne Effect in the Twentieth Century

RICHARD SHIFF

"Everything"

Early in 1908 André Lhote received discomforting news: his Paris dealer, Clovis Sagot, had no enthusiasm for the new paintings that Lhote had sent; his work had lost its character, its originality (see fig. 13.2). "Lhote does Cézanne," were Sagot's words; "the whole Salon d'Automne was full of Cézanne from top to bottom."[1]

Everyone was "doing" Cézanne, and everyone, it seems, was aware of the fact during the years immediately preceding and following the painter's death in 1906. The newly famous Cézanne—more than Paul Gauguin, Georges Seurat, Vincent van Gogh, or Pierre-Auguste Renoir—was influencing, even overpowering, the younger generation, few of whom appeared equal to his challenge.[2] When the 1904 Salon d'Automne featured Cézanne with more than thirty paintings, critical reaction was mixed. In his review Raymond Bouyer referred to the work of Henri Matisse (see fig. 13.3) as "more Cézannean than Cézanne"—no compliment in this context, in which the writer characterized Matisse's source of inspiration as "feeble-minded" and "infirm." Bouyer regretted that Matisse and other former students of Gustave Moreau were adhering to a new dogma of *Cézannisme,* exchanging rational teaching for a cult of naive genius.[3] In 1905 Kees van Dongen shared at least some of Bouyer's concern; he rated Cézanne "the greatest painter of his time," but with one reservation: "How many moths are burning their wings in this light!"[4] Jacques-Emile Blanche held a similar opinion: "Cézanne's color charms me when it is in his canvases and disgusts me when it is in others."[5] Van Dongen and Blanche, both painters, were responding to an enquiry into the state of visual art conducted by the critic for *Mercure de France,* Charles Morice. Morice asked an open question: "What do you make of Cézanne?" He himself had seen that the entire 1905 Salon des Indépendants (Matisse included) amounted to a "vast homage to Cézanne."[6]

During the twentieth century Cézanne's influence—or, to put it more accurately, Cézanne's "effect," the Cézanne effect—never truly waned or dissipated.[7] From its initial outburst it became successively transformed and often difficult to recognize.

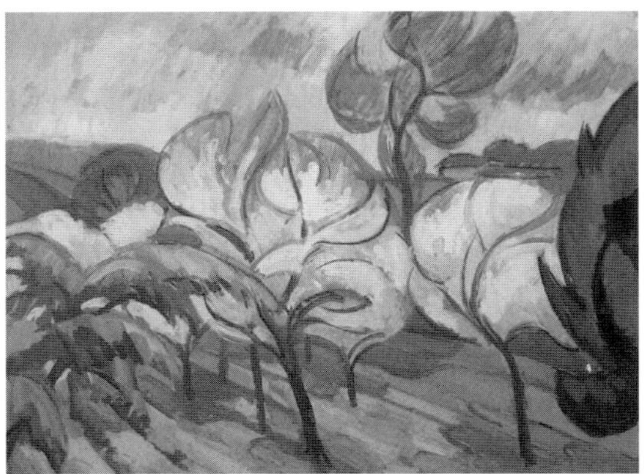

FIGURE 13.2. André Lhote, *Flowering Trees*, 1907, oil on paper. Musée National d'Art Moderne, Centre Georges Pompidou, Paris. © 2007 Artists Rights Society (ARS), New York/ADAGP, Paris. Photo: CNAC/MNAM/Dist. Réunion des Musées Nationaux/Art Resource, NY.

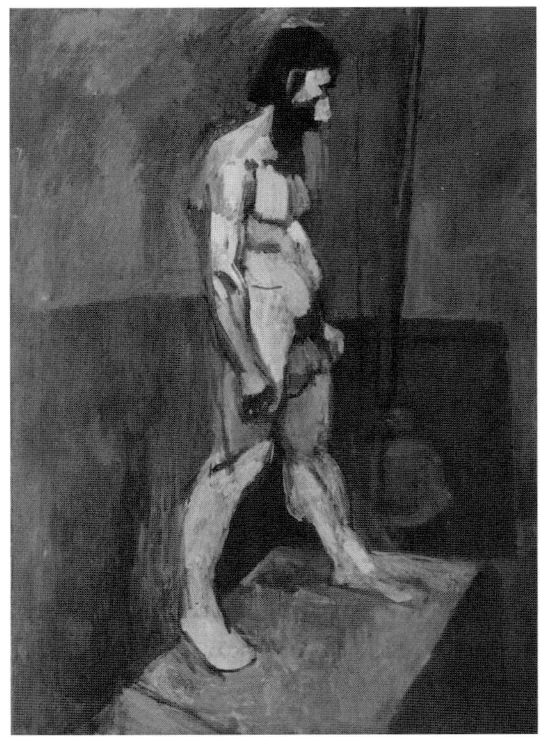

FIGURE 13.3. Henri Matisse, *Male Model*, c. 1900. The Museum of Modern Art, New York; Kay Sage Tanguy and Abby Aldrich Rockefeller Funds. © 2007 Succession H. Matisse, Paris/Artists Rights Society (ARS), New York. Digital Image © The Museum of Modern Art/Licensed by Scala/Art Resource, NY.

In someone like Lhote, however, with his dual occupation as Cubist painter and historically minded art theorist, the effect remained easy enough to detect throughout an entire career. In his studio work Lhote typically used sequences of parallel brushstrokes and angled patches of color to create a faceted Cézannean surface, and in his theoretical writings he was entirely unapologetic concerning the persistent Cézanne factor in the art of his generation. Instead of stressing the master's idiosyncrasies, Lhote (like many other theorists) linked Cézanne to the search for universal "plastic" or "pictorial" values, viewed as the fundamental goal of every artist at any moment regardless of personal orientation and historical exigencies.[8]

In a retrospective account from 1946, in which he explained the importance of the Cubist technique of *passage,* Lhote added that this device could be found in "Cézanne, *who contains everything*" (Lhote's emphasis).[9] Yet Lhote did not equate Cézanne's methods with those of his Cubist admirers. He implied instead that much of the "everything" found in Cézanne was there only in embryo—incomplete, intuitively grasped, perhaps somewhat confused, to be continued and developed by successors sensitive enough to comprehend the potential for aesthetic liberation.[10] This was the ultimate view of Maurice Denis, a major early supporter committed to aesthetic order who regarded Cézanne as an inspiring but incomplete autodidact: "This great artist had a singular weakness in being unable to practice any art of which he was not the creator."[11] Cézanne was compelled to do "everything" in his own way, to invent, or reinvent, every technique. He began; he did not finish: "I'm too old, I haven't realized, and now I won't realize. I remain the primitive of the way I've discovered."[12] To the American Clement Greenberg at mid-century, Cézanne was "the most copious source of what we know as modern art. . . . Because he had exhausted so little of his own insights, he could offer the Cubists all the resources of a new discovery."[13] His painting was an enduring promise of freedom, despite the amount of pastiche it seemed to induce.

This essay will not attempt to identify "everything" that younger generations derived from Cézanne, nor will it track their innumerable appropriations of his technique and imagery. I will be selective in the extreme, limiting my focus to two closely related aspects of his art that I believe have been critical to the development of a practice of painting designed to satisfy twentieth-century concerns. Both are features of a do-it-yourself artist, the Cézanne who every day made a new beginning from the pictorial materials at hand (even though he always acknowledged his interest in the Old Masters). Both enforce a sense of the painter's inherent incompletion or "unfinish" by implying the continuity of a process that has no natural end. The first is the discrete, digitized character of his brushstroke, his interminably additive "mark"; the second, the essential pictorialism—some would call it "abstraction"—of his mode of representation.

Pictorialism and Motif

The second of these features requires immediate clarification. By "pictorialism" I mean the tendency of a Cézanne picture to be organized by a self-generating, self-sustaining "motif." By 1900 it was common for critics and theorists to oppose pictorial motifs to narrative and allegorical themes derived from nonpictorial sources, such as religion, politics, and literature. Although pictorial, the "motif" never functioned as illustration. By extending its sense of specificity, some critics even opposed the "motif" to all *visual* models, whether picturesque views taken directly from nature or patterned after images from the history of art. The "motif" was something distinctively other, something unique; it would find no true analogy in a nonpictorial medium or even in a similar visual image.[14] Analogies to music were nevertheless tempting, not only because painting acquires its descriptive vocabulary from music ("rhythm," "harmony," "movement"), but also because musical composition has no precise literary equivalent. Like painting, its expression relies on nothing beyond the qualities of its own medium, as the Cubist Jean Metzinger argued in 1910: "Music does not attempt to imitate Nature's sounds, but [embodies] emotions awakened by Nature through a convention of its own . . . we [painters] construct decoratively pleasing harmonies and symphonies of color, expression of our sentiment."[15]

A motif is sometimes called a "motive." As the term implies, an artistic "motif" can both "move" (rhythmically) and be "moving" (emotively). It both motivates (moves or stimulates the artist) and is self-motivating (indicates and induces its own continuation). We might reason, however, that a materialized art never arises from nothing: it would have an origin or some prior existence in nature, in the mind of the painter, or in the natural inclinations and ingrained habits of the painter's hand. This is to conceive of the motif as an originary trace, a potential path of movement always available to be followed but not manifest until an artist actually does follow it, producing a picture: to be seen and known, a trace-motif must be traced. Although this distinction between actual motif and potential trace-motif can be articulated, it has no clear experiential dimension. Rendering a motif will not show whether it now exists for the first time or has existed in some sense previously. This is why we have such a difficult time deciding whether the coherence of a visual order, such as that perceived in one of Cézanne's landscapes, is a phenomenon that belongs to the landscape, to the painting tradition, to the painter, or to us.

Cézanne knew the same problem. One of the most detailed witness accounts, which records the visit by R. P. Rivière and J. F. Schnerb to the artist's studio in 1905, is typical in leaving a great degree of ambiguity: "Composition, according to Cézanne, should be the result of the working process *[du travail]*. Every motif recorded *[copié]* as it falls before the view of the painter should, through his study, become a perfectly balanced whole, not by mere choice, nor by selectiveness inspired by decorative taste, but according to the logic of the reproduction, by the

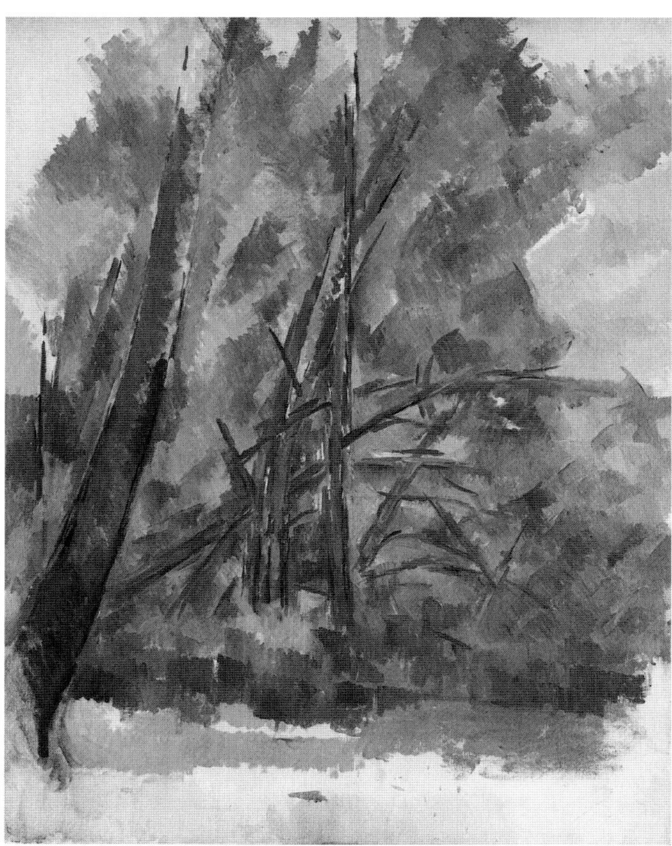

FIGURE 13.4. Paul Cézanne, *Arbres au Tholonet (Trees at Le Tholonet)*, 1900–1904. The Menil Collection, Houston. Photographed by Hickey-Robertson, Houston.

effort to balance the illuminated parts and the shaded parts."[16] Does such "logic" reflect a preconceived method of the artist? Or would it become evident only as the "working process" moved along, creating the picture? If Rivière and Schnerb had used the word *représentation* instead of *reproduction* (we will see that Cézanne himself may have done so), their sentence would still be ambiguous, but would tilt Cézanne's practice in the direction of a particular understanding of "motif"—the motif as true not only to the internalized sensation of the artist, but also to the internal development of the picture.

Late in his career, around the time he was visited by Rivière and Schnerb, as well as by Maurice Denis, Emile Bernard, and other interested artists and writers, Cézanne painted *Trees at Le Tholonet* (fig. 13.4). There he traced the position of tree trunks with multiple, segmented contour lines. ("Trace" is the natural term to use. To "trace" is to follow an existing course, but also to mark a course for the first time. The trees already existed, but Cézanne's picture was new.) These strokes or traces of paint, tentatively positioned and entirely characteristic of Cézanne's technique, are more like extended touches than conventional contours. He might have used them to seek out the perfect compositional arrangement and balancing of the elements of the forest. In terms of a "motif," however—much more of a process than a fixed order—these lines do not supplant but supplement one another. Each line, each stroke, is coordinated with all other colored marks, both angled patches and angled lines; and the whole is developed

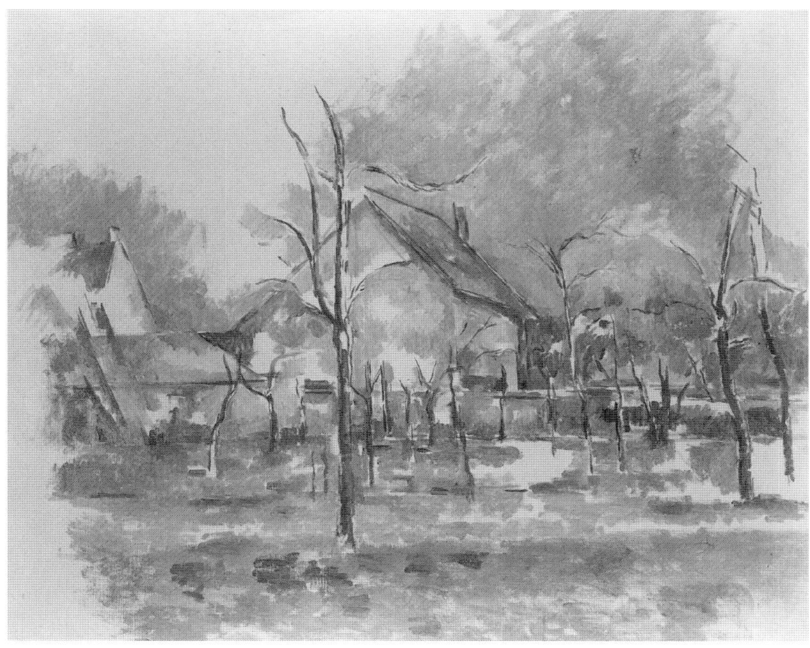

FIGURE 13.5. Paul Cézanne, *Winter Landscape, Giverny*, 1894. The Philadelphia Museum of Art; Gift of Frank and Alice Osborn, 1966. Photo: The Philadelphia Museum of Art/Art Resource, NY.

as a single, continuing rhythm and comprehensive harmony. Each mark traces the indications of some other mark, drawing out their mutual implications. It is the same with Cézanne's figure compositions: the instances of repetitious outlining in his late *Bathers* (plate 8) or the much smaller *Study of Bathers* (Rewald 874) establish a coordinated pictorial motif, as much as and even more than they define human bodies in action. The painted lines live and move, not the represented bodies.

This kind of pictorial "motif" also operates in a somewhat earlier landscape with a different type of surface structure, *Winter Landscape, Giverny* (fig. 13.5). Here the image seems to grow outwards, extending in a blocky, segmented fashion, until its movement is arrested, presumably when the artist ceased to work on the painting. (If Rewald's ascription of this work to Cézanne's November 1894 visit to Giverny is correct, then the abrupt end came when the painter decided to leave Monet's company.)[17] Although the termination of the motif (Cézanne's process of marking) would have been unforeseen and arbitrary, his discrete strokes remain integrated at every moment of his effort, with their order independent of any description of the scene in nature. It is as if the organic movement of *Winter Landscape, Giverny* belonged to the painting rather than the landscape and had simply been broken off, without becoming any less organic.

I am emphasizing the difference between one understanding of "motif" and another. A motif might be regarded as a scene in external nature, a choice of subject matter available to be captured in a rectangle by an artist adept at hand rendering, or captured equally well by a camera, or even in writing. Perhaps this is how Rivière and Schnerb actually understood the word, and Cézanne himself may have applied this meaning to *motif* in his everyday speech: "here, along the river, the motifs multiply."[18] Yet even in a statement such as this the meaning becomes insecure, because the "motifs" in this instance—a set of very similar views of trees, a stream, and a bridge (fig. 13.6)—were already more of an evolving visual theme than a fixed subject. Those who had direct

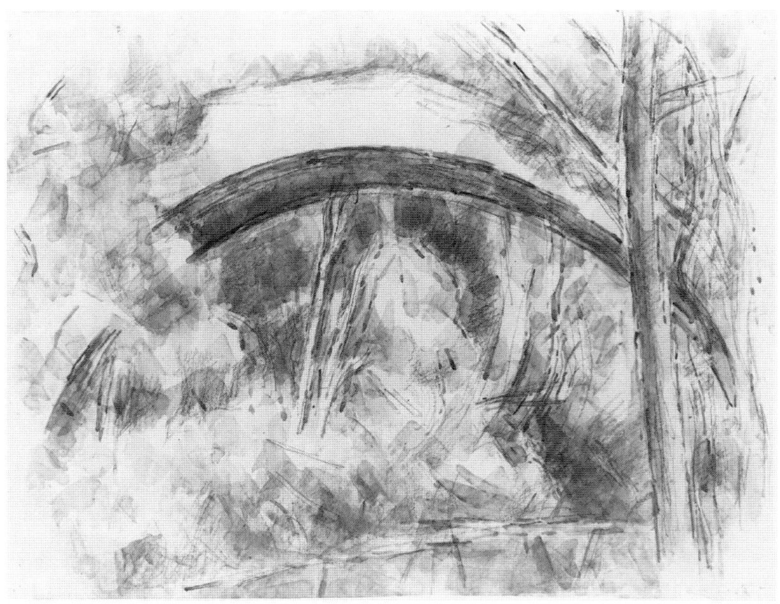

FIGURE 13.6. Paul Cézanne, *The Bridge of Trois Sautets*, 1906, watercolor and pencil. Cincinnati Art Museum, Gift of John J. Emery, 1951.298.

knowledge of Cézanne usually interpreted him as distinguishing little, if at all, between model and motif; and because the word itself acquired a special resonance in his case, it was often set off by italics or quotation marks: "He could do nothing without the model, or the 'motif.'"[19] The look of Cézanne's art convinced many of his viewers that his "motif" was in essence a pattern, harmony, or rhythm specific to his medium—a sensation or movement that became fully available to the painter only through his work. Whether or not it felt so to him, the "motif" was his creation.

This notion of an independent motif is the foundation of Maurice Denis's distinction, first elaborated in 1890, between "pictorial" form and preconceived, "literary" subject matter. Both terms encompass more than one might suspect. Initially, Denis used the example of a Byzantine Christ (formal, abstracted, emotive) in opposition to a typical modern painting of the same subject (naturalistic, literary, literal-minded).[20] Eventually, the critic applied this same distinction to Cézanne and his rediscovery of classical pictorial values: "He is so naturally a painter and so spontaneously classical. . . . He assembles colors and forms outside of any literary preoccupation . . . 'the subject [matter] disappears, there is only a *motif*.'"[21] Although Cézanne's "classicism" connoted tradition and stability, his "spontaneity" was consistent with the organic character of the "motif." With Cézanne, a classical order reemerged in harmony with the empirical facts of nature and an artist's sensations; this order was alive, unlike its "dead" or defunct academic counterpart.

Cézanne intuited that "you can't reproduce the sun but you can represent it" (a remark documented only by Denis). "The contrast of these two words, *reproduce* and *represent*," wrote Denis in 1906, "sums up our doctrine of a pictorial *[pictural]*, nonliterary Symbolism."[22] Denis also stated that the contrast of two other Cézannean terms, *modulation* and *modeling*, established something analogous: to modulate color was to unify and order the entirety of the pictorial surface, whereas the modeling of color was designed to recreate the look of a particular object under illumination.[23] With modeling, the motif would seem to derive from (or "reproduce") a view of nature; with modulation, the motif would become purely pictorial, a self-generating construction.

Abstraction and "Nothing"

All these distinctions—associated at the beginning of the twentieth century with what I will call "pictorialism"—were made with respect to paintings of traditional subjects: portraits and figure compositions, landscapes, still lifes, even genre scenes, and romantic fantasies. How did "pictorialism" convert this type of subject into "abstraction"?[24] For the moment, let this complicated matter rest on the fact that Denis himself asserted the connection through an account of his artist-critic colleague Charles Guérin. Guérin created scenes of Second Empire life with a technique of squarish, discrete marks of color. Although the narrative theme might be "literary," the method was essentially "abstract" because the paint application did not vary according to the subject matter, nor had it been developed through a study of nature. Given his contemporary's example, Denis reasoned that subject matter was becoming a mere "pretext for picturesque [or pictorial] inventions. . . . Painting tends no longer to be an art of imitation. . . . [Guérin] deliberately restricts himself to rendering the precise coloration of things, the logical relations of their tones, in sum, to painting only abstractions." The inspiration here, Denis duly noted, was Cézanne.[25] In a brief reply to Morice's 1905 inquiry into the state of modern art, Denis laid down a general principle: "I believe that the representational arts *[les arts d'imitation]* are evolving toward abstraction."[26] It was ironic that Cézanne, who usually disapproved of what he understood as "abstraction," was regarded as the most "evolved" in this direction, yet could not know it.[27]

One further irony: from a broader perspective, the generational shift from "reality" to "abstractions"—Denis's words[28]—was an aspect of a certain social pathology, a defense against the declining humanity of "real" everyday life (I will return to this issue). Denis disapproved of many of the more extreme pictorial responses to Cézanne and soon altered the valence he gave to "abstraction," disassociating it from his revered master. He wrote in 1907 that Cézanne "does not compromise [his synthesis] with any abstraction."[29] By 1920 Denis made certain to distance Cézanne from those who entertained "Cubist or post-Cubist theories," became "impassioned over abstractions," or would "systematically deform" objects in a misguided attempt to follow the master's still lifes.[30] Denis had had enough of "polyhedrons, tubular forms, women without heads, faces without a nose"; he now rejected any practice premised on "the concept of the picture as such" if it excluded "the imitation of nature."[31]

As Denis's wary commentary implies, the idea of pictorial abstraction—or, what he had once seen favorably as "pure painting," "la conception vraiment 'peintre' du tableau"[32]—had lodged in the minds of younger twentieth-century artists. It remained there, a problematic matter regarded as both a symptom and a cure for the malaise of modernity and the modern individual's diminished soul. The concept had appeared initially with another influential Cézanne proselytizer who, like Denis, was also to have second thoughts, Emile Bernard: "He opened to art this amazing door: painting for itself. . . . The more [Cézanne] works, the more his work removes itself from the external view [and] the more he abstracts the picture."[33] A final irony: Bernard's description may have better fitted his own early painting (see fig. 13.7), which resembled the style of Cézanne but also that of Gauguin and a number of Symbolists and Neo-Impressionists—work Cézanne disdained.[34]

Subsequent critics commonly associated abstraction with Cézanne, for better or worse. Francis Carco wrote in 1924: "In his 'Bathers' there is not the slightest sexual attraction. . . . Cézanne presents bodies modeled [or formed, *pétris*] from abstract color [and] torsos that become two parallel lines."[35] Here the descriptive term *pétri* evokes particularly strong, physical manipulation. As Carco contrasts Cézanne to Renoir, the former's image of bathers assumes the purely *material* properties of its constituent colors and lines, with any potential eroticism (as well as any spirituality) being muted, as if everything other than brute matter had been beaten down or flattened by the force of the painter's handling. Carco's statement contradicts the more typical view of abstraction as either intellectualizing or spiritualizing.[36]

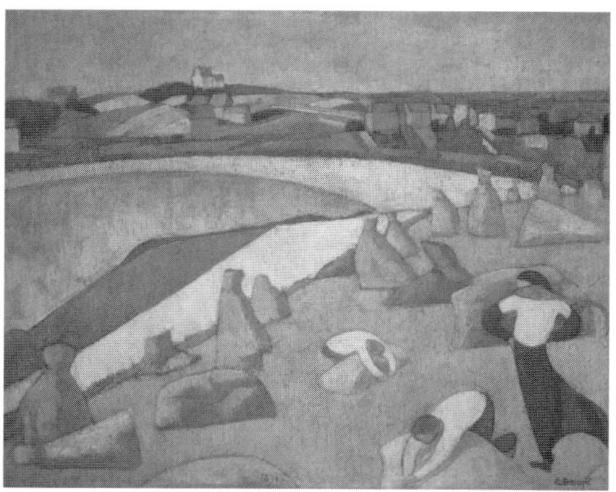

FIGURE 13.7. Emile Bernard, *Harvesting at the Sea Shore*, 1891. Musée d'Orsay, Paris. Photo: Réunion des Musées Nationaux/Art Resource, NY. Photographed by Hervé Lewandowski.

The complex reaction to Cézanne's art calls for more than a mere characterization of his "mark" and "motif." The historian risks confusing the terms of Cézanne's late nineteenth-century painting with a kind of abstraction and pictorial materialism that grew ever more familiar as the twentieth century advanced. Such confusion actually has substantial historical validity. By citing early critical commentary, I want to suggest that Cézanne's viewers were preoccupied with the "mark" and the "motif"—and with the "abstraction" of the picture, its material self-sufficiency—from the time the painter first gained a public audience. The impact of these features on later twentieth-century art can hardly be exaggerated. Critics acknowledged Cézanne's deep attachment to his landscape sites. Yet, whether promoting or resisting him, they concentrated on his technical innovations and idiosyncrasies. The attention given to his marks and strokes of color caused the specifics of his model in nature to become an ever less essential factor in the cultural significance of his art.

When Ambroise Vollard exhibited Cézanne in 1895 critics remarked, often with derision, that the image was incomplete.[37] Viewers inferred that the painter had failed—either in rendering the character of nature or in converting his chosen view into an acceptable composition. Like others, Thadée Natanson noted the lack but reached a more subtle conclusion: although Cézanne's pictures failed to convey many of the naturalistic and thematic elements people were accustomed to see, the artist provided instead an essential remainder: "all the rest that is nothing but painting." Natanson did not intend his remark as mere witticism, for he set it in italics as his central observation: "*tout ce reste qui n'est que peinture*."[38] This remainder, the "nothing," was "everything" to generations who followed.

Painting and Living

Cézanne, it was believed, had been a fanatic of painting. Georges Braque, who particularly identified with him, made the typical comment: "He bound his life into his art, his art into his life."[39] Little but painting ever held Cézanne's attention. Although wealthy, he lived simply and reclusively; he was suspicious of others' motives and determined not to let anything interfere with his work.[40] "I always found him completely alone," recalled one young admirer.[41] Another speculated that the artist was shrewd enough to have dissembled: "He often exaggerated the strangeness of his conduct in order to protect his freedom."[42] It was loosely implied that Cézanne died in the very act of painting, fulfilling a desire or a prophesy he had once made explicit.[43] In 1907, just a few months after this death, Morice—formerly Gauguin's literary collaborator and well acquainted with the ironies of mythologized lives—captured Cézanne's character poignantly: "We hardly dare say Cézanne lived; he painted. . . . [His is] painting estranged from the course of life, painting with the aim of painting. . . . [His art constitutes] a tacit protest, a reaction—was this fully conscious? I don't know—[his work] remains a gesture, a sublime indicator [of modern society's problems]."[44]

Morice's 1907 summary is particularly informative because it suggests, more directly than most early commentaries, that the interest in Cézanne's achievement was related to tensions in bourgeois life under the conditions of modernity. Perhaps it was ill humor, but in 1902 Cézanne himself had complained of modern "progress," which he identified with the installation of electric street lighting.[45] Morice in 1905 used much broader terms: "The tyranny of science oppresses modern humanity."[46] Rather than carping about technology, he was referring to a pervasive materialism, a positivist mentality, and a misplaced faith in scientific method. One troubling sign was the seemingly mechanistic technique of Seurat and the influence of his Neo-Impressionist followers such as Henri-Edmond Cross, whose art was "cold and artificial" (see fig. 13.8).[47]

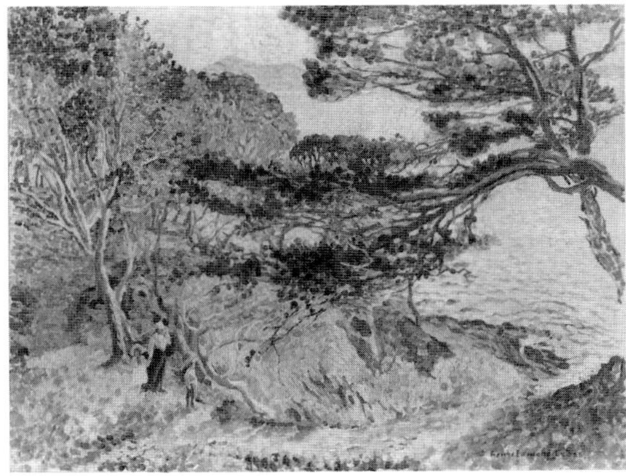

FIGURE 13.8. Henri-Edmond Cross, *Cap Layet (Large Version)*, c. 1904. Bayerische Staatsgemäldesammlungen, Neue Pinakothek, Munich.

Morice's analysis was true to a certain pattern shared by a great number of critics: if Impressionism (despite a pretense to accuracy of effect) was disorganized and "anarchic," then Neo-Impressionism went too far in the other direction, becoming "scientific." Within this framework Cézanne was regarded by some as sharing the worst dehumanizing qualities of both movements, and viewed by others as effecting a revitalizing synthesis.[48] To Morice himself, Cézanne appeared as a symptom of the same forces that were driving Neo-Impressionism. He reduced painting to "pure technique," to coloristic "values": "He is anxious, but only over knowing whether his values are right, and the humanity in his pictures has only the [moral] value of a [color] value."[49] This is a truly acid comment, perhaps directed more at the inane vogue for Cézanne (Morice was writing in 1905) than at the quality of the painter's work. In any event, Morice took Cézanne's apparent withdrawal from humanistic culture as a signal that conventional notions of art were failing present human needs: art would no longer be effective in revealing either universal or personal truths; it would no longer express the spirit of a race, nation, or era; nor would it embody a collective beauty, suitable for public decoration. In 1907 Morice called Cézanne's aesthetic one of "separation," so thoroughly did it break from these traditional ideals, cutting itself off from life, whether everyday life or a more idealized existence. Yet a different sense of living, of continuity, would emerge: life experienced not as a narrative sequence of human events, but as a continuity of pure aesthetic sensation, intensely personal. Although the artist never actually ceased to be concerned with the outside world, his peculiarity was to take "no more interest in a human face than in an apple . . . people and things impassioned him only with regard to their quality as objects to be painted. . . . [His concern was] painting in itself."[50] (Here I have combined Morice's statements of 1905 and 1907, before and after the death of the artist.)

It should not be surprising that, on balance, Morice's account is neither clearly positive nor clearly negative. The strongest artists—at once lauded and condemned—excite the entire range of feeling that surrounds the debates of a generation. Intelligent critics are likely to recognize competing values and have conflicted responses. Was Cézanne finding salvation through personal and aesthetic isolation? Or did his painting offer only escapism and denial? As if to moderate his persistent doubts, Morice cited a proven friend of Cézanne's generation, Théodore Duret, whose *Histoire des peintres impressionnistes* appeared in 1906, timely for Morice's purposes. There Duret described Cézanne as someone uninterested in either literary subjects or the expression of a human soul: "He devotes himself to

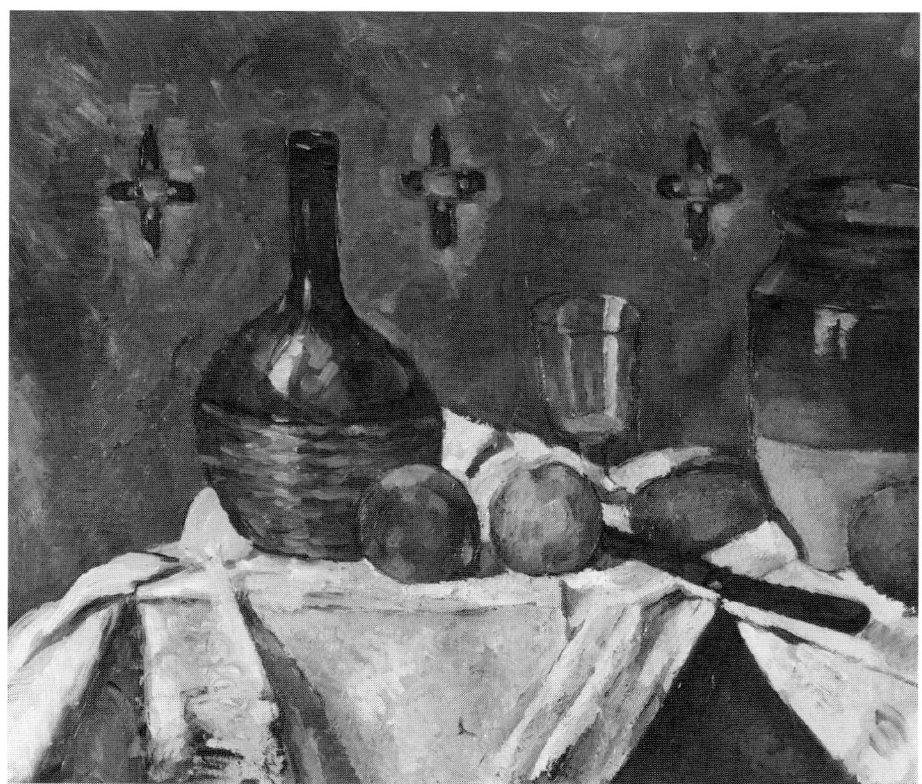

FIGURE 13.9. Paul Cézanne, *Still Life: Flask, Glass, and Jug*, c. 1877. The Solomon R. Guggenheim Museum, New York; Thannhauser Collection, Gift, Justin K. Thannhauser, 1978. Photo © The Solomon R. Guggenheim Foundation, New York.

painting what can be seen with the eyes . . . figures are set side by side without conveying any specific actions, above all to be painted."[51] Duret presented Cézanne's technique without passing judgment on it, yet indicated its provocation by alluding to a typical viewer's expectations: "For those who would want surfaces to be covered evenly, his execution, rough in spots and elsewhere leaving patches of canvas uncovered, may appear to be that of an incompetent; his application of colors of like value, juxtaposed or superimposed to result in a concentrated thickness, may seem gross, barbarous, monstrous."[52]

This is accurate description. Consider a relatively "finished" still life of the late 1870s, *Still Life: Flask, Glass and Jug* (fig. 13.9). It has a facture that ranges from a taut network of rectilinear marks in the apples and the flask to sections of loose patchwork and even scribbling in the tablecloth and the background wall—sometimes stiff, sometimes fluid, the combinations can seem arbitrary. In rendering the wall, Cézanne blended ochres and greens of similar value to no obvious mimetic purpose, creating the impression of a surface not flat but warped (because the variation in hue implies analogous variation in depth). Perhaps this effect, a common feature of the painter's work, can appear "gross, barbarous, monstrous"; yet the wall surface has been activated and enlivened, and projects itself forward as the object of a significant amount of artistic attention. This surface corresponds to the patterned wallpaper in Cézanne's Paris studio of 1877; it appears in a number of other works, including *Madame Cézanne in a Red Armchair* (fig. 13.10),

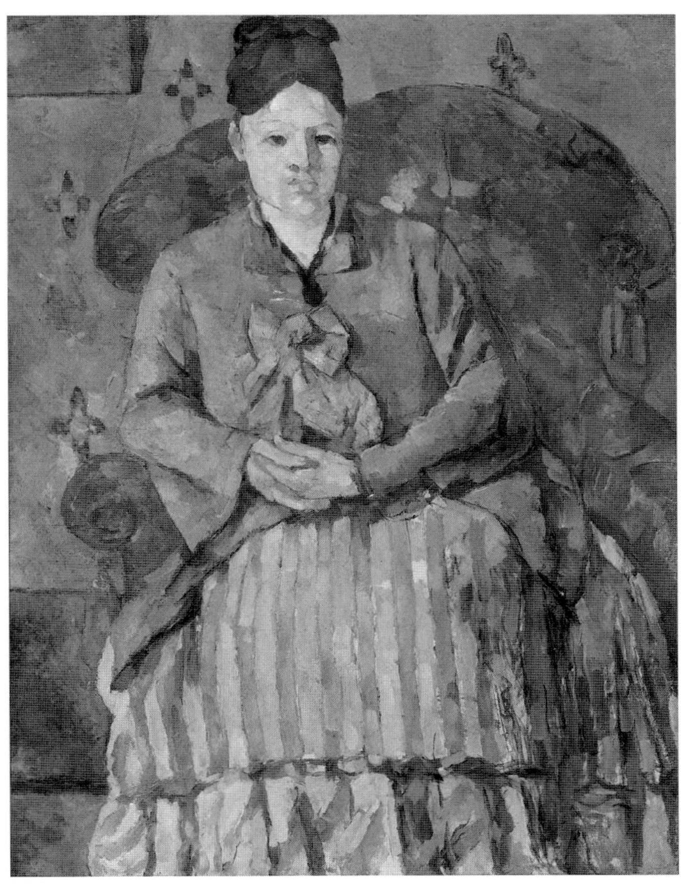

FIGURE 13.10. Paul Cézanne, *Mme. Cézanne in a Red Armchair*, c. 1877. Museum of Fine Arts, Boston; Bequest of Robert Treat Paine, 2nd, 44.776. Photo © 2007 Museum of Fine Arts, Boston.

which (by Cézannean standards) is also relatively "finished." It is less so, however, toward its lower edge, where several thin strokes of unmixed brilliant red can be seen along with patches of primed but otherwise unpainted canvas, indications of incompletion.

The initial viewers of *Madame Cézanne in a Red Armchair* would have been faced with yet another problem, one that Duret happened to address: in Cézanne's art "some apples and a napkin on a table assume the same grandeur as a human head."[53] Indeed, here the head has been rendered with the same blocky facture that the artist typically applied to his inanimate apples; and it exhibits about the same degree of articulation as the ornamental medallions punctuating the expanse of wall behind it. The figure's nose and eyes have a curious affinity to those medallions, which Cézanne distilled from what was, in reality, a more elaborate pattern. The Cubist generation considered such effects as Cézanne's discovery of "universal dynamism . . . the reciprocal modifications that inanimate material objects project upon one another."[54] The "motif" becomes a hybrid of the perceptual effects of these disparate real objects; it represents their interaction in human experience.

To take another pair of examples, two small portraits of the painter's son, Paul, from the early to middle 1880s: one is quite finished (fig. 13.11); the other is obviously incomplete (fig. 13.12).[55] A description of the former, attending to the way Cézanne structured the image, will reveal the motif: it is not to be found in the boy but in the picture. Pictorially, a set of interlocking ellipses defines the crown of the boy's

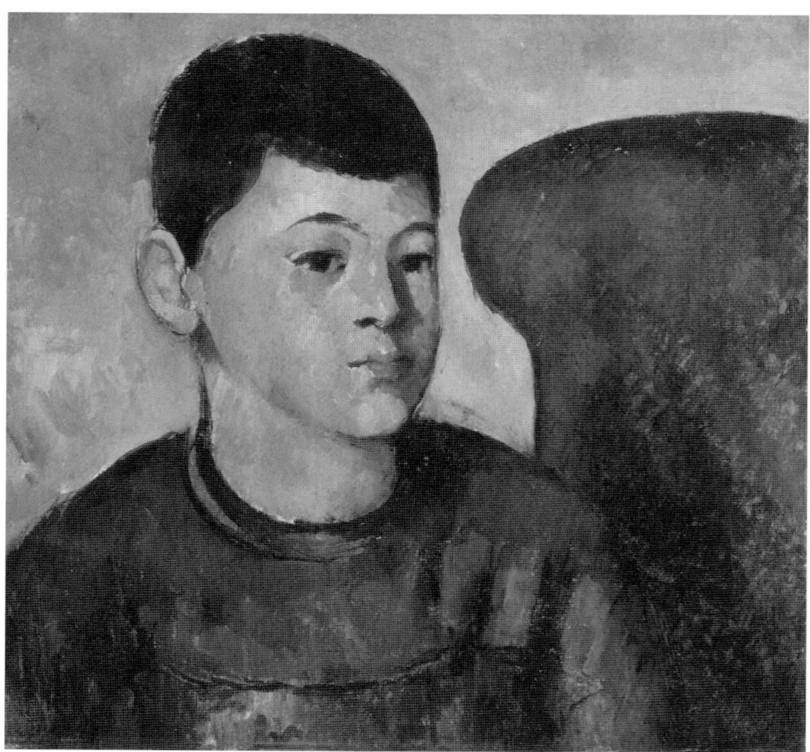

FIGURE 13.11. Paul Cézanne, *Portrait of the Artist's Son, Paul,* c. 1883–85. Musée de l'Orangerie, Paris. Photo: Réunion des Musées Nationaux/Art Resource, NY. Photographed by Arnaudet.

head, the roundness of his shoulders, the scoop of his collar, the back of the chair beside him and even, on a finer scale, the arcs of his eyebrows, ear and chin. These analogously curved forms, which constitute the motif, derive as much from the artist's gestures of painting as from his observation of physiognomy. The motif arrives through the medium on the surface of the painting itself, perhaps stimulated by the presence of the boy, but not dependent on any particular aspect of him. Although much less "finished" and resolved, the other portrait also displays a motif—just now emerging. A broad band of dull green strokes to the right of the figure echoes both the curvature of the head and its axial tilt. Whether this band of hatchings in the background represents an object is as yet unclear. Paintings of this sort are likely to have inspired the compliment Renoir paid: "[Cézanne] can't put two strokes of color on a canvas without it [already] being very good." In reporting these words, Denis added that every work by Cézanne, no matter how unstable or disjointed, was "full *[plein]*."[56] "From the moment he begins to put down a stroke, the painting is already there," Pablo Picasso was to remark much later, contrasting this to traditional methods, which attained fullness of effect only in their final state.[57] Works by Cézanne required no termination; the motif was "already there."

As I have noted, observers acknowledged that Cézanne felt compelled to paint in the presence of an external model *(sur le motif)*, to which he would give continuous, rapt attention.[58] The motif was his stimulus and could be anything from Mont Sainte-Victoire to a mere photograph or, in the case of the Bathers, his own drawings after works by masters he admired.[59] Although opinions differed over details, it was argued that Cézanne's picture was coordinated with appearances, yet ultimately not dependent on them. He did not imitate apples, wrote Natanson in 1895, but would "make them his own [as] an object is to its creator."[60] Other writers recognized that the ob-

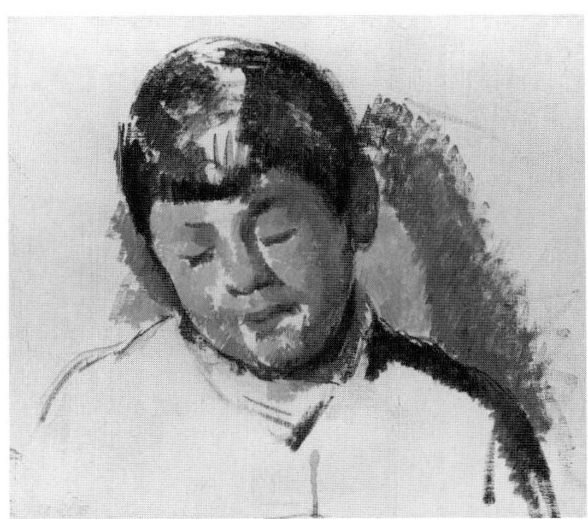

FIGURE 13.12. Paul Cézanne, *A Child (Sketch for a Portrait of the Artist's Son)*, c. 1883. Wadsworth Atheneum Museum of Art, Hartford, Connecticut; The Ella Gallup Sumner and Mary Catlin Sumner Collection Fund.

ject at which formal expression is directed need not be as solid and secure as an apple. It could be a movement, a sensation, a feeling—something intimately identified with the transient life of the artist-creator and the actual painters' materials he animated. This was the implication of Gustave Geffroy, who salvaged Cézanne's "mark" from any loss of humanity, as if anticipating the kind of complaint Morice and others would soon be making.

Mark, Sensation, Picture

It was Geffroy's brilliance to convert Cézanne's failings into virtues. Most of the artist's pictures were neither signed nor dated, which only added to the suspicion that they were unfinished. When he reviewed the 1895 exhibition Geffroy insisted that Cézanne's paintings were "better marked than by a signature."[61] Perhaps he had been inspired by Charles Baudelaire's famous essay "Le Peintre de la vie moderne," which concerned Constantin Guys, another artist who neglected to sign. Signatures, Baudelaire wrote, are "easy to counterfeit . . . but all of [Guys's] works are signed by his dazzling soul [upon] these murky studies"—"*ébauches*," literally, underpaintings that lack finish and polish.[62] Geffroy's Cézanne was like Baudelaire's Guys; his touch was "emotionally moving *[émouvante]*" and distinctive enough to establish a unique identity, signed or not, finished or not.[63] Cézanne's accentuated mark recorded and even enhanced a sensation that could be his only. If Natanson personalized the motif of apples, Geffroy personalized the very marks of which they were made, a motif in itself. This was a reason to value, as Renoir did, the placement of every single stroke.[64]

In 1901 Geffroy took his analysis further. He justified the perceived incompletion by alluding to the impossibility of stabilizing sensation or, for that matter, life itself—whether the life of nature's object or of the artist's motif. Our sensations never cease to change, to move: "Art does not proceed without a certain incompletion, because the life it reproduces is in perpetual transformation."[65] Geffroy acknowledged the movement, mutability, and temporal duration proper to artistic representation, a life force captured but not stilled by Cézanne's marks.

I have referred to Cézanne's repetitious marking of contours, as in *Trees at Le Tholonet* (fig. 13.4). This practice might relate to his troubled acknowledgment that successive views of a chosen motif in nature were not alike: "The motifs multiply, the same subject seen at a different angle takes on the greatest interest, and there is such variation that I believe I could work away for months without changing position but just by leaning a little to the right and then a little to the left."[66] Instability of this kind might be recorded (rather than resolved) in a living image in which all parts assume pictorial equivalence without respect to what they represent. The artist would suspend any final judgment regarding theme, design, or composition. Perhaps this explains why the objects in Cézanne's still lifes often meet the framing edges of the canvas in an unusually casual or even awkward way, as if cut off by a compression of the view (for example, fig. 13.13).[67]

One wonders whether the initial framing of the view was simply chosen arbitrarily because Cézanne believed that a picture could be created from anything

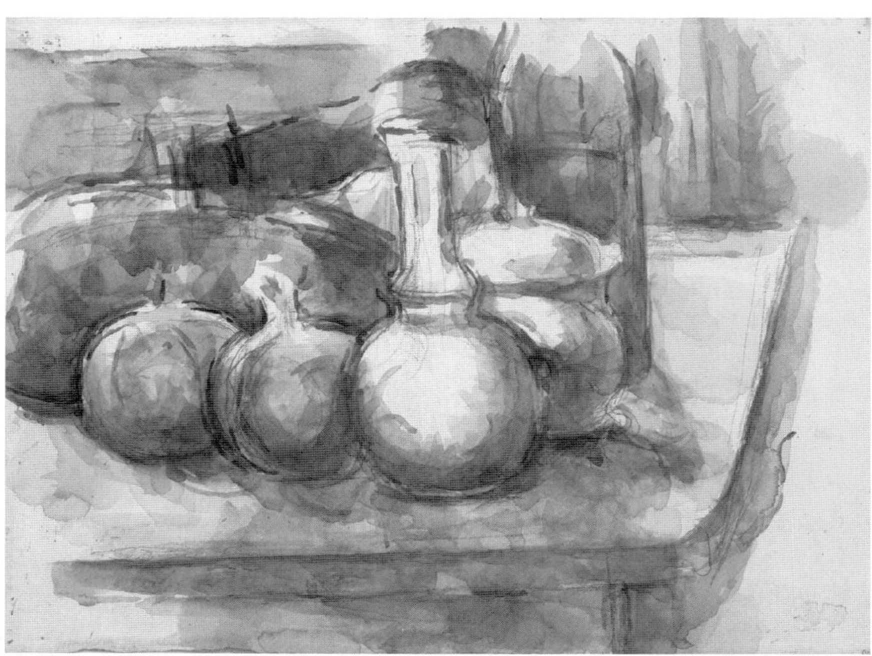

FIGURE 13.13. Paul Cézanne, *Still Life with Fruit, Carafe, Sugar Bowl, and Bottle*, c. 1900–1906; watercolor and graphite on white paper. Musée du Louvre, Paris. Photo: Réunion des Musées Nationaux/Art Resource, NY. Photographed by Michèle Bellot.

("the motifs multiply"). Yet he also carefully arranged objects in his studio as if struggling to find the suitable motif in advance, "tipping, turning, balancing the fruits as he wanted them to be," a witness observed in 1898.[68] His perceptual flexibility (or insecurity) may also explain why Cézanne's marks sometimes cluster and accumulate along the contours of represented objects (see the girl's head and hands in fig. 13.14) and sometimes seem to fade out (see fig. 13.15, especially the glass). Such effects dominate in watercolors, in which they define much of the character of the technique. At these overarticulated or disarticulated edges the model turns away from the eye, becoming particularly susceptible to minor shifts in the painter's own position, his own sense of himself seeing. "In my case," Cézanne wrote to Bernard, "sensations of color . . . are the cause of abstractions that prevent me from covering my canvas or from pursuing the delimitation of objects where the points of contact are tenuous and delicate."[69]

In his later years Cézanne's "abstractions"—products of his lively, transient "sensations"—became more and more pronounced. A diabetic, he complained of bad vision that caused planes to appear to overlap.[70] Obviously, it is impossible to know what he actually saw (or even what he thought he saw). In his paintings he allowed strokes that represented background elements to assume the material force of those in the foreground and to impinge on the foreground, as in views of Mont Sainte-Victoire in which he rendered the light, flat sky with as much substance as the dark, volumetric rock (for instance, fig. 13.16). In images of bathers it seems that branches, foliage, and sky are constructed from color patches all of the same general type (see plate 8). The more restrained brushwork of Cézanne's earlier years had produced similar tensions, often a play of strokes of "sky" laid over foliage (for example, fig. 13.17). Once Cézanne became engaged with the "life" of a sensory motif within a picture he was creating, all marking

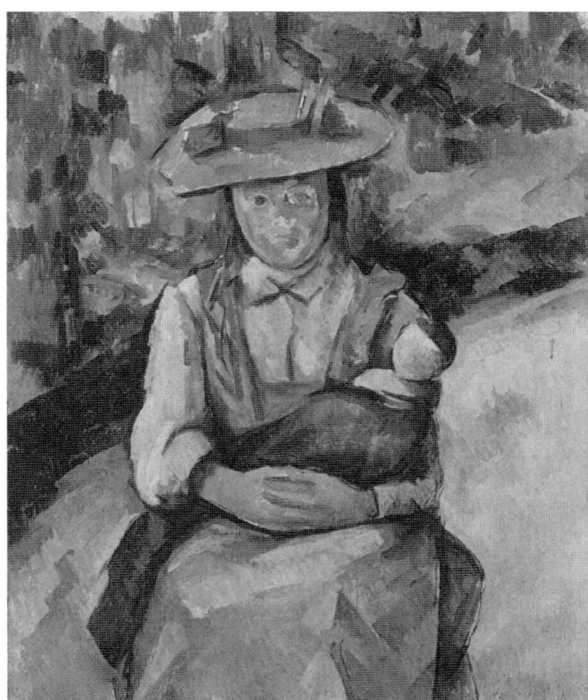

FIGURE 13.14. Paul Cézanne, *Girl with Doll*, 1902–4. Nationalgalerie, Museum Berggruen, Staatliche Museen zu Berlin. Photo: Bildarchiv Preussischer Kulturbesitz/Art Resource, NY.

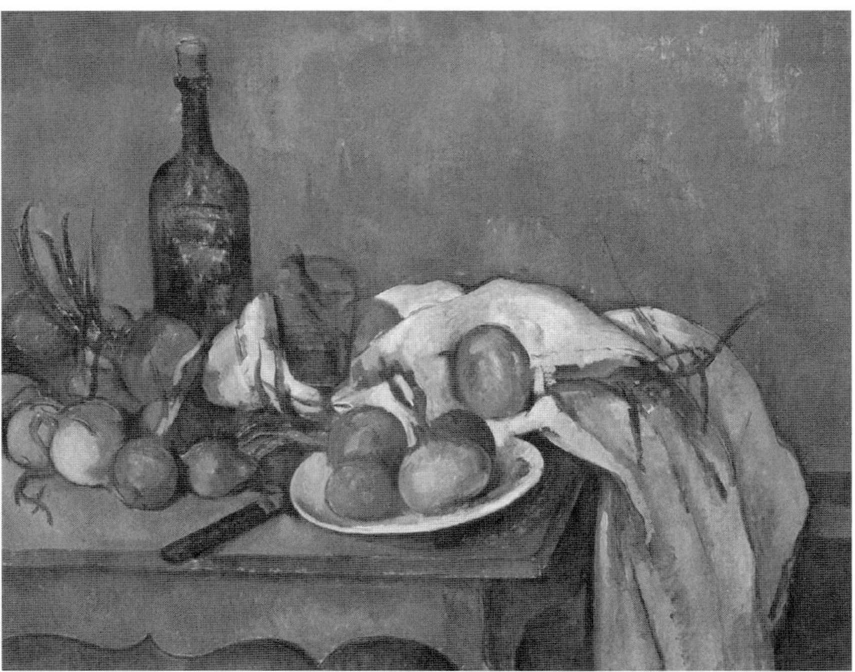

FIGURE 13.15. Paul Cézanne, *Still Life with Onions*, c. 1895. Musée d'Orsay, Paris; Bequest of Auguste Pellerin. Photo: Réunion des Musées Nationaux/Art Resource, NY. Photographed by Hervé Lewandowski.

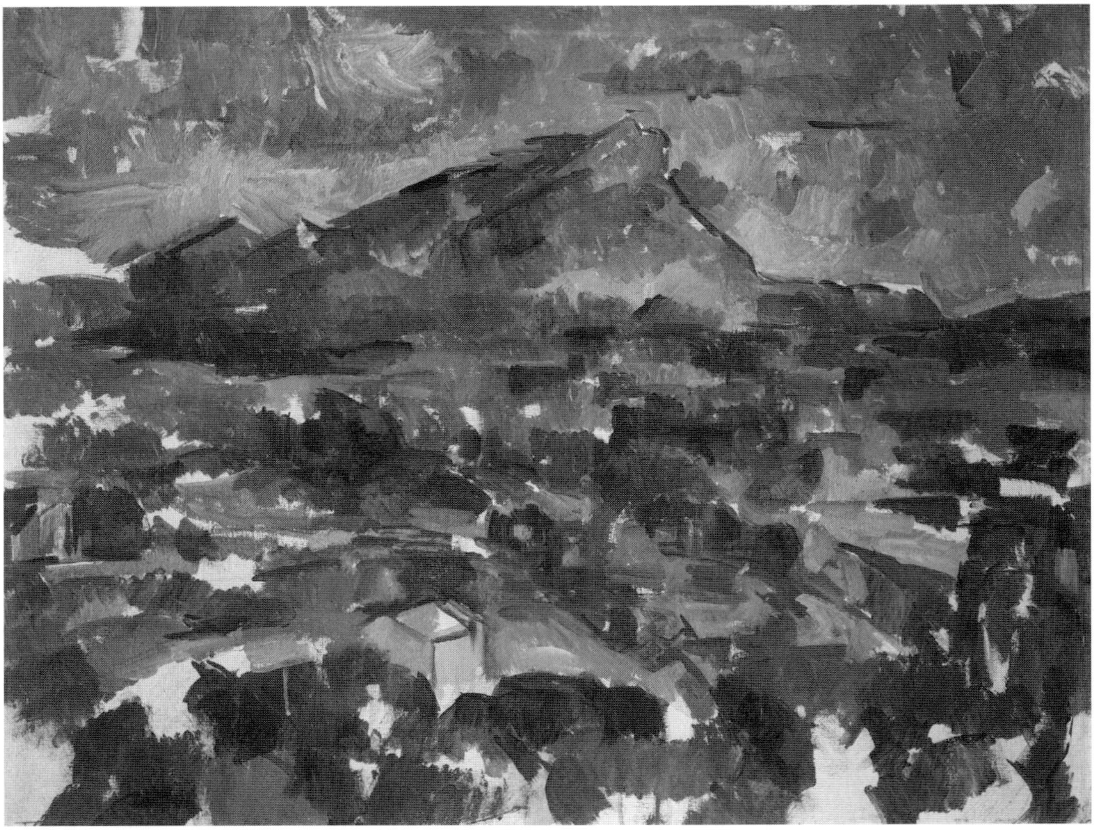

FIGURE 13.16. Paul Cézanne, *Mont Sainte-Victoire Seen from Les Lauves,* 1902–6. Kunsthaus, Zurich. Photo: Erich Lessing/Art Resource, NY.

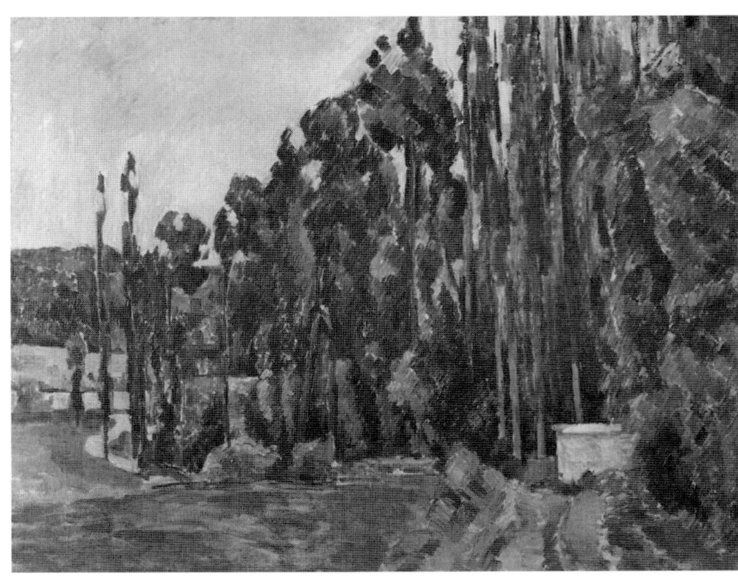

FIGURE 13.17. Paul Cézanne, *Les Peupliers (The Poplars),* c. 1879–80. Musée d'Orsay, Paris. Photo: Erich Lessing/Art Resource, NY.

extended this organic quality, no matter how much it might seem to contradict the conventional structural logic of the model in nature. In Denis's terms this was the sign of Cézanne's escape from "literary" constraint—his act of "representation" as opposed to literal reproduction. It was even his "abstraction" (at least during the period that Denis used this word with favor).

Among the most enthusiastic Cézanneans of the first decade of the twentieth century, Matisse best pursued the master's art as at once organic and abstract. "Think of the firm lines of the stretcher or the frame; they influence the lines of your motif," he told his pupils in 1909, as they worked from a live studio model.[71] It was Matisse's way of arguing that the construction of a picture should take its cues not only from nature, but perhaps even more from the physicality of its materials and the specific dimensions of its format. No compositional device, no canon of proportion, was preordained to apply in every situation. Matisse's stress on this point may relate to early criticism from A.-W. Bouguereau for his failing to center a drawing of the model in the conventional manner.[72] Cézanne himself, a painstaking worker, would become frustrated when the instability he perceived in his painting appeared to result from his model's movements and changes, whether the stirring of branches, the shifting of a studio pose, or the wilting of flowers. He complained that Vollard would not keep still while sitting for his portrait; and, as for flowers, he often resorted to paper ones.[73] Regarding Cézanne's efforts, Matisse thought that everything hinged on the artist's feelings, as opposed to the subject's tics: "After a certain time, Cézanne always painted the same canvas of Bathers. . . . A Cézanne is a moment of the artist, [not] of nature. . . . Despite the continual use of the same means, there are different effects; it's the man, Cézanne, that has changed."[74]

Matisse understood that he, as the artist, would change along with each successive work and in the course of completing any particular work, even when he repeated a stock repertory of subjects: "For me, it is impossible to copy nature slavishly, because I feel compelled to interpret and to submit to the spirit of the picture. . . . To someone who said that I didn't see women the way I represent them, I replied . . . I don't create a woman, I make a picture. . . . I'm driven by an idea that I really grasp only as it grows with the picture."[75] This is Matisse's pictorialism. He quickly reaches the point at which his emergent picture motivates him more than any specific aspect of his model.

In 1899 Matisse purchased a small Cézanne from Vollard, a composition of three female bathers (fig. 13.18). Whether "finished" or "unfinished," he regarded it as "heavily worked . . . very dense, very complete."[76] He revered this painting and spoke of it on a number of occasions. At first encounter, his statements may seem to indicate that he was appreciating Cézanne's compositional rigor, as if the painter of *Three Bathers* were Poussin reborn: "All is so well arranged that, no matter what the distance and how many figures are there, you will clearly distinguish the bodies and understand which limb belongs to which . . . all confusion has disappeared."[77] Indeed, Matisse often makes a general argument for the necessity of a guiding conception of the picture, something that must be present from the beginning: "everything is in the conception."[78] But this "conception" or systematic order is analogous to what others regarded as the motif and what Matisse himself was calling "the spirit of the picture." Human spirit and pictorial spirit join through the physical process of painting, each affecting the other: "I cannot distinguish between the feeling I have of life and the way I translate it."[79] When Matisse views Cézanne—and himself—his emphasis on concept, spirit, and feeling readily shifts to a *material* order, one that emerges in the making of the painting, with all parts receiving equal attention. Each mark or stroke of color is equal in concentration and density to every other mark, and each responds to the other.

In 1943, when Matisse described *Three Bathers* in an interview, the direction of his understanding became most evident: "I remember that everything there was set in order *[hiérarchisé]*, that the hands and the trees assumed equal significance *[comptaient en même temps]* with the sky." Matisse refers to the three

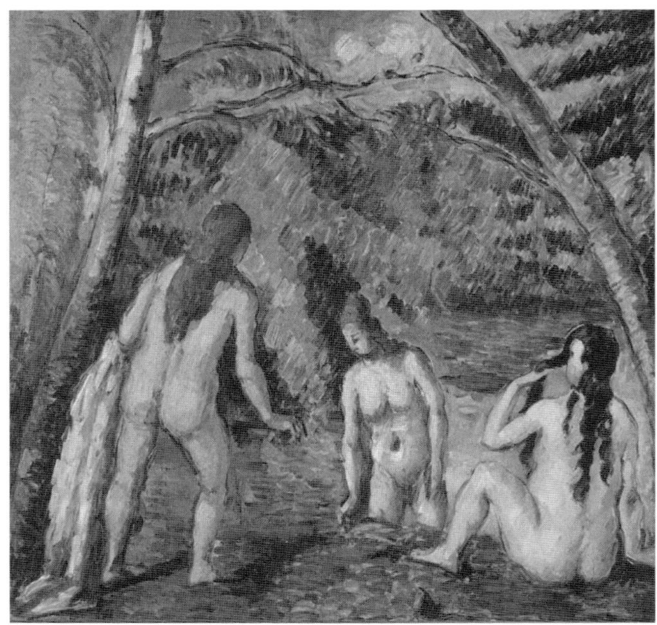

FIGURE 13.18. Paul Cézanne, *Three Bathers*, c. 1879–82. Musée du Petit Palais, Paris. Photo: Erich Lessing/Art Resource, NY.

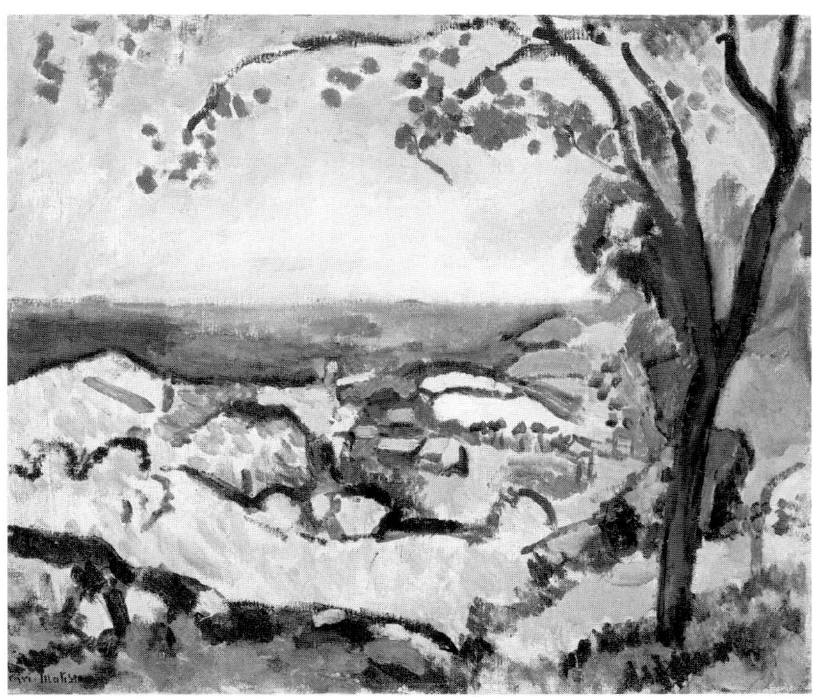

FIGURE 13.19. Henri Matisse, *View of the Sea, Collioure*, 1906. The Barnes Foundation, Merion, Pennsylvania, BF #73. © 2007 Succession H. Matisse, Paris/Artists Rights Society (ARS), New York. Photo © The Barnes Foundation.

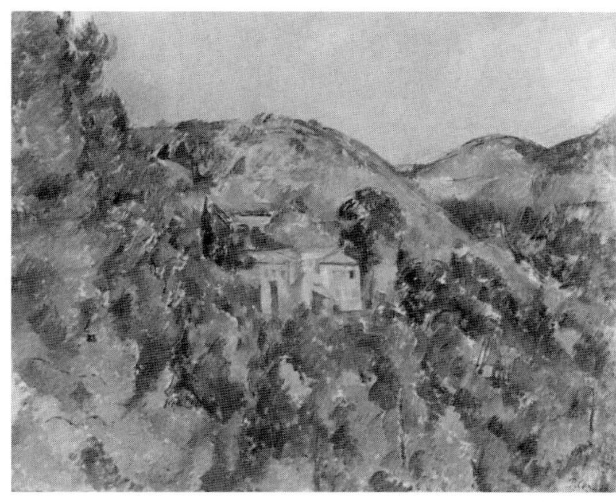

FIGURE 13.20. Paul Cézanne, *View of the Domaine Saint-Joseph*, 1888–90. The Metropolitan Museum of Art, New York; Catharine Lorillard Wolfe Collection, Wolfe Fund, 1913 (13.66). Photo: The Metropolitan Museum of Art, all rights reserved.

representational elements (hands, trees, sky) as if they were syntactical equivalents, joined not by an allegorical or naturalistic theme but by a formal structure of marking. His French location suggests simultaneity, everything working together in measured harmony—as if to say that the parts were at once fixed and moving, that they "moved to the same rhythm."[80]

Matisse appreciated the way that the various elements of Cézanne's representation became clearly articulated variations of each other. He saw that Cézanne coordinated the leg of the striding bather with her towel and with the tree beside her, that he integrated segments of sky into the patterns of the trees and foliage, that he also linked these combinations back to the figures. Such connections were established by the rhythm of individual strokes of color as much as by composite shapes and linear patterns.

Matisse's own application of color often resembles Cézanne's in the looseness of its mimeticism. He lets the blue of a daytime sky extend into passages of bluish green or pinkish violet—an effect likely to have been suggested by the chromatic range of the rest of his picture, not by any specific feature of nature. Compare his *View of the Sea, Collioure* (fig. 13.19) to Cézanne's *View of the Domaine Saint-Joseph* (fig. 13.20): In these paintings of similar palette one hue leads to another; but the Matisse is coarser, with individual blocks of color proportionately larger and less diffuse. He described his experience around 1905–6, the time of *View of the Sea, Collioure:* "I would lay down a color, the first color on the canvas. I would juxtapose a second color; and then, instead of reworking if the second color did not seem to agree with the first, I would put in a third to make them harmonize. So I had to continue like this until I felt I had created a complete harmony within my canvas."[81] The description approaches the appearance of any number of unfinished landscapes from Cézanne's final years (for example, fig. 13.1).

A bold or exaggerated line in a painting, describing no particular contour, might be the clearest sign of the motif; it might indicate that the artist's attention had been transferred from model to picture. Matisse's *Portrait of Olga Merson* (1911; fig. 13.21) exists in a highly irregular state of finish, exhibiting not only obvious signs of adjustment in the position of the figure, but also abrupt shifts in the quality of paint surface. Still more noticeable, however, is a different kind of adjustment. Two dark arcs—one running from the figure's chin and crossing the torso and lap to reach the base of the thigh, the other extending from the armpit across the forearm to the hip—mark the disposition of the central image within its rectangular format. These two lines reflect or parallel each other. The shorter line seems more plausibly descriptive; it approximates a possible contour for the figure, confirming the position of the buttocks in relation to the torso. The longer line appears more

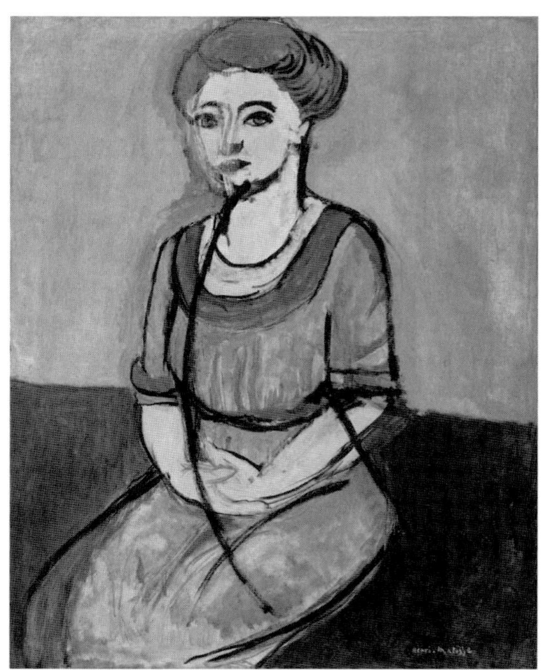

FIGURE 13.21. Henri Matisse, *Portrait of Olga Merson*, 1911. Museum of Fine Arts, Houston; Agnes Cullen Endowment Fund. © 2007 Succession H. Matisse, Paris/Artists Rights Society (ARS), New York. Photo: The Bridgeman Art Library.

"abstract," its presence somewhat puzzling; it might be regarded as establishing the figure's axis or torsion, defining a force field for the figure's dynamism. Or, having set the smaller arcs of head and thighs tangent to the top and bottom picture edges, perhaps Matisse was reconceiving the torso as one long arc extended between these two pictorial anchors.[82] This is his motif.

Matisse noticed details of marking and coloring in Cézanne as much as such generalities as sweeping arcs of branches and the broad rhythm of a group of bathers set against a screen of foliage; the one might lead him to paint *View of the Sea, Collioure*, while the other might sanction the freedoms taken in *Portrait of Olga Merson*. Many others joined Matisse in finding "everything" in Cézanne; they included Wassily Kandinsky, who saw his paintings exhibited at the Munich Secession in 1909. That year Kandinsky read Matisse's "Notes d'un peintre" in its German edition, illustrated with two of Cézanne's works.[83] Kandinsky acknowledged Cézanne as Matisse had, as an artist who could create from any subject in nature something "abstract" and spiritualized—"an internally resonating painterly object, what we call a picture *[Bild]*."[84]

Passage

Many features of Cézanne's art led in opposing directions. Indeed, they suggested "everything." Morice worried over Cézanne's "abstract" manner, which threatened to dehumanize painting at a time when society itself was undergoing an analogous process; but Kandinsky saw in this abstract pictorialism the highest human spirituality. Even the more specific technical details of Cézanne's art evoked complementary, oppositional readings, as in the case of his *passage*, recognized as his legacy to Cubism.[85]

What is *passage?* The Neo-Impressionist Paul Signac attributed the term to Pissarro, who would "reduce the distance between two colors by introducing intermediary elements within both of them"; these, he said, were *"passages."*[86] (For example, if touches of red-violet were added to an area of red, while blue-violet was added to an adjacent area of blue, this would "reduce the distance.") As for Cézanne, Bernard reported that "the *passage* of color values" was an issue that "tormented" him.[87] No doubt it evoked the difficulty Cézanne experienced in "delimit[ing] objects where the points of contact are tenuous and delicate"; to Bernard's suggestion that *passage* could be understood as the reflection of a color within the shaded area of a neighboring one, the older man responded with approval.[88] When the Cubist Lhote wrote later that subtle color transitions between adjacent forms tend to efface contours, he was referring, like Bernard, to capturing a worthy naturalistic effect—the enveloping atmosphere.[89] This is clearly different from the method more frequently attributed to Cézanne (here, in Denis's description) of representing isolated volume by applying "a number of squarish strokes to indicate rounded form by subtle passages *[doux voisinages]* of hue."[90] Lhote was among those who saw that both of the earlier senses of *passage* could be extended. He stressed the unbounded "flow" of the color transitions, their capacity to join one represented object to another so as to give an appearance of interpenetration (which Cézanne may never have intended).[91] With *passage* the passive presence of the ubiquitous atmosphere energized the represented objects, adding unexpected pictorial movement. Given the Cézannean precedent (Lhote argued), Braque and Picasso could conceive of their "Cubist" *passage:* it created an "atmosphere" that circulated (as in Impressionism and Neo-Impressionism) while also "gnawing away" at individual represented objects, a kind of modeling process applied in reverse.[92] Cubist technique fragmented the conventional sense of appearances yet integrated the material surface in its own version of "pictorial" space. Like Denis's *tableau* and Kandinsky's *Bild,* this "abstract" space was physically real; it countered illusionism and any tendency to dematerialize the visual field.[93] Cubist pictorialism may have been a form of "pure painting," but it also became a sensory hybrid—it made touch visible and vision tangible.

As traditionally conceived, *passage* eliminated breaks and gaps introduced by other technical devices, such as overlap. But by calling attention to itself in unfinished or boldly structured paintings, Cézanne's version of *passage* did something quite different. Rather than producing rarefied nuance or mechanistic "abstraction" (as Neo-Impressionist pointillism supposedly did), Cézanne's coarsely grained technique, "abstract" as it was, demonstrated that human feeling could be conveyed by painting in itself, in its sheer material presence. Lhote's commentary of 1920 is very much to the point: "A great part of the emotive power of Cézanne's canvases derives from the fact that, rather than hide them, the painter *shows his means* . . . the purely pictorial thought is less and less camouflaged" (Lhote's emphasis).[94] Cézanne's *passage* could be observational, structuring, emotive in its material and sensory immediacy, incomplete in its suspended process—all at once. Ironically, this art of *passage*—with the word referring first to a technique of observational and material transition—was itself, in its historical effect, transitional. It developed its own artistic future.

Cézanne did not pretend to refine what he only barely understood, an attitude that caught Braque's attention: "At long last, Cézanne! He cleansed painting of the idea of mastery."[95] Braque's modest *Houses at L'Estaque* (1908; fig. 13.22) follows from Cézanne in its illusionistically irregular, but pictorially effective manipulation of planes and their edges. Some of Braque's contours are suppressed (by converging tonal values and *passage,* as at several of the architectural joins). Many others are accentuated coloristically (by highlights and contrasts of hue) or by more directly material means (by hatchings and linear overlays, as along the base of the tree trunk). Braque recalled that he "had wanted to make of the [painter's] touch a form of matter." He meant that the quality of a color should be specific to the means of its application, whether by a particular type of brushstroke or (eventually) by the technique of collage: "What pleased me very much was precisely this 'materiality.'"[96] Cézanne's individual mark of the brush remained aggressively visible in sequences of *passage,* ignoring the margins of represented objects. In this way, it cultivated its inherent "materiality." And it pleased Braque.

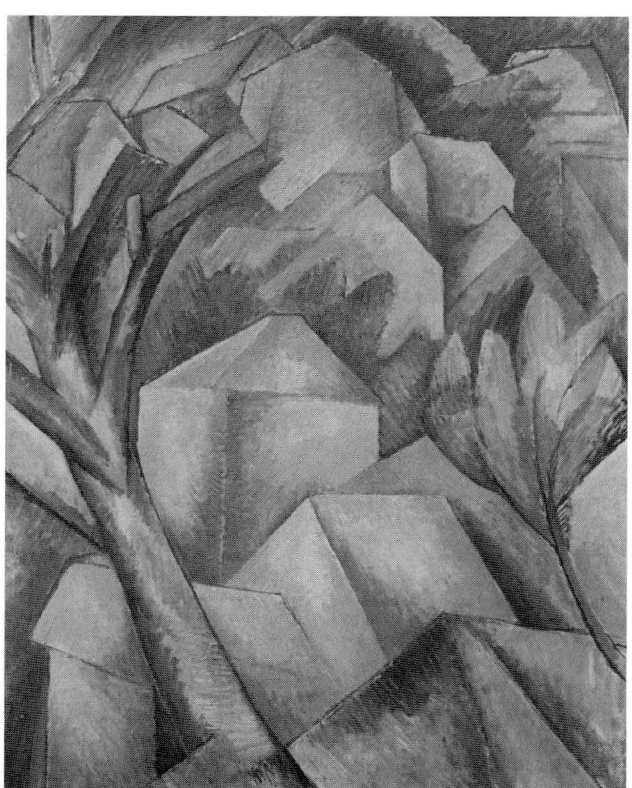

FIGURE 13.22. Georges Braque, *Houses at L'Estaque*, 1908. Fondation RUPF, Bern, Switzerland. © 2007 Artists Rights Society (ARS), New York/ADAGP, Paris. Photo: Bridgeman-Giraudon/Art Resource, NY.

Materiality

Late in his life Picasso, who owned Cézanne's *The Sea at L'Estaque* (fig. 13.23), rapped his hand against its densely structured marks of blue, blue-green, and blue-violet, saying: "Look at the sea, it's solid as a rock."[97] One wonders whether to accept his metaphor at face value or as the literal truth: Cézanne composed the atmosphere at L'Estaque "solidly" (a metaphor), but also allowed his canvas and paint to retain and even enhance their materiality, their literally solid substance. Indeed, Picasso's initial *Cézannisme* took a very material turn, at odds with the sense of *passage* as airy, nuanced transition. In paintings of 1907 and 1908 he accentuated the application of paint along the contours of volumetric objects, with the strokes and hatchings sometimes running parallel to the contour and elsewhere striking it from the perpendicular. The effect is part Fauvism, part primitivism, part sculptural bas-relief, but also part Cézanne. An example is *Green Bowl and Black Bottle* (1908; fig. 13.24), especially at the neck and mouth of the bottle and at the left edge of the table, where alternating parallel and perpendicular strokes of red compete with each other. Such marks depict no objects, "nothing." Perhaps they represent an effect of illumination or spatiality; if so, their assertive material presence becomes ironic.

Cézanne's paintings overflow with ironies of this sort. Many of his still lifes have aggressive background markings that contradict the illusionistic space one expects to see.[98] His *Still Life: Flask, Glass and Jug* of c. 1877 (fig. 13.9) sets horizontal strokes against the vertical neck of a flask and projects three wallpaper medallions forward by means of accentuated marks surrounding them. His *Still Life with Glass and Apples* of 1879–80 (fig. 13.25) allows a wallpaper pattern of leaves, absolutely flat in the reality

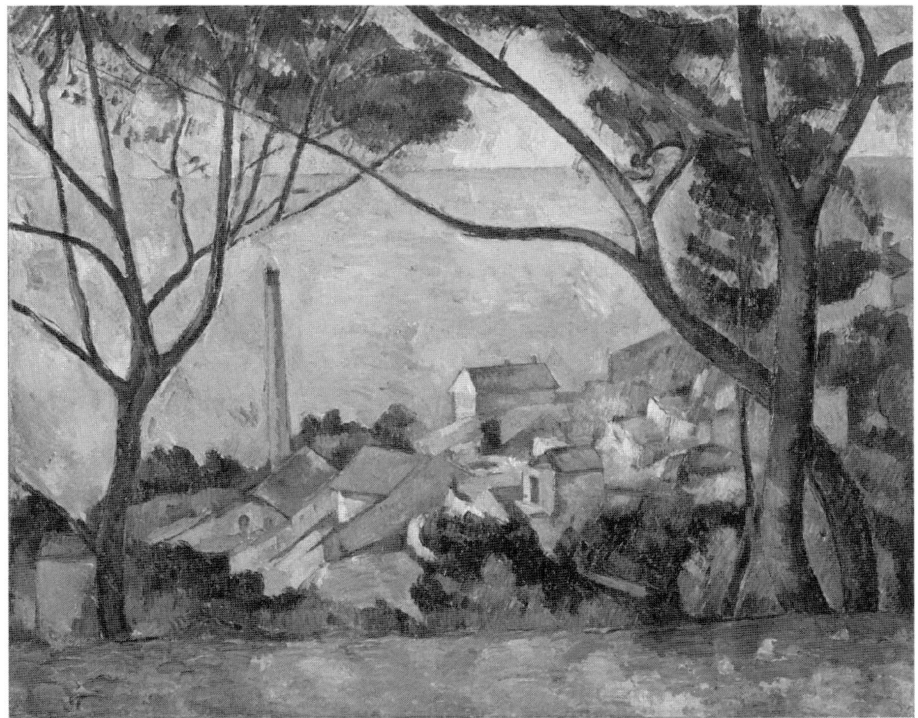

FIGURE 13.23. Paul Cézanne, *The Sea at L'Estaque,* 1878–79. Musée Picasso, Paris. Photo: Réunion des Musées Nationaux/Art Resource, NY.

of the studio, to acquire an effect of volume like that of the apples and glass placed before it in the pictorial foreground. To the right and left of the leaves, across the expanse of background wall, a rhythmic pattern of comparably active marks continues, with its own subtle transitions of hue and value. But here the marks and their nuanced variation appear to describe nothing. It is the "nothing" to which Natanson referred in 1895—nothing but painting in its purest pictorial and material force.[99] Picasso made much of Cézanne's "nothing," inserting pure painting—marks of varying density, fluidity, and texture—into the corners of his Cubist images, such as *Portrait of a Woman* (1910; fig. 13.26). His pictorialism activates the background emptiness that surrounds the fullness of the body, a field of analogous activity. Indeed, Picasso's empty spaces are full, just as Cézanne's are—not full of illusion, but of substance, an accumulation of matter.[100]

The most influential American critic of the twentieth century, Clement Greenberg, understood the implications of Cézanne's materiality, with its "solid flatness [the backgrounds], or flat solidity [the bodies and objects] . . . that Picasso and Braque, as Cubists, took [as] their point of departure."[101] Greenberg saw that an art with no concern for "human interest," one that referred to nothing beyond itself, had an advantage: it made every sensation "equally important" and an entire picture "dense, not in detail but in feeling."[102] He was describing a kind of emotive abstraction that he associated with the most typical and genuine of modern desires—not a mystifying spiritual yearning, but a concrete, materialist passion. Accordingly, he linked Cézanne's dense formal structure to the social and psychological malaise of which some of his early French critics had warned (recall Morice's "tyranny of science"). As someone born into the twentieth century, however, Greenberg

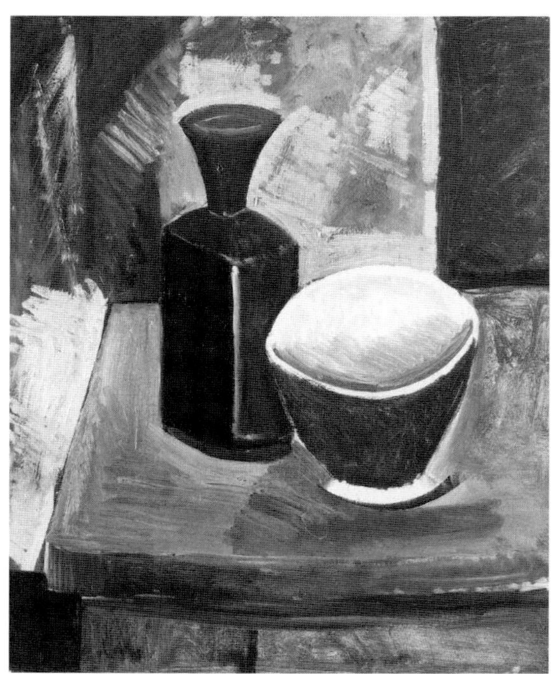

FIGURE 13.24. Pablo Picasso, *Green Bowl and Black Bottle*, 1908. The State Hermitage Museum, St. Petersburg. © 2007 Estate of Pablo Picasso/Artists Rights Society (ARS), New York. Photo: The Bridgeman Art Library.

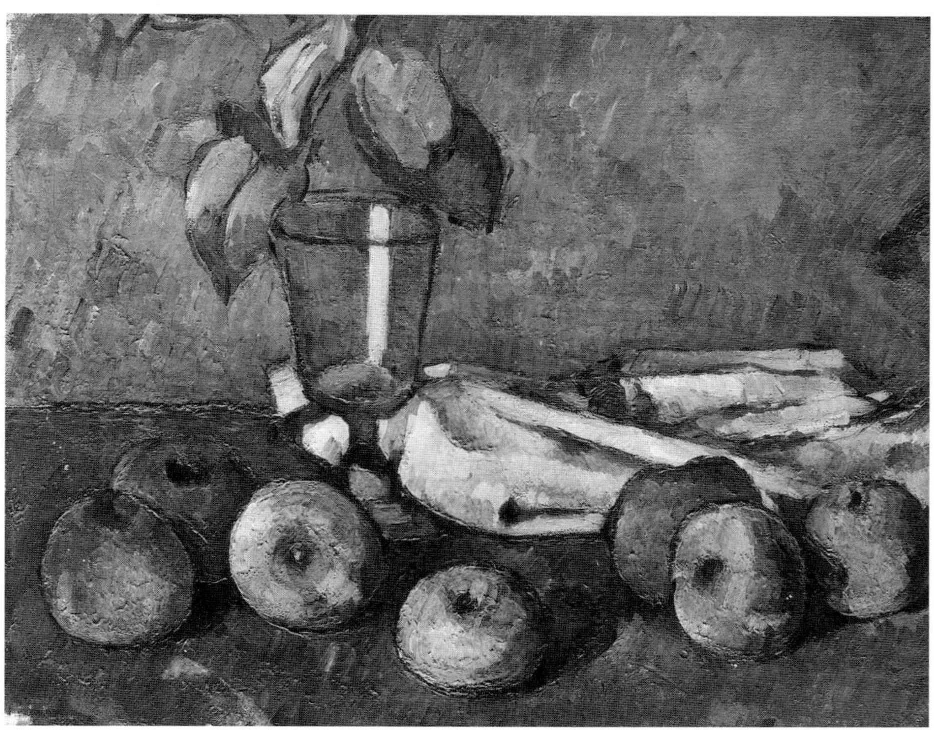

FIGURE 13.25. Paul Cézanne, *Still Life with Glass and Apples*, 1879–80. Collection Rudolf Staechelin, permanent loan to the Kunstmuseum Basel. Photo: Kunstmuseum Basel, Martin Bühler.

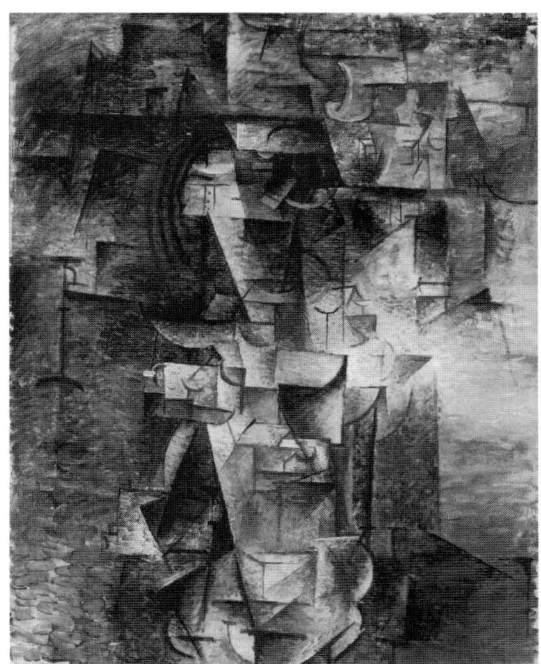

FIGURE 13.26. Pablo Picasso, *Portrait of a Woman*, 1910. Museum of Fine Arts, Boston; Charles H. Bayley Picture and Painting Fund, and Partial Gift of Mrs. Gilbert W. Chapman, 1977.15. © 2007 Estate of Pablo Picasso/Artists Rights Society (ARS), New York. Photo © 2007 Museum of Fine Arts, Boston.

encountered the consequences of the industrial revolution, its positivist mentality, its utilitarian ethic, and its urban culture of commodities as permanent features of the environment. To regret what had "been lost [would be] futile."[103]

Pictorial (or aesthetic) materiality and cultural materialism: the two concerns were not to be separated. In 1905 Denis had observed that his contemporaries preferred "abstractions to reality." Abstraction represented a materiality of the artists' own making—an *idealized* materiality—their defense against the detestable "real" conditions that beset them: "Increasingly our sensibility requires pure aesthetic emotions [because] life loses each day a little more character. Our streets are cold and ugly, our interiors vulgar; comfort destroys the picturesque charm of private life, regulations suppress all fantasy in the spectacle of public life."[104] Artists soon took abstraction too far, however. This was no liberation, no salvation, as Denis admonished Matisse: "Ah! Matisse! Damn the pedants who have taught us to distinguish prose from poetry in our pictorial language! . . . It's the materialism of our professors that has led us by reaction to seek Beauty outside Nature, and Nature through [intellectualized] Science, and art in theories."[105] The desirable classical balance of reason and instinct, thought and feeling, had been lost to Matisse's generation, which was also Denis's.

The premises of Greenberg's argument were very similar. In a number of reviews published during the 1940s and 1950s, he identified modernity's materialism (which he also called positivism) as a "dulling," "flattening" factor in life. But with the hindsight of fifty years of modernism, he saw too that Cézanne, Douanier Rousseau, Matisse, Picasso, and Joan Miró had all acted as if the condition of cultural "flatness" demanded some kind of acknowledgment rather than simple negation, even from those who wished to resist.[106] With "cold, hard heads" these artists would privilege "the medium over whatever it figures." Events occurred in them as if in the form of brute material objects; they represented their experience in terms of "the concrete sensation, immediate return, tangible datum."[107] Whereas Denis grew to distrust this kind of materialist or pictorialist abstraction as an effective artistic response to the conditions of modernity, Greenberg embraced it, although somewhat reluctantly. He detected a logic (perhaps unconscious in the artists) that Denis either never quite imagined or simply refused to accept. It seemed to Greenberg that anyone sensitive to art had been receiving a homeopathic cure from the modernist avant-garde: society's crass materialism had inspired an equally materialistic art that found aesthetic nuance in the crudest physical matter; in turn, it forced its viewers to acknowledge the real character of their social and cultural life, that is, its objectification and even degradation.[108] Although the revelation might be painful, the feeling was "dense" (as Greenberg said of Cézanne) and offered a formal beauty to those capable of intimate appreciation. A viewer could learn from this art because it concealed nothing: technically, it displayed the medium; ethically, it enacted the truth.

Finished or unfinished, Cézanne's art—from one view crude, from another refined and uplifting—stimulated Greenberg's thinking as it had Denis's. When Greenberg addressed the topic of "abstract art" in 1944 he wrote of "Cézanne's parallel, roughly rectangular touches of the brush [which] echo the outline of the canvas." The image became one with its material components. Perhaps this was to see Cézanne through Picasso, who more self-consciously attended to the physical interplay of paint and support surface. Greenberg nevertheless credited Cézanne with a certain prescience, noting that the "distortions" of his drawing were "compelled" by a "new realization of the importance of every physical factor."[109] Here was an appropriate aesthetic response to the positivism and scientism of nineteenth-century culture, the source of the vulgarity that had struck Denis's generation before Greenberg's. All advanced art after Eugène Delacroix and Gustave Courbet, Greenberg argued, "spoke positivism or materialism: its essence lay in the immediate [physical] sensation."[110] The situation had hardly changed over the intervening century: "Only by reducing themselves to [their proper medium] can the arts communicate that sense of concretely felt, irreducible experience in which our sensibility [in 1949] finds its fundamental certainty."[111] If artists—Cézanne in 1899, Jackson Pollock in 1949—were to deal with the realities of modern experience, they would have to "show their means" (as Lhote had already suggested), expressing themselves "only in material terms."[112] The precise results might be inadvertent: when Cézanne used *passage* in *his* way, to bring distance and volume to Impressionism's atmospheric light, he "got 'solidity,'" Greenberg wrote, but it was "as much a two-dimensional, literal solidity as a representational one."[113] Aiming for depth, the artist found a familiar, reassuring, material flatness. Picasso sensed the same irony: Cézanne had painted *The Sea at L'Estaque* so "solidly" that one was led to touch as much as look, inspecting the image by knocking against it.

Image and Matter

American artists of the later twentieth century, like their European counterparts, often attempted to reinvent painting after an initial period of institutional training; they aimed to isolate their personal experience from a social environment they rejected.[114] Although some turned to a dematerializing conceptualism, others sought an ever more immediate sensation and a fundamental physicality. Like the Cubists, they found the example of Cézanne liberating, especially with regard to his straightforward materiality. Whether working from a "motif" in nature or from the Old Masters, Cézanne's essential pictorialism seemed to derive from next to nothing; he extracted his art from no more than what was immediately before his eyes—or in his hands. His mark was distinct from that of other artists (as Geffroy had insisted), but also conveyed a look of anonymity. It remained true to the nature of paint—undisguised, without pretense to the "artistic." It could be trusted.

Jasper Johns states that he has always admired Cézanne the most among modernists, his works as "alive and contemporary" as ever.[115] Johns is the owner of Cézanne's *Bather with Outstretched Arms* of 1877–78 (fig. 13.27), a small painting with the type of aggressive marking that, as he puts it, "makes looking equivalent to touching" (a description that might fit Picasso, too, another favorite of Johns).[116] Whereas Cézanne's mark appears active, Johns's seems passive—yet just as physical, which is his interest. Much of Johns's art, especially his earlier works, features a rather deadpan, repetitious stroking of paint, almost to the exclusion of any other quality. He enhanced the pointed materiality of many of his surfaces by using encaustic (a wax medium) to which he added bits of collage (usually newspaper). A viewer can recognize such marking as Johns's but is also struck by the fact that the marks seem only to represent themselves—materially, they are what they are. A number of Johns's works go one step further by attaching easily recognizable objects to the working surface. *Canvas* (1956; fig. 13.28) puns on its literal identity by displaying a stretched canvas facing

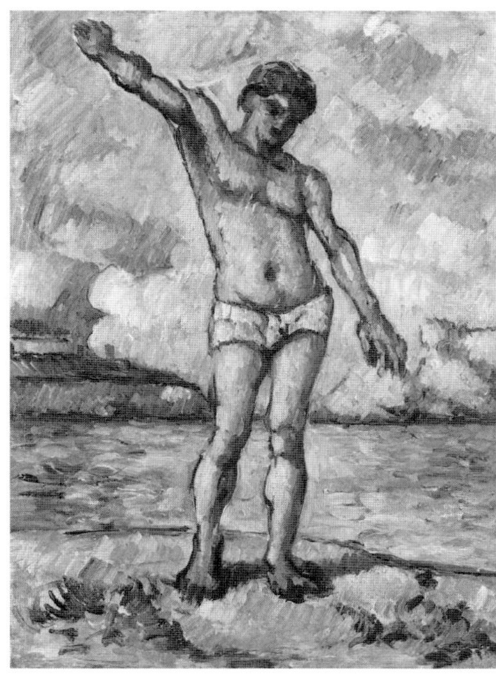

FIGURE 13.27. Paul Cézanne, *Bather with Outstretched Arms*, 1877–78. Collection Jasper Johns. Photographed by Dorothy Zeitman.

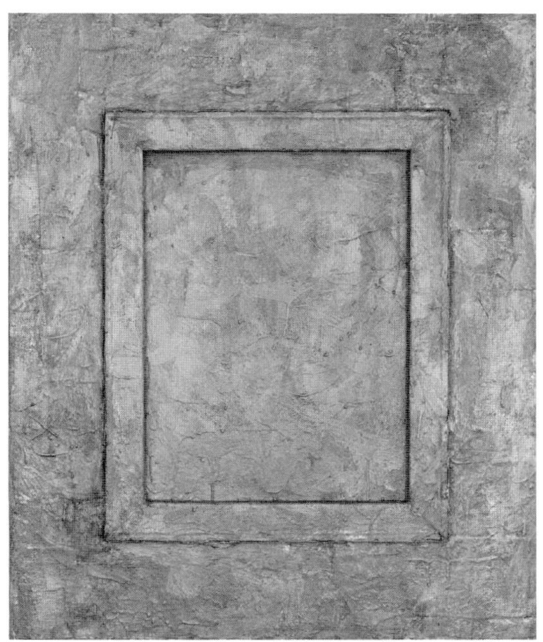

FIGURE 13.28. Jasper Johns, *Canvas*, 1956, encaustic and collage on wood and canvas. Collection of the artist. Art © Jasper Johns/Licensed by VAGA, New York, NY. Photographed by Zindman/Fremont.

into a larger, surrounding one; one canvas contains the other as the picture or image it presents. Yet this "image" remains real in its evident substance, neither virtual nor illusionistic.[117] As for the gray encaustic surface, it passes over everything equally and, like Cézanne's marks, ignores internal boundaries.

Just as Cézanne was a model for Johns, so Johns became a model for artists who matured during the 1960s; and both were crucial for Brice Marden. His *Three Deliberate Greys for Jasper Johns* (1970) consists of three monochromatic, oil-and-wax panels that derive their dense materiality from these two sources. The Cézanne element is not particularly obvious, although Marden hinted at it when first asked to comment on this work: "Jasper Johns paintings showed me paint dispersed on a surface being a surface [as well as] much about Cézanne."[118] We find another hint in some jottings from Marden's *Grove Group Notebook* of 1971–74, which he composed during visits to Greece. In connection with a sketch for a horizontal two-panel work, Marden wrote, "Cézanne gets the weight of the sea in Louvre view from Estaque. The airy weightyness of it . . . do a big heavy sea painting."[119] Through his sketch, Marden thinks of "heavy" layers of pigment, whether light ("airy") or dark ("weighty"), as he accumulates a dense network of penstrokes. The "Louvre view" must have been *The Gulf of Marseille Seen from L'Estaque* of 1878–79 (Rewald 390), with its area of blue sea as "solid" as that in Picasso's Cézanne. Beside another drawing of a similar type—this from *Suicide Notes* of 1972–73—Marden wrote, "Planes made of planes, diminishing planes, molecular, Cézanne plane study."[120] It seems that Marden marveled at the way Cézanne's mark could mark "nothing"—a plane constituted of other planes. As for himself, he imagined configuring a given surface plane in terms of its fundamental materiality—a molecular grain of pure paintmark, pure color, pure matter, having the potential to be extended throughout a surrounding environment.[121] Such reductive "abstraction" (associated with a concrete sensation, like that of the sea) allowed Marden to view all imagery as having equal pictorial potential but also equal emotional potential. Like Cézanne, he was able to find a "motif," whether humble or grand, virtually anywhere; and its organicism might continue uncompleted, "on and on and on and on," as Marden said in 1991 with regard to his drawings.[122]

That same year the kind of material freedom seen in Cézanne's art inspired a project Marden executed for the Museum of Fine Arts, Boston. He selected two small, predominantly gray figure paintings by the Spanish Baroque artist Francisco Zurburán, removed them from their frames, and spaced them to stress their verticality and also activate the vertical slice of wall between. From Zurburán's art emerged a "motif" related to Marden's own, seen in abstract works he hung in the same gallery (his vertical, gray panels often took their proportions from a human body).[123] In an adjoining gallery, Marden displayed a number of anonymous Chinese objects along with more of his own works and a single Cézanne, *Still Life with Fruit and Jug* (Rewald 741). For the project's catalogue he wrote, "Rows of charged mysterious objects. A room of things with no known author, excepting Cézanne, my hero."[124] From the density of Cézanne's surface of marks, intended to represent objects and spaces, Marden derived his "pure" (but evocative) abstraction, equally dense.

Let Sylvia Plimack Mangold—a painter of the same 1960s generation as Marden and one who has just as thoroughly absorbed Cézanne's substance—close this essay. Plimack Mangold returns us from abstraction to representation. Cézanne is especially apparent in her work of the late 1980s and 1990s, in paintings of trees in the vicinity of her studio. Emotionally as well as pictorially, her art connects to his. She repeats views of favored sites, works with great deliberation and explores vision through tactile materiality.[125]

Some of Plimack Mangold's tree studies retain a device she developed much earlier—the incorporation of an illusionistic band of semitransparent masking tape, as along the bottom margin of *The Elm Tree (Summer)* of 1991 (fig. 13.29). This strip of paint, which imitates both tactile and visual properties of tape, functions as an ironic reference to the material process of its own construction. Like accentuated Cézannean marks or elements of Cubist collage and trompe-l'oeil, the "tape" indicates the human intervention that picture-making demands. Yet its presence is hardly necessary, given the masses of brushstrokes, often rubbed or scraped, that Plimack Mangold assembles to represent foliage. All her marks are in some obvious way both image and matter. Accordingly, her most recent tree paintings, such as *Summer Pin Oak* of 1998, lack the "tape," which has become superfluous. Here, as with Cézanne, marks make, and are, the motif. Such art largely eliminates the distinction between representation and abstraction. What results is a gain in sensation, always Cézanne's concern.

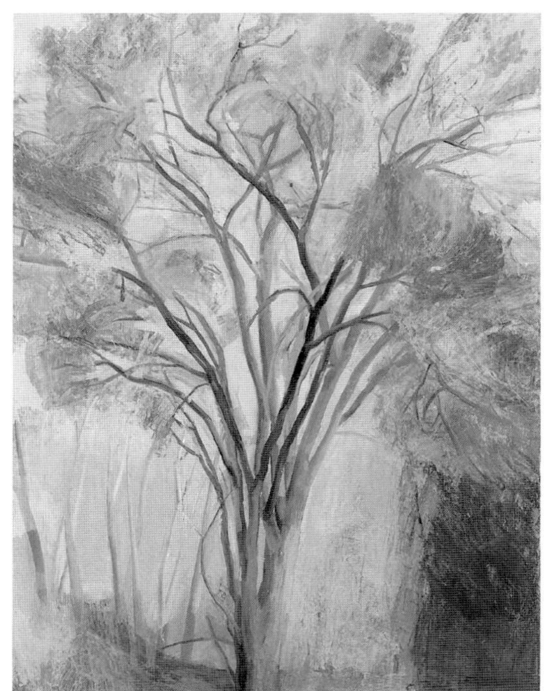

FIGURE 13.29. Sylvia Plimack Mangold, *The Elm Tree (Summer)*, 1991, oil on linen. Courtesy Alexander and Bonin, New York, and Annemarie Verna Galerie, Zurich. Photograph © D. James Dee.

Notes

Originally published in *Cézanne: Finished/Unfinished*, exh. cat. (Vienna: Kunstforum, and Zurich: Kunsthaus, 2000), 99–123. All translations are by the author unless otherwise indicated.

Editor's note: Parenthetical references within this essay to Rewald are to images in John Rewald, with Walter Feilchenfeldt and Jayne Warman, *The Paintings of Paul Cézanne: A Catalogue Raisonné* (New York, 1996).

1. Clovis Sagot, quoted in a letter of 9 January 1908 from Jacques Rivière to André Lhote, in André Lhote, Alain Fournier and Jacques Rivière, *La Peinture, le cœur et l'esprit: Correspondance inédite (1907–1924)*, vol. 1 (Bordeaux, 1986), 39. In fact, Cézannean facture had appeared in Lhote's work at the latest by 1906, when the painter was just twenty-one years old. I thank Terence Maloon for alerting me to the significance of Lhote's various responses to Cézanne, Alexander Dumbadze for essential aid in researching this essay, and Jean-Pierre Criqui for locating a work.
2. See George Lecomte, "La Crise de la peinture française," *L'Art et les artistes* 12 (October 1910): 27–28; Octave Mirbeau, "Preface," *Cézanne* (Paris, 1914), 8–9; and Mirbeau, "Interview d'Octave Mirbeau par Paul Gsell"(1907), in idem, *Combats esthétiques*, ed. Pierre Michel and Jean-François Nivet, vol. 2 (Paris, 1993), 419. According to Lhote, Cézanne's influence, always strong, was "universal" from 1908 to 1914; André Lhote, "De l'influence de Cézanne" (1947), in Lhote, *La Peinture liberée* (Paris, 1956), 231.
3. Raymond Bouyer, "Le Procès de l'art moderne au Salon d'Automne," *Revue politique et littéraire [Revue bleue]* 2 (5 November 1904): 604–5. In contrast, Roger Marx offered a positive appraisal of the same situation, in Roger Marx, "Le Salon d'Automne," *Gazette des beaux-arts* 32 (1 December 1904): 464. On early critical perceptions of Matisse vis-à-vis Cézanne, see Roger Benjamin, *Matisse's "Notes of a Painter": Criticism, Theory, and Context, 1891–1908* (Ann Arbor, Mich., 1987), 79–122. In the 1904 exhibition Matisse chose not to show his most recent work, such as *Place des Lices, Saint-Tropez* (Statens Museum for Kunst, Copenhagen).
4. Kees van Dongen, statement in Charles Morice, "Enquête sur les tendances actuelles des arts plastiques," *Mercure de France* 56 (1 August 1905): 352.
5. Jacques-Emile Blanche, statement in Morice, "Enquête," 357.
6. Morice, "Enquête," 349; and Charles Morice, "Le XXIe Salon des Indépendants," *Mercure de France* 54 (15 April 1905): 541. "Nearly every artist was in agreement" over Cézanne's importance; Morice, "Le XXIe Salon des Indépendants," 551. For commentary on Morice's "Enquête," see Philippe Dagen, *La Peinture en 1905: L'Enquête sur les tendances actuelles des arts plastiques de Charles Morice* (Paris, 1986), 3–46.
7. On the tendency of creative productivity to generate a continuing cultural discourse (an "effect") and on the need of a generation simultaneously to respond to and resist that discourse, see Roland Barthes, "From Work to Text" (1971) in idem, *Image–Music–Text*, ed. and trans. Stephen Heath (New York, 1977), 155–64; and Harold Bloom, *The Anxiety of Influence* (New York, 1973). On aspects of the Cézanne effect, see Denis Coutagne, *Paul Cézanne* (Paris, 1990), 121–85; and Christian Geelhaar, " 'The Painters Who Had the Right Eyes': On the Reception of Cézanne's Bathers," trans. Dorothy Kosinski, in Mary Louise Krumrine, *Paul Cézanne: The Bathers* (New York, 1990), 275–303.
8. See, for example, André Lhote, "Conseils à l'èbéniste" (1936), in Lhote, *Peinture d'abord* (Paris, 1942), 9–16, and Lhote, "L'Enseignement de Cézanne," *La Nouvelle Revue française* 15, no. 86 (November 1920): 649–72.
9. André Lhote, "Petite Histoire du cubisme" (1946), in Lhote, *La Peinture liberée*, 129.
10. "Every discipline implies a liberty, every rule an exception"; André Lhote, "Totalisme," *L'Elan*, no. 9 (February 1916): n.p.
11. Maurice Denis, "L'Impressionnisme et la France" (1917), in Denis, *Nouvelles Théories: Sur l'art moderne, sur l'art sacré 1914–1921* (Paris, 1922), 67–68.
12. Cézanne's words as reported in Emile Bernard, "Souvenirs sur Paul Cézanne et lettres inédites," *Mercure de France* 69 (1 and 16 October 1907): 614. For related statements and reports, see Richard Shiff, *Cézanne and the End of Impressionism: A Study of the Theory, Technique, and Critical Evaluation of Modern Art* (Chicago, 1984), 194.
13. Clement Greenberg, "Cézanne and the Unity of Modern Art" (1951), in Greenberg, *The Collected Essays and Criticism*, ed. John O'Brian, vol. 3 (Chicago, 1986–93), 82–83.
14. On the concept of "motif," including Cézanne's own use of the term, see Georges Roque, "Au lieu du sujet, le motif: La Quête des peintres depuis l'impressionnisme," *Ethnologie française* 25, no. 2 (1995): 196–204; and Richard Shiff, "Sensation, Movement, Cé-

zanne," in *Classic Cézanne*, ed. Terence Maloon, exh. cat. (Sydney: Art Gallery of New South Wales, 1998), 13–27. Cézanne appears to distinguish between subject matter (*sujet*) and motif (*motif*) in his letter of 8 September 1906 to his son, Paul; John Rewald, ed., *Paul Cézanne: Correspondance* (Paris, 1978), 324.

15. Jean Metzinger, quoted in Gelett Burgess, "The Wild Men of Paris," *Architectural Record* 27 (May 1910): 414 (punctuation added for clarity). Cf. the remarks made by Roger Fry, Cézanne's great British critic: "The logical extreme of [the method of Cézanne and the French Post-Impressionists] would undoubtedly be the attempt to give up all resemblance to natural form, and to create a purely abstract language of form—a visual music"; Fry, "The French Group," in *Second Post-Impressionist Exhibition*, exh. cat. (London: Grafton Galleries, 1912), 14–15. Lhote referred to Cézanne's nuances of warm and cool hues as "pictorial musicality"; André Lhote, *Cézanne* (Lausanne, 1949), 9.
16. R. P. Rivière and J. F. Schnerb, "L'Atelier de Cézanne," *La Grande Revue* 46 (25 December 1907): 816.
17. See Rewald, *Paintings of Paul Cézanne*, vol. 1, 470. Because Cézanne "worked very slowly, his picture was often left off halfway"; Bernard, "Souvenirs sur Paul Cézanne," 399. "His simplest canvases required a considerable, often enormous number of sessions . . . he would abandon many of these paintings in progress [when] the desired effect could not be achieved or circumstances prevented his bringing them to term"; Théodore Duret, *Histoire des peintres impressionnistes* (Paris, 1906), 184. In a letter of 6 July 1895 to Monet, Cézanne referred to abandoning his portrait of Gustave Geffroy (Rewald 791) because of the "meager" results achieved after many sessions; Rewald, ed., *Paul Cézanne: Correspondance*, 246.
18. Letter of 8 September 1906 to his son, in Rewald, ed., *Paul Cézanne: Correspondance*, 324.
19. Maurice Denis, "L'Influence de Cézanne" (1920), in Denis, *Nouvelles Théories*, 128.
20. Maurice Denis, "Definition du néo-traditionnisme" (1890), in Denis, *Théories, 1890–1910: Du Symbolisme et de Gauguin vers un nouvel ordre classique* (Paris, 1920), 9–10. See also Denis's "L'Exposition de Renoir" (1892), ibid., 17, where "expression by the subject matter" is distinguished from "expression by the work of art [itself]."
21. "Cézanne" (1907), in Denis, *Théories*, 251–53 (Denis attributes the final observation to his fellow painter Paul Sérusier). See also "L'Influence de Cézanne," in Denis, *Nouvelles Théories*, 129: "he wanted to make pure painting, that is, painting without literature, without signification, without subject." Denis repeatedly credited Sérusier with this understanding of Cézanne's achievement; see "Paul Sérusier" (1908), in Denis, *Théories*, 147–49. Responding in part to Denis's account of Cézanne, Roger Fry explained the classicism of the French Post-Impressionist painters in relation to their avoidance of "associated ideas," his term for the "literary"; Fry, "The French Group," 16.
22. "Le Soleil" (1906), in Denis, *Théories*, 223. See also Denis, *Journal*, vol. 2 (Paris, 1957–59), 29, 48; "Cézanne," in Denis, *Théories*, 253; and "L'Impressionnisme et la France," in Denis, *Nouvelles Théories*, 67. On the political and religious beliefs factored into Denis's aesthetic theory, see Jean-Paul Bouillon, "The Politics of Maurice Denis," in Guy Cogeval et al., eds., *Maurice Denis, 1870–1943*, exh. cat. (Lyon: Musée des Beaux-Arts; Cologne: Wallraf-Richartz Museum; Liverpool: Walker Art Gallery; and Amsterdam: Van Gogh Museum [Ghent, 1994]), 95–109; and Bouillon, "Le Modèle cézannien de Maurice Denis," in Françoise Cachin et al., eds., *Cézanne aujourd'hui: Actes du colloque organisé par le Musée d'Orsay, 29 et 30 Novembre 1995* (Paris, 1997), 145–64.
23. "Cézanne," in Denis, *Théories*, 258; and "L'Influence de Cézanne," in Denis, *Nouvelles Théories*, 125. See also Emile Bernard, "Paul Cézanne," *L'Occident* 6 (July 1904): 24, "One should not say *modeler*, one should say *moduler*." Louis Le Bail had the same memory of Cézanne's words; see John Rewald, *Cézanne: A Biography* (New York, 1986), 228.
24. On the twentieth-century distinction between painting a model *(modèle)* and painting a picture *(tableau)*, leading to the question of abstraction, see Jean-Claude Lebensztejn, "Les Textes du peintre" (1974), in *Zigzag* (Paris, 1981), 161–88; and Lebensztejn, "Sol" (1971–72), in *Annexes: De l'œuvre d'art* (Brussels, 1999), 41–58. On the "pictorial" as it developed in nineteenth-century painting and criticism, see Richard Shiff, "Corot and the Painter's Mark: Natural, Personal, Pictorial," *Apollo* 147 (May 1998): 3–8. On related issues of imitation (representation) and copying (reproduction), see Shiff, "The Original, the Imitation, the Copy, and the Spontaneous Classic," *Yale French Studies*, no. 66 (1984): 27–54; and Shiff, "Original Copy," *Common Knowledge* 3 (1994): 88–107.
25. Maurice Denis, "A propos de l'exposition de Charles Guérin" (1905), in Denis, *Théories*, 142–43.
26. Denis, in Morice, "Enquête," 356.
27. "The literary type expresses himself with abstractions, whereas the painter makes his sensations [and] perceptions concrete"; Cézanne, letter of 26 May 1904

to Bernard, in Rewald, ed., *Paul Cézanne: Correspondance*, 303.

28. "A propos de l'exposition de Charles Guérin," in Denis, *Théories*, 144.
29. See Maurice Denis, "La Réaction nationaliste" (1905) and "Cézanne," in Denis, *Théories*, 196, 260.
30. "L'Influence de Cézanne," in Denis, *Nouvelles Théories*, 123–24.
31. "La Mort de Renoir" (1920), in Denis, *Nouvelles Théories*, 116.
32. "A propos de l'exposition de Charles Guérin," in Denis, *Théories*, 143.
33. Emile Bernard, "Paul Cézanne," *Les Hommes d'aujourdhui* 8, no. 387 (February–March 1891): n.p., and Bernard, "Paul Cézanne" (in *L'Occident*), 21. Bernard's views had been affected by those of Gauguin, who, at a still earlier date, argued that the expressive power of Cézanne's painting (and other great art) derived from an essentially abstract use of color and line; see Gauguin's letter of 14 January 1885 to Claude-Emile Schuffenecker, in Paul Gauguin, *Correspondance de Paul Gauguin (1873–1888)*, ed. Victor Merlhès (Paris, 1984), 87–89.
34. See Cézanne's letters of 23 October 1905 and 21 September 1906 to Bernard and of 22 September 1906 to his own son, Paul, in Rewald, ed., *Paul Cézanne: Correspondance*, 315, 327.
35. Francis Carco, *Le Nu dans le peinture moderne (1863–1920)* (Paris, 1924), 48.
36. Where Carco regarded abstraction as a somewhat unnatural impulse, Roger Fry found it entirely proper to painting: "The preoccupation with the female nude is [not] a result of sexual feeling. It is simply that the plasticity of the female figure is peculiarly adapted to pictorial design"; Fry, *Letters of Roger Fry*, ed. Denys Sutton, vol. 2 (New York, 1972), 548.
37. For details of the exhibition and its reception, see Isabelle Cahn, "L'Exposition Cézanne chez Vollard en 1895," in Cachin et al., eds., *Cézanne aujourd'hui*, 135–44.
38. Thadée Natanson, "Paul Cézanne," *La Revue blanche* 9 (1 December 1895): 498.
39. Georges Braque, in André Verdet, "Avec Georges Braque," *XXe siècle* 24, no. 18 (February 1962): n.p.
40. "Having become rich [in his later years], he changed nothing of his way of life. He continued, as in the past, to paint assiduously, never interested in anything but his art"; Duret, *Histoire des peintres impressionnistes*, 189.
41. Charles Camoin, letter of July 1941 to Henri Matisse, in Claudine Grammont, ed., *Correspondance entre Charles Camoin et Henri Matisse* (Lausanne, 1997), 157. On living alone, cf. Cézanne's letter of 31 May 1899 to Egisto Paolo Fabbri, in Rewald, ed., *Paul Cézanne: Correspondance*, 270.
42. Edmond Jaloux, *Les Saisons littéraires, 1896–1903* (Fribourg, 1942), 75–76. On Cézanne's character, see John Rewald, *Cézanne, Geffroy et Gasquet* (Paris, 1959); Lebensztejn, "Persistance de la mémoire," *Critique* 49 (August–September 1993): 609–30; and Richard Shiff, "Introduction," in Michael Doran, ed., *Conversations with Cézanne* (Berkeley, 2001), xix–xxxiv.
43. See Cézanne's reference to death (letter of 21 September 1906 to Bernard) and Bernard's commentary on the actual event, in Bernard, "Souvenirs sur Paul Cézanne," 624–25.
44. Charles Morice, "Paul Cézanne," *Mercure de France* 65 (15 February 1907): 577, 593–94. "Was it fully conscious?": this is a qualification made by the majority of Cézanne's critics, both for and against, who hesitate to say that the artist intended the results attributed to him (cf. the remarks on Roger Fry in Shiff, *Cézanne and the End of Impressionism*, 146–52).
45. Cézanne, letter of 1 September 1902 to Paule Conil, in Rewald, ed., *Paul Cézanne: Correspondance*, 290.
46. Morice, "Le XXIe Salon des Indépendants," 553.
47. Ibid., 542–52.
48. The quoted words and the notion of a successful synthesis are found in Elie Faure, *Les Constructeurs* (Paris, 1921 [1914]), 247, 267. See also Carco, *Le Nu dans le peinture moderne*, 45. Cf. Morice, "Le XXIe Salon des Indépendants," 552. The "anarchic" and "scientific," however much opposed to one another, could be regarded as similar threats to religious values, both representing atheistic extremes of secularism.
49. Charles Morice, "Le Salon d'Automne," *Mercure de France*, vol. 58 (1 December 1905): 390; cf. Morice, "Le XXIe Salon des Indépendants," 552, 555. Morice was probably aware that Paul Signac had associated Cézanne's rectilinear marks with "the methodical *division* of the Neo-impressionists"; Signac 1898, 128. His statements were also informed by Denis's commentary on Guérin's "abstraction" (discussed above), quoted in Morice, "Le XXIe Salon des Indépendants," 546.
50. Morice, "Le XXIe Salon des Indépendants," 552; and Morice, "Paul Cézanne," 592–93. Morice and a number of other critics were drifting toward the kind of analysis later offered from a philosophical perspective by Maurice Merleau-Ponty (Merleau-Ponty, "Le Doute de Cézanne," *Fontaine*, no. 47 (December 1945); reprinted in idem, ed., *Sense et Non-Sense* [Paris, 1948]).
51. Morice, "Paul Cézanne," 592; and Duret, *Histoire des peintres impressionnistes*, 173. Cf. "Cézanne," in Denis,

Théories, 252: "nude figures, unrealistically grouped in a nonexistent landscape."

52. Duret, *Histoire des peintres impressionnistes*, 179.
53. Ibid., 180.
54. Albert Gleizes and Jean Meizinger, *Du cubisme* (Paris, 1912), 9.
55. John Rewald discusses the question of finish/unfinish in his commentary on the latter work; Rewald, *Paintings of Paul Cézanne*, vol. 1, 314–15.
56. Statement reported by Denis, who visited Renoir just after seeing Cézanne in 1906; "Cézanne," in Denis, *Théories*, 252; and "La Mort de Renoir," in Denis, *Nouvelles Théories*, 114. See also Joachim Gasquet, *Cézanne*, 2nd ed. (Paris, 1926), 101. A variant of the statement, referring to only one stroke, is found in Georges Rivière, *Cézanne: Le Peintre solitaire* (Paris, 1936), 19.
57. Picasso, quoted in Hélène Parmelin, *Picasso dit . . .* (Paris, 1966), 85.
58. For a rather extreme account, see Gasquet, *Cézanne*, 101.
59. See Bernard, "Souvenirs sur Paul Cézanne," 609. Complaining of Cézanne's lack of imagination, Bernard believed that his attempt at an allegorical *Apotheosis of Delacroix* was feeble: "he does not know how to give anything form *[dessiner]* without the model, a serious obstacle to any valid creation"; ibid.
60. Natanson, "Paul Cézanne," 500. "He is and remains the painter of apples" was Natanson's characterization of Cézanne, several years before Denis gave this notion pictorial form in his *Hommage à Cézanne*, exhibited at the Salon of 1901.
61. Gustave Geffroy, "Paul Cézanne" (1895), in Geffroy, *La Vie artistique* (Paris, 1892–1903), vol. 6, 215.
62. Charles Baudelaire, "Le Peintre de la vie moderne" (1863), in Baudelaire, *Oeuvres complètes*, ed. Claude Pichois (Paris, 1975–76), vol. 2, 687–88.
63. Geffroy, *La Vie artistique*, vol. 6, 215.
64. Geffroy had referred to Cézanne's "famous apples" in a previous essay: "Paul Cézanne" (1894), in Geffroy, *La Vie artistique*, vol. 3, 259. Indirectly, the attitude of Geffroy and Renoir addressed another of Natanson's issues: the public's desire to get their money's worth by demanding "the greatest number of marks [or strokes, *traits*]"; Natanson, "Paul Cézanne," 497. Cézanne's "unfinished" paintings contained relatively few marks. In 1925 Matisse observed that, had there been no photographs of the works, "people would not have failed to 'finish' all the Cézannes, just as they were in the habit of adding trees to all the Corots"; Henri Matisse, *Ecrits et propos sur l'art*, ed. Dominique Fourcade (Paris, 1972), 87.
65. "Salon de 1901" (1901), in Geffroy, *La Vie artistique*, vol. 8, 376.
66. Cézanne, letter of 8 September 1906 to his son, Paul, in Rewald, ed., *Paul Cézanne: Correspondance*, 324.
67. On this effect, see Friederike Kitschen, *Cézanne: Stilleben* (Ostfildern-Ruit, 1995), 116–18.
68. Louis Le Bail, as recorded in Rewald, *Cézanne: A Biography*, 228.
69. Letter of 23 October 1905 to Bernard, in Rewald, ed., *Paul Cézanne: Correspondance*, 315.
70. See Bernard, "Souvenirs sur Paul Cézanne," 626. The issue of Cézanne's failing eyesight has been raised, but inconclusively, by George Heard Hamilton, "The Dying of the Light: The Late Work of Degas, Monet and Cézanne," in John Rewald and Frances Weitzenhoffer, eds., *Aspects of Monet* (New York, 1984), 230–37.
71. As reported in 1952 by Matisse's ex-student Pierre Dubreuil; Gaston Diehl, *Henri Matisse* (Paris, 1954), 42. See also Henri Matisse, "Notes d'un peintre" (1908), in Matisse, *Ecrits et propos*, 43: "[When] I trace a drawing, it assumes a necessary relationship to its given format." It is significant in this context that Denis became critical of Matisse just as Matisse was developing the "abstract" sense of Cézanne's methods; see Benjamin, *Matisse's "Notes of a Painter,"* 87–99, and Shiff, *Cézanne and the End of Impressionism*, 139–40, 274 n. 85. Denis wrote that Matisse's works at the 1905 Salon d'Automne placed the viewer "fully in the realm of abstraction [and] artificiality. . . . It is painting apart from any contingency, painting in itself, the pure act of painting"; "De Gauguin, de Whistler et de l'excès des théories" (1905), in Denis, *Théories*, 207.
72. See Pierre Schneider, *Matisse*, trans. Michael Taylor and Bridget Strevens (London, 1984), 720 (citing Pierre Courthion's 1941 interview with the artist). Cézanne associated the success of Bouguereau with traditional norms; see Bernard, "Souvenirs sur Paul Cézanne," 609.
73. See Denis, *Journal* (Paris, 1957–59), vol. 1, 157; vol. 2, 34; and Léo Larguier, *Le Dimanche avec Paul Cézanne* (Paris, 1925), 107.
74. Matisse's comments in 1925, 1950, and 1952; Matisse, *Ecrits et propos*, 44 n. 7, 83; and Dominique Fourcade, "Autres propos de Henri Matisse," *Macula* 1 (1976): 101. "It's the man that has changed": Matisse understands that Cézanne's "sensation" must be internal (an emotion) as well as external (a vision). In the present essay I have minimized reference to the important concept of "sensation" because I have investigated it elsewhere; see Richard Shiff, "Sensation, Movement, Cézanne," in *Classic Cézanne*, exh. cat. (Sydney: Art

Gallery of New South Wales, 1998). On Matisse's attitude toward Cézanne, see also Yve-Alain Bois, "Matisse and 'Arche-drawing,'" in *Painting as Model* (Cambridge, Mass., 1990), 3–63; and Isabelle Monod-Fontaine, "Cézanne chez Matisse," in Cachin et al., eds., *Cézanne aujourd'hui*, 165–73.

75. Matisse, "Notes d'un peintre" (1908) and "Notes d'un peintre sur son dessin" (1939), in Matisse, *Ecrits et propos*, 46, 163.
76. Matisse's comments in 1935 and 1936; Matisse, *Ecrits et propos*, 133, 134 n. 104.
77. "Notes d'un peintre," in ibid., 48.
78. Ibid., 47.
79. Ibid., 42.
80. Matisse, quoted in Gaston Diehl, "Avec Matisse le classique," *Comoedia*, no. 102 (12 June 1943): 1. A less idiomatic variant of the same statement appears in Diehl, *Henri Matisse*, 17. Denis used forms of the verb *hiérarchiser* just as Matisse did: "to submit the painting *to a single rhythm*, a dominant, to sacrifice, subordinate, generalize"; "Cézanne" in Denis, *Théories*, 260 (emphasis added).
81. Statement of 1941, in Matisse, *Ecrits et propos*, 71–72 n. 48. On Matisse's sense of the relation of the pictorial quality of a given hue to its quantity (or surface extension), see Bois, "Matisse and 'Arche-drawing,'" 22–23.
82. Matisse's work on this painting may have been interrupted; see Jack Flam, *Matisse: The Man and His Art, 1869–1918* (Ithaca, N.Y., 1986), 498 n. 36.
83. Henri Matisse, "Notizen eines Malers," *Kunst und Künstler* 7 (1908–9): 335–47.
84. Wassily Kandinsky, *Über das Geistige in der Kunst, insbesondere in der Malerei* (Munich, 1912); trans. as "On the Spiritual in Art" (1912), reprinted in Kenneth C. Lindsay and Peter Vergo, eds., *Kandinsky: Complete Writings on Art* (New York, 1994), 34.
85. Because *passage* is a French word used in a technical sense, I will continue to italicize it; its English cognate "passage" would introduce further ambiguities.
86. Paul Signac, "Les Techniques impressionniste et néo-impressionniste," *La Revue blanche* 16 (15 May 1898): 123. In 1889 Pissarro had discussed the theory of *passages* (a word he placed within quotation marks) at the request of the Neo-Impressionist advocate Félix Fénéon; see Pissarro's letter of 20 February 1889 to his son, Lucien, in *Correspondance de Camille Pissarro*, ed. Janine Bailly-Herzberg (Paris, 1980–91), vol. 2, 266. See also William Rubin, "Pablo and Georges and Leo and Bill," *Art in America* 67 (March–April 1979): 146–47 n. 38. Use of the word *passages* at this time was becoming common; see, for example, Jules Christophe, "Dubois-Pillet," *Les Hommes d'aujourd'hui*, no. 370 (1890): 4.
87. Bernard, "Souvenirs sur Paul Cézanne," 400.
88. Ibid., 400, 623. See also Rewald, ed., *Paul Cézanne: Correspondance*, 315.
89. "Consells á l'ébéniste," in Lhote, *Peinture d'abord*, 14. See also "Seurat" (1948), in Lhote, *La Peinture liberée*, 225, where Lhote's reference to "*teintes de passage*" corresponds to the Pissarro-Signac-Bernard definition.
90. "Cézanne," in Denis, *Théories*, 259.
91. Lhote, "L'Enseignement de Cézanne," 669.
92. "Petite Histoire du cubisme," in Lhote, *La Peinture liberée*, 129. Many others gave alternative descriptions, which contain similar elements: "The Cézanne formula led up to cubism . . . a geometrical arrangement of masses in their *rhythmic continuity*, with intervals of shadow and *passages* of tones automatically regulated"; Adolphe Basler and Charles Kunstler, *Modern French Painting: The Modernists from Matisse to de Segonzac* (New York, 1931), 32 (emphasis added). In 1978 the definition of *passage* became a topic of debate between William Rubin and Leo Steinberg. Rubin's sense of *passage* was consistent with Lhote and others who used the term in its broad, traditional sense: see William Rubin, *Picasso in the Collection of the Museum of Modern Art* (New York, 1972), 51; Rubin, "Cézannisme and the Beginnings of Cubism," in *Cézanne: The Late Work*, exh. cat. (New York: Museum of Modern Art, 1977), 165; and Rubin, "Pablo and Georges and Leo and Bill," 137, 139. Steinberg sought a definition specific to Cézanne. He concluded that *passage* occurs where the representation of a projecting or receding plane ceases to appear as such (illusionistically) and refers back to the fundamental materiality of the underlying canvas plane: Leo Steinberg, "The Polemical Part," *Art in America* 67 (March–April 1979): 121–23. In other words, *passage* occurs where a visual metaphor or figure reverts to its literal materiality. Steinberg's alternative to the traditional definition of *passage* may be somewhat anachronistic—Cézanne, like Pissarro, was more concerned with the representation of "atmosphere"—but it suggests why this painter's technique had such a powerful effect on twentieth-century art, so preoccupied with materiality.
93. As much as their twentieth-century heirs, nineteenth-century artists and critics experienced conflict between illusion and pictorial or material effects; but the priorities tended to be reversed. Charles Blanc worried over the actual size of the painter's stroke, lest it interfere with the appreciation of the representational

image; Blanc, "Salon de 1866," *Gazette des beaux-arts* 21 (July 1866): 38. Félix Bracquemond stated a general principle: "The more the mark *[tache]* assumes importance in itself, the more the modeling disappears"; Bracquemond, *De dessin et de la couleur* (Paris, 1885), 42. See also Joseph Masheck, "The Carpet Paradigm: Critical Prolegomena to a Theory of Flatness," *Arts Magazine* 51 (September 1976): 82–109.

94. Lhote, "L'Enseignement de Cézanne," 43.
95. Braque, quoted in Verdet, "Avec Georges Braque," n. p.
96. Georges Braque, quoted in Dora Vallier, "Braque, la peinture et nous: Propos de l'artiste recueillis," *Cahiers d'art* 29 (October 1954): 17. For further investigation of "touch," see Richard Shiff, "Cézanne's Physicality: The Politics of Touch," in Salim Kemal and Ivan Gaskell, eds., *The Language of Art History* (Cambridge, 1991), 129–80.
97. *"Regardez la mer, c'est solide comme la pierre"*: Pablo Picasso, quoted in Rubin (interviewed by Milton Esterow), "Visits with Picasso at Mougins," *Artnews* 72 (Summer 1973): 44. The word "solid" *(solide)* resonates with the famous remark reported by Denis that Cézanne "wanted to make of Impressionism something solid and durable like the art of the museums"; "Cézanne," in Denis, *Théories*, 250. Like Matisse, Picasso spoke reverentially of Cézanne on numerous occasions.
98. Geffroy and other early critics frequently remarked on the tendency of Cézanne's backgrounds to project forward; see "Paul Cézanne" (1894), in Geffroy, *La Vie artistique*, vol. 3, 259. Subsequent critics said the same; see Clement Greenberg, "Cézanne: Gateway to Contemporary Painting" (1952), in Greenberg, *Collected Essays and Criticism*, vol. 3, 117.
99. In the context of Seurat's art, Lhote referred to this same kind of "nothing," a powerful form of pictorialism; "Seurat" (1948), in Lhote, *La Peinture liberée*, 223–24.
100. Picasso differs from Matisse in insisting that his choice of marks is controlled by his will, as opposed to being induced by inherent pictorial forces and tensions, whether arising from the model, the medium, or the artist's own emotions. This difference structures Françoise Gilot's memory of being represented by both artists in 1946: "It was fascinating to see that Matisse's flowing lines became somewhat less flowing but more incisive and sharper under Pablo's hand"; Françoise Gilot, *Matisse and Picasso: A Friendship in Art* (New York, 1990), 27. Cf. Picasso's statement of 1923: "Whenever I had something to say, I have said it in the manner in which I felt it ought to be said"; Dore Ashton, ed., *Picasso on Art: A Selection of Views* (New York, 1977), 5.
101. "Cézanne: Gateway to Contemporary Painting," in Greenberg, *Collected Essays and Criticism*, vol. 3, 117.
102. See "Cézanne and the Unity of Modern Art," in ibid., vol. 3, 87.
103. "The Necessity of the Old Masters" (1948), in ibid., vol. 2, 250–51.
104. "A propos de l'exposition de Charles Guérin," in Denis, *Théories*, 143–44.
105. "De Gauguin, de Whistler et de l'excès des théories," in ibid., 209–10. See also note 71 above.
106. Greenberg's comments on positivism in the context of American art are particularly trenchant in two essays he wrote for European consumption: for England, "The Present Prospects of American Painting and Sculpture" (1947), in Greenberg, *Collected Essays and Criticism*, vol. 2, 160–70 (originally published in *Horizon*); and for France, "L'Art américain au XXe siècle," *Les Temps moderne* 3 (August–September 1946). On Greenberg's sense of positivism, cf. Thierry de Duve, "The Monochrome and the Blank Canvas," in Serge Guilbaut, ed., *Reconstructing Modernism: Art in New York, Paris, and Montreal, 1945–1964* (Cambridge, Mass., 1990), 244–310; and de Duve, *Clement Greenberg between the Lines* (Paris, 1996). See also Yve-Alain Bois, "The Limit of Almost," in William Rubin, ed., *Ad Reinhardt* (New York, 1991), 14–17; and Bois, "Greenberg's Amendments," *Kunst & Museumjournaal* 5, no.1 (1993): 1–9.
107. "Henri Rousseau and Modern Art" (1946), in Greenberg, *Collected Essays and Criticism*, vol. 2, 94.
108. Ibid., 95. See also Shiff, "Breath of Modernism (Metonymic Drift)," in Terry Smith, ed., *In Visible Touch* (Chicago, 1997), 184–213.
109. "Abstract Art" (1944), in Greenberg, *Collected Essays and Criticism*, vol. 1, 202. See also "Cézanne and the Unity of Modern Art" and "Cézanne: Gateway to Contemporary Painting," in ibid., vol. 3, 86–88, 117.
110. "Review of an Exhibition of School of Paris Painters" (1946), in ibid., vol. 2, 88. See also "The Crisis of the Easel Picture" (1948) and "The Role of Nature in Modern Painting" (1949), in ibid., vol. 2, 224, 274.
111. "The New Sculpture" (1949), in ibid., vol. 2, 314–15. A revised version of this essay refers to "our increasing faith in and taste for the immediate, the concrete, the irreducible"; "The New Sculpture" (rev. 1958), in Clement Greenberg, *Art and Culture* (Boston, 1961), 139. In addition to Cézanne, Greenberg

applied this understanding to Matisse, to his "cold hedonism and ruthless exclusion of everything but the concrete, immediate sensation"; "Review of an Exhibition of Joan Miró" (1947), in Greenberg, *Collected Essays and Criticism*, vol. 2, 155.

112. "The Present Prospects of American Painting and Sculpture," in Greenberg, *Collected Essays and Criticism*, vol. 2, 164.

113. "Cézanne" (rev. 1958), in Greenberg, *Art and Culture*, 54. Critical terms can be deceptive. In Greenberg's context "literal" should not be associated with an artist's use of "literary" thematics, as it would be in Denis's theory. Cézanne's commitment to the traditional means of representing volume and spatial distance was a standard feature of the early accounts: according to Bernard, the painter said that he "would never accept the lack of modeling or of gradation"; Bernard, "Souvenirs sur Paul Cézanne," 400.

114. Recalling the situation of his generation during the 1940s, Barnett Newman spoke of having had "to start from scratch . . . to examine the whole process. . . . We couldn't build on anything. The world was going to pot"; "Interview with Emile de Antonio" (1970), in Newman, *Selected Writings and Interviews*, ed. John P. O'Neill (New York, 1990), 303–4.

115. See Geelhaar, " 'The Painters Who Had the Right Eyes,' " 297–98; Roberta Bernstein, "Seeing a Thing Can Sometimes Trigger the Mind to Make Another Thing," in *Jasper Johns: A Retrospective*, ed. Kirk Varnedoe, exh. cat. (New York: Museum of Modern Art, 1996), 42; and Johns, quoted in Edmund White, "MoMA's Boy," *Vanity Fair*, no. 433 (September 1996): 304. In 1994 Johns made a series of drawings *(Tracings)* after the Barnes Foundation's *Large Bathers* of 1894–1905 (Rewald 856), discussed in Bernstein, "Seeing a Thing," 63.

116. Jasper Johns, quoted in Grace Glueck, "The 20th-Century Artists Most Admired by Other Artists," *Artnews* 76 (November 1977): 87. Given the context, Johns appears to be claiming that Cézanne's touch captures the look of an object so as to convey something of its tactile nature, yet also retain a palpable materiality of its own. See also Shiff, "Cézanne's Physicality," on touch in Cézanne and Picasso, and Shiff, "Breath of Modernism," 207–13, on touch in Johns.

117. "If the painting is an object, then the object can be a painting"; Jasper Johns, in Walter Hopps, "An Interview with Jasper Johns," *Artforum* 3 (March 1965): 35.

118. Brice Marden, "Three Deliberate Greys for Jasper Johns," *Art Now: New York* 3, no. 1 (March 1971): n.p. Marden stated that the dimensions of his painting surface were derived directly from Johns. See also Marden, "Brice Marden in Conversation with William Furlong," *Art Monthly*, no. 117 (June 1988): 4. "Jasper has influenced me [regarding] painting as a reality rather than depiction."

119. On *Grove Group Notebook* and the paintings related to it, see Robert Pincus-Witten, *Brice Marden: The Grove Group*, exh. cat. (New York: Gagosian Gallery, 1991).

120. Brice Marden, *Suicide Notes* (Lausanne, 1974), 40 (punctuation added). On the circumstances surrounding *Suicide Notes*, see Alan Moore, Edit de Ak, and Mike Robinson, "Conversation with Brice Marden," *Art-Rite*, no. 9 (Spring 1975): 40. On Marden and Cézanne, see also Bois, "Greenberg's Amendments," 53–67.

121. Cf. Marden's statement from 1978: "I think the grid is an arbitrary measure to put on space; it's like a molecule next to a molecule. These paintings *[Annunciations]* are particles of the grid which is space, and they can be dissonant or they can be cordial"; quoted in Jean-Claude Lebensztejn, "From," in *Brice Marden: Recent Paintings and Drawings*, exh. cat. (New York: Pace Gallery, 1978), n.p.

122. Quoted in Pat Steir, "Brice Marden: An Interview" in *Brice Marden: Recent Drawings and Etchings*, exh. cat. (New York: Matthew Marks Gallery, 1991), n.p. Believing that work need not be finished to be shown, Marden often resumes a painting after its exhibition; see Marden, statement in "Interview by Robin White at Crown Point Press, Oakland, California, 1980," *View* 3 (1980): 22.

123. See Trevor Fairbrother, *Brice Marden: Boston*, exh. cat. (Boston: Museum of Fine Arts, 1991), 7.

124. Ibid., 30.

125. Plimack Mangold's practice has been related to statements by Cézanne in Cheryl Brutvan, *The Paintings of Sylvia Plimack Mangold* (New York, 1994), 42–44.

Select Bibliography

Additional works are cited in the notes to each chapter.

Primary Sources and Criticism

About, Edmond. "Le Salon de 1868." *Revue des deux mondes,* 1 June 1868, 714–45.

———. "Le Salon de 1869." *Revue des deux mondes,* 1 June 1869, 725–58.

Astruc, Zacharie. "Salon de 1868 aux Champs-Elysées: Le Grand Style—II." *L'Etendard,* 27 June 1868.

Babou, Hippolyte. "Les Dissidents de l'exposition." *Revue libérale* 2 (1867): 284–89.

Baudelaire, Charles. *Ecrits sur l'art,* 2 vols. Paris: Livre de Poche, 1971.

———. "Exposition Universelle 1855: Beaux-arts, I: Méthode de critique. De l'idée moderne du progrès appliquée aux beaux-arts." *Le Pays,* 26 May 1855; reprinted in Baudelaire, *Ecrits sur l'art,* 1.

———. *Oeuvres complètes.* Paris: Gallimard, 1961.

Berson, Ruth, ed. *The New Painting: Impressionism, 1874–1886: Documentation.* 2 vols. (vol. 1 reviews; vol. 2 exhibited works). San Francisco: Fine Arts Museums of San Francisco, and Seattle: University of Washington Press, 1996.

Bigot, Charles. "Causerie artistique: L'Exposition des 'impressionnistes.'" *La Revue politique et littéraire,* 28 April 1877, 1045–48.

Blanc, Charles. *Grammaire des arts du dessin: Architecture, sculpture, peinture.* Paris: Vve J. Renouard, 1870.

———. *Rapport au Ministre de l'Instruction Publique, des Cultes et des Beaux-Arts, sur l'Exposition Nationale de 1872,* December 1871; reprinted in catalogue of the Salon of 1872.

———. "Salon de 1846, IV." *La Réforme,* 19 April 1846.

———. "Salon de 1866 (2e article)." *Gazette des beaux-arts,* 1 July 1866, 28–71.

Bouillon, Jean-Paul, ed. *La Critique d'art en France, 1850–1900.* Saint-Etienne: CIEREC, 1989.

Bouillon, Jean-Paul, Nicole Dubreuil-Blondin, Antoinette Ehrard, and Constance Naubert-Riser, eds. *La Promenade du critique influent: Anthologie de la critique d'art en France, 1850–1900.* Paris: Hazan, 1990.

Brookner, Anita. *The Genius of the Future.* London: Phaidon, 1971.

Burty, Philippe. "Chronique du jour." *La République française,* 16 April 1874.

———. "Exposition de la Société anonyme des artistes." *La République française,* 25 April 1874.

———. "L'Hôtel des ventes et le commerce de tableaux." In *Paris Guide,* vol. 2. Paris: A. Lacroix, 1867.

———. "Les Paysages de M. Claude Monet." *La République française,* 27 March 1883.

———. Preface to sale catalogue, *Tableaux et aquarelles par Claude Monet, Berthe Morisot, A. Renoir, A. Sisley.* Hôtel Drouot, Paris, 24 March 1875; reprinted in Riout, *Les Ecrivains devant l'impressionnisme.*

———. Preface to sale catalogue, *Tableaux et dessins par M. Amand Gautier*. Hôtel Drouot, Paris, 1 April 1875.

———. "Le Salon, I, III, V, IX." *Le Rappel*, 2, 11, and 20 May; 12 June 1870.

Castagnary, Jules-Antoine. "Exposition du boulevard des Capucines: Les Impressionnistes." *Le Siècle*, 29 April 1874.

———. *Salons (1857–1879)*. Paris, 1892.

Champier, Victor. *L'Année artistique, 1879*. Paris, 1880

Chaumelin, Marius. "Salon de 1868, III." *La Presse*, 11 June 1868.

———. "Le Salon de 1869, V." *L'Indépendance belge*, 21 June 1869.

———. "Salon de 1870, VII." *La Presse*, 17 June 1870.

Chennevières, Philippe de. *Souvenirs d'un directeur des beaux-arts*, new edition with preface by Jacques Foucart and Louis-Antoine Prat. Paris: Arthena, 1979.

Chesneau, Ernest. "A côté du Salon, II." *Paris-Journal*, 7 May 1874.

Chevalier, Frédéric. "Les Impressionnistes." *L'Artiste*, 1 May 1877, 329–33.

Claretie, Jules. *L'Art et les artistes français contemporains*. Paris: Charpentier, 1876.

———. *Peintres et sculpteurs contemporains*. Paris: Librairie des bibliophiles, 1882–84.

Crouzet, Marcel. *Un Méconnu du réalisme: Duranty*. Paris: Nizet, 1964.

Denis, Maurice. *Théories, 1890–1910*. Paris: L. Rouart and J. Watelin, 1920 (1st ed. 1912).

Denvir, Bernard. *The Impressionists at First Hand*. London: Thames and Hudson, 1987.

Du Pays, A. J. "Salon de 1859 (neuvième article)." *L'Illustration*, 2 July 1859, 19–22.

Duranty, E. *La Nouvelle Peinture*. Paris, 1876; reprinted in Moffett, ed., *The New Painting*, and Berson, ed., *The New Painting*.

———. "Le Salon de 1870, III, XII." *Paris-Journal*, 5, 19 May 1870.

———. "Sur le Physionomie." *Revue libérale*, 10 July 1867.

Duret, Théodore. *Critique d'avant-garde*. Paris, 1885; reprinted with introduction by Denys Riout, Paris: Ecole Nationale Supérieure des Beaux-Arts, 1998.

Duvergier de Hauranne, Ernest. "Le Salon de 1874." *Revue des deux mondes*, 1 June 1874.

Enault, Louis. "Mouvement artistique: L'Exposition des intransigeants." *Le Constitutionnel*, 10 April 1876.

Ephrussi, Charles. "Exposition des artistes indépendants." *Gazette des beaux-arts*, 1 May 1880, 485–88.

Exposition internationale de peinture, deuxième année, exh. cat. Paris: Galerie Georges Petit, 1883.

Fénéon, Félix. *Oeuvres plus que complètes*, 2 vols. Geneva: Droz, 1970.

Flint, Kate, ed. *Impressionists in England: The Critical Reception*. London: Routledge, 1984.

Fromentin, Eugène. *Les Maîtres d'autrefois*. Paris, 1876.

Gantès, F. de. "Courrier artistique: L'Exposition du boulevard." *La Semaine parisienne*, 23 April 1874.

Gautier, Théophile. *Abécédaire du Salon de 1861*. Paris, 1861.

———. "La Rue Laffitte." *L'Artiste*, 3 January 1858, 10–13.

———. *Tableaux à la plume*. Paris, 1880.

Geffroy, Gustave. *Pays d'ouest*. Paris, 1897.

———. *La Vie artistique*, vol. 1. Paris, 1892.

Goncourt, Edmond de, and Jules de Goncourt. *Journal: Mémoires de la vie littéraire*, ed. Robert Ricatte, 3 vols. Paris: Robert Laffont, 1989.

Greenberg, Clement. *The Collected Essays and Criticism*, 4 vols., ed. John O'Brian. Chicago: University of Chicago Press, 1986.

Harrison, Charles, and Paul Wood, eds. *Art in Theory, 1900–2000: An Anthology of Changing Ideas*. Oxford: Blackwell, 2003.

Henriet, Frédéric. "Le Musée des rues, 1: Le Marchand de tableaux." *L'Artiste*, 15 November 1854, 113–15, and 1 December 1854, 133–35.

———. *Le Paysagiste aux champs*. Paris, 1876.

Houssaye, Arsène. "Les Petites Expositions de peinture." *Revue des deux mondes*, 1 March 1880, 193–202.

Huysmans, Joris-Karl. *L'Art moderne*. Paris, 1883.

Isaacson, Joel. "Constable, Duranty, Mallarmé, Impressionism, Plein Air, and Forgetting." *Art Bulletin* (September 1994): 427–50.

"Jacques." "Menus propos: Salon impressionniste." *L'Homme libre*, 11–12 April 1877.

Jowell, Frances Suzman. *Thoré-Bürger and the Art of the Past*. New York: Garland Press, 1977.

Laforgue, Jules. "L'Impressionnisme," 1883. First published in *Mélanges posthumes* (Paris, 1903). Reprinted in Laforgue, *Textes de critique d'art*, and Richard R. Brettell, *Impression: Painting Quickly in France, 1860–1890* (New Haven: Yale University Press in association with the Sterling and Francine Clark Art Institute [Williamstown, Mass.], 2000).

———. *Textes de critique d'art*, ed. Mireille Dottin. Lille: Presses Universitaires de Lille, 1988.

Leroy, Louis. "L'Exposition des impressionnistes." *Le Charivari*, 25 April 1874, 79–80.

Mantz, Paul. "Salon de 1868, V." *L'Illustration*, 6 June 1868.

———. "Salon de 1869, II." *Gazette des beaux-arts*, July 1869, 5–23.

Martelli, Diego. *Les Impressionnistes et l'art moderne*, ed. Francesca Errico. Paris: Vilo, 1979.

Massarani, Tullo. *L'Art à Paris*, 2 vols. Paris, 1880.

Maupassant, Guy de. "La Vie d'un paysagiste." *Gil Blas*, 28 September 1886; reprinted in Riout, *Les Ecrivains devant l'impressionnisme*.

Montifaud, Marc de. "Exposition du boulevard des Capucines." *L'Artiste*, 1 May 1874, 307–13.

Moore, George. *Impressions and Opinions*. New York: Scribner, 1891.

Neiss, Robert J. *Zola, Cézanne, and Manet: A Study of "L'Oeuvre."* Ann Arbor: University of Michigan Press, 1968.

Nochlin, Linda, ed. *Impressionism and Post-Impressionism, 1874–1904: Sources and Documents*. Englewood Cliffs, N.J.: Prentice Hall, 1966.

Olby, G. d'. "Salon de 1876: Avant l'ouverture—exposition des intransigeants." *Le Pays*, 10 April 1876.

Orwicz, Michael, ed. *Art Criticism and Its Institutions in Nineteenth-Century France*. Manchester: Manchester University Press, 1994.

Parsons, Christopher, and Martha Ward. *A Bibliography of Salon Criticism in Second Empire Paris*. Cambridge: Cambridge University Press, 1986.

Perrier, Charles. "Du réalisme." *L'Artiste*, 14 October 1855, 85–90.

Planche, Gustave. *Etudes sur l'école française (1831–52)*. Paris: M. Levy, 1855.

Privat, Gonzague. *Place aux jeunes! Causeries critiques sur le Salon de 1865*. Paris: F. Cournol, 1865.

Prouvaire, Jean. "L'Exposition du boulevard des Capucines." *Le Rappel*, 20 April 1874.

Reclus, Elisée. "Du sentiment de la nature dans les sociétés modernes." *Revue des deux mondes*, 15 May 1866, 352–81.

Renoir, Edmund. "Cinquième Exposition de la Vie moderne." *La Vie moderne*, 19 June 1879, 174–75.

Riout, Denys, ed. *Les Ecrivains devant l'impressionnisme*. Paris: Macula, 1989.

Rivière, Georges. "L'Exposition des impressionnistes." *L'Impressionniste*, 6 May 1877, 2–6, and 14 May 1877, 1–4, 6.

———. "Les Intransigeants et les impressionnistes: Souvenirs du Salon libre de 1877." *L'Artiste*, 1 November 1877, 289–302.

Roos, Jane Mayo. "Aristocracy and the Arts: Philippe de Chennevières and the Salons of the Mid-1870s." *Art Journal* (Spring 1989): 53–62.

Schop, Baron. "La Semaine parisienne: L'Exposition des intransigeants—L'Ecole des Batignolles—Impressionnistes et plein air." *Le National*, 7 April 1876.

Silvestre, Théophile. "Salon de 1874, III." *Le Pays*, 20 May 1874.

Simpson, Juliet. "Bourget, Laforgue, and Impressionism's Inside Story." *French Studies* 55, no. 4 (2001): 467–83.

Snell, Robert. *Théophile Gautier: A Romantic Critic of the Visual Arts*. Oxford: Clarendon Press, 1982.

Stock. "Le Salon par Stock." *Album Stock*, 20 March 1870.

Thoré, Théophile. *Salons de W. Bürger, 1861 à 1868*, 2 vols. Paris: Renouard, 1870.

[Vassy, Gaston]. "La Journée à Paris: L'Exposition des impressionnistes." *L'Evénement*, 6 April 1877.

Venturi, Lionello. *Les Archives de l'impressionnisme*, 2 vols. Paris, 1939.

Vinet, Ernest. "Correspondence: Letters from Paris." *Fine Arts Quarterly Review* (October 1866): 431–46.

Weinberg, Bernard. *French Realism: The Critical Reaction, 1830–1870*. New York: Modern Language Association of America, 1937.

White, Barbara Ehrlich, ed. *Impressionism in Perspective*. Englewood Cliffs, N.J.: Prentice-Hall, 1978.

Wrigley, R. *The Origins of French Art Criticism: From the Ancien Régime to the Restoration*. Oxford: Clarendon Press, 1993.

Wolff, Albert. "Le Calendrier parisien." *Le Figaro*, 3 April 1876.

Zemel, Carol. *The Formation of a Legend: Van Gogh Criticism, 1890–1920*. Ann Arbor, Mich.: UMI Research Press, 1980.

Zola, Emile. "Les Chutes." *L'Evénement*, 15 May 1866; reprinted in Zola, *Mon Salon, Manet*.

———. "Edouard Manet." *Revue de XIXe siècle*, 1 January 1867; reprinted in Zola, *Mon Salon, Manet*.

———. "Le Moment artistique." *L'Evénement*, 4 May 1866; reprinted in Zola, *Mon Salon, Manet*.

———. *Mon Salon, Manet: Ecrits sur l'art*, ed. A. Ehrard. Paris: Garnier-Flammarion, 1970.

———. "Le Naturalisme au Salon." *Le Voltaire*, 18–22 June, 1880; reprinted in Zola, *Mon Salon, Manet*.

General and Period Studies

Adams, Steven. *The Barbizon School and the Origins of Impressionism*. London: Phaidon, 1994.

Assouling, Pierre. *Discovering Impressionism: The Life of Paul Durand-Ruel*, trans. Willard Wood and Anthony Roberts. New York: Magowan and Vendome Press, 2004.

Bodelsen, Merete. "Early Impressionist Sales 1874–94 in the Light of Some Unpublished 'Procès-verbaux.'" *Burlington Magazine* (June 1968): 331–48.

Boime, Albert. *The Academy and French Painting in the Nineteenth Century.* London: Phaidon, 1971.

———. *Art and the French Commune: Imagining Paris after War and Revolution.* Princeton, N.J.: Princeton University Press, 1995.

Brettell, Richard R. *Modern Art, 1851–1929: Capitalism and Representation.* Oxford: Oxford University Press, 1999.

Broude, Norma. *Impressionism: A Feminist Reading: The Gendering of Art, Science, and Nature in the Nineteenth Century.* New York: Rizzoli, 1991.

———. *World Impressionism: The International Movement, 1860–1920.* New York: Abrams, 1960.

Bürger, Peter. *Theory of the Avant-Garde.* Manchester: Manchester University Press; and Minneapolis: University of Minnesota Press, 1984.

Callen, Anthea. *The Art of Impressionism: Painting Technique and the Making of Modernity.* New Haven: Yale University Press, 2000.

———. *Techniques of the Impressionists.* London: Orbis, 1982.

Champa, Kermit. *Studies in Early Impressionism.* New Haven: Yale University Press, 1973.

Clark, Timothy J. *Farewell to an Idea: Episodes from a History of Modernism.* New Haven: Yale University Press, 1999.

———. *The Painting of Modern Life: Paris in the Art of Manet and His Followers.* New York: Knopf, 1985.

Clayson, Hollis. *Painted Love: Prostitution in French Art of the Impressionist Era.* New Haven: Yale University Press, 1991.

———. *Paris in Despair: Art and Everyday Life under the Siege (1870–71).* Chicago: University of Chicago Press, 2002.

Cottington, David. *Cubism in the Shadow of War: The Avant-Garde and Politics in Paris, 1905–1914.* New Haven: Yale University Press, 1998.

Crary, Jonathan. *Suspensions of Perception: Attention, Spectacle, and Modern Culture.* Cambridge, Mass.: MIT Press, 1999.

———. *Techniques of the Observer: On Vision and Modernity in the Nineteenth Century.* Cambridge, Mass.: MIT Press, 1990.

Crow, Thomas. "Modernism and Mass Culture in the Visual Arts." In *Modernism and Modernity: The Vancouver Conference Papers,* ed. Benjamin H. D. Buchloh, Serge Guilbaut, and David Solkin. Halifax: Press of the Nova Scotia College of Art and Design, 1983; revised version in Crow, *Modern Art in the Common Culture.* New Haven: Yale University Press, 1996.

Dawkins, Heather. *The Nude in French Art and Culture, 1870–1910.* Cambridge: Cambridge University Press, 2002.

Distel, Anne. *Impressionism: The First Collectors.* New York: Abrams, 1990.

Eisenman, Stephen F., et al. *Nineteenth-Century Art: A Critical History.* London: Thames and Hudson, 1994.

Ferguson, Priscilla Parkhurst. *Paris as Revolution: Writing the Nineteenth-Century City.* Berkeley: University of California Press, 1994.

Fidell-Beaufort, Madeleine, and Jeanne K. Welcher. "Some Views of Art Buying in New York in the 1870s and 1880s." *Oxford Art Journal* 5, no. 1 (1982): 48–55.

Fowle, Frances, and Richard Thomson, eds. *Soil and Stone: Impressionism, Urbanism, Environment.* Aldershot: Ashgate, 2003.

Frascina, Francis, et al. *Modernity and Modernism: French Painting in the Nineteenth Century.* New Haven: Yale University Press, 1993.

Garb, Tamar. *Bodies of Modernity: Figure and Flesh in Fin-de-Siècle France.* London: Thames and Hudson, 1998.

———. *Sisters of the Brush: Women's Artistic Culture in Late Nineteenth-Century Paris.* New Haven: Yale University Press, 1994.

———. *Women Impressionists.* Oxford: Phaidon, 1986.

Green, Nicholas. " 'All the Flowers of the Field': The State, Liberalism, and Art in France under the Early Third Republic." *Oxford Art Journal* 10, no. 1 (1987): 71–84.

———. "Circuits of Production, Circuits of Consumption: The Case of Mid-Nineteenth-Century French Art Dealing." *Art Journal* (Spring 1989): 29–34.

———. *The Spectacle of Nature: Landscape and Bourgeois Culture in Nineteenth-Century France.* Manchester: Manchester University Press, 1990.

Harrison, Charles. *Painting the Difference: Sex and Spectator in Modern Art.* Chicago: University of Chicago Press, 2005.

Herbert, Robert L. *From Millet to Léger: Essays in Social Art History.* New Haven: Yale University Press, 2002.

———. *Impressionism: Art, Leisure, and Parisian Society.* New Haven: Yale University Press, 1988.

Hobbs, Richard, ed. *Impressions of French Modernity: Art and Literature in France, 1850–1900.* Manchester: Manchester University Press, 1998.

House, John. "Die französische Landschaft 1877: 'Le Village de Lavardin (Loir-et-Cher)' von Charles Busson." In *Jenseits der Grenzen* (festschrift for Thomas W. Gaehtgens), ed. U. Fleckner, M. Schieder, and M. F. Zimmermann. Cologne: Dumont, 2000, 11.

———. "The French Nineteenth-Century Landscape." In

Culture, Landscape, and the Environment: The Linacre Lectures 1997, ed. Kate Flint and Howard Morphy. Oxford: Oxford University Press, 2000.

———. *Impressionism: Paint and Politics*. New Haven: Yale University Press, 2004.

———. "Impressionism and History: The Rewald Legacy." *Art History* (September 1986): 369–76.

Hutton. John G. *Neo-Impressionism and the Search for Solid Ground: Art, Science, and Anarchism in Fin-de-Siècle France*. Baton Rouge: Louisiana State University Press, 1994.

Jensen, Robert. *Marketing Modernism in Fin-de-Siècle Europe*. Princeton, N.J.: Princeton University Press, 1994.

Mainardi, Patricia. *Art and Politics of the Second Empire: The Universal Expositions of 1855 and 1867*. New Haven: Yale University Press, 1987.

———. "The Double Exhibition in Nineteenth-Century France." *Art Journal* (Spring 1989): 23–28.

———. *The End of the Salon: Art and the State in the Early Third Republic*. Cambridge: Cambridge University Press, 1993.

Mayeur, Jean-Marie, and Madeleine Rebérioux. *The Third Republic from Its Origins to the Great War, 1871–1914*. Cambridge: Cambridge University Press, 1984.

McQuillan, Melissa. *Impressionist Portraits*. London: Thames and Hudson, 1986.

Melot, Michel. *The Impressionist Print*. New Haven: Yale University Press, 1996.

Nochlin, Linda. *The Politics of Vision: Essays on Nineteenth-Century Art and Society*. New York: Harper and Row, 1989; London: Thames and Hudson, 1991.

———. *Realism*. Harmondsworth: Penguin Books, 1971.

———. *Women, Art, and Power and Other Essays*. New York: Harper and Row, 1988; London: Thames and Hudson, 1989.

Nord, Philip. *Impressionists and Politics: Art and Democracy in the Nineteenth Century*. London and New York: Routledge, 2000.

Poggioli, Renato. *The Theory of the Avant-Garde*. Cambridge, Mass.: Harvard University Press, 1968.

Pollock, Griselda. *Avant-Garde Gambits, 1888–1893: Gender and the Colour of Art History*. London: Thames and Hudson, 1992.

———. "Modernity and the Spaces of Femininity." In *Vision and Difference: Femininity, Feminism, and the Histories of Art*. London: Routledge, 1988.

Pool, Phoebe. *Impressionism*. London: Thames and Hudson, 1967.

Rewald, John. *The History of Impressionism*, 4th ed. New York: Museum of Modern Art, 1973.

———. *Post-Impressionism from Van Gogh to Gauguin*, 3rd ed. New York: Museum of Modern Art, 1979.

———. *Studies in Impressionism*. New York: Abrams, 1985.

———. *Studies in Post-Impressionism*. New York: Abrams, 1986.

Roos, Jane Mayo. *Early Impressionism and the French State, 1866–1874*. Cambridge: Cambridge University Press, 1996.

Rubin, James H. *Impressionism*. London: Phaidon, 1999.

Schapiro, Meyer. *Impressionism: Reflections and Perceptions*. New York: Braziller, 1997.

———. *Modern Art: Nineteenth and Twentieth Centuries*. New York: Braziller, 1978.

Shiff, Richard. *Cézanne and the End of Impressionism: A Study of the Theory, Technique, and Critical Evaluation of Modern Art*. Chicago: University of Chicago Press, 1984.

Smith, Paul. *Impressionism: Beneath the Surface*. London: Calmann and King, 1995.

Thomson, Belinda. *Impressionism: Origins, Practice, Reception*. London: Thames and Hudson, 2000.

———. *The Post-Impressionists*. Oxford: Phaidon, 1983.

Thomson, Richard, ed. *Framing France: The Representation of Landscape in France, 1874–1914*. Manchester: Manchester University Press, 1998.

Wadley, Nicholas. *Impressionist and Post-Impressionist Drawing*. London: Studio, 1991.

Ward, Martha. *Pissarro, Neo-Impressionism, and the Spaces of the Avant-Garde*. Chicago: University of Chicago Press, 1996.

White, Barbara Ehrlich. *Impressionists Side-by-Side: Their Friendships, Rivalries, and Artistic Exchanges*. New York: Knopf, 1996.

Selected Recent Catalogues: Group Exhibitions

Bailey, Colin, Joseph Rishel, et al. *Masterpieces of Impressionism and Post-Impressionism: The Annenberg Collection*. Philadelphia: Philadelphia Museum of Art, 1989.

Bazaine, Jean, et al. *Claude Monet [. . .] up to Digital Impressionism*. Berlin: Fondation Beyeler in association with Prestel (Munich), 2002.

Bomford, David, et al. *Art in the Making: Impressionism.* London: National Gallery, 1990.

Brettell, Richard R. *Impression: Painting Quickly in France, 1860–1890.* New Haven: Yale University Press in association with the Sterling and Francine Clark Art Institute (Williamstown, Mass.), 2000.

Brettell, Richard R., et al. *A Day in the Country: Impressionism and the French Landscape.* Los Angeles: Los Angeles County Museum of Art, 1984.

Brettell, Richard R., and Anne-Birgitte Fonsmark. *Gauguin and Impressionism.* New Haven: Yale University Press in association with the Kimball Art Museum (Fort Worth, Tex.), 2005.

Champa, Kermit. *Monet & Bazille: A Collaboration.* Atlanta, Ga.: High Museum of Art in association with Harry N. Abrams (New York), 1999.

Champa, Kermit, et al. *The Rise of Landscape Painting in France: Corot to Monet.* Manchester, N.H.: Currier Gallery of Art, 1991.

Clarke, Michael. *Lighting Up the Landscape: French Impressionism and Its Origins.* Edinburgh: National Gallery of Scotland, 1986.

Dayez, Anne, Michel Hoog, and Charles S. Moffett. *Impressionism: A Centenary Exhibition.* New York: Metropolitan Museum of Art, 1974.

Des plaines à l'usine: Images du travail dans la peinture française de 1870 à 1914. Dunkerque: Musée des Beaux-Arts, 2001.

Les Femmes Impressionnistes: Mary Cassatt, Eva Gonzales, Berthe Morisot. Paris: Musée Marmottan, 1993.

Gunnarsson, Torsten, et al. *Impressionism and the North: Late 19th-Century French Avant-Garde Art and the Art in the Nordic Countries, 1870–1920.* Stockholm: Nationalmuseum, 2002.

Herbert, Robert. *Neo-Impressionism.* New York: Guggenheim Museum, 1968.

Homburg, Cornelia, et al. *Vincent van Gogh and the Painters of the Petit Boulevard.* St. Louis: St. Louis Art Museum in association with Rizzoli (New York), 2001.

House, John. *Impressionism for England: Samuel Courtauld as Patron and Collector.* London: Courtauld Institute Galleries, 1984.

House, John, et al. *Landscapes of France: Impressionism and Its Rivals.* London: Hayward Gallery; Boston: Museum of Fine Arts, 1995.

———. *Monet's London: Artists' Reflections on the Thames, 1859–1914.* St. Petersburg, Fla.: Museum of Fine Arts, 2005.

Isaacson, Joel. *The Crisis of Impressionism, 1878–1882.* Ann Arbor: University of Michigan Museum of Art, 1979.

Johnston, Sona, John House, et al. *Faces of Impressionism: Portraits from American Collections.* Baltimore: Baltimore Museum of Art, 1999.

Lochnan, Katherine J. *Turner, Whistler, Monet.* London: Tate Publishing in association with the Art Gallery of Ontario, 2004.

Moffett, Charles, et al. *Impressionists in Winter: Effets de Neige.* Washington, D.C.: Phillips Collection, 1998.

———. *Impressionists on the Seine: A Celebration of Renoir's "Luncheon of the Boating Party."* Washington, D.C.: Phillips Collection, 1996.

———. *The New Painting: Impressionism, 1874–1886.* San Francisco: Fine Arts Museums of San Francisco, 1986.

Le Néo-impressionnisme de Seurat à Paul Klee. Paris: Musée d'Orsay, 2005.

Pissarro, Joachim. *Pioneering Modern Painting: Cézanne & Pissarro, 1865–1885.* New York: Museum of Modern Art, 2005.

Rathbone, Eliza E., and George T. M. Shackelford. *Impressionist Still Life.* Washington, D.C.: Phillips Collection, 2001.

Robins, Anna Gruetzner, and Richard Thomson. *Degas, Sickert, and Toulouse-Lautrec: London and Paris, 1870–1910.* London: Tate Publishing, 2005.

Roos, Jane Mayo. *A Painter's Poet: Stéphane Mallarmé and His Impressionist Circle.* New York: Hunter College, 1999.

Shackelford, George, and Fronia E. Wissman. *Monet, Renoir, and the Impressionist Landscape.* Ottawa: National Gallery of Canada, 2000.

Thomson, Richard. *Monet to Matisse: Landscape Painting in France, 1874–1914.* Edinburgh: National Gallery of Scotland, 1994.

Tinterow, Gary, et al. *Splendid Legacy: The Havemeyer Collection.* New York: Metropolitan Museum of Art, 1993.

Tinterow, Gary, and Henri Loyrette. *Origins of Impressionism.* New York: Metropolitan Museum of Art, 1994.

Tucker, Paul H. *The Impressionists at Argenteuil.* Washington, D.C.: National Gallery of Art, 2000.

Wattenmaker, Richard J., et al. *Great French Paintings from the Barnes Foundation.* New York: Knopf in association with Lincoln University Press, 1993.

Wayne, Kenneth, et al. *Impressions of the Riviera: Monet, Renoir, Matisse, and Their Contemporaries.* Portland, Maine: Portland Museum of Art, 1998.

Wilson-Bareau, Juliet. *Manet, Monet, and the Gare Saint-Lazare.* Washington, D.C.: National Gallery of Art, 1998.

Recent Monographic Exhibitions

BAZILLE

Jourdan, Aleth, et al. *Frédéric Bazille: Prophet of Impressionism*. Brooklyn: Brooklyn Museum of Art, 1992.

Marandel, Patrice. *Frédéric Bazille and Early Impressionism*. Chicago: Art Institute of Chicago, 1978.

CAILLEBOTTE

Distel, Anne, et al. *Gustave Caillebotte: Urban Impressionist*. Chicago: Art Institute of Chicago, 1995.

Gustave Caillebotte. Paris: Grand Palais, Réunion des Musées Nationaux, 1994.

Varnedoe, Kirk, et al. *Gustave Caillebotte: A Retrospective Exhibition*. Houston: Houston Museum of Fine Arts, 1976.

CÉZANNE

Baumann, Felix, ed. *Cézanne: Finished, Unfinished*. Vienna: Kunstforum, 2000; Ostfildern-Ruit: Hatje Cantz, 2000.

Cachin, Françoise, et al. *Cézanne*. Paris: Grand Palais; London: Tate Gallery; Philadelphia: Philadelphia Museum of Art, 1995–96.

Conisbee, Philip, et al. *Cézanne in Provence*. Washington, D.C.: National Gallery of Art in association with Yale University Press (New Haven), 2006.

Gowing, Lawrence, et al. *Cézanne: The Early Years, 1859–1872*. London: Royal Academy of Arts, 1988.

Krumrine, Mary Louise. *Paul Cézanne: The Bathers*. Basel: Museum of Fine Arts in association with Abrams (New York), 1989.

Rubin, William, ed. *Cézanne: The Late Work*. New York: Museum of Modern Art, 1977.

Verdi, Richard. *Cézanne and Poussin: The Classical Vision of Landscape*. Edinburgh: National Galleries of Scotland in association with Lund Humphries (London), 1990.

DEGAS

Boggs, Jean Sutherland, et al. *Degas*. New York: Metropolitan Museum of Art, 1988.

———. *Degas at the Races*. Washington, D.C.: National Gallery of Art in association with Yale University Press (New Haven), 1998.

Kendall, Richard. *Degas: Beyond Impressionism*. London: National Gallery Publications in association with Art Institute of Chicago, 1996.

———. *Degas and the Little Dancer*. Omaha, Neb.: Joslyn Art Museum in association with Yale University Press (New Haven), 1998.

———. *Degas Landscapes*. New York: Metropolitan Museum of Art in association with Yale University Press (New Haven), 1993.

Kendall, Richard, and Jill De Vonyar. *Degas and the Dance*. Detroit: Detroit Institute of Arts in association with Abrams (New York), 2002.

FANTIN-LATOUR

Fantin-Latour. Paris: Grand Palais, 1982; Ottawa: National Gallery of Canada, 1983.

GAUGUIN

Brettell, Richard R. *The Art of Paul Gauguin*. Washington, D.C.: National Gallery of Art, 1988.

———. *Gauguin and Impressionism*. Fort Worth, Tex.: Kimball Art Museum in association with Yale University Press (New Haven), 2005.

Druick, Douglas, and Peter Zegers. *Van Gogh and Gauguin: The Studio of the South*. Chicago: Art Institute of Chicago, 2001.

Pickvance, Ronald. *Gauguin and the School of Pont-Aven*. Künzelsau: Museum Würth, 1997.

Shackelford, George, et al. *Gauguin, Tahiti*. Boston: MFA Publications, 2004.

Zafran, Eric. *Gauguin's Nirvana: Painters at Le Poldu, 1889–90*. Hartford, Conn.: Wadsworth Atheneum, 2001.

MANET

Cachin, Françoise, et al. *Manet, 1832–1883*. New York: Metropolitan Museum of Art, 1983.

Conzen, Ina. *Edouard Manet und die Impressionisten*. Stuttgart: Staatsgalerie Stuttgart in association with Hatje Cantz (Ostfildern-Ruit), 2002.

Marques, Manuela B. Mena, ed. *Manet en el Prado*. Madrid: Museo Nacional del Prado, 2003.

Mauner, George. *Manet: The Still-Life Paintings*. New York: Abrams in association with American Federation of the Arts, 2000.

Reff, Theodore. *Manet and Modern Paris*. Washington, D.C.: National Gallery of Art, 1982.

Wilson-Bareau, Juliet. *The Hidden Face of Manet: An Investigation of the Artist's Working Processes*. London: Burlington Magazine, 1986 (catalogue of exhibition held at Courtauld Institute Galleries, London, also published as supplement to *Burlington Magazine*, April 1986).

Wilson-Bareau, Juliet, and David Degener. *Manet and the Sea*. Chicago: Art Institute of Chicago, 2003.

MONET

Clark, Michael, and Richard Thomson. *Monet: The Seine and the Sea*. Edinburgh: National Galleries of Scotland, 2003.

Hommage à Claude Monet. Paris: Grand Palais, 1980.

Pissarro, Joachim. *Monet and the Mediterranean*. Fort Worth, Tex.: Kimbell Art Museum in association with Rizzoli (New York), 1997.

Stuckey, Charles F. *Claude Monet, 1840–1926*. Chicago: Art Institute of Chicago in association with Thames and Hudson (New York), 1995.

Tucker, Paul. *Monet in the '90s: The Series Paintings*. Boston: Museum of Fine Arts in association with Yale University Press (New Haven), 1989.

———. *Monet in the 20th Century*. Boston: Museum of Fine Arts in association with Yale University Press (New Haven), 1998.

MORISOT

Berthe Morisot, 1841–1895. Paris: Réunion des musées nationaux, 2002.

Delafond, Marianne, et al. *Berthe Morisot, or Reasoned Audacity*. Paris: Marmottan Monet Museum, 2002.

Stuckey, Charles, and William P. Scott. *Berthe Morisot, Impressionist*. South Hadley, Mass.: Mount Holyoke College Art Museum in association with Hudson Hills Press (New York), 1987.

PISSARRO

Bretell, Richard R. *The Impressionist and the City: Pissarro's Series Paintings*. Dallas: Dallas Museum of Art in association with Yale University Press (New Haven), 1992.

Thomson, Richard. *Camille Pissarro: Impressionism, Landscape, and Rural Labor*. Birmingham, England: City Museum and Art Gallery in association with Herbert Press (London), 1990.

RENOIR

Bailey, Colin. *Renoir's Portraits: Impressions of an Age*. Ottawa: National Gallery of Canada in association with Yale University Press (New Haven), 1997.

Benjamin, Roger. *Renoir and Algeria*. Williamstown, Mass.: Sterling and Francine Clark Art Institute in association with Yale University Press (New Haven), 2003.

Renoir. London: Hayward Gallery; Boston: Museum of Fine Arts, 1985.

SEURAT

Cachin, Françoise, Robert Herbert, et al. *Georges Seurat, 1859–1891*. Paris: Réunion des musées nationaux; New York: Metropolitan Museum of Art, 1991.

Herbert, Robert. *Seurat and the Making of "La Grande Jatte."* Chicago: Art Institute of Chicago, 2004.

Lee, Ellen A. *Seurat at Gravelines: The Last Landscapes*. Indianapolis: Indianapolis Museum of Art in association with Indiana University Press (Bloomington), 1990.

Leighton, John, and Richard Thomson. *Seurat and the Bathers*. London: National Gallery, 1997.

VAN GOGH

Bailey, Martin. *Van Gogh in England: Portrait of the Artist as a Young Man*. London: Barbican Art Gallery, 1992.

Dorn, Roland, George S. Keyes, et al. *Van Gogh Face to Face: The Portraits*. Detroit: Detroit Institute of Arts, 2000.

Ives, Colta, et al. *Vincent van Gogh: The Drawings*. New York: Metropolitan Museum of Art, 2005.

Pickvance, Ronald. *Van Gogh in Arles*. New York: Metropolitan Museum of Art, 1984.

———. *Van Gogh in Saint-Rémy and Auvers*. New York: Metropolitan Museum of Art, 1986.

Welsh-Ovcharov, Bogomila. *Van Gogh à Paris*. Paris: Musée d'Orsay, 1988.

Contributors

CAROL ARMSTRONG is Professor of Art and Archaeology and Doris Stevens Professor of Women's Studies at Princeton University. She is the author of *Odd Man Out: Readings of the Work and Reputation of Edgar Degas* (1991), *Scenes in a Library: Reading the Photograph in the Book* (1998), *Manet/Manette* (2002), and *Cézanne in the Studio: Still Life in Watercolors* (2004), as well as coeditor (with Catherine de Zegher) of *Women Artists at the Millennium* (2006).

T. J. CLARK, who teaches at the University of California, Berkeley, is the author of a series of books on the social character and formal dynamics of modern art, including *The Absolute Bourgeois: Artists and Politics in France, 1848–1851* (1973), *Image of the People: Gustave Courbet and the 1848 Revolution* (1973), *The Painting of Modern Life: Paris in the Art of Manet and His Followers* (1985), and *Farewell to an Idea: Episodes from a History of Modernism* (1999). He is the coauthor (with Iain Boal, Joseph Matthews, and Michael Watts) of *Afflicted Powers: Capital and Spectacle in a New Age of War* (2005). His most recent book is *The Sight of Death: An Experiment in Art Writing* (2006).

STEPHEN F. EISENMAN is Professor of Art History at Northwestern University. He is the author of *The Temptation of Saint Redon: Biography, Ideology, and Style in the Noirs of Odilon Redon* (1994), *Gauguin's Skirt* (1997), and *The Abu Ghraib Effect* (2007), as well as coauthor (with Richard Brettell) of *Nineteenth-Century Art in the Norton Simon Museum* (2006). The third, revised edition of his popular textbook, *Nineteenth-Century Art: A Critical History*, is forthcoming.

TAMAR GARB is Durning Lawrence Professor in the History of Art at University College London. She is the author of many books on nineteenth-century art, including *Sisters of the Brush: Women's Artistic Culture in Late Nineteenth-Century Paris* (1994), *Bodies of Modernity: Figure and Flesh in Fin-de-Siècle France*(1998), and *The Painted Face: Portraits of Women in France, 1814–1914* (1997).

NICHOLAS GREEN, a Lecturer in Art and Cultural History in the School of Art History and Music at the University of East Anglia, was the author, most notably, of *The Spectacle of Nature: Landscape and Bourgeois Culture in Nineteenth-Century France* (1990).

ROBERT L. HERBERT is Andrew W. Mellon Professor Emeritus of Humanities at Mount Holyoke College. Among his publications are *Seurat's Drawings* (1962), *Impressionism: Art, Leisure, and Parisian Society* (1988),

Monet on the Normandy Coast: Tourism and Painting (1994), *Nature's Workshop: Renoir's Writings on the Decorative Arts* (2000), *Seurat: Drawings and Paintings* (2001), and *Seurat and the Making of "La Grande Jatte"* (2004).

JOHN HOUSE is Walter H. Annenberg Professor at the Courtauld Institute of Art, London. He is the author of *Monet: Nature into Art*(1986), *Impressionism: Paint and Politics* (2004), and many essays and articles on French nineteenth-century painting. He has also been involved in the organization of many exhibitions, most recently *Impressionists by the Sea* (London, Washington, Hartford, 2007–8).

MARY TOMPKINS LEWIS, whose publications on Impressionism include *Cézanne's Early Imagery* (1989) and *Cézanne* (2000), teaches art history at Trinity College, Hartford.

MICHEL MELOT is the author of numerous studies on the graphic arts in late-nineteenth-century France, including *The Impressionist Print* (1996).

LINDA NOCHLIN is the Lila Acheson Wallace Professor of Modern Art at the New York University Institute of Fine Arts. She recently published *Bathers, Bodies, Beauty: The Visceral Eye* (2006), and a new edition of her essays on Courbet is forthcoming. She has co-curated (with Maura Reilly) the 2007 exhibition *Global Feminisms* for the Brooklyn Museum.

RICHARD SHIFF is Effie Marie Cain Regents Chair in Art at The University of Texas at Austin, where he directs the Center for the Study of Modernism. He is the author of *Cézanne and the End of Impressionism: A Study of the Theory, Technique, and Critical Evaluation of Modern Art* (1984) and coauthor of *Barnett Newman: A Catalogue Raisonné* (2004).

DEBORA SILVERMAN holds the Presidential Chair in Modern European History, Art, and Culture at the University of California, Los Angeles. She is the author of *Selling Culture* (1986), *Art Nouveau in Fin-de-Siècle France: Politics, Psychology, and Style* (1989), and *Van Gogh and Gauguin: The Search for Sacred Art* (2001).

PAUL HAYES TUCKER is The Paul Hayes Tucker Professor of Art at the University of Massachusetts Boston. He is the author or coauthor of five books on Claude Monet and the curator of numerous international Impressionist exhibitions.

MARTHA WARD, Associate Professor of Art History at the University of Chicago, is the author of *Pissarro, Neo-Impressionism, and the Spaces of the Avant-Garde* (1996) and compiled (with Christopher Parsons) *A Bibliography of Salon Criticism in Second Empire Paris* (1986).

Illustrations

All works are oil on canvas unless otherwise indicated.

Plates (following page 156)

Figures

Index

Page numbers in italics refer to illustrations.

SPONSORING EDITOR	Deborah Kirshman
ASSISTANT EDITOR	Sigi Nacson
PROJECT EDITOR	Sue Heinemann
EDITORIAL ASSISTANT	Lynn Meinhardt
INDEXER	Ruth Elwell
DESIGNER	Claudia Smelser
PRODUCTION COORDINATOR	John Cronin
TEXT	10.5/12.75 Fournier
DISPLAY	Berthold Akzidenz Grotesk Condensed, Fournier
COMPOSITOR	Integrated Composition Systems
PRINTER AND BINDER	Thomson-Shore